PEOPLE OF THE LAKES

Stories of Our Van Tat Gwich'in Elders/
Googwandak Nakhwach'ànjòo Van Tat Gwich'in

THE UNIVERSITY OF ALBERTA PRESS

PEOPLE OF THE LAKES

*Stories of Our Van Tat Gwich'in Elders/
Googwandak Nakhwach'ànjòo Van Tat Gwich'in*

VUNTUT GWITCHIN FIRST NATION & SHIRLEEN SMITH

Published by

The University of Alberta Press
Ring House 2
Edmonton, Alberta, Canada T6G 2E1

Copyright © 2009 Vuntut Gwitchin First Nation and Shirleen Smith

LIBRARY AND ARCHIVES CANADA CATALOGUING IN PUBLICATION

People of the lakes : stories of our Van Tat Gwich'in elders = googwandak nakhwach'ànjòo Van Tat Gwich'in / Vuntut Gwitchin First Nation, Shirleen Smith.

Includes bibliographical references and index.
ISBN 978-0-88864-505-0

1. Vuntut Gwich'in Indians—Yukon Territory—History. 2. Vuntut Gwich'in Indians—Yukon Territory—Biography. I. Smith, Shirleen, 1953- II. Vuntut Gwitchin First Nation

E99.V8P46 2009   971.9'1004972   C2009-902145-5

All rights reserved.
First edition, first printing, 2009.
Printed and bound in Canada by Friesens, Altona, Manitoba.
Copyediting and Proofreading by Meaghan Craven.
Indexing by Elizabeth Macfie.
Maps by Wendy Johnson.

No part of this publication may be produced, stored in a retrieval system, or transmitted in any forms or by any means, electronic, mechanical, photocopying, recording, or otherwise, without the prior written consent of the copyright owner or a licence from The Canadian Copyright Licensing Agency (Access Copyright). For an Access Copyright licence, visit www.accesscopyright.ca or call toll free: 1-800-893-5777.

The University of Alberta Press gratefully acknowledges the support received for its publishing program from The Canada Council for the Arts. The University of Alberta Press also gratefully acknowledges the financial support of the Government of Canada through the Book Publishing Industry Development Program (BPIDP) and from the Alberta Foundation for the Arts for its publishing activities.

CONTENTS

Foreword VII
    JOSEPH LINKLATER, *Chief, Vuntut Gwitchin*

Preface XI
    A Note on the Structure of the Research and Book

Acknowledgements XXI

Introduction XXV
    Van Tat Gwich'in Oral History

1 | Long-ago Stories   1
    Yeenoo d'ài' googwandak

2 | The First Generation   59
    The 19th Century

3 | The Second Generation   157
    Early 20th Century

4 | The Oral History of Today   265
    Van Tat Gwich'in Commentary on the Past, Present, and Future

Notes   313

Glossary   325
    Gwich'in to English   326
    English to Gwich'in   339

Bibliography   355

Index   365

FOREWORD

"*TRY*"—This word has been a part of my vocabulary for as long as I can remember.

I have never before been asked to do a foreword for a book, much less done one, but I consider it a great honour. I began by reading the draft manuscript, still quite nervous about doing something new. And there in the early pages appeared that word, "...the mandate from the Elders was to *try*." If anyone were to ask me to describe in one word the best advice I've ever received from my parents and Elders it would be: "*try.*"

That simple three-letter verb, when spoken by the generations of Elders who have contributed to this wonderful body of work, is said with a deep quiet passion. It speaks to me; it says, "Don't ever give up!" "Don't be afraid." "No matter how difficult life seems, do what is right." "Look after your family." "Look after yourself good." Most important, it is spoken by the generations that know the very essence of the word: those who have lived epic lives in this harsh and at times unforgiving land; those who have travelled the lands of this Gwich'in Nation and beyond by dog team, not riding on the back of a sled but out front breaking trail with snowshoes for their dogs; those who have chased down caribou while wearing snowshoes and shot them from a standing position, shooting as fast as they could reload, a feat that would put any Olympic athlete to shame (no special gear, no special rifle, just conditioning and skill); those who have lost almost every member of their family and yet had to get up every day and work hard in order to survive, men and women equally, because the land has no prejudices.

It's interesting to read in these pages so many stories I have heard over my lifetime and not get the same feeling I have when hearing the spoken word, although as a Gwich'in person I am able to make the connections and put the words into context. It may be difficult at times for those reading this book to relate to some of the stories if you haven't heard them first-hand in the oral storytelling tradition of our people, but those connections to our day-to-day lives are definitely there. I have read books about our people written by researchers in various fields of study, and I have been able to transcend their written words and hear the voices of our people, in many cases getting more out of it than simply what was written on the page. In this book, the words are quoted directly from our Elders and the connection is that much closer and therefore so much more special in every sense. I believe that is what our Elders are expecting, that our inherent knowledge as Gwich'in will breathe life into these pages and provide the foundation and context for the stories of our people. This body of work, like so many other things in our lives, is done by the Elders for the grandchildren, first and foremost. If others are able to get something positive out of this book, so much the better.

I recall a story Charlie Peter Charlie told me about him and my father trapping in the Ogilvie Mountains/Eagle Plains area. They were running low on food, so my father went to hunt caribou and Charlie Peter continued trapping. They agreed to meet at a certain spot in exactly one week and on that precise day, they both arrived there. They shared everything equally, the work and the reward. It was a business arrangement that was never written or spoken about. All my life I've heard Gwich'in refer to each other as "partner"; only in the last ten years or so, I've come to realize the significance of that word by that generation. I can honestly say that I've never heard any Gwich'in speak badly of their "partner." It seems to me to be one of the highest compliments one can pay to another.

This story made me understand why it is so important to our Elders that we not just talk about doing something, but we actually do it or at least *try*. "Don't just talk about it, do it," my father used to say. He was always emphatic on that point. To our Elders, survival could hinge on the commitments they made and therefore it is important that we follow through on our commitments. Today, when we fail to honour some of our promises the consequences may not be very dire, but to our Elders' trained minds, this is a dangerous sign. Being prepared for hard times means more than having the right equipment and good skills but also understanding the importance of following through on commitments and working as a team in order to survive on the land. These traits are still strong in our people when they are on the land, but they have to be understood and carried on by future generations. It is our Elders who understand first-hand why it is so important.

In the ten years I have had the honour of serving my people as the chief, I have also had the great fortune to be counselled and guided by these amazing Elders, some of whom are no longer with us today except in spirit. They told incredible stories of strength of body, mind, and spirit; stories of triumph and heartbreaking loss; stories of love and laughter—all with the ease and grace of true storytellers. They weren't bragging, which is bad form; they were passing along information in the way it has always been passed on by Gwich'in. The incredible hardships and toughness of the people was simply a backdrop to the lessons or information they were sharing. It still overwhelms me to think of how tough these Elders I see today must have been in their prime. Their instincts for survival are still honed and sharp, but now it is the survival of our culture and history that must be carried on by future generations. Our Elders saw what needed to be done, spoke about it, and then did it. They had our oral history put into writing so that it could be passed to future generations, so we will never forget who we are and where we came from.

This single piece of work will not ensure our cultural survival, but it is our Elders' contribution toward that survival. We must all do our part to honour this gift from them.

To honour our Elders, we have to try.

JOSEPH LINKLATER
Chief, Vuntut Gwitchin
February 2009

PREFACE

A Note on the Structure of the Research and Book

Well, [this story] is from old people, early days people. They tell that story to us. They carry the story out here and there and then like newspaper, just like newspapers. They carry this story from one generation to the other. That's how they know.

(MOSES TIZYA, August 20, 1979, VG2000-8-22:112-114, Gwich'in and English)[1]

Lots of times, elders, their grandfathers told stories in front of them. They told those same stories again. Me, too, my grandfather Peter Moses, he told lots of stories in front of me. I remember some of his stories really well. Whatever I don't really remember, I could never talk about. Maybe I would tell my friends, but if I don't remember good, I wouldn't tell stories out loud to anybody. This was put in my ears. Not long ago the elders, when they were gathering their stories, maybe two or three times it was translated. One was William Nerysoo; he said this when they gathered his stories: "My grandfather and my uncles told stories in front of me. 'Where did you get these stories?' I asked them. 'Long ago our grandfathers gave us these stories. That's what we talk about. They are carried on and will not be changed. If we change them, then they will all be mixed up.'" This is why when elders talk with us we are to keep their stories good. We try to keep it that way.

(ROY MOSES, November 15, 1998, VG2003-3-7:012-025, Gwich'in)

Van Tat Gwich'in Oral History Research

IN JANUARY 1999, at a community meeting in Old Crow, Yukon, on an evening that was -50°C, Van Tat Gwich'in elders, community members, Vuntut Gwitchin First Nation (VGFN) Heritage Manager Megan Williams, and anthropologists Shirleen Smith and Murielle Nagy came together to plan a project to gather and document Van Tat Gwich'in oral history. Those who attended the meeting were passionately determined that the work be done promptly and well. They set out their priorities: they wanted to document their history on all of their traditional lands, not just part (for example, the area that was to become Vuntut National Park or the Dempster Highway area). They wanted the considerable body of interviews recorded in the past by a variety of researchers and held at a number of archives brought back to Old Crow. The group also agreed that current elders needed to be interviewed as soon as possible.

The overriding concern of the people in Old Crow was to pass the history and knowledge of the elders, across the barriers of language and changing lifestyles, to the youth and future generations. Everyone recognized the risk that the history and knowledge of the elders, the last generation to have spent their entire working lives on the land, would be lost before it could be passed on to the youth. The elders emphasized that their experience and knowledge could also be vitally important to the younger generation: life can be difficult, and they firmly believe that hard times are coming again, and that the next generations must be prepared. As this oral history illustrates, the framework the elders used to structure their knowledge was predominantly historical: where they or their elders went during their lifetime to make a living, what they did there, who lived where, what happened in the past.

> What I know, what I heard, I'll tell you about that. You want to learn everything, that's why you're taking the elders around here. It's really good that's being done. It's for our children and our grandchildren in the future. They will hear this and they'll use it. That's why when you tell me to come to places like this, I obey you. People would not come around here. Me, I know a little about this place so I will sit here with you....
>
> That story is long. Then, who would know? Around Old Crow, not one person knows. Andrew Tizya was raised around here, Johnny Ross, too. Even they don't know this kind of big story about this area. But me, Peter Moses told me stories about how people lived around here. That's why I come here now and that's what I talk about. I never saw it, that's what I mean.
>
> (ALFRED CHARLIE, Black Fox Creek, June 24, 2001, VG2001-2-44:006-012, 060-065, Gwich'in)

The Van Tat Gwich'in have had considerable experience with researchers over the years, and at the meeting they expressed their views about the conduct of this research. As a result, the Van Tat Gwich'in Oral History Project was structured according to the following mandate from the elders and the community. They stressed the importance of doing interviews in context: on the land and in the language with which the speaker is most comfortable (Gwich'in approximately 90 per cent of the time). As much as possible, all phases of the research—from planning to interviewing, filming, and transcribing—should be done by Van Tat Gwich'in so that the people would themselves guide and own the project, as well as grow with it. Finally, the project and the information should first and foremost benefit Van Tat Gwich'in and not be directed toward fulfilling outsiders' research goals.

As well as passing their knowledge and stories to their youth, Van Tat Gwich'in have a tradition of sharing their stories, culture, and history with non-Gwich'in. Old Crow is perhaps unique as a First Nations community whose voice has been widely heard, particularly through Edith Josie's column, Here Are the News. Josie was the Old Crow correspondent to the *Whitehorse Star* for 31 years beginning in 1962, and her column was reprinted in the *Edmonton Journal* and the *Toronto Telegram*, translated into German, Italian, and Spanish, and it attracted readership from as far away as New Zealand, Texas, Florida, and the Philippines. The column represents one of a number of Van Tat Gwich'in public expressions of their history and culture. Another, and perhaps the most significant recent example of Van Tat Gwich'in public commentary is their highly publicized worldwide lobby to protect the Porcupine caribou herd from oil drilling in their calving grounds in the American Arctic National Wildlife Refuge.

With the guidance of the heritage committee, the Van Tat Gwich'in Oral History Project was conducted by community members from Old Crow from 1999 to 2004, followed by the Van Tat Gwich'in Cultural Geography Project (2004-2007), which centred on toponyms (place names) and associated information, as well as developing educational materials.[1] While the interviews for these projects were being conducted and previously recorded interviews assembled, a number of themes and foci became apparent. The elders were extremely serious in their objectives to have their knowledge of Gwich'in oral traditions and history recorded for the future. They welcomed tape recorders and video cameras and were enthusiastic to travel on the land, often specifying where the research team needed to go to conduct specific interviews.

> So, tomorrow, at *Tanch'ohłii* mountain, when you fly there with me, I will talk about the first time the Van Tat Gwich'in people came on this land, stories from that time. How they lived off the caribou fences—all

> I have heard, I will talk about it. Crow Flats, too, how they lived off the small animals in the summer. In the small streams they made fish traps and they fished there. Tomorrow on that mountain across there, if they land there with me I'll talk about all that.
> (ALFRED CHARLIE, Black Fox Creek, June 24, 2001, VG2001-2-44:180-195, Gwich'in)

The elders were careful to describe their sources—who originally passed stories on to them, for example—and how they came to know what they knew. They made it clear whether they heard something from someone else or witnessed it themselves through repeated expressions translated as "this I remember" or "this happened in front of me," meaning "in my presence" or "I experienced (or witnessed) this." Some elders also described the process of passing on stories so that they remain accurate. Others emphasized the limits of their knowledge, beyond which they would not attempt to speculate.

> Now, my friends, for the Vuntut Gwitchin Nation, I came here to tell stories. This is all I know about long-ago caribou fences. What they did, I know….My grandmother told me stories, I remember, when I was a child. That way, I know this much. This is about all I know, that I can tell you about.
> (CHARLIE THOMAS, Old Domas's Caribou Fence [Thomas Creek Caribou Fence], July 27, 2000, VG2000-4-3:035-45, Gwich'in)

The elders were interested in accurate history. Telling the stories properly, refusing to go beyond what they knew either from their own experience or a qualified witness (who they named) were important factors that contributed to their accuracy. They also distinguished between stories that were historical and stories that were not primarily about history, such as some elements of *yeenoo dài' googwandak* (long-ago stories) that are more akin to legends and myths:

> Long-ago stories, some of them are not true. Even so, what is said is storytelling, that's why it's told. Some of it I don't remember too well, but I will talk about it. Two old women were living at the fish trap in the summertime….
> (SARAH ABEL, April 19, 1980, VG2000-8-32:003-004, Gwich'in)

Thus, Van Tat Gwich'in elders took care that both the historical and non-historical stories were told by the elders best qualified to do so.[2] The history presented in this book represents their sincere efforts, priorities, and values about passing on their history and other stories to the future. This collection of oral history is intended to highlight the Gwich'in perspective on the importance and role of their oral history and to fill the gap in the body of writing and information about Van Tat Gwich'in.

Structure of the Research and Structure of the Book

There are many ways to approach researching and compiling oral history. As a primary source of information, oral history interviews and transcripts form the foundation for research for myriad purposes. For example, the Yukon Native Language Centre and Alaska Native Language Center have used oral history as an important source for preserving and furthering Aboriginal languages and have produced verbatim transcriptions in a number of Indigenous languages. Other researchers looked at the performance element of oral history and suggested mechanisms, such as "the treatment of oral narratives as dramatic poetry" and "sensitivity to verbal art as performed 'event' rather than as fixed 'object' on the page," to bring a dramatist's perspective to oral narratives (Tedlock 1983:54–55). Scholars William Schneider (1995, 2002) and Ruth Finnegan (1970, 1992) emphasized that much is lost by removing oral history from its original spoken context by working with recordings and transcripts. A number of others examined the nature of the speech event or communication, differences in the ways speech is used by men and women in different speech communities, the speech conventions in different cultural settings and roles, and how speech contributes to constructing identity, ideology, and cultural ideals and norms (Bauman and Sherzer 1989; Hensel 1996).

Looking at oral history in various cultures, past and present, researchers identified the use of devices, such as repetition, emphasis, alliteration, and rhyme, to aid the speaker-performer's memory (Ong 1982; Vansina 1961, 1985). Others, such as Peter Nabokov (2002), explored the myriad ways history is collected, expressed, transmitted, maintained, celebrated, integrated into American Indian societies, and even projected into the future. Still other researchers examined oral history for its ability to preserve historical accuracy through time in an oral medium (Cruikshank 1990, 1996, 1998; Helm and Gillespie 1981). They identified means, such as authorizing particular individuals (or groups, such as castes like griots, professional praise-singers, and tellers of accounts in West Africa), to hold and transmit history, and how oral historians routinely identify their sources (Vansina 1985:37). Other mechanisms, such as the use of physical objects to represent ideas or group decisions, were identified as a conservative force in oral history that promoted historical accuracy: for example, the use of wampum belts to represent the terms of agreements made by the Iroquois confederacy (Morgan 1963[1877]:142).

Taken together, these and numerous other studies have drawn upon oral traditions as a rich source of history, along with other elements that are not specifically historical (such as oral traditions related to beliefs, rituals, philosophy or world view, humour or entertainment) but that hold important contextual information for understanding history. As with previous oral history research, the Van Tat Gwich'in oral history projects were directed toward clear goals, in this case determined by the community (Old Crow) and its research needs. The primary objectives set out by the heritage committee for a clear, easily readable, accurate oral history guided the structure of the manuscript. All the interviews (both from archival sources and newly recorded) were indexed, translated into English, and transcribed by current Van Tat Gwich'in translators Mary Jane Moses, Brenda Kay, and Florence Netro under the direction of Jane Montgomery, a Van Tat Gwich'in language expert trained in the modern Gwich'in orthography. As well, translators were fortunate to be able to verify the various dialects and usages of the language with living elders, whose first, and continuing, language is Gwich'in. From these translated transcripts, the heritage committee desired that the words of the elders and others be represented in correct, standard English usage (rather that colloquially or in the local Old Crow dialect), which would best represent the fluency of Gwich'in speakers in their own language and render their ideas—the content—as clearly and accessibly as possible.

Translation is an exacting and highly skilled task and the Van Tat Gwich'in were fortunate to have sufficient skilled personnel to take on the massive task of translating (or re-translating) over 400 taped interviews. In a few instances, written transcripts of interviews from previous research projects were all that was available at the time this manuscript was being prepared (e.g., the LaPierre House Oral History Project). In such cases, the translations were done in the past in accordance with different objectives than more recent projects. The older transcripts were summaries of the statements of the speakers rather than verbatim translations and don't represent the original speakers' words or manner of speaking. Nonetheless, these translations are valuable sources of information.

Following translation and transcription, the interviews were grouped by generation and then by theme or topic. Highlighting the generation of the speakers brought to light similarities in vision and experiences within generations and interesting differences between generations. Also, the references by speakers to their elders and contemporaries was clarified once the generation of the speakers was shown. In excerpting passages from the interviews and grouping these according to themes, some lengthy excerpts set the tone and provided background to a topic, while other briefer segments supplied details or additional points of view. The main reason for organizing the material this way was practical. Many interviews were encyclopedic in their scope, covering a wide range of topics and providing thoughtful commentary. Others were fragments of longer stories or assumed a fair familiarity with the topic at hand on the part of the listener. In both cases, collecting similar thematic material from many interviews made it considerably easier to appreciate and remember the words of the elders.

Each step in the process of translation, transcription, excerpting, and grouping transcripts by generation and theme is an editorial reworking of the voice of the original speaker and a step away from the original context of the interview. However, the speakers' distinct identities still emerge in reading the excerpted transcripts. Furthermore, rendering their words as appreciable as possible was our approach to respecting the original intent of the speakers: that their words be understood and go forth into the future for the generations to come.

Structurally, at its heart, this book is about the history and culture of Van Tat Gwich'in in their own words. There is also significant use of non-Gwich'in sources, which often served to introduce or contextualize the Van Tat Gwich'in texts. The objective was to introduce the Van Tat Gwich'in and their oral history in context so the oral history was as accessible as possible. The non-Gwich'in references and brief introductions to the Van Tat Gwich'in passages endeavour to supply context, fill in gaps, and essentially provide sufficient stitching to draw together the patchwork of interviews, in as unobtrusive and respectful a manner as possible.

Much is lost in putting oral history on paper: the nuances of meaning, physical expression, gesture, speech, the interaction between speaker and audience, and the cultural knowledge shared by the community. Likewise for Van Tat Gwich'in oral history, the written version of the elders' words pales in comparison with hearing them speak, especially on the land where they and their stories are truly at home. However, the elders fear what will be lost if their words are *not* put into print. They are aware that the unbroken chain of transmission from generation to generation from far, far back in their history is more fragile now than it has ever been. They worry that young people who do not speak Gwich'in are not hearing the words of their elders and will not know their history. So, imperfect though the medium of writing may be for adequately expressing all there is in oral history, the mandate from the elders was to try. This book is the result.

This tape we're talking into, hopefully some day the young people will listen to it and they may look after the land better.

(JOHN JOE KYIKAVICHIK, 1980, VG2000-8-26:048)

Right now what I talk about, a lot of older men told me stories. That's how I know the stories. So now I'm an Elder, all this comes back to me; that's what I talk to you about. If you don't do this, how are the stories going to be passed on? No way. Right now down there, our children, even when they're a bit older, they won't talk about this stuff. They don't know about it. They never see the elders. How are they going to know? You're really doing a good job [the Oral History Project]. Right now, what you're doing, it's for our children's future.

(ALFRED CHARLIE, Crow Mountain, July 29, 2000, VG2000-4-8:315-326, Gwich'in)

Conventions Used in the Book

References and Quotations

Central to this book are the quotations from elders, other Gwich'in, and published sources. The quotation style for published works follows common conventions, with the author's name, date of publication and page number following the quotation, and the full reference in the bibliography. The oral history interviews are referenced slightly differently. The speaker's name is followed by information about the interview: the location (if known and other than Old Crow), date, catalogue number (for example, VG2000-4-8:315-326 indicates the tape is part of the Van Tat Gwich'in collection, added in 2000, series #4 that year, the eighth tape in the series, and at 315-326 on the tape), and language of the interview (usually Gwich'in or English). The reference can be relevant to the information in the interview, such as when the speaker refers to the context of the land where the interview took place. As well, interviews in English are quoted essentially directly, while those in Gwich'in have been translated into standard English and edited for comprehension and to represent the speaker's fluency in Gwich'in. Consequently, an individual quoted in both English and Gwich'in may appear to have a different "speaking voice" depending on their fluency in each language, many elders being much more comfortable and expressive in Gwich'in. Occasionally we lacked the original interview and only had a transcript where the translator described what was being said usually in the third person (for example, "She said her father raised her") rather than translating word for word, a system often used when an immediate translation is needed. These cases are also noted in the reference.

Within the quotations from oral history interviews or translations of interviews, words enclosed in square brackets [ ] are not part of the original quotation. Instead, they are usually words added by the translator or editor to provide further information or clarification. Parentheses ( ) indicate digressions, explanations, or ancillary information spoken in the interview by the original speaker. Ellipses … indicate words or sounds in the original interview that have been omitted. Em-dashes — are used to indicate the speaker made a longer break than what is normally represented by a comma, or that the speaker made a parenthetical comment of greater emphasis than indicated by enclosing it in parentheses, such as an exclamation in the middle of a sentence. In the modified example below, the items in square brackets were not spoken by Mary Thomas but added later to clarify her comments. The sentence in parentheses was spoken by her as background information to her main story. The ellipsis at the end indicates that she continued her narrative but it is not included here:

> We got down to John's [John Thomas, her husband]. Only he had a motor and he came all the way up Potato Creek with a canvas boat and gas. Coming down [the Crow River] he picked up all the canvas boats and brought them to Old Crow. (He had a boat like what we have today [wooden scow] and he brought all the people down from *Van Tat* with it.)…
>
> (MARY THOMAS, February 20, 1980, VG2000-8-16:054-230, Gwich'in)

Orthography—Spelling

While we have striven for accuracy, consistency, and simplicity, we employ a number of different names and spellings for Van Tat Gwich'in in this book. For the most part, the reasons are historical. Until relatively recently, Gwich'in was not a written language. The first major written representation of Van Tat or Dagoo Gwich'in was by the missionary and later Archdeacon Robert McDonald, who produced a written Gwich'in version of the Bible, a hymn book, and other religious material in about 1898. McDonald used English as his model for representing Gwich'in, while at the same time, other missionaries were translating the Bible into languages such as northern Slavey (É. Petitot in Fort Good Hope, NT) based on French. However, neither English nor French are consistent in their rendering of sounds: for example, in English "ot" and "ought" are used to spell the same sound, as in "cot" and "bought," and three different spellings are used in "their," "there," and "they're" for the same sound. Fluent speakers learn to read the different spellings—and understand the meanings—through practice, and similarly many fluent Gwich'in learned to read written Gwich'in based on the idiosyncratic English ways of writing sounds. The modern Gwich'in orthography, on the other hand, is based on a standardized system for representing sounds so that readers can sound out the written Gwich'in words with greater accuracy, which is especially important for students of Gwich'in who are not fluent speakers. In practice, many older Gwich'in continue to use the system devised by Archdeacon McDonald, with which they are familiar, while the modern orthography is taught to younger people and children, and is the primary method used in this book.

There are a number of names and spellings for Van Tat Gwich'in, and all of them are used here when quoting the original sources. "Van Tat Gwich'in" is currently the preferred name written in the modern orthography. The name is a reference to the heartland of Van Tat Gwich'in (people of the lakes), or *van* (lakes) *tat* (many) *Gwich'in* (people), referring to Old Crow Flats (or just Crow Flats). Other names and spellings include: Vuntut Gwitchin, used in the official name for the Vuntut Gwitchin First Nation, which follows the older orthography; Loucheux, a name given Gwich'in by French fur traders; Kutchin, an earlier rendering of Gwich'in often found in social science literature; Rat Indians (an allusion to the abundance of muskrats in Van Tat, which Van Tat Gwich'in trapped and traded), represented today in place names such as Rat Indian Creek; and Tukudh, the spelling used by Archdeacon McDonald for the Dagoo Gwich'in of the upper Porcupine River (who now primarily reside with Van Tat Gwich'in and Teetl'it Gwich'in of the Fort McPherson, NT, area).

The question of whether to capitalize the "e" in "elder" as a mark of respect was resolved by using capitals when referring to a specific elder but not when referring to one or more elders in general.

Gwich'in-English translation and pronunciation guidance is provided in notes and in a glossary at the end of the book.

ACKNOWLEDGEMENTS

FIRST AND FOREMOST, we wish to express our gratitude to the Van Tat Gwich'in and Dagoo elders, past and present, and their families, for their generosity and foresight in sharing their knowledge. In addition, their stories tell of other Van Tat Gwich'in, and thereby we learn of the experiences and characters of countless others who contributed to Van Tat Gwich'in heritage. *Mahsi' Cho* to these elders and their families: Sarah Abel, Ellen Bruce, Alfred Charlie, Charlie Peter Charlie, Lazarus Charlie, Donald Frost, Stephen Frost Sr., Bella Greenland, William Itsi, Dolly Josie, Edith Josie, Mary Kassi, John Kendi, Myra Kaye-Kyikavichik, John Joe Kyikavichik, Charlie Linklater, Effie Linklater, Irwin Linklater, Annie Lord, David Lord, Neil McDonald, Myra Moses, Peter Moses, Hannah Netro, Joe Netro, Mary Netro, Dick Nukon, Kenneth Nukon, Stanley Njootli Sr., Abraham Peter, Lazarus Sittichinlii, Charlie Thomas, Lydia Thomas, Mary Thomas, Andrew Tizya, Clara Tizya, Martha Tizya, Moses Tizya, and Peter Tizya.

We also wish to acknowledge the contribution of the middle-aged and younger elders for sharing their knowledge and that of their elders: Robert Bruce Jr., Freddy Frost, Roger Kaye, John Joseph Kyikavichik, David Lord, Joel Peter, Esau Schafer, and Marion Schafer.

Special thanks are due to Van Tat Gwich'in youth for their enthusiasm for learning the elders' stories and sharing their insights into the world of Van Tat Gwich'in today. *Mahsi'* to: Frances Bruce, Mylinda Bruce, Cheyanne Charlie, Cheryl Charlie, Kathie Marie Charlie, Myranda Charlie, Amanda Frost, Natasha Frost, Sherrie Frost, Travis Frost, Tammy Josie, Kecia Kassi, Michelle Kendi-Rispin, Brandon Kyikavichik, Melissa Frost, Lance Nagwan, Jeffrey Peter, Phillip Rispin, and Erika Tizya-Tramm.

This book and the many years of work that preceded it would not have been conceived and accomplished without the dedication of the Heritage Committee in Old Crow: long-term members Jane Montgomery, Robert Bruce Jr., Mary Jane Moses, and more recently, Marion Schafer, and past members Brenda Kay and Florence Netro. They are unsurpassed at providing the link between the elders, the community, and the research project, and steering everyone so that our joint objectives are realized. Most of all, they have a rock-solid handle on what is truly important, the values that we should strive for in our work. Particular thanks are due to Jane, Robert, and Mary Jane for many years of very hard work.

Very special thanks are due to Megan Williams, VGFN Heritage Manager, who contributed immensely to all facets of the research and production of this book: project management; editing; co-ordinating community members, researchers, and pilots; shepherding team members and their gear; and juggling often hair-raising quantities of detail with dexterity, grace, and humour.

Community supporters in Old Crow helped us during the research conducted for the book with everything from cooking meals to driving boats, taking us to their lands, video filming, and typing transcripts. Our thanks go out to: Rosalie Abel, Frances Bruce, Shawn Bruce, Darius Elias, Bertha Frost, Freddy Frost, Harold Frost, Marvin Frost Sr., William Josie, Danny Kassi, Roger Kaye, Randal Kendi, Robert Kyikavichik, David Lord, Georgie Moses, Roy Moses, Curtis Netro, Justin Netro, Dorothy Rispin, Tracy Rispin, Esau Schafer, Randall Tetlichi, and Dorothy Thomas.

Many individuals and agencies provided essential support in terms of finances, co-operation, information, and advice. We wish to express our heartfelt thanks to the following for their generous support: Yukon Aboriginal Languages Service (Cheryl Mclean and Jeannette Poyton); Canada Council for the Arts (Aboriginal Media Arts Program); Canada: Museums Assistance Program (Michelle Genest, Colleen Craig, and Phillipa Syme); Canada: Aid to Scholarly Publications Programme; Canadian Museum of Civilization (Judy Thompson and Dennis Fletcher); Cultural Industry Training Fund; Northern Native Broadcasting, Yukon (Vic Istchenko); Parks Canada (Robert Lewis, Darius Elias, David Neufeld, Rhonda Markel, Jane Park, Brenda Frost, and David Henry); Polar Continental Shelf Program (Bonni Hrycyk, Dave Maloley, Martin Bergmann, Mike Kristjanson, Barry Hough, and Kari Borris); Yukon Archives (Clara Rutherford); Yukon Heritage Resources (Ruth Gotthardt, Doug Olynyk, and Grant Zazula); Canada: Aboriginal Languages Initiative (Gayle Corry); Library and Archives Canada—Canadian Culture Online (Krista Peterson and Kristina Lillico); Gathering Strength: Canada's Aboriginal Action Plan; Yukon Department of Tourism and Culture; Yukon Historic Resources Fund; Shaunessy

Investment Counsel Inc.; Yukon Department of Education; Yukon Environmental Assistance Fund; Yukon Native Language Centre (John Ritter); Yukon Protected Areas Secretariat (Katy Hayhurst); and Vuntut Gwitchin First Nation (Chief Joe Linklater, council, and staff).

Many individuals have supported us in our research, which resulted in this book—sometimes accompanying us, sharing their knowledge, and offering their encouragement. In addition to those already mentioned, we would like to thank: researchers Dr. Ray Le Blanc, Barney Smith, Dr. Duane Froese, Dr. Paul Matheus, Sheila Greer, Murielle Nagy, and Colin Beairsto; computer mapper Jeff Hamm; educators Bob Sharpe and Mark Stevens; film instructors Ross Burnett, Andy Connors, and Richard Lawrence; and helicopter pilots Jim Broadbent, Steve Rickets, Wayne Sorge, and Jim Watson.

Finally, we would like to express our appreciation to the staff of the University of Alberta Press: Alan Brownoff, Linda Cameron, Cathie Crooks, Michael Luski, Peter Midgley, Mary Lou Roy, and others for guiding us safely through the publication process. Our thanks also go to the anonymous peer reviewers for their generous and helpful comments.

Introduction
Van Tat Gwich'in Oral History

Van Tat (Crow Flats), heartland of Van Tat Gwich'in country.
[Shirleen Smith ©VGFN 2000 (VG2000-6-39)]

THE COMMUNITY OF OLD CROW, population 300, is in the heart of the traditional lands of the Van Tat Gwich'in: the people of the lakes. Their traditional territory in the northern Yukon is vast. Van Tat Gwich'in routinely made their living and travelled as far west as the Yukon River (now Fort Yukon, Alaska), Herschel Island in the Arctic Ocean to the north, east to Fort McPherson across the mountains in the Northwest Territories, and south to the remote headwaters of the Porcupine River near today's Dempster Highway. There are stories of people travelling even farther under special circumstances. Van Tat Gwich'in accounts describe not only where people lived and travelled throughout the year, during times of feast and famine, but also where noteworthy, ordinary, or even fantastic events took place. Some stories tell of incidents that may have occurred thousands of years ago, others from a few hundred years past, and still others from the 19th and 20th centuries, when newcomers began to arrive with their own objectives for the land and their exotic ideas and things. This book is about those stories.

Van Tat Gwich'in are Aboriginal people of northern Canada whose roots go back millennia in the area. Their homeland is the farthest reaches of northern human settlement but for the Inuit peoples of the Arctic coast. In this fragile land the sun shines around the clock in summer but only presents a few hours of pink dusk in the middle of winter, and permafrost is less than a foot below the soil surface. Much of Gwich'in lands are mountainous, forested primarily with spruce but also some deciduous trees and shrubs, and other parts are tundra and vast areas of lakes and convoluted rivers and creeks. The main waterway flowing through Van Tat Gwich'in country is the Porcupine River, which begins on the west side of the Richardson Mountains, which flows north and west, joining the Yukon River to cross

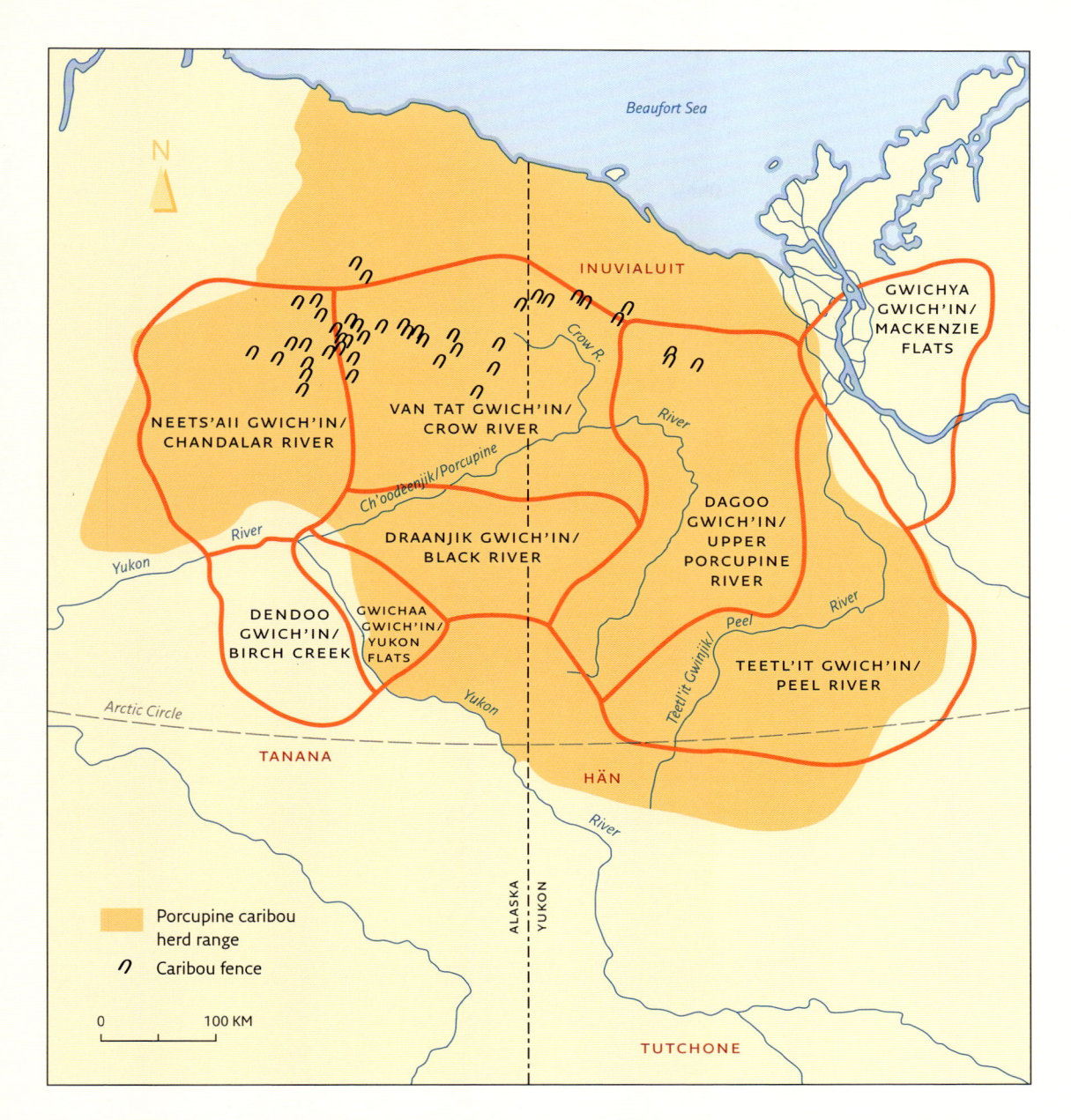

MAP 1 *Gwich'in and Caribou in Northern Yukon and Alaska*

Cultural boundaries from Osgoode 1970[1936].
Caribou fences from Jakimchuk 1974.
Caribou range from North Yukon Planning Commission 2006 (www.nypc.planyukon.ca).

Alaska and empty into the Pacific Ocean. Numerous species of salmon make the extremely long upstream voyage to Gwich'in country to feed the people and their dogs, as well as bears, eagles, and other wildlife. The northern area of their lands extends into the British Mountains north of the broad flat basin dotted with hundreds of lakes that feed into the meandering Crow River and ultimately the Porcupine River. This region, known as Van Tat (Crow Flats), is cherished by Van Tat Gwich'in for its waterfowl, fish, muskrats, and moose, as well as for the beauty of the land itself. Just north of Crow Flats, the trees disappear and the land rises again into hills and mountains before tipping into the vast coastal plain, the North Slope, stretching across the Yukon and Alaska to meet the Arctic Ocean.

Although distant from the homes of Van Tat Gwich'in, the North Slope is critical to their survival, for it is here that the 160,000-strong Porcupine caribou herd, one of the world's few remaining grand amalgamations of wildlife, each spring birth and rear their young. Like a living tide, they flow north in the spring from their wintering grounds in and around the lands of Van Tat Gwich'in and ebb south again in the fall with their new generation of offspring. For countless centuries the caribou have made their annual journeys, and Gwich'in have watched for their arrival, observed their behaviour, monitored their numbers and health, hunted them to feed their families and build shelters, clothed themselves, and made tools from their hides, antlers, and bones. The importance of the Porcupine caribou herd to the Van Tat Gwich'in cannot be overstated.

Elder Alfred Charlie spoke of the relationship between Gwich'in and the Porcupine caribou herd on June 29, 2001. He was on a hill called *Tanch'ohłii* in the British Mountains, looking south over Crow Flats:

> Now they will see the mountains in the picture, the lakes down there, too. I heard the stories of [early times] around here when there were lots of Van Tat Gwich'in [and] the caribou, in those days.
>
> Today there are many caribou. Then there weren't so many. Even so, the caribou migrated down [northwest to the Alaska North Slope] to the calving grounds. They went there in the spring.... After that, when the young ones were raised, they came up this way in the month of August. They migrated...through the mountains.... Some of them came over the mountains, over that big mountain. Some of them, by the ocean coast, up on the grass [the Yukon North Slope, above the treeline].
>
> Around Arctic Village [Alaska], when they migrated over the mountains, some of them stopped there. There the Arctic Village people lived off them.
>
> From there, they came this way through the mountains. At Firth River, Thomas Creek, through there, they migrated over the mountains, then at Thomas Creek, they came down. Back there at a place they called *Dzan Ehłai'* [Timber Mountain], they crossed Crow River and went right to King Edward Mountain, over that and down. Some of them came straight down Ear Mountain. They went down at the creek, at the mouth of *Dzêenjik*, then down to Old Crow.
>
> Some of them went over King Edward Mountain, straight down they came. They went across [the Porcupine River] at the caribou trail. From there all the way to Old Crow, way down [downriver] at Canyon, they

crossed there, and at *Tl'oo K'at*. Then some of them crossed way up [upriver] at David Lord Creek, at Fish Lake. The caribou did that all the way upriver, they migrated across.

Some of them [migrated east] up at the ocean, up that way, on the mountains. Some of them went up that way. Then the Aklavik people, in the summer, them, too, they took their meat from them.

Some of them went way up at Bell River,...then way up where they call Loon Lake, above there they went over the mountains. Then...the Fort McPherson people, they ate good from it, too.

Then at a place called James Creek all the way to Eagle Plains, that's how the caribou migrated before winter.

All winter they stayed up there.[1] Sometimes some of them came down this way. They knew where they were going to stay for the winter and they went back there. Way up above Eagle River, above *Ch'ihilii Chìk*, they say it's really big. Below there is the Eagle River. They're going to stay there for the winter, so they crossed *Ch'izhìn Njik* [Eagle River].... There they stayed for the winter.

Some of them came across White Snow Mountain and there, too, were caribou all winter. From there, the caribou crossed *Ch'aghootl'i* and then Lone Mountain. They stayed on that mountain for the winter, they gathered all around there. Today, they don't do that anymore. Now, for a long time, I know there hasn't been caribou on Lone Mountain.

A long time ago, all winter there was caribou around here. The Old Crow people really depended on them after New Year's. Now, the caribou don't stay here anymore. I wonder how their food is? Maybe it's because of that.

So, that's how these caribou migrated. They did that, and the people knew. Where there were caribou trails, they knew it, and they made caribou fences there for the caribou. The caribou fences were up this way, on the mountains. [They were used when] the caribou migrated up this way, and also when the caribou migrated back down. They didn't have guns. They only used bows and arrows in those days. So, they made caribou fences. They fixed it all up in the springtime.

(ALFRED CHARLIE, *Tanch'ohłii*, British Mountains, June 29, 2001, VG2001-2-62:015-083, Gwich'in)

Today the Van Tat Gwich'in include a number of people who identify some of their ancestors as Dagoo (or Tukudh) Gwich'in, a regional First Nation that lived in the country drained by the upper reaches of the Porcupine River to the east and south of the Van Tat Gwich'in. The Dagoo dispersed in the early 20th century to live among the Van Tat Gwich'in and

Ch'oodèenjik *(Porcupine River)* upstream of Old Crow.

[Shirleen Smith ©VGFN 2004]

the neighbouring Teetl'it Gwich'in in the Fort McPherson area. In Old Crow, the history of people with Dagoo heritage has been joined with Van Tat Gwich'in. For example, Elder and former Chief Alfred Charlie, whose father was Dagoo and mother was Van Tat, considers himself Van Tat because membership-identity is determined matrilineally. He is knowledgeable in the history of both peoples:

> Before white man came there has always been Gwich'in people right here. Dagoo, Van Tat Gwich'in they kept this area open. And then Dagoo: from Bell River up towards Blackstone, right up to Fishing Branch [River] and Miner River and across to the head of Cody Creek,

> all this was Dagoo country. That's where they used to make their living. Even us, we used to do that. We used to cover all that country. There was no country around this area without people; there were always people on it making a living. Just like here: Crow River right up to Bell River, right across [to] the head of Bluefish [River], right down to the [U.S.–Canada] border around Rampart House, right up to the head of Caribou Bar and back this way: that's Van Tat Gwich'in country. They covered the whole thing. So that's how people used to keep their land. Every year they used a different place so this country has never been without people, even before white men came.
>
> (ALFRED CHARLIE 1995 in VGFN1995B:4)

Like Alfred Charlie's history, Van Tat Gwich'in have passed their history from generation to generation to generation for centuries by word of mouth. They also told their stories to some of the newcomers, and some of these wrote out the accounts. Later travellers, scientists, historians, ethnographers, missionaries, and a variety of researchers employed tape recorders (described in more detail in the historical review, below). And Van Tat Gwich'in recorded their elders themselves and produced a small number of written accounts (such as Edith Josie's many publications: *Whitehorse Star* 1963, 1965, 1966, 1970, and 1973; Sherry and VGFN 1999).

Over the past 25 years, measures have been proposed to protect the unique natural and cultural resources of the Van Tat Gwich'in and their traditional lands. In the mid-1970s, the most thorough and detailed social and environmental impact assessment in Canadian history, the Mackenzie Valley Pipeline Inquiry, was conducted. Between 1974 and 1977, Justice Thomas Berger visited the communities of the Mackenzie Valley and Yukon and recorded testimony about the impact of the proposed pipeline on people's lives, First Nations' societies, and the natural environment, particularly the Porcupine caribou herd. In 1977, Justice Berger concluded the inquiry by recommending:

> There should be no pipeline across the Northern Yukon. It would entail irreparable environmental losses of national and international importance. And a Mackenzie Valley pipeline should be postponed for ten years. If it were built now, it would bring limited economic benefits, its social impact would be devastating, and it would frustrate the goals of native claims.
>
> (BERGER 1988[1977]:28–29)

Since that time, a number of Berger's recommendations have been fulfilled. No large-scale pipeline was built to "provide a corridor across the Yukon for the delivery of Alaskan gas and oil to the lower 48" (Berger 1988[1977]: 19). In 1980, the United States designated and protected much of the area of the North Slope of Alaska to the west of the Old Crow Flats as the Arctic National Wildlife Refuge, although successive American administrations have threatened to open the area to oil and gas development. In Canada, a number of comprehensive land claims and other kinds of agreements have been initiated with First Nations. In the Yukon, the Yukon First Nations *Umbrella Final Agreement* took effect in 1993, and agreements with individual Yukon First Nations were negotiated and a number of northern parks and protected areas have been created.[2]

Although Berger's recommendation that no pipeline be built across the northern Yukon offered the Porcupine caribou herd protection in Canada, the very survival of the herd has been imperilled from another quarter in the past three decades. Oil companies in the United States and Canada discovered deposits in the Beaufort Sea and Prudhoe Bay, and they made plans to develop oil reserves beneath the caribou calving grounds. Development is feared because the far north is fragile, with few species and very long time periods required for the often frozen land to heal itself. The risk to the caribou is great and there is nowhere else for them to go, no earthly way to repair the damage if their habitat is harmed. Van Tat Gwich'in (and their Gwich'in neighbours) continue to rely on the caribou as high-quality food and as essential to their cultural survival. Given that all imported foods are transported by air at great cost, they stress that their ability to continue to live on their lands into the future is inextricably linked to the survival of the Porcupine caribou herd. This has been expressed by Van Tat Gwich'in elders and leaders for decades in their efforts to protect the caribou. In Canada, as part of the comprehensive claim that Gwich'in and other First Nations negotiated with the federal government, Vuntut National Park and Ivvavik National Park were established in part to protect part of the herd's range. These national parks border on the Arctic National Wildlife Refuge (ANWR) in Alaska and together comprise a large preservation area. However, this move to protect the caribou's sensitive calving grounds on the North Slope of Alaska was put into jeopardy when some of the restrictions on petroleum development in ANWR were loosened in the Reagan years, and again by the government of George W. Bush in the early 2000s. Van Tat Gwich'in conservation and lobbying efforts continue.

Comprehensive claims agreements in the Canadian North are closely tied to the development of parks, protected areas, and heritage conservation. In the northern Yukon, Ivvavik National Park and, more recently, Vuntut National Park have been established, and Rampart House and LaPierre House historic sites are co-owned and co-managed by the Vuntut Gwitchin First Nation and the Yukon government under the terms of the *Vuntut*

Gwitchin First Nation Final Agreement of 1995. As well, through this agreement a number of "Special Management Areas" within Van Tat Gwich'in traditional territory, such as the Old Crow Special Management Area, were designated (Canada et al. 1998). In addition, part of the Fishing Branch River area was established as the Niinlii Njik Protected Area under the *Yukon Parks Act* and the *Wildlife Act*.

A necessary component of the protection of Van Tat Gwich'in traditional lands, heritage and culture, co-management with national and territorial agencies, and First Nations self-governance is the collection and preservation of the rich oral history and knowledge of the Van Tat Gwich'in about the enduring relationship between their people and their lands.[3] To that end, the Vuntut Gwitchin First Nation negotiated support through their *Comprehensive Claim Final Agreement* (signed in 1993 and in effect in 1995) and the establishment of Vuntut National Park to embark on a major four-year project to document their oral history of their lands.

In a community meeting in January 1999, Old Crow elders and community members discussed their priorities and concerns about the oral history project, which were interlinked with their concerns about their people and lands. Elders described how the research should collect information about how they lived on the land and how the land should be looked after so that it could help the young people in the future because, they said, "there are hard times coming." They directed that the history be collected soon, while elders remain capable of sharing their knowledge. Elders emphasized that the land, water, and caribou are very important to Van Tat Gwich'in. They also stressed that the water remain clean and that Crow Flats be protected and used only with Van Tat Gwich'in permission. The caribou fences are also a concern as they are deteriorating and may soon be difficult to see. Elders suggested selecting one or two of them for preservation and protection, and involving youth in that project.

Other elders guided the vision of assembling their oral history by sharing their views of how such efforts should be conducted. The information would need to be in both Gwich'in and English, to promote teaching the Gwich'in language and to ensure the knowledge is easily accessible to those who speak only English. They felt it was important that young people be involved in collecting their oral history and that interviews should take place on the land as much as possible. Van Tat Gwich'in have been participants in other peoples' research projects about their lands and culture. This time, they said, Van Tat Gwich'in should have a central role in all facets of the research, its direction, conducting the research, and producing the end products, involving outside expertise only as needed to produce a professional quality study. They felt that Gwich'in oral history of the traditional lands should be taught in schools, as well as through other public education initiatives,

Van Tat Gwich'in Heritage Committee discussing place name research, 2006. (L–R) Robert Bruce Jr., Jane Montgomery, Marion Schafer, Mary Jane Moses.
[Megan Williams ©VGFN 2006]

and to facilitate education, books and other publications and videos should be produced. Many elders have been involved in other research projects, and some stated that they wished to protect their traditional stories from leaving the community and from outsiders, rather than community members, profiting from them.

Building on research going back to 1995, the Van Tat Gwich'in project to collect their oral history began in earnest, concurrent with the development of a management plan for a national park on an important fragment of their traditional lands. They sought the widely scattered tapes of interviews with their people recorded by a panoply of visitors over the decades, as well as photographs, film footage, and other sources of history from their elders, past and present. As well, they began systematically recording the history held by current elders, the last generation to have grown up and lived most of their lives on the land. Elders and Van Tat Gwich'in researchers, directed by the VGFN Heritage Committee, journeyed to the most important locations on their traditional lands to conduct interviews and record them on audio tape, video, and in photographs. The result of these efforts

David Lord's family leaving for Crow Flats, April 1943.

[Yukon Archives, Frank Foster fonds 82/415 #308]

is a collection of over 300 audio tapes, meticulously translated into English for the benefit of young Gwich'in not fluent in their language, as well as non-Gwich'in. The collection includes an extensive video and photography archive, along with maps of Gwich'in place names, trails, locations of camps and villages, and other significant places.

The Van Tat Gwich'in Oral History Collection is a treasure. The stories it contains are from four or more generations of Van Tat Gwich'in who were born in the century from the 1880s to the 1980s. The fascinating histories they relate are from their own experiences or those of their elders and span the 19th and 20th centuries. The stories they describe as "long-ago stories" take the history back centuries and even millennia.

The time-span is not the only, or even the most significant, attribute of the collection. Taken as a whole, the stories reveal a unique and compelling perspective. The language of the speakers is predominantly Gwich'in, and their cultural perspective—their narrative voice—is remarkably consistent and recognizable throughout the generations. This perspective affords a fascinating commentary on the events of their lives: how Van Tat Gwich'in

Introduction XXXV

approached the changes—and continuities—in life over the past two or more centuries. They reveal their thoughts about the people and events of their time, as well as their often surprising insights about ways of life that, increasingly, many people would have difficulty even imagining. Through this Gwich'in oral history, what emerges is not only a sense of the sweep of history and events of a people from ancient times to the present but also a detailed portrait of the people themselves. Moreover, the history that is told through Gwich'in oral accounts constitutes both chronicle and commentary on historical events, as well as a counterpoint to the writings of others about the Van Tat Gwich'in.

The history presented here is a representative sample of the oral history collection transcripts, which run to over 2,000 pages of transcribed, translated interviews. The heart of this work (the four central chapters) is drawn almost exclusively from the transcripts, and here the voices of generations of Van Tat Gwich'in emerge as directly as possible. The most significant modifications of their actual words are their translation into English. About 80 per cent of the interviews were originally in Gwich'in, and the English translations were a daunting task. There are considerable linguistic differences between the two languages. Gwich'in is an Athapaskan language structured primarily on verbs and modifiers, a tonal language without English-style pronouns to identify gender, and with regional variations and different forms of complexity, indicating change over time. To enhance their accessibility, the interviews have been excerpted and edited to downplay the interview structure, repetition, redundancy, and occasional lack of clarity stemming from references to shared experiences between elders and interviewers. As well, certain aspects of the Old Crow dialect of English have been transformed into standard English according to the desire of community heritage experts for the elders' words to be in proper English for clarity and to reflect the fluency of the original speakers in their own language. Throughout these transformations of the interviews, we have sought to preserve the original voices and intentions of the speakers. In general, we have found that the distinctiveness of each person's way of telling history remains recognizable in the translations.

Like any history, Van Tat Gwich'in history tells some stories in great detail. Others are more general and assume some knowledge of the Van Tat Gwich'in world on the part of the listener. As well, the sweep of the history—the time depth—is of a magnitude unfamiliar to most North Americans of non-Aboriginal origins. European-derived histories generally cast a few centuries past as familiar history, a millennium is more murky, two millennium Biblical, and three millennium ancient and archaeological. The European stories of even a hundred years ago often feature great upheavals and dislocations more than continuity. In the dark distant corners of their history, Europeans may have difficulty relating those who are the subjects of history as their ancestors except in a symbolic sense. For example, Greek and Roman cultures may be touted as important influences on European and North American culture by people who certainly would not claim Greek or Italian heritage. Distant history may more closely resemble what folklorists and anthropologists call origin myths, legends, or fables.

Van Tat Gwich'in history stretches back to the very distant past, although it is difficult to determine the actual age of particularly ancient accounts. However, from other sources of information, such as archaeology and geology, it is evident that people have lived in Van Tat Gwich'in territory on a continuous basis for tens of thousands of years, and ultimately people who can be positively identified as Van Tat Gwich'in ancestors existed in the same location over a millennium ago.

Historical Overview

The primary focus and bulk of this book is Van Tat Gwich'in history from their own perspective. The objective is to bring their views on their own past and culture to the foreground essentially without interruption or intrusion from other perspectives. Each individual Gwich'in oral historian presented a discrete segment of history, or a number of these in a series of interviews. When assembled, they reveal a larger picture like an exquisite patchwork quilt. Some of the accounts assume a certain level of familiarity with basic historical events on the part of the listener. Consequently, a brief historical overview taken from a number of sources, both from Gwich'in and outside researchers, is provided here as a guide and introduction to the Van Tat Gwich'in history that follows and to reduce the need for interruptions and clarification. The intention is not to diminish Van Tat Gwich'in authority by beginning with non-Gwich'in perspectives. Rather, this historical summary is intended to augment the context, chronology, and other information needed to weave together the many Van Tat Gwich'in voices into a readily comprehensible statement of their history.

In a 1992 report summarizing and discussing past ethnographic and archaeological research in the area, Sheila Greer and Raymond Le Blanc draw attention to the importance of Van Tat Gwich'in oral history while noting that most outside researchers did not base their work on it (although some researchers included aspects of oral history that pertained to their projects).

> The human presence in the Old Crow area has incredible time depth; the region has probably the longest record of human occupation found anywhere in Canada. Moreover, its aboriginal people, the Van

Page XXXIX: Annie Fredson and baby Roger Kaye.

[Corporal Kirk/Eloise Watt fonds #9 (VG1998-1)]

Tat Gwich'in, have maintained strong ties with the land, despite the changes they have faced in the past 150 years. These two situations, the great time depth and a vibrant aboriginal culture, present great opportunities for human history interpretation. There are many, many stories to be told about the region's past.

(GREER and LE BLANC 1992:4.1)

The major early written sources on the Van Tat Gwich'in are the reports of early explorers, traders and missionaries. The most extensive of the explorers and traders accounts are those of John Hardisty (1872), Strachan Jones (1872), William Kirkby (1865), and Sir John Richardson (1851). The Anglican missionary Robert McDonald (1869) developed a writing system in Tukudh (his spelling of Dagoo), the language of the Gwich'in of the upper Porcupine River, some of whom have intermarried and live with Van Tat Gwich'in. In 1898, McDonald translated the Bible and other religious materials into Dagoo (Tukudh), and his transcription system is still in use, along with a modern orthography. Other early visitors and researchers mentioned Vuntut and Dagoo Gwich'in as part of their documentation of neighbouring groups, such as the Oblate missionary Émile Petitot (1876, 1889).

Early studies by professional ethnographers of Vuntut and Dagoo were conducted in 1932 by Cornelius Osgood (1936), followed by Douglas Leechman (1949), Asen Balikci (1963), and Anne Welsh Acheson (1977). Geographers Robert McSkimming and John Stager conducted interviews into the effects of a proposed large-scale pipeline across the Northern Yukon in the early 1970s. In addition, a considerable body of research has been conducted with neighbouring Gwich'in, such as the work of Richard Slobodin (1962) with the Peel River Gwich'in (referred to as Kutchin), and Frederick Hadleigh-West (1963) and Robert McKennan (1965) with the Chandalar Gwich'in. Thus, by 1978 the Gwich'in were among the best-documented Aboriginal peoples of the western subarctic (McClellan 1981:40).

Van Tat Gwich'in have been referred to by different names in literature about them: Vantat or Vanta Kutchin, Loucheux, and, in older traders' and missionaries' journals, Rat Indians.[4] The word *Gwich'in* refers to the specific people. *Dinjii* is the Gwich'in word for "man" or "person," differentiating them from other northern Athapaskan speakers, such as those to the east where the word *dene* has the same meaning and is a term of cultural identity (for example, the Dene Nation). Van Tat Gwich'in constitute one of a number of regional Gwich'in groupings whose lands stretch into mid-Alaska and the Mackenzie Delta in the Northwest Territories (see pp. XXVIII and LVIII). Van Tat Gwich'in regularly associate with and intermarry into neighbouring Gwich'in regional groups. There are some differences in dialect between the groups, but linguistic differences are not nearly so great as with the other

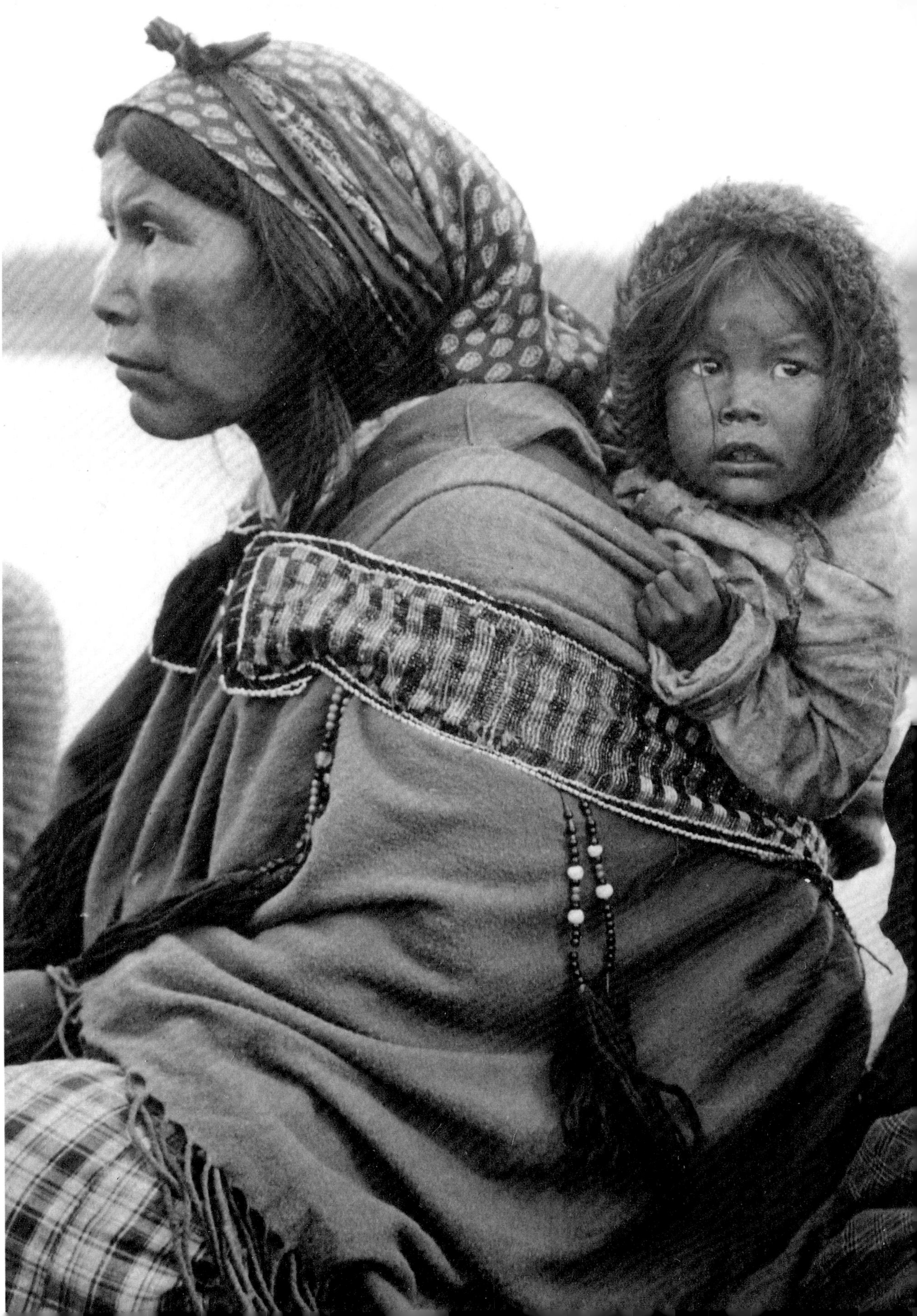

Athapaskan speaking peoples in the North, nor with the other language groups, such as the Inuvialuit to the north.

Archaeological investigations in the Old Crow–Northern Yukon area date from a more recent time, with research beginning about 1966 and continuing into the early 1980s, peaking with the Northern Yukon Research Program from 1975 to 1979 (for example, Richard Morlan 1973; William Irving and Jacques Cinq-Mars 1974; Raymond Le Blanc 1984). Many studies drew upon the aforementioned journals of explorers, traders, and missionaries. Archaeological research has pointed to great antiquity of occupation and use of the northern Yukon and has determined the area to be highly significant for reconstructing the cultural history of North America. As well, numerous more recent and historic sites have been investigated, such as dwelling sites and caribou fences and the trading posts at LaPierre House and Rampart House. These latter two fur-trading sites are co-owned and co-managed by the Vuntut Gwitchin First Nation and the government of Yukon department of Tourism and Culture. All activities at the sites, including research, building stabilization, and site interpretation are guided by a jointly developed management plan. They are set aside as historic sites under the *Vuntut Gwitchin Final Agreement* and are to be designated as Yukon Historic Sites under the *Historic Resources Act*.

To summarize, the primary perspectives and objectives of early researchers were to examine such themes as reconstructing Aboriginal Gwich'in culture (Osgood 1936), Van Tat Gwich'in adaptation to their environment (including ethnographic and archaeological research on caribou fences by A.M. Clark 1975; Irving and Cinq-Mars 1974; and Le Blanc 1984), cultural change caused by contact with Euro-Canadian society (Acheson 1977; Balikci 1963; McSkimming 1973; and Stager 1974), the antiquity of human habitation of the northern Yukon and its implications for the peopling of the New World (Irving and Cinq-Mars 1974; Harrington et al. 1975), related research on palaeoenvironments, questions of ethnicity in archaeological remains, and recording traditional stories and place names (Cruikshank 1990; Leechman 1949) (Greer and Le Blanc 1992; McClellan 1981).

Some oral history was collected in the course of these investigations, and part of this major research project brings together oral history from previous research to create a record of Van Tat Gwich'in oral history that is as complete as possible.

> For the fur trade and recent periods, there are a wealth of sources which should be tapped in order to assemble a more accurate understanding of how this land was used. In addition to the obvious government game harvest records, the most important and untapped data sources are the community's Elders. A program of land use history

research with these resource specialists is needed to document abandoned sites, key resources areas, harvesting practices and historically important landscape features.

(GREER and LE BLANC 1992:2.35)

Since Greer and Le Blanc's assessment, some oral history or traditional environmental knowledge research has been conducted with Van Tat Gwich'in elders, most recently on the use of the Dempster Highway area (Sherry and the Vuntut Gwitchin First Nation 1999). As well, Van Tat Gwich'in have documented aspects of their oral history and produced a number of publications (Josie 1966; Netro 1973; Te'sek Gehtr'oonatun Zzeh 1997). However, to this date, no comprehensive study has been undertaken to document Van Tat Gwich'in oral history of all of their traditional lands.

Van Tat Gwich'in history is reflected in the land. Their traditional land in what is now the northern Yukon and Alaska is a unique area of North America that geologists inform us was not covered by glaciers in the past when much of the surrounding country was encased in ice.[5] Consequently, the land surfaces in the Old Crow area are more ancient than elsewhere in Canada, where glaciers wiped the slate clean both figuratively and literally. Scientists have named the area "Beringia," which at one time included the land now submerged under the Bering Sea between Alaska and Siberia and extended as far west as the Kolyma River in Siberia. As well as a subcontinent-sized oasis in a sea of glaciers, Beringia was the home of dramatically exotic animals during the Pleistocene era, from scimitar cats to mammoths and mastodons, short-faced bears, giant beaver, moose, horses, giant bison, and camels.[6] Gwich'in oral history contains a very old and long story of the culture hero *Ch'ataiiyuukaih,* known as the Man who Paddled a Different Route or the Traveller, who fixed the animals so that they were as they are today, smaller and no longer a threat to humans (see *Ch'ataiiyuukaih* story, Chapter One).

The glaciers surrounding Beringia caused great changes in the land. At one time the Porcupine River flowed eastward through the Richardson Mountains at McDougall Pass to drain into the Arctic Ocean. This route was blocked by ice during the last glaciation, causing the river to back up and form a large lake that filled Crow Flats and the low area around Bluefish River. A similar ice blockage on the Bell River basin caused a large lake to form in the valleys of the Porcupine, Eagle, and Bell rivers. Farther south, the Peel River was blocked and a lake formed in its lower reaches (Hughes 1989; Morlan et al. 1990). Today, evidence of the lakes can be seen in the layers of sediments in the rock bluffs around Old Crow.

Gwich'in oral history tells stories of the flood.[7] E.E. Cass, a medical doctor who worked in the northern Northwest Territories and Yukon in

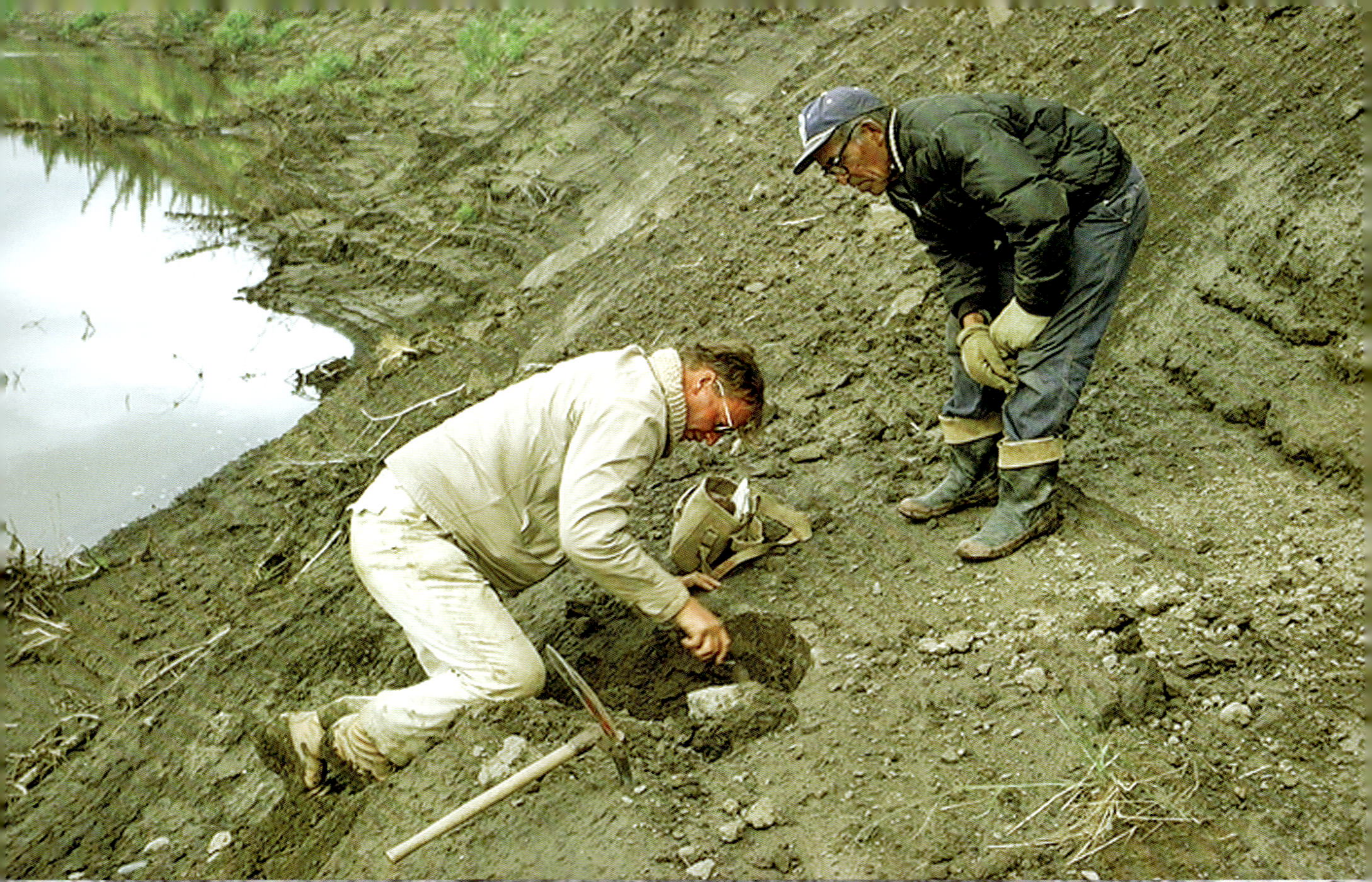

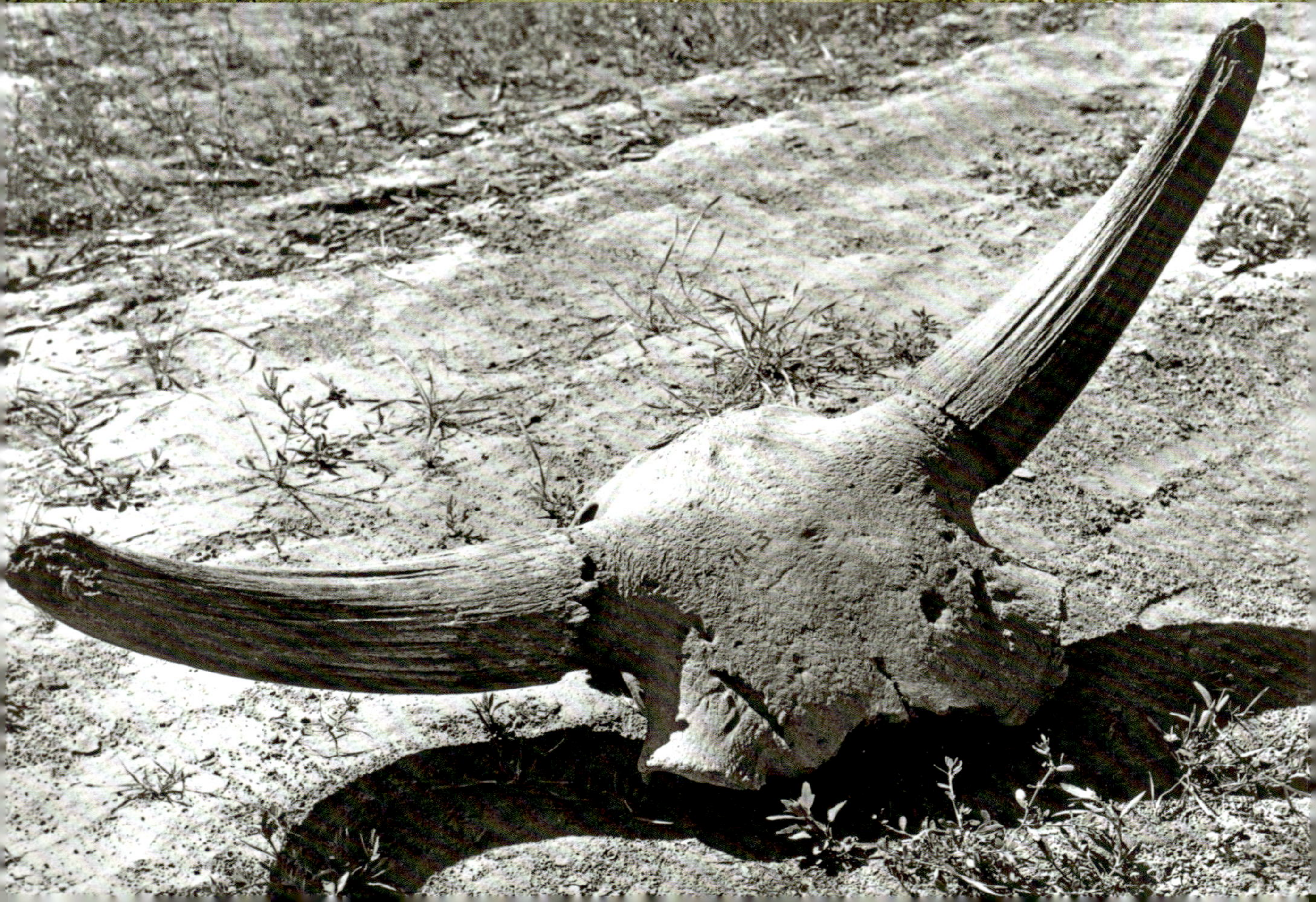

1958, recorded a description of a flood that includes a reference to the cause: melting glaciers (unfortunately she doesn't identify her source for this story):

Page XLII (top):
Palaeontologist C.R. Harrington of the National Museum of Canada and Charlie Thomas.
[Gerald Fitzgerald photo]

Page XLII (bottom):
Pleistocene bison skull, Crow River area.
[Yukon Archives, Richard Harrington fonds 85/25 #26]

This is the Loucheux story of the flood. The Loucheux say that many years ago, all the North of Canada was covered with ice, but one day, due to the heat of the sun, the ice melted and there was a great flood. Now one Indian had time to build himself a raft and he and his wife were on the raft, and they even had a little wigwam there. Many animals swam toward them and tried to get on the raft; they took as many as they could but they had to stop because of the danger of sinking. Now, among the animals who swam to the raft was the beaver, and the beaver saw a poor little ground squirrel who was clinging to a branch. The ground squirrel begged the beaver to take him on his back and the kindly beaver did so. There was also a large porcupine there and the porcupine also requested a ride but the beaver told him that he could not possibly take them both. However, the great big porcupine jumped on the ground squirrel's back and the little beaver was nearly submerged. He tried to argue but he couldn't, for if he had opened his mouth, he would have drowned. So with great difficulty, he managed to get to the raft. Now that is why the beaver has a flat back with no fat on it. All his fat is on his belly. And the ground squirrel is flattened above and below because he was on the beaver's back and he had the weight of the porcupine above him. The porcupine has no fat on his belly because he was resting on the ground squirrel and he only has fat on his back. Also they say that because the beaver and the porcupine are now such enemies, you must never, never go hunting the two of them on the same day because you will be unlucky.

The floodwaters still continued rising and rising and the man got very worried. So he called to the duck, and he said "Please, duck, will you dive—I know you can do so—will you dive as deep as you can and see if you can find any earth under the flood waters?" Well, the little duck did his best; he dived and dived repeatedly until he was exhausted. But he could not find any earth. Then the man turned to the muskrat and he said, "Oh, muskrat! I know you will help me if you can. We must do something about this. Do you think you can try?" So the little muskrat dived over the side and he stayed down a long, long time and everyone became very worried about him. Finally, he floated to the surface more dead than alive and they pulled him on the raft. And there in his little paw was a little bit of earth. The man revived the poor muskrat and then he took the earth in his hand and he molded it. As he started to mold it, the earth started to grow so that soon he could put it in the water. And when it grew sufficiently large, he landed the raft on it and he and his wife and the animals left the raft. The land went on growing until there was a big piece of land which is now northern Canada.

(CASS May 10, 1959:Tape 4)

Another such version, recorded in Fort McPherson just after the turn of the century, tells of the beginnings of life in the Old Crow area:

In the days when the earth was all covered with water, the animals lived on a large raft. The Crow said, "Had I any earth, even so little, I would make it grow large enough for all the animals to live upon." Muskrat, Otter, and many other divers went down under the waters and tried to bring up some earth, but they were all drowned. Last of all, Beaver dived with a line attached to his body. He went so deep that he was almost drowned when he reached the bottom. In his death-struggle he clutched some mud in his paws, and the mud was still there when he was drawn up lifeless by the line. Taking it and running his walking stick through it, the Crow planted the stick in the water in such a way that the bit of earth rested at the surface of the water. The earth grew larger and larger. When it was big enough to hold all the animals, they stepped from the raft. Crow's walking stick is still supporting the land; and, as it has never rotted, it is still to be seen somewhere about the junction of the Old Crow and Porcupine Rivers [the site of present day Old Crow].

(BARBEAU and CAMSELL 1915:253)[9]

Eventually (around 12,500 years ago) the volume of the lakes increased until they joined and the flow of water succeeded in cutting a channel to the west at the Ramparts on the Porcupine River to establish the modern flow of the river into the Yukon River drainage in Alaska (Schweger 1989:31).

Archaeologists have found remains of people's activities during this time, as well, and have been assisted in their research by Van Tat Gwich'in for many years. An early find in the Old Crow basin, the "Old Crow flesher," was the cause of controversy. Its darkly stained appearance was much like the remains of extinct mammoths and bison, from 33,800 to 22,600 years old, but was later dated to only about 1,000 years (Nelson et al. 1986:750). Archaeologists debated whether people lived in the area at such an early date. The archaeological remains that have contributed to the discussion are bones of mammoth, bison, horse, and caribou, which were modified by human hands by striking off flakes to shape and sharpen tools. These bones are about 40,000 to 25,000 years old and appear to have been modified or shaped by people while they were fresh. Similar patterns of breakage and flaking are not evident on bones older than 40,000 years, suggesting a hypothetical time period for the arrival of people into the area (Morlan et al. 1990:87).

After 25,000 years ago, the Old Crow basin was filled by glacial lake Old Crow and was uninhabitable. In caves in high country overlooking the Bluefish River were found the remains of people's activities, some of which may date to as old as 24,000 years ago. More interesting, the stone tool fragments, worked bone (including mammoth bone), and other debris in the Bluefish Caves are in their original context (except for some movement of the sediments due to frost), unlike many of the remains from the Old Crow basin, which have been moved and redeposited by erosion and river action. The Bluefish Caves and other similar caves in the Ogilvie and Bear Cave Mountain areas are exciting sources of information about ancient ways of life, as well as early environmental conditions and extinct animals (Cinq-Mars 1979, 1990). Van Tat Gwich'in are familiar with archaeological remains at Bluefish Caves and other areas through many years of assisting with the research and taking an active interest in its interpretation.

Traditional Gwich'in stories refer to creatures, such as the giant beaver, (Cass 1959:Tape 7; Greer 1989:88) that don't exist today. As mentioned previously, the Gwich'in culture hero *Ch'ataiiyuukaih* is understood to have rid the land of dangerous animals, making it safe for humans. He also is credited with giving the modern-day animals their dispositions and habits. Stories, such as those of the flood and *Ch'ataiiyuukaih,* suggest that Gwich'in were aware that the animals and land underwent significant changes in the past.

Following the time of the last glaciers and glacial lakes, from 12,000 to 7,000 years ago, some of the large animals later to become extinct may still have been available for people to hunt, such as mammoths, horses, bison, and elk (Harrington 1989). Archaeologists have found the remains of a number of different kinds of tools in the Van Tat Gwich'in area and have given the different tool styles various names, such as Northern or Arctic Cordilleran (dated to 7,000 to 8,000 years ago) and the Palaeo-Arctic Tradition (7-8,000 to 3-4,000 years ago) (Gotthardt 1990). Archaeologists aren't certain who may have made Palaeo-Arctic tools and who their descendants (if any) might be. They caution that it is extremely difficult and risky to try to determine ethnicity from material remains, such as stone and bone tools and the ruins of living structures. However, tools from the next time period, 3,400 to about 1,250 years ago, may have belonged to the precursors of modern Inuit and "Indians" (i.e., unspecified Aboriginal people who are not Inuit). Sites of Inuit ancestors have been found north of Crow Flats and in the Rock River area. "Indian" precursors occupied places along the Porcupine River, not far

Daniel Fredson in skin boat with caribou.
[Yukon Archives, Father Jean-Marie Mouchet fonds 91/51R #34]

from Old Crow, and farther up the river at Rat Indian Creek. Archaeologists can't determine from the remains if the people were ancestors of Van Tat Gwich'in, another northern First Nation, or other peoples who left no descendants in the area. Like current Gwich'in, the people who lived in these places 3,000 to 4,000 years ago relied heavily on caribou (Irving and Cinq-Mars 1974; Gotthardt 1990).

Sites from the time period 1,250 years ago and younger are clearly identified as those of ancestors of Gwich'in.[10] For example, along the Porcupine River at *Tl'oo K'at* (above Old Crow) and upriver at Rat Indian Creek, artifacts of stone, bone, and antler (preserved by permafrost) are the same as those used by Gwich'in in the recent past, prior to adopting European manufactured goods. There are many similar details in both the oral history and archaeology of the past few centuries to a millennium ago, such as the descriptions of "moss houses," dwellings that pre-date canvas tents, and widespread use of log cabins. The remains of the animals Gwich'in of that time period were hunting were also preserved at these sites: primarily caribou, hunted in the springtime (Morlan 1973; Le Blanc 1984).[11]

The long-term importance of caribou to the Gwich'in is evident in oral history. Old stories, such as "Boy in the Moon," illustrate the dependence on caribou for survival (see Chapter One). Some stories emphasize the close link with the caribou through descriptions of people who transform themselves into caribou. In numerous other stories, hunting caribou is the background to the narrative, the way people were making a living while other events occurred. More recent historical accounts describe hunting methods, changes, unusual occurrences (such as how two old women at a fish trap accidentally come by a large group of caribou, see Chapter One), and other events that reiterate the ongoing relationship between Van Tat Gwich'in and the Porcupine caribou herd.

Caribou were not the only important resource, however. Crow Flats was a critical area for fish, waterfowl, moose, and muskrats, and was often resorted to in times of scarcity. Archaeological remains of these hunting activities have been found there, as well. Sites of fishing and muskrat hunting have been found in Crow Flats in later times, indicating continuity between historic and recent Gwich'in land use (Le Blanc 1997). As well, archaeological sites in Crow Flats show that in the past the area was used by peoples other than Gwich'in, such as Inuvialuit, which echoes Gwich'in stories of their history of living with neighbouring peoples.

Gwich'in describe their relations with a variety of people of other nations, such as their Hän neighbours (two current Old Crow elders speak Hän) and Inuvialuit to the north. Both Van Tat Gwich'in and Inuvialuit have used Crow Flats and the mountains to the north and have a long history of war and peace together. More recently, Gwich'in oral history chronicles accounts of the coming of strangers glossed as "white men," generally Russians, English, Americans, or Canadians of European extraction (see Grass Pants story, Chapter One), and of life thereafter. Just prior to the coming of traders to the Van Tat Gwich'in area was a period of movement and disruption due to various groups jockeying for position as middlemen in the fur trade, a widespread phenomenon (Slobodin 1963:23-26). There are numerous Gwich'in stories of hostilities with *Ch'ineekaii* (likely Inuvialuit of the Mackenzie Delta or Alaska), which, according to oral history, occurred prior to the coming of white men (see Moses Tizya's story in Chapter One).

Trade was not a new import of the European fur trade, but as everywhere else, Gwich'in traded with their neighbours. Exotic items traded into Van Tat Gwich'in country, such as native copper and non-local stone types were traded into Van Tat Gwich'in country and have been uncovered in archaeological excavations, as as at *Tl'oo K'at* near Old Crow, indicating that trade has been an important activity there over many millennia (Greer 1999:8).

*"A Loucheux dance."
Colourplate from an original sketch by Alexander Hunter Murray, 1848.*

Published in Richardson, Sir John, 1851 (in bibliography).

Before traders came to their lands, Van Tat Gwich'in travelled to distant posts to trade. Elder Moses Tizya tells of two such travellers: *Olti'* brought spears (likely iron spearheads) to his people by trading with *Ch'ineekaii*,[12] who in turn were trading with Russians, and this trade had negative consequences (see Chapter One). Later, *Khach'oodaayu'* journeyed up the Mackenzie River and brought metal tools, such as axes, chisels, and pots, which are remembered in a beneficial light.[13] Van Tat Gwich'in are reported to have been astute middlemen traders. Slobodin notes, "The 'Mountain Indians' who in 1826 violently resented the threatened competition of the British exploring party led by Captain (later Sir) John Franklin of the Royal Navy in their trade with the Eskimo (Richardson in Franklin, 1828:175 ff.) were Crow River or Porcupine River Kutchin" (Slobodin 1962:16).

The first non-Aboriginal traders on or near Van Tat Gwich'in lands were from the Hudson's Bay Company (HBC). John Bell reconnoitered the lower Peel area for the company in 1839 and established Peel River Post (later named Fort McPherson) on the Mackenzie River in the Northwest Territories in 1840, and for some time this was the nearest trading post for Van Tat Gwich'in. In 1845, Bell crossed westward into the Bell and Porcupine river systems as far as the junction with the Yukon River (Simpson 1845). Then in 1846, Alexander Murray built an outpost of Peel River Post at LaPierre House on the LaChute River (later moved to the Bell River in 1851–52 due to a shortage of wood), and at Fort Yukon in 1847 at the confluence of the

Yukon and Porcupine rivers (Coates and Morrison 1988:2). Murray's drawings of Gwich'in people, dances, and round houses, made at the request of his employer, have been reprinted often and serve as intriguing images of the people at that time. Murray was also charged with describing what he found at Fort Yukon, the country of Van Tat Gwich'in and their neighbours. Excerpt from Alexander Murray's *Youcan Journal*:

> On the 6th of July [1847] the "Letter Carrier," chief of the "Vanta Kootchin" (people of the lakes) arrived with twenty men. This Indian is well known at Peels River having visited that place annually since its establishment, he sent a message in the spring that he would meet me here [Fort Yukon] in the summer. They brought some dried meat, geese and babiche according as desired, but the object of their visit was principally to receive some ammunition for the summers hunt and to see where we were building. The Letter Carrier said this place was much more convenient for him and nearer his country than Peels River and he would prefer trading here if I wished it, he had a debt at Peels River but had furs to pay for it. I told him he was at liberty to trade wherever he chose, but that we had very little goods this year, and he could get no advances except in ammunition, and as there were plenty of Martens and Beaver in this country we would trade no rats at least for the present, but if he came here we would be well pleased, as we looked upon him and his people as our particular friends, etc. etc. What they brought was paid for in ammunition, tobacco, and knives, and a few of them only got credit although they all asked for it. The Youcon chief and his brother were here when the band arrived, and next day they had a bit of a row, which nearly ended in bloodshed: their quarrel was, as all their quarrels seem to be, about the women. One of the Letter Carrier's party had taken to wife a sister of the young chief, and he had heard that they had killed her. The chief demanded payment in beads for his sister's death, which was refused, and something said that insulted him, when he drew his knife and walked boldly up to the others, who would soon have cut him to pieces but for our intervention. A few words of explanation from an Indian Hunter, who was acquainted with the merits of the case, brought matters to a better understanding—the woman had not been killed, but was drowned in crossing a river by her canoe upsetting, the Letter Carrier made the brother a present of a large Esquimaux spear, valued ten skins, and friendship was again restored. They remained here four days during which time a party of Youcon Indians arrived and we witnessed some of their great dances, and gymnastic games between the two parties: such a dancing and singing, leaping and wrestling,

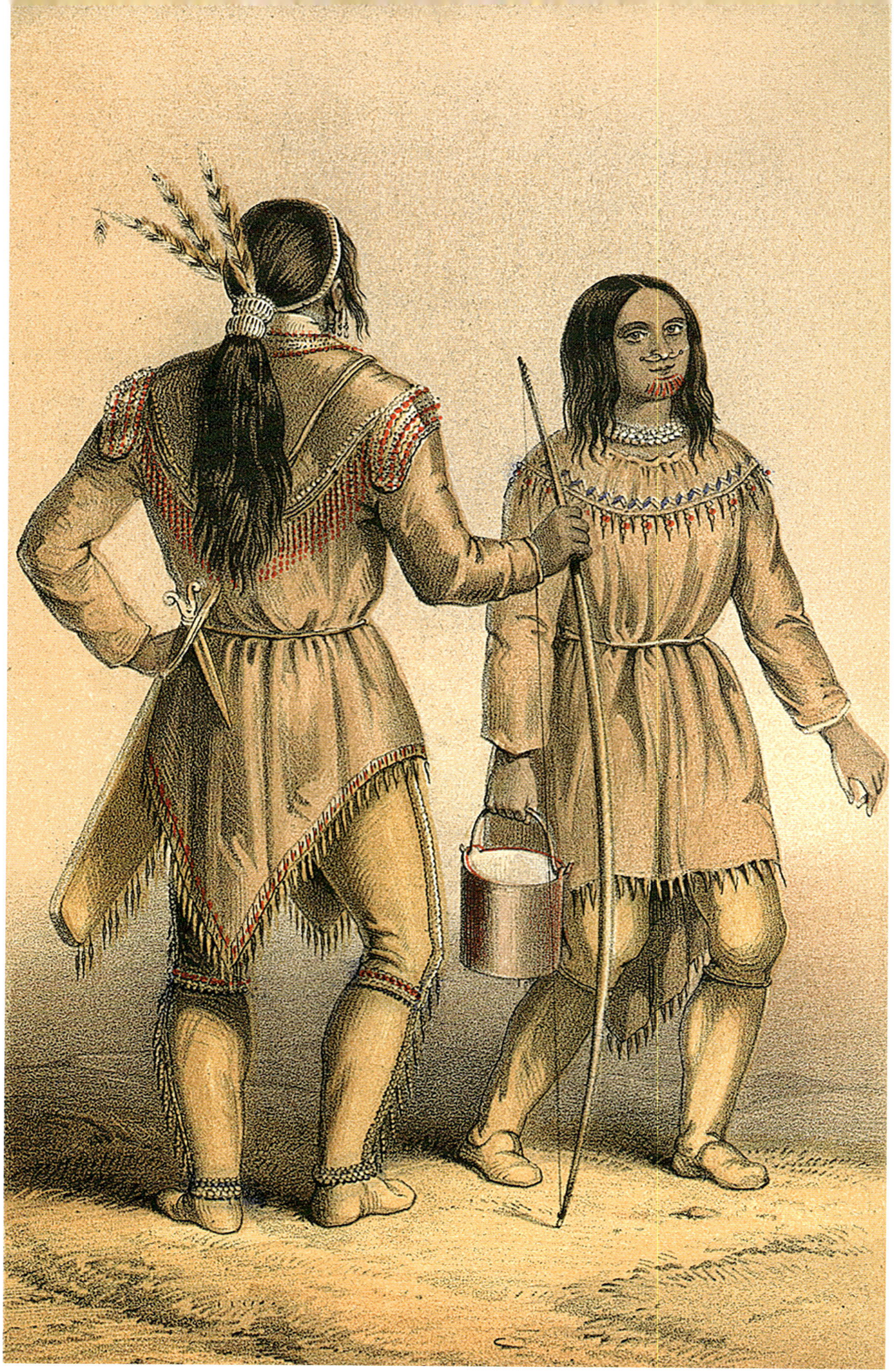

whooping and yelling, I have never before heard or seen. This was always persevered in all night and although amusing to us at first, by being continued became very tiresome, we could not sleep at night for the noise they made, although requested by the men, I would not ask them to desist in case of giving offense: these people consider it the greatest treat they can give us, by carrying on their games in our camp, they said they had not been so happy for many years. We were heartily glad when they all left, and allowed us to enjoy peace and quietness for a few days. No more of the Rat Indians (as the men of the lakes are called at Peels River) arrived until the beginning of August..."

(MURRAY 1910[1848]:56–58)

Above: Sketches by Alexander Hunter Murray, 1848.
Page L: Colourplate based on Murray's sketches, published in Richardson, 1851.

Sketches: Murray 1848;
Colourplate: Richardson 1851

Murray found Fort Yukon was a hotly contested location, not only between rival Gwich'in groups but also between the Russians and the British (Hudson's Bay Company). He feared the Russians might attack the fort with cannon to drive out the competition (Murray 1910[1848]:97). As it turned out, it was a different nation that expelled the British. The Americans purchased Alaska from Russia in 1867, causing a series of eastward moves of the Hudson's Bay Company's Fort Yukon post. In 1869, Fort Yukon was abandoned and James McDougall built Howling Dog Post at the foot of the Ramparts on the Porcupine River (also the first location to be called Rampart House).[14] A year later, it was moved, the buildings left behind were burned, and the company established Rampart House near the mouth of Salmon Trout River, which became known as Old Rampart House once U.S. surveyors found in 1889 that this post, too, was on American ground, engendering yet another new post.[15] In 1890, (New) Rampart House was established on the upstream end of the Ramparts at the mouth of Shanaghan ("Old Women's") (Sunaghun on maps) Creek, just east of the border (Coates 1982).[16] Gwich'in gave the name *Jiindehchik [Gindèh Chik]* to their camp near this location (Van Tat Gwich'in Place Name database 2005).

Initially, Gwich'in did not take up fur trapping for trade as a major economic activity. Both Gwich'in oral history and traders' and missionaries' records report that early HBC traders had very few goods to barter: some tobacco and tea, pots and muskets. It wasn't until other traders arrived much later that a wider selection of goods was available. In the early trade, Gwich'in supplied mainly meat and a few furs. In Murray's time, traders weren't interested in muskrat fur, valued less than the preferred beaver and marten, due to prohibitive transportation costs at remote posts (Murray 1910[1848]:57).

Trade between the Gwich'in and the Hudson's Bay Company followed the system developed for much of this area of the North. Gwich'in "trading chiefs"—high status and wealthy—interfaced between their people and the traders (Slobodin 1981:522). Early Gwich'in trading chiefs were shrewd and

Introduction LI

demanding traders who knew what goods they wanted in trade and took advantage of rivalry between HBC and Russian traders. After one trading session, Murray reported:

> Settled with the indians [sic] after breakfast & had some trouble to satisfy them. *Beads, Beads* is all they cry and we have none to give.[17] These Gens du Fou are the most unreasonable fellows to trade with that I ever came across. They say as we have not what they want it is unlikely that the band will come here this fall as they can always get what they want from the Russians. As for cloth and capot they will have none of them. Beads, Axes, Knives and Guns we must hereafter have in plenty, or there is no use trying to compete with the Russians.
>
> (MURRAY September 21, 1947)

A number of HBC traders, and later trappers, missionaries, and NWMP-RCMP, married Gwich'in women, and the surnames of their descendants recall this period of history. For example, while Andrew Flett was a trader at LaPierre House in 1864-65, he married Mary Flett, who was Gwich'in. Their son, William Flett, was later the factor at Fort McPherson. In 1880-84, John Firth traded at LaPierre House and also married into the Gwich'in community.[18] He later took over Old Rampart House and then the new Rampart House, which closed in 1893. He then moved to Fort McPherson (Greer 1999:24). In the Old Crow area there are numerous descendants of marriages, such as that between Archdeacon McDonald and Julia Kutug (described below). Descendants of families of traders, such as Robert Bruce, Victor Peterson, and Ab Schaeffer, and former NWMP Harold "Jack" Frost and Archie Linklater continue to live in Old Crow.

The area was also competitive ground for the churches. Stories of religion, specifically Anglicanism, occupy a prominent place in Van Tat Gwich'in history. In the 1860s, the first Christian missionaries came to LaPierre House, both Roman Catholic Oblate Father Seguin and Church of England Reverend Kirkby. Kirkby continued west to Fort Yukon, while Seguin remained at LaPierre House to establish the first parish in the Yukon: St. Barnabas Mission (Duchaussois in Vyvyan 1998:277). The Anglicans ultimately prevailed in the northern Yukon and among Gwich'in in the Northwest Territories with the exception of Arctic Red River (Tsiigehtchic), where the Oblates of Mary Immaculate were ascendant (as they were along the Mackenzie River from Tsiigehtchic south).

The Church Missionary Society, part of the evangelical element of the Church of England, sent Anglican missionaries to the North armed with the policies of the day. The prevailing philosophy emphasized individual

Archdeacon Robert McDonald and his sons (Neil on right).

[Yukon Archives, Anglican Church of Canada General Synod fonds]

salvation and strove to put Christianity at the centre of Aboriginal life. Henry Venn, secretary to the Church Missionary Society, promoted a policy of respect for Aboriginal culture, the appointment of Native catechists (lay readers), and translation of the Bible into Native languages (Coates 1991:116–17).[19]

The missionary with the most lasting legacy for Van Tat Gwich'in was Reverend (later Archdeacon) Robert McDonald. Known to Gwich'in as *Giikhii Danahch'i* (Old Man Minister), he was of Métis heritage from St. Andrew's parish in the Red River Colony of Manitoba. He arrived in Gwich'in country in 1862 and travelled extensively between Fort Yukon and Fort McPherson. Over his forty years in the area, McDonald translated the Old and New Testaments, Book of Common Prayer, and a hymn book into Gwich'in, and he deputed a network of Gwich'in lay readers and catechists, many of whom were Gwich'in leaders. In 1877, he married Julia Kutug, a Gwich'in woman from Fort McPherson, and their descendants are among the elders who contributed to the Van Tat Gwich'in Oral History Collection (Slobodin

Introduction   LIII

Page LV (top):
Traders in the Van Tat Gwich'in area, 1930s-1940s. (L-R) Frank Foster, Reuben Mason, Harry Healy, Joe Netro, Harry Strom, Waldo Curtis, Bill McAuley.
[Corporal Kirk/Eloise Watt fonds #36 (VG1998-1)]

Page LV (bottom):
International survey parties setting out for Fort Yukon, September 9, 1911.
[International Boundary Commission]

1962:25; Sax and Linklater 1990; Van Tat Gwich'in Oral History Collection). McDonald was not the lone Anglican cleric in the area. As well as the lay readers he trained, he was joined for a time by his colleagues W.C. Bompas (in 1865) and I.O. Stringer; both later became bishops (Cody 1913:20).[20]

Oral history and missionaries' writings both record changes brought about through contact with outsiders. Moses Tizya reported that a scarlet fever epidemic occurred the year McDonald arrived, one of a series of epidemics that significantly reduced the population (Vuntut Gwitchin First Nation 1995b). As well, the missionaries immediately set about encouraging Gwich'in to abandon polygamous marriages and their belief in their medicine men, refrain from work on Sundays, and adopt regular worship.

The system of trade at LaPierre House and Rampart House, at the farthest reaches of the Hudson's Bay Company's far-flung network, moved traders, goods, and missionaries up and down the Porcupine River and over the mountains to Peel River (Fort McPherson). The setup was drastically altered in 1893. That year, due to competition from whaling ships at Herschel Island and middlemen Inuit and/or Inuvialuit traders, the Hudson's Bay Company closed both LaPierre House and Rampart House and quit the area (Ingram and Dobrowolsky 1989:148-149). Van Tat Gwich'in were left without a post in their territory and travelled for trading and supplies to posts in American territory on the Yukon River, to the Hudson's Bay post at Fort McPherson on the Mackenzie River, or to Herschel Island in the Arctic Ocean. There American whaling ships overwintered from 1890 until the crash of the whalebone industry in 1907, although some former whalers and whaling captains returned to trade at posts on the Mackenzie Delta until 1928 (Bockstoce 1986:338).

The hiatus in convenient trading opportunities for Van Tat Gwich'in ended with the dramatic influx of people and goods flocking into the Dawson area to seek their fortune in the Klondike Gold Rush (1897-1910). During this time, Dagoo traded at Dawson or Eagle, Alaska. In 1903-04, they were joined by Vuntut and Teetl'it Gwich'in, Hän, and Tutchone to hunt caribou to supply Dawson and at the mouth of the Firth River to trade with Herschel whalers (Slobodin 1962:31).

Some of the men who "rushed" to the Klondike remained in the northern Yukon to try their hands at trapping or trading, while others were drawn to the area specifically by attractively high fur prices early in the 20th century. In 1904, the year Archdeacon McDonald retired to Winnipeg, Dan Cadzow opened a store at Rampart House and remained in business there until his death 25 years later (Netro in McClellan 1987:285). Others who trapped in the area had their names attached to local geographical features: Rube and Billy Mason and his wife Shirley, David Lord, Ab Schaeffer, Andy Johnson, Paul Nieman, and Nap Norville. Some, such as Archie Linklater, David Lord,

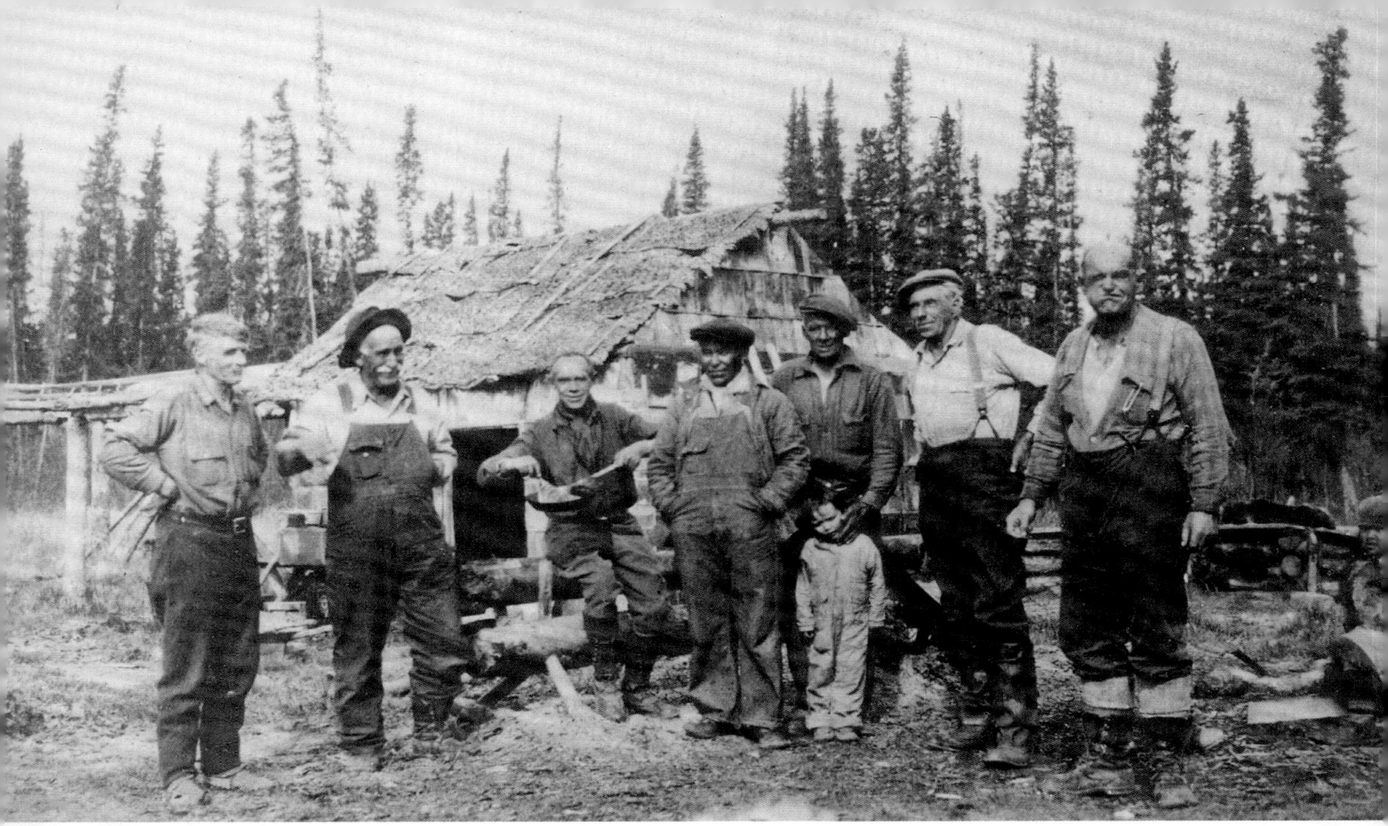

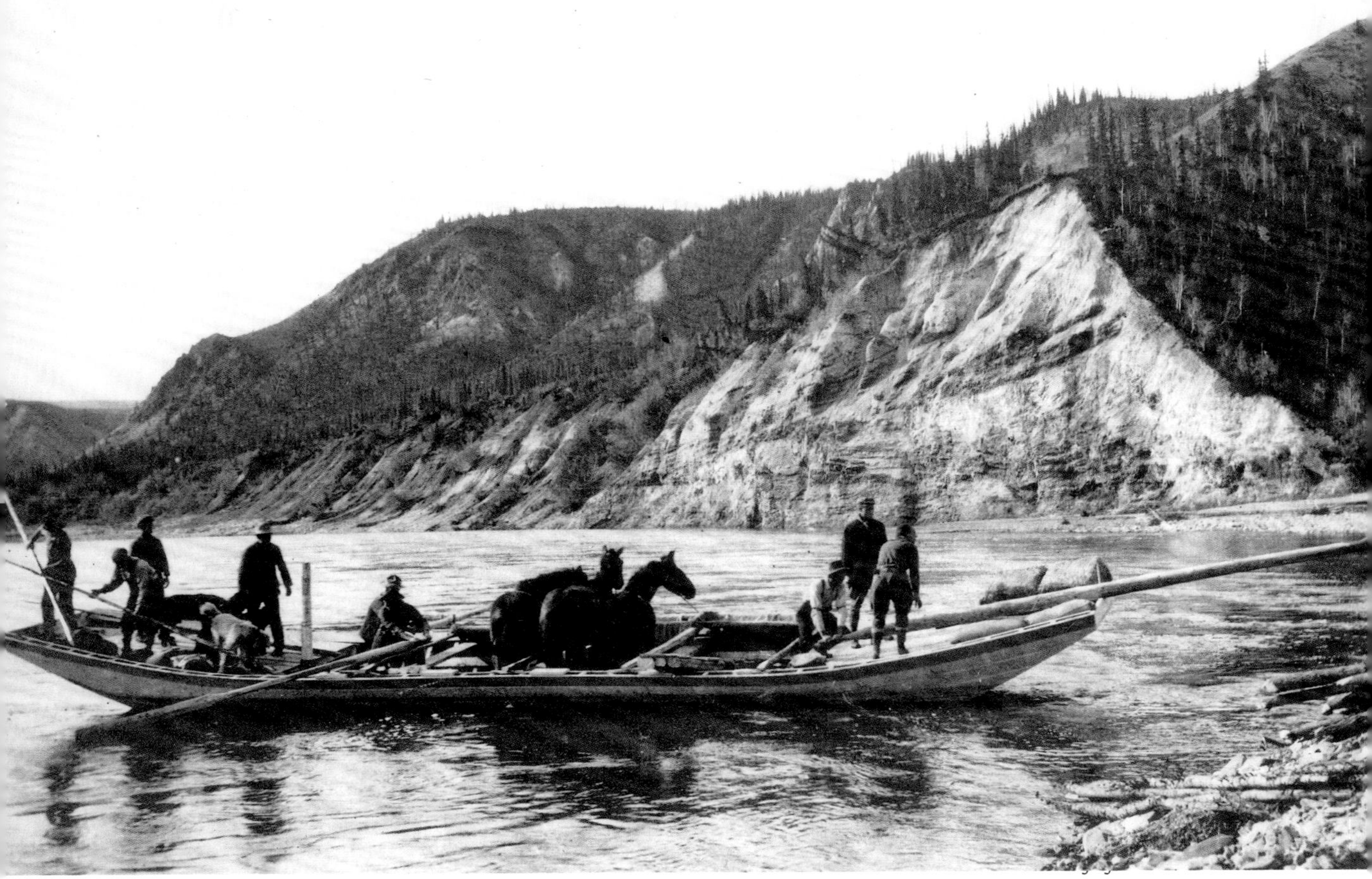

The first airplane to land in Old Crow, ca. 1920.

[Yukon Archives, Bob Sharp fonds 82/326 #6]

and Harold "Jack" Frost, married into Gwich'in families. According to Van Tat Gwich'in oral history, relations with non-Gwich'in trappers and traders were predominantly amicable but for a few problematic situations: certain areas were trapped out, due at least in part to use of poison bait by outsiders, and the influx of trappers put pressure on some areas and strained Gwich'in management practices. Gwich'in trapping was compromised by encroachment on their areas and rare instances of conflict (for effects of problematic trapping practices, such as use of poison bait, see oral history in Chapters Two and Three; McCandless 1985:101, 105, 123).

In 1911, the International Boundary Survey sent a survey party of 105 people and 166 pack horses to Rampart House to extend the survey of the U.S.-Canada border on the 141st meridian. The party arrived equipped with supplies and a doctor who diagnosed some form of disease after a young Gwich'in girl became ill. Smallpox was suspected and a quarantine station was set up on an island by Rampart House. The Canadian government brought in vaccine and medical supplies and conducted widespread vaccinations. Gwich'in oral historians relate being quarantined on the island and their dwellings and possessions being burned, which caused additional hardship. The epidemic ran all winter and into the following spring, and 22 people were quarantined on the island. In April of 1912, the epidemic was declared over and the hospital was then burned to the ground (Riggs 1945:41-42). In all, one infant died and there is some dispute about whether

Launching boats, Old Crow, May 23, 1946. (L–R) James Francis, Peter Charlie, Frank Foster, John Charlie.
[Yukon Archives, Frank Foster fonds 82/415 #302]

the disease was smallpox or chicken pox (see Chapter Two). The longer term effect of the boundary survey, disease, and burning of cabins was that some people chose to rebuild their seasonally used homes in the traditional fishing and hunting locale of Old Crow rather than at Rampart House, in part because of newly restricted access to their traditional territory on the Alaskan side of the border. This was an important consideration given Gwich'in were not sedentary but made their living throughout their traditional lands at this time. Later regulations and duties served as a significant impediment to freely crossing the line that bisected their lands (Netro in *Te'sek Gehtr'oonatun Zzeh*, Students 1997).

Around 1917, muskrat fur prices began to climb, except for a brief slump after World War II, from 40 cents in 1914 to an all-time high of $4.00 in 1945 (for analysis and summary of fur price trends, see Slobodin 1962:38–39). This created great interest in spring muskrat hunting in Crow Flats, already a common traditional activity. In 1917, the federal department of Mines and Resources established a muskrat trapping season in 1917 from March 1 to June 15. Winter trapping for fine furs, such as marten, mink, lynx, and fox, continued in the upper Porcupine area by Whitestone Village and Johnson Creek Village, drawing both Dagoo and Teetl'it Gwich'in (Fort McPherson people). From the 1920s to 1935, independent Canadian traders, brothers Jim and Frank Jackson, operated a store at LaPierre House. Marten trapping was important at Johnson Creek Village and downstream along the

Introduction LVII

MAP 2 *Van Tat Gwich'in Homeland*

Chief Peter Moses wearing British Empire Medal, and wife Myra, August 19, 1946.

[Canadian Museum of Civilization, photo D. Leechman 1946 #100601]

Porcupine through the 1930s and 1940s. Small settlements were strung along the Porcupine River, from Rampart House to Bluefish River, Old Crow, David Lord Creek, Salmon Cache, Johnson Creek, and Whitestone Village, as well as LaPierre House (Sarah Abel in Vuntut Gwitchin First Nation 1995a:77; Greer 1999:27).[21] As well, during this time Van Tat Gwich'in entrepreneur John Nukon had a store for a few years at Whitestone Village. The affluence of this period for Van Tat Gwich'in trappers enabled an expression of their generosity that was international in scope. Chief Peter Moses collected a sizeable donation to assist World War II war orphans in England, for which he later received a British Empire medal from the British government.

Against the richly recalled backdrop of many Gwich'in families and white trappers (some with families) busy throughout the land trapping, travelling, and trading, one of the more dramatic events of the early 20th century occurred. Albert Johnson, the "Mad Trapper of Rat River," was accused of interfering with other trappers' traplines and subsequently shot the RCMP officer sent to investigate. News of the ensuing manhunt and its end not far from Old Crow was spread across the North by newly available radio technology, and the suspense, fear, and after-effects are well-remembered (see Chapter Three) and spawned a number of published accounts, as well (Anderson 1994; Downs 2000; Kelley 1972; North 1972).

Introduction LIX

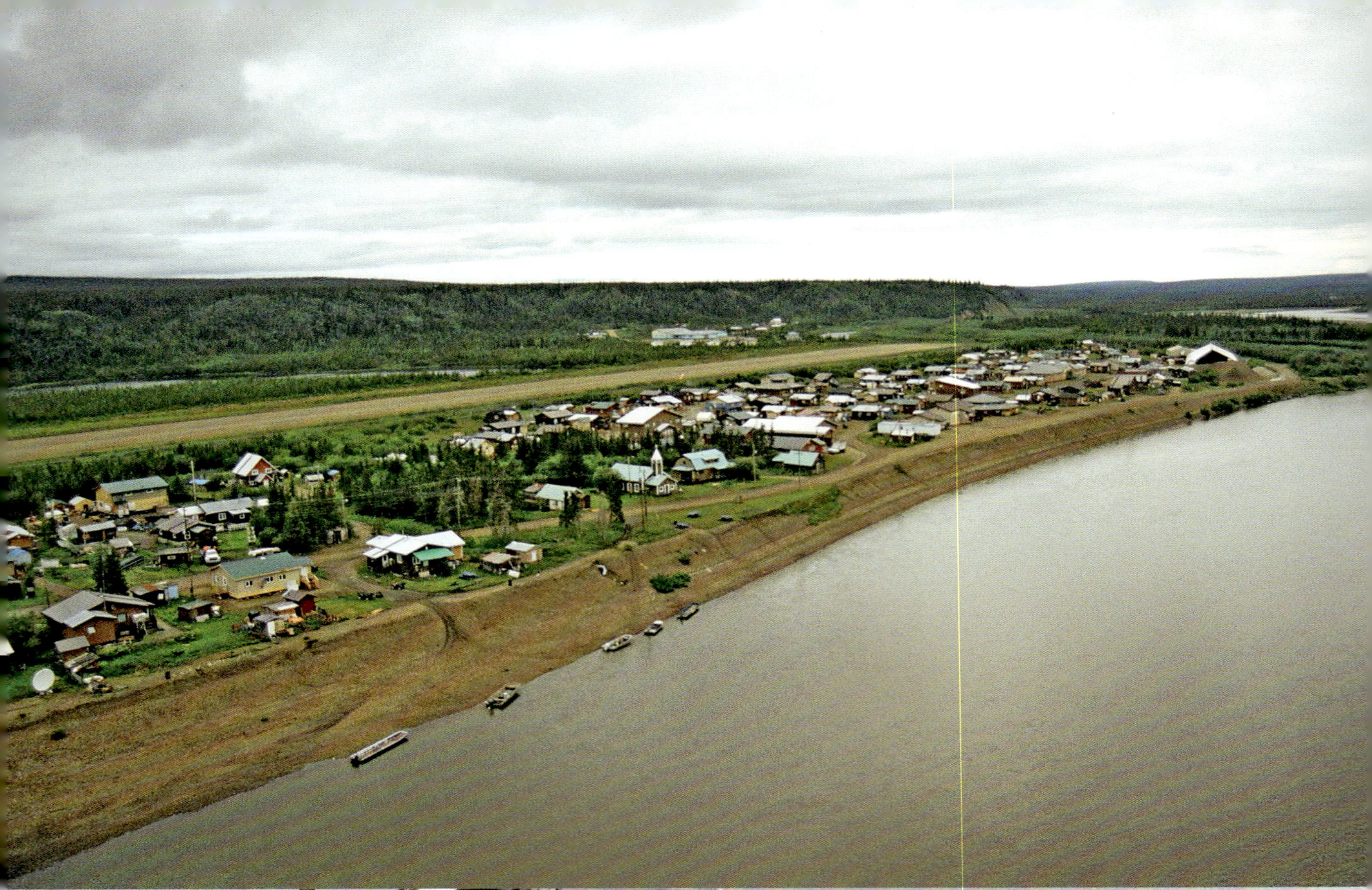

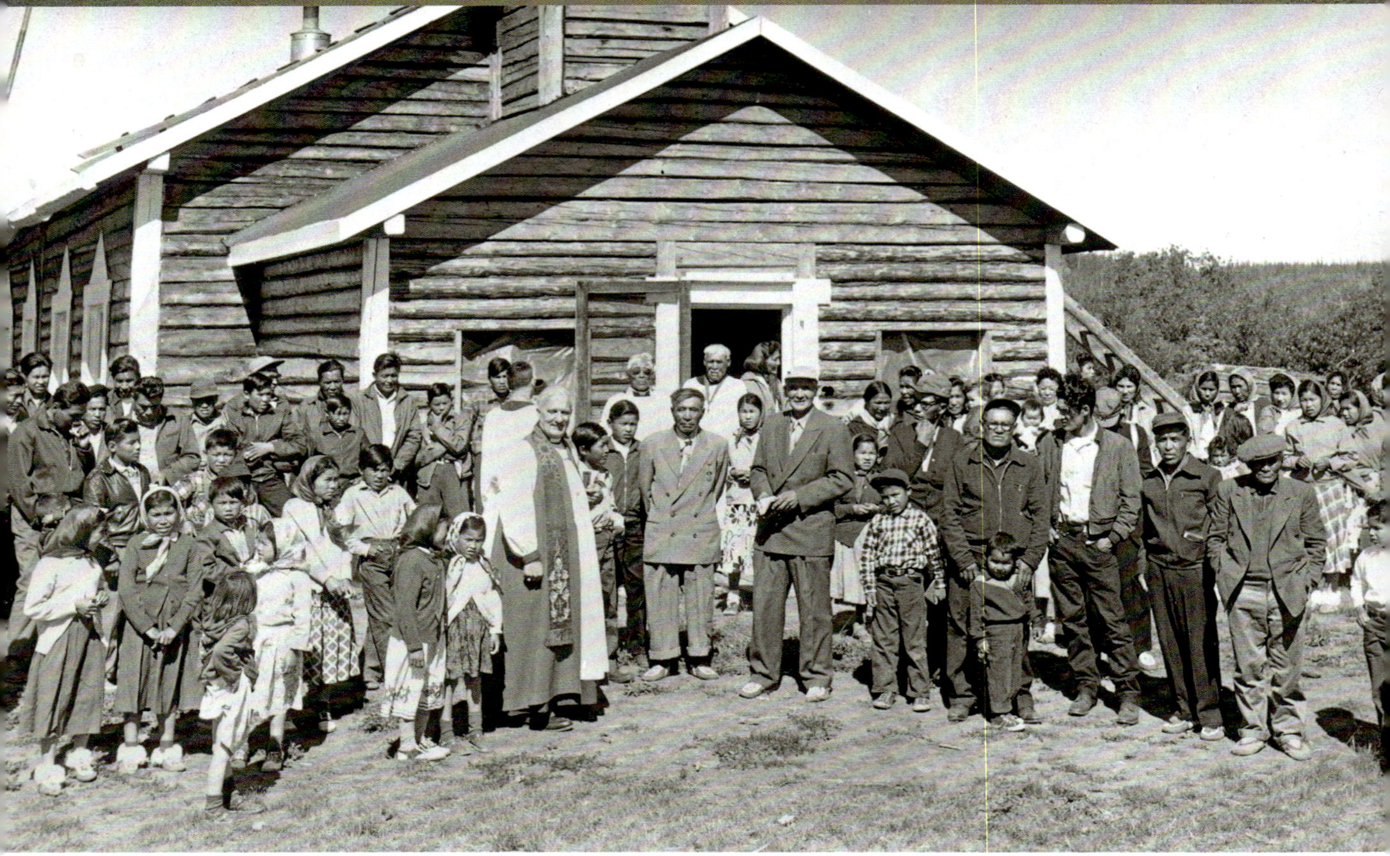

Page LX (top): Old Crow on Ch'oodèenjik *(Porcupine River), summer 2005.*
[Shirleen Smith ©VGFN 2005 (VG2005-03-211)]

Page LX (bottom): Old Crow community after church, July 10, 1960.
[Yukon Archives, George and Margaret Hamilton fonds 89/38 #37]

During the first half of the 20th century, the seeds of the community of Old Crow were planted and gradually took shape. The junction of the Crow and Porcupine rivers had long been the heartland of Van Tat Gwich'in country, evidenced by the thousand-plus-year-old archaeological sites found nearby at *Tl'oo K'at* and *Dahah T'ee* (Caribou Lookout), and in Van Tat Gwich'in oral history. The location is said to be where the old chief, *Zzeh Gittlit* or Walking Crow, had his fish camp. John Tizya built the first house at the confluence of these rivers in 1905. In 1921, the Anglican Church moved to Old Crow from Rampart House, followed in 1928 by the RCMP detachment, which had been at Rampart House for 14 years (Thornthwaite, Yukon Archives 61-62). Trader Dan Cadzow died in 1929, and in 1940 his widow, Rachel Cadzow, the last resident of Rampart House, moved to Old Crow. As well, near this time the last residents of LaPierre House, the Chitzes, moved to Fort McPherson. In the late 1940s, Harry Healy operated a store in Old Crow, later taken over by a man named Phillip Diquemare. In 1950, the first day school was opened in Old Crow (as in many other northern Canadian communities) and the vagaries of the fur economy at that time (falling fur prices and rising commodity prices) prompted many Van Tat Gwich'in to move to town.[22] As well, by 1950 the country around Johnson Creek Village and Whitestone Village was "cleaned out" of fur and food animals, spurred by the influx of trappers from elsewhere: other Gwich'in trappers and white trappers who used poison overwhelmed the conservation and management practices of the people whose traditional territory it was (primarily Dagoo). The area didn't recover until late in the 20th century. Van Tat Gwich'in families living there moved to Old Crow, and Dagoo families dispersed between Fort McPherson, Old Crow, and Dawson (Alfred Charlie, personal communication, 2000). In the subsequent three decades, other services, such as a nursing station and airport, as well as electrical and water systems, were built in Old Crow.

In the 1970s, resource exploration and development, especially by the petroleum industry, came to the North. American companies actively extracted oil at Prudhoe Bay on the Arctic coast of Alaska, and a huge pipeline was proposed to bring Arctic petroleum to southern markets by crossing the Yukon east to the Mackenzie River and then south to join the continental pipeline grid. Van Tat Gwich'in, along with other northern First Nations, were immediately concerned about their lands and animals—particularly the Porcupine caribou herd. They participated in the Mackenzie Valley Pipeline Inquiry (Berger Inquiry) in the early 1970s, a process that influenced the federal government to negotiate and settle the *Yukon Comprehensive Claim Umbrella Final Agreement* in 1993 and led to the establishment of Ivvavik and Vuntut National Parks in the northern Yukon in the late 1990s.

Van Tat Gwich'in continue to use their lands from their homes in the community of Old Crow. Their diet revolves around caribou, fish, moose, and other local wildlife, as well as plants, such as berries, wild rhubarb, and various medicinal herbs. They trapped and hunted muskrats at Crow Flats and the area of lakes south of the Porcupine River from Old Crow well into the 1980s. Now, in addition to making spring trips to Crow Flats, people maintain camps for use at various times of the year along the Porcupine River. The land and animals remain central to Van Tat Gwich'in economy, culture, and identity. They strongly desire this connection to remain in the future.

The best source for their values, history, and culture are the Van Tat Gwich'in themselves. What follows in this book are Van Tat Gwich'in accounts of their history, first their "Long-ago Stories." This category of stories is based on material that the speakers did not witness nor hear about from someone who experienced the incidents first-hand. Rather, these stories are from a more distant, in some cases mythical, past. The stories grouped as *Yeeno dài' googwandak* are diverse, ranging across a spectrum of Western categories (legends, folktales, myths, parables, and ancient history). The stories that the elders have deemed most important to know are presented here. As well, "Long-ago Stories" gives the essential backdrop to the more recent history in the subsequent chapters, thereby enriching the overall picture of Van Tat Gwich'in and their history.

1 | Long-ago Stories
Yeenoo dài' googwandak

Contents

5   **THE NATURAL WORLD**
5   *Dzan, Tsèe hah*—Muskrat and Beaver
6   *Ts'ałvit, Deetrù' hah*—Loon and Crow
7   *Daatsoo, Trùh hah*—Mouse and Otter

8   **SUPERNATURAL EXPLOITS**
9   *Chyaa Zree Zhit Dhidii*—Boy in the Moon
12 *Ch'ataiiyuukaih*—Paddled a Different Route
17 *Shih Gwandak*—Young Man and Grizzly Bear
19 *Dinjii Dèe Ehdanh Ts'ałvit hah*—Blind Man and the Loon

21 **LEGENDARY FIGURES**
21 *Kò' Ehdanh*—Man Without Fire
35 *K'aiiheenjik*—Willow Man

41 **STORIES OF HEROIC ROLES AND ARCHETYPES**
41 *Shanaghàn*—Old Women
48 *Tr'iinjoo Vigwizhi' Goonlii*—Smart Woman

51 **LONG-AGO HISTORY**
51 War with the *Ch'ineekaii*
56 First Contact with Europeans: *Tl'oo Thał*—Grass Pants

Well, this story is from the old people, early days people. They tell that story to us. They carried the story here and there,...like a newspaper, just like newspapers. They carried this story from one generation to the next. That's how they know.

(MOSES TIZYA, August 20, 1979, VG2000-8-22:003-113, Gwich'in and English)

GWICH'IN LONG-AGO STORIES include a variety of kinds of narrative, from explanations of aspects of the natural and social world to exploits of people and beings with supernatural powers, and to adventures of legendary heroes and of Gwich'in ancestors and predecessors. The timeframe of long-ago stories is from ancient or indeterminate time to the time of early contact with Europeans in the early 19th century.

Here the category of *yeenoo dài' googwandak* (long-ago story) is used because it is the way Gwich'in elders identified these kinds of stories: an "emic" (internally imposed) category, to use the anthropological definition. It is interesting to note the variety of kinds of narratives Gwich'in categorize together, essentially all the oral forms produced prior to the speaker's direct observation of events or that reported to them by another eyewitness, such as a parent.[1] These stories are peppered with the expression "*akoo diginuu*" or "they say," denoting that they were passed on by generations of people prior to the specific individual from whom the speaker heard the story. *Yeenoo dài' googwandak* encompass folktales, myths, legends, as well as "long-ago history," and each of these analytical groupings have some bearing on history. The conventional definitions of each term are as follows. Legendary narratives are generally secular or sacred, occur in the present world, feature human characters, and are often considered factual and historical (such as, *Kò' Ehdanh*). Myths are usually sacred narratives that involve non-human characters, occur in an earlier world or a different world, and may be treasured as absolute truth (for example, the creation of the world). Folktales are secular, commonly happening outside of any time or place, involve human and non-human characters, and are regarded as fictional stories with entertainment or educational value (like "Loon and Crow") (Bascom 1965:3–20). In addition, Gwich'in include some "long-ago history," such as *Tl'oo Thał* (Grass Pants), the story of first contact with whites, in *yeenoo dài' googwandak*. These kinds of stories appear to be history that has been handed down repeatedly, coming to the elder narrating it not from a first-hand observer or as direct experience but through a chain of tellings, where the original observer may be far removed.

In total, the body of long-ago stories held in current Van Tat Gwich'in oral history includes a number of well-known stories that are icons of Gwich'in cosmology. They were handed down through generations, as Moses Tizya describes at the beginning of this chapter, and were essential stories every Gwich'in would know.

Among the extensive body of *yeenoo dài' googwandak* are some key stories that have been selected to represent those most widely known and to exemplify the different types of stories. Some of the original stories, such as the epics of the legendary figures *Kò' Ehdanh* (Man Without Fire) and *K'aiiheenjik* (Willow Man), are very long and likely would have been told over a number of episodes. While many stories are specific to the Van Tat Gwich'in area and people, others in the collection are told amongst many peoples across northern North America and reflect the interconnectedness of the people and their world. *Dinjii Dèe Ehdanh Ts'ałvit hah* (Blind Man and the Loon) is an excellent example, a tale that Craig Mishler describes as being diffused across cultures all over northern Canada, Alaska, Greenland, and portions of the western United States, dating perhaps to an archaeological site in Point Hope, Alaska, from the first few centuries A.D. (Larsen and Rainey 1948), and first published by Hinrich Rink in 1866 in a collection of Greenlandic stories recorded prior to 1828. In 1973, Mishler recorded a Gwich'in version from Maggie Gilbert of Arctic Village, Alaska, a community that, along with the Van Tat Gwich'in of Old Crow, is part of the Gwich'in Nation (Mishler 2003:50).

As discussed previously, aspects of some of the stories vary. In some cases, the precise identity of protagonists and antagonists differ between versions of the story, as well as a number of other alternative explanations. These variations will be noted and often provide interesting insights to Gwich'in history and culture.

Edith Josie writing her column, Here Are the News.

[Yukon Archives, Richard Harrington fonds 85/25 #3]

THE NATURAL WORLD

According to Gwich'in legend, there was a time when things were not as they are now. Certain animals did not exist, others had yet to move to their now familiar locations, and others have since altered their appearance and behaviour. These stories feature animals that can converse with each other and with humans and exhibit human behaviours and motivations.

***Dzan, Tsèe hah*—Muskrat and Beaver,** told by Edith Josie
The complex of hundreds of lakes and marshes north of the Porcupine River that makes up Crow Flats is a richly productive muskrat, fish, and waterfowl habitat. In the mid-20th century, Van Tat Gwich'in utilized Crow Flats as a rich source of muskrats *(dzan)*. Beaver *(tsèe)* live along the Porcupine River rather than in sparsely treed Crow Flats.

Beaver [*Tsèe*] was swimming up the river and the Muskrat [*Dzan*] was swimming down; they met each other. And the Muskrat told the Beaver, "I will go up. You rest here." And the Muskrat left. He was gone a long time. He climbed to the top of the mountain and looked around. It looked good. On the other side of the mountain there were lots of lakes, and across the [Porcupine] river there were lots of lakes. This story happened here in Old Crow. The Muskrat climbed to the top of Second Mountain and looked toward Crow Flats and across the Porcupine River. And then he came back down. "My feet are sore....I can't walk and I'm thirsty for water." He pretended that his feet were sore. "It's really no use. It's better that you go upstream. It's better upriver. There's no use to look for a place on the land." The Muskrat told the Beaver this.

And the Beaver swam upstream. Muskrat said he would stay and heal his feet there. While the Beaver swam upstream, he went back up the mountain and stayed in Crow Flats.

The Beaver was told to look for a place along the river, but the Muskrat decided to live in Crow Flats, across the river or wherever there is a lake.

(EDITH JOSIE, VG2000-8-18:024-047, Gwich'in)

Ts'aɬvit, Deetrù' hah—Loon and Crow, told by Stephen Frost Sr.
The story of Loon (*Ts'aɬvit*) and Crow (*Deetrù'*) explains the colouring of the two birds and also uses the common element of trickery.

This was told to me by my uncle John Moses several years ago. And Peter Thompson also told it to me other night. Maybe I'm not telling it exactly right but [I'll] try anyway.

They say the reason why, anyway how it starts:...Loon [*Ts'aɬvit*] and Crow [*Deetrù'*], one time they sat together and at first they were just like the seagull. They were all white. They said, "We should paint each other." So the Crow, he's first. So the Crow sat behind the Loon and the Loon face away from him and he painted that Loon really fancy. That's how come that Loon is fancy now, all different colours on its wings. And after he finished, he turned around looked at himself, "Oh, gee," he's really fancy. But he still didn't like that Crow little bit.

So it was his turn to paint that Crow. He told that Crow: "Sit in front of me, look that way, and don't look back. I'm going to paint you really fancy." So some charcoal there, he rubbed his hand in that. He took both hands, he just rubbed it right across that Crow, the whole thing, he made it black. Then he got scared so from there he jumped in the lake.

Stephen Frost Sr. at Black Fox Creek.
[Shirleen Smith ©VGFN 2001]

And that Crow turned around. He was mad but that Loon was gone.
Pretty soon that Loon came up in the lake over there. That Crow, he picked up a rock and threw it. It hit that Loon right on top of the head. That's why today yet that Loon has grey on top of its head. That is the end of this story.

(STEPHEN FROST SR., VG2000-8-19J, English)

Daatsoo, Trùh hah—Mouse and Otter, told by Edith Josie
The *Daatsoo* (Mouse) and *Trùh* (Otter) story describes how many members of the weasel family (*mustelidae*, which includes mink, marten, weasel, wolverine, and otter) came into being by emerging out of otter. The Mouse and Otter story is one of a series of stories about how the world was ordered so animals, such as otters, would no longer eat humans.

They both lived together. The Mouse [*Daatsoo*] had a tidy house but Otter [*Trùh*] was not very tidy. The Mouse kept clean. And they lived along the river together. Whenever they had a visitor, the female Mouse served them well, while the Otter would bring the visitor's canoe ashore and hide the canoe. And he killed the people.
A man came with a canoe. The Otter bossed the man around. The female Mouse gave the man pemmican made from roots, and

Long-ago Stories   7

meanwhile the Otter gave the man pemmican....The Mouse whispered to the man, "Don't eat that pemmican. It's made from humans." The man pretended to eat the pemmican, but he poured it into his coat. The Mouse served pemmican made from roots; they enjoyed it. And then the man wanted water. The Otter said, "I will get water for you." He started to go toward the river, but the man said, "I've never drunk river water in my life. When I was paddling down I saw a creek where I drank water." He started to walk up.

In the meantime the Mouse repaired the canoe. While the Mouse was sewing the canoe, [he said to] the Otter..."Up around the bend, there is the creek, go up there." While the Otter disappeared around the bend, the man put his canoe into the river and paddled away. The Otter came back but the man was paddling away. He dove into the river and swam after the man. He cried after the man and said, "my husband."

The man landed downriver where he hid his canoe in willow brush. The man killed a beaver and put the beaver beside himself and went to sleep. He woke up and heard a noise. He saw the Otter was roasting the beaver on a fire, and he had also tanned the beaver hide and hung it up.

The man got a long skinny dry willow and put the end into the fire....When it was hot, he put this hot willow up the Otter's rear end....It felt like something was chewing it. The man pulled it back out and it looked like something chewed it up. He had a skinny steel [rod] that he put into the fire. It got red hot. He put this into the Otter's rear end, and from his mouth came Marten, Mink, and Weasel. He rubbed ashes onto the Marten and said, "You be Marten." After that he did the same to the Mink. The Weasel came out and he said, "You be Weasel." When the Weasel ran the man hit it with charcoal and that is why it has black on its head.

The man took his pack, put the roast beaver in it and paddled away. The man killed the Otter but there are still otters around. The Mouse said to the Otter, "You killed humans. Don't ever kill humans again: only eat roots." This is what happened.

(EDITH JOSIE, VG2000-8-18:060-125, Gwich'in)

SUPERNATURAL EXPLOITS

Some of the longest and best-known Gwich'in stories feature a person who encounters challenges and resolves them utilizing his or her supernatural abilities or with the assistance of a being with supernatural powers. At times, a normal person is married to a supernatural one and thus encounters danger not only from the mundane obstacles of life but from the powerful spouse or fearful and suspicious neighbours. Such stories are commentaries on right and wrong ways to live and interact with others and are detailed discourses on interpersonal and intercultural relations and values.

***Chyaa Zree Zhit Dhidii*—Boy in the Moon,** told by Effie Linklater
Gwich'in see a boy [*chyaa*] with a dog and a sack when they observe the land forms on a full moon [*zree*]. How the boy came to be there is the subject of a story about caribou fences, sharing, and magical powers.

> Ah, the Boy in the Moon. One cold winter day, people were hungry and even starving. There was no meat or fish. A man with strong medicine tried to make the caribou come their way, but nothing worked.
>
> All the time, one small boy asked and asked, wanting to work with his medicine, but no one paid any attention to him. They thought that he was just a baby. Finally, however, a man decided to let the boy do as he wanted, just to see if anything would happen. The boy ordered a caribou fence to be built. After this was done, the boy told the men to set all their caribou snares in the fence, although there were no tracks of any kind to be seen. Five hundred or more snares were set in a single day.
>
> Then the boy split the men into two groups, one group to go one way and another group to go another way. They were to go quite a distance, then circle toward each other to come to where the fence had been built. This was done. Out of nowhere, a herd of caribou was driven into the caribou fence. Caribou were caught in every snare.
>
> After the herd was killed, the boy asked his father to carry him around to see all the caribou. The boy asked the hunters to find the fattest caribou and to give him the fat from that caribou. However, the boy's uncle found the special caribou but would not give the fat away. The boy begged and begged. Other men offered their caribou fat but the boy wanted only the fat from this special caribou. He cried when he did not get it. All the hunters went home. Finally the boy's father pulled him home on the load of meat.
>
> At home they cooked some meat. The child put aside one shoulder and tripe half full of blood, caribou blood. Then he went to bed. The next morning, the father called his son but he did not answer. He had disappeared during the night. His marten-skin pants, which he always wore, were hanging by the smoke hole at the top of the tent, but nowhere was the boy to be found.
>
> That same morning, the hunters went to haul meat. When they came to the caribou fence, no meat was left. It had all vanished. There

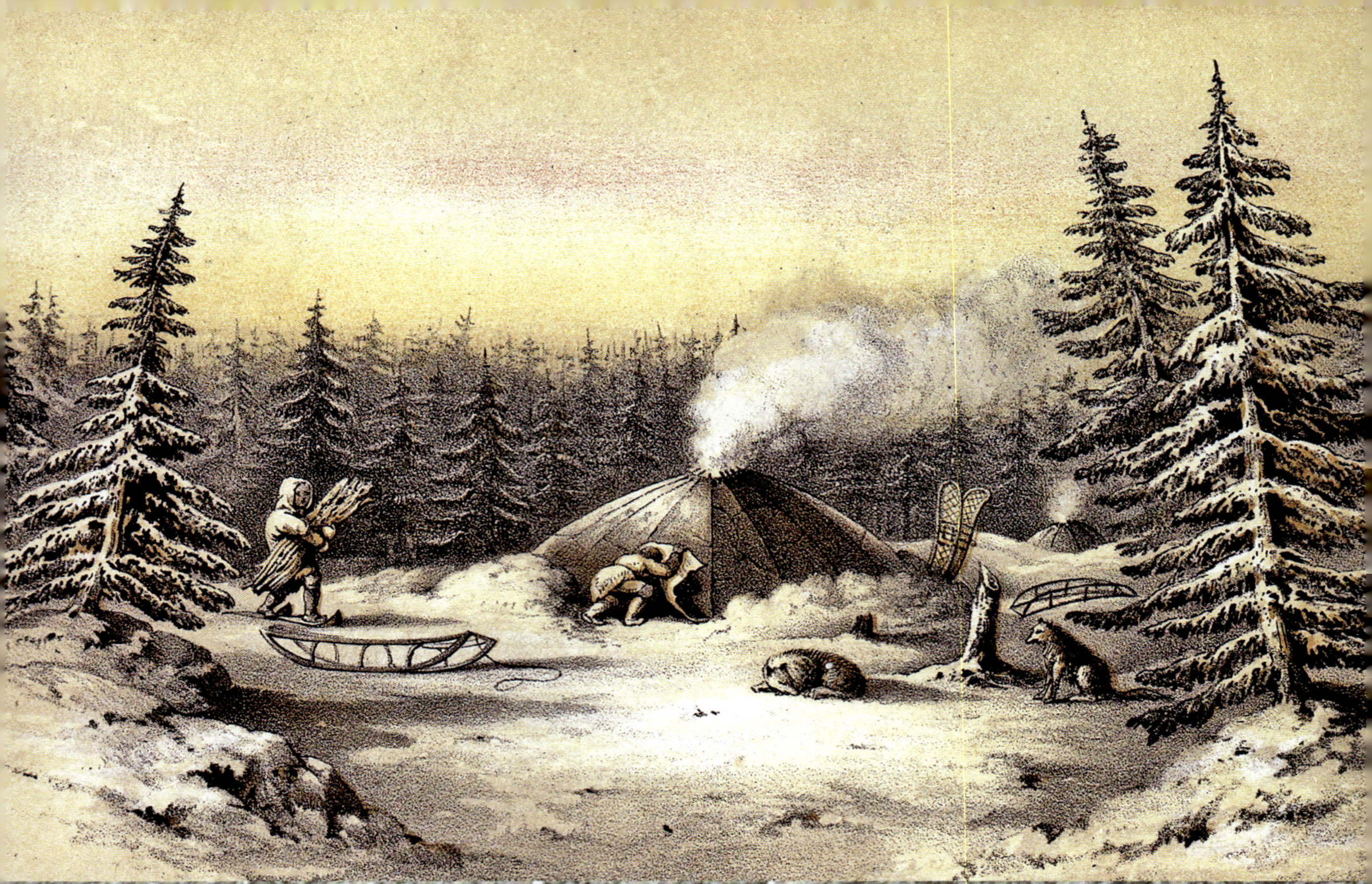
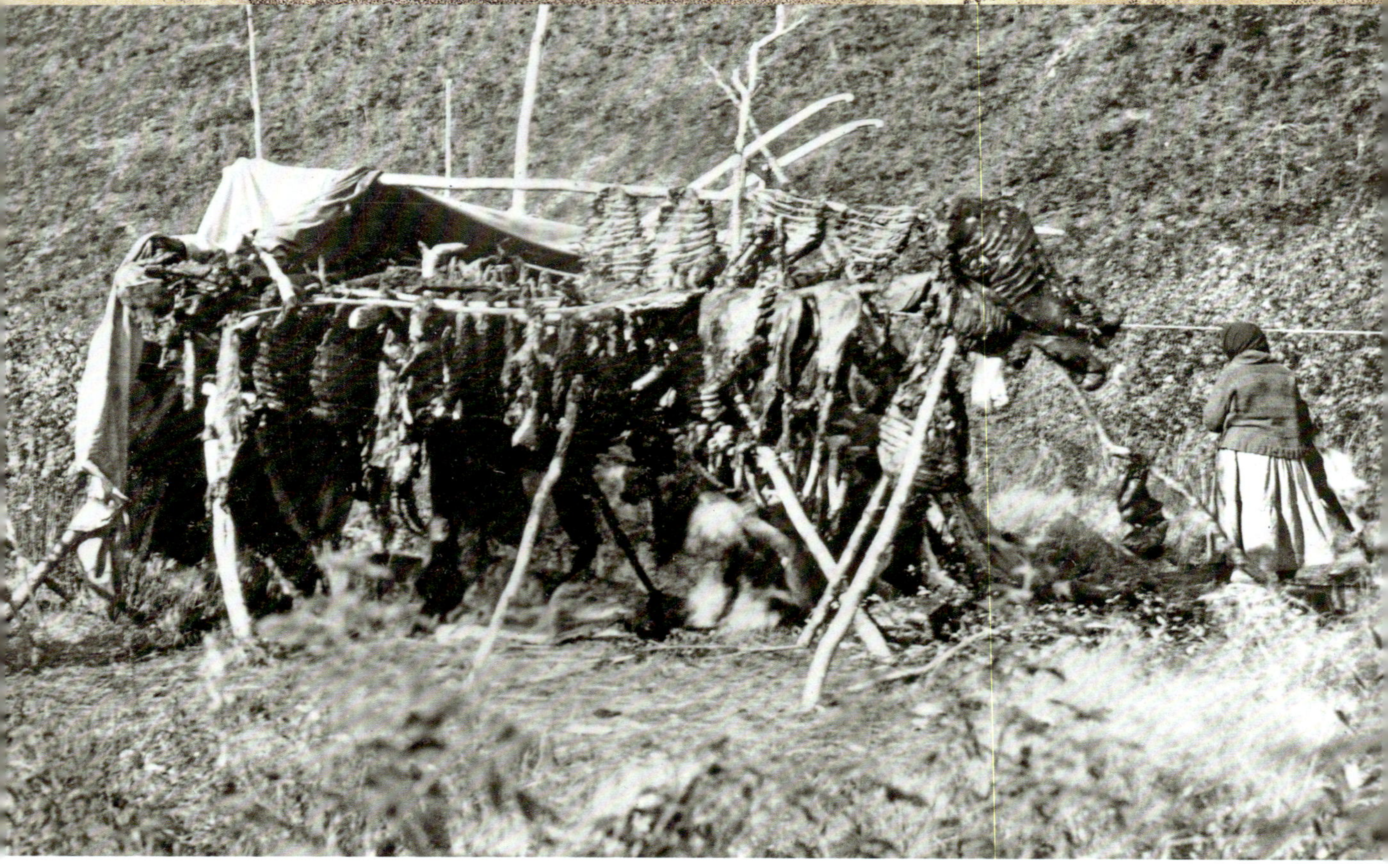

Page 10 (top): Gwich'in winter lodges, from a drawing by Alexander Murray, 1848.

[Yukon Archives, Catharine McClellan fonds 90/57 #6]

Page 10 (bottom): Gwich'in woman with drying caribou.

[Yukon Archives, Arthur Thornthwaite fonds 83/22 #320]

Above: Remains of meat cache at Antl'it (Thomas Creek Caribou Fence).

[Shirleen Smith ©VGFN 2000]

was not even a sign of blood. Everyone cried because of the loss of the child and the meat. They knew this had happened because the boy had not been given a piece of fat from the fattest caribou.

One night not long after, the boy appeared to his surprised parents. He told them to keep the caribou shoulder he had set aside and to cut off some meat to the bone for eating, but not to break the bone or tear off a strip. His parents did as he instructed. Every morning the bone would have lots of meat on it, like before. Every day the parents cut off meat and ate it. They did this for a long time.

Then the boy told his parents that he would vanish into the moon and live there until the end of the world. He said that at the eclipse of the moon, if the moon seems to be on its back, there will be a good winter with lots of caribou. But if the moon should face down, it will be a sign of a cold winter and starvation. He told his parents that in time of plenty, all the people should sing, dance, and feast. He said that he would be watching from the moon. Today, if people look at the shadow on the moon, they will see the boy with his bag of blood in one hand and a dog on the other side. This is the end of the story.

(EFFIE LINKLATER, *December 3, 1979, VG2000-8-39:006-060, English*)

Alfred Charlie on Ch'ii Ch'àan *(Bear Cave Mountain).*

[Shirleen Smith ©VGFN 2000]

Ch'ataiiyuukaih—Paddled a Different Route

The story of *Ch'ataiiyuukaih*[2] is considered a very old story. In 1947, Van Tat Gwich'in William Itsi told anthropologist Richard Slobodin that it may be the oldest story (Slobodin 1971:261). The hero *Ch'ataiiyuukaih* (Paddled a Different Route) travelled around in his canoe "fixing" the world, placing the land and animals in their proper places and functions. The story is analogous to stories from other regions of men with supernatural powers who ordered the world, such as Yamoria on the Mackenzie River to the east in the Northwest Territories. In this story, Alfred Charlie described how *Ch'ataiiyuukaih* ordered a feature of the Gwich'in social world, the clan structure, and in the process gave the Crow his allotted number of toes. Joe Netro gave an abbreviated account of how *Ch'ataiiyuukaih* fixed the seagull, otter, and bear so they no longer ate humans. Edith Josie wrote a longer version, parts of which are reproduced below, in the distinctive style for which she became known and loved in her column, Here Are the News.

Ch'ataiiyuukaih: Crow and the Clan System, told by Alfred Charlie

The way I understand it, _Ch'ataiiyuukaih_ was coming down the Peel River, and when he got to Arctic Red River, there was nobody there.[3] But there's a bluff around the bend and there was the sound of lots of people: it was pretty noisy up there. So he went up there. Gee, people were having a good time....

He met Crow [_Deetrù'_] there. It was summertime so he paddled to where [the community of] Arctic Red [River] is right now, the little bluff there. He wanted to do something to that Crow. He told Crow, "we're going to sleep on the bluff because it's windy there so there will be no mosquitoes." Crow knew what _Ch'ataiiyuukaih_ was thinking. When they were going to bed, he told _Ch'ataiiyuukaih_, "Don't kick me over the bluff. If you do, there will be a big noise and I'll take all the people away and make them disappear." _Ch'ataiiyuukaih_ didn't believe him.

Pretty soon, Crow starting snoring. _Ch'ataiiyuukaih_ kicked him over the bluff. All he could see was feathers blowing all over because Crow's body was all smashed. It hit here and there and when it got to the bottom of the cliff, just his head was there. Then [the sound of all the people stopped]. _Ch'ataiiyuukaih_ went back up again and saw there was not a soul—not even one single person was there.

So _Ch'ataiiyuukaih_ came back to where he killed the Crow. I don't know how he was going to put him back together. "Oh," he said and he fooled around. With a little driftwood, he made a little house. He collected the pieces of the body and began to put it back together like a puzzle. Oh, it took him a long time for it was just like hamburger. He put together all the little pieces and pretty soon he had part of the head. He put the head on and I don't know how the heck he stuck it together.

Anyway he put Crow back together so the next thing he had to do was make him breathe, come back to life. He didn't know how but he figured it out. He took a little piece of driftwood and opened Crow's mouth wide and put that little stick in his mouth to hold it open. He took his pants down and put his butt into that opening and let out a big fart. That's the way he made Crow breathe. Yeah, that's how he made Crow breathe.

Then Crow said, "There's one piece of me missing. You've got to look for it." _Ch'ataiiyuukaih_ held the missing piece but pretended he couldn't find it. He told the Crow, "I can't find it. I looked all over and can find every piece of your meat but one toe. I can't find that." That's why Crow has only three toes.

So *Ch'ataiiyuukaih* got away with it, even though Crow tried to talk his way out of it. Crow asked him, "How do you live there? People are noisy up there. Do you see anybody?" *Ch'ataiiyuukaih* said, "No. Not even one single man is up there. I told you. You did that."...So Crow told *Ch'ataiiyuukaih* to paddle him up to where the people had been and when they got there, he told *Ch'ataiiyuukaih*, "I see a big *chèhlùk* [fish: loche/burbot] going toward the shore. Take me to the shore." ...

So he did that. He saw the big loche coming to shore, upside down. Crow told him to step on his belly. So he did. Then all the people came out; most people came out of his mouth. All those people came back.

So that's how the *Ch'ichyàa* [Wolf Clan] and *Neetsaih* [Crow Clan] came to be. I don't know how *Teenjiraatsyaa* [the middle clan] started. That's how they started, the way I understand it. It's a true story.

(ALFRED CHARLIE, January 29, 1998, VG1998-2-1A:015-080, Gwich'in)

Ch'ataiiyuukaih Fixed the Bad Animals, told by Joe Netro

Yeah, that one [who fixed the bad animals], a long time ago, a guy named...[*Ch'ataiiyuukaih*]. He's the one who killed all the bad animals. He came through the country from the Mackenzie River, Yukon.

Seagull used to live on people, eat anything, [he was] so big. He [even ate] human beings. He lived on that, but this man [*Ch'ataiiyuukaih*] killed them. So he got the young [Seagull] there and told him, "Get gopher or birds before he fly." He give it to him, "That's all you're going to eat from now on, no more eating people."...He fixed that. He killed them. Just like the otter, he ate people, too. He killed him, so he fixed all the bad animals.

Brown bears, in the wintertime, they didn't go into the hole [hibernate], they just wandered around all winter. To cover himself, he went into the open water, rolled in snow, and got full of ice so an arrow can't do anything. [When he] saw a person, he just killed him and ate him.

(JOE NETRO, August 10, 1977, VG2001-4-2:317-354, English)

Ch'ataiiyuukaih and *Ohdik*, written by Edith Josie

In old days the boy born and after week the girl born and the parent start to tell their kids to be wife and husband. So *Taachuukaii*[4] born and after a week the girl born so those parent start to say that their kids will get marriage after they grow up.

So this girl name is *Ohdik* and she was a brave little girl. In old days when girl get their first period and the parent have to make a little brush camp so they let them stay their until their first period. They let them stay little farther away from people. Also they won't let them look around and first stay in their brush camp.

So *Taachuukaii* left in canoe and this girl, she stay for awhile. While she sleep she stretch her leg and push little rock and middle of river a big rock on the river. The people saw the rock on the middle of the river and they tell her mother if she could move it to the cross of river. Because people go on river with raft and the rock is on the way. So next morning it was other side of river and I hear the rock is still there. And they call it Women Rock, and it still there forever.

After that next day she was disappear. Nobody know what happen.

She walk and she camp at Dawson, where Dawson is now. Every place she camp it was mark and people know where she went....One day she run into *Taachuukaii* and she was happy as she could be. They were together in Ottawa and they want to get marriage so they did and after marriage, they give them a name. *Taachuukaii* is King Edward and his wife *Ohdik* is Victoria. So they got a name and they were together for a while.

All this is what going to be happen and tell the people what is bad or what is good.

So he killed all the bad animals and when he going to leave some animals, he told them not to kill man, is not right to kill people. He travel all way down the Yukon River and go all around part of the state [United States] and arrived to Ottawa. He travel all summer and take his time and camp many places.

And his name is *Taachuukaii*—he was a smart man and a magic guy....So he start down the river with his birch canoe.[5]...He came to bear and this bear, he kill man. When *Taachuukaii* land and went up the bank, bear had a camp there. And he was good to the man and start to call a man "my son-in-law." So his daughter stay near a big lake but she never come to camp.

So next day he tell man he had a good place for moose hunting by the lake. So he told him to make a bow arrow. How could he make it? He told him there lots of birch down on the hill so he went down and he bring birch back and he was kind afraid the man.

Next, what string could I use? [A]nd he told him to go down to the hill, that where I always get string. All this danger was around, that is what they kill man. He went down. There was a big skinny moose got up. The little mouse came to man and he tell mouse run over to the moose and ran up on his leg and go in and chew all his vein. And the skinny moose fall down so he skin it and took a thread and went back. Next what could I use for feather? [A]nd he tell him to go down to the

Long-ago Stories

hill, there lots of feather. So he went down, and here a big Eagle nest on the hill, so he look. There two young Eagle was there and ask them, "[W]here are your father and mother?" They say, "[T]hey went out hunting." So he kill one little Eagle and he ask other one, "[W]hen your mother coming, what kind weather is with her?" "When she come, a big black cloud coming with her." "How about your father?" "That one, [too,] a big storm and hail come with him."

So he told [the Eagle,] "[W]hen your mother [comes], don't tell I was here. If he ask where your brother, he say he had a strong headache so he went down under hill to rest."

And Eagle mother say, "[H]ow come I smell man?" And that little Eagle told her, "[Y]ou bring man back. That is what you smell."

While that, the man hit her with a big stick and kill her and he throw her over the hill. And next Eagle father coming with a man body and he tell the same to little Eagle. While that the man hit him with a stick and he kill them all. After that he went out to hunt and got rabbit and ptarmigan for him [little Eagle] and he told him, "just eat this kind and don't ever eat man. That is not good."

He came back. He got feather and start to tell him to hunt but he told him his moccasin had a big hole. "Give it to me. I give it to my daughter." So he follow him and see him....Where he say it was good for moose hunting, he got there and tell the man, "go this way and I go this way." Where his daughter stay, he sent man that way. Soon he came around the lake. Here a big Bear coming to him. He had sharp spear and hit her in the chest and kill her. He start to go for [the] man, but he snuck away from him. There was a big running river. He put the snare for men. All this he (*Taachuukaii*) see but he don't know. He had a skin pant. He took it out and put some moss in it and put [it in] his snare. When [the man] went to see his snare, something [was] in it so he start to make fire place. And he went to snare a big pant with moss in it. Gee, he really got mad.

While that, *Taachuukaii* run to his canoe and paddle down river. From there on all he do is travel and at last he got to Ottawa. So where he camp a place and they name it, all this places where he camp.

Sure a big and long story for him and nice to read it. In the olden days lots of things happen and write about it be good.

So this is how to be careful with some animals. Like Crow, we can kill it and so with Wolf, just if he try to go after us, it's only time they kill it, but people shouldn't kill it for nothing.

(EDITH JOSIE, handwritten manuscript on file, Vuntut Gwitchin First Nation)

Sarah Abel, showing a tanned hide.

[Yukon Archives, Richard Harrington fonds 85/25 #19]

Shih Gwandak—Young Man and Grizzly Bear, told by Sarah Abel
In this story [*gwandak*], people can converse with animals, and through their shared social mores, issues such as the importance of keeping your word, loyalty to one who helps you, vengeance for betrayal, and "speaking well" as an ingredient in making peace, are elucidated.

In the days when man had only arrows, the *Shih* [Grizzly Bear] was a nuisance, especially an angry Grizzly Bear. In the spring, April I guess, a creek flowed just below his den. His den was somewhere on the hill above. People were walking below.

In the fall, in the month of October when the ground froze, three boys [young men] went hunting on the mountain. They came upon the den and the bear killed two of the boys. The female Grizzly grabbed the third boy and brought him into the den. She put him under the grass she slept on. And he stayed under the grass all winter. What gopher meat they had that her husband got, she would give the boy some.

Long-ago Stories   17

She kept him under the grass in her den all winter. She took care of him. Finally, the male Grizzly said, "How come I smell man?" She replied, "You never killed anything that smells. Why do you say you smell man?" The male Grizzly never said a word. The winter passed. The winter passed and in the month of April, bears come out of their dens. Meanwhile just below the den, near the creek, people were travelling with dog teams. Lots of men were looking for moose on the hard snow. People came by dog team so [the male Grizzly said], "I will go out, I will go down to them. If you see big smoke…" He went out.

His wife watched him. He planned on killing the people but the people killed him with arrows. The female Grizzly pulled the boy out from under the grass. But the Grizzly's two cubs might kill the man so she killed her own children.

The man took care of her all summer. In the fall, around the time when the ground freezes and the Grizzlies return to their den, it snowed a little. She told the boy, "I took care of you a long time. Now look for your people. If you find them, don't go to your wife right away. Wait until the next day. When you arrive there, only go to her the next day." He was happy so he left.

He crossed the river and not far from there was a camp. His wife was there. People thought her husband was dead a long time ago. Her husband came back. But he didn't obey what the Grizzly told him: "When you get there, only go to your wife's place the next day," he didn't obey. The female Grizzly knew. And she came in the night, came into their home and killed him. The Grizzly didn't bother the wife. The Grizzly came in the night and killed the boy who returned, people said.

There were many people. When the Grizzly returned to its den, the people went looking for it. They followed the Grizzly back to its den. The Grizzly sat in front of its den crying. Ah, the Grizzly's tears flowed down the hill. "I took care of my husband and miss him. I will not bother you. Look at me." The people said there was no use killing the Grizzly so they left her. The Grizzly spoke well so they didn't kill her.

In the past, the Grizzly helped people many times. People always tell of it. The female Grizzly, they didn't kill her. The people left her. "Really, I will not bother you guys again and I hope you guys do the same." They didn't do anything to the grizzly.

(SARAH ABEL, VG2000-8-1:041–125, Gwich'in)

John Joe Kyikavichik and his sister Reverend Ellen Bruce, overlooking Van Tat Gwatsàl *(Little Flats).*
[Shirleen Smith ©VGFN (VG 2000-6-322)]

Dinjii Dèe Ehdanh Ts'atvit hah—Blind Man and the Loon,
told by Ellen Bruce

The Blind Man and the Loon [Literally: *dinjii* (man), *dèe* (eye), *ehdanh* (without), *ts'atvit* (loon), *hah* (and)] is a widespread story across the North, with shared elements, such as the way the blind man kills the moose, diving beneath the water three times, and the offer of a vessel of water containing bugs. The story deals with deception, betrayal, the intervention of an animal helper, retribution, the disposal of the dead, and the resolution of the story.

> Long ago, one man was blind; I don't know his name. Those kind [of people] live amongst other people and they kill people. Sometimes one man gets loose; that is what they mean, I guess.
>
> One man who was blind lived with his wife and children. They lived alone. His wife hunted for small game...for their children. They lived on that, anywhere. All of a sudden they heard a moose coming. The woman told her husband, "A moose is coming." So he said to her, "Wife, put me in front of it and aim an arrow toward it for me." She did all that. "Now" she probably told him. He let go of the arrow and heard the arrow hit the moose. "Ah, I heard it clearly," he said.
>
> What she was going to do to him, she was mad....They both went inside. He knew she was going to work on the moose. Even so, she said that the moose went [the other] way. She followed it [to where] the moose was dead, butchered it and cut it up. Then she told her children, "Don't tell your father," so they went over to the moose. "I'm going to go with the children then we'll come back for you. Just stay here,"

Long-ago Stories 19

she told her husband. Then they went to the moose and she dried the moose meat. She knew she wouldn't see her husband again.

[Her husband] crawled in the direction he thought they went. He crawled for a long time. All of a sudden while he was feeling around in front of him, he heard a voice nearby, talking. I wonder what he told him? [The Loon] landed and asked, "How are you?" "I can't see anything and this is what happened to me," he said. [The Loon] told him, "Put your head in my armpits," and he dove in [the water] with him. They went quite a ways and, amidst that, [the Loon] asked how he was doing. [The man] said, "Again." So they dove under the water and again they came out. [The Loon] asked [the man], "How is it now?" He replied, "Still a little more." So they went back the same way. Now he could see everything clearly. So he said "I can see," and the Loon left him.

[The man] walked along the lakeshore for a long time and he saw a cache with lots of food. He sneaked close to it and started crawling, pretending to be blind. He crawled, peeked a little until he was close then made like he couldn't see. His children saw him. They said, "Our father is coming." "Ah, my children, I'm really thirsty for water," he said; he was just lying. They grabbed the birchbark container but the woman said, "I will get water for your father." He crawled by the fireplace, while she took the birchbark container and ran down to the lakeshore for water. What they call water bugs, there's all kinds in lake water. She poured some into the container.

The man knew the water was close and he asked, "How come your mother is gone so long getting the water? I'm thirsty for water." Meanwhile, she was roasting a [moose] ham. "Is that a moose ham?" he asked.

Finally, she came back and said, "Here is the water" and sat down. He took a big gulp and swallowed a water bug. They say he poured the water on top of her head. He grabbed the ham and clubbed her with it and killed her. The children were yelling and crying and running around. With that moose ham he killed them all, too. Not one of them was alive, they said.

In those days, when people did this, they made big fires and burned them all. They never buried anyone. Any human who we deeply care for and died was put on a high cache in those days, they said. He killed all of them. He threw all the moose meat into the fire with them and burned it. He didn't take any meat. He left there and wandered all over. He came upon his younger and older brothers and lived amongst them, *akoo diginuu* [they said].

(ELLEN BRUCE, 1980, VG2000-8-30:101–190, Gwich'in)

LEGENDARY FIGURES

Stories of legendary heroes who prevail due to their perseverance, moral character, and physical strength are among the longest and most complex *yeenoo dài' googwandak*. These stories also afford a detailed look at the interplay of conflicting values in Gwich'in society and how social conflicts might be resolved.

Kò' Ehdanh—Man Without Fire, told by Sarah Abel, Moses Tizya, and Myra Moses

Kò' Ehdanh [Literally: *Kò'*, "fire" and *ehdanh*, "without,"] is an important and old Gwich'in story. In 1947, William Itsi, a Van Tat Gwich'in living with Teetl'it Gwich'in, related the story to anthropologist Richard Slobodin in a hunting camp in the Richardson Mountains. In the context of World War II, Mr. Itsi described "Man Without Fire" as a significant story of war.

> You want to talk about war. I'll tell you a story of war. Some of you know this story, but hear me. This really happened. This happened maybe a thousand years ago, maybe ten thousand. It is perhaps the oldest story. Maybe *Atocok'ái* is older.[6]
>
> (WILLIAM ITSI [ITTZA], 1947, in Richard Slobodin 1971)

There are a number of other recorded/published versions of "Man Without Fire." Slobodin reported hearing other recitations in 1938 and 1961 (Slobodin 1971:261). The 19th-century Oblate missionary Émile Petitot published a version in 1888 (Petitot 1888) and anthropologist Cornelius Osgood included a brief synopsis in his *Contributions to the Ethnology of the Kutchin* (1970[1936]:166–167). More recently, the *"Kwan ehdan"* story from the Gwichya Gwich'in of Tsiigehtchic, Northwest Territories, was published by the Gwich'in Social and Cultural Institute in 2001.[7] A detailed comparison of different versions of this Gwich'in classic legend would be fascinating.

This version of the *Kò' Ehdanh* epic is drawn from the recorded stories of Sarah Abel, Moses Tizya, and Myra Moses. These highly respected Elders were all born between 1884 and 1900 and lived to a great age (90 to 100 years), which enabled their stories to be recorded in oral history projects of the late 1970s and 1980s. Their detailed accounts are presented in combination, using Sarah Abel's version of the story as the basis, drawn from her telling of the story to Jim Fell in 1977 with Alice Frost as interpreter,[8] and her later account recorded by her grandson, Roy Moses. Sarah Abel's *Kò' Ehdanh* was augmented by Moses Tizya's briefer version recorded in 1979, supplemented by two interviews with Myra Moses recorded in 1980 by Henry Nukon.[9] All of

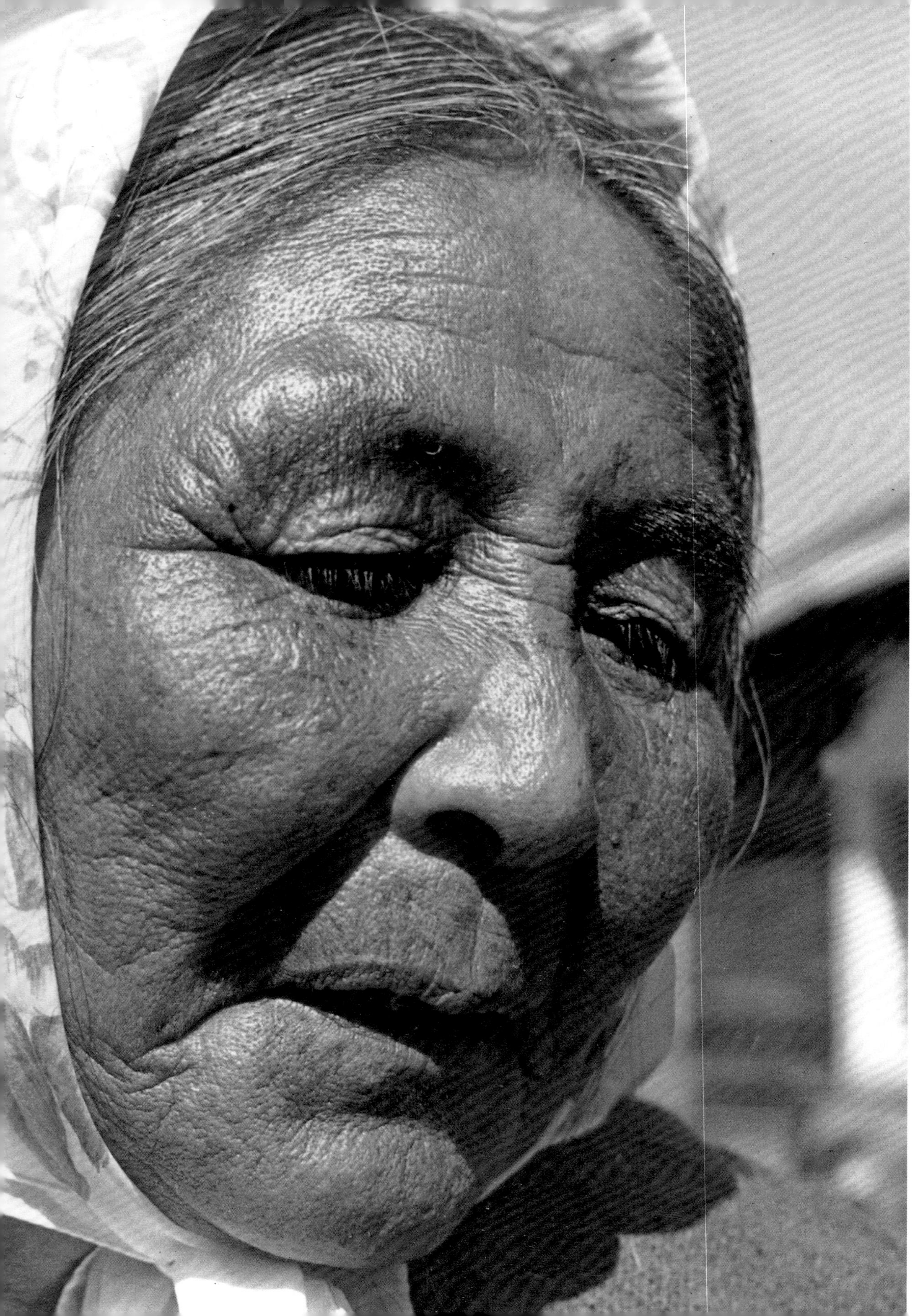

Page 22: Myra Moses, 1960.

[Yukon Archives, George and Margaret Hamilton fonds 89/38 #41]

the recordings were retranslated by Mary Jane Moses and Jane Montgomery between 2000 and 2003. The resulting account is an elaboration of the individual stories that serves to accentuate the key themes, reveal some of the classic variations, and showcase the richness of Van Tat Gwich'in elders' oral tradition of this epic. Other Elders have contributed additional detail to Sarah Abel's story.

> Grandchild, the man they call *Kò' Ehdanh* [Man Without Fire], I will tell you about that, some of it. That story is really long. Some of it I remember. The one they call *Kò' Ehdanh*, he was a Gwich'in like us, a Van Tat Gwich'in.

Myra Moses adds that the story of *Kò' Ehdanh* begins around the Black River-Fort Yukon area and that he had two wives (VG2000-8-21).

> They lived in Crow Flats, around there. In October they had settled down by what they call a caribou fence.[10] There was meat. They had shot a moose also, they said, and made a feast with it.

In Moses Tizya's version, they were at some springs at the head of the Porcupine River having a feast of rabbits, possibly after a rabbit drive: "Anyway, he hunted rabbits with his crew. They killed rabbits and he was cooking all the rabbits they brought together, and all the people were there when an army came and killed them" (Moses Tizya, August 20, 1979, VG2000-8-22, Gwich'in and English). Myra Moses concurred that they were feasting after a rabbit drive (Myra Moses, VG2000-8-14, Gwich'in).

> While they were there, the *Ch'ineekaii* [Inuvialuit or Inuit] found out about them. *Kò' Ehdanh* was making a feast. His wife was a really smart woman, *akoo diginuu* [they said]. And his brother was staying across from him.

Moses Tizya describes a more southerly enemy: "Well, it took about six months before they caught up to them, and I figure that was around Great Slave Lake. They came from there. That's a long way" (Moses Tizya, August 20, 1979, VG2000-8-22, Gwich'in and English). Myra Moses's description concurred: "They say it was strangers from way up the river [Mackenzie]. They would come across this way and kill people, they say" (Myra Moses, VG2000-8-14:120, Gwich'in).[11]

> [They lived] in skin tents. They wouldn't have canvas tents: skin tents, round skin tents. Two round skin tents were beside each other. All the people, all of them were going to go in there to eat. No one was sitting outside. But Grandchild, in those days, the people didn't have many dogs. *Kò' Ehdanh* had only two dogs.
>
> The *Ch'ineekaii* were going to kill them and surrounded them. The Gwich'in didn't notice.
>
> So the *Ch'ineekaii* attacked *Kò' Ehdanh's* house. He was giving a feast and serving food, and only had on caribou-skin pants. He wasn't wearing a coat. It was warm so he took off his coat. He had put it down when the *Ch'ineekaii* jumped them. He cut a hole and crawled out of the skin tent and ran off, they said. His brother went with him, too. Just those two escaped from there. All the rest were killed. And his wife, they knew she was a smart woman so they took her. In October this happened.

Myra Moses identifies the man who took *Kò' Ehdanh's* wife as "*Chii Choo,* Big Stone" (Myra Moses, VG2000-8-14A:131, Gwich'in).

> His brother's wife hid under the snow, they said. The *Ch'ineekaii* headed toward where she was hiding; they started off in that direction also. Oh, when they talk about this part, I don't like it! Underneath their snowshoes, the *Ch'ineekaii* had tied sharp stones. And the woman that was under the snow, they went right over top of her and the stones cut the tendons in her ankles. The tendons: the rocks cut them right off.
>
> So the *Ch'ineekaii* followed *Kò' Ehdanh* and his brother. They followed them. Even high rocky hills, he climbed them. He had no coat! He only wore caribou-skin pants.
>
> His brother was trying to follow him but they grabbed the back of his snowshoes and knocked him down.

Moses Tizya states that *Kò' Ehdanh's* brother couldn't run and jump as well as *Kò' Ehdanh* and his snowshoes got wet and iced up, slowing him fatally. Other versions report that the binding on his snowshoes broke or that the *Ch'ineekaii* were able to poke sticks through the webbing and impede his progress.

> And down there in front of *Kò' Ehdanh*, they killed his brother. That man, he really went through lots of hard times, they said. They killed his brother in front of him and they had his wife.

Moses Tizya adds a further grisly detail, "*Kò' Ehdanh* went up a rock cliff where they couldn't get him. He was sitting there, naked, and they [enemies]

Gwich'in hunters, colourplate from a sketch by Alexander Murray, 1848.

Published in Richardson 1851:377

all went past. All those who went past—you know his brother's body was down there—they hit his body with their horn clubs, just hit him once, like that. They kept on going and pretty soon there was nothing left, not even blood" (Moses Tizya, VG2000-8-22).

When all the *Ch'ineekaii* had passed, the last one was a friend. Grandchild, long ago, whoever was friends with each other, they said they wouldn't fight each other. His friend sat below him and cried for him, "My friend, come down to me." But *Kò' Ehdanh* didn't want to. His friend was called "*shijaa*." That's what they called it.

Long-ago Stories   25

Moses Tizya refers to this partner relationship as *shitlih,* also translated as "partner."[12]

> His friend had long mitts tied with strings. They were tied behind him. He left these there for *Kò' Ehdanh*.

Other versions, including those of Moses Tizya and Myra Moses, note that the long mitts were made of beaver skin.

> So *Kò' Ehdanh* didn't even have a coat. He had no hat either, but even so, he called out to his friend, "My friend, in September when the bull caribou has a white neck, at that time, don't stay in your house." He was talking about next September. When the bull caribou sheds its summer coat, the fur on its neck is white. He meant that time. Although he didn't know whether he was going to live, he said that.
>
> So then, Grandchild, *Kò' Ehdanh* went back to where they had killed the people. He saw smoke coming from the tents. His sister-in-law who had crawled under the snow, all her tendons were cut but even so, she had made a fire, they said. She told him, "Brother-in-law, I'm alive."
>
> *Kò' Ehdanh's* two dogs were wise. They had run into the bush. When they heard their grandfather [master], they came out.
>
> Grandchild, when that woman crawled out from under the snow, there were ashes from the fire in the middle of the skin house. She put lots of wood on it and lots of mud on top of that, and then she put some branches on it—she didn't put much.
>
> So then her brother-in-law came back to her. In a stump there was some rotten wood. They took it all out. In there he put a bunch of dry branches. He put a little mud down there first and then on top of that, he put some coals from the fire. He put it there for her, "like this, keep it good and don't let snow fall inside. Keep it good," he told his sister-in-law.
>
> *Kò' Ehdanh* had two sisters who had gone to a different place, and he decided to go that way. He gave his sister-in-law the stump. What was she going to kill meat with? She did not have anything to kill meat with. In those days they had long caribou fur skin coats. And so his sister-in-law cut off some of her caribou skin coat for him. They say he wrapped himself in it.

Moses Tizya recounts the death of the sister-in-law: "Anyway *Kò' Ehdanh* had three dogs. They ran away when the fighting started, the battle. Then the dogs came back and this woman had a caribou-skin blanket, and he put the lady in it and the three dogs pulled her behind him. So that woman told *Kò' Ehdanh*, "if your dogs come behind you alone, don't come back and look for me," she said, "because I'll be gone anyway" (Moses Tizya, August 20, 1979, VG2000-8-22:265-270, Gwich'in and English). Myra Moses concurred: "'Brother-in-law, when your dogs go behind you alone, that's because I will be dead. Don't look back for me, just keep on going to where the people stay. Try hard, maybe you will live,' they said she told her brother-in-law. Only his dogs went behind him, they say, so he just went on his way, carrying the fire. That's why they call him *Kò' Ehdanh* [Man Without Fire]" (Myra Moses, VG2000-8-14A:207-215, Gwich'in).

> So he made two wooden sticks strong. He carried only that. Only two dogs were walking with him. Whenever he saw a rabbit, he put that stick above it and it ran underneath. Then he stepped on it with his snowshoes and grabbed it in the snow.
>
> So, Grandchild, this was in October. All he did was walk and walk until the winter was nearly over. He cooked the rabbits. Some of it he gave to his dogs, the two of them. Those dogs, he did not have any blankets so when he was going to sleep, he put them on each side of himself and he slept between the dogs.
>
> So, Grandchild, from the rabbit snares, the first thing he had made was a rabbit-skin hat, they said. After that he made rabbit-skin clothing for himself, they say.
>
> Now he was alive and well.
>
> Whenever he saw a rabbit, he would put the stump with the fire down very carefully. Then he would work on the rabbit. Then, in the middle of winter, in January I guess, when he was killing rabbits, he didn't do it properly. Snow fell inside and the fire went out.
>
> From that time, he would kill rabbits. It was hard for him to eat them raw, so he ate the skin, a little piece of it, the liver, he swallowed it raw, they say.
>
> He'd just kill rabbits, but he couldn't eat them. They say one thing, rabbit, nobody can eat it raw. So he just threw them away. He just ate the guts or something, just a little at a time.
>
> (MOSES TIZYA, August 20, 1979, VG2000-8-22:285, Gwich'in and English)
>
> *Kò' Ehdanh* lived this way all winter, and in March he finally found other people. Grandchild, finally, finally he got to a trail. There was an old campsite. The snow was very deep on it. He found a trail and an old camp, and the packed snow on top measured just about a foot.

From there he followed a trail. Now there wasn't much snow on it. Then he found a camp where people had stayed for a long time. They had just moved on that morning. There was still fire burning.

As he was going along, he came to a place that looked like where everybody, hunters, had been there together. There was a big place, hard packed. He checked it and pretty soon he saw a snowshoe trail. He followed it and, sure enough, there was camp that people just left that morning. That meant not just a few hundred people, that meant thousands and thousands of people.
(MOSES TIZYA, August 20, 1979, VG2000-8-22:291, Gwich'in and English)

So he put lots of wood on the fire, they said. There were lots of caribou feet around the camp. He put one under the fire to cook. He hadn't seen fire all winter so when he saw fire again, he felt tired. So he put branches under his head and put his mitts on top and fell asleep. He slept all day and close to the evening, he woke up. He took the caribou foot out of the fire and it was cooked really well, soft.
...
He started walking again, following the people who made the trail.
The hunters killed lots of caribou that day. When those who hunted were coming back to camp, they saw smoke at their old camp from *Kò' Ehdanh's* fire.

So as they were approaching the camp, they called out. In those days, one man always called out. Now they say it was the Chief. Whoever was smart they had for their leaders. He was the one who called out and all the people heard him. The leader told everybody to watch closely because they saw smoke coming from the campsite.

Then *Kò' Ehdanh* started walking to a little snow house, where an old woman stayed. He took off his snowshoes and went into her house.

In Moses Tizya's version, the role of the old woman resembles other stories about their watchfulness and ingenuity, and he adds the character of her child (in other versions the child is a smart daughter):

One woman was way behind the camp. When they went over what they call a divide, the top of a mountain, the woman was way behind having a rest and she saw smoke coming from the camp they left that morning. So, that's danger, you know. In those days, there was nothing but wars all over.

Kò' Ehdanh had started to follow. When he got to where the old lady had rested, he rested, too. The old lady told the people so they talked about it and said, "watch out all night around the camp." So they did. "Stand and listen to see if anybody is coming or anything like that."

Anyway, *Kò' Ehdanh* snuck in. The old lady was camped way behind and in the camp was her grandchild, girl or boy, I don't know. So the old lady and this girl, they talked together and said, "We're going to eat this now and we're going to eat that for breakfast." So *Kò' Ehdanh* said, "Well, why don't you do that." Gee! They got scared. They thought they heard something. The old lady turned to go out and *Kò' Ehdanh* said, "No!" He told them a little of his story and said, "Give me something to eat before you tell my story." So they gave him a little, I guess. He ate one bite maybe. Anyway, everybody started to go after him. He got away. Later, he came back and then they found out *Kò' Ehdanh's* story of the massacre.

(MOSES TIZYA, August 20, 1979, VG2000-8-22:302–339, Gwich'in and English)

He said, "Whatever my name was before this happened, you won't call me that. You'll call me *Kò' Ehdanh*—Man Without Fire." He told her to say this, so the old woman turned to go outside, but he grabbed her. "If you have some good bone juice, then give me some before you go," he told her.

Myra Moses noted that *Kò' Ehdanh's* previous name was known at one time: "*Kò' Ehdanh*, his other name, I don't know it, Grandchild. Grandfather used to call it out; I don't remember it" (Myra Moses, VG2000-8-14A:255, Gwich'in).

"All my relations, the enemy killed them all and only I am alive," he told her. So, she gave him some good bone juice and some small pemmican balls. He ate them and drank the juice with it. Then he told her to say, "Now, you can tell them that all *Kò' Ehdanh's* people have been killed and only he is alive."

There were a hundred people there in the camp. When they heard the story they all began crying. Two of *Kò' Ehdanh's* sisters were there. Everyone ran toward him—in those days people did that, you know. Even though he hadn't eaten all winter nor seen fire,[13] he kicked off his snowshoes and ran away from them.[14] No one caught him. He stopped before them and said, "Fight with me." He told them he had to revenge the deaths of his relatives. So they said yes.[15]

In those days, for what we now call money, they used big beads, long and coloured.[16] His two sisters kept them for him. He paid people with these, they said.

This took place in the month of March. All summer they harvested meat and made arrows. The meat was for the women to use when they stayed in camp.

Long-ago Stories   29

Myra Moses emphasized this aspect of going to war, the necessity of making weapons and storing food for those left behind: "They made lots of arrows. They say they made them out of [caribou] bones....Finally they killed lots of caribou for the women who were left at camp" (Myra Moses, VG2000-8-14A:309-317). In another interview, Sarah Abel explained that men who were good hunters also would be left behind, "There were lots of women. They will depend on drymeat, I guess, they left. People like Andrew Tizya will hunt, that's why they were left behind. So they went to fight" (Sarah Abel, VG2003-03-01:111). Andrew Tizya (1921-2005), son of Moses Tizya, never married and was known for his ability to hunt and support many families.

> In the month of August, they left. The men left and went to where *Kò' Ehdanh's* friends were killed. They saw where the *Ch'ineekaii* (Inuvialuit or Inuit) went and set off after them.
>
> This was in October when their tracks didn't show. The *Ch'ineekaii* had *Kò' Ehdanh's* wife whose name was *Ts'at T'atha'at*, Caribou Skin Blanket. She had two *Ch'ineekaii* women with her, one on each side, whenever she went anywhere. They watched her so she couldn't leave any signs for her people to follow. Even though she had a caribou blanket wrapped around her and two people watching her, sometimes when she passed a bush, she would rub her arm on it. Those who followed traced her by that. She also stepped on willows to break them, they said.

Moses Tizya reiterates *Kò' Ehdanh's* warning to his partner and explains the name and position of *Kò' Ehdanh's* wife. "When *Kò' Ehdanh* was on that cliff, he told his partner, 'When the caribou's hair is changing...' that means part of September. 'When they get different hair,' he told him, 'don't stay home.' So, *Kò' Ehdanh* started following them. He followed all spring and then summer came, and they went where the *Ch'ineekaii* took *Kò' Ehdanh's* wife. They called her *Srehteetr'aadyaa*, meaning 'one who changes,' because they took that wife. She was the only woman they took with them, and she was wise" (Moses Tizya, August 20, 1979, VG2000-8-22:353-360, Gwich'in and English).

> So, way down at the coast, all the *Ch'ineekaii* gathered at one place and they took *Kò' Ehdanh's* wife there. They made their camp on the other side of a big lake.

Moses Tizya identifies the enemy as eastern Dene rather than *Ch'ineekaii* and therefore ascribes a different location as their home territory: "I figure that was around Great Slave Lake" (Moses Tizya, August 20, 1979, VG2000-8-22:374, Gwich'in and English). The enemy in Myra Moses's version was also from up the Mackenzie River: "It was a long way to the strangers' country. I think maybe they mean around Fort Simpson [Northwest Territories]" (Myra Moses, VG2000-8-14A:325, Gwich'in). All versions (and published accounts) agree that the enemy camp was beside a long lake reached by crossing a mountain.

> On the mountain above the lake, the snow never melted. It became ice. The followers lost the trail and didn't know which way they went. It was hard for *Kò' Ehdanh's* wife to leave signs while they were going over the ice mountain. So she said "my moccasins are torn," and she purposely tore them. She had a bag of red ochre pigment for colouring hide/leather. She sewed it on the soles of her boots. When it got wet, it made red marks on the ice. That's how she left markers on the ice.
>
> *Kò' Ehdanh's* people climbed the mountain. They had lost the tracks. The people told Man Without Fire they would have to turn back. "From here we're going go back home. We can't find those people," they said. *Kò' Ehdanh* really cried, they said.
>
> But while they were there, one man saw a rock and dug it out and there were wood shavings under it so they knew *Kò' Ehdanh's* wife had been there. Then they climbed over the mountain and way down on the lake shore, they saw *Ch'ineekaii* tents, skin tents, lots of them.
>
> They went down the mountain, and when they came close to the camp, they made a sign to *Kò' Ehdanh's* wife. So she responded and threw water in the direction that was the shortest way to go around the lake.
>
> (SARAH ABEL, August 11, 1977, VG2001-4-5#2:014-391;008-206, Gwich'in)

> They crawled through the willows to the bottom, they crawled. Around the lake big bushes grew. *Kò' Ehdanh's* wife knew about him and waited for him. The old *Ch'ineekaii* woman was always with her. Even when she went for water, they wouldn't let her go alone. Ah, she looked across for a long time and she listened. Well, that lake was big and she knew which was the closest way to go around. She went for water and threw it that way. They asked her "What did you throw water on?" She said, "Ah, I'm killing these mosquitoes, I'm spilling water on them. What do you think I am doing?"

"When they got to that lake, they saw a big camp on the other side. At night, pitch dark, they snuck to the lake and covered themselves with moss so nobody would see them. By that time, *Kò' Ehdanh's* wife, she watched, you know, she watched. She went down to get a pail of water. She saw one of the men. The lake is long, a couple hundred miles, you see, and she threw water in the direction of the shortest way around the lake, and they knew it. Her (captor) husband jumped up and asked, 'What are you doing?' She said, 'Oh, I was just throwing water on mosquitoes'" (Moses Tizya, August 20, 1979, VG2000-8-22:270-280, Gwich'in and English). Myra Moses's more personalized version featured *Chii Choo* [Big Stone], her abductor, asking why she threw the water (Myra Moses, VG2000-8-14A:342).

> Then, that night, while it was getting dark, [*Kò' Ehdanh's* people] went into the bushes and came up along where there were caches in the thick brush. [*Kò' Ehdanh's* wife] got wood with the *Ch'ineekaii* women and they kept watch on her from far away. There she came upon [*Kò' Ehdanh's* people]. They hadn't eaten for a long time. "What can you do?" they asked her. As she was carrying wood, she tore the soles of her shoes. "I poked my feet so I'm going to sew my soles," she told her captors. She made like she was doing something, she never took her blanket off. She put grease in her jacket even though they kept a good watch on her. It was snowing out; she dropped the grease on the trail.
>
> That night, as they played games, she said to them, "This is how my people played games." She tired them out and they fell asleep right away. They were spread all around, sleeping. Even then, a *Ch'ineekaii* woman and two girls listened really well and looked in all directions, going in and out. Finally, they went back inside and while the sun was still rising.... They never took notice of *Kò' Ehdanh* and he stood up and [made a noise]....He only had a club—they mean he wasn't carrying a gun. They told an old ragged man to tell them where the house *Kò' Ehdanh's* wife was in was located. "A piece of red cloth hangs on it," he said.
>
> "Make a mark on your house," her husband told her. They say she had a white caribou skin on her house.
>
> (MYRA MOSES, VG2000-8-14A:383)

> Now the man she saw told her to put a flag up. That means to put moose skin up so they'll know where she was staying. They said, "Tomorrow morning, you're going to hear an owl down that way. You're going to hear a ptarmigan this way, just before daylight. That's the time we're going to come." Well, the woman knew, so she was awake. Sure enough, they came into town. They came into the village and killed everybody and took the woman back with them.
> (MOSES TIZYA, August 20, 1979, VG2000-8-22:030-0040, Gwich'in and English)

> He grabbed his [*Chii Choo's*] hair and knocked him over and clubbed him, and *Òe'teerahdyaa*,[17] *Kò' Ehdanh's* wife, ran out....They killed

everyone. *Kò' Ehdanh* said, "A bunch of caribou is going to escape." His friend's brother had his hair braided, long, hanging down. *Kò' Ehdanh* grabbed that and swung him around. "This is in place of my brother [who you killed]," he told him. He knew his friend's brother was going to get away. They killed everyone there....He said "Look for my friend." They were looking for his friend but he was gone. *Kò' Ehdanh* had said "Don't stay in one place in the month of...when the bull caribou's neck hair is white and long." He meant September.

They told *Kò' Ehdanh*, "Your friend is gone." "Then put all his belongings up on a stick." They were almost ready to leave when amongst the grass, the friend got up. He had a white club tied to his gun case. They said, "I wonder how many thousands of people they [the enemy–*Ch'ineekai*] killed." Grandchild, even so, *Kò' Ehdanh* never revenged his brother, they said. He suspected something and he stood there. He went to meet him. He was carrying the clothes for him. He said, "*Shijaa* [friend], don't come to me." The *Ch'ineekaii* cried, "My friend, my brother: did they kill him too?" *Kò' Ehdanh* knew they wouldn't get him. "*Shijaa*, your brother ran away. I was the one who got your brother." They said both of them cried. *Kò' Ehdanh* cried for his brother and his friend cried for his brother. They both grieved. *Kò' Ehdanh* said, "*Shijaa*, they sewed this for me to give to you. I will leave it here. After, you can take it. I will be leaving you now with my people. *Shijaa*, you are going to your people. Are you going to be okay?" "My friend, not far down is the ocean and there is a mountain. Near there are five families. I'm going there. When it gets dark, I'll rest. Tomorrow afternoon and all night if I travel, then I'll see them."...

Moses Tizya, too, told how *Kò' Ehdanh's* friend was going to live with a few of his people: "So *Kò' Ehdanh* gave the same kind of coat or something to him, whatever he had. So *Kò' Ehdanh's* partner told him about the Slave Lake people; he said, 'You just killed everybody. Now there are no more. There's only one house and one half left, that's all.' *Kò' Ehdanh* told him, 'Well, go there, go and stay with those people anyway'" (Moses Tizya, August 20, 1979, VG2000-8-22:360-370, Gwich'in and English).

Grandchild, after many years those five families gathered [with *Kò' Ehdanh's* people]. Everybody became friends and they gave each other gifts. Everything was good. Even so, *Kò' Ehdanh* killed some people there. They said he killed his friend. He grieved again, I guess, he grieved again. They said they killed lots of caribou and he cooked for the *Ch'ineekaii* in the evening. They had a good time. He was hot and took off his caribou skin parka. His friend was staying in front of him. "*Shijaa*, why don't you talk with me sometimes? Why are you always tired?" he asked his friend. "*Kò' Ehdanh*, why don't you talk another way?"

Grandchild, in those days, when they killed people, they did this [on their body], "My friend, how many times I [killed someone] and [made scars], you can see it." *Kò' Ehdanh* remembered his brother so he grabbed the club and jumped over the fire beside him and clubbed him. His [friend's] wife was going to run out and *Kò' Ehdanh's* wife grabbed her. They killed her also....Now *Kò' Ehdanh* thought about the past to animals [dreamt to animals—had shaman's powers], they said. They stood together on one side. They never thought they would fight; the place was filled with dust. While it was dark they killed all the *Ch'ineekaii*. *Kò' Ehdanh* said he wanted to stay with the Van Tat Gwich'in.

(SARAH ABEL, VG2003-3-01:163-365, Gwich'in)

Moses Tizya described how men made scars on their bodies to represent the number of people they had killed, and how this motivated *Kò' Ehdanh* to kill his "enemy-partner." He provided an additional reason: his partner lied to him.

Years and years after, *Kò' Ehdanh's* partner came back again. *Kò' Ehdanh* had a big bunch of people camped with him but they were scared of each other. They camped a short distance apart; the Slave bunch was there, and *Kò' Ehdanh's* bunch was here. *Kò' Ehdanh*, knew his partner had lied to him. He said there were no more people and then he came with a big bunch of people. So he knew that those people were going to try to kill him.

So anyway, those *Ch'ineekaii* knives, you ever see one? They call them *vih* but I don't know what the name is in English. *Kò' Ehdanh* sent his son to his partner, telling him, "Just run up there and open the door. Just throw this knife to that old man and tell him you want to make peace. My father asks you to make peace together and live happily together." His son said, "Alright."

So the next day or that same day, same evening maybe, they put their camps together. They all camped together and *Kò' Ehdanh* was singing that he won the war, he sang. The others didn't understand him but our people knew it. So they were really all happy. Everybody was happy.

Toward the evening, *Kò' Ehdanh's* partner, like a crazy fool, said something he shouldn't say. They were together, camped together. *Kò' Ehdanh* told him that evening, "Ah, *shitlih*, why don't you tell me some kind of story." So this darn fool, he just pulled up his sleeve and showed the marks on his arms for how many times he had killed people. He had all these marks; he showed that to *Kò' Ehdanh*, while *Kò' Ehdanh* had a club with him there. He said, "What can I tell you?" He told the old man, "Look," he said, "look how many times I killed people." At that time *Kò' Ehdanh* had his club and he knocked him out and killed him, killed the whole bunch. So he went out and he hollered, he said, "He wants to fight now, just go right across and kill him," he said. People didn't know what had happened. He just jumped out and killed the whole works.

(MOSES TIZYA, August 20, 1979, VG2000-8-22:383-380, 040-067, Gwich'in and English)

K'aiiheenjik—Willow Man, told by Dick Nukon

K'aiiheenjik [Literally: Willow Creek] is a story of a highly respected Van Tat Gwich'in man of legendary stature and power who used his strength to provide for his people, as a "big man" should, and then he became a target of envy and a dangerous threat. He possessed powerful brothers (like many "big men") to whom he was loyal and embarked on a campaign of retribution after one brother was killed. He proved impossible to kill except by his own hand. Unlike the *Kò' Ehdanh* story, *K'aiiheenjik* is associated with specific places on the land between Old Crow and the upper Porcupine River. The site of his death is a bluff in the Fishing Branch area that appears permanently stained red by his blood and marks his end to all who know his story.

This version of the story is by Dick Nukon, a current Elder. In his parents' generation, Myra Kaye recorded an oral version and Joe Netro produced a written version, and excerpts of these are referred to here, as well.

Whoever was the smartest and strongest, they just wanted to kill them. Long ago, *K'aiiheenjik* lived amongst them. He was smart; moose were just like nothing to him [he was very strong]. His brothers were the same and they followed him.

"That *K'aiiheenjik* is too smart. We should kill his brother instead," [the people] said, so they killed him. Then they were going to kill *K'aiiheenjik*, too. That's why they followed him but they made a mistake. He had killed a moose and was skinning it when they came upon him. He asked them, "Have you seen my brother?" "Up there not far, he was skinning a [moose]. We passed him," they said.

He figured it out right then....He cooked the moose head for them. While they were eating that, he was going to kill them....When he was

Dick Nukon holding his daughter, Christine.

[Canadian Museum of Civilization, photo Father Jean-Marie Mouchet s2004-1328]

roasting the head, one man was so scared he shivered. *K'aiiheenjik* found out that way: "What happened in front of him that he shivers so much?" *K'aiiheenjik* said, and he killed the man.

Other versions, such as that of Myra Kaye and Joe Netro, report that *K'aiiheenjik* killed the people using the jaw from the moose head as a club (Myra Kaye, 1980, VG2000-8-21, Gwich'in; Netro n.d.:16).

K'aiiheenjik was as strong as two men. *K'aiiheenjik* went back on the trail following them. He was close to home. *K'aiiheenjik* knocked [one man] down and killed him. The other one was going to tell the news, but he made a mistake. *K'aiiheenjik* killed him....The boy that was going back to camp was screaming and they heard him. "A moose just went by here," *K'aiiheenjik* told them. *K'aiiheenjik* went after the moose, followed the moose tracks....Those who were at the camp went with *K'aiiheenjik* far into the woods. He followed them and while the people were walking, one tripped and the rest of the people followed. He killed them.

> All the people started to run to the moose. Willow Man was behind and pushed the man in front of him. This man then stepped on the next man's snowshoes and everyone in front fell down so he killed them all with a good dry wood club, except the ladies. Then the ladies led him to another camp. Apparently he killed a lot of people.
>
> (NETRO 1973:16)

> From there, how *K'aiiheenjik* made out and where he went, nobody knew. Down this way [toward Crow River] *K'aiiheenjik* rafted down the Porcupine. He pulled out big trees; he tore them out of ground. In the big hole in the ground, he hid. They were coming downriver to where they stayed; *K'aiiheenjik* saw all that. He went back upriver and killed them.

Both Myra Kaye and Joe Netro reported events that occurred upstream of Old Crow, at *Tl'oo K'at*, where two young men were trained to defeat *K'aiiheenjik*: "From Rat Indian Creek to *Tl'oo K'at* they had spring camps. Two young boys, one of them could jump over a fishnet and the other could run across the river on a stick sticking out of the river...." (Myra Kaye, 1980, VG2000-8-21, Gwich'in). Netro writes:

> Willow Man's sister was married to a man. Apparently she went for wood and came upon Willow Man. His sister told him everything. She said two boys were being trained to challenge him. One can jump over a net and one can walk across the river on sticks. The girl told Willow Man that she didn't want to lose her husband so he told her to put a feather on his head so he could see that this particular man with a feather on his head was his sister's husband. When this man was jumping over the net, Willow Man killed him and he also killed some of the people. This other man was running across the river and the people told Willow Man that it was his brother that was running away from him. These are the people who killed his brother apparently. He killed all the people and walked away. This was the last time he killed people.
>
> (NETRO 1973:17)

> Then where he went, nobody knows; upriver at Bear Cave Mountain, around there. One man was following a sheep there. The sheep disappeared and the man followed the sheep and walked right into *K'aiiheenjik*. The man quickly retreated. He crawled under big spruce branches.... I guess he was a medicine man. He got out of there. How come *K'aiiheenjik* never found him? His brother was with him, too. With big rocks from around there, he pounded the big spruce trees and there were chips flying all over. The man was sitting underneath the trees

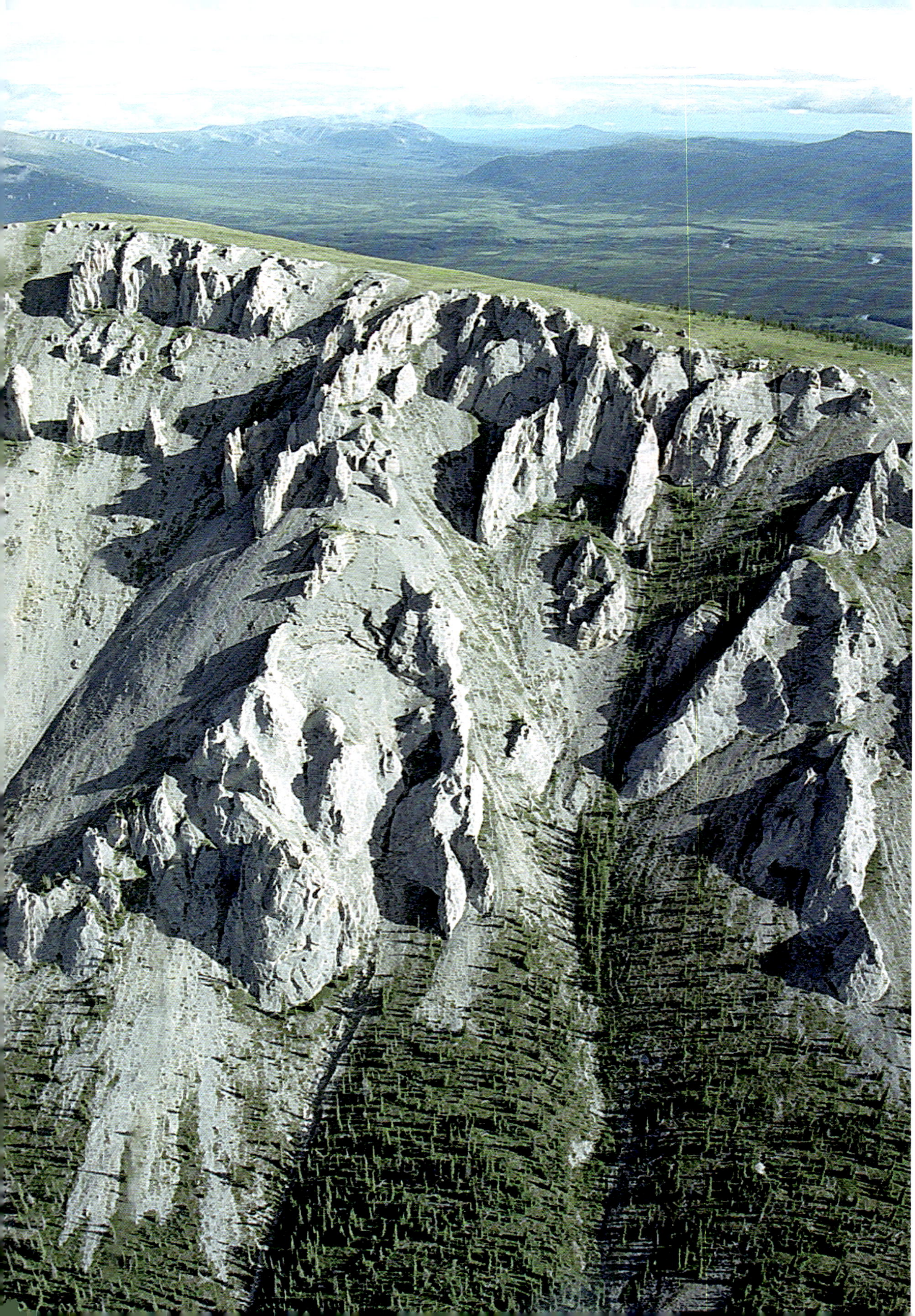

Ch'ii Ch'à'an *(Bear Cave Mountain)* and Fishing Branch River in the distance.
[Shirleen Smith ©VGFN 2000]

and *K'aiiheenjik* hit [near] him two times, but he was left untouched. I guess he was a medicine man.

That man saw *K'aiiheenjik* so they found him. The man went to his people down[river] this way [Crow River area]. The man and his people went back up to kill *K'aiiheenjik*, but they made a mistake. At Bear Cave Mountain, when he hunted, they say he made himself look like a grizzly bear. One of his brothers went with him and one of them sat back at camp. They came upon him [at camp]. He was just scared looking. "What does your brother say when he comes back?" they asked him. "I say *Gwikhih* and I jump over the fire," [he said]. All the boys said the same thing, and one of the boys said exactly what he said. They put [the boy] in *K'aiiheenjik's* brother's place and killed him.

In the evening *K'aiiheenjik* was coming back. The man sitting at camp looked scared. [Laughter] *K'aiiheenjik* said, "*Gwikhih, Gwikhih.*"

His sister was there in his absence, they asked her, "When your brother is coming, what sound do you make?" He called his sister, "*Shihshuu Deechan, Shihshuu Deechan,*" she said, and I answer "'*Gokheh*' and I run out to him." Out of all those people who tried to imitate her,...just one could imitate her. That woman [*K'aiiheenjik's* sister] was killed....[*K'aiiheenjik*] told her, "I thought I told you to make fire for me." He knew something was wrong, and they attacked him.... His brothers yelled, and he told [them], "I am not defeated yet, my brothers." And they killed his brothers....They were not smart people. Two strong men tried to attack him and he grabbed them; he had them both under his arm and said, "These two will replace my nephews." And jumped off the cliff, and when he hit bottom his intestines fell out and he grabbed his intestines and moved them over a little further and died. And in that area there is red ochre that is said to be his blood, they said. It turns really red when you burn it; it turns to powder to paint with.

(MYRA KAYE, January 21, 1980, VG2000-8-21, Gwich'in)

The man never replied and that's how *K'aiiheenjik* found out. They had lined up in view of on the trail [and shot *K'aiiheenjik* with arrows]. His body was covered with arrows like porcupine quills. It didn't hurt him. He was going to kill them all but they had killed his brothers. Because of that, he killed himself. He went up amongst the rocks and pretended to be dead. The two leaders of the people who had beaded headbands came down to him. He was lying up there and they came toward him. They thought he was sleeping. He woke up. One of them grabbed him by the arm because he was going to go over the cliff. Those that were down there, he talked down to them, they say. *K'aiiheenjik* said, "Don't say you killed me, say you *dhaadlii*[18] [froze me; or orphaned me]....," he said, and jumped off the cliff. He killed himself.

He killed too many people so the people wanted to kill him so they moved to the head of the Porcupine. He hid at Fishing Branch....The news spread to other tribes of people so they all planned to move in on him and kill him. So all the people came to his camp but he was gone. Only his brother was home. The brother's name was *Shoo-da-chun*—Smart One. The people asked him, "What kind of sign do you make when your brother comes home?" He made a noise and jumped back and forth over the fire. The people chased two boys to imitate him. They killed *Shoo-da-chun* and put the two boys in his place. It was getting a bit dark when he came home. He called his brother but the boys were so scared they made a different noise. Willow Man said to his brother, "I told you to make fire to dry my clothes," but a different voice came so he turned back. The people started shooting arrows at him. All his brothers were dead but he didn't even feel the arrows hit him....All his body was covered with arrows. After he removed the arrows from his body, on a bluff, he made a fire with them. Actually, one arrow could kill a moose in those days.

(NETRO, N.D.:17)

Then he laid down by the fire and pretended to die. He had a head band made of bones and beads. He rubbed this against a rock. The people said to each other, "We shouldn't let him wear those expensive bones out. Let's go and get them." So two boys went to him but he got up and picked the two boys up and put each one under each arm and said, "I'm happy, I'm going to kill these two." He also said, "Don't say you killed me, say you froze me to death." He then jumped over the bluff and almost killed himself. After he fell on the ground, he picked up his intestines and moved them a little further away and died there. His blood turned to paint and this paint is used to paint snowshoes—Indian Ink [red ochre].

(NETRO, N.D.:18)

There where he fell, the ground is just red, you know. Where his body landed, I saw it one time from a helicopter. Funny, he died there, but those geologists, how come they never looked around there? If they looked there maybe they'd find his bones.

That is the way *K'aiiheenjik* said beforehand he was going to kill himself. They probably ran home, I guess. Now the white people and

> Native people would have him for a great leader ["king"], but instead they killed him, they said.
>
> *K'aiiheenjik* was a real big man, you know. In the fall, when he hunted, his brothers with him, when the grizzly bear went into his den, he just kicked a hole and spoiled the den. The grizzly bear gets angry easily. He just grabbed its head....He never hurt it. He put it inside his jacket, they say.
>
> Long ago when I was a child, my old man [father] always talked about him. I never saw *K'aiiheenjik*.
>
> (DICK NUKON, Crow Flats, June 11, 2001, VG2001-2-34:007-110, Gwich'in)

STORIES OF HEROIC ROLES AND ARCHETYPES

There is a body of Gwich'in stories about heroic deeds by a type or social category of person, rather than specifically named individuals. Common examples are the tales about the beneficial deeds of *shanaghàn*—old women who often outwit danger and overcome great obstacles to protect and provide salvation for their people. There are also many stories in which a smart young woman (much like *Kò' Ehdanh's* wife) plays a key role through her intelligence and industry, and because her value is widely recognized, she often has to apply her skills in escaping captors.

Shanaghàn—Old Women

Looking at Gwich'in stories of *shanaghàn* and similar stories from other subarctic peoples, Slobodin observed: "Since, as in so much of the world's folklore, 'the last shall be first,' poor old widows, who occupy the least enviable statuses in subarctic American society, frequently play critical roles. Their daughters are boreal Cinderellas..." (Slobodin 1971:282).

Old women, especially widows, were relatively powerless physically and vulnerable members of Gwich'in society. Long-ago stories highlight how they were able to overcome great difficulties in spite of their weakness and limited resources.[19] The value of their experience, ingenuity, and moral steadfastness proved their greatest assets. Generally there is an ironic twist, whereby instead of being feeble liabilities, their actions feed the people in times of famine or protect them from significant threats.

How a Smart *Shanaghàn* Saved People Who Were Starving,
told by Sarah Abel

In this two-episode story, Sarah Abel described the virtue of sharing food and the importance of attending to the warnings of elders. The old woman

Above: Sarah Abel with her grandson, David Lord.

[Canadian Museum of Civilization, photo Father Jean-Marie Mouchet S2004-1343]

Page 43: Eliza Steamboat, Gwich'in Elder.

[Canadian Museum of Civilization, photo Father Jean-Marie Mouchet S2004-1426]

in this story saves people through her kindness, industriousness, and observation. The story also mentions details of the social position of old women.

One man had no food. There was no food and he had a young child. The child was big enough to eat food and his grandmother was living. The man was married to the *shanaghàn's* [old woman's] daughter but she died.

Grandchild, *ch'idrèedhòh vał* is a toboggan made from the skin of the caribou leg bones. They made one, put in a fur blanket, and in it he pulled the child, they said.

The *shanaghàn's* other daughter had a big family, too. She had lots of children. They had a hard time hunting so that man hunted. They did something; it's bad. While he pulled his child in the dark they said, "You are not coming in here. Don't come in," the other daughter told him from inside.

Well, Grandchild, if he went inside, she would kill him. Long ago it was like that. So he couldn't go in. So even though it was dark, he put on his snowshoes and he pulled his child.

He walked in the dark beside a small valley and came to a small spruce tree all by itself. He leaned against it with his head. He put branches in it, put the baby in there and went away, they say. He walked a ways and ptarmigan came out from under some brush. He

42   PEOPLE OF THE LAKES

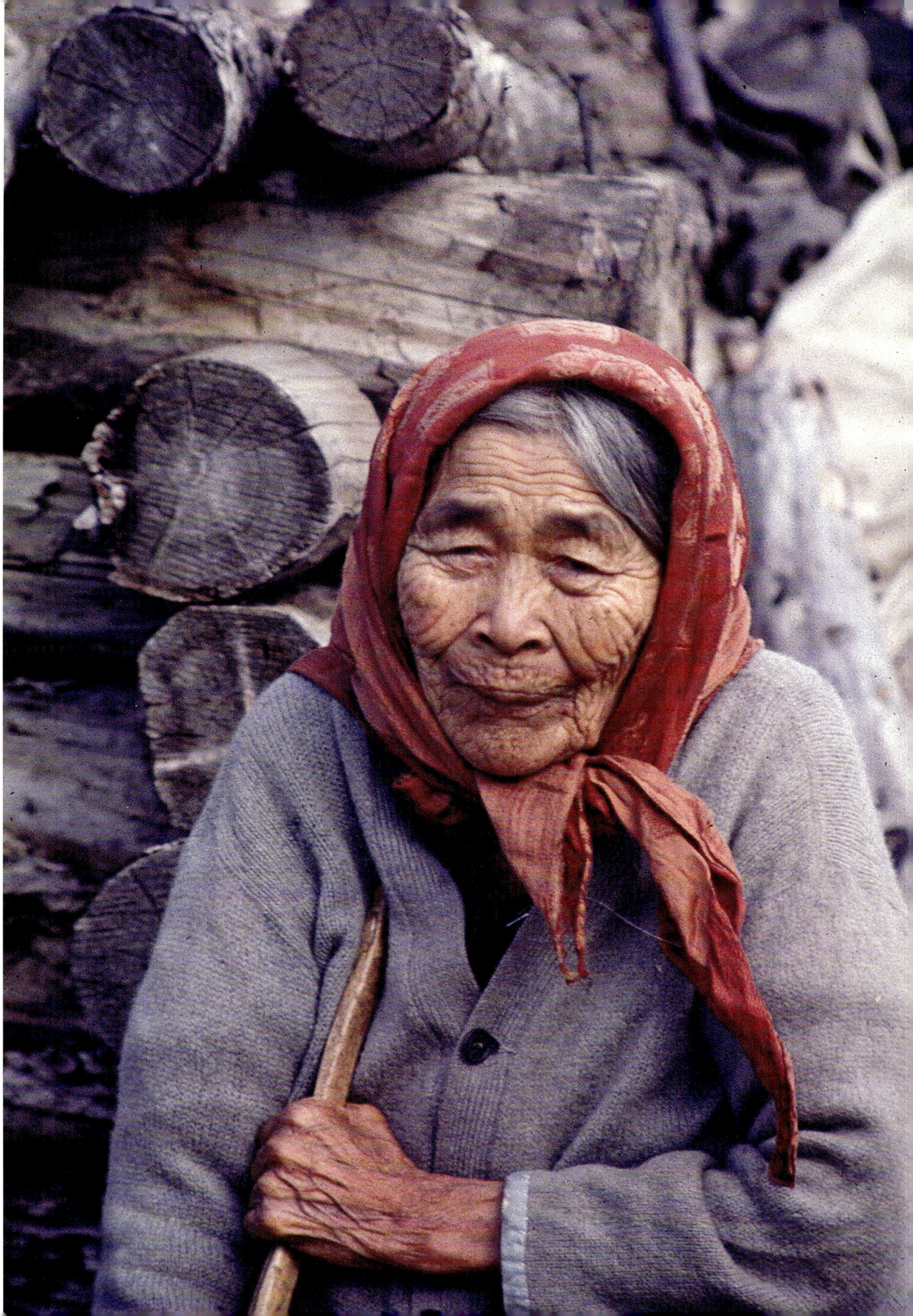

stepped on one of the ptarmigan with his big snowshoes and killed it. That was his food and he took it back to his child.

The *shanaghàn*, mother of his wife who died, had followed him. She pulled a small tent after the child. They say she was a smart *shanaghàn*. She came upon the child sitting there. She dug out the snow, laid branches in there, and put the little tent over him to make a shelter. Then, she collected wood and made a fire while her son-in-law was coming back, the child's father. "Ah!" she told him. "I am going to warm the child inside, that's what I'm doing." He asked her, "Why did you come after me?" "I'm going to teach him everything," she told her son-in-law, and she did. He gave her hot ptarmigan and made ptarmigan broth for his child, so the child ate. Him, too, he ate a little but he made the child drink the ptarmigan broth. After that, in the early morning, he left, saying, "Follow and where I make a mark, stop with the child and make a fire."

Near there was a river and lots of wood. He made a sign and there they camped. He killed winter caribou, they said. The *shanaghàn* gathered blood for his child. They made broth from the blood and gave it to the child to drink. He did that for him and he ate; then the child grew.

Ah, the child grew up to be smart. All the people used him for killing food. The woman who told him "Don't come in here" froze, they say, because they had no food.

In those days the people lived through really hard times, Grandchild. Today, every person can survive. They can't camp one night without food, either. Then, we would get weak and wouldn't live well. At that time, sometimes there was no meat for a long time. Even so, not knowing how soon they were going to see meat, they moved around, moved around. Finally they came to where there was meat. The *shanaghàn* made *ch'idrèedhòh vał* [caribou-leg toboggans]. They pulled their little tents with them, walking on the trails, in those days. Then, Grandchild, the *shanaghàn* on the trail stayed with the people.

Lots of people who had no food stayed with the child, his grandmother, and his father. There were lots of people, but there was not much food.

In those days, the *shanaghàn* would never camp in the middle of the people. When the people were moving down from high country on a hard trail, they would camp away from the main camp and make fire. They camped by the river. As they were moving down over the mountain, the snow was melting so it was good. Even from a long ways away, their tracks were white. She knew that, the *shanaghàn*. She was pulling behind on the trail. Behind, she was tired and cold.

Margaret Blackfox with a load of firewood, June 1946.

[Yukon Archives, Claude and Mary Tidd fonds 7644]

The *shanaghàn* kept looking back. Just then, way up on the mountain they had come over, she saw a big black thing on the trail. She really got scared, so she made a small fire the middle of the trail, and then she spoke out. She spoke out to the people: "Way up there on the melting snow we came over, I looked back. Really, I think I saw an animal walking. Be alert. Don't sleep tonight," she told them.

Well, Grandchild, amongst us sometimes are those who are not wise. Those people laughed at her. They thought she was lying. But the *shanaghàn* knew she saw something. She made her doorway small and narrow. She tied rope all over her house and made it really strong.

Now, all the people went to sleep. Then there was a big noise. In those days, when a *shih* [grizzly bear] lived in the winter,[20] his fur was

Long-ago Stories   45

all iced up and he made a lot of noise when he walked, they say. While the old *shanaghàn* was warning the people that he was coming, the *shih* was walking down through the timber. She found a large stump and hollowed out the top of it. She tied it with rope so it wouldn't break. Then she put lots of dry branches, kindling, and cinders in it. Just as she finished, the bear arrived, noisy. She lit the stump. In the middle of her house, she built up the fire to see him clearly. She looked outside, and then he tried to come in but the doorway was too narrow. He couldn't come in, the *shih*. While he was trying to get in, she put the stump on his head. She kept pushing it on his head, that old woman. The stump didn't break because she had tied it well with rope. Then he went away, and he was angry when it ignited. It didn't come off his head; his head was really stuck. It blew up, far up. She never heard it, they say. It didn't make a noise.

In the morning when everybody was still sleeping, the old woman made a fire. She untied her door and went outside to look around for the *shih*. He was laying there, they say. The old woman spoke out loudly. "You told me I was lying! Come and see!" she told them. Ahh! Everybody got up. "What is the *shanaghàn* talking about up there?" They gathered around her. The big *shih* lay there, dead. It was all covered in ice. Well, Grandchild, they didn't have much meat, and she fed the people.

The...*shanaghàn* did this, they say.

(SARAH ABEL, April 19, 1980, VG2000-8-32:085-230, Gwich'in)

Two *Shanaghàn* and *Nanaa'in'* at a Fish Trap, told by Sarah Abel
Elders emphasize that in long-ago times people travelled a great deal. For the elderly and infirm who could neither manage such strenuous activity nor easily be transported by others (such as in summer when sleds could not be used), settling at fish traps during the season when many fish species spawn was a valuable alternative. This story describes the situation of two such women who not only accomplished their own survival but that of their people, as well, while relying on their limited physical resources but considerable experience and ingenuity.

Long-ago stories, some of them are not true, even so what is said is storytelling, that's why it's told. Some of it I don't remember too well, but I will talk about it.

Two *shanaghàn* [old women] were living at the fish trap in the summertime. They were poor and weak. There was lots of meat, caribou. The people moved around; it was hard for the *shanaghàn* to move

Gwich'in fish weir.

[Canadian Museum of Civilization, photo Father Jean-Marie Mouchet S2004-1417]

from camp to camp, so the people made them a fish trap and left them there. If they killed fish, that way they would eat. In those days it was hard to get store-bought things. They just had one small knife, which they shared. They cut and dried fish. They had a fire in the middle and slept beside it. When they fished, sometimes they got only two or three fish. No matter how few fish they caught, they would dry them. "If there's not enough meat for a lot of people, then they can help themselves to this fish." They worked for that.

When they had killed quite a lot of fish a *nanaa'in'* [bushman; troublesome, semi-wild man] came upon them and ate their fish. They had a fire outside. He didn't come in but tormented them from outside. One of the *shanaghàn* had a good mind. She set rabbit snares for him and they got rabbits. As they caught each rabbit, he would eat it. He took all the rabbits out of their snares, too. All that they caught, only he lived on it.

Finally he was sleeping, I guess. While he was sleeping somewhere, they found one of the rabbits. They cut its stomach and they carefully removed the guts. At the fireplace, they put it on the hot ashes.

Long-ago Stories 47

Then the *nanaa'in'* came and visited them. He poked his head inside the doorway and all night as they slept, he would make them mad. Of course, they didn't have an axe either so they burned long dry willows. Some of the wood was outside and he shook the ends so the coals sparked. He really gave those old women a hard time.

Finally the *shanaghàn* was going to kill him. She was prepared. The rabbit guts were really hot. She had put them on hot ashes, mixed with coals, and the guts were boiling. As it was getting dark, he came again to harass them around the doorway. Just when the *nanaa'in'* poked his head in the door opening, she placed the hot rabbit guts on the palm of her hands, on the mitts she wore. As he was looking down at them, she threw it on his face. She killed him, my grandchild.

They fell asleep. All the previous nights the *nanaa'in'* bothered the *shanaghàn* and they had never slept well. The fish hung above them and he would take that, too, while they slept. The *shanaghàn* threw the hot rabbit guts on him and then they heard a big noise. They tried to wait for him, in case he came back. They waited for him but a long time passed, so the *shanaghàn* fell asleep.

They woke at dawn. They looked down the way he had gone. It was around September, I guess. They had been at the fish trap since the month of June. So, they looked for the *nanaa'in'* and where he had fallen down, he was laying dead. They saw him.

So now the *shanaghàn* killed lots of fish. They made a cache for them, too. They made grease from the guts and dryfish; all that they put in there. When it began to freeze, they hung up the fish, sometimes one or two. This way it froze, and they put it in the cache. They did this with the rabbits, too.

Grandchild, meanwhile lots of people travelled in the mountains and never killed any food. They checked on the *shanaghàn* and they had killed a lot of fish. The people depended on them, they said.

(SARAH ABEL, April 19, 1980, VG2000-8-32:003-077, Gwich'in)

Tr'iinjoo Vigwizhi' Goonlii—Smart Woman

In Gwich'in folklore, smart women often became "stolen women" because, as highly valued individuals, they were kidnapped by rivals, enemies (for example *Kò' Ehdanh*'s wife), supernatural beings, or animals, such as *nanaa'in'* [bushmen]. In 1888, Petitot described smart women as women who are stolen back and forth (1888:199), which Slobodin calls "Prize Women" (1971:285). They were beautiful, well-dressed, and adorned, and if they were also clever, they would escape from their captors to return to their own people. They were valued not only for their beauty and skills but as prizes of high-ranking leaders in war. Slobodin cites a humorous side to the Prize Woman story. A woman who was captured back and forth between two or more groups of people eventually came to have children and grandchildren in many camps. Ultimately, when a war party led by her original husband came for her yet again, she told them that since she was now old, they could continue to fight if they wished, but she was not going to move again. Her refusal caused the combatants to turn to verbal rivalry and, ultimately, trading instead of battle (1971:287).

Nanaa'in' or bushman stories also comprise a category in themselves. *Nanaa'in'* stories are widespread: for example, Slavey and Hare stories of *nakah* stealing young women and sabotaging traps among the Dene throughout the Mackenzie River valley to the east and south. The *nanaa'in'* lived apart from society and were known to steal girls and women as their partners whenever the opportunity arose, as well as wreaking havoc by stealing food and being intentionally bothersome. There is a body of stories about how the stolen women were able to defeat the *nanaa'in'* by relying on their intelligence and guile and return to their people while removing the threat. Attitudes expressed in these stories about the hostile and unpredictable *nanaa'in'* reflect the distrust and suspicion of people not integrated into Gwich'in kin-based social institutions. In this story, Moses Tizya supplied additional information on the nature of *nanaa'in'* as essentially ordinary men who became *nanaa'in'* by violating the social obligation to share food.

Story of *Tr'iinjoo Vigwizhi' Goonlii* [smart woman] and *Nanaa'in'* [bushman], told by Moses Tizya

Anyways, there was one bushman, we call him *nanaa'in'*. McPherson people call him *nana'iih*, different again. Well, ours is really the right word.

Anyway this *nanaa'in'* stole a girl from one family. They fished between the lakes with a fish trap. Years after, this *nanaa'in'* was bringing good fish all the time. So the young girl became suspicious. It looked to her like it was her parents fishing for her. It looked like the same fish. So she got wise and told her husband, *nanaa'in'*, "This is good fish. To get ready for winter, why don't we move closer to where you got these fish." So they moved to the creek.

This was the creek between the lakes, where the girl and her family used to fish, in the early days. He only fished at nighttime, that *nanaa'in'*. He only fished at nighttime, and to the girl, it looked like where her parents used to fish every year. The fish looked the same.

Martha and Moses Tizya by their tent. Upright log in foreground is notched for bending toboggan boards.

[Yukon Archives, George and Margaret Hamilton fonds 89/38 #7]

Anyway, one day *nanaa'in'* was sleeping and the girl heard her mother cry for her from one of the nearby creeks. She heard her mother cry so she knew where she was when they got up in the evening to start fishing again. So the girl followed him, followed behind him.

Sure enough, the camp was there, and her parents were fishing. At the bridge across the fish trap,[21] *nanaa'in'* fished in the fish trap while everybody slept....He was naked and he got fish. While he fished the girl snuck into the camp and woke the people. She told them that bushman, *nanaa'in'*, was fishing out there.

In those days, they say, know this: expect war all the time. So when they fished...they had a bridge this way and one that way; and they had a bridge here, too. So *nanaa'in'* was out there and it was nighttime, dark, you see. And they came across here, some across there. He didn't know it. That's the way they fooled him and they killed him. That's the way she fooled *nanaa'in'*, that girl. That's that way it happened.

In those days, people were always travelling and sometimes they got so hungry they didn't want to give what they had to eat to their own friends, their own relations. That's why they would sneak away, run into the bush and hide and make their own living, and they say they made a den....They just lived in dens, those *nanaa'in'*, in those days.

After that, they would only get wood and everything in the summer. They didn't go out in the wintertime. They just stayed in their dens all winter. That's the way *nanaa'in'* lived in those days. There were lots of them. They never lived in the open. Just in summertime, they came out and hunted bear, gophers, ptarmigan, anything, moose, caribou, and dried them in their dens. They packed it up for winter. They lived on drymeat all winter, that's how they lived.

(MOSES TIZYA, August 20, 1979, VG2000-8-22:117-176, Gwich'in and English)

LONG-AGO HISTORY

Yeenoo dài' googwandak—long-ago stories—include accounts that are believed to be accurate representations of first events (history). The stories are considered historical (consciously distinguished from mythological or legendary stories) but of considerable antiquity, such that there is no known link between the narrator and original participants or eyewitnesses, usually important Gwich'in criteria for accuracy.

War with the *Ch'ineekaii*

In this story of war and peace, Moses Tizya made it clear that he was talking about relatively recent events, "about 300 years ago" or in 1500 or 1600. One of his contemporaries, Myra Kaye, provided another clue to the time of the war: she noted that *Dahjiłti* (a variant pronunciation of *Daachilti'*) was an old man when Bishop Bompas travelled to Fort Yukon, in 1865 (Sax and Linklater 1990:14):

> [Bishop Bompas] arrived in Arctic Village and gave the elders tobacco, pipe, and matches....*Dahjiłti* was still living....He stayed with his daughter. His daughter was working and she heard her father pounding. He was blind and had no teeth. He only ate pounded meat. Once in a while he laughed so she looked to see: he was pounding [tobacco] leaves. "The tobacco...was given to you to smoke, what are you doing? Why are you laughing?" she asked. He said, "I can't see. Why don't they give us something we are familiar with?" and he threw the pounded leaves away. That is how little we knew about tobacco.
>
> (MYRA KAYE, VG2000-8-37, Gwich'in)

The event she described from 1865 when *Dahjiłti* was elderly suggests that the story Moses Tizya told of him likely occurred 40 to 50 years earlier, in *Dahjiłti's* younger years, which would put the "war" sometime between

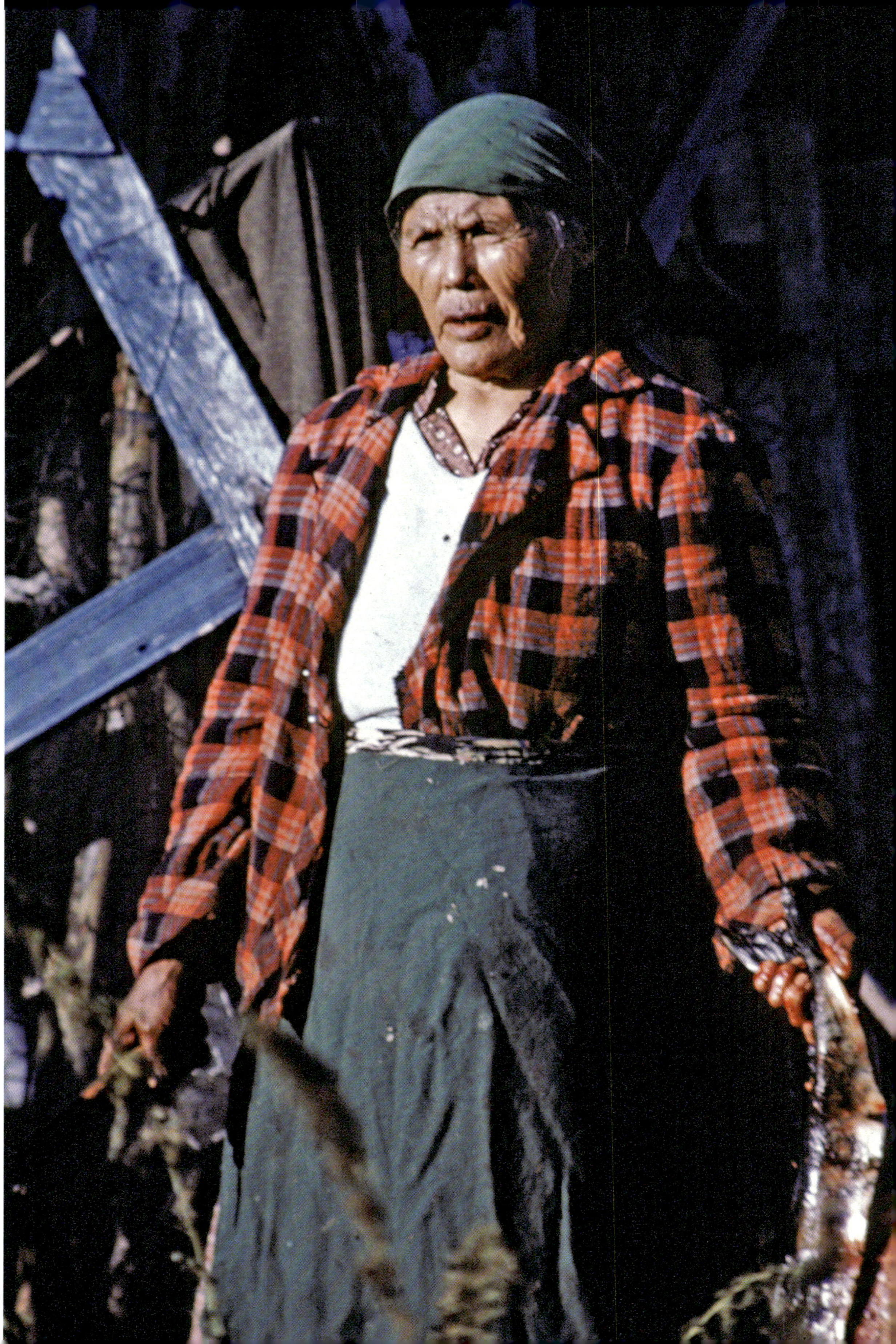

Page 52: Myra Kaye, wife of Reverend Joe Kaye.

[Canadian Museum of Civilization, photo Father Jean-Marie Mouchet s2004-1350]

Above: Inuvialuit camps on the spit near Shingle Point, northern Yukon.

[Shirleen Smith ©VGFN 2000]

1815 and 1825. The anthropologist Richard Slobodin compiled a list of published reports of hostilities between "Eskimo" and "Kutchin" of the lower Mackenzie River between 1817 and 1856, which he noted were a continuation of pre-contact conflicts. He commented that, "Although unwritten tradition is said to be of little direct historic value, it may be remarked that most of the incidents after 1840 are preserved in Kutchin tradition" (Slobodin 1962:24-25). Moses Tizya's story represents part of the historical facet of this tradition.

Moses Tizya drew an analogy between the way elders passed on the story of these events to the function of newspapers today. He also asserted that this history would be familiar to both sides in the former dispute, "Rat Indians" [Gwich'in] and "*Ch'ineekaii*" [Inuvialuit].

War with *Ch'ineekaii*: *Daachilti'* and *Hanadaandaii*, told by Moses Tizya

Ah, this fellow had a war with *Ch'ineekaii*, Herschel Island *Ch'ineekaii*.... His name was *Daachilti'*; that means something like Hook. He was...a General [leader] in those days....Two [Gwich'in] boys went down to visit the *Ch'ineekaii*, down to Herschel Island. They went into the *Ch'ineekaii* camp and [the *Ch'ineekaii*] killed these two guys from Crow Flats, Rat Indians. Then they had a war over that, but the Rat Indians killed

Long-ago Stories 53

thousands and thousands of *Ch'ineekaii* and [the *Ch'ineekaii*] never killed one after that.

Daachilti's brother's name was *Hanadaandaii*: that means "He Works Hard to Survive." *Hanadaandaii* fought *Ch'ineekaii* at Shingle Point and his brother *Daachilti'* fought them down at Herschel Island....

One time *Daachilti'* went down to Herschel Island. [The *Ch'ineekaii* had made a] protective building for themselves. I don't know how long it was but a good many thousand *Ch'ineekaii* were in it....The Indian army went there.

The *Ch'ineekaii* thought they were going to kill people. They made a hole up there and one *Ch'ineekaii* lay on the floor. He thought he was just going to go down and kill all the army. He made a mistake. But *Daachilti'* went on top. He went quick, you know, his arrow came fast. While the *Ch'ineekaii* got everything ready, it hit him right in his chest and killed him. Then the Indian family put wood on [the *Ch'ineekaii* shelter]. They piled it up and...pretty soon, there was no more room... so the Rat Indian army...put fire to that shelter and burned the whole works. Burned the whole *Ch'ineekaii* army. I don't know how many thousand were in there...they burned them all.

And then another time, the Rat Indians were going down the Firth River and it was springtime....They couldn't even see footprints on the ice, and when they...came out of the mountains...they had two boys sitting there, watching the *Ch'ineekaii*....They just kept quiet. There happened to be a big kind of den there; they call it a big hole in the rock [cave]. The whole army was in there. When all the *Ch'ineekaii* started to come up, they pounded them with rocks. With gravel, you know: Eskimo Pass, good gravel there. Some *Ch'ineekaii* passed but then, after that they saw nobody and no sign or anything, no tracks and no footprints. As they passed, they had moved a [piece of gravel to one side]. That's the way they counted them, see.

So they determined there were two [*Ch'ineekaii*] left. They thought they made a mistake, but still they waited....Late in [the] morning, two more came back....All this time these boys just...sat there and never say a word, because that's the way the family did it, you know, in those days. And then everyone went up there and looked. Gee! There were twice as many as their army! Anyway they killed them all....They went up the Firth River and *Daachilti'* told them: "Better beat it right away because those *Ch'ineekaii* made a noise that means...a signal." Maybe lots of *Ch'ineekaii* were near and would hear him, that's what he meant.

Anyway, in those days, *Ch'ineekaii* didn't use snowshoes....The Indian army went back to the head of the Firth River and put on their snowshoes and...started to go up the mountain. Lots of *Ch'ineekaii* were coming. They say that there was a big glacier there. Oh, I don't know how many miles...but that army came behind him, the *Ch'ineekaii* army. Well...they couldn't go in deep snow without snowshoes, so they turned back.

And after that, another time, Gwich'in were at the head of the Firth River and a big bunch of *Ch'ineekaii* were there and they killed them all, too. They say they lived in snow houses and the Gwich'in had what they call war clubs. They mean caribou-horn war club, I guess, long. They say when they hit them, snow houses are ice inside. The *Ch'ineekaii* had a fire going in there, and it was full of ice. They say when they hit it, all that ice fell down and killed them. They sleep naked and the ice dropped on them and killed them, the whole works.

There were three brothers who killed people around the other way....*Hanadaandaii's* brother went to Herschel Island and did the same thing, too, but there's no story about him.

And that's the way they had a war with the Rat Indian in those days....The *Ch'ineekaii* made a mistake, and they never killed anyone.... Before that, I think the *Ch'ineekaii* had [a] big war with the McPherson Indians for a long time, and later on they told the story. They say the McPherson people, their bows are not very strong. Sometimes, they hit a *Ch'ineekaii* with an arrow and they just took it out and cured that man. But they say that [Rat] Indian arrows, when they hit a *Ch'ineekaii*, the arrow went right through them: just, like, no chance.

So, after that *Daachilti'* told his people..."Ah, there's no use killing the people. We're going to make peace with them." Anyway, they went back...to Herschel Island and started to make peace, and his brother did the same thing at Shingle Point. They made peace with the *Ch'ineekaii*. They said that both sides had armies; the *Ch'ineekaii* army and the Indian army....Well, I don't know what they paid them with in those days. There was no iron of any kind. That was way before white men ever came to the country. We don't know what year that was, probably, we'll say 1500, 1600....Anyway, *Daachilti'* made peace with them. He told them, "There's no use killing each other. We might as well make peace and be happy and be good friends together." So they did, and they made good friends with them.

After that, there was no more trouble between Rat Indians and Herschel Island *Ch'ineekaii*....That's the way they had a war with the Rat Indian one time but that was just between Herschel Island *Ch'ineekaii* and Rat Indians.

This is how much I know. I heard the story from old people, early days people. They told that story to us. They carried the story out here

Long-ago Stories

and there...like a newspaper, just like newspapers. They carried this story from one generation to the next. That's how they know. If you guys ask all the old *Ch'ineekaii*, they're going to tell you the same story. They know all about it, even those young ones. They know all about it.
(MOSES TIZYA, August 20, 1979, VG2000-8-22:003-113, Gwich'in and English)

First Contact with Europeans: *Tl'oo Thał*—Grass Pants,
told by Sarah Abel

Stories of early encounters with Europeans or white men are included under the Gwich'in category of "long-ago stories." The story of *Tl'oo Thał* is a humorous account of the first experiences of new people and their belongings.[22]

Many times my dad told stories but I don't remember all of them. A long time ago the first white people came down the Yukon River in a wooden boat. At that time people around here had never seen a white person before.

It was *Tl'oo Thał*—Grass Pants. He went down to the river. He had a fire along the river when the white people came down in wooden boats. *Tl'oo Thał* wore tanned pants and a jacket. It was a warm summer day. When the white people arrived, *Tl'oo Thał* was afraid. He had never seen people like this before. Then the people lived on ground squirrel, caribou, moose, and small game. *Tl'oo Thał* did not know of any other kind of food besides meat. The white people poured flour; he said it looked like *cheezrilchit* [ashes]. Then they put something into the flour. After this they put a big black pan on the fire. He didn't know how to say fry pan. The mixed flour was cooked in the black pan with a long handle.

When rice was poured into the pot, he didn't know what it was. He thought it was *daatsoo trìn* [mouse droppings], and then they put raisins in the rice. He said it looked like *ddhah dee* [mountain berries]. All this food was cooked. The bannock was served with yellow grease on it. The mouse poop with raisins was given to him. He was told to eat it. He was afraid so he ate it all.

"They took my bow and arrow and put it in their boat. The men brought me a gun from the boat. They taught me how to make the bullets, too, and they took off all my clothes. These they put into the boat. In those days there was black pants made from thick material. They also gave me a shirt. My caribou-hide clothes were tied up into a bundle and thrown into the boat."

Tl'oo Thał had flint [*tl'yah vah tr'ichyaa*] in his bag. The men took the flint from him. He thought he would freeze without the flint. At the time it was called "*ko tanh*" meaning frozen matches. I remember it was big. I saw it. It was in Cadzow's store. Fire was made with this: you strike it and light the fire. This was put into his bag and he felt much better. They also put shells into the gun and told him to shoot.

The man's name was *Tl'oo Tha*ł in the Indian way. His people were living up in the mountains. He returned home and the people gathered around him. He brought out the gun. He had been taught how to use the gun. He said when he shot the gun it sounded like a fart. The people were afraid. He shot the gun; they were afraid of the bang.

This is the first time the white people met the Natives. And then the white people came. Because of this we got things like food. Sometimes in the winter when it's cold there was no food. With the gun of *Tl'oo Tha*ł the people lived good that winter.

The people travelled down the Yukon River toward Dawson. At that time people were having a hard time. It was about the time I was a small child. This story was told to me, and I am retelling it. When there was no food it was very hard. We never killed rabbits, caribou, or moose. It was hard. Just when people were going to starve, one member of the group would be lucky at hunting. This prevented starvation. Now the people live a wealthy life.

(SARAH ABEL, March 4, 1983, VG1997-4-3:074-165, Gwich'in)

2 | The First Generation
The 19th Century

Contents

64 **LIFE LIVED FROM THE LAND**
65 Travel, Hunting, and Fishing
68 The Seasons
78 Tools and Techniques
84 Values
86 Caribou and Caribou Fences (*Tthał*)
97 The Importance of *Van Tat* (Crow Flats)
106 Relations with Neighbours
108 Leaders
116 Celebration, Music

118 **NEWCOMERS AND NEW THINGS**
119 Gwich'in Long-distance Traders
 Before the Arrival of the Hudson's Bay Company
121 The Hudson's Bay Company
127 New Tools
129 When the Hudson's Bay Company Pulled Out
131 The Succession of Private Traders
137 Beliefs and Missionaries
151 Education and Schools
153 The Border
154 The Settlement of Old Crow

They lived like one family, all the people on this earth.

(MYRA KAYE, February 2, 1980)

When I was a child, I will tell you about it. My Grandchild, it was hard times then. The Hudson's Bay store was here but there were not many goods: only tea, and tobacco, guns and gun supplies. People were poor. We travelled on the land and killed caribou. Moose, too, fish, too, we killed any small animal. That is how we survived.

In the winter all the people travelled together. The leader came with us; he told us what to do. All the people worked together as one. It was really good. All the people did what the leader wanted; they listened to the leader. When we killed caribou, the meat was given out to everybody. The people who killed the caribou were not the boss of the meat. It was good this way. Any small animal that was killed was for all the people. And when we travelled, if there was an old man or old woman, we took care of them. They couldn't hunt so we took care of them. That was how they lived. And people worked together.

In the summer we fished together. When we got fish, it was given out to all the people. All the people had fish. The person who got the fish didn't keep it for himself. When we travelled…some of them stay in Crow Flats. They got fish. All the people worked together. Everyone stayed together. They took care of each other. It was good, even though we were poor.

In the winter all the people travelled a long ways. The men hunted. When they killed caribou, everyone got meat. Because of this we

> survived. We were never the boss of ourselves. This is what we did when we travelled. The women all worked together and the men, too. If someone didn't have firewood, we would get wood for that person, and cut it, too. We helped the poor. The people all worked together as one and it was really good.
>
> (MYRA MOSES, January 1980, VG2000-8-19A, Gwich'in)

The Nukon family and dogs travelling. Kenneth Nukon on left and John Nukon holding paddle.

[Yukon Archives, Bob Sharp fonds 82/326 #13]

THE EARLIEST INTERVIEWS in the Van Tat Gwich'in Oral History Collection were recorded in the 1970s with seven Elders. Sarah Abel was born in 1899 in Alaska and lived until 1998; Moses Tizya was born in 1900, likely in the vicinity of Old Crow. Martha (Ch'idzee) Tizya was Dagoo, born in 1898 in the Dagoo territory toward the Northwest Territories. Myra Moses was born in Alaska in 1884 and lived until 1984. Myra Kaye was born in Alaska and was a contemporary of the others. Neil McDonald was born July 9, 1889, in Fort McPherson, NT, and spent much of his 90-year life in the Old Crow area. Joe Netro was born in 1889, possibly in the vicinity of Rampart House (T. Rispin-Kassi pers. comm. 2003), and he died in 1980. They were very elderly when interviewed in the 1970s; many reached nearly 100 years of age. The history of events in their own lives, together with the legacy passed on to them by their immediate elders, spanned much of the 19th and well into the 20th centuries.

The history of Van Tat Gwich'in goes back countless generations, to the edges of memory and beyond. The Van Tat Gwich'in Oral History Collection is the recorded history of the most recent generations of elders. The accounts related by the first generation are a fascinating history, rooted in the time when people lived in many ways, as they had for millennia. They tell of a life of travelling on the land, living solely from their own efforts in hunting and fishing, utilizing tools of their own manufacture, and wearing clothing made from hides and furs. As well, they acquired early exotic goods from the Russians, Americans, and English and Canadians, and they chronicled their encounters with the newcomers, who they often aided in their early efforts to survive in the Van Tat Gwich'in homeland.

The first generation of elders also described the novel ways, tools, and ideas brought by the visitors, some having an unassuming beginning but an enduring impact. For example, elders reported the unreliability of early guns, whereas the first stoves and tents were immediately appreciated for the lack of smoke indoors and their surprising warmth despite the thinness of the tent fabric.

Notably, this generation's stories of change do not centre on an abundance of new goods: they emphasize that the early traders carried very little and relied on local food. Many of the long-term changes from that period were of a legal, political, or religious nature, rather than technological or

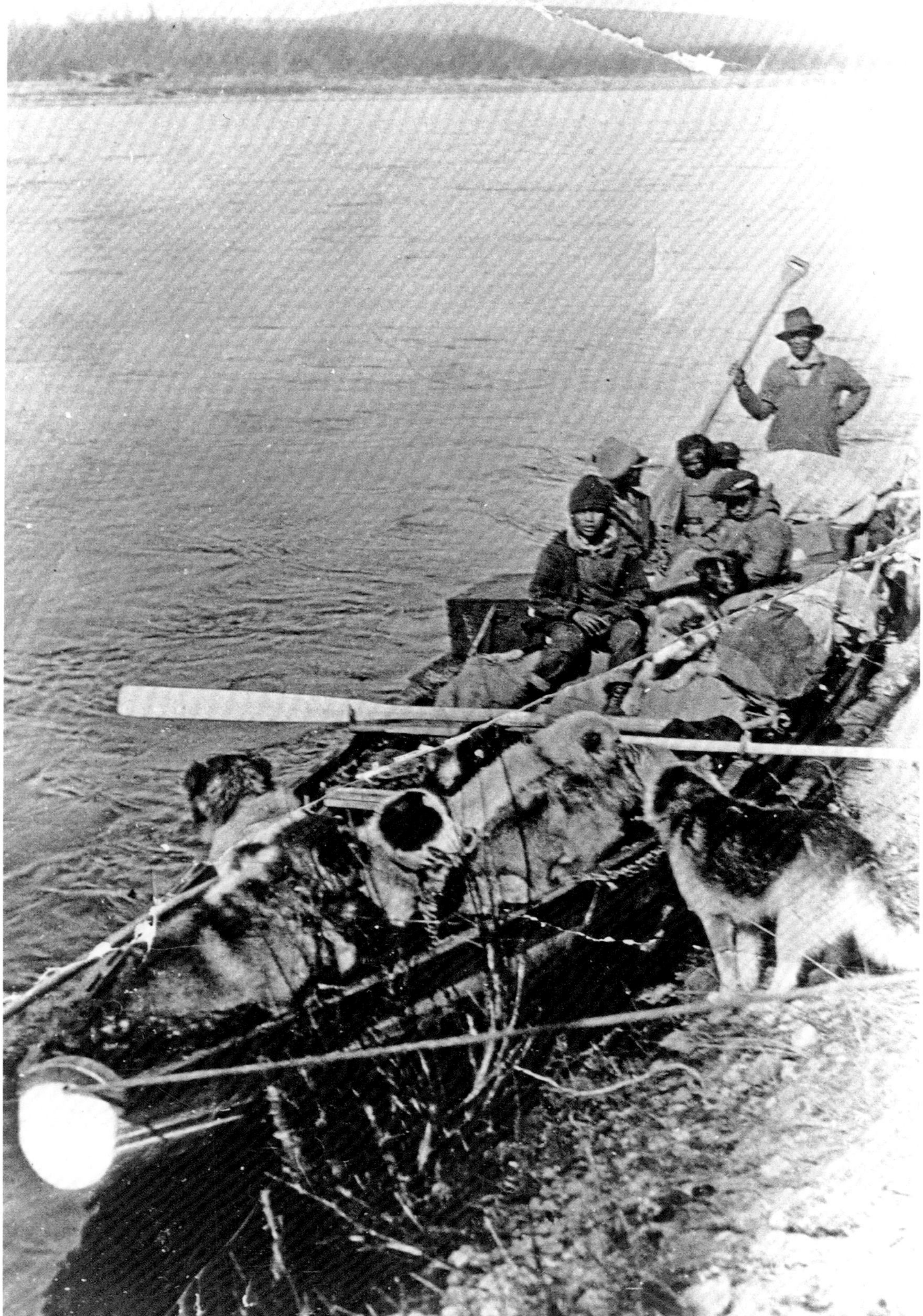

economic. Elders refer to the reduction in the Gwich'in population due to disease, the coming of the first missionaries (Church of England) who began what was to be an extended tenure, as well as the creation, survey, and eventual enforcement of the Alaska-Canada border.

This history of change is set against a backdrop of continuity, particularly the continuity of values such as sharing and helping one another. People in the early days were accustomed to hard work, much travel, co-operation, and great self-reliance. Children were taught how to live from the land, as well as generosity and respect for their elders. New technology and ideas did not overturn the way of life but were incorporated into people's lives and were generally perceived to make things easier.

From the perspective of the 1970s when these interviews were recorded, those interviewed were elderly and reflective. They emphasized that life had become considerably easier but also, consequently, people were less capable of coping with hardship. They described the beginnings of many new things but also what was important to carry over from the past. Reflecting their central themes, the Elders' stories are grouped below under two main topics: life lived from the land, and newcomers and changes.

LIFE LIVED FROM THE LAND

> So then I got married and I had 17 children. My husband trapped and worked for meat. Me, too, I worked at home. All the women in those days did that. At home I set snares for rabbits and ptarmigan. I set traps around there, too....Our husbands and ourselves, whatever we harvested, that's what we raised our kids on.
>
> (SARAH ABEL, August 11, 1977, VG2001-4-5:121-126, Gwich'in)

Elders Sarah Abel, Myra Moses, Moses Tizya, Myra Kaye, and Martha Tizya spoke in detail about how people lived on the land. They described hunting, food preparation, and travel, and, occasionally, the difficulty of life. They emphasized the importance of sharing and working together, along with the satisfactions of that life. Many of these Elders also described their seasonal round of activities.

The stories of life on the land undoubtedly have links to previous history: they are not "time out of time." While they include elements of continuity with the past, these stories refer to specific incidents, as well as significant changes. The major foci of this body of history are hunting, fishing, and travel, along with associated values and experiences. Myra Moses and Sarah Abel gave a sketch of how people lived in the last half of the 19th century, as evidenced by Myra Moses's comment that the Hudson's Bay Company was in the area (which places the time period between the company's arrival in 1846 and its departure in 1893). As Sarah Abel points out, these Elders knew stories from before their time:

> In those days, there were no white people so it was hard to get things. We managed. Even me, I never saw it but it was spoken about in front of me. That is what I talk about. This is how I know, but really it happened before them.
>
> (SARAH ABEL, July 1979, VG2000-8-10A:67-71, English and Gwich'in)

Travel, Hunting, and Fishing

Myra Moses and Sarah Abel described how life in the late 1800s meant relying entirely on the land for food, clothing, and other necessities: a more difficult way of living than in later years but with its own rewards, as well. Myra Moses also suggested there were more Gwich'in in the mid- to late 1800s. Neil McDonald gave details of distant history and compared them to the long-ago story, "Boy in the Moon."

Myra Moses's Life as a Child

> Down that way [Alaska], my mother and those people lived. At that time there were still hard times. There was a Hudson's Bay store down there but it was hard to get supplies. When I was a child, sometimes it was hard to get food. Sometimes, too, there were no supplies. We had skin tents.
>
> They fished and hunted for meat, too. That's the way they ate, that's how they lived. Sometimes there was no food. My father and mother, my father was lucky when he hunted for meat. Those poor people around, when he killed meat, he would give them meat. My mother did that also. In the summer, some of the people did not even have tents. Not all people had tents. There were lots of mosquitoes, but there were no tents for some people. Really, I remember it was hard times they came through.
>
> So, wherever they went on the land, they had to kill meat, for sure, to eat. They looked for it and the family did as well....
>
> On the river, they didn't even have fishnets. Sometimes they made fish traps [with willows]; there they killed fish. Around here, it's really good [for fish]. The fish traps catch more fish than fishnets.
>
> (MYRA MOSES, August 10, 1977, VG2001-4-4:020-057, Gwich'in)

The First Generation

We also stayed in Crow Flats. We trapped for muskrats and your grandfather [Chief Peter Moses] hunted for caribou. We helped lots of people, too, when I was young, me and your grandfather. You see all the people around here; they were all born after us. There's no one older than me in Old Crow....

Long ago people used to travel around. What we call a teepee, we made our home in there and we all wore skin clothes. At that time and it was all fur, rabbit-skin coats, too. We made fire in the middle of the teepee; in those days there were no stoves. There were no towels then, and no soap. I remember I washed with rabbit feet. I wet the rabbit feet and I wiped my face with it....

Also there was no flour, no grub [store-bought food], only meat, fish, rabbit, and other animals. What we killed we ate....Lots of people used to travel all over the land and sometimes there was no meat. When there was no meat we never ate all day; meanwhile, we still travelled. Finally we killed caribou or moose. That's the only way we ate. We never saw grub in those days. And down at Rampart House there was a Hudson's Bay [store] there but there was no food there either. They also ate only meat; they had no grub either. In those days people had a hard time you know, my grandchild.

Today we sure live good. In those days, there were lots of old people. I remember them all. Up along the river: Salmon Cache, Driftwood, LaPierre House, all the way upriver were lots of people. And all the way down to Fort Yukon. There were lots of people along the river, and all over Crow Flats were lots of people, and at Rampart House and Old Rampart [House], lots of people, too, and also at Old Crow. All of those people passed on in my time.

(MYRA MOSES, VG2000-8-8:035-067, Gwich'in)

Sarah Abel's Life as a Child

Grandchild, first of all, when I was being raised, I'll tell about...those days, what I know. Those days were really hard, you know. From then to not long ago, it was hard....In a small village there were stores; even so it was hard to get what we wanted.

There was no school then either. The children never had school. They moved around in the bush to kill meat: caribou, moose, rabbits. That's how they ate. They searched for food. Grandchild, those children didn't go to school. One of them was me....

In those days, they moved in the early morning while it was still dark. Then they set camp before it got dark in the evening. While they

Three dog teams en route to muskrat hunting on Crow Flats (1925–32).

[Yukon Archives, Arthur Thornthwaite fonds 83/22 #298]

did that, the men went hunting. But those women setting up camp, they had a lot of work to do. Their children were sitting in the toboggans, too. The men out hunting were still gone. Sometimes they wouldn't kill any meat and come back. But sometimes, when they killed meat [caribou], all the people gathered together in one place and worked good with it [butchered, prepared it].

(SARAH ABEL, August 11, 1977, VG2001-4-5:017-048, Gwich'in)

A Time Without Dogs

Long ago, long before the white man came, the way I hear it, they had no dogs. They had no toboggans, but they used sleighs. They had to pack their stuff and pull their sleighs. And then they had a story about the man [boy] in the moon. This boy had a little dog, took this little dog up [to the moon], I hear. They...say it was about twenty thousand years ago....So there must have been dogs at that time. A long time ago.

Well, later on, [they learned to hitch the dogs], I guess [when the] Hudson's Bay Company came down and the Northwest Company.

(NEIL MCDONALD, August 12, 1977, VG2001-4-7:019-033, English)

The First Generation

The Seasons

Elders Sarah Abel, Myra Kaye, Moses Tizya, and Myra Moses emphasized that life on the land had a seasonal rhythm. People moved to specific places, season by season, to fish camps, caribou fences, snaring locations, and good places to find moose. Myra Kaye's story of two old women is clearly among the archetype included with the long-ago stories, here told in the context of seasonal activities. Moses Tizya graphically illustrates how many more Gwich'in there were before unfamiliar diseases were introduced. The Elders comment that life then was more difficult and, alternately, that seemingly difficult tasks were not problematic for the people. Finally, Myra Moses painted a particularly detailed picture of the seasonal round of life in the late 19th century.

Autumn and Winter

> Grandchild, in those days it was hard....In the summer, it was hard for them to get around with toboggans, so they made dog packs for the dogs to carry. The dogs carried the packs and travelled along with them, and they would hunt for caribou....In the warm summer when they killed meat, they dried it and the dogs packed some of it. They made lots of meat. Little by little, they made lots.
>
> In the month of September they settled down. Wherever there were many caribou, they would find out and settle down there. Then they made fences for the caribou, [*tthah*] they called them. So then, Grandchild, they settled down, and before winter, they made snowshoes and toboggans.
>
> In November, in October, they all settled down. In the Native language, they call October "Caribou Month" [*Vadzaih Zrii*], you know. That month they settled in. Then in November when they didn't have much food, even though it was cold they moved around hunting for caribou.
>
> Grandchild, they all did that all winter; they did all that. Really, after the people had suffered, supplies became available....Only when I was around fourteen or fifteen years old, lots of goods came here.
>
> Grandchild, when I was fourteen years old was when they took children out to schools, to Whitehorse, by the Yukon River. I remember. That's how hard it was. Even my children didn't make it to school.
>
> (SARAH ABEL, August 11, 1977, VG2001-4-5:068-105, Gwich'in)

Mary Nukon butchering caribou.

[Yukon Archives, Father Jean-Marie Mouchet fonds 91/51 R #112]

Hunting Caribou in the Summer and Spring

In the summer we killed lots of caribou and dried lots of meat. The women hunted ground squirrels and dried them. Girls your age[1] made ground squirrel strips and dried them. They put sticks in them to spread them so they dried properly. Their mothers put it in a bag later. They also had a big pile of food; that was what we lived on.

Before August, those who had a caribou fence travelled back there. When there were lots of caribou in August, people went back to their caribou fences and set snares....

In March, before the caribou came, we set up camp in the mountains. Here the elders pulled these toboggans and snowshoes. It was hard to get birch [for toboggans] so the old sometimes pulled their blankets. This is how hard it was in those days.

I only saw some of it, what I'm talking about. I will not talk about things that happened before my time.

After spring passed, we went over the mountain pass. The old men travelled as I said. Somewhere along the creek, it was said that two *shanaghàn* [old women] had two snow houses [*zhoh kahn*] beside each

The First Generation   69

other. There were lots of glaciers around there. On the glacier, there were lots of ptarmigan in the willows. There were no rabbits there, only ptarmigan. They made snare fences to capture the ptarmigan. Sometimes...they killed lots of ptarmigan. This is what they did.

In the meantime, people travelled in the timber. Up around *Nichìh Ddhàa* [Rosehips Mountain], in the valley there was a glacier where these two *shanaghàn* set snares. The rabbits and ptarmigan knew the snares were there so the old women didn't catch any. They set the snares somewhere else. They set snares along the creek where they got rabbit and ptarmigan. Just when they set the snares near the valley, caribou came onto the mountain ridge. At that time it was difficult to get guns.

One had shaman abilities, I guess...."Up there," she said. Up the valley, on top of the snow crust was a bunch of caribou. Just then—you know when on a bluff there's a mudslide—this happened with snow [avalanche]. All the caribou were like the wind blew them. And the snow was like, you know, when snow is mixed with water [slush]. Some of the caribou were pushed across the creek. They were taking out the caribou from the snow. The two *shanaghàn* had a cache full of drymeat when the people returned. This is how the elders were cared for. They were only snaring ptarmigan and instead they each had two caches full of drymeat.

(MYRA KAYE, February 2, 1980, VG2000-8-19C, Gwich'in)

A Time When There Were Many More People

After New Year or when they ran out of meat, then they started to move. That's the time they...made that fence I told you about: winter fence. Oh yes, [they got lots of caribou]. They had to, big bunch [of people]. Three to four thousand people had to have lots of meat to keep them going.

In my father's time, like I told you, they made four roads to move one camp to the other....[They had] no dogs them days, just driving sleigh. Well, they had nothing to haul, just a little drymeat. They used caribou skins for camp, [they're] light, too, and they used nothing but caribou clothing [which] weighed nothing. Well, that's all they pulled, caribou-skin blanket. It's light, see, it's light.

No pots or nothing. Those days they had wooden pots and they got big rocks....They carried rocks and put those rocks in the fire and they put meat and snow in there and then they threw the rocks in there. Pretty soon that meat boiled....That's how they cooked meat in them days. And summertime, they dug a hole. They put caribou skin and then they put water, then they threw hot rocks in there, red hot rocks. And pretty soon they boil their meat. That's hot. That's how they boiled their meat in those days, you see.

They used [wooden bowls] sometime [in the summer], I guess. And like I say, they dug a hole in the ground, they put caribou skin in there, they boil their meat. The caribou skin was no good after that, so they... got to have a lot of skins to do that. [They used each skin only once] Yeah. That's what they said, anyway.

In olden times I guess...[they snared moose] too....[The best places to hunt moose were] around where you call a dry lake, around the lakes. In summertime, even wintertime, they stay in one place. They have a trail to where they feed around the lake. You see the grass. That's where they set snares for it. That's how they got them...They killed lots of them with bow and arrow, too.

In summertime they had a fish trap between lakes, that's where they fished....Wintertime they speared them through the ice, bone spear...

(MOSES TIZYA, August 11, 1977, VG2001-4-6#1:276-381, English and Gwich'in)

Myra Moses's Predecessors

I think I am the only one who's living out of them all:...your [Linda Netro's] grandfather, your father, his father and mother, your grandmother Martha Blackfox's father. At that time there were lots of old people. Old *Gwatl'ahti'*,[2] Old *Gwatl'ahti'vinh*, *Ch'eeghwal*, Old *Cheesih*—there were lots of old people and now they're all gone. I remember them all; they all lived in my time....I am really old now, too....Your grandmother Mary Charlie and Peter Charlie, they all looked young, and now they all look older than me....

At one time me and your grandfather [Old Chief Peter Moses] trapped in Crow Flats. Sometime we had no food. Your grandfather killed caribou and moose; that's how we ate. Now you all live good. In those days, young and old, everyone looked for small game to kill just so we could eat....All the people who used to live passed away. And at Rampart House there were lots of people and they all died, too. Old Crow, too, all of them die, too. Right now all them young people are living, not many living.

(MYRA MOSES, July 26, 1979, VG2000-8-8:073-107, Gwich'in)

Peter and Mary Charlie (Tetlichi) family in the 1940s. (L-R) Peter, Andrew, Mary holding baby Dorothy, Lazarus, Charlie Peter, Alfred.
[Corporal Kirk/Eloise Watt fonds #22 (VG1998-1)]

The men would hunt, that way they got meat. They killed caribou and moose; that way they lived. They would do this and move around the country. There were lots of people.

Along this river [Porcupine River] lots of people were living, and all over the country back at Crow Flats and all around there were lots of people. They would always go amongst each other and the people really looked after each other well.

(MYRA MOSES, August 25, 1980, VG2000-8-34:072-076, Gwich'in)

Detailed Seasonal Round

In the wintertime, only around [the Old Rampart area] there were always lots of caribou, Grandchild, way across on the mountains. The people all moved there with their families. There were no tents, too, no stoves. They sewed caribou skins with the hair still on into big pieces. They made houses with those, with wood. They made fire in the middle. The smoke went up through the smoke hole. Even so, smoke

Fall caribou hunting on the Porcupine River east of Old Crow.

[Canadian Museum of Civilization, photo Father Jean-Marie Mouchet s2004-1425]

bothered us....and our eyes were really sore. We even cried. [Laughter] I remember all that.

All the people stayed across where there were lots of caribou. Gee, they killed lots of caribou! Caribou skin, caribou leg skin, caribou sinew: they made sinew and all those things. Some of the Fort Yukon people [went there] too. At a place called Black River, people came from around there, and from down this Porcupine River, Old Rampart, those living there, too.

Sometimes, at Chandalar [River] where grandma Big Myra[3] [Kyikavichik] stayed, people all went around there, too. Back at Crow Flats, those living around there, too, they all stayed across there in the wintertime. Ah, they killed lots of caribou. Sometimes they made a feast. They pounded up the [caribou] bones, they took the bone marrow out: they call it "boil up everything" [bones and gristle]. You wouldn't know it; you ever see it? They boil it up in a pot, *ch'itsùh* [pemmican], pemmican grease. Ah, it was really like cake....I mean good....Even though there are lots of caribou [now], and it would be good, nobody does it.

The First Generation 73

The caribou skin, caribou blood, they wouldn't leave that behind. Even caribou guts, they wouldn't leave that behind, either. They took it all to eat, also for dog feed. Around there, they stayed there; ah, it was really nice.

They just ate meat, and there was no grub [store-bought food]. Sometimes somebody had a little tea. Sometimes there was tobacco, too. They boiled meat on the fire. That's all they ate. Nothing, even the Hudson's Bay store had nothing. There was no stuff [trade goods]. What they call muzzle-loader gun, that was the only gun. The things [parts and ammunition] for it were hard to get. Those who were poor didn't have guns. I remember they had arrows.

People who were strong killed lots of meat. They gave it out to all their relatives. All the people treated each other good. Nowadays, it's not like that. They stayed there all winter. Sometimes where they built a house, then another house [was built] over there, then another house, then another house, and the smoke would go up like that. Even there, all the people took good care of each other. They always made feasts for each other.

But at Old Rampart, when they killed animals [for furs for sale], it was cheap [low prices]. Even marten, at first it was only 50 cents. Was that good? [No!][Laughter] They made dried meat and also bone grease. Caribou skins, too, they tanned the skins and sold them. They also made babiche. All that, they sold at the store. With heavy sleds, they went down to Old Rampart, they said. A little tea, little tobacco, matches, those muzzle-loader guns, their parts and shells: they only had a little stuff there. They wouldn't have flour or sugar, either.

Even so, it was no problem for them. They moved around [on the land] from there all winter. After that it warmed up. It's warm in the month of May, so they went way up [the Porcupine River] above Crow Point. Up there at *Tl'oo K'at* where the rock sticks out, what do they call it, I wonder?...*Tl'oo K'at*, right there, the caribou cross there....

There were no [store-bought] canoes. Sometimes with skin, they made canoes. Sometimes they took the bark off the birch trees and sewed it up and made canoes. With that, they killed caribou. The few shells that they had, they were careful with them, too. They made a long pole and tied sharp tin on the end. When the caribou crossed the river, they paddled out to them in the canoes, and with the pole, they speared them and killed them. They killed lots of caribou that way.

At *Tl'oo K'at*, up along the bank for one mile up that way, there were people. Big caches, behind lots of the houses: ah, there were lots of people. It was really nice. Then, they played ball and jumped around with each other. While they brought in caribou, they dried meat, and

Harold ("Jack") Frost Sr., former RCMP, making a canoe for muskrat hunting.

[Canadian Museum of Civilization, photo Father Jean-Marie Mouchet 52004-1433]

fixed the caribou skins. The women pounded bones to make bone grease. They made lots of dried meat. After that, June arrives and then there's no more caribou.

Then they went way upriver with a big raft....Sometimes the boys had wood rafts....On it were places for paddles [oars] and they made paddles [oars]. They make a big raft and put all the dried meat on the raft, the caribou skins, too. They tied them together and made a raft. Then they piled stuff on it.

Meanwhile, back in Crow Flats, people living there made dog packs....They went to Crow Flats. The people living out on the lakes packed stuff and their dogs packed stuff, too. They packed kids, too. They all went to Crow Flats.

After that, sometimes the Fort McPherson people went to LaPierre House....All the people lived along the Porcupine River below [Bell River] there, *Chiitsiighe'*, Salmon Cache. At LaPierre House there was a Hudson's Bay store. There was a church there also. All the people living along the shoreline walked with dog packs. They packed stuff and children, but the men also went up the river in canoes. Then the people rowed the big raft down to Old Rampart [House]...to the Hudson's Bay store in summer. They bought whatever they were going to use from the store. They sold all the meat, caribou, hides, babiche. [They didn't buy] much. They bought muzzle-loader guns, shells, and whatever you

The First Generation 75

need for it to shoot, just that, and tea and tobacco, just a little of each. You wouldn't see flour.

Then, in the summer they made caribou hide clothing. They wore that. Those who really had lots of money, only they had material clothing. [Chuckles]

When they got to Old Rampart, they really had a good time. They had a feast with drymeat and bone grease. They danced to fiddles at the Hudson's Bay store. Ah, they had a good time....Nothing was wrong. They were having a good time.

The people staying below [downstream; west on the Porcupine River], even to Fort Yukon, they went down with rafts. People from down that way, from Arctic Village where grandma stays, those people travelled with dog packs....Even so, they all had a good time. Only some of them had tents. Those who didn't have tents made skin houses.

Even in summer, some of the people were really poor. The Hudson's Bay had fishnets, but they were not big. They gave them to people. There's lots of fish in the little rivers in Crow Flats. Around there, they made fish traps. They killed lots of fish. But this river, sometimes the people have one net. They set the fishnet and then fish. All the people ate it. They did this and people looked after each other.

Then they all started moving all over. The Fort Yukon people went back downriver. In summer and winter, they didn't stay home at all. Only the Hudson's Bay had a house. They also had a store. In the house, they made a fire. They had a big hole in the house and they fixed it with mud [chimney]. In there, they made fire. It was nice. They never worried about a stove. They lived on berries. In the fall, they picked berries. They dried fish, and everything they killed, they dried.

In winter they tanned skins and made clothing. Rabbit, too, when it comes to winter, rabbit-skin parkas are really good for kids. Lots of times I had a rabbit coat, rabbit pants. That's how I lived a long time ago. That's why I never felt cold.

After that, at the start of winter and then again sometimes, [they went] over to Black River. It's past the Yukon River, not far down that way. People moved there from all over, Grandchild, people from around here, down the river people, too, all of them. They all moved over that way. Sometimes there were no caribou, sometimes no moose. In those times they were really hungry. When they killed even one rabbit, they boiled it in a big pot, its juice and its little meat. Ah, there were lots of houses; even so, all of them got a small portion of meat and juice of the rabbit. All the people gave it to each other. We never ate by ourselves. Sometimes they killed one caribou or one moose, and the

Barge Brainstorm *arriving in Old Crow with supplies from Dawson.*

[Canadian Museum of Civilization, photo Father Jean-Marie Mouchet 52004-1425]

people had a meal just for one night only; tomorrow there is no meat. They did this and they moved here and there.

The family would have no meat. The dogs didn't eat so they died, too. Sometimes, some people wouldn't have even one dog. Then they pulled their stuff on a toboggan. Even so, it's nothing [no hardship] for us. Around there, one old woman couldn't walk so they pulled her. She nearly died: there was no meat and they didn't eat. They cleaned caribou skins or moose skins and boiled it. They ate it; it's really good.

Finally over there, close to the Yukon [River], there were caribou and moose. They killed them. Finally there was lots of meat. The people without even one dog got one, sometimes two....They moved to Circle [Alaska], it's close to the Yukon. Around Black River, they killed lots of caribou and moose. They made drymeat. over there. Circle is below Eagle. Below Dawson, Eagle is located and below that is Circle. Over that way is the way people went. There at Circle, they found meat.

At that time, there were lots of white people in the Yukon.[4] The steamboat travelled there. There was lots of stuff [trade goods, supplies] in the Yukon. From there, they brought things back over. They sold skins and meat. Lots of people from Circle, there was no toboggan, they just packed stuff there. So there was lots grub [store-bought food]. Flour, sugar, they brought these back home. Then they had a big feast. It's really good with pemmican grease. Meanwhile, it got warm.

> Then in April, [they travelled] a long way. With no dogs, the women pulled all the stuff, sometimes packing kids and pulling [toboggans] at the same time. They moved back over this way, to *Tl'oo K'at*, [near Old Crow]. There were lots of caribou....In May, they came, when the caribou cross [the Porcupine River]. In May the ice moves out. Then the caribou cross. They made caribou drymeat there.
>
> (MYRA MOSES, July 1979, VG2000-8-10B:014-295, Gwich'in)

Tools and Techniques

The elders who grew up in the late 1800s gave detailed descriptions of the many ways they made a living without store-bought tools and supplies. They emphasized the changes that occurred in their lifetimes and the ingenuity of people in the past. Unlike the elders in 2000, they do not express concern that the skills necessary to life on the land were being lost, just changed. A few of the many techniques they described are: boiling meat without kettles, washing without soap and cloths, making drinking vessels, preserving food, making fire with flint, clothing and tents made of skins, snares, deadfalls, fish hooks and nets, fish traps, knives of caribou bone or stone, and birch-bark canoes.

Boiling Meat, Melting Snow

> Grandchild, in those days when they killed meat [they had] a kettle. They didn't have this kind of kettle [metal]. They carved one out wood and put rocks in it. They put the rocks in the fire and, when they got hot, in that wooden pot. They put meat and the hot rocks in there. That boiled the water. That's how the people did it long ago.
>
> Sometimes, too, they put meat in a caribou stomach, when they made ground caches. They put lots of meat in there...The water, the hot rocks, they put them in and it boiled. The meat broth, they would never throw it out. They had it for tea....
>
> They had wooden plates also.
>
> So, Grandchild, when men were hunting and got thirsty, it was hard for them to put water in something. So they had a dried caribou stomach bag in their pocket. They hung it [by a fire] where it wouldn't burn, where the snow melted and dripped into the dry bag. They drank that. That's how hard it was in those days.
>
> (SARAH ABEL, August 11, 1977, VG2001-4-5:240-274, Gwich'in)

Washing

Really, when I was a child, it was hard to get stuff [supplies] and make a living. There was no soap and no towel. What were we to wash with? The rabbit's foot, they kept that. They kept lots of rabbit's feet. They wet them and washed their faces. Me, I did that, too. It was hard in those days, the days I was a child.

(MYRA MOSES, interpreted by Alice Frost, August 10, 1977, VG2001-4-4:141–143, Gwich'in)

Cups

...Squirrel cup,...[we used to use a squirrel's head for a cup, long ago. We used to clean it and then use it.]

(MYRA MOSES, interpreted by Alice Frost, August 12, 1977, VG2001-4-4:285, Gwich'in)

Preserving Food

Fish, in summertime they dried it. Around August when they got caribou, they dried that....As soon as it started to get cold, they had a big meat cache....Ground cache, slab cache....[They] just made a big cache and put willows [in it] so it's kind of cold in there. That's where they hung all the meat. Even in summertime, they hung meat and it never spoiled in the mountains. When they travelled in the mountains, that's where they used to keep their meat...they dried meat. They took the rocks on the mountain...and put the drymeat under those rocks and mud. It never spoiled. They could use it for two years like that.

(MYRA MOSES, interpreted by Edith Josie, VG1999-6-7:072–085, English)

Making Fire with Flint, and Making Caches, Toboggans, and Snowshoes

At that time we used flint to start fires. This is what we did. Ah, fire [sparks] all over. We made shavings, a big pile. We held it while working the flint. Eventually the shavings lit from the spark. Then we put dry branches in with the shavings, which caught fire. Finally the fire got bigger. We made more shavings and added them to the fire. Once there was flame, we made fire. All our lives we did this. Whoever was going to make fire did this with the flint. When we travelled, that is what we did.

The First Generation

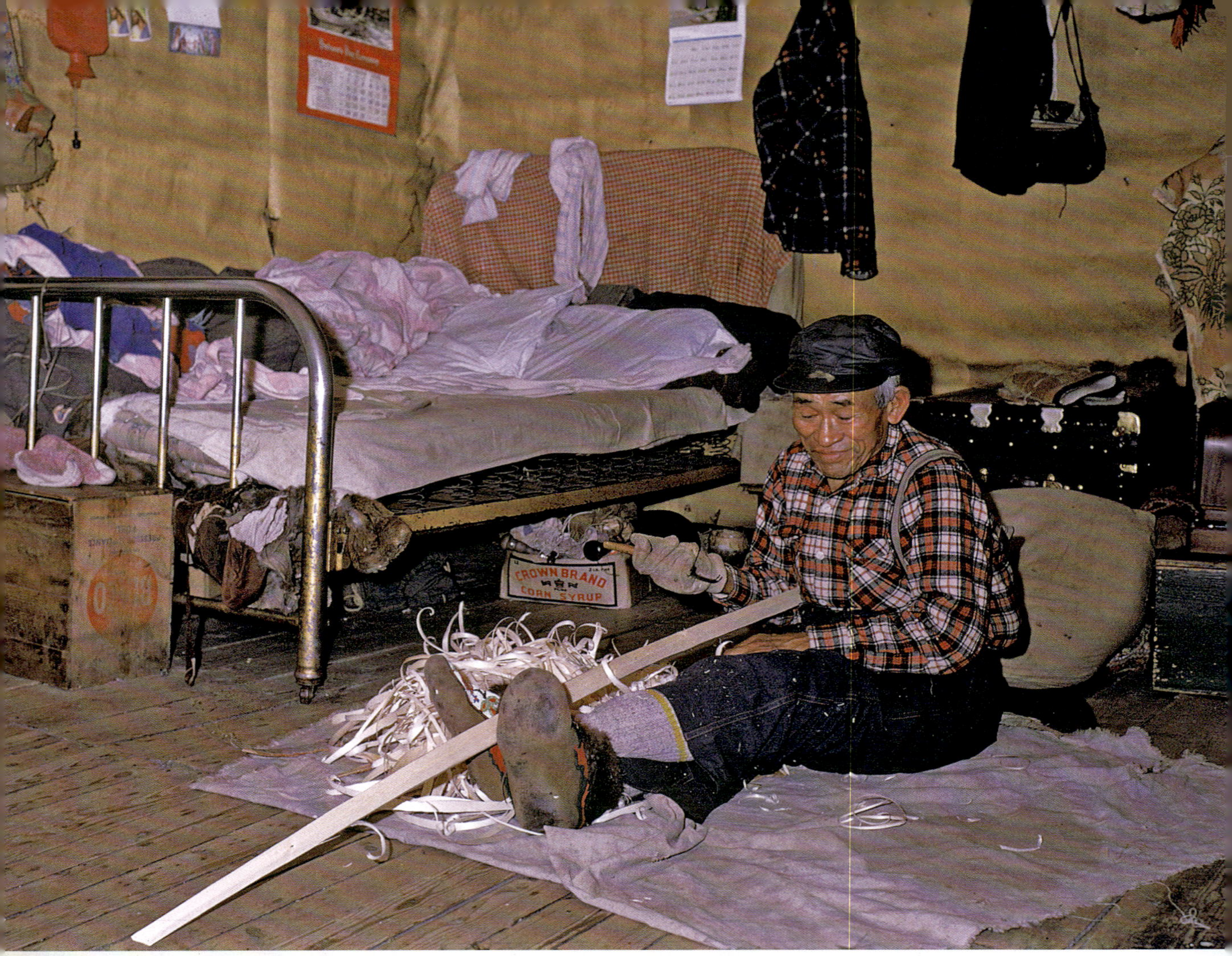
CROWN BRAND
CORN SYRUP

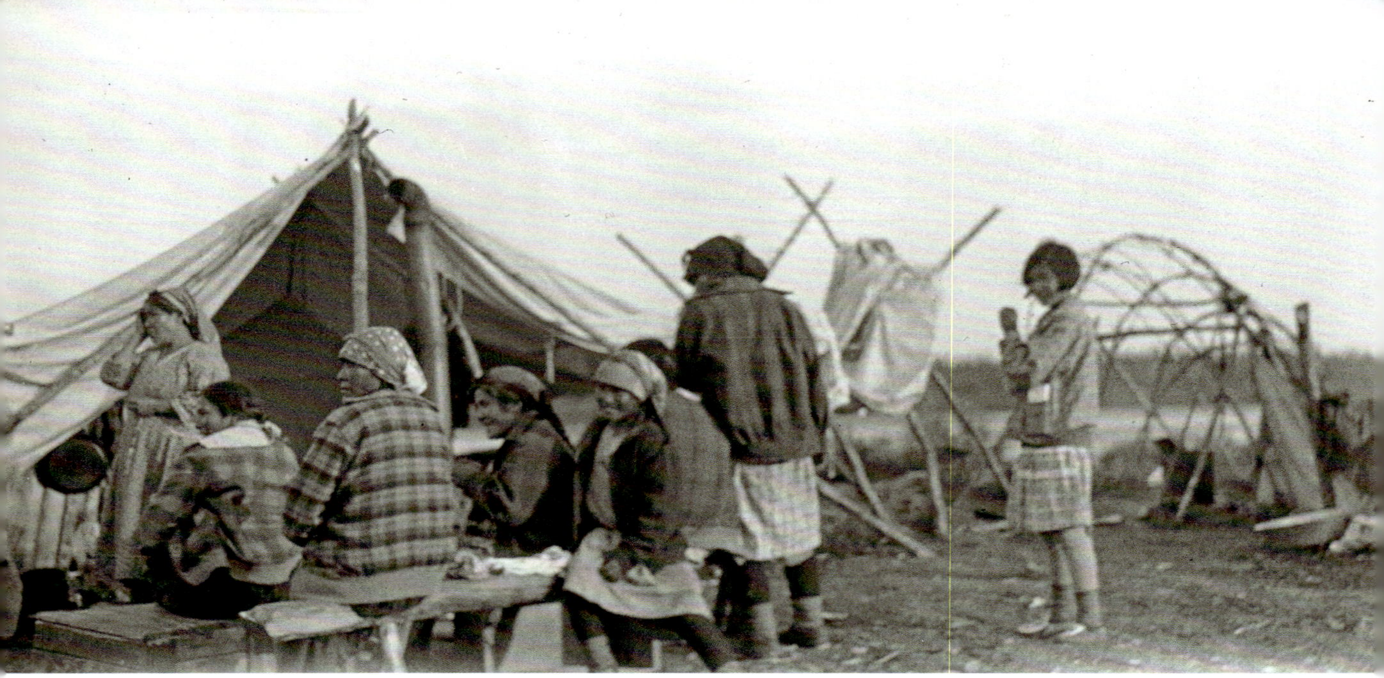

Page 80 (top): Peter Charlie Sr. making snowshoes.

[Canadian Museum of Civilization, photo Father Jean-Marie Mouchet S2004-1377]

Page 80 (bottom): Women by Mrs. Blackfox's smoke frames (1926–32).

[Yukon Archives, Arthur Thornthwaite fonds 83/22 #1412]

Then Mr. Firth came by here with supplies.[5] He landed in Fort Yukon. And guns, fishnet. The fishnet was not knitted. He gave these out and taught the people how to knit fishnets. This is what they did.

We dried only with willow. When we travelled we made a drying place with willows to dry meat. We also laced the drymeat onto the willows. This is the only way we lived. When we killed lots of caribou in a caribou fence, we cut the ground into squares....And they split wood in half. This is what they put on the outside of the hut and the squares of mud [earth] were put up against this split wood. This is how it was [sod house].

When we went inside, the women tanned summer caribou hides and there was lot of work. Men made snowshoes. And after New Year was celebrated, we went to a mountain just above Fort Yukon where there were lots of caribou. There is no birch down that way so while people were hunting for caribou, the elderly men went to the river and got birch to make toboggans. They split it in half and planed it with an axe. They made it thin; that is what they made toboggans with. They did the same for snowshoes: they also planed it and tied it into the shape of a snowshoe. A file was put into the fire and when it was hot, they burned a hole in the toboggan with it. They put babiche through there.

(MYRA KAYE, February 2, 1980, VG2000-8-19C, Gwich'in)

Skin Clothing and Tents

They used to wear fur parka, caribou-fur parka, in wintertime. The mountain sheep they kill, they used to make fur boots and pants and fur parki. They wore that in winter. In summertime woman smoked [hides] and some of [the hides] were white. They made jackets and pants out of it. They wore nothing but skin clothes, that's about all.... Everybody [women] worked hard on skins.

Men, all they did was hunt for game or fish. Before winter started they worked on the toboggans, things like that.

People never had cabins like this. The women tanned caribou skins, over 20. They were just busy tanning skins. Twenty caribou skins, and they sewed them together and made just like a *Ch'ineekaii* igloo house. They made it with willow, a round house. They sewed the 20 caribou skins together and put it over that [frame]....That's where people stayed, summer and winter.

(MYRA MOSES, interpreted by Edith Josie, VG1999-6-7:245-278, English)

The First Generation

Tents, Snares, Deadfalls, Fish Hooks, and Willowbark Fishnets

Yeah, they had caribou-skin tents. They sewed lots of caribou skins together. They made them big and stayed in them, and made a fire in the middle.

I snared rabbits down there. I made snares with [caribou skin] and I set them down there. Then, I made a deadfall, and I caught marten in it. That's how they trapped marten. Then they found a little tin and made little hooks with it and hooked for fish with that. Now, we really live good, you know, Grandchild. The government gives us everything.

Before my time...they took the bark off the willows. It's long, used for making fishnets, they say. They kill fish with that. That, too, is good. That was the days there were no fishnets. That was before my time.

(MYRA MOSES, August 10, 1977, VG2001-4-4:159-200)

Caribou-skin House, Toboggan, Clothing

Grandchild, your grandpa [Moses Tizya, her husband], he talked with me. That way I know a little. [Long ago they used to sew ten caribou skins together to make a tent, skin house.] Just like a house, they made it really big. Where they were going to make a fire in the middle they [had a space or gap on top and they dug a hole in the ground for the fireplace].

When they were going to move camp. [They used to use caribou skins for toboggans. They shaped it like a toboggan while it was wet, I guess.]

[They used to make snares out of caribou skins. They had to clean it and make snares with that.] That way they snared the caribou. Your grandfather said that.

Calf-skin clothing, the people used only caribou calf-skin clothing and caribou-skin pants, too. They didn't have cloth material. You wouldn't see cloth pants.

(MARTHA TIZYA, interpreted by Alice Frost, August 11, 1977,
VG2001-4-6#1:270-363, Gwich'in)

Snares, Arrows, Awls, Knives, Spears, Dishes, Rafts, and Fishtraps

When I was a child, around that time, there was a Hudson's Bay Store around here, Grandchild. Some of the people had guns, and some only had arrows. That was the poor people. They would never kill meat with

Chief Charlie Abel in boat.

[Yukon Archives, Father Jean-Marie Mouchet fonds 91/51 R #126]

that. They really made use of and depended on snares, Grandchild. They twisted caribou sinew and made rabbit snares with that. And the caribou skin, with that they made caribou snares and they set them for caribou.

Bones, too, they used them. Some of them made awls. They made everything [bone scrapers, awls, the tips of arrows], and what they knit snowshoes with, they made that from bone, too. They even make knives with it.

Long ago, even in my time, some people lived like that, the poor people. They made knives, and from the time there were files, they started making knives from files. They call it *tl'ilghoo*. I saw them use files, long ago.

When we went to look for caribou they made a sharp metal point and tied it on the end of a long stick. They hunted with that from a canoe, in front of me, in those days. They stabbed the caribou with that and killed it.

The bark on birch trees, they took it off and made canoes, you know. That, too, was done in my time, long ago. They even made plates with it. Whoever didn't have plates used birchbark. They made pots and plates with it. They sewed them together with spruce tree roots: they pulled them out and used them to sew it together. And that birch, too…they make dishes with it. They call them wooden dishes….

> They made wooden rafts. They made canoes out of the bark of spruce. The spruce gum, they stuck it on and no water got in.
>
> On the shores, too, there's skinny willows. [They made a kind of net out of it and caught fish in creeks or along the rivers. They called it *chihvyàh*.]
>
> (MYRA MOSES, interpreted by Alice Frost, August 10, 1977, VG2001-4-4:298-388;001-009, Gwich'in)

Values

> Grandchild, long ago, a really long time ago when the earth first came about, the people on this earth knew how it was to be good. In those days, some of the people, now they call them smart. These people, sometimes they made lots of people live by killing the bad ones. Sometimes lots of people had no meat and they were going to die. Sometimes the smart people saved them.
>
> (SARAH ABEL, August 11, 1977, VG2001-4-5:218-232, Gwich'in)

Elders Sarah Abel, Myra Kaye, Martha Tizya, and Myra Moses emphasized that in the past, people cared for each other as if everyone were members of the same family. In particular, food was shared with everyone who lived together, even in times of scarcity. They illustrated the various ways that the old and infirm and the destitute were cared for and how surpluses were stored for times of need. The values of generosity, sharing, and caring for everyone that guided the people in those days were of paramount importance.

The Arctic Village People

> The Arctic Village people were like one big family. If one person killed an animal, everyone was served like one family. That is how they lived. They were never stingy. When we moved, we filled the dog packs with dryfish. When we had lunch, we boiled enough fish for everyone. When it was time to eat—we never had tea then—fish was served. That was how they lived. Whoever got food would always cook. Blood soup was like gravy. When we told the minister, he said soon you won't have to make blood soup, you will use flour for gravy. Now we make gravy with flour. That was how hard the times were in the past.
>
> (MYRA KAYE, February 2, 1980, VG2000-8-19C, Gwich'in)

Caribou hunters, 1930.

[Yukon Archives, Arthur Thornthwaite fonds 83/22 #276]

Sharing When Food was Scarce

If you killed even one ptarmigan, lots of people were fed from it, they said, even though there was so little. My grandfather...made snares with sinew. They set snares with those [for rabbits and ptarmigan and animals like that].

(MARTHA TIZYA, August 11, 1977, VG2001-4-6#1:320-317, Gwich'in)

How People Looked After Each Other

When I was a child, my dad was not a lazy person. He killed everything. When he killed lots of rabbits, he gave them out to the people, not only our family. Everyone did this. When people killed an animal, it was [shared] with everyone. We helped each other....

We took good care of our elders, old women and old men. Orphans, too, we took them in and took care of them. This is what we did. People took care of each other at that time.

Ah, Grandchild, when there was no food it was difficult. What were we going to eat? We soaked hides and ate that. It was good. Moose skin, too. That is what we did. At that time people took really good care of each other.

(MYRA MOSES, January 1980, VG2000-8-19A, Gwich'in)

Small Feasts

> She said that when they had meat, [they put it in the cache]. They cached meat and fish: some of the people dug ground cellars outdoors and they put their meat in there. When some people had no meat, they took all the meat out and just gave meat to whoever had no meat. They boiled the meat...and invited the people and all those people went to their house with their dishes. That's how they just made little feasts, like that. That's the only way they could do it.
>
> (MYRA MOSES, interpreted by Edith Josie, VG1999-6-7:148-157, English)

Caring for Elders

Speaking of the time people lived at Rampart House during missionary Bompas' time:

> The old women lived alone in small round houses. I used to pick up wood chips for them outside their houses. The other little girls did that with me. In those days the poor people told the children what chores to do, their parents their fathers and mothers, those. That is what they did. We would haul water for them [old women]. We would bring snow indoors for them. This is what they did for them. At that time there were no saws; they would just chop wood, that's all. At the Hudson's Bay store there were lots of wood chips. We picked them up. The old women who lived alone in small round houses had fires inside. There were no stoves. They would sit alone there. We visited with them. We picked the wood chips for them. For payment, we sat with them. When we made tea, all the old women saved the tea leaves. They remade tea with it again, and they give us some. [Laughter]
>
> (MYRA MOSES, ca.1980, VG2000-8-31:071-083, Gwich'in)

Caribou and Caribou Fences (*Tthał*)

Van Tat Gwich'in speak of making two kinds of caribou fence, one for summer[6] when the big herds migrate en masse from their calving grounds on the Alaskan North Slope, and a second type used in winter when the herds are dispersed in the timber country to the south. Of the two kinds, the summer fences are the most famous, due to their spectacular size and elegant design. They were hairpin-shaped with arms up to a kilometre long built of logs, which were increasingly stout and sturdily constructed toward the "pocket." Herds of caribou could be intercepted from different directions, herded between the arms toward the pocket where they were ultimately snared and speared. Building these caribou fences and using them required

Two caribou fence drawings.

[Raymond Le Blanc 2007. Adapted from R. McFee 1975]

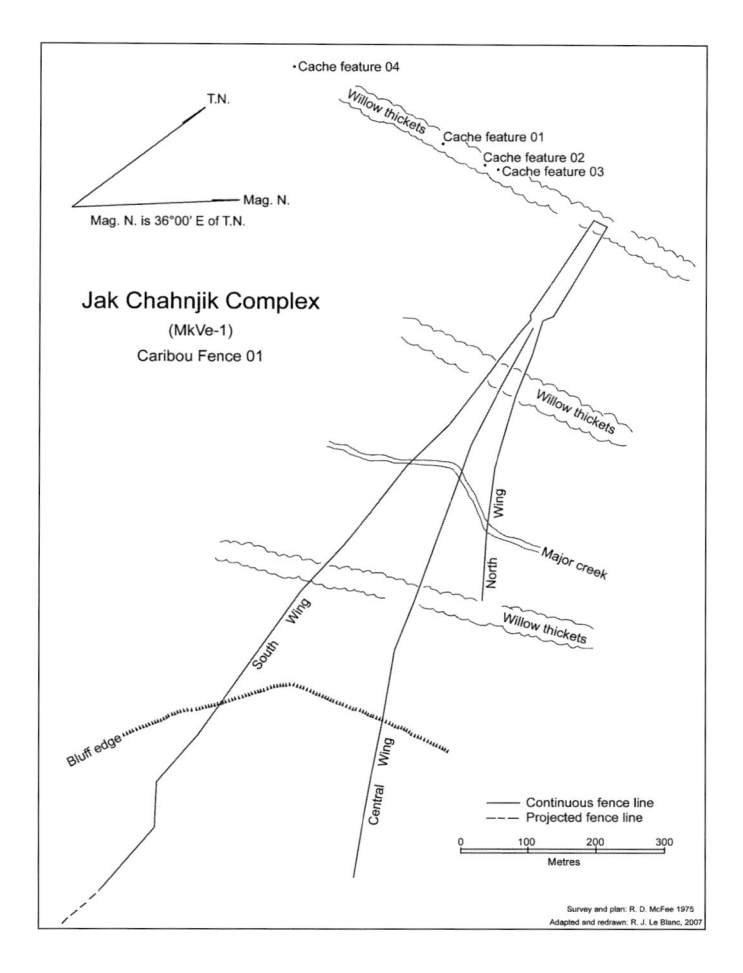

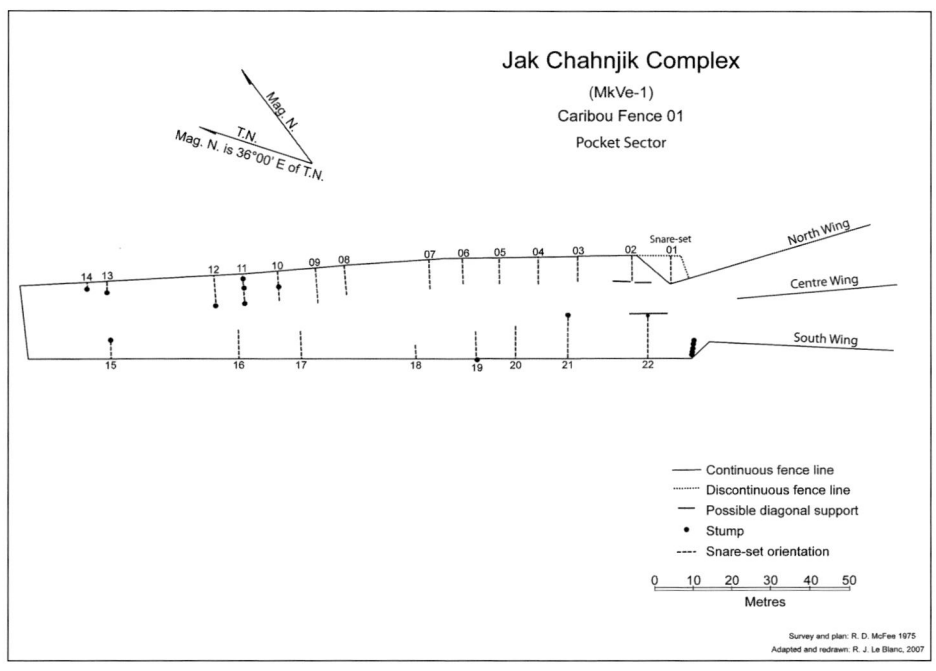

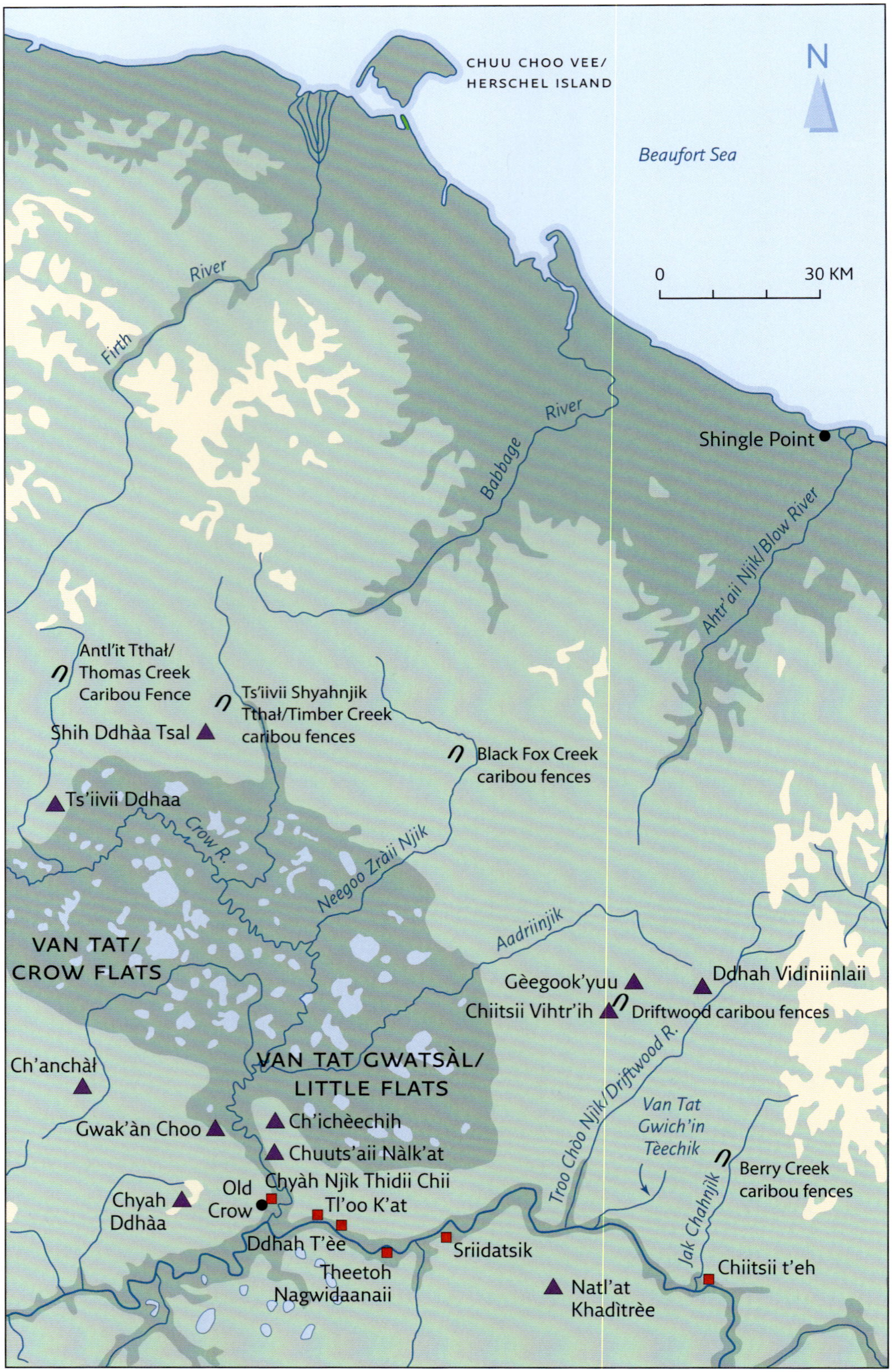
CHUU CHOO VEE/
HERSCHEL ISLAND
N
Beaufort Sea
0
30 KM
Firth
River
Babbage
River
Shingle Point
Ahtr'aii Njik/Blow River
Antl'it Tthał/
Thomas Creek
Caribou Fence
Ts'iivii Shyahnjik
Tthał/Timber Creek
caribou fences
Shih Ddhàa Tsal
Black Fox Creek
caribou fences
Ts'iivii Ddhaa
Crow R.
Neegoo Zràii Njik
Aadriinjik
VAN TAT/
CROW FLATS
Gèegook'yuu
Ddhah Vidiniinlaii
Chiitsii Vihtr'ih
Driftwood caribou fences
Ch'anchàł
VAN TAT GWATSÀL/
LITTLE FLATS
Troo Chòo Njik/Driftwood R.
Van Tat
Gwich'in
Tèechik
Gwak'àn Choo
Ch'ichèechih
Chuuts'aii Nàlk'at
Berry Creek
caribou fences
Chyàh Njìk Thidii Chii
Old
Crow
Chyah
Ddhàa
Tl'oo K'at
Ddhah T'èe
Sriidatsik
Jak Chahnjik
Theetoh
Nagwidaanaii
Chiitsii t'eh
Natl'at
Khadìtrèe

MAP 3 *Routes from Porcupine River and Van Tat (Crow Flats) to Herschel Island/Arctic Ocean*

the efforts of many people and, if successful, provided a great amount of food. According to recent elders, the last summer fence in use was run by Old Domas (the Thomas Creek caribou fence), likely up until the end of the 19th century.

Nineteenth-century visitors, such as Sir John Richardson, who undertook an expedition to the Mackenzie area and beyond searching for the missing Sir John Franklin in 1848, drew on the observations of the Hudson's Bay Company traders Bell and Murray to describe the "Kutchin" and the caribou fences. Richardson's account is valuable despite some facets that are at odds with the oral history of the use the fences, which he appears not to have observed personally. For example, he reports that the caribou were driven onto sharpened stakes, whereas oral history tells of the use of snares and spears:

> Mr. Bell informed me that, on the open hilly downs frequented by reindeer, the Kutchin have formed pounds, toward which the animals are conducted by two rows of stakes or trunks of trees extending for miles. These rows converge, and as the space between them narrows, they are converged into a regular fence by the addition of strong horizontal bars. The extremity of the avenue is closed by stakes set firmly in the ground wither the sharp points sloping toward the entrance, so that when the deer are urged vehemently forwards they may impale themselves thereon. The hunters, spreading over the country, drive the deer within the jaws of the pound; and the women and children, ensconced behind the fence, wound all they can with arrows and spears. These structures are erected with great labour, as the timber has to be brought into the open country from a considerable distance. Some of the pounds visited by Mr. Bell appeared to him, from the condition of the wood, to be more than a century old. They are the hereditary possessions of the families by whom they were constructed.
>
> (RICHARDSON 1851:393–394)

Bell's comments speak to the antiquity of the caribou fences, and Archdeacon McDonald wrote of both the summer and smaller winter "deer barriers" and their importance for provisioning both Gwich'in and traders (and missionaries) (see McDonald's journal 1869). Elder Moses Tizya described the two different kinds of caribou fences and how they worked. He explained why they were eventually abandoned in favour of different hunting techniques when effective guns were acquired and, he emphasized, when there were too few Van Tat Gwich'in to make use of the fences, a comment echoed by Myra Kaye. Sarah Abel, Myra Moses, and Myra Kaye told of the amount of work and co-operation required to make and use a

The First Generation

caribou fence, and how the food was shared among everyone afterward, echoing the values of caring for others and sharing. They also described women's roles in using caribou fences, such as making and caring for the hundreds of snares that were required.

Winter and Summer Caribou Fences

> They used nothing but bow and arrows and snares. Just bow and arrows in those days. What they did was in the wintertime, they made fences with trees, brush, things like that, and then they set lots of snares. [They made the fences by] Old Crow, anywhere, any place in the country, not only in one place. [They drove] a big bunch of caribou in those snares.
>
> But the other caribou fences [summer] were different altogether. There are lots of them over there now, they say [north of Old Crow in the hills surrounding Crow Flats, west into Alaska and east to the Northwest Territories]. If you go to Crow Flats with Dr. Irwin,[7] you're going to see lots of them, old things. They're a different thing again, that's Native poles or something [made from cut poles]. They're still there.
>
> [There were two different kinds of fences.] The first one was only for wintertime. When they saw a big bunch of caribou, they put a fence around it, and then they set lots of snares inside and they chased the caribou in there. That's how they got lots of caribou. [They saw the caribou first and then they made the fence and chased them in?] Yeah, that's the way they did it.
>
> [The second kind was the summer fence.] Well, the summer fence, we used them here and there, big fences. They had poles across this way, the middle was open, you know. They say they had over a hundred snares in there. From that fence they made arms, four arms. They just dug here and there and then tied something on it so the wind would move it. And when they chased the caribou, they followed it in and the caribou got scared. Pretty soon they went inside the fence. When they went right to the end of the fence and started to come back, that's how they got caught. [It's a] story; I haven't seen it. Not very long ago they still had fences. Some of them are pretty good yet, but some of them fell down. Still, they see lots of them, those Dr. Irwin. [archaeologists]
>
> Well, after they got guns in the country, that's how they quit [using caribou fences]. And then by that time, people were all finished, all died off anyway.

[You needed quite a lot of people to hunt with a caribou fence.] Yeah, my father told me [in] his time there was so many people, he had to make four trails, wintertime, when they moved. You know what I mean....And after that, through Archdeacon McDonald, we know when what they call scarlet fever came to [this] country. That's what killed all the people off. That's what my old man told me, died off, everybody died off with it. [This happened] a way long time before I was born. All these things were in the 1800[s]. 1800[s] was my father's time.

[The person that owned the fence] just gave one [caribou] here and all over, whoever was around there. He divided them up. A lot of people had to work on the fence. They got poles and [fixed the] place.

[They drove rabbits, too.] That's what they did. Well, they like a strip of brush, lots of rabbits in there. They set snares in one end, same as they do with caribou. They set lots of snares and then drove all the rabbits in there and got lots of rabbits that way. Women and all, women help with caribou fence, too....

Babiche snares, that was all they used. I think one caribou skin made one snare. My father had lots of them but now there's no more in town, I think. All gone. Lots of geologists came around and they got hold of them and that's why there's no more, I guess. They bought them, paid five dollars for one snare, just about this size [door opening]. They made babiche out of [caribou hide]. Then they twisted it and twisted it, oh, maybe six, seven, eight. And then they twisted them again and tied them to a pole and stretched them.

Sometimes [the caribou got choked in the snares]. After they went in the fence, those caribou were alive. They had long spears, bone spears, on the end of a long stick. They stabbed them here someplace and that's how they killed them in the snares. Then they threw them over the fence. They probably got 100 caribou, something like that. They threw them over the fence right away and reset the snares in case there's another bunch coming. And then everybody, women, all cut up the meat and they had big cache there, maybe the size of this place, but logs just like that. Yeah, they threw all the meat in there.

They took home what they could use. They left all the meat in that cache...They just packed home so many and watched for another bunch. Another bunch came, then they chased them there again. That way they [got lots] of caribou, you see. That's the time, they [hunted] the caribou...not every day of the year, just when the caribou are running [migrating] like they do now, you see. That's the time they got them. They lived off that meat until, oh, probably after New Year, when they ran out of meat. Then they started to move. That's the time they made the [other] fence I told you about, winter fence.

Dog sleds heading downriver (1914–1940).
[Yukon Archives, Frank Foster fonds 82/415 #100]

[They got many caribou in the wintertime fence, too.] Oh yes, they got a big bunch. Three to four thousand people need lots of meat to keep them going.

(MOSES TIZYA, August 11, 1977, VG2001-4-6#1:131-283, English and Gwich'in)

Ch'eeghwalti's Tthał [caribou fence]

Me and Tabitha [Kyikavichik] and Johnny Ross's father went to *Chanlaii Laii* for trapping and we forgot tea....We moved to *Aadriinjik* and I made some Labrador tea. [Not] far from our camp *Ch'ahuu'oh'* had his camp, so we went [there]. We went on *tan daagaii* [white ice] and when we got to his camp, they made tea for us.

While I stayed at that camp with the kids, him and Peter *Ch'ahuu'oh'* came down for supplies and from that camp we went to *Chiitsii vihtr'ih tthał*. On the way there somebody had a tent set and we set camp up there at *k'ohnjik* [a creek]. We camped there two nights. We set traps there and I made a round house with willows and from there he set traps for fox at *Chiitsii vihtr'ih tthał*.[8] Long ago *Ch'eeghwalti'* had a [caribou] fence around there but they all left.[9]

> There used to be a lot of people there but they all died from starvation.
>
> (MYRA KAYE, February 20, 1980, VG2000-8-20B:015-040, Gwich'in)

Life During the Time When Caribou Fences were Used

> A long time [ago there] was no white man....We just used moose, caribou, all kind of little animal [to live on]. And at that time there was no gun, either.
>
> ...In those days the people looked for and lived on caribou, moose, rabbit, ptarmigan, ground squirrel, all small animals, ptarmigan, all of them. Moose skin, they made snares with it, to snare caribou. The caribou skins, they made caribou snares with them. Whenever there was a lot of caribou, when the caribou all went to one place, they made a caribou fence around there. They put the caribou-skin snares and moose-skin snares on the fence. They snared them, and then lots of people lived by the caribou fence. They all worked together, how good. They helped each other. All the people gave each other lots of meat....
>
> They used arrows to kill meat; moose, caribou, they killed with arrows. Grizzly bear, black bear, sometimes they killed them with arrows.
>
> In the summertime, but when it gets cold, at that time it's hard to kill meat. When people were moving from place to place, they moved without food. No matter how far, they moved to where they were going to see meat. Those who had lots of children had a really hard time. How hard it was for them. Sometimes when they didn't kill meat, lots of people froze to death without food. Even so, the people didn't perish. In those days on the land, there were lots of people....
>
> Then, those people who were good helped the other people around them. Sometimes when they got meat, they went to the different places where lots of people travelled around and they helped the people there. Sometimes people who were going to die were saved by those people. So that's how people helped each other lots of times. Long ago it happened....
>
> In those days, there were no white people so it was hard for everything. I never saw it but it was talked about in front of me. That is what I am talking about. This is how I know it, but really [it happened] before me.
>
> Sometimes the people killed each other. The *Ch'ineekaii* people and Native people fought and killed each other. Around that time, sometimes only one of the people was left living, sometimes two. Sometimes, really, all the people were killed.
>
> (SARAH ABEL, July 1979, VG2000-8-10A:028-075, English and Gwich'in)

Myra Moses Tells how She Learned about Caribou Fences

When she was born, her mother passed away. Everybody looked after her because she was small. At that time it was hard to get baby bottles. All they did was feed her from the breast and her father give a little flour, tea, things like that to those woman so they could feed her from their breast. She said she sucked lots of women's breasts and that's how she grew. Her father came up to Rampart House, where Mr. Firth had a store and he took flour, sugar, and tea, and his father just fed her some porridge. Her father raised her. Other kid[s] grow after they're born, they grow good, but she had a hard time. Her father had a hard time raising her.

When she was about five or six years old, her father passed away and then all her grandparents looked after her. They used to go out in the woods. They set nets and all that. Her grandfather just stayed in the woods with her and raised her on caribou. You know that a long time ago they made big fences for caribou. The caribou went in and they had snares on both ends. The caribou came through to the gate end[10] there were snares there, too, so they could get another caribou. That's what her grandparents did....Long ago it was hard to get things [store-bought supplies] and they just made snares out of caribou skin. The skin is hard and strong...

(MYRA MOSES, interpreted by Edith Josie, VG1999-6-7:005-029, English)

Snaring Moose and Caribou

They made snares from skins and set them for caribou. Sometimes they snared caribou and sometimes they snared moose. Long ago, when the Hudson's Bay was around [they had guns that only took one or two shells]. That was really hard.

Caribou fences, they are back on the mountains. There are lots on the mountains, lots of old ones. Many people lived around there. They made lots of snares. They set them and made caribou fences and with that they killed lots of caribou. [All the people who killed the caribou divided that meat between the people.] That's how it was good.

(MYRA MOSES, VG2001-4-4:080-094, Gwich'in)

Rawhide snare for moose or caribou, near Old Crow.

[Yukon Archives, Arthur Thornthwaite fonds 83/22 #1313]

Women's Roles and Making and Preserving Snares

Around that time women never tried trapping or fishing. Only the men set snares for caribou. You know when they set snares, they put willow at the end. That's the only time the women helped. They packed willows for their husbands. The only time she helped her grandmother, she packed willows with her. Women never used to trap or fish, she said.

When they set snares on a stick, sometime caribou would break the stick and then they had to pull wood to that gate [block the gate with wood]. Some women cleaned the skins and made babiche; they made a lot. They kept it under the ground [cold, on permafrost]. For many years they kept it underground and soaked it in winter. After they soaked it and stretched it out, they used it for snares. That's how people made their snares.

(MYRA MOSES, interpreted by Edith Josie, VG1999-6-7:173-193, English)

Caribou Fences, Snares, Arrows, Traps, and Guns

When someone saw tracks and which way was the best, we made a caribou fence with trees. We set snares inside; we only depended on snares then. I remember people still used bows and arrows then. After we made the caribou fence and set snares, everyone rounded up the

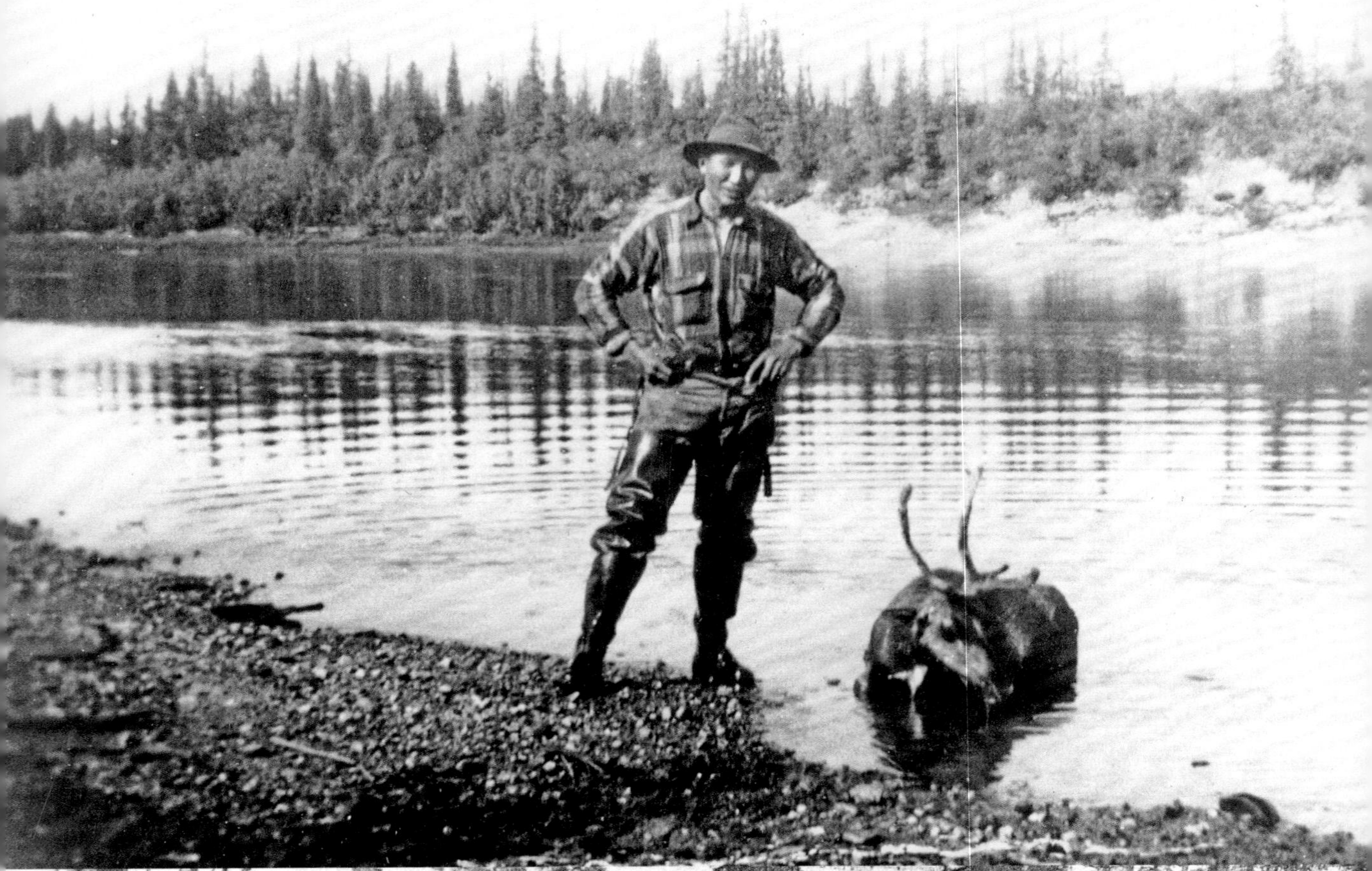

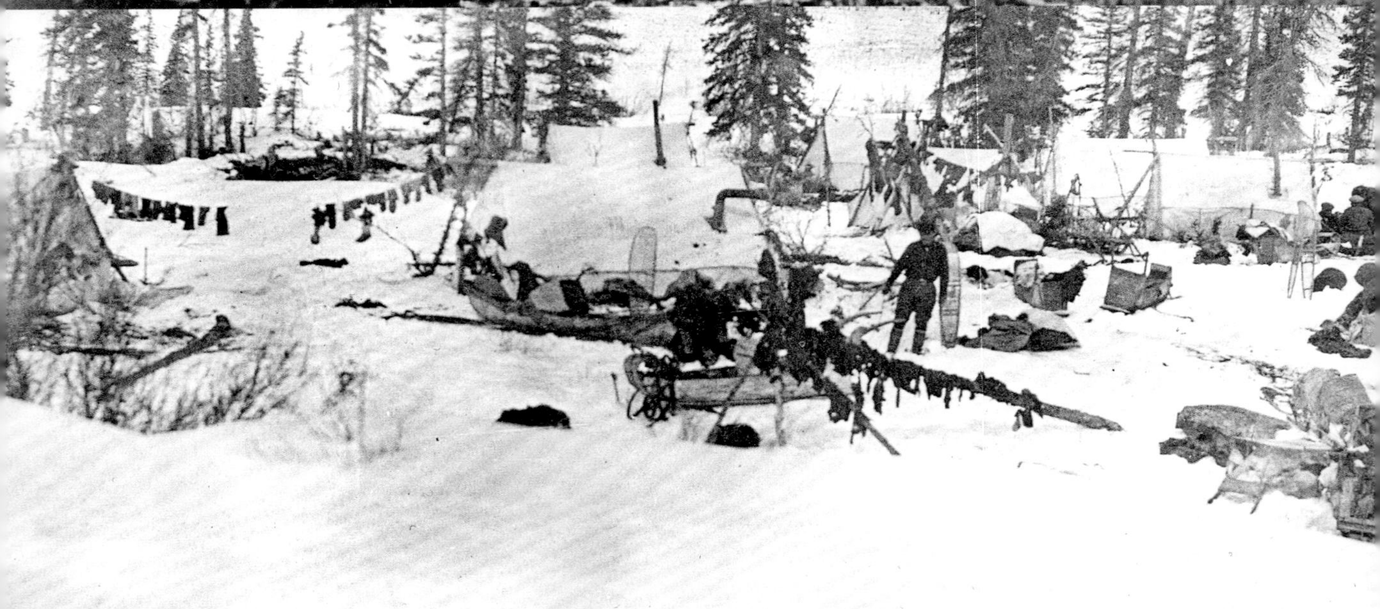

Page 96 (top): Peter Tizya with caribou, ca. 1920.

[Yukon Archives, Bob Sharp fonds 82/326 #1]

Page 96 (bottom): Muskrat hunting camp at Van Tat *(Crow Flats).*

[Yukon Archives, Arthur Thornthwaite fonds 83/22 #229]

caribou. When the caribou heard us they all scattered. How many times we snared lots of caribou!

Sometimes the caribou were shot with bows and some with guns. At that time there was only skinny guns. The trader who came by here brought shotguns; that is what we used later. It helped the people. We didn't know about [steel] traps. We made deadfall traps. Eventually we started using traps. In the winter we set wolverine traps in the valley. We could get one gun with all the supplies to last one year [bullets] with one wolverine pelt. That was what we did. That was when we got 30 [.30-.30 rifle].

(MYRA KAYE, February 2, 1980, VG2000-8-19C, Gwich'in)

The Importance of *Van Tat* (Crow Flats)

That's why they are stingy about [protective of] *Van Tat*. It's easy to kill meat there. Grandchild, I saw all around, you know: Fort Yukon, I was all over this land. All around Black River, I saw there, too. I saw all around Fort McPherson, too. Even so, only in this *Van Tat* is it easy to kill small animals to eat. On account of that, they don't like anyone to bother *Van Tat*.

(MYRA MOSES, VG2001-4-4:066-072, Gwich'in)

Van Tat [Crow Flats] is the jewel in the heart of Van Tat Gwich'in traditional lands. It is a large flat area of lakes, rivers, and streams between the Porcupine River and the British Mountains. Criss-crossed with caribou trails, it is also rich in muskrats (explained in the Muskrat and Beaver story, Chapter One), fish, moose, and, seasonally, waterfowl. As well as a valuable area for food and furs, and the place people went in times of scarcity, *Van Tat* is beloved for its beauty and a variety of other emotional and spiritual reasons. In the Gwich'in language, *Van* is "lake," *Tat* means "among," and *Gwich'in* means "people," hence *Van Tat Gwich'in* refers to "lake people" or "people who live among the lakes." *Van Tat* or Crow Flats is an area of thousands of lakes and it is from this place that the Van Tat Gwich'in, "People of the Lakes," derive their name.

Sarah Abel and Neil McDonald told of one of the most important aspects of *Van Tat*: a place to go in time of need, to prevent starvation. Sarah Abel described how people relied on fish in the small creeks and rivers, and Neil McDonald related how people would hunt for muskrats in the wintertime. Myra Moses added another aspect: how old men and women for whom travel was difficult would stay and fish in *Van Tat* while the younger people were on the move to other locations. Mary Thomas told of muskrat trapping

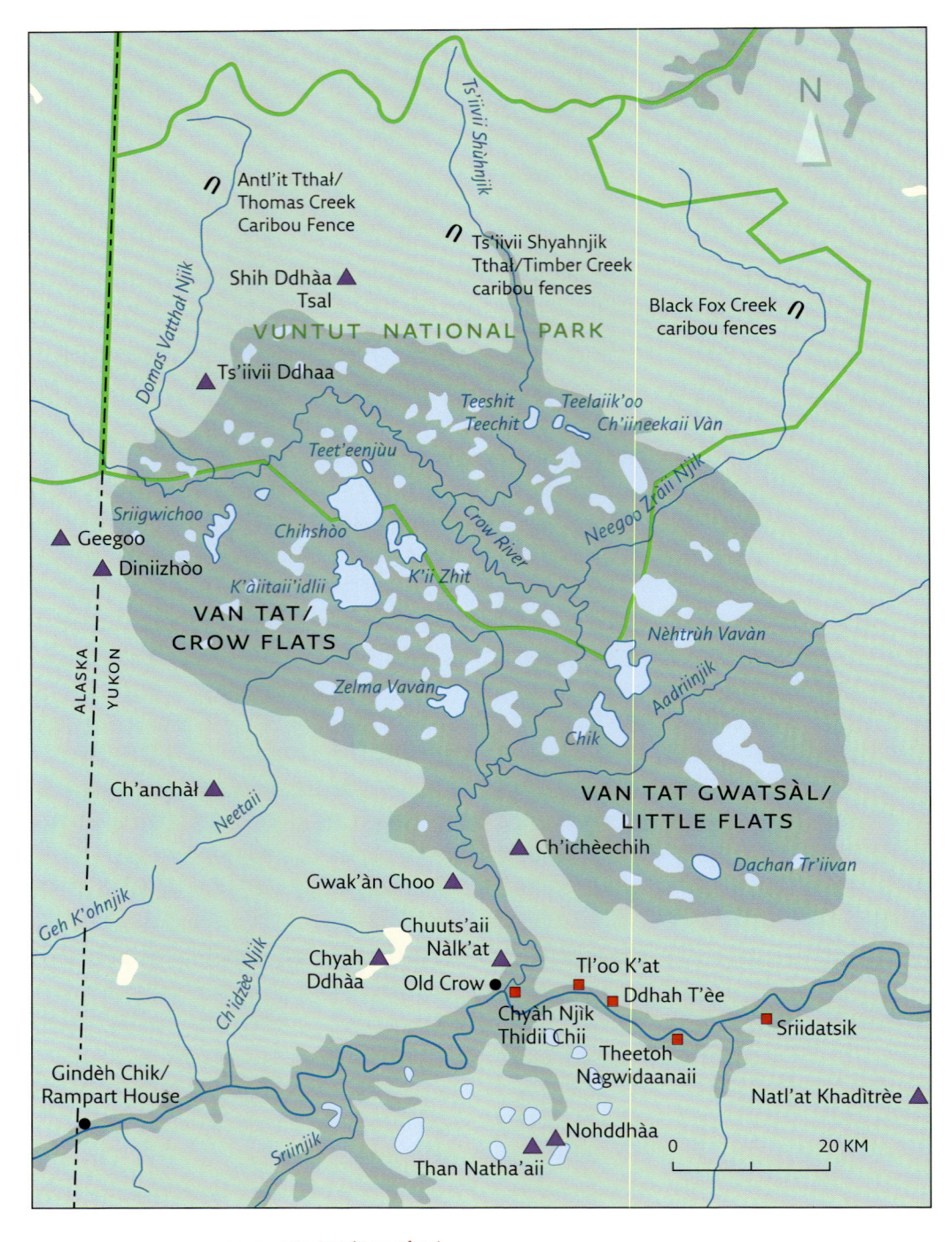

MAP 4 *Van Tat (Crow Flats)*

in the western part of *Van Tat*, the various neighbouring people who used the area, and returning to Old Crow for funeral services.

Crow Flats was a Destination in Time of Need

> Grandchild, in those days there were hard times. Even so, all the people on earth were friends toward each other. That's how people sometimes survived. But when there was no meat, when it was hard for them to kill meat, about a hundred people froze to death up there, that mountain called *Chyah Ddhàa* [Second Mountain]. Lots of people froze to death on it. That's why it's called *Chyah Ddhàa*.[11]
>
> So then, Grandchild, at *Van Tat* and up there at Crow Point, those two [places], a long time ago, when there was no food, people depended on those places, they said....When people had no food, they moved to *Van Tat* [for fish], where there's creeks by the lakes. In those days there were no fishnets. They tore off the willow bark and knitted them as big fishnets. They set these in the creeks. They got lots of fish and ate really good, they said. With its broth, they used every bit of it.
>
> Grandchild, many years ago, maybe a thousand years ago, they did that. Still today, the people continue to live off of *Van Tat*. The people raised now, those being raised, they still use it. They still depend on *Van Tat*.
>
> So, Grandchild, *Chyahnjik*, that is Crow River, they call it. It flows through the middle of *Van Tat*. The fish from the lakes went through there and the people used it.
>
> (SARAH ABEL, August 11, 1977, VG2001-4-5:312-389, Gwich'in)

Hunting Muskrats in *Van Tat* during Times of Scarcity

> Yes, they had a hard time, you know, sometimes...A long time ago, when they used to go south, in the fall, [they dried] fish and meat. They travelled south. When there was no game, they had to rush back to Crow Flats for [musk]rats. The way they hunted [musk]rats in wintertime:...I guess they had bone chisels. All along the shore of the lake, they had camps....[by] the rat runways back to the lake. You open that place up and they put a [snare/trap/net]. When they fish they use that net...made out of roots or babiche. As soon as [a] little stick in front [moved], like [something] touched the stick...[they] pulled it up. So, they got quite a few that way.
>
> (NEIL MCDONALD, August 12, 1977, VG2001-4-7:073-089, English)

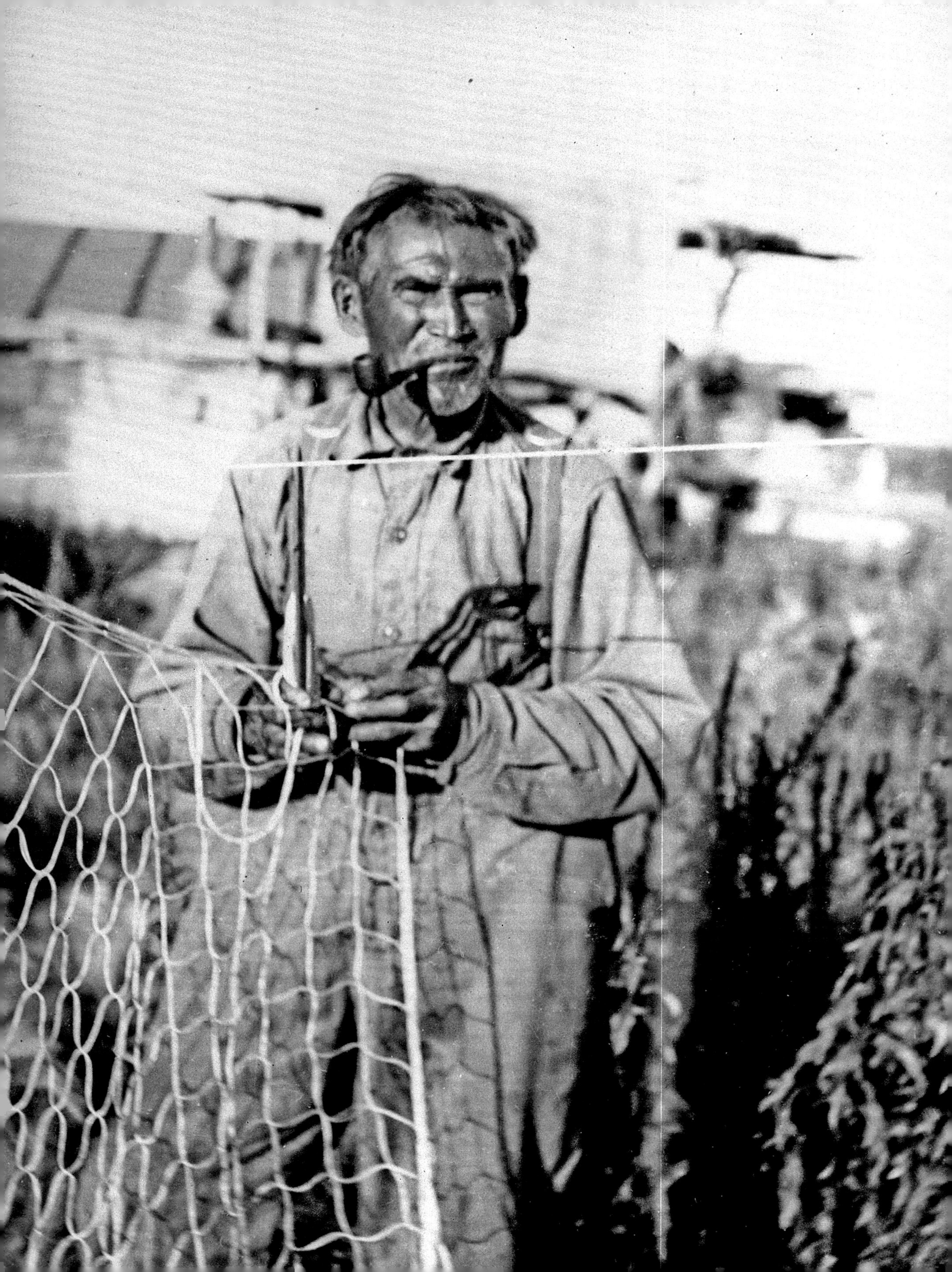

Page 100: "Old Steamboat" making a fishnet, Old Crow, August 10, 1946.

[Canadian Museum of Civilization, Leechman fonds #100597]

Above: Neil McDonald cutting wood (1965–69).

[Exham fonds (VG2008-01-189)]

In the olden days, the people used to fish on Crow River with fish traps and they got enough fish, dryfish and they freeze it up. Then when the cold weather came, they moved south for caribou and for moose. And there [were] times when there were no caribou. They had to come back. They would be running short on food and they had to come back from the south to Crow Flats. There's lots of times some of the people were starving, starving to death....

Then when the people, those that are left, got to Crow Flats and with the ice chisel, bone chisel, they used to walk around the edge of the lake and tap the ice. Where [there was a] hollow sound, that meant that's where the rat comes out to go onto the lake, to their houses to feed. When they find that, they open it, then they put, sort of a scoop net in. When the rat gets in that scoop, they dip it out and that's how the Old Crow people used to live, right up to today.

Crow Flats is the mainstay of the people in Old Crow. Now today, the people in Old Crow get most of their fur from Crow Flats: that is rat skins. That is the reason why the first time the oil people wanted this Crow Flats, there was a meeting here. Only one man spoke about

Old Crow, Joe Kaye, and what he said was to explain why the people depended on Old Crow [Flats]. The white man, they got banks in buildings. The Indians got no banks; Crow Flats is their bank. That's what Joe Kaye said and a lot of people could have spoke, [but] nobody spoke.[12] Today the people want that. Old Crow, all the Old Crow, after all, we'll still own all the Old Crow [Flats] after land settlement. That's what the people want.

(NEIL MCDONALD, June 27, 1979, VG2000-8-4:034-085, English)

How Old Men and Women Spent the Summer in *Van Tat*

Sometimes this happened to old men. During the summer when people travelled...these two old men had a fish trap. And in a different area two old women had a fish trap, too. The land was good and there were lots of *tthaa* [ground squirrels]. They hunted for the *tthaa* and there were lots of roots, too. They got lots of fish and when it was all cut and hung up, they would get roots. After bringing the roots home, they were peeled, cut up into small pieces, and pounded. This was put into fish oil and they made something like pemmican with it. When they got birch to make toboggans, they also got birch[bark] to make plates or bowls. These are what they made the fish pemmican in. This was how people lived.

It was difficult to get fishnets in *Van Tat*; there were only fish traps. Downriver [there were] fish trap places. Upriver, there is a hole where the fish came through. When there was lots of fish, the trap was closed. The wood was knitted with willow to close the trap. They came down and said *"Yaagha' nak'oo iinjil"* ["there are lots of fish in your fish trap"]. And everyone ran across the creek. There were so many fish it sounded like rocks hitting each other. Then they would spear the fish. Ah, it was lots of fun. Meanwhile the wives would go for roots. After the fish was cut, the guts were cleaned and cooked with the roots. Whoever got lots of fish would boil fish, and the roots mixed with fish guts were served.

(MYRA KAYE, VG2000-8-19C, Gwich'in)

Hunting Muskrats at Potato Creek

Potato Creek is long way from here, the other end of this mountain, back of Rampart House. [From] Rampart House we went over the mountain [*Ch'anchàl* or King Edward Mountain]. The wind was strong

Canvas boats rafted together returning from muskrat hunting in Crow Flats.

[Yukon Archives, Gordon and Lorna Walmsley fonds #13480]

and we tied the kids to the sled and went for muskrats. That's how we went over the mountains.

At Potato Creek there used to be lots of muskrats....When we travelled over the mountains, at that time we had too many kids so I went first and then came back, and then we went over the mountain all by ourselves. I am talking about when there was lots of muskrats. Now there are no muskrats in *Van Tat*. There was lots of caribou at that time, too. We dried meat and with it we came to Old Crow down the Crow River with canvas boats. When they went to the village, they went over the mountains to Rampart House.

At that time people from Fort Yukon were in *Van Tat*, too: lots of people, when [there were] lots of caribou and muskrats....They hunted muskrats with canoes under the mountain. All they carried were the skins and they carried lots. They carried canoes, too, and sometimes they camped out for two days. All that time they shot muskrats, and they carried big packsacks of muskrats, and muskrats were a good price.

We made canvas boats with birch [frames] at the head of Potato Creek. Canvas boats had a blunt [square] prow and that's how we came down [the Crow River]. We stayed for awhile and then we went

Sarah Baalam and Mary Thomas.

[Canadian Museum of Civilization, photo Father Jean-Marie Mouchet S2004-1372]

to Rampart House and we stayed there. The river was a long trip and a long way and when we were coming down, we shot lots of small game. That's how we ate. They saw moose on the way down but we couldn't kill it because there was no room in the boat. We had all our dry muskrat skins in one big canvas boat. If we killed a moose, where were we going to put it?

We got down to John's [John Thomas, her husband]. Only he had a motor and he came all the way up Potato Creek with a canvas boat and gas. Coming down [the Crow River] he picked up all the canvas boats and bought them to Old Crow.[13] He had a boat like what we have today [wooden scow] and he brought all the people down from *Van Tat* with it. I don't know how they paid him. My uncle Ben was waiting for us. I told him I was going to pay but he said, "No. This is the first time we're going to help you. Why are you going to pay? You're not going to pay; we will take you down." And it rained hard and we all got wet. We set tents on the mud and camped and it was a hard time.

The *Ch'ineekaii* [Inuit] came from the ocean: they knew there were lots of caribou and they came down the river. They hunted and killed caribou and trapped muskrats.

I pulled my kids around with a dog team. While [my husband] went to town, I killed lots of muskrats. When he went to Rampart House for more food, all the women who stayed around [did] nothing and I took muskrat skins to them. While I worked hard, they all had no food.

At Potato Creek there were big muskrats. I used to stay at this lake and it went dry, no water in the lake, just bare ground. All the lakes that had big muskrats went dry. We moved around and that's the way we used to trap. When we killed caribou, we dried the meat.

We went to town to Old Crow and Rampart House, too. Over the mountains is a long way. My dog team, it was just like nothing for them at that time. Lots of people from Alaska stayed with us. One man named "Big Head" stayed with us and some of the Fort Yukon people stayed with us, too. They never trapped or shot muskrats. Meanwhile we hunted muskrats and John really laughed at them, at his relatives, anyway. I had kids in the sled and I used one dog and I brought home a big packsack of muskrats while they just sat around. Before he went back to Rampart House, he killed caribou; [they] went to the mountains for caribou. My brother made him work hard while they were gone. When they came back, just when they started to sleep, two people were coming. I told them there were two people coming and asked what they were doing. They said, "Katherine [Linklater] drowned. We're going down to town with her so we came to see you....While she was setting a trap, the ice broke and she fell in." They brought some food. Me, I was drying meat, and I told him, "Put the dry muskrats in your sled and give them to people in Old Crow."...

All the snow started to melt and [there was] a lot of water, and lots of people went to town with her. Often [when someone] died, they buried them there. They went back to *Van Tat* and everything was over....Before that one of our kids died and we brought him to town, too. Everyone went with him. [His father] killed a moose and took it to town for a feast at the burial site.

That's all I remember. The mountains behind Rampart House, we also went over them. We had good dogs at that time. They travelled like the wind. We all sat on the big sled and they pulled us around. And we spent the spring in *Van Tat* and came down with canvas boats. Everyone had come to town already and I thought our boat might sink. We had a paddle behind the boat; that's why it didn't sink. I had lots of kids and they brought them all down. You see all the canvas boats around, he brought all of them down with his motor. That was the way we used to live.

(MARY THOMAS, February 20, 1980, VG2000-8-16:054-230, Gwich'in)

Relations with Neighbours

Van Tat Gwich'in were surrounded by other Gwich'in groups for the most part, with the exception of their northern neighbours, the *Ch'ineekaii* or "Eskimo," now known as Inuvialuit and Inuit.[14] As well, Van Tat Gwich'in had contact with Hän in the more distant southwest. Records of early traders (such as Murray) and oral history from other locations records some hostility between Gwich'in groups at various times, however the first generation of Van Tat Gwich'in elders speak mainly of peaceful relations with other Gwich'in. Their stories of their encounters with their *Ch'ineekaii* neighbours are more complex, as seen in the previous chapter. The accounts of hostility between the two nations are followed by more recent history of peaceful coexistence. Both peoples used *Van Tat* (Crow Flats) and the country to the north, and they traded at Herschel Island and Rampart House.

Neil McDonald described the various neighbours of Van Tat Gwich'in and their relations with each other. Myra Moses related stories of fighting between Van Tat Gwich'in and *Ch'ineekaii* from a time when both people used stone and bone tools. Moses Tizya gave a more recent opinion of *Ch'ineekaii* people from his own experience.

Neighbours of Van Tat Gwich'in and how They Coexisted

> These people here now, Arctic Red River, Peel River, McPherson people…, LaPierre House (and there's that Peter Charlie, he's a Dagoo [Tukudh] [or] LaPierre House Indian) and the Rat Indians, Fort Yukon Indians, Chandalar, Vuntut talk the same language but some of the languages, some of the words [are different], but [they know] what it means. Same as the southern Cree: Crees in the south and Crees in the north, their languages are a little different.[15] They [Gwich'in] got no songs or war songs or dance songs.
>
> From Fort Yukon down, the people have their own songs and their war songs. On the Tanana, across from Fort Yukon, Tanana people, from Eagle up all the way up to southern end [of the] Yukon, they all got their dance, feast songs and war songs. And these six tribes [Gwich'in], they got no war songs, they got no dance songs. They copy from others. The Peel River Indians: Teetl'it Gwich'in, that means "head of the water."
>
> LaPierre House, they call them, Dagoo [Tukudh]…and the Rat Indians, they call them "lake dwellers" [Vuntut]. Fort Yukon Indians, they call country dwellers, Gwichaa Gwich'in….And Chandalar people are [Neets'aii] Gwich'in….They never fought each other.

The Gwich'in and the Eskimos, they used to...fight each other. The Eskimos used to steal one woman, smart woman. They captured her and then she ran away. She came back and she told her people where they were. She went to the Eskimo camp....They're always there. One man, the Eskimos saw him, they were all coming up the river in the canoe and this one man went up the creek. They saw him going up the creek and no! They didn't see him. They saw, the foams and bubbles coming down, they know that it was somebody. So they went up there where the boat is coming out behind the brush and they brought a lot of sticks. Every canoe pass he put the stick to one side, that's how they counted and then when they were all coming back, he return all the sticks, but [there were] two sticks left. He waited and waited [until] those two came back down [and then] went up to the camp. They returned just this side of the camp, the Eskimos. So when he got there he told the people and they all went down and they always fight, just before they came there. They went down and the Eskimos were camping on the beach, and these Indians, they were in the brush and they, from one end to the other, they, two men, they called out like an owl. So they knew each other...and they all rushed down.

Yes [this was before guns]. They used spears a lot.

Later on they [were] all at peace. No more fighting, they used to trade with each other.

(NEIL MCDONALD, August 12, 1977, VG2001-4-7:059-158, English)

Warfare with the *Ch'ineekaii* in the Time of Bone and Stone Arrows

People around here, these Van Tat Gwich'in, fought with the *Ch'ineekaii*. The Van Tat Gwich'in killed lots of *Ch'ineekaii*, they said. The people around here had arrows and the *Ch'ineekaii* also had arrows but not as many, I guess. The bone arrow is really sharp, they say....Ah, Grandchild, they used stones [to make the bone arrow tips]....There were lots of stone axes, too. Everything was made of stone.

[They fought with the *Ch'ineekaii*]...over trade goods. When they couldn't agree over something to buy, they would be mad with each other, they said.

(MYRA MOSES, August 10, 1977, VG2001-4-4:224-242, Gwich'in)

Moses Tizya, Old Abel Chitze, and a third man prepare to skin and butcher a moose, 1930.

[Yukon Archives, Arthur Thornthwaite fonds 83/22 #1386]

Relations with *Ch'ineekaii* in More Recent Times

Yeah I saw it, *Ch'ineekaii*, what they made: fish hooks. They even put little eyes in it. Boyee! They're good, you know, those *Ch'ineekaii*. Smart people.

(MOSES TIZYA, August 11, 1977, VG2001-4-6#1:018, English and Gwich'in)

Leaders

According to their historical accounts, Van Tat Gwich'in had leaders who guided their economic activities, acted as their emissaries with other groups, were good providers, sponsored feasts, provided for the sick and destitute, and had other leadership attributes. Some of their actions were harsh by modern standards (sometimes they killed people), but this is often interpreted as necessary to ensure the survival of their people. Elders also comment on the institution of "chief," noting that some leaders were trading chiefs, as well, a status created by the Hudson's Bay Company fur-trading system.

Elders described leaders from before their time, such as "Old Crow," for whom the town of Old Crow and the Crow River are named. In Gwich'in, his name was *Deetru' K'avihdik* (Crow May I Walk), and he was also known as Chief *Zzeh Gittlit* ("in the corner") from his habit of sitting near the smoke hole of his tent.[16] He is believed to have lived from the early 1800s to before

Shahnuuti', an important Gwich'in leader of the late 1800s.

_{Dall, William Healey 1898 The Yukon: Narrative of W.H. Dall, leader of the expedition to Alaska in 1866–1868... Downey, London}

the Hudson's Bay Company left the country and is said to have died around 1869 along with John Kyikavichik (grandfather of present Elder John Joe Kyikavichik) and another man after drinking poisoned water from a muskrat house while trapping in Crow Flats. In his lifetime, he was the only trading chief for the Hudson's Bay Company in the 800 kilometres between Fort Yukon and LaPierre House, and he would collect furs from trappers to trade for goods, which he then distributed among the people. He was known for his honesty, diplomacy, and ability to settle disputes. The school in Old Crow is named for him, Chief Zzeh Gittlit School.

Other well-remembered leaders from around the same time as *Deetru' K'avihdik* were the three influential brothers *Shahnuuti'*, *Shahvyah*, and *Ch'eeghwalti'*. They were important leaders whose skills included shamanic abilities. *Shahnuuti'* is said to have lived in the Fort Yukon area and was associated with fish traps; *Shahvyah* (Sunsnare, or Rainbow) was known for his relationship with moose in the Circle, Alaska, area; and *Ch'eeghwalti'* lived in Van Tat Gwich'in territory and east and had special abilities with caribou and freshwater fish. *Ch'eeghwalti'* is remembered as an important leader and ancestor of many people in Old Crow and Fort McPherson. There is reputedly a fourth brother who is not well-recalled (Stanley Njootli, VG2002-3-20:045). These leaders were described by early traders and missionaries, such as Alexander Murray, who drew a portrait of "*Sreevyàa*" (*Shahvyah*) in 1847-48, and English artist Frederic Whymper, who drew him in 1867. Whymper travelled with a party led by American naturalist William Dall,

The First Generation

who sketched "*Shahnahti'*."[17] *Shahnuuti'* is particularly remembered in Alaska as *Shahnyaati'*. William Schneider described the qualities of a leader embodied by *Shahnyaati'*, as told to him by Alaskan Elder Sophie Paul:

> In all accounts, *Shahnyaati'* takes responsibility for feeding and supporting a large number of people, a major accomplishment at a time when people sometimes starved to death. This message has particular meaning for today's elders, who recall difficult times in their own lives when they didn't have enough to eat. Because *Shahnyaati'* was a provider, the Yukon Flats Gwich'in supported him. They hunted and trapped, and he did the trading. People wanted to be around him. Old Birch Creek Jimmy told me, "*Shahnyaati's* sons weren't going far for wives."...*Shahnyaati'* himself had many wives, a sign he was able to provide. When he wanted to make war, his band stood by him....I recall Sophie Paul saying that when the minister[18] told *Shahnyaati'* to give up all his wives and keep only one, he said he'd take his first two, but he still gave food to the others.
>
> (SCHNEIDER 1995:191)

The elders also credit their contemporary, Chief Peter Moses, as an important leader, a generous and just man. During his tenure as chief, he and the community gained recognition when the people of Old Crow contributed money to assist orphans in England during World War II, for which he received the British Empire Medal.

Old Crow–Crow May I Walk

> Yeah they had [chiefs]. They elected one man for chief, before the missionaries. This Old Crow [is] named after a chief. That chief [was] always fishing up here, [at the] mouth of Crow [River]. Hudson's Bay went by here; they trade with fish, ammunition, tea. Before that chief they called it *Chyahnjik*[19] [Crow River; derived from *njik* (river) and *chyah* (long braided hair)], Old Crow. After the chief stayed there for long time, they called it Crow River [after] this chief named Crow, Walk[ing] Crow. So they made [it] the name [for] this village in 1912.
>
> (JOE NETRO, August 10, 1977, VG2001-4-2:91–104, English)

The Three Brothers: *Shahnuuti'*, *Ch'eeghwalti'*, and *Shahvyah*

> I will talk about where we came from with you.

The one they call *Ch'eeghwalti'* was a man from long ago. His story is a long one. Lots of times my father talked about him in front of me but I don't remember all of it.

He was a man from long ago...along with *Shahnuuti'*, his brother. Their older brother was called *Shahvyah*. They were really depended on for getting food. In that way, their names were important.

Now, even today, people come from other countries. There were lots of people who descended from *Ch'eeghwalti'* from Fort Yukon. He came up this way and around Van Tat Gwich'in country. He slept [dreamt] to caribou.[20] In those days, they didn't know religion or God. They said the people really depended on him for caribou. Wherever he moved on the land, all the people moved along with him. He knew where the caribou were; in that way people harvested their food. He made it possible....

[Once] *Ch'eeghwalti'* was fighting with one of his wives and his wife died. Also, one of his brothers fought with one of their wives and she died. *Shahnuuti'* did the same thing; the same thing happened to him. But other than that, the people really depended on them for caribou.

They really helped their people. Today, us, we have friends and we do good to each other, that is good. The people were not like that long ago. People were poor and worked to eat and they had good luck in everything. There are lots of good about how they helped their people, together.

Really, on this earth today, there are a lot of descendants from *Ch'eeghwalti'*. *Chitzi*, his wife, is called *Ts'ihgwat'i'*....*Chitzi's* children, all of them are from *Ch'eeghwalti'*. Down around Fort Yukon there's lots of descendants from him. My auntie May, their father was called Roderick, he and *Ts'ihgwat'i'* were brothers. They were *Ch'eeghwalti's* sons. My auntie May, she has lots of descendants down Fort Yukon and *Ch'eeghwalti'* has many here in Old Crow. He's got lots of descendants in Van Tat Gwich'in country.

My grandfather *Chitzi*...my sister-in-law Mazun, Mary Kunnizzie they called her, she and her children and others who have married off [their line] are descendants. My brother-in-law Edward [Itsi] and all his children come from him [*Ch'eeghwalti'*]. John Itsi, all of them, they're *Ch'eeghwalti's* grandchildren. Really he has a lot of descendants on this earth. They probably don't know they are descendants of *Ch'eeghwalti'*. Down in Fort Yukon, my auntie May all her children and John Itsi's family, all of them [are descendants of *Ch'eeghwalti'*]. There's lots of them down it Fort Yukon....Really, now, my grandfather *Chitzi*, his children don't know they're direct descendants from *Ch'eeghwalti'*.

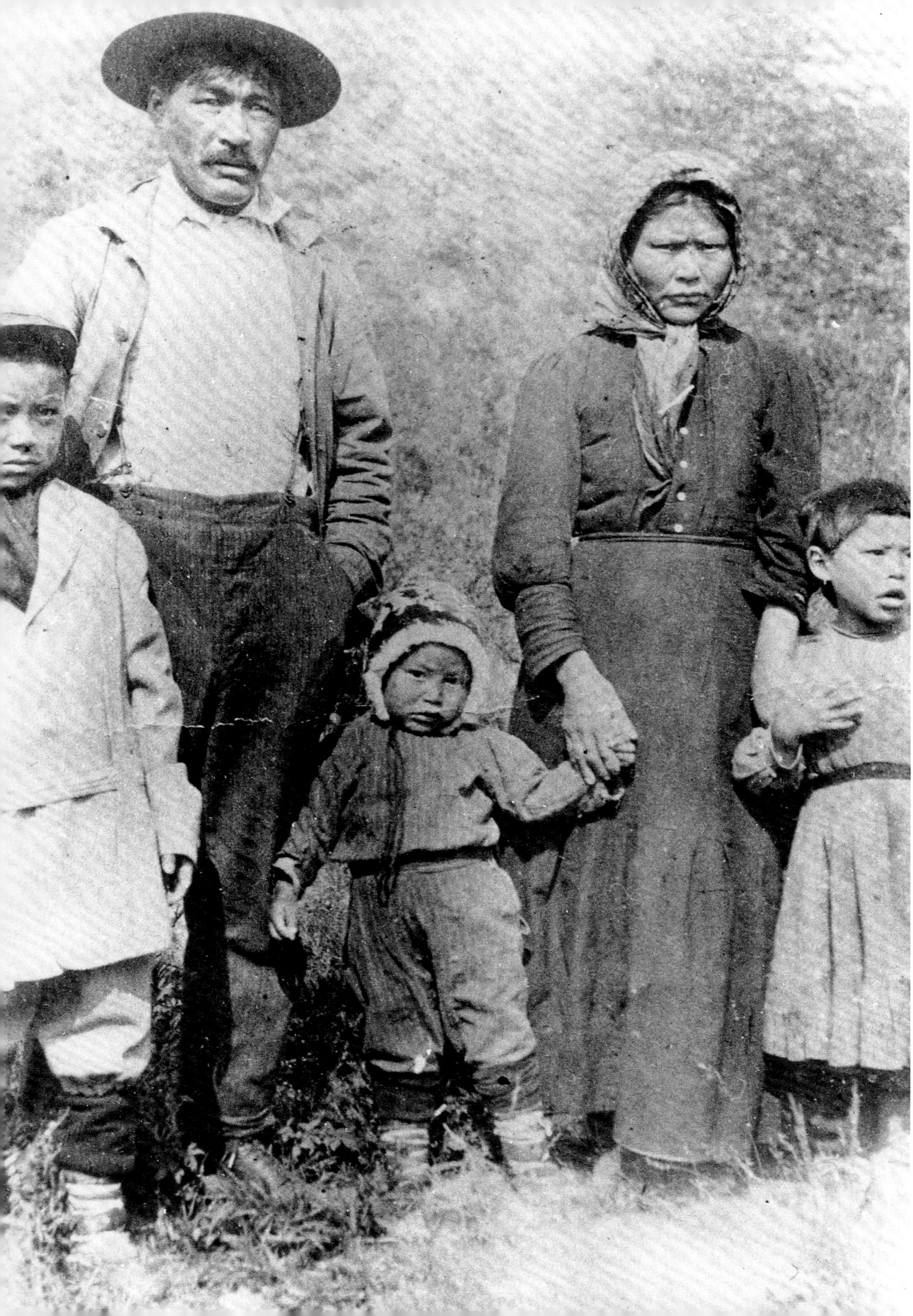

Ben and Eliza Kassi family in 1917. (L–R) Charlie Kassi, Ben Kassi, Paul Ben Kassi, Eliza Ben Kassi, Hannah Kassi.
[Yukon Archives, Bob Sharp fonds 82/326 #11]

Stephen Frost, his wife Ethel, she is a descendant of my auntie May. All her children are *Ch'eeghwalti's* descendants.

It was like this and long ago, from the beginning of time, of the earth. The elders tell stories of it and this is how they know each other good. Today it is not like that. When a child is raised up they don't know where they come from....In the future, after us, however the earth will be, we don't know that. Only He knows, from above. This is all about *Ch'eeghwalti's* descendants, so that they will know. That's why I give my grandchild a short story, what I remember....

Shahnuuti' really looked after the orphans, they said....My grandfather [*Chitzi*] said it seems that there are not too many descendants from him, but *Ch'eeghwalti'* had many descendants. But his brother *Shahnuuti'*, my grandfather said he did not treat his people well; his work was not good. He helped orphaned children giving them a little food to eat. "Lots of times I made mistakes, but doing this I made it good for myself," they said he said this when he was going to die. He died up there; by the rock cliffs by Eagle, around there somewhere is his burial site. When the steamboats came up the Yukon River the first time, they knew where his burial site was. When the boat went around the point by the site, they say the steamboat honked its horn in honour of him....

When he [*Shahnuuti'*] lived, he had many wives they say....By all that [he did], people will remember him. In those days they never [knew about God—before missionaries], but even so they [leaders] knew what was best and worked that way. The people depended upon them, they say. That's how *Shahnuuti's* story goes.

Ch'eeghwalti', he's from Fort Yukon. At that time Fort Yukon was really big; now all that land is gone. They said there were lots of people there. *Ch'eeghwalti'* became an elder, that's what my father talked about. *Ch'eeghwalti'* told them, "Take me back to Fort Yukon." That's what they did and he died there...in the fall time. The old man was going to die during the night. In the bushes behind Fort Yukon, the caribou came around, they said. They said it was just noisy during the night. They thought Fort Yukon was going to get trampled over. He died that night. Then the next day, all night the caribou made noises; they all heard it....In the morning the smart men, they looked to kill meat, but there was no tracks on the snow.

...Today it's not like that. Today they use God's word on earth; it looks like people live only on that. People long ago didn't know about heaven. Some of them were dreamers....

But after that, *Giikhii Danahch'i* [Old Man Minister, Archdeacon McDonald], was going to talk to him about it. *Giikhii Danahch'i* said,

"If you dream about heaven, tell me about it."...Long ago, before they found out about God, some of the people were dreamers. That was how they knew of things to come.

(SARAH ABEL, VG2003-3-1:005-173, Gwich'in)

Our great, great grandfathers, *Shahnuuti', Shahvyah*, we came from them. From there, my mother's grandmother Eliza Biederman...and my mother's mother [descended]. My mother is from *Ch'eeghwalti'*. I use to keep fire for some of the women. She died in 1943. She was an old lady. She was over 100 years old. Grandmother *Gwatl'ahvinh*, another where the Netros are from, and in Old Crow there are two generations from her. We are from two blood, two generations. I remember the old people used to sew clothes with beads. There are pictures of them with these clothes on, about thousands of years ago. These are the people I am from and also my children.

(Second-generation Elder MARY KASSI, VG1997-4-16B:112-125, Gwich'in)

Myra Moses on the Life of Her Husband, Chief Peter Moses

He was born in 1882, it said on his card...on the American side. They used to move around down that way all the time....He was an orphan from when he was small. When they had a hard time for meat, he killed meat for the people....Way down[river], around Fort Yukon, we were raised around there....

Around then they were going to war. At that time they only travelled by dog team. You would never see an airplane or an engine. An inspector and the police hired him to walk ahead of the dogs [break trail in the snow]. They really wanted him to go with them to the outside [to the south—the city]....

In those days he was a real Indian. Nobody knows it....Down the Yukon, [he broke trail] ahead of the dogs [with his father]. Then he came back up with the dog team. After that, the mailman hired him to walk ahead of the dog teams. Wherever there was an emergency they would take him. While doing all that, he would kill meat and trap. He lived a good life from the land.

When your grandfather was living, he used to go to Herschel Island all the time for supplies. He worked a long time at Herschel Island, many years. He made patrols with the police. He even went to Aklavik with dog teams and all the down to Fort Yukon, too, when he was making patrols with the police. Your grandfather did a lot of work in this country.

(MYRA MOSES, August 25, 1980, VG2000-8-34:113-118, Gwich'in)

Peter Moses, chief at Old Crow, stretching muskrat furs over wire frames, June 1946.

[Yukon Archives, Claude and Mary Tidd fonds #8242]

He grew up and...in 1901 we got married. We went back through Black River [Alaska]. Lots of people went with us. That winter he trapped around *Draanjik* [Black River]. I don't mean the time we carried around a tent and stove, Grandchild: we just carried our blankets. There were also no steel traps. We made deadfall traps. We got marten, mink, those kinds of animals. We stayed there three years. In 1904, we came back up the Porcupine [River].

Cadzow[21] was coming up this way, so we went to Rampart House and lived around there. There were lots of people there from this area and Fort Yukon because Cadzow had a store there. After that, we came up to Old Crow and stayed. We started raising a family, other people's children. We raised eight children; one was our child.

Then we went over [the mountains] to Fort McPherson with our family. We stayed for two years. We know the country all around there, too....The people were poor, poor elders. [Chief Moses] would kill meat and give it out, just give it freely to the people. Finally, we came back over this way and just lived right here in Old Crow. There and here, too, we stayed with our relatives a long time.

Meanwhile, they made him a chief. He was chief for 18 years. We trapped in Crow Flats and killed lots of mink around here. We saved our little money. When the war started your grandfather sent money out. That time he made his name big. All the people around here and us, too, we collected the money and sent it out...Then they sent him a medal....They came here to see him and put the medal on him.[22]

The First Generation   115

> He was chief for a long time. He was very old when he died...Lots of times he killed meat for poor people wherever we stayed. When we lived with our relatives at Fort McPherson there was lots of caribou. The old men and women stayed with us. He would kill caribou for them and they would dry it. Many times they went to Arctic Red River. At the end, he was never sick and he died. He said he was going to do that and it happened that way.
>
> (MYRA MOSES, July 17, 1980, VG2000-8-41:013-114, Gwich'in)

Celebration, Music

Elders often spoke of the difficulty—and rewards—of their lives on the land. They emphasized the satisfaction they experienced from working and playing with their families and friends. Certain celebrations became regular annual events: among these, the New Year's dance and feast at Rampart House is recalled fondly. A number of accounts suggest that Gwich'in did not use drums like the Inuit/Inuvialuit to the north and Dene on the Mackenzie River to the east, nor did they have their own distinctive body of music (songs). However, they enthusiastically adopted music and the fiddle (violin) brought by the early Scottish-heritage traders, as well as dances such as jigs and square dances, for which they are renowned to this day (see Mishler 1993). Myra Moses reviewed which neighbouring groups had various musical instruments and described a New Year's celebration in the 1800s. Neil McDonald spoke of the years 1905-30 and the more routine practice of organizing feasts when a moose was shot, as well as the special skill of dreaming described earlier.

Celebration in the late 1800s

> The Hän Gwich'in, only they have lots of songs. Way downriver the ones they call *Òeechii* Gwich'in [an Alaskan village], they have lots of songs, too. The up-the-river-people and the *Ch'ineekaii*, [Inuit or Inuvialuit] too. We didn't have [skin drums], only the *Ch'ineekaii* had them. The Native people around here just played fiddle at all the dances. When there were lots of skin tents, they paid one man who played the fiddle with his mouth. He played fiddle music with his mouth. They brought a toboggan into that caribou-skin tent and on that they danced.
>
> The old man made New Year's [feast], too. He made New Year's and they ate. That, too, was in a skin house. At that time, in the Hudson's Bay that kind of small [bowl or dishes]. Only some of the people had

them. So he made New Year's, but really it was good. The dish, he would hit it while they danced to him, I heard. [Laughter] He hit that dish for a long time and banged it all up. [Laughter] He only had that dish, just one. The old man, he just had one dish and he lost it but it was nothing to him.

(MYRA MOSES, August 10, 1977, VG2001-4-4B:022-068, Gwich'in)

Dancing at Rampart House and Moose Feasts

[At Rampart House, they danced in] the old church...same kind of dances as they dance here: jig, rabbit dance, brandy, [the Crow Dance that Old Chief used to do]. Oh, that Old Peter [Moses], I don't know where he got that from. [Laughter]...

If somebody killed a moose, he gave it to one person and that person cooked the moose and put up a dance....Well, [they gave it to] whoever they think will make a good feast. Peter Charlie, Joe Kaye made quite a few feasts. Peter Moses made quite a few feasts.

We went down to Goose Camp: me, Peter Tizya, Moses Tizya, John Kendi, David Njootli, and Peter Charlie. We took Peter Charlie's launch and put long poles on each side—that's where we put our canoes— and I shot the moose. Peter Charlie told me, you should give it to John Charlie. He never made a feast so we brought the moose up for him.

So here's what I'm going to tell you: you have to believe it. I used to dream about moose, [but it was] no dream I had. If I dreamed about that, I [would] kill moose. Once up at David Lord Creek where we were staying, a cold day, and I dreamt. So I went up the mountain back of David Lord Creek, the little mountain. I saw moose a long way off. So I went a little way, I took my snowshoes off and God, it was a cold day! I managed to walk up to the moose and kill it. I had to make fire while I was skinning it to keep warm.

That morning, I dreamt that if I was to hunt, I was going to kill something, I knew. I didn't know which way to go, downriver or upriver. While I was thinking of that, Peter Tizya—the old Peter Tizya—came in. I said, "You and I and Moses [should] buy gas, go down to the Goose Camp." Even if I was amongst a hundred people, I'd be the one to kill that moose.

We landed this side of the Goose Camp. None of them said anything. They were still shaking dice for shells. So I put my canoe behind the willow and then I built a little smudge, [there were] lots of mosquitoes. After awhile, Moses and Peter came up....There's a lake back here; I walked halfway around it. There were lots of moose track. I came back and Moses was sleeping. I went down to the bank and there was nothing.

So later on Peter Tizya and Peter Charlie went down, "Moose down here," he [Peter Charlie] said. So, he grabbed the gun, and he shot first. [He indicated I should shoot] but I told him go ahead. And that man is a good shot. The moose had its head in the water, feeding. When [the moose] lifted his head up, he shot at it. It hit the water, about this much from the moose. And I shot the moose. [Surprised expression] I dreamt I was going to shoot that moose. And he [usually] never missed. He was just across the slough. I shot the moose, and gave it to John Charlie. [Laughter] [Did he make a feast?] Oh yes, why certainly. [Laughter]...

(NEIL MCDONALD, VG2000-8-40:295-020, English)

NEWCOMERS AND NEW THINGS

For the fur trade, Van Tat Gwich'in territory was arguably one of the most remote destinations in North America. Although fur traders with an eye on the riches of the North had an established trading presence for many decades, Gwich'in travelled great distances and traded through intermediaries until about 1840. There were three possible avenues for commerce to the Porcupine: up the Yukon River system through present day Alaska, down the Mackenzie River system from eastern Canada, or by ship to the Arctic Ocean coast. At various times each route was used by traders seeking to purchase furs or meat from the Gwich'in in exchange for basic tools and, later, foodstuffs. The first traders in Van Tat Gwich'in country were from the Hudson's Bay Company, which had a post at Peel's River (Fort McPherson) from 1840 and moved west across the mountains to establish an outpost primarily for provisioning at LaPierre House in 1846 and Fort Yukon (in Russian territory) in 1847. Both posts were later moved, the latter a number of times (to Howling Dog and the two locations of Rampart House) after Russia sold Alaska to the United States in 1867.

The logistics of travel to Van Tat Gwich'in territory, as well as competition from whaling ships at Herschel Island, convinced the Hudson's Bay Company to withdraw to Fort McPherson on the east side of the Richardson Mountains in 1893. There followed a series of private traders, some originally coming with the Klondike Gold Rush or with the whaling ships. They established stores at Rampart House, LaPierre House, Whitestone Village, Johnson Creek Village, and later at Old Crow. Van Tat Gwich'in elders from the generations born in the late 1800s to early 1900s remember these individuals and the time when groups of Gwich'in and traders were established at various places throughout the territory, and hunting and trapping were the universal pursuits.

As well, the coming of the Anglican missionary Robert McDonald is well-remembered, along with the lasting influence of the ministers and lay readers he ordained. Other newcomers brought a variety of changes, from medical supplies, a different education system, new boundaries and legal obstacles to travel throughout their territory, the decimation of fur-bearing and food animals from certain areas due to outside competition and trapping practices, and changes in the locations of settlements.

Gwich'in Long-distance Traders
Before the Arrival of the Hudson's Bay Company

Prior to the coming of foreign traders to Gwich'in country, Gwich'in traders travelled to distant places to trade. Moses Tizya told of two such traders: *Olti'* and *Khach'oodaayu'*. *Olti'* went to Herschel Island to trade caribou skins for spear heads with the *Ch'ineekaii*, who in turn were trading with the Russians.[23] He suggested that *Olti's* activities (trading for spears), and possibly his attitude toward status (the "big shot"), caused discord with the Tanana. In any event, Moses Tizya offered his own opinion of such values. The second Gwich'in trader, *Khach'oodaayu',* crossed the mountains to the east to travel up the Mackenzie River to Fort Simpson (a Hudson's Bay Company post) to exchange furs for a variety of useful trade goods, to the approval and benefit of the people. Joe Netro spoke of travel from Crow Flats to distant Point Barrow to trade for Russian goods with middlemen *Ch'ineekaii* [Inuit or Inuvialuit].

Olti' and *Khach'oodaayu'*

> I will tell you about *Olti'*....He brought spears [to the] country. That's the first time spears came to this country. He [was] called *Olti'*, Big Shot.
>
> With lots of people, he went down [the Porcupine River] with a raft. They didn't even reach Fort Yukon. They met people in canoes coming up. There was another chief who brought all those spears. You know what spears are?...*Olti'* bought all the spears from that chief....They sold mostly caribou skins for all those spears.
>
> That chief, he took all the caribou skins, maybe a thousand skins. He took them down to the coast to sell to the *Ch'ineekaii*. That's where they got their fur, see. They were trading with Russians in those days. Only spears, that's all, nothing else: no pots, no axes, no nothing....

Olti' had a war, down below Tanana somewhere. He went down with an army and killed all the people for nothing. He had no business [there]. After that he came here. They fought amongst themselves. The spears didn't mean nothing. And somebody killed him.

...After they killed *Olti'*, [there was a] big war over it. All *Olti's* [people] fought. They just went around with spears and started to kill people. Pretty soon people got together and some from Fort McPherson, another bunch from Whitefish Lake, they killed them. They killed them all. McPherson, they done something. There was a law for killing people, just [because of] *Olti'*....They used spears—no gun, no nothing—just spears. That's what *Olti'* produced. When Big Shot *Olti'* went someplace, he took married women or married men, or not [married], he just took them. Took them by force, a big bunch of them....

After that was *Khach'oodaayu'*. He is the guy that used to go up the Mackenzie River, way up to Fort Simpson or whatever you call it. He brought stuff: axes, files, chisels, pots, tobacco. All that stuff he brought here. He traded for it with furs. He had a real great name because he brought all that stuff into this country [for the first time]. He was the one that got that name; they called him *Khach'oodaayu'*.... It means look out....He was a big shot. He used to bring all that stuff from the Northwest Territories, up the Mackenzie River....He brought axes, files, chisels, guns, ammunition, tobacco, but he never sold tobacco. He kept all that for himself.

Once *Khach'oodaayu'* made a feast. He gave everybody smoke [tobacco]. It was hard times in those days. [There was] no Hudson's Bay [store], not any kind of trading in the country. He was the only one.

(MOSES TIZYA, January 1980, VG2000-8-19B, English and Gwich'in)

Trading with *Ch'ineekaii* at Point Barrow for Russian Goods

Before the Hudson Bay, my father and all the old people in Crow Flats, they got muskrats in the spring, before the lakes opened up [ice melted] and they [muskrats] had no place to go. They had to go way down to Point Barrow [Alaska]; that's a long way, maybe three or four hundred miles. They took the rat skins down there. They say there were lots of Eskimos down there. From Crow Flats, they killed some [mountain] sheep before they got to Point Barrow. They sold all that to the Eskimos and the Eskimos gave them tents from around Russian country, I think, and gun, ammunition. [It took] all summer to go down and come back, walking with packsacks....[They didn't stay in Point

Barrow] very long: went down, got their supplies and stayed down a little while, [got] what they wanted and came right back.

Well, I don't know, [how long the trip took], not a very long time. They never told me how long. Anyway, they said [it was a] hard trip. The women stayed behind. [While the] men made the trip down there, the women lived off fish in Crow Flats. They made fish traps in Crow Flats. [There's] lots of little creeks all full of fish, that's where we fished. Lots of ducks, too. They killed these ducks in summertime. You see, ducks can't fly [when they're] getting new wings and feathers. At that time we used arrows to kill those ducks.

About the time of year [the ducks] flew from Crow Flats, the people went up in the mountains. They had a fence there, a caribou fence, and they waited for caribou. Before the caribou came they lived on whatever they could get. When the caribou came to the caribou fence, they set lots of snares in it, caribou snares. When a bunch of caribou went in, they caught them all [and dried the meat there]. The skin, hides, they used for tents. Women tanned the skins with the hair on and sewed them together. Maybe ten caribou skins were sewed together for a winter tent.

(JOE NETRO, August 10, 1977, VG2001-4-2:118-175, English)

The Hudson's Bay Company

The Van Tat Gwich'in were active in the fur trade for a considerable length of time before any traders came to their territory. The Hudson's Bay Company was the first formal trading company to reach the area, although Russian traders had penetrated much of Alaska previously. In 1839, the Hudson's Bay Company extended its network to Peel River (later Fort McPherson) and expanded to Fort Yukon in 1847. Subsequently, Fort Yukon was moved a number of times (Howling Dog Village, Old and New Rampart House) before the company pulled out of the area altogether in 1893. Joe Netro showed his keen understanding of the fur trade (he was a trader at Whitestone Village for a time) in his telling of early travel on the extensive Hudson's Bay Company trade route along the Mackenzie-Athabasca river system. Myra Kaye remembered early Hudson's Bay factor John Firth. John Joe Kyikavichik (Kaye), son of first-generation Elder Joe Kaye, recalled a story of when the Dagoo supplied meat to the outpost at LaPierre House. Myra Moses described the time of Howling Dog Village and what people did when there was famine. Moses Tizya told of how Hudson's Bay Company employees lived much the same as Gwich'in at LaPierre House in the late 1800s.

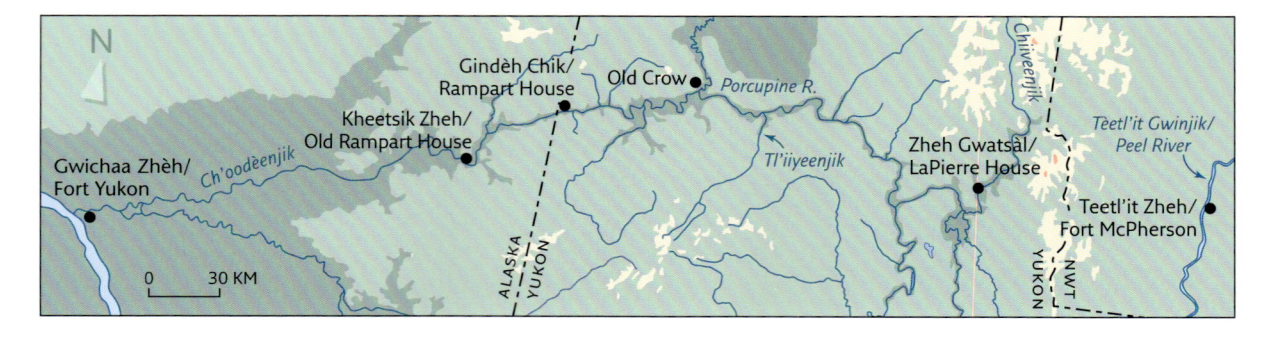

MAP 5
Inland Fur Trade Routes

Moving Trade Goods to Van Tat Gwich'in Country

When the Hudson's Bay first came to the country, we'll say that 1840, these people right here went over to [Fort] McPherson to trap and [hunt] up about a thousand miles [on the] Mackenzie. Sometimes they hauled boats over portages, sometimes paddled up, down. They brought supply in for McPherson and up here, too. Even the Hudson's Bay boat went down to Fort Yukon. There was medicine, tobacco, and tea; that's all they had.

My father told me one time they went up the Athabasca. I don't know. How far is that?...Every spring they went up the Mackenzie [River]. All the boats went over the portage; there's some bad water up there somewhere.[24] You had to do portaging. [Those who] worked for Hudson's Bay, all they ate was drymeat. That's all they [ate]; they had tea, I guess.

All winter, all summer the deck hands made one kettle [in payment]. They had to work all summer for that. If somebody wanted a gun, they got one gun for an [entire] summer's work. If...one person wanted a gun, he got a double-barrelled muzzle-loader. The Hudson's Bay [stood the gun] up and whoever wanted it, piled beaver [pelts] flat like this [until] the beaver reached even with the gun....The Hudson's Bay, they say they got about a pound of flour a year, [each] winter. I don't know how much sugar, but people just had tea and tobacco.

The Hudson's Bay, I don't know where they shipped their furs to. They sent it out. They had to wait three years before they got their return. People sold meat to the Hudson's Bay, one half they dried it. They oven-dried it, one ham, one shoulder measure, they paid 25 cents....And the fur price...I think marten was 50 cents in them years.... Oh yeah [bad price]....I don't know what the price was outside, maybe low out there, too.

(JOE NETRO, August 10, 1977, VG2001-4-2:052-115, English)

Early Hudson's Bay Company Trader John Firth

The people from Arctic Village didn't get Western food right away. The McPherson people called Canadians "English." English people were travelling down by boat with trade goods. They helped all the people along the Porcupine River....

Then Mr. Firth came by here with supplies. He landed in Fort Yukon with guns, fishnet. The fishnet was not knitted. He gave it out and taught the people how to knit fishnets. This is what they did.

(MYRA KAYE, February 2, 1980, VG2000-8-19C)

At that time there was a fur trader named *Kheh Kai' Zhoo* ["Bearded Chief" John Firth] who bought food. He said, "You guys killed all the caribou before me," and he cried. "We killed a lot of caribou. Skin as much as you want. It's no use for you to cry. It is your fault that your work is poor. Why do you cry?" That's what was said about him. They didn't know how many caribou he skinned. While we were returning home, he didn't load his sleigh right. His wife had made drymeat and he was bringing it home. At that time, we had no sacks. We made meat sacks from babiche. On his way down he lost one meat sack. The person behind him found it. While he was unloading the meat from his sleigh into the house, *Kheh Kai' Zhoo* noticed one meat sack was missing. The person behind him threw it to him in the house.

We sold meat at that time for gun shells. We never had white man's food. Even the fur trader *Kheh Kai' Zhoo* had little white man's food. It was like that long ago.

When they built *Kheh Kai' Zhoo's* house, they used dry white caribou skin on his window. That's what they used for curtains. At that time it was hard, we only bought what we needed. They built him another house called *nishuunii*.[25] He had fire in there. They brought him food. In the house they called *nishuunii*, there were a lot of caribou heads hanging. He was married to a Native woman. He did all that and eventually he became chief. He was a fur trader for people from Fort Yukon and up this way.

He travelled back and forth and his last trip was to New Rampart House. From there he went to LaPierre House at the head of Bell River. By then he had lots of kids. We made a raft and that is how we got his supplies across the Bell River. *Nagwachoonjik* [Mackenzie River] was where they brought his stuff with a canoe, and over the mountains. We carried his stuff with packsacks, people from Fort McPherson and Old Crow. And that's what he traded in the winter. By spring, he ran out of supplies, and he would go back over the mountains to get some more. And again, we brought his supplies over. That's what he did and that's why he was the chief. After he crossed over the mountains from LaPierre House to *Chii Tsal Dik* [Fort McPherson, Northwest Territories] they built him a house there and that's where he settled. That is where he died, the fur trader named *Kheh Kai' Zhoo*.

Now we have a lot of things. At that time we didn't think about what little we had and we still had a good life.

(MYRA KAYE, February 20, 1980, VG2000-8-20:025-078, Gwich'in)

Hudson's Bay Company Times at Howling Dog, Rampart House, and LaPierre House

My dad [Joe Kyikavichik] told me that at the time when Gwich'in people were having a hard time living off the land, the Hudson's Bay Company had a store at LaPierre House, and people used to dry meat for sale. My dad told me, at that time, when somebody killed caribou and gave it away, they wouldn't give the head away. They took the tongue because it was good money. People used to dry meat and sell it for good money....

(JOHN JOE KYIKAVICHIK, *LaPierre House Oral History*, 1995:131)

Way down the river there was a village at Howling Dog, below Old Rampart House. They called it Howling Dog Village. The Hudson's Bay had houses there. I never saw the place; that was before my time. After that, they made a village at Old Rampart House. When I was a child, there was the Hudson's Bay store and church there. It was really nice then.

There was lots of fish here; it was good for the people. My mother and father always stayed around there. My father always fished and he caught lots of fish. He also provided fish to the Hudson's Bay. My mother dried the fish. Sometimes he would shoot moose and they would dry the meat and give it to the Hudson's Bay. Not only they did that: lots of people lived with them and would give some to the [Hudson's Bay].

There was a village there for a long time. After that, when I was bigger, I remember it all. Those ministers had big boats, and the Hudson's Bay also. We would never see an engine in those days. They would only track and walk [along the shore] with the boats. Big boats with ropes, lots of people walked and pulled the ropes. Fort Yukon is where they would bring the minister's freight. Lots of boys and men would bring it for the minister. But the Hudson's Bay man would go to the Mackenzie [River] for supplies. From there, the big boats would bring in supplies. There were lots of people there.

At a dance when I was a child, I saw them dancing, I remember. There was a church there, [Old Rampart House] too. I went to the church often. I went to the church service with my mother. Gee, the church was really nice. The window in the church, some of it was red, some of it coloured, the window there was in the church. That was really nice. When my mother got ready for church, I would go with her, right now! That window was really nice and I always looked at it. I never listened to the minister. [Laughter]...

The Hudson's Bay lived there [Old Rampart House] a long time, [and] the ministers, too. Bishop Bompas was there, too [with Archdeacon McDonald], I remember. The men chopped and hauled wood for him. At that time, the ministers had lots of things. The people really liked the tea and tobacco. The minister gave them tea and tobacco, sometimes a bit of sugar and flour, too. They looked after the ministers very well. When there was meat, they give them meat, too.

The Hudson's Bay man didn't have many supplies. A hundred pounds of flour lasted one year, they said, and sugar, too. Even so, they give a little to their relatives. At New Year's they made bannock and fed people from their hundred pounds [of flour]. They, too, never ate it: just a little sometimes. This is what they did. I remember them.

Then, there was lots of meat [and] fish, too. In the store warehouse was frozen fish, dried fish, dried meat, and [frozen] meat. The Hudson's Bay bought all that....They, in turn, gave it out to the people. How many times, whoever was staying there, they would give them again. They did that because they had no meat. Those poor old women, all of them, too. It's not far to the mountains and there were lots of caribou at Rampart House and lots of fish. It was good, but one winter, there was no meat, no caribou. So, they set rabbit snares, men and women, all set rabbit snares, so it was good.

At that time, my mother had a big pot with handles. In the evening, my mother boiled rabbits because my father killed lots of rabbits. After that, she would take [the meat] out of the pot, sometimes if she had some flour, she would make gravy. After that, whoever was staying around there, she would give each of them a small piece. We walked around with [the pot], even to the Hudson's Bay man. Even he was given rabbit.

(MYRA MOSES, 1980s, VG2000-8-31:008-050;95-130, Gwich'in)

LaPierre House as it was in the 1800s

LaPierre House is from the 1800s. The Hudson's Bay had a store there at that time and Gwich'in people used to have a big village at LaPierre House. People from Arctic Village even used to come and trade. There was a mission house and Bishop Bompas used to stay for awhile....

At that time, the Hudson's Bay had a store down the Porcupine River in Alaska [at a place called] Howling Dog. The Hudson's Bay had store there but the Americans chased them away. Then they brought that store up to Old Rampart...for a while. That's where Bishop Bompas and other ministers used to stop because...where they had store, that's where people used to stay and the minister used to follow and have services for people in those villages.

At that time it was hard to get boats. The only people who had boats was the Hudson's Bay Company. At that time...they had stores here and there along the Porcupine River. The Hudson's Bay had a store in Fort McPherson. There they got their groceries and outfit from Fort Smith with boats because they're the only ones had boat. They brought their groceries and outfit from Fort Smith, along the Mackenzie to Fort McPherson, in the summer. That was [the wintertime supplies] for all the Hudson's Bay stores, wherever they had stores [along] the Porcupine, LaPierre House, and down the Porcupine, Rampart....Then when wintertime came, after freeze-up, they hauled it over the mountains with dog teams.

All the stores they had along the Porcupine River down to Alaska—they closed all their stores. The only place they had a store after that was LaPierre House, for quite a while. The Gwich'in people really depended on them....

At that time, Bishop Bompas used to travel back and forth to every Hudson's Bay store and he said even in Fort Yukon there was no one there. There was no Fort Yukon—there was no village there and all the way up to Whitehorse, there was no town or village. People stayed here and there....

When the Hudson's Bay had a store at LaPierre House, people used to dry meat and sell it to the employees. The employees used to live like the Gwich'in people; they used to live off the land. Gwich'in people used to sell them meat and that's how they lived. At that time Hudson's Bay didn't have too much—the main stuff was flour, tea and stuff like that, guns and some clothing, that's about it. They didn't have too many groceries themselves. If they had 100 pounds of flour, that would last them for one year. But they had fried bannock and stuff like that on Sundays, and the rest of the time they lived off meat the Gwich'in people sold them—drymeat and the good parts of the caribou. At the time the Hudson's Bay had the store at LaPierre House, they didn't even have stoves. They made fireplaces in the house with rocks and clay and built it up, that's how they used to keep fire. There were no stoves at that time. There were not even tents then and when Hudson's Bay employees travelled, they used to have open camps.

(MOSES TIZYA, *LaPierre House Oral History*, 1995:136-138,139)

New Tools

Gwich'in considered many of the new tools as great advantages, yet not all worked out quite as promised. Myra Kaye illustrated how the trade goods were integrated into the peoples' lives at the time of the well-known ancestor of many present Gwich'in: Elias *Gwahtl'ahti'*. Her story of *Gwahtl'ahti'* is an amusing incident that occurred in her youth that illustrates how the promise of new technology sometimes failed to live up to expectations. Balaam Jhudi's experience with innovation was more successful, according to Alfred Charlie. Sarah Abel recalled the first tents from the Arctic coast.

Gwahtl'ahti' and a New Gun

> *Gwahtl'ahti', Gwahtl'ahti'.* They got married when not many people were around. They used to move around all the time....
>
> We stayed at *Tl'oo K'at* and they moved there with us. We were chasing caribou and moose by one mountain. He was with us; he was running with the caribou and the stock of his gun fell off. [Laughs] The stock of his gun fell off and he was just running with the barrel. When we were close to the caribou, everybody started shooting. He aimed his gun and realized that the stock was gone. He grabbed it and hollered, "The stock on my gun is gone." He stood up while we were shooting caribou and went back to look for the stock of his gun. It was not far from where he lost it. Meanwhile we killed all the caribou.
>
> (MYRA KAYE, February 20, 1980, VG2000-8-20:011-022, Gwich'in)

The First Canvas Tents

> The first tent that came to [the people of the upper Porcupine]: there was one guy named Balaam, everybody knew him. He had been down to Eagle [Alaska]. He bought a tent and stove. When he came to where

Elias and Annie Kwatlatyi departing from Old Crow to Crow Flats, 1946.

[Yukon Archives, Claude and Mary Tidd fonds #8263]

those people stayed, he set the tent. Everybody thought he was going to freeze. Well, they'd never seen a tent before, eh? A skin tent is warm, with fire right there, good heat, they figured. They don't know the stove heat, too, eh? That's what I heard. But the young people, they always sat with him. His house was full all the time because there was no smoke. [The fire in the] skin house, you know [it was] sometimes smoky. The tent and stove, [there was] no smoke there so they say he had a full house all time.

(ALFRED CHARLIE, August 11, 1994, VG1997-7-06, English)

Grandchild, in those days we would never see a tent. Only Father, my oldest brother [were] in a tent, in a round tent, they said. But we [younger children] never saw round tents. Father [travelled to what] they called *Chuu Vee* [coast] at that time. They never called it anything else. From that time tents [became available]. They weren't ready-

> made, that's what they mean, Grandchild. They would bring back heavy tents [canvas]. All the woman would sew it. My father had a big tent set, I remember. I wasn't too big [but even so], I remember.
>
> (SARAH ABEL, VG1997-2-2A:166-173, Gwich'in)

When the Hudson's Bay Company Pulled Out

When the Hudson's Bay Company withdrew to Fort McPherson in 1893, Gwich'in had to travel much farther to trade. They travelled to American posts on the Yukon River, Fort McPherson, and Herschel Island on the Arctic coast. American whaling ships had overwintered there since 1890 and were able to compete successfully in the fur trade due to their cheaper transportation costs and wider variety of goods. The whalebone industry crashed in 1907, but some former whalers and whaling captains continued to return to trade at locations on the Mackenzie Delta until 1928.

Myra Moses sketched the distribution of Gwich'in on the land and how they responded to the sudden absence of traders in their territory. Joe Netro described trade and travel to some of these alternate locations, such as the whaling ships at Herschel Island. He also spoke of near famine conditions in 1903. Moses Tizya talked of the general opening up of the fur trade following the Klondike Gold Rush (1898) and the options that faced Van Tat Gwich'in seeking to trade. Myra Moses pointed out that the Herschel Island whalers brought goods that were formerly scarce, such as ammunition, and noted the amicable relations with Inuit and Inuvialuit traders.

A Time without Local Traders

> Finally, the Hudson's Bay left for [Fort] McPherson. [At that time], up there at LaPierre House there was a Hudson's Bay store and also a church. At that time, there were lots of people around there: all the way down this river there were lots of people. There were also lots of people in Crow Flats, at Johnson Creek [Village] and Whitestone [Village]. All around there were lots of people. There was no stores: where were they to buy supplies? Over at Dawson and Eagle [Alaska], lots of people went there. Some people from here went to [Fort] McPherson. Then down to Fort Yukon, lots of people went there.
>
> Meanwhile in Crow Flats, the Van Tat Gwich'in they're called, they stayed there. Below there, at Herschel Island, American ships landed all the time. [Van Tat Gwich'in] got supplies from there. They never went any [other] place, those Gwich'in people.
>
> Moses Tizya, his father and mother, all of them, their grandparents, too, Netro, *Gwahtl'ahti'*, they made caribou fences and killed lots of

caribou in them. In Crow Flats there were lots of fish in the summertime. So they always stayed up there. It was not far to Herschel Island, too. They would go down and get supplies from there. So, they never went anywhere [else], you know.

(MYRA MOSES, 1980s, VG2000-8-31:138-160, Gwich'in)

Trading at Herschel Island, Point Barrow, and the Mackenzie River

I remember a few stories from 1903. At Herschel Island there were seventeen whalers there from outside. That's where our father went to get the supplies we lived on: tea, tobacco, ammunition, guns, tents. That winter, people had tough luck, no caribou, so they pretty near lost their lives. But they never gave up, kept on going, even though they had nothing to eat. They went down to Alaska and ran into bunch of people [who] saved their lives. Once in awhile they killed one moose. They say a big bunch of people together, one moose, they had just one meal out of it, skin and all. And no dogs left: all the dogs froze to death. The women hauled the toboggans and their camp supplies and the men went out hunting all the time.

Later on, around March I guess, they moved back to Crow Flats. In summertime they lived on fish, lived on ducks, and of course caribou and sometimes moose.

That summer, 1904, Dan Cadzow came up to New Rampart [House] down there at the border, with trading supplies. He tracked up from Fort Yukon. [He had an] eight- or ten-mile tracking line.[26] He hauled about five loads with that scow and that's where the people got their supplies from then on, right up to today. People just trapped in this country. You can't even grow potatoes here, nothing. If somebody tried it, they couldn't make it. So we just lived off the country: fur, fish, birds.

(JOE NETRO, August 10, 1977, VG2001-4-2:013-050, English)

Opportunities for Trade after the Hudson's Bay Company

Once they found gold in Dawson [1898], that's when a lot of people came and started [a lot of] stores. After that they started developing villages here and there. They started building where Fort Yukon is located now. The Hudson's Bay left. There was a store in Fort Yukon, Alaska, and in Fort McPherson, they had a store. The Hudson's Bay moved away from LaPierre House. After that, the Gwich'in people in the Old Crow area had a hard time and they started going to Herschel Island and getting groceries from there. The main basic stuff, tobacco, tea, flour, and stuff like that—they used to go to Herschel Island to get that. One year they say there were seventeen ships there.

The Van Tat Gwich'in people at that time used to live around Crow Flats and go to Herschel Island from there. Not only Van Tat Gwich'in; people from different villages like Arctic Village [Alaska] and those areas used to go to Herschel Island.

After [that time], Dan Cadzow brought a store up to Rampart House. There was a village there at that time. Dan Cadzow's [store] made it easier for the Van Tat Gwich'in and they started buying from Dan Cadzow. He owned a boat and he used to bring his groceries up in the summer to Rampart House. He brought enough groceries and things people needed to last until springtime....He used to bring things like for Christmas, what he thought people needed—what they could use for Christmas....

Fort McPherson people used to come around LaPierre House area and trap. There used to be hundreds of families moving around to dry meat and trap around there and Jim Jackson [private trader] made a little bit of money around there, but not too much....

(MOSES TIZYA, *LaPierre House Oral History*, 1995:138-140)

Travel and Trade at Herschel Island

They [whaling ships] brought lots of shells [for guns]. They made the shells, too. They brought [goods] from Herschel Island. That's how it became good for the people, you know, [because of] the American people. In the summer, they went down with dog packs to Herschel Island. But in the winter, they went by dog team. [Did you like the *Ch'ineekaii* at that time?] Yeah, really!

(MYRA MOSES, August 10, 1977, VG2001-4-4:243-255, Gwich'in)

The Succession of Private Traders

After the Hudson's Bay Company withdrew and whaling ships left after depleting the supply of bowhead whales in Arctic waters (and replacements for whale oil and baleen were developed), a variety of private traders served Van Tat Gwich'in for the remainder of the duration of the fur trade. Sarah Abel spoke of the time of the private traders: when people had to accumulate surplus food in order to go to trade. Neil McDonald gave a richly detailed inventory of the private traders in the area. Moses Tizya and Joe Netro spoke of the later era of the private traders. The names of these traders and white trappers are familiar to this day because they became the official names for many places dotted about the land.

How People Lived at the Time of Private Traders

At the time Amos Njootli[27] was the minister, we had really hard times. There was lots of trade goods, but when they didn't kill animals it was really hard.

When they killed two animals they would go to town. The man who killed the animals would go right away. It was difficult to get supplies: flour, sugar, rice, raisins, butter, even that was really lots of food. While [the men went to trade] the women set rabbit snares. They hunted and trapped for animals, too. They set snares for lynx and traps. They tried to help their husbands as much as they could....

About the hard times in those days, wherever there was meat, they would move with their families. They would camp and then the next day, they would move again. Those who carried lots of children, they did a lot of work. The smart women, it was nothing for them. They were used to it. But those who weren't like that, it was really hard for them. I remember some of it was hard.

[Around Old Crow] at that time there weren't many houses, only about three houses. We moved here around that time. There were two stores here, too....We really snared lots of rabbits and ptarmigan. That way, our children never went hungry in those days....

The people who had good strong dogs, their dogs really helped them out. Even when they went long distances with their dogs, it was nothing for the dogs from Rampart House.

(SARAH ABEL, April 22, 1980, VG2000-8-33:001-047, Gwich'in)

Experiences with Early Free Traders

[Dan Cadzow's store was built] must be around 1909 or '11, July....He had a store before. It's on this side....It's a long building, so Cadzow built a new church, across [the] creek, on this side, and there was a village. He got a new church built, around 1909 or '10, he had this one built by Bill Mason and a fellow named Bill Cody. Cody was the captain, and Archie Linklater and Old Bruce built it.

[Ab Schaeffer and Bill Mason] He didn't come, up he...escaped from Herschel Island, from the ships. No, he came up from Dawson to Rampart House....They came to trade and trap....Well, there's no other place for them to go to. [Laughter]

They used poison, the white people, the white trappers. One time, one [party] of them, name of Martin and Schaeffer, were on Schaeffer

Creek. [There were] lots of traps out there and Elias and his old father,[28] were trapping close to there. Old Elias father [found] a dead silver fox. Schaeffer or Dick Martin caused [its death] because it fell down, you see. The law...took it away [from the] old man, so the old man got the blame for it, for the silver fox. He found it so it's his. The other two fellows, they can't very well claim it....Well the poison, they can't say, when it comes to the law [illegal]...

Well, they [Gwich'in] didn't like it [white trappers using poison] but they never said nothing. There was no police around at that time. The first police were at Rampart House during the smallpox [epidemic, 1911]. It was chickenpox not smallpox. They thought it was smallpox so they built a hospital at Rampart House. There was a nurse and the first policeman, Jimmy Five. He came from Dawson. He was a Mountie, and in the First World War; where the Germans had a [prison camp], he was killed there; well...they just [starve] them all to death.

[Dan Cadzow moved to Rampart House] from Black River. Before he came to Rampart House, he was on Black River, on the American side, in Alaska, but he used to get the Canadian goods. Of course, at that time, lots of Fort Yukon people still wanted Hudson's Bay goods, blankets....Yeah, Rampart House was a gathering place. Until '19, around '20, they all moved to Rampart House. Just few of them stayed down there. They all moved up.

[I worked for Cadzow] for two years....His nephew and I looked after his store in Old Crow for one year and then his nephew left. The next year I looked after the place. Some of them moved down to Rampart House; there wasn't much going on in Old Crow at that time. So he had that place [Old Crow] closed [and just traded in Rampart House]

Cadzow's nephew looked after store while I went out to [go to] all the traders with mostly dry goods. [I just went] out to Crow Flats; most of the people lived around Crow Flats....

Well, it all depended on the price of the fur. At that time five pounds of tea was four dollars; five pounds of sugar, one dollar; flour, $15.00 [100 pounds]. So even if your fur was low, you still got that much: cheap. Now, how much are you going to pay for a hundred pounds of flour in the store? Well, 10 pounds of flour is over $10.00 [price ca. 1980].[29]

The fur trader [only traded for furs], that's all....He went up to Dawson and brought a scow load down to Fort Yukon. He had two or three men with him. Floating down from Fort Yukon, he had to hire eight to ten men to track that big scow up to Rampart House. [He brought] dry goods, mostly: men's suits, underwear; women's and men's underwear and scotch pants, shawls, handkerchiefs. He was the only trader there until 1912, and then [from the] trading post in Fort Yukon, they sent two men up to Old Crow in 1912 to look after the store here. That store is still standing, the one Freddy Frost lives in.

[Horton and Morris Company] were only here about two years, I think. They had a little sternwheeler and [one trader] went back to the stern to do something and the engineer started the engine. One of the wheels came down and broke his two legs. Yeah, two fellows had to paddle him down to Fort Yukon, but I think he got [blood] poison[ing] and he died. They quit, and then later on, Johnson [and another man] were the ones that traded for them up here.

[They were here] but [people traded with] Cadzow mostly. He must have been around 50 years old or more. He never drank all his life. He just started drinking. Gallstones, that's what killed him. Oh yes, he was well-liked. In the fall, he gave [people] credit and then they came back in the winter with [furs]. Oh yeah, there were problems, some of them didn't pay up their debt; they didn't get enough fur. Well, he had to give them tobacco, tea, ammunition.

Later on, [Cadzow] married. They had [no children], but they got two—Rachel Cadzow had two girls.[30] The oldest one died and the other one, Nellie, she's down in Fort Yukon, Nellie Carroll....

[Rachel Cadzow] was his second wife. She died there. Quite a few years ago, I don't know what sickness they had, it kind of chokes them to death....There was her, Myra Edward and Donald Fredson died that spring. By that time, they had medicine, otherwise it would have killed more. The medicine came in time to save the others. The medicine came while Pete Lord was out in Crow Flats. He came in and they gave him the medicine to take to people. By that time it was mostly over. As he went down, he went to Peter Charlie's place to give them medicine, and Mary Charlie, two more days and she would have been gone. He gave them the medicine, told them how to drink lots of water. Peter was sick, too. He was the one that saved them, with the medicine. The plane brought it in. The RCMP were the ones who went after the medicine. The minister here...he was the one that the Indian agent sent the medicine, Reverend Wheeler....No, not too long ago.

[Cadzow left Rampart House], oh, I don't remember, in the [19]20s. He had to go out to Dawson—that's where he died—because he was sick [gallstones]. Nobody took over [at Rampart House]. Well, most of the people were up here then [Old Crow]. [The trader here was] Shultz. Later on I bought Shultz out, and I only traded three years. Then I [worked] with the Jackson brothers and Joe Netro at that time: [he had a store at] Whitestone [Village]. They joined him, Healy and Strom, but he bought them out and then he traded here.

Neil McDonald and Joe Netro, managers of the store in Old Crow.

[Canadian Museum of Civilization, photo Father Jean-Marie Mouchet S2004-1467]

[David Lord] traded for Horton...in Fort Yukon.

Well, [Joe Netro] had a log building [at Whitestone]. Wherever you go, you had log houses. [Laughter]...[There was a little village there]: the Nukon family and Paul Josie's family....They traded with Joe Netro, [as did] some of the Johnson Creek bunch, the Charlie family. And he trapped himself: Joe [Netro] is a good trapper....

[Cadzow] just traded. He came down during the gold rush....Up around David Lord Creek there's lots of good whitefish. So he stopped there and fished and sold the fish to the miners that were going through there. From here he went to down to Fort Yukon and up to Black River [Alaska]. Well, he made money with the fish. I don't know whether he trapped or not but I know he started a trading post at a place they call Fish Hook Town on Black River. And then he moved up to Rampart House in 1904 and he always talked about what wonderful stuff he's got. [Laughter]...

[When Cadzow left Rampart House, there was Horton and] the Jackson brothers. [Joe Netro, too], he was up at Whitestone....Hardly anybody [stayed] in Rampart House.

(NEIL MCDONALD, VG2000-8-40:031-295;000-072, English)

The First Generation 135

Joe and Hannah (Kyikavichik) Netro and daughters Minnie, Elsie, and Kathy.

[Canadian Museum of Civilization, photo Father Jean-Marie Mouchet s2004-1424]

Later Traders

That's about all I did [hunt and trap after returning from school]. Every summer, we [hauled] freight for all the traders like Joe Netro, who been trad[ing] for a long time, you know. After that, they told Neil McDonald to run the store for little while [on] his own. And he told him [Cadzow], he didn't make no headway. So the Jackson brothers bought the store. They ran it quite awhile. Well, they didn't run it; they were up at LaPierre House, the Jackson brothers. [At first] their store was up at LaPierre House. There was nobody there, so I don't know how they made out. They didn't make much, I guess.

In between times, the NC Company [Northern Commercial Company] was here [Old Crow] two times. Both times they couldn't make nothing, so they pulled out. The last time NC came, the Jackson brothers sold out to [them]. That was second time. Before that, Joe Netro and another fellow named Harry Anthony sold out to NC Company and they never made no headway. And after NC come in, first time NC came, he pulled out of here. Then Joe Netro was there again, him and Harry Healy. They ran the store here and bought all the furs. At that time, Joe Netro was trading way up at Whitestone,

136 PEOPLE OF THE LAKES

by himself though. When NC came he was here again. Joe bought the Jackson brothers out. They [NC] were here then, the second time, and this time Joe Netro bought them out, and Joe Netro ran store for quite a long time.

[It was a little bit easier with the stores here.] Before you had to go to Fort Yukon or else Fort McPherson for a little tea and tobacco. [Finally] Joe Netro sold that store to the store there now, the Co-op. Joe is back there, you could talk to him.

(MOSES TIZYA, August 11, 1977, VG2001-4-6#1:203-259, English and Gwich'in)

Yeah for fifty years, I think, I ran store. I haul my own freight. I got my own launch, you see, haul my own freight from Fort Yukon to here. And then, between times, I trapped, wintertime, fishing, hunting. Yeah, I [ran my] business; [I was] never educated, but still I learn my own way. I don't know where I got it from. I read [a] little, write, type on my paper. I even type, picked it up on my own.

(JOE NETRO, August 10, 1977, VG2001-4-2:034-050, English)

Beliefs and Missionaries

In the 1860s, Christian missionaries from both the Oblates of Mary Immaculate—Father Seguin—and the Church of England—Reverend Kirkby—travelled to Van Tat Gwich'in country. The Anglicans were to prevail, and Reverend Robert McDonald (later Archdeacon) had a lasting legacy. He spent 40 years in the area between Fort McPherson and Fort Yukon, from 1862 to 1904 when he retired to Winnipeg. In his time in the North, he travelled with the Hudson's Bay Company and by dog team to the far-flung camps of Dagoo and Van Tat Gwich'in, translated the Bible and prayer and hymn books into Dagoo (Tukudh), married Gwich'in Julia Kutug from Fort McPherson, and raised a number of children. His primary objective was to convince the Gwich'in to abandon their previous beliefs and some of their practices (such as polygamy) and take up Christianity, and his efforts included creating a number of ministers and lay readers among the Gwich'in from the Yukon and Alaska. Most Van Tat Gwich'in elders are devout Anglicans to this day, and many are ordained ministers.

Elders remember some Gwich'in beliefs before the missionaries brought news of God. These included belief in the powers of their medicine men and women, who had shamanic powers. While some new beliefs and practices were adopted from the missionaries, some earlier Gwich'in beliefs were maintained. As Myra Moses pointed out, these included rules of ethical behaviour, such as the importance of sharing food and looking after the weaker members of society. Neil McDonald recalled some stories of the exploits of medicine people, including events he experienced personally, such as predicting future events, healing, and their special relationships with certain animals. Joe Netro related stories about medicine men healing themselves and others. Moses Tizya emphasized that Gwich'in did not violate the Christian principle of having many Gods, and the medicine men were important in feeding the people.

The first missionaries to come to Van Tat Gwich'in country arrived in the generation of the parents or grandparents of this generation of elders, in the 1860s. However, given that the early Anglican Robert McDonald was to remain for four decades, he and his work were known personally to many elders—some, such as Neil McDonald, were his direct descendants. Consequently, Elders such as Myra Moses, Joe Netro, Moses Tizya, Neil McDonald, Sarah Abel, and Lazarus Sittichinlii related many and detailed accounts of missionaries, catechists, and lay readers, the Women's Auxiliary, the practices of the new religion, and the difficult life on the land for the missionaries and their supporters.

Gwich'in Beliefs other than Christianity

Long ago, before the ministers came, they didn't believe in anything, but when the children did foolish things or talked foolishly, the old people [said], "Up above the marten looks after us." They told the children, I heard that. That's how they spoke to their children and then, "If you're good people, you'll live long," they told them. That's all! And, "Look after the poor people and you'll live long." And then, meat, when they killed meat, they [shared the meat]. Even in my time, they did that. When there was no meat, if they killed one rabbit they would boil it and its juice and give it out to all the people. They did that. They ate all small animals in those days. But the wolf is not good to eat, they said. All small animals are good to eat but wolf.

(MYRA MOSES, August 10, 1977, VG2001-4-4:113–150, Gwich'in)

One thing they believed in was the medicine man. I know of two. I heard about medicine men: they kill each other through sleep [dreaming], from one country to another country....

Edward, his Indian name is *Dajiinuh*. There's one mountain back here, Scow Mountain. They call it King Edward Mountain now.

Well, this man, his wife told me [about him]. She was a woman that didn't tell lies, a religious woman. He told her, "My medicine, [it's going to leave.] They told me. That means I'm not going to last through the winter and after I pass away, a man will propose to you. You'll talk nice to him and tell him he can't marry you. Later on, another man will propose to you, you'll get mad and scold him. And later on, years later, you'll go blind." That's exactly what happened. She refused two men who proposed to her, and then quite a few years later, she went blind. Now, how did he know?

Another time, we heard about this Mad Trapper, Albert Johnson. I came back from the Flats. There was a big storm while I was out in the Flats, so I came home about 10 o'clock at night. I was tired, the dogs were tired, and the Mountie came in and said, "Tomorrow we're going up to Johnson Creek to head off Albert Johnson—he passed LaPierre House." And I said "Tomorrow! Can't you see that I just came back? I'm tired, dogs are tired." "Get ready tomorrow, or we'll go the next day." There was only one man [left in town], the rest of them were all on the trapline. I said, "What's matter with Elias?" He said, "He got sick as soon as we told him we're going up there."

So, next morning at about eight o'clock, a woman came into our house. "This afternoon they're going to get that man. They're going to kill that man. He's going to wound a man and the man will live." So, I told the police so he won't leave. I didn't believe it but I tried to make him believe, make him believe that I believed it. Well, by that night you heard on the radio that they got Albert Johnson. Then I believed what she said. Around eight o'clock he rushed in. "They got Albert Johnson," he said. "He wounded a man but they took him to Aklavik and he's going to live." "Well, that's exactly what I told you this morning," I said.

How did she know? It might have been dreams but I asked her one time how she knew these things. She hollered at me, you know, to ask her that question.

Yes [they cured people]. A strong medicine man [healed a man who was] skin and bone, just about ready to die. They say he made a wooden knife and cut this man's breast open, pulled his lung out and washed him inside and rubbed the inside of him, then put the ribs back together. He just rubbed it on, spit on it in his hand and rubbed well. I saw that man. He lived for a long time after that. That's what I heard, but I don't know. But a lot of them say that it's true.

And another story, [about a man who] belongs to here, what they call Fish Lake, 25 miles up the river. They used to fish there in the spring, these people here, but one man, a medicine man, was getting more fish than the others. There were some [people] came over and he refused to sell them fish. So the medicine man from over there he worked on [the medicine man from here], and out in the Crow Flats, the medicine man from here said, "If you see anything [an animal],

The First Generation 139

don't try to do anything to it." He started to cross the lake and a big storm came up. And a moose was swimming across that lake and a man at the camp shot this moose. And they said the moose screamed out. It was one of his medicine [medicine animals], this moose. They found his canoe but they never found him.

(NEIL MCDONALD, August 12, 1977, VG2001-4-7:191-318, English)

Medicine Man? I don't know how they worked that medicine. I know one medicine man, he got hurt in the chest so they brought him inside the house. He couldn't stand so he told the people, "The only way I'll be better is to shoot me. Shoot me." So, people didn't want to shoot him. He was a wonderful person. Anyway, pretty soon his relation said, "Okay, I'll shoot him." [The medicine man said], "Here's a muzzle-loader, my own shotgun, and everybody in the camp, they're all going to watch. I'm not going to get shot." They watched. He told his brother, "Hurt me right here." So he wore his skin coat. He showed the people, he loaded the gun, put the powder in the gun, put a wad and behind it a ball, another wad and behind that he put another ball. [So it was] good, I guess. He pulled the trigger back and handed that gun to who was going to shoot him. "If you're going to shoot, hit me right here," he say. He fell down, upside down, and he lay there for awhile. They thought he got killed, I think. He lay there for awhile; pretty soon he moved. He got up. [Laughter] That's a medicine man....[He only did this to himself], just himself.

Another medicine man up here, it happened about 30 miles [upriver]. One boy got sick and his father, his poor father, was a medicine man. "Fix my son." He turned around. I guess the boy needed an operation. He split dry wood with straight grain and made a knife. Then he got the boy—I don't know what happened, [whether] he put him to sleep or I don't think so—with that wooden [knife] he cut the boy open, right in the chest. Sure enough, [there was] lots of blood inside the boy's chest. He cleaned him up, cleaned the blood out and that boy got better....His name was Henry Nospeak. He has a graveyard down at New Rampart. That's medicine....Yeah that happened when he was a little boy and he lived to over seventy....

[Nobody can do that today because they're] religious. Religious, yeah. Well, maybe somebody has a little medicine but it's not good enough, hah?...

They had to give him something. [Pay the medicine man.]

(JOE NETRO, August 10, 1977, VG2001-4-2:210-297, English)

[Before missionaries], they believed mostly in what they call medicine people. The Old Crow Flats people, they believed in the above, which they did the right thing. They didn't believe in no images, they just believed in the above....They didn't know it [Christianity] [until] the missionaries came in the country.

They believed in medicine man if they want [no Gods or spirits], that was just like their God. They say if they were out of food or something, the medicine man, they talked to him and people altogether made just like a service [church service]. People, everybody, went there, and sometimes those medicine people went to sleep, see, and while they sleep, they go someplace. They see a big bunch of caribou and then they lead the caribou across to camp. That's how they kill them. That's what they called medicine people in those days. That's the way they did it.

[They led the caribou right] to the camp, close to the camp. And then in the morning, they told the people to go there and sure enough, there was a big bunch of caribou. That's how they got their meat in those days, most of the time, anyway.

(MOSES TIZYA, August 11, 1977, VG2001-4-6#1:102-130, English and Gwich'in)

The Attitude Toward the First Ministers

At that time there was lots of ministers. We saw a minister who said there was a God. We really respected that. We took good care of the minister when he visited. We worked for them for nothing. We gave them everything free and we took good care of the minister. When we saw ministers, they taught people to read and so some people can read.[31] There was no school, only ministers. The minister told us about God and taught us how to pray. That is how people learned to pray. People really respected this. Now it's the same.

(MYRA MOSES, January 1980, VG2000-8-19A, Gwich'in)

When the missionary come to the country, the people [were] good enough to believe them right away. These people told me that. [The] minister [who] came into the country first, that's...Neil McDonald, his father Archdeacon McDonald. He did lots of work for the people. You see the Holy Bible translated into our language, the prayer book, hymn book? That man did a lot of work. I didn't see him; [he was] before my time.

(JOE NETRO, August 10, 1977, VG2001-4-2:73-80, English)

Moses Tizya's Father, Catechist John Tizya

My father [John Tizya] was a catechist. [The church] told him move down here to the mouth of [Crow River] and so they moved and they stayed ever since. He was under Archdeacon McDonald....

[My father was] born in Arctic Red River somewhere. Those people, they call them Gwichyah Gwich'in. *Gwichyah* means "flat country." ...Yeah, that's where he belonged to, [Arctic] Red River, some place around there.[32] That's what he told me anyway.

Well, he met him [Archdeacon McDonald] over at Archdeacon McDonald's camp in Fort McPherson and then he travelled around the country, summer and winter.

Archdeacon McDonald [was] stationed down at Howling Dog around 1800.[33] The Hudson's Bay Company, they were first stationed in Fort Yukon....From there, the Americans got hold of Alaska, you know that, and then they chased them away. They moved up to Howling Dog, that's where they call Howling Dog. They were stationed there for so many years. Archdeacon McDonald and his brother [Kenneth McDonald] were there. Archdeacon was minister then....The surveyors chased them again. Later on they [were] stationed at Old Rampart. That was 35 miles below New Rampart House. From there they chased them some more. They moved up, this time...to New Rampart. [The] missionaries followed them. That's all in 1800, [the 1800s] of course. Then after that they pulled out [of] the country.

The missionaries followed them, [Hudson's Bay Company] too, [when] they moved out the country. The last station they had was LaPierre House. That's where Bishop Bompas was at that time. Of course, Archdeacon McDonald was in the country way before that.... He was stationed all over, he travelled all over. He [was] stationed at Howling Dog; after that, he moved to McPherson. That's where he finished. He was in the country for 40 years, missionary for 40 years.

(MOSES TIZYA, August 11, 1977, VG2001-4-6#1:048-098, English and Gwich'in)

Archdeacon McDonald and Bishop Bompas at LaPierre House

I know all that happened. Bishop Bompas worked hard around here. And Archdeacon McDonald stayed in Fort McPherson in the summertime with his family. He came over the mountains and someone was with him.

Do you know LaPierre House? Two boys packed all his stuff over the mountain to LaPierre House with a canoe, Indian canoe [birchbark]....

The two boys paddled him downriver. They started at LaPierre House and stopped at Salmon Cache, Driftwood [River], and David Lord Creek, Old Crow, Rampart House, New Rampart, Old Rampart, and all that time, he baptized children and he also married people. Then he went to Fort Yukon and Old Rampart, too, and down below the *Òaii Treezheh* [Howling Dog Village]....From there all the way downriver there were people staying along the river. He healed all of them on his way down.

After they got to Fort Yukon with the big canoe, the two boys paddled him all the way up the Yukon River to Fairbanks and Dawson. He worked for the people all summer. It started to get cold, and down below Old Rampart House my father was staying there to fish and they dried fish while my mom picked berries. Meanwhile, Archdeacon McDonald was travelling around; sometimes his wife was with him and sometimes one of his kids. All day long they sat in the canoe; the Yukon River is strong water where they paddled [upriver]. They worked very hard....

He worked around Dawson. He saw lots of gold down in the water but he didn't touch the gold. At that time he was working for God so when he saw money, he never took it. After that they went back to LaPierre House with the canoe and the two boys. They started packing stuff over the mountains to Fort McPherson and it's a long way and there's lots of rivers. When they came to the river, there was lots of water so the two people who travelled with them packed them across the river, Bishop Stringer, your grandfather Big Joe [Kyikavichik], and Jacob Tizya and their wives. There's two rivers: one is at LaPierre House, and over the mountain there's two more rivers to cross. When they came to a river they carried them across, two of them held one person up and took them across the river.

And then they got to Fort McPherson. All this took place close to wintertime. His wife told me, sometimes it was raining hard while they were travelling and they all got wet. She didn't want the matches to get wet so she put them under her arm. So I kept the matches under my arm and when we landed to camp, the boys started to make fire and all their matches were wet. I had matches under my arm, with them we made fire. This is how old people made their living. His wife was a young women and she knew lots, all about Indian work.

You see that big Bible sitting up there? Archdeacon McDonald made that, this is what they said. He sure beat a lot of people, ha? Grandchild, there was a lot of ministers who worked around here but Archdeacon McDonald worked the hardest. He worked for 40 years. At McPherson was the first place they built a church, that's what they said. And Archdeacon McDonald worked there. After that,

Bishop Bompas, I wonder where he came from. England, someone said. I don't know where he came from, that Bishop Bompas. I think [Archdeacon McDonald] was born in Manitoba in Winnipeg, in the month of May.

[Bishop Bompas] was coming from the south and he got to McPherson after it was cold, [and it was] winter over at LaPierre House [when he arrived there]. The Hudson's Bay store was there and a mission, too. A lot of people stayed there. They made a skin fur parka, pants, mittens, and fur boots for Bishop Bompas. Somebody went with him with a dog team. From there, you see the big mountains on the other side of Crow Flats. Lots of people stayed there and he travelled there, too. He gave them baptism, Bishop Bompas. In the wintertime, he travelled by dog team all the way down from Crow Flats to above John Oliver's place.[34] There is a mountain there and people stayed all along it at that time.

All down that way he worked for the people, healing them. From there my father and Old Moses went with him, and Old Donald's dad, Dozriikaii, too. Old Archie [Linklater] [and his] mother, too, were with them....Down toward Shuman House, they packed their belongings. They had no dogs; they used backpack, packing their blankets. That's what they ate. After that, toward Shuman House they came to the river, and over toward Black River there was an Indian chief. There were lots of people there and Bishop arrived there, too. There was no meat. They were packing only their blankets. They came to a lot of people and Bishop Bompas was there, and there was [only] a little meat there. At that time we never had any grub [store-bought food], we only had meat and fish. One person went to Fort Yukon—*Jałk'iichik*—it's called Fishing Town. There are still people living there, you know.

The Bishop arrived there and the men shot a moose. While they did that, one man went to Fort Yukon with just snowshoes. He walked day and night...and arrived there while the Bishop was there....That man [had] camped only one night....Bishop Bompas was staying there with the people. [Another] man had good dog team; on his way he killed a moose and brought some moose meat. He took Bishop Bompas to Fort Yukon with the dog team. The man who walked to Fort Yukon by snowshoes arrived there. People living out on the land were told to go to Fort Yukon. All the people gathered at Fort Yukon; there were lots of people there. The Bishop arrived there and everyone was baptized. He worked for them all. He completed his work and the man with dog team brought him back up and took him to where he was staying. A lot of people were staying there now. People arrived with the Bishop. My father was one of them. They returned home, packing their belongings. They were given meat. From there my dad knew about the Bible. All those who were with the Bishop were taught about the Bible by campfire light. They all were taught, the old men, they were not yet old men: my grandfather Old Moses and my father [John Englishoe] and others.

The [Bishop] spoke about what will happen in the future. Eventually there will be lots of white people. At that time we didn't have flour, we ate blood soup. [The Bishop] didn't like it but he couldn't say no. He said, "Soon there will be flour and you can make gravy. Then you won't eat blood soup." Now we can't eat blood soup. Gravy mixed with sugar is tasty. After that a lot of people travelled to Black River with Bishop Bompas. They killed caribou and moose. All the families dried the meat. They arrived at LaPierre House, all the families, and returned. They brought Bishop Bompas back in the springtime.

(MYRA MOSES, August 29, 1979, VG2000-8-9:000-195, Gwich'in)

The Church in the Early Days of Old Crow

This [building] here is the first church [in Old Crow]. The people moved up from Rampart House to here. The minister came up and stayed in one of the old houses of mine...and he used another man's house for services....If you go inside the church in the front you'll see Archdeacon McDonald Memorial Church. You'll see what time it was built. [The first one they built was] a little too small, so they built this one, some people themselves. They're not carpenters, most of them....They made toboggans, snowshoes, canoes, paddles, all these they make it themselves.

[Moses Tizya's father John Tizya] was the catechist in 1904. The catechist from Fort Yukon, William Loolah, three young men brought him up as far as what they call Circle Rock, that's below LaPierre House. From there they went to McPherson.

There was about seven of them altogether [cathechists] and Moses's father came from here—not from here [town] but just the mouth of Crow [River]. That's where they all used to gather. All along here was nothing but timber. There were seven of them: one from LaPierre House and the rest from McPherson. They went through the examination: two made it. They were ordained priests, those two.

And that was the year we [Archdeacon McDonald and family] left for Winnipeg. He [Archdeacon McDonald] told John Tizya, "You've got a big family now and you can't go among the people. You go down

Reverend John Kendi making fire at the church (1965–69).
[Exham fonds (VG2008-01-188)]

below the mouth of Old Crow [River] and build yourself a house where the people, when they come from Crow Flats, you could hold service for them there. Him and his son [built a cabin]. There was another cabin over here someplace. That's all [there was]. The traders from Fort Yukon came up and built a big house, up in front. That was a store they made. They didn't have to pack logs, they just chopped them down… When I first came up in 1913, you couldn't see the mountain [Crow Mountain, behind Old Crow]. All this was big timber.

Yeah, [John Tizya was the only person staying here for awhile]. The [people] used to all gather here and then go down to Rampart House. That's where the store was.

Just around the bend down here there's a bluff. The river runs into the bluff, down here. That [where] his [John Tizya's] fish camp was. That's where he fished.

(NEIL MCDONALD, August 12, 1977, VG2001-4-7:104-165, English)

Hard Times and Early Church Services in Camp

There were seven of us [children] when my mother died. While [she] was still living, William Njootli [was] down in the Arctic Village area, my father was living alone....His brother used to stay with him but he was staying alone. My father was hunting, [and] my brother saw a man's footprints and came back and told my father about it. "He was not walking strongly, it looked that way," he said. So the next day, my father made a load of meat. Drymeat he loaded at home, to look after us. But then, Minister William Njootli was moving. There was no meat there. My father went to them with meat. Then the dogs were not strong so many times they had to camp and then they could move to us....

"Ah, Grandchild, now my brother next to me," I said. He was walking; he was just about as big as me. He was not baptized yet but the minister was going to move to us. But my father put the child in [his toboggan] and went to the minister. He went again for a load of meat, so he met the minister, and there my brother was baptized and then he came back.

The next day, only then William Njootli moved beside us. Ah, my grandchild, there were lots of people all the way down the island. It was just noisy outside. My brother and me, it was fun for us to see. But my father, they moved over beside us with no meat. There was a big meat cache out there....He left with my brother, ah, they killed lots of caribou, him and Brother. That was what the minister was going to live on as they moved down further. Grandchild, from when I was a child, that's the first time I saw a minister.

My father came back; they had killed lots of caribou....My mother, too, gave out meat in the village. She was fixing a toboggan and the minister moved right beside us. Our grandmother, *Cheesih*, was still a strong woman at that time.[35] She was a big help to ministers, that's why she stayed across from the minister. With the round tent, they set them on either side of the minister. My father [from] a new store had it set up that if the minister [has service in his tent, he had candles] and candle containers, too. "In the evening when they're going to have church service, you give it to the minister," he told my mother.

Grandchild before that, they made that *łùh jik*—today they call it kindling. They made lots and burned it in the middle, and it lit up the whole tent. Then they made church service. Finally, in the evening, William Njootli, was going to have church service and they made kindling candle sticks. There were candles all along the front, across there in front of their tents.

Reverend Joe Kaye.

[Canadian Museum of Civilization, photo Father Jean-Marie Mouchet S2004-1374]

They were ready to have service. In those days bells would never ring, Grandchild....They hit a fry pan; [Laughter] that was the bell....The minister's oldest son was named Esau. He went amongst the people. He made church service, he told people there's going to be church service; he went all over the village. Ah, my father, the minister was right beside them. "If there's church service, they're going to sit on it." It was a summer [caribou] skin. My mother gave that and on that they sat, my father and my brother.

They took us all to the church service, Grandchild, for how long they made church service. My brother just kept looking up at the house ceiling. Before that, he never saw that kind of house, I guess.

(SARAH ABEL, VG1997-2-2A:160-260, Gwich'in)

Early Ministers in the Old Crow Area, LaPierre House, and Fort McPherson

From the time I remembered the ministers' names, I'll talk about that. The minister's wife, Old McDonald's ministers, from the time the ministers came here, I'll talk about that.

Long ago, the first ministers, there were two of them, one was a minister, for LaPierre House. He was the first minister there; the people gathered there, Minister William [Njootli]. After that they made him minister for Old Crow and downwards [downriver, west]. I don't remember how long he stayed around there. When he got sick he came back over the mountains [east]....

So Minister John [Tizya], they called him, he was a minister from a long time ago....He stayed around LaPierre House. From there he would teach down as far as Fort Yukon, he would go down there. William Njootli did that also....After that he came back here and the Old Man Minister [*Giikhii Danahch'i*] made lots of people lay readers. I remember there were six of them.

That winter my poor father [Edward Sittichinlii] was a lay reader. I remember their picture from that time. From there they went different ways. Minister John, they sent him to Mayo. On the way there he died. Minister William lived in town the winter my father first taught there. He was sick so he had to stay in town. We moved up the river. Minister William went up with us, too, with his children to Trail Creek, and from there he went to Fort McPherson. My father went up farther and stayed around there for the spring. They went down to town that spring and they said William died. I don't know how big a minister he was but they called him minister at that time. That was Minister William.

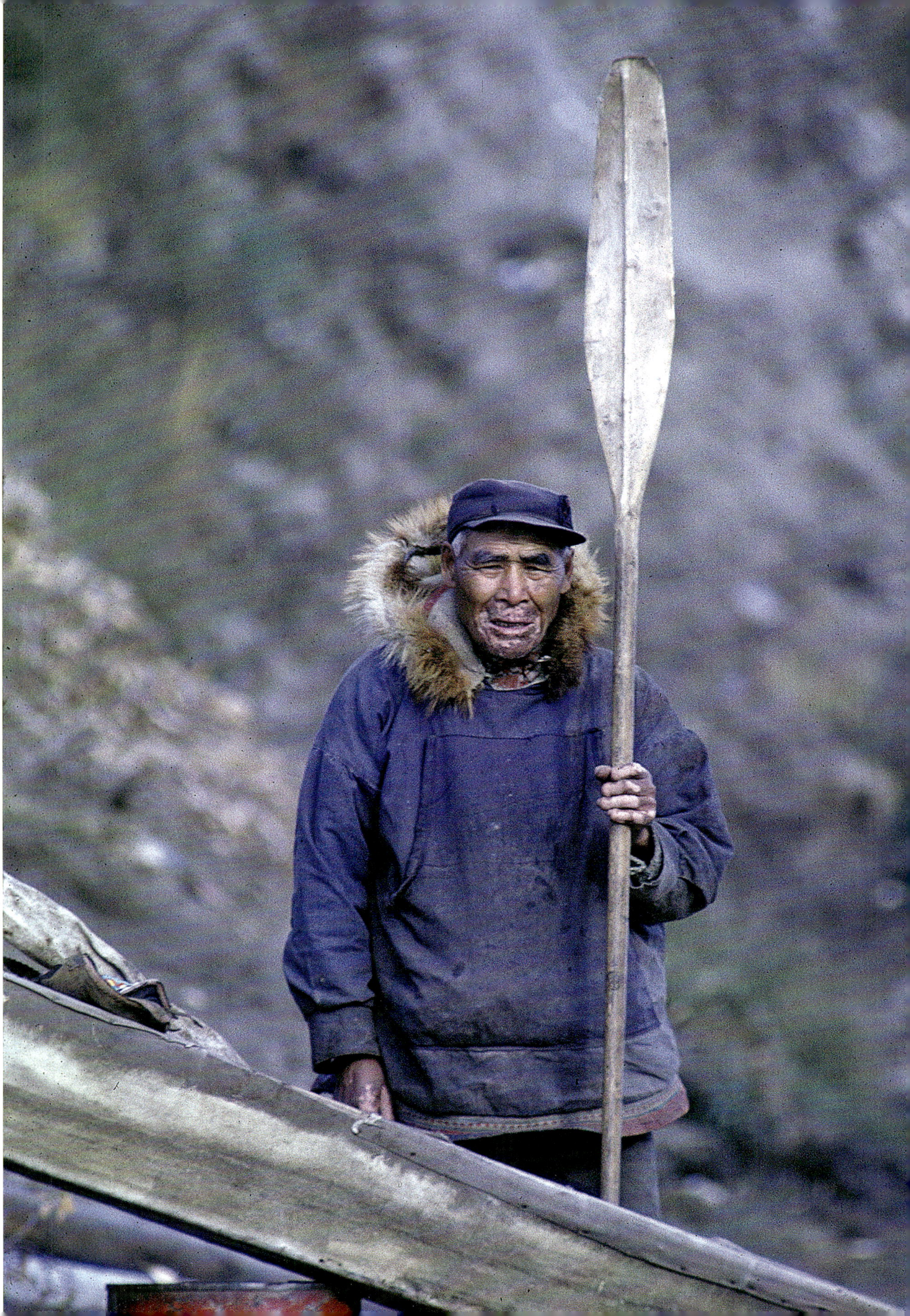

Not long after, they finally started teaching my father and he stayed in town. He was taught for three years in town. Then in the spring, the Old Man Minister...sent them out to different places in the country. From there they went to town in the spring and then he would teach them again. They were taught for three years. After that, they made him minister, my father, Old Sittichinlii. I don't remember when they made him a minister, but in 1918 or '19, he was a minister.

Around 1919, he would travel around with the people after that they made him a minister. In 1911, he first went to Fort Yukon. At that time I was so big [a boy]. I would work for nothing for the people where my father was. He worked for the mission but I just worked for them voluntarily.

Archdeacon Whittaker was staying in town then. They called for him: his wife was getting sick steadily. So that's why my father took his place. He went to Old Crow in 1911. Then in 1912, after New Year's he finally came back up [to Fort McPherson]. The white people were stingy to him down there. We came Christmas before Christmas and then after New Year, we left.

We came back to town and in the fall the police that went to patrol to McPherson froze to death.[36] Nobody knew about it....In the springtime around *Chuu Tl'it*[37] [Whitestone Village], the people moved over the mountains to visit Dawson. Only then did they find out the police were gone. That was in the spring. Well me, I thought, when those police froze in December, they didn't travel around. We never travel with meat in our toboggan for long periods of time. They had only gone with [the load of food in their toboggans]. Way up where they had put a food cache for them, there was no sign of it. So that's why they froze to death.

Not long afterward, my father was a minister and he travelled all over the country. Wherever he went, I went with him. Around Old Crow, only that place he didn't go. In Dagoo [country], there were lots of them there. He worked among them for three years. Around Fort McPherson, he walked amongst the people. After that he was an Elder so he just stayed in town. Then there was no ministers so he stayed a long time in Fort McPherson and took the minister's place. Around there, he performed weddings for the white people and Native people.

In those days, it was still hard. In the spring the people were poor for meat in town. My father had a good life. He was lucky. His name was Sittichinlii: that is a spruce tree standing. In those days a spruce tree standing, its branches spread out, that is called *sittichinlii*. That is why they gave him that name in Gwich'in because he's going to have a good life....

My brother who was in school, they made him minister. He was good. Me, I never went to school, so we helped the ministers. We just stayed in Aklavik. My wife, too, she swept up in the church and tidied up. Me, too, all the ministers who came and went, when the people couldn't understand [the white ministers], then I helped out with the church services a bit. Only now I have no strength so I make fire in the church....

Before me, ministers travelled in the bush with the people and they worked, too. That's the way we lived our lives in those days....Long ago, there were lots of lay readers. The Old Man Minister, him, too, he would go over the mountains and up the Yukon [River] in the summertime. Sometimes he would go down to the coast.

This was the way the Old Man Minister lived in those days. In the fall, before November, he would go to LaPierre House. Only then he would make a big day for them. They would be moving so before Christmas, on November 16, 17, and onward they would celebrate Sunday. He would make Communion service for them. Way up at Trail Creek and down this way, the elders went to LaPierre House. They came if they wanted something at the store and then he gave them Communion. In those days, people didn't know money. They got a little tobacco and small things. Whatever they could afford they put in the dishes [at the service]. After the people left the church, Old Man Minister would take it to the old people. That's how it was in those days.

(LAZARUS SITTICHINLII, VG1997-2-15:006-166, Gwich'in)

Education and Schools

Van Tat Gwich'in educated their children in life on the land, social behaviour, ethics, beliefs, environmental knowledge, and all aspects of what it is to be Van Tat Gwich'in. Missionaries and early traders brought additional things to learn, including reading in their language. Early in the 20th century, a residential school was established in Carcross, Yukon. Later, ministers' wives and nurses provided instruction in basic subjects. However, most elders in this generation, and even the next, did not receive any non-Gwich'in schooling. Some elders learned English through their participation in fur trading. Moses Tizya spent many years at the residential school and spoke English, and Myra Moses learned some literacy from missionaries.

Carcross School

[I went to] Carcross School. Bishop Stringer came through here in 1912. They were just starting to haul logs over for that store. He picked us up. There were nine of us [who] went to school together to Carcross.... [From aged] six to eighteen, I lived there. I left in 1918....I never [visited home during that time]. I only went to Campsell Hospital for nine months one time, and I never went no place, only stayed here. [I went] to school steady. We had only two weeks holiday when it was harvest time, cutting hay....It's not bad, it's good....

From the time [I spoke no English], all of us done pretty good, too! Some of us went up to eighth grade in six years. All of them died now, though....Only one I see, few days ago in Whitehorse. I see one of my school[mates].

[The school] was run by the mission [so] of course it had to be strict, just like jail. One time I see newspaper, it said "Children been to jail that time," which is right. They were so strict, those missionaries.... They're so strict we can't even talk to girls. They wouldn't let us chew gum, even. I'm not kicking about food though. Pretty good manager there. He fed us pretty good. He got maybe five tons of grub at a time, lots of meat anyway. Like Sunday, we had good dinner, maybe chicken dinner or beef dinner or something like that, vegetables, all kinds of it. Of course we grew all that ourselves....We did all the work. No, I never missed home. My first year, I missed home. After that I didn't care.

On Saturday afternoon, no school, we work. We go to town and work for 25 cents an hour, well over a dollar, which is good. One dollar was big money that time. If we don't work, we hunt rabbits, shoot gopher. We sell gopher for five cents apiece and rabbit for 10 cents apiece, make few dollars. In school we had about five twenty-twos [.22 calibre rifles]. Number two was my gun there. Hard to get them good and clean, though. Then they give us 12 shells each to hunt with, but we buy our own shells. It cost not much anyway. Forty cents for 22 long rifle, 35 cents for 22 long, and 25 cents for 22 short, one box. That's cheap...

Yes, [after I finished school I came right back to Old Crow]. A power boat, good gas boat brought us up from Fort Yukon. We came to Fort Yukon with steamboat. In 1912 we went up in steamboat, too. At that time, [the] steamboat [was] running, but from here we rowed down, rowing a boat all the way down [to] Fort Yukon.

(MOSES TIZYA, August 11, 1977, VG2001-4-6#1:092-196, English and Gwich'in)

Learning from the Ministers

> When I was a child, I will talk about what I remember. Old Rampart [House], I really remember about around there. Bishop Bompas and Archdeacon McDonald were the church ministers there. They travelled all over the country. I remember them all, you know. Down at New Rampart House, they called it, there, too, he was a minister. I remember Bishop Bompas! He made school for us children. What I mean is he taught us [ABCs]. After that, Archdeacon McDonald would visit all the people and he worked for the people. He and Bishop Bompas were the first ministers. At that time my mom and my dad were still living.
>
> (MYRA MOSES, August 25, 1980, VG2000-8-34, Gwich'in)

The Border

Various European countries claimed ownership of First Nations' land in North America. Russia sold its interests in Alaska to the United States in 1867, and British-Canadian interests were ejected over the course of the next 44 years. In 1911, a formal American survey party delineated the border and it became more formally enforced, including collecting customs and duties. Ultimately, the border became a barrier between Gwich'in communities and families, restricting access to Gwich'in lands. Myra Kaye told of how the unity of Gwich'in was affected by the externally imposed boundary. Myra Moses described moving the Hudson's Bay trading post farther east.

Problems Caused by the Border

> A long time ago we had hard times....When elders travelled, we travelled every day. We lived from the land and travelled for food. We hunted for everything. We travelled every day....My relatives and people from downriver lived like this, too. And I only knew this; I didn't know anything else.
>
> On this land, when people gathered a long time ago, when there was no boundary, the people from Arctic Village stayed near a herd of caribou, down near a mountain, they stayed there. At that time there were no caribou around here. That's where people went for caribou. All the Gwich'in people were like one. They lived like one family, all the people on this earth.
>
> Now the Americans put a boundary up and it's hard to visit. Even so we travel down, it's not far. That's how it is and we continue to live on.
>
> (MYRA KAYE, February 2, 1980, VG2000-8-19C, Gwich'in)

Old Rampart House and New Rampart House

> Old Rampart was still on the American side at that time. Then, the surveyors arrived and the Hudson's Bay still lived in the American side. So then at the new Rampart House, the [Hudson's Bay Company] moved there.
>
> The houses that were there [Old Rampart House], they took them down. They brought them up with boats. They had big boats. They put the house timbers in the boats, the church and all, the Hudson's Bay store and houses, all that. They brought it up to New Rampart [House]….and built the houses there. The Hudson's Bay man lived there a long time. The minister, too, had a mission there….I was big and I remember.
>
> (MYRA MOSES, 1980S, VG2000-8-31:056-070, Gwich'in)

The Settlement of Old Crow

In the lifetime of this generation of elders, the community of Old Crow was formed and Van Tat Gwich'in, along with some Dagoo, came to base their trading and livelihoods in Old Crow. The duration and relocations of the trading posts and other services over the course of the late 19th and early 20th centuries have been woven through many elders' accounts. Elders describe how the location of Old Crow at the mouth of the Crow River was a traditional fishing site, near a number of major caribou hunting locations, and convenient to the rich Crow Flats area. The community is named after their ancestor *Deetru' K'avihdik*, meaning "Crow May I Walk" (also known as Chief *Zzeh Gittlit*). Moses Tizya's father had a fish camp and was the first resident of what was to become Old Crow. Myra Moses recalls the move from New Rampart House.

Arriving in Old Crow

> I'm gonna talk about since 1905. I landed here in 1905 and been here since. I was only five years old then. I was going Crow Flats, but we came back. We were over [at] McPherson for two years, from there we came back. We landed here in 1905, according to a fellow named Big Joe Kaye, and we fooled around here ever since. There was nothing here that time, nobody, just brush that's all. [Laughter]
>
> There were three families [who] came down on one raft from what they call LaPierre House. [We] came over the portage from McPherson to there and after we land here, we were [on the] other side [of] this mountain, we camped there. From there we saw four people on this

hill here, on top of the hill here. A few years ago I found out that was Camsell, Charlie Camsell, with his crew...surveying. He was a mining manager and surveyor....He was one of first men to explore when they found Klondike. He was there to see how much is there....

[We came to Old Crow from LaPierre House because] my father [John Tizya] was a catechist. [The church] told him move down here, [to the] mouth of [Crow River], so they moved and they stayed ever since. He was under Archdeacon McDonald....

[The other three families who came with my father from Fort McPherson:] Yeah, this fellow named Old John Kwatlatyi, [meaning] trapping father or something like that. Not untidy, something like that....And his son, he was married, too, Elias Kwatlatyi, was with us.... But they didn't stay with us here. They stayed down at Rampart House mostly. And my father stayed here until we were grown up....Even around 1920 there were not many people here yet, mostly at Rampart House. That was the main town in those days. Around 1920, they hadn't moved the church here yet. That little church down here was just put up in 1926....

First a white missionary was stationed here before 1920. He had no church; he just held services in another Native building. There were not many people here, anyway. In 1926, another missionary came here. That's when we put the little church up. They had a church down at Rampart House but nothing is there now.

I don't know how come everybody moved here. I guess everybody moved up here after Dan Cadzow died, hah? Dan Cadzow was a trader down there. He got to Rampart in 1904. He was the only trader in the country.

Yeah, somebody else [made a store there]...from Fort Yukon, they put this big store over here. That's the one they put here in 1912, and [its] still up. And then, after [Horton and Morris], they were partners. Well, he got hurt with a wheel. He had a little steamboat. He got broken up with the wheel and he died.

And then after that [Johnson]...bought that store over here. He was here in 1918 when I come home from school. He ran the store.

(MOSES TIZYA, August 11, 1977, VG2001-4-6#1:012-050;023-089, English and Gwich'in)

The End of Rampart House

At that time, Cadzow, the white man store manager, arrived at Rampart House. He brought in supplies. There were no engines in those days. They just had big scows that they pulled [with] ropes and walked along the shore. Lots of boys drove it. He arrived at Rampart House. All those who stayed up there, all of them went down [to Cadzow's store], and those below there, too...all of them. So all the way downriver, there were lots of people.

Then here, too, a store opened. A white man, named Billy Moore had a small steamboat. He would bring supplies upriver with his boat. Here at Old Crow, down where there's a big house, they built [a store]. But Billy Moore got hurt with the boat and he died and other white people were traders here. So everyone moved up here and built houses. Eventually they built the church here.

So there were no more people down at Rampart House. They just started living here [Old Crow]. Those people staying at Old Rampart House all moved here, too.

(MYRA MOSES, 1980S, VG2000-8-31:164-180, Gwich'in)

3 | The Second Generation
The Early 20th Century

Contents

162 **HARD WORK AND PROSPERITY**
163 Hunting, Trapping, and Trading Round
173 Trapping, Hunting, Trading, and Village Areas
176 The Old Crow–*Van Tat* (Crow Flats) Area
184 The Mountains Surrounding *Van Tat* (Crow Flats)
192 Upriver on *Ch'oodèenjik* (Porcupine River)
  Driftwood Village, LaPierre House, Johnson Creek Village, and Whitestone Village
213 Downriver on *Ch'oodèenjik* (Porcupine River)
  Bluefish River, Rampart House, and Alaska
219 Farther Afield
  Fort Yukon, Dawson, Fort McPherson, and Herschel Island

223 **NEIGHBOURS, NEWCOMERS, AND VISITORS**
224 Inuvialuit in Crow Flats and the Upper Porcupine
226 White Trappers and Other Visitors
230 Ministers and the Church

233 **EVENTS AND TRENDS**
234 The Dagoo Disperse
240 The Effects of the Border with Alaska
243 Moving to Town
247 The Mad Trapper Incident
251 Endurance and Change

I saw it from a plane, that calving ground.[1] *It's just wide and grassy, green grass. Around there is a small lake; that is where the caribou drink. This land, how big it is! It's a beautiful land; it's all good. Really, it's such a beautiful land. Everything we live off, everything [animals], plants, water, everything, He put it [here] for us, Grandchild. We live on that now.*

But...other people bother us for our land. That's why there has been lots of work about that. Down at the dance hall, you see the pictures up there on the walls [of elders]. All of them fixed everything for us long ago. Around 1940, they had meetings, Old Chief [Peter Moses], Joseph Kaye, Johnny Kaye from over Fort McPherson way; chiefs, all of them. They would come over for meetings. They were really smart people. All of them have passed away. "In the future, they will not bother you for the land." That's still to come, they said. "That's why we fix it for you," they told the people. We are in that [time] now. But I really thank the Lord. I [came] here for that. You all do lots of work for our land. By God, it's going to be good, we hope. I always worry about that.

(HANNAH NETRO, *Diniizhòo* [Game Mountain], August 1, 2000, VG2000-4-13:320-350, Gwich'in)

IN THE EXTENSIVE BODY OF INTERVIEWS that make up the Van Tat Gwich'in Oral History Collection, the second generation of elders are those currently active in the late 20th and early 21st centuries. They are the sons, daughters, nieces, and nephews of the first generation and were born in the early 1900s. They were interviewed from the 1980s to the present. Their history comprises a century of great changes, from hunting, trapping, and living across the breadth of Van Tat Gwich'in traditional lands, to staying in Old Crow for much of the year. For the most part, they still travel on the land when opportunities and their health permit, and they continue to derive much of their food (meat, fish, berries, some plants) and heat (firewood) from the land by their own efforts and those of their children and other community members.

The vast majority of Van Tat Gwich'in in this generation spoke Gwich'in as their first language and continue to speak it as their primary language. Many emphasize that in their early lives they did not have the opportunity to attend school and consequently picked up some English only later in life. The translated interviews reveal the comparative richness of their expression in Gwich'in over English. A number of Elders, such as the Frost and Tizya families, spoke English in their youth either due to having one non-Gwich'in, English-speaking parent (Harold "Jack" Frost) or because one parent was educated in English outside the community (Moses Tizya and Clara Frost).

As with the previous generation, the second generation spoke primarily of the life they had experienced themselves, as well as what they had learned from their parents, including some of the well-known long-ago stories. While very generously sharing the history they know well, they were reluctant to speculate on events that occurred before their time but about which they hadn't been informed by a reliable source, such as an eyewitness or someone with a direct link to such a person. For example, this generation did not experience the use of the celebrated caribou fences, which are still visible across the northern reaches of their lands and were relied upon by their grandparents and previous generations. They have been interviewed repeatedly about these impressive structures by a series of assorted researchers (archaeologists, geologists, anthropologists, biologists) and other visitors, and most recently, National Parks managers, and they adamantly refuse to speculate about the use of the fences beyond the specific areas of knowledge that have been passed on to them.

The two overriding themes of this generation of elders are their satisfaction with their lives on the land, and change. They began their lives living much as their parents and countless generations of ancestors did, with perhaps a few changes in technology (firearms, metal traps, wire snares, fishnets, canvas tents, and stoves) that made their lives on the land easier

Hannah Netro and Mary Kassi.

[Canadian Museum of Civilization, photo Father Jean-Marie Mouchet S2004-1456]

but didn't cause significant alterations to that way of life. The larger changes happened as a result of events in the outside world, such as the Depression of the 1930s, which brought many Euro-Canadian trappers to their land, and the rapid decline of fur prices after World War II, coupled with dramatic inflation in the cost of trade goods. At the same time (around 1950), the federal government adopted a policy of tying social programs and benefits to inducing First Nations people across the North to move off of their lands and into permanent communities. Consequently, a recurrent theme of this generation of elders is the differences in the way Van Tat Gwich'in live today compared to their own lives and a great concern for the future of their grandchildren's generation and beyond.

    Taken together, the interviews of the second generation are extremely detailed. They described where they used to live, what they did, who they knew, and memorable anecdotes, as well as how to look after the land and animals, how people should treat each other, and how life has improved or declined. They touched on many topics and many different summaries could be made of their information; for present purposes, twelve topics have been selected to give a sense of the breadth of their history and knowledge. This selection of excerpts in no way exhausts the wealth of information they

The Second Generation 161

Cache and tent frame at Stanley Njootli's camp at K'ii Zhìt (Schaeffer Lake) in Van Tat (Crow Flats), 2006.
[Shirleen Smith ©VGFN (VG2006-11-242)]

have to offer. Their experiences overlap in some regards with those of their predecessors yet their perspectives differ; consequently some topics are similar to those spoken of by the previous generation.

HARD WORK AND PROSPERITY

The second generation of elders represented in the Van Tat Gwich'in Oral History Collection spoke at length about the way they made a living during their lifetimes. They emphasized the hard yet satisfying work during their youth and middle-aged years when they spent most of their time working and travelling on the land. They often compared this life to that in Old Crow, particularly the differences between their youth and the life of young Gwich'in today, and frequently they expressed concern for the distinctly different and uncertain future facing the youth.

Like the first generation, most of this group of elders speak their own language, Gwich'in. Only a small number attended any formal schools and most picked up the English they know throughout various experiences in their lives, such as performing wage labour for traders. They were well-instructed in hunting, trapping, and myriad related skills, and they possessed a detailed knowledge of great expanses of country.

While their life experiences contrast with those of their grandchildren in many ways, certain aspects of the lives of this generation differ from that of the previous generation, as well. Particularly as they grew older, they spoke of changes in areas like economic arrangements, prices of furs, areas that became devoid of furs and meat and were abandoned for the remainder of their lifetimes, technology, the role of Euro-Canadian outsiders, the role of outside governments and agencies (Canadian, Yukon, American) in their lives, border restrictions, trading locations, and, ultimately, the move to a single base community, Old Crow. Following the decline of fine fur species (notably marten) in some parts of the territory, this generation of elders depended on muskrats in Crow Flats to a greater extent than previously. Through these changes, they reiterate that they experienced both times of plenty and of hardship, yet by hard work and looking after each other, they prevailed. They continued this generosity into their elder years by their commitment to sharing their history and knowledge with the youth, their community, and beyond.

Hunting, Trapping, and Trading Round

Like their predecessors, the second generation of elders followed a round of different activities in various locations on the land throughout the year. There was some variation in the locations and activities, particularly the inclusion of wage labour or trading, among the elders. For example, the Kyikavichik (Kaye) family resided primarily upstream from Old Crow at Driftwood Village during the winter, whereas the Frost family lived downstream in the Bluefish River area. The Tetlichi-Charlie family resided upstream at Johnson Creek Village in the winter, and the Nukons were farther south, toward the headwaters of the Porcupine River at Whitestone Village. The family of Charlie Thomas lived in the northwestern part of the territory, in Alaska and the Potato Creek part of Crow Flats, and it was not until his early adulthood that Charlie Thomas moved to Whitestone Village. Many families travelled to Crow Flats for muskrat hunting in the spring and early summer beginning early in the 20th century, while others did not take up this activity until later (or, in the case of one family, not at all), when the upper Porcupine was no longer a good hunting and trapping area.

Elders often spoke of their trapping locations, prices for furs, and other details of the trapping lifestyle, including families' base-camp locations in Crow Flats for muskrat trapping. However, they also emphasized that until relatively recently, there was very little food to be had at the trading posts

Ben Charlie making a raft of logs.

[Canadian Museum of Civilization, photo Father Jean-Marie Mouchet s2004-1468]

and their sustenance was derived from hunting, fishing, gathering, and trapping, supplemented with occasional treats of flour, fruit (often dried), sugar, and other "staples" of agricultural-southern diets. Consequently, the seasonal round of activities focussed on both trapping and hunting, as well as trading excursions and non-economic events, such as gatherings for celebrations (feasts and dances at Christmas and New Year's Day), at which times they also chose their leaders. Well into the second half of the 20th century, drying meat and fish was a major economic activity.

Hunting and Trapping at Driftwood Village and Rampart House, and Men's and Women's Activities

> My father [Big Joe Kyikavichik (Kaye)[2]] lived around [Rampart House] and up at Driftwood [Village]. Cadzow had a store [at Rampart House]. Sometimes they would go there, at Christmas and New Year....And so, when I was about to be born, he took my mother down and I was born there in 1911. They just went there for short periods of time and lived off the land, worked for their living. My father just stayed at Driftwood.
>
>   They made rafts and landed at Rampart House and stayed there for the summer, they say. I was a child yet. In the fall time, I wonder how they came back up this way [up the Porcupine River, to Old Crow,

Driftwood River and beyond], maybe with dog packs, by the mountains, I guess....In the summer when they moved around, they travelled only with dog packs, even until not long ago.

Now when there are caribou up [on Crow Mountain], they go up with four-wheelers.[3] In the past they really depended on the caribou and its skin, too. That's why in the month of August, when there were caribou, they looked to kill lots of caribou for the skins. They made caribou-skin pants; and with calf skins, they made dresses. With the slightly larger skins they made mitts and caribou-skin mukluks. The August [caribou] skins are very good for making winter clothing. They killed lots of caribou in August. In those days, when they found there were caribou [on Crow Mountain], the men went up the mountain. Up there where Randall Tetlichi lives [halfway up the mountain, at a spring], they made fire. All the men gathered there and the elders would tell them, "Go this way." They would tell the men, "You go that way, too," they would say, and they would [follow these instructions and hunt] the caribou.

Elders gave directions. The elders told the [hunters] what to do and just like the fence they made, the men, would do as they said....That way they killed lots of caribou. Afterward, they would come back down [from the mountain]. Then everybody would go up; the women and children. The bigger children ran; the smaller ones were packed. Now there's a road up there [to the top of Crow Mountain]...lots of times, I get mad.

[Caribou fences], I never saw, Grandchild. They only had those on the mountains...They made a big caribou fence, and corralled the caribou. They killed them with arrows. In those days, they went through hard times. [It was] just like nothing for us. They would go up and put all the meat [in] one place.

All the people didn't stay together. Families stayed here and there... on this side of the mountain and all over. We saw all the tents and we just watched. In the evening, they had fires and cooked. At that time... the willows weren't very big, nor the trees. Everybody could see each other clearly and what they were doing. When I remember, all of a sudden I wish for all that.

There were no freezers then so we dried all the meat. We even dried caribou heads....They put all the caribou in one place, and our mothers dried the meat. Then, after all our work was done, we picked berries.

We picked berries and brought our pails home; we had that for fruit. In those days, we never knew fresh fruit. Only recently, my children, when you were raised, only then, [a supply boat came only] once a year. Before that, [we had] dried fruit sometimes. They didn't boil it;

The Second Generation

they just gave a little to their children. They ate it as candy. Candy: we never knew that, either.

Finally, when everything was dried, they put the meat into dog packs and brought it down and put it in caches. We did that in August and into September. Then, my poor father, he [went to his] net, [in his canoe] holding a paddle, he said. Not only one, all the people set nets downriver...and killed lots of chum salmon. All over, they put dry chum salmon in the caches.

In mid-September, they didn't cut [the salmon] up. They [put them on] sticks and hung them up before winter. [My father] always had fifteen dogs. He did lots of work for them; not only him, everyone who had dogs. They made dog food for the winter. They made dryfish. They cut out the bones and dried that, too. When it got cold, they hung it up. Sometimes there were one thousand fish. All around there were big fish caches, for all winter. As well, there was caribou meat, too. [When it was] cold, they made frozen caribou meat. That's what they lived off.

At the beginning of October the women tanned the fall caribou hides and they smoked it in a round house....Afterward they sewed caribou-skin parkas for the children. First they made parkas for the people who were going to travel. Every year they made new caribou skin clothing, I guess. They say the old ones got cold. They had not one day of rest....

After they finished, the ice was frozen by then and then the women went around on the rabbit trails. They set snares for rabbits; they made long snare lines. All over this country, up the mountain, across the river, and downriver, the women set snares for the winter. All winter they looked at their snares and kept putting fresh willows on them.

Meanwhile, they set fishnets under the ice in October, sometimes up to January, to springtime. They caught fish and rabbits, too, and so we lived well, and our dogs, too. That is how we lived.

In the fall when we went rabbit snaring, the men went overland, I remember. They went to the steep banks across [the river]; sometimes they wouldn't kill any meat and would come home with nothing. When they killed meat, they came home with meat. When they came home without meat, it was bad. Us at home, what we caught [fish, rabbits] we lived on. All our lives we never had a rest.

(ELLEN BRUCE, March 12, 1997, VG1997-8-7:020-106, Gwich'in)

Alice Abel with her brother, Johnny, holding muskrat skins.

[Canadian Museum of Civilization, photo Father Jean-Marie Mouchet S2004-1342]

Trapping Round in Northwestern Crow Flats, 1920s

I will talk with you about how people around here made their living from muskrat trapping and hunting. Long ago, this was Neil's [McDonald] country. This is where he came to the river. Up there, his lake is called *Ts'iivii Zhit*...down there, too, *Ta'ałshaa*—in English I don't know the name. [Phillip] *Tsal Vavan* is called Phillip Lake in English.

Those people living on the river in 1921, I know about that. They lived at Rampart House. The little old man really worked hard, he did. He lived all around here. His lake is up there. This part of Crow Flats, from that time it became Neil's place, I guess. He had it as his place for

The Second Generation

a long time when his wife was still living with him....From when Archie Linklater became his son-in-law, he was with him here. Steamboat and his wife stayed with him here. He had this place for a long time. When we came around here, there were signs of all that but it's grown over with brush. Well, that's how the land is.

I will talk about Neil. This is where he came to the river.[4] He had strong dogs. They pulled on the bare ground. Really! It wasn't hard for them. They hauled loads of stuff ahead to the river. Muskrat skins are heavy, too. Around here in Crow Flats, some families would get thousands of muskrats, 1,500 muskrats, 900 muskrats, 1,900 muskrats. They killed that many muskrats, all the way [through Crow Flats]. Pete Lord, he's the one that killed 3,000 muskrats a year in the springtime, in March....Schaeffer taught him how to trap. That's how all the people lived, by trapping.

Even so, they never killed that much. The people lived off Crow Flats. There was lots of everything: caribou, the birds were noisy singing all over the land, all kinds of them. Now, here, I just hear one small bird. When we came in the spring, we saw seagulls flying up high in Crow Flats. It started to warm up. Ah gee, it really sounded good! All over the birds were singing; the old squaw ducks too, on the lakes....

At Black Fox [Creek], close to the lakes, [Victor] Peterson [Sr.] had a house there. There he raised his children....Peterson was a good man. He liked people. In those days, when the people came to *Van Tat*, there wasn't much food. Sometimes the dogs were hungry before the muskrats came out on the ice. He gave out fish for dog food. He really helped the people, Peterson. After he raised his children, he died. He was a Dane.

After that it was time to stop trapping down this way.[5] People lived all over, to the mountains, all along [the river]. There are lots of lakes on this side, too....This river is really long.[6] Julia McDonald [wife of Archdeacon McDonald] worked as hard as a man for her livelihood, trapping. In the winter, they trapped up this way from Old Crow for fox, mink, and that....Down at Rampart House, Thomas, David Njootli, Paul Ben [Kassi], all those people trapped far up in *Van Tat*. In those days, the Eskimos trapped for muskrat at the head of Crow River. Across from Old Crow, [is] marten country: in 1936, there were no marten. They cleaned them all out. The people lived off them.

That was how the people lived off the land around here. They made it, you know. The last year Joe [Netro] had a store, all the people living in *Van Tat* killed 55,000 muskrats. Joe gave credit for all that. When we trapped for muskrats, [and] winter trapping, Joe billed up [credit was repaid]. Not only Joe, [traders] Jim Jackson and Harry Healy, [extended credit for] what [people] needed to go trapping muskrats. After that they paid them back. This is the way the people lived. You wouldn't see money in our pockets. We only lived off the land.

Over to Fort McPherson [Northwest Territories] and up farther to Dawson, they trapped and lived off the land....In the springtime, in March was muskrat trapping....Only in the summer did they go to Fort Yukon to see their relatives. This is how it was....I made a canvas boat, way up there....One time my wife and I stayed here...with Norman. He paddled with me up to that point and I split the logs apart. Joseph was with us, too. He split them apart while I brought dry wood for the cross-pieces inside. In six hours' time I landed a canvas boat down here. That was how all the people lived up this way. They made canvas boats just like scows. After that, they paddled down. It's a long way. Somebody was at the back with a paddle [to steer]. When it came time to camp, they camped. There were lots of dogs in the boat.

From here [it took] about three days [to go to Old Crow with canvas boats] I guess. From way across at Potato Creek, it took one week. My father used to do it.

(CHARLIE THOMAS, *Van Tat*, June 10, 2001, VG2001-2-20:005-145, Gwich'in)

People from Distant Locales Gathered at *Van Tat*

When I was a child, there was a lot of fish in Fort McPherson. I was born over there, when they went over....They brought me here [Driftwood Village]. I'm Teetl'it Gwich'in; [but] I was raised here. I call this my home. When I was growing up...they went to *Than Natha'aii* [Lone Mountain] after New Year's for meat. Ah, they dried lots of meat. In those days there were no freezers; whatever meat they got, it was all dried.

After that, the people would go to *Van Tat*. It was really nice around my father's country. People also stayed around Schaeffer Creek, Schaeffer Lake, and upstream [north, northwest]. Dogs were always barking and we heard gun shots. When there was a crust [on the snow], dog teams were always coming to camps. They had feasts together; I remember that.

As children, we played outside, a game called *yuu, yuu*.[7] That's the only game we knew. We really liked playing outdoors. Meanwhile, inside the tents they would eat good. I guess we were happy outside playing *yuu, yuu*.

In *Daii* [springtime] they make canvas boats. Before those canvas boats, they used to come down with rafts. I never saw that. After the

Elder Lydia Thomas demonstrating a deadfall trap for ground squirrels at K'ohdàkna'òok'ii (Top of the Hill Mountain), 2000.

[Shirleen Smith ©VGFN (VG2001-6-238)]

Page 171: Charlie Peter Charlie, former chief and recipient of the Order of Canada, building a boat.

[Canadian Museum of Civilization, photo Father Jean-Marie Mouchet S2004-1412]

canvas boats were made...everyone would gather on the riverbanks by their camps, waiting for each other. Together they all came down [the Crow River]. When they came to the canyon, they got out of the boats and made a big [church] service. Then they continued on down. In those days the canyon was very dangerous. There was swift water. From there on it was good; there were no big waves. I remember that. Now I am older, [this is] what I remember.

(LYDIA THOMAS, August 7, 2000, VG2000-4-19:082–108, Gwich'in)

Looking After the Land
How People Organized Their Work and Chose Their Leaders

My father told me about times people lived in Rampart House in 1926. The late Peter Charlie, Old Daniel [Fredson] were some I was acquainted with....Back then they did not know or use the word "chief." They don't know about chiefs [only the] head of people or well-to-do person, is all. Whoever will be the leader is decided in a group, somewhat like a meeting to discuss matters. They [would] meet, discuss and decide on a qualified person. Then the person is claimed to be head of his people. Also a second person, next in charge is chosen. They are the boss. How they live on the land, how they handle food, how they hunt, how they care for themselves, that is the way they looked after it.

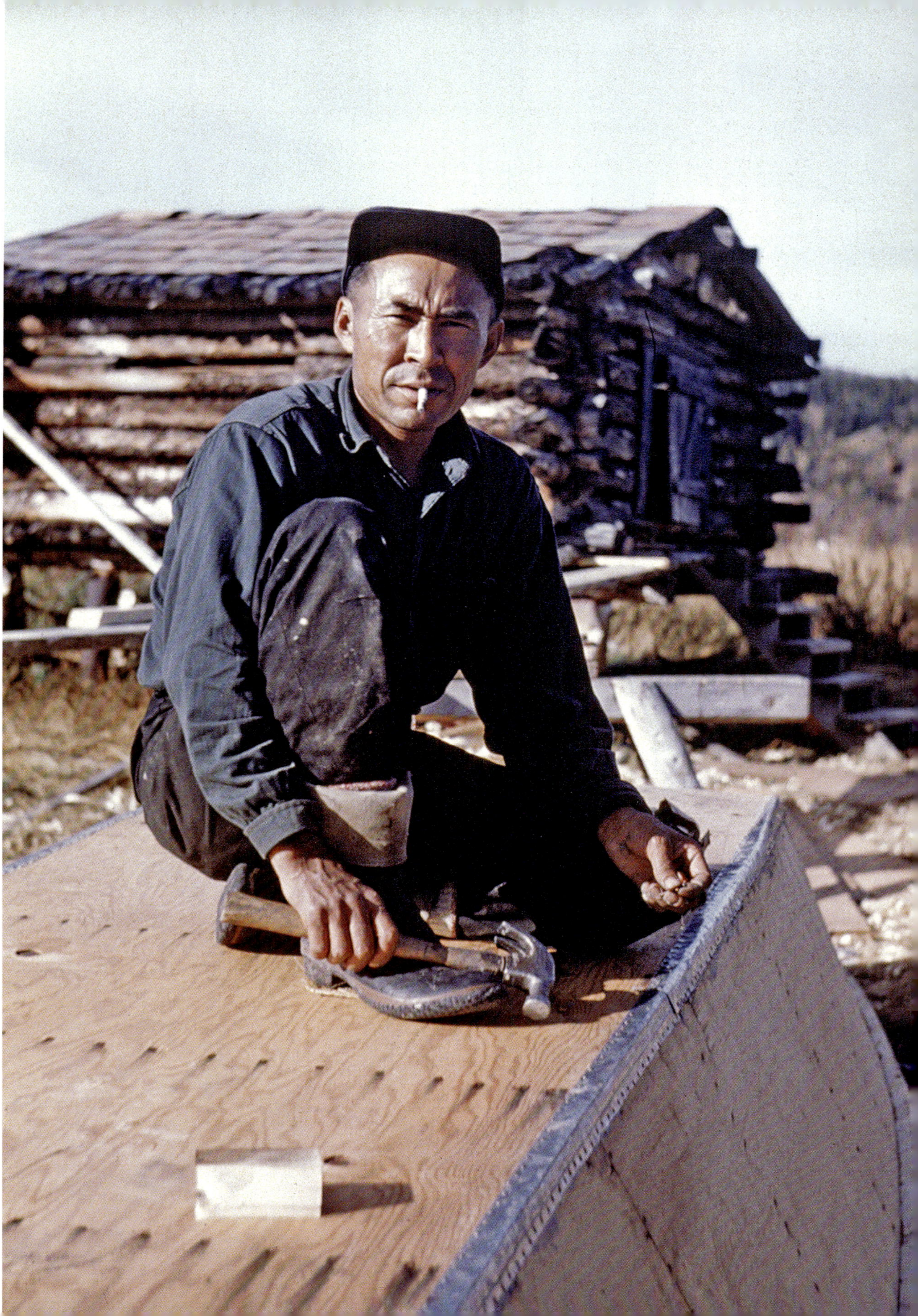

It is the same since 1930, Old Chief [Peter Moses]. My father [Joe Kyikavichik] was told he will be leader and they appointed him. Second was Moses [Tizya]. They were head of the people. Later on Old Chief became chief, my father left and the people told [Old Chief] he will take his place. Moses Tizya was told he will work with the chief [Peter Moses]. You see? That's the way.

Later on they started making Xs. That was on account of Corporal Kirk. Since then it was established that the leader of the people is called chief. They did not know chief before that. They established councillors, too: second, third, and fourth. They looked after this land, like the old way. Long before Christmas, they held a meeting with the chief and discussed how people will work for themselves. At that meeting, everyone told each other where they are going, how long they will be gone, each in a different direction. Back in those days supplies were hard to come by. They went out on their trapline with what little they could get from the store, taking a chance, hoping to harvest fur and wildlife. They explained this at the meeting.

Trappers on the land know where others are. That way if someone gets stuck, [having difficult times] others can help out. Also if a trapper happens upon some caribou and shoots them, if others hear this then they would gather. When all the trappers gather back home, they buy goods with the fur they harvested and contribute to a collection for celebrating Christmas and New Year. This practice still goes on; it was a long time ago that it started.

(JOHN JOE KYIKAVICHIK, March 12, 1993, VG1997-6-7:106-148, Gwich'in)

Drying Meat

In the winter, we stayed all over for food. [In the summer,] we only dried meat, that's all. At that time they didn't have [cellars]....In the springtime, we stayed in *Van Tat*, that's about all. In those days we would never stay in Old Crow. In the summertime and fall time we stayed at fish camps and dried fish. In the winter, too, we went around after the caribou, we dried meat. With that we went to *Van Tat*....Before summer, we made only dried meat. We dried everything. In the spring, we dried lots of muskrats, too. That was for dog feed in the summer. Oh, we did lots of work.

(MARY NETRO, February 20, 1997, VG1997-8-6:050-058, Gwich'in)

Trapping, Hunting, Trading, and Village Areas

Prior to the availability of canvas-wall tents, Van Tat Gwich'in used round "moss houses" and caribou-skin tents and moved throughout their traditional lands. During the lifetime of the second generation of elders in the oral history collection, families continued to travel for hunting and trapping, use portable dwellings (canvas-wall tents and portable stoves), as well as building more enduring log cabins in some of the areas where they previously had camps. Individual cabins (usually with outbuildings), as well as aggregations known as villages, were built around the 1920s and onward, some in association with trading establishments (such as at Rampart House), while others were residential centres that attracted traders only for brief durations. The ruins of some of these buildings are visible into the early 2000s. In some instances, such as at Driftwood Village, cabins were dismantled and moved so no ruins are reported at the site. In other locations, people continue to use cabins or have built new ones, for example at Whitestone Village and a variety of family cabins in Crow Flats and along the Porcupine River. Some villages were built around trading posts, such as at Rampart House. At others, the locale was a long-time habitation and the traders came later (for example at LaPierre House), or the trading was secondary and temporary (such as at Whitestone Village). In other trading centres, such as Fort Yukon, Fort McPherson, and Herschel Island, Van Tat Gwich'in made periodic visits but did not maintain residences. In any case, hunting, trapping, and trading were organized into a seasonal rhythm based on availability of game, furs, and traders' supplies. In later years, the traders also provided wage income, mostly in transportation: packing goods from distant suppliers, working on steamboats, and cutting wood for steamboat fuel.

Elders related their experiences at the various village, cabin, and camp locations, and the history of people and events at these places. They described the most important areas for Van Tat Gwich'in in the 20th century: *Van Tat*; the mountains north of *Van Tat*; up the Porcupine River at its confluence with the Driftwood River, Salmon Cache, the Bell River-LaPierre House area, Johnson Creek Village and the Whitestone Village area, including Bear Cave Mountain and the Miner River to the present Dempster Highway area; down the Porcupine River at Bluefish River and the Rampart House area; the lakes area south of the Porcupine River from Old Crow; and, finally, the Old Crow region, including the ancient caribou hunting places at *Tl'oo K'at* and Caribou Lookout.

Van Tat Gwich'in traditional lands are extensive. They are divided here into the central Old Crow-*Van Tat* region, the mountainous areas surrounding *Van Tat* (mainly to the north and west), the territory up the Porcupine River from Old Crow (to the east and south), and the region downriver from

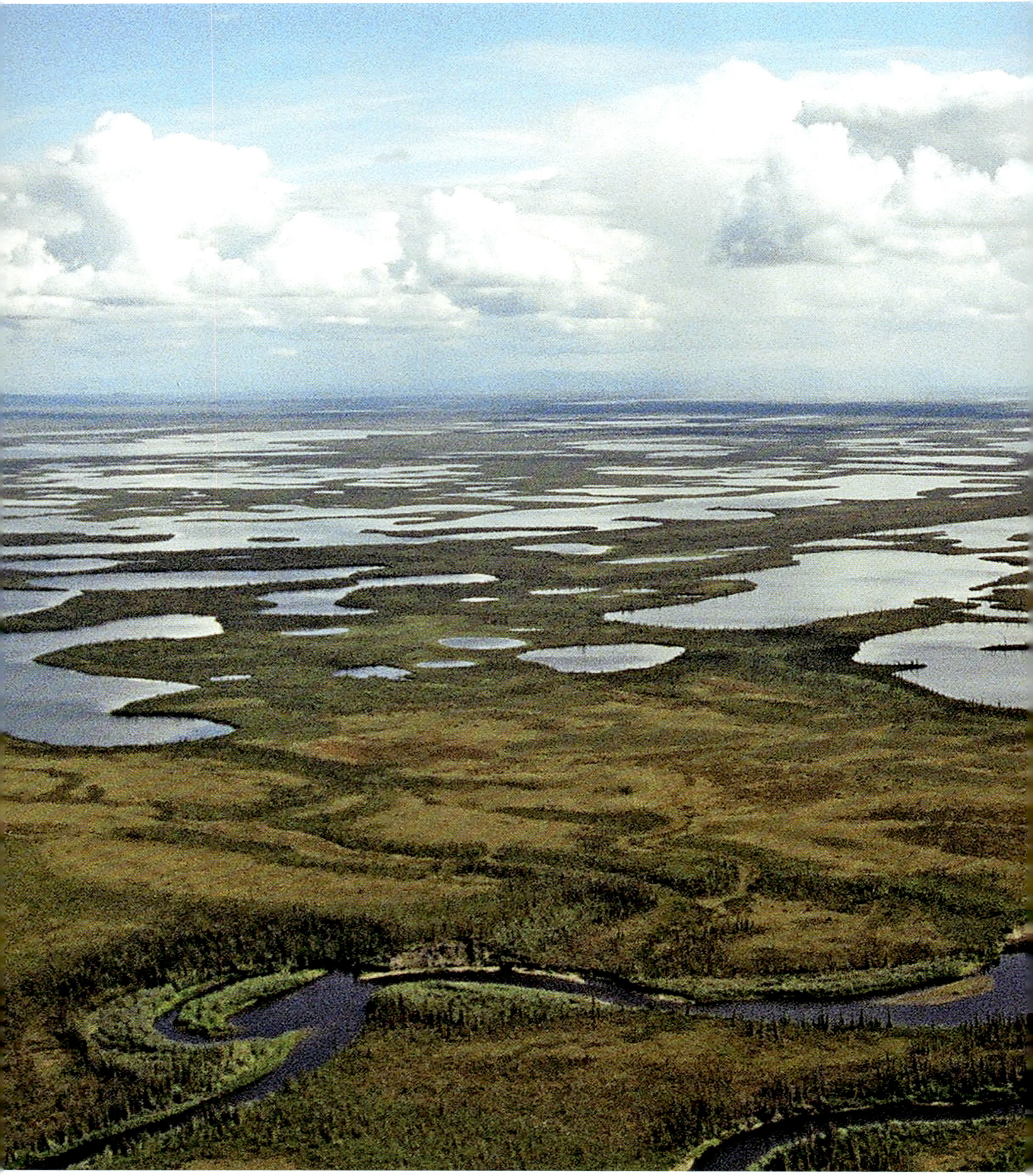

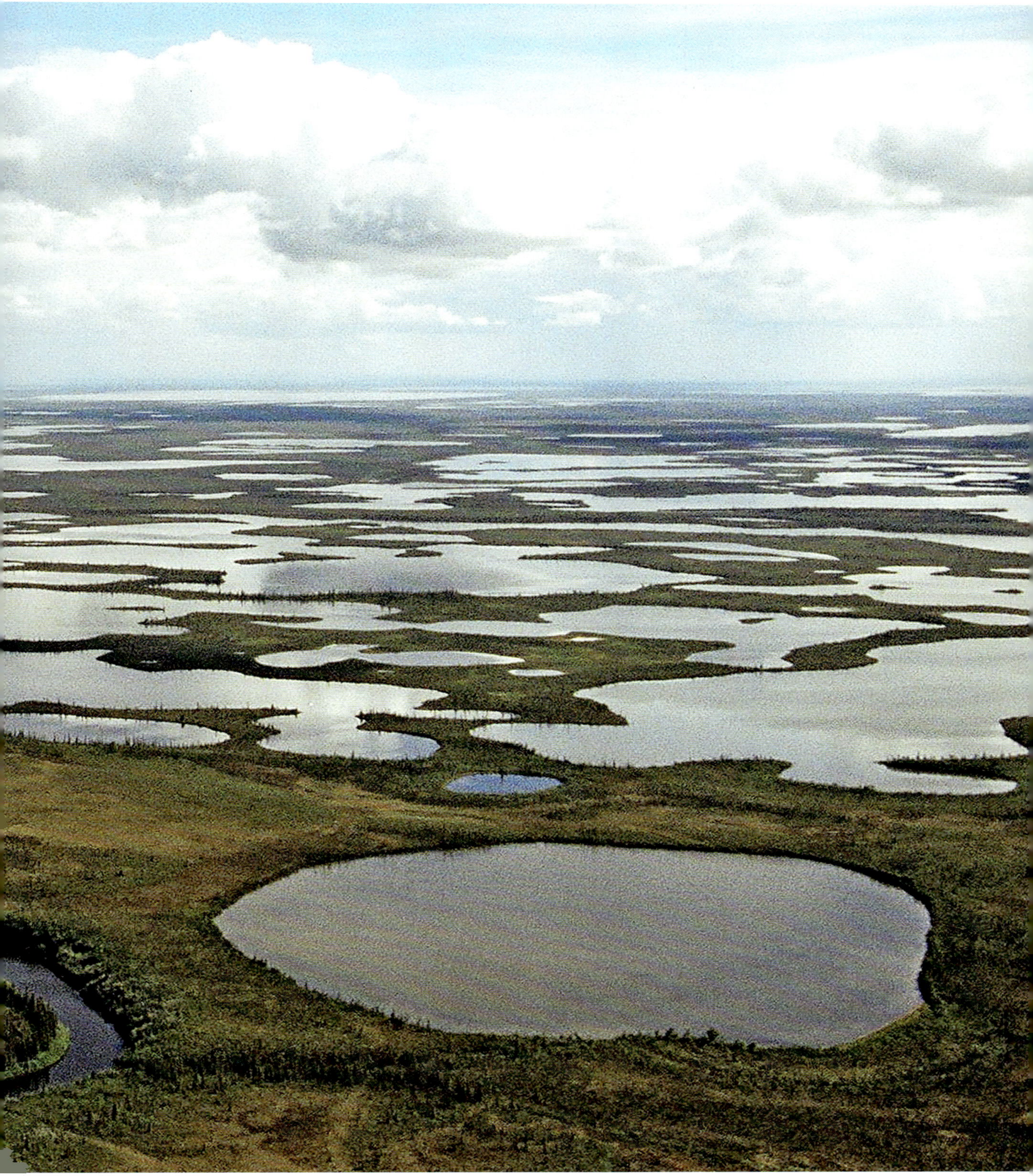

Pages 174–175: Van Tat
(Crow Flats) and Chyahnjik
(Crow River), 2005.
[Shirleen Smith ©VGFN 2005]

Old Crow (west). Van Tat Gwich'in also travelled to more far-flung locations, such as Herschel Island, Fort Yukon, and Fort McPherson.

The Old Crow-*Van Tat* (Crow Flats) Area

Van Tat (Crow Flats) remains literally and symbolically central in Van Tat Gwich'in geography, identity, and history, and it is from this area that they take their name.[8] Elders speak of the importance of the myriad lakes north of the Porcupine River, how the Crow River meanders through these lakes, and the wealth of food and furs available there. Like the generations before them, second-generation elders identify the strategic importance of *Van Tat* in times of starvation. By the end of the 20th century, the collapse of the fur trade and establishment of a more centralized village life in Old Crow meant that all the families didn't spend every spring in *Van Tat* as they did up to the 1980s. Yet Gwich'in still believe that *Van Tat* will see them through hard times yet to come.

Because of its abundance, *Van Tat* was important both in times of plenty and scarcity. People hunted, trapped, and fished there, and elders recall travelling back and forth between the Porcupine River and *Van Tat*. The many landmarks in *Van Tat* are associated with well-remembered history, echoing the stories of the previous generations, yet told in the distinctive manner of this generation. John Joe Kyikavichik, Charlie Thomas, Alfred Charlie, and Ellen Bruce recalled these stories and added to them their own experiences of living, working, and travelling in *Van Tat*.

Van Tat in Time of Need

> When there were no muskrats long ago, I'll talk about that time....1934-35, there was no [musk]rats in *Van Tat* [Crow Flats] and I stayed with my father at Driftwood Creek. Day and night people were going up to the headwaters....At LaPierre House, there's a little flat there, and that's where they were going for beaver at that time when there were no [musk]rats. When it was hard times people would come here to *Van Tat* for small animals. There were lots of rabbits and ducks, too. That's why people would come here to *Van Tat*. Fish, they made...fish traps and put those in the water and fished. That is the way our elders made their living long ago. From not that long ago, we also did that ourselves.
>
> Now in recent times, people don't go out to *Van Tat*. We come up with boats sometimes. Really, we don't know how it will be in the

176   PEOPLE OF THE LAKES

Elders John Joe Kyikavichik, Alfred Charlie, Mary Kassi, Dick Nukon, and Donald Frost on Chyahnjik (Crow River), 2001.

[Shirleen Smith ©VGFN (VG2001-6-370)]

future. In 10 years, 20 years, from now, people may not come back here to *Van Tat*.

(JOHN JOE KYIKAVICHIK, *Van Tat*, June 11, 2001, VG2001-2-31:079-086, Gwich'in)

Van Tat in Abundance

It's like this: that's why from the beginning of time, they took the kids around [on the land]. It would be a big help. Long ago, our fathers told us all this. They went with us children on this land; we travelled all around. That's how we know the land. They used to kill lots of caribou around here [Van Tat]...[and] lots of muskrats. My father, my mother, too, my grandmother stayed...even she killed lots of muskrats. That's how many muskrats there were.

In 1946, when I first got married, I used to stay around here. At that time, there were lots of muskrats. Me and my wife travelled all over around here. [We shot a hundred] muskrats. Then we went home.... The next day, we went back again...and there was the same amount of muskrats. That's how many muskrats there were. After that, in 1949, '48, I stayed with my inlaws. Even around that place, there were many muskrats. There were also lots of people. Even with that many people, some got a thousand, 1,500. That's how many muskrats there were in those days....

But now there's not very many muskrats around here. Now, there's still lots of ice [on the lakes] but in different places, we saw only about four muskrats. I wonder how it will be in the future. In the future, how our children are going to be, nobody knows....

From there people would go in all different directions to the different lakes. There were lots of people. In May on hard ice, they would [visit]. They would have a good time. Way over there is a long lake.... In 1930 Peter Moses sold a little stuff here. He would go down through that valley to Shingle Point for trade goods. From here he would go to Fort Yukon...[to get trade goods]. That's how hard our elders long ago worked so that people could live well.

Down that way the white man lived, too; his house was down there. Now it's fallen down; that was in 1940....[At] Black Fox [Creek], Peterson [Victor Peterson Sr.], they called him, raised his children. Long ago, the white people lived around here on the land.

(JOHN JOE KYIKAVICHIK, Crow Flats, June 11, 2001,
VG2001-2-31:020-070, Gwich'in)

Land and Travel Between *Van Tat* and the Porcupine River

This creek is called King Edward Creek; in Gwich'in it's called *Tsii'ideh Njik*. Way up there, that mountain is called King Edward Ridge in English. In the Gwich'in language, it's called *Tsii'ideh*. The mountain down below there, it's a high mountain, in Gwich'in it's called *Ch'anchàł*. In English it's called King Edward Mountain. There, my grandfather *Deetru'*, it was his country. At *Ch'anchàł*, he trapped muskrats. Then he would go down to Rampart House with dog packs. Old Donald [Fredson] used to do that, too. He stayed below King Edward Mountain with Annie [Fredson] for muskrat hunting. She had a young girl and all of them went down the mountains with dog packs. They came into [the Crow] River [here].

I stayed with grandfather Elias [Kwatlatyi] one time on the other side of King Edward Ridge. It's a long way to here overland from the top of King Edward Ridge. When dogs were good, we hauled our stuff to the river with dogs; dogs were strong then. It was nothing for them on bare ground. I took loads ahead halfway. At that time my wife was living with me. We had not adopted Willie and Florence yet. We got to the river then the next night I went back for more stuff with the dogs. It's a long way overland. At that time, the people living around Schaeffer Lake landed here when they were coming downriver. I still had to make a boat. Grandfather Elias made a boat and then I did, too. Then we pushed out and it was really good.

Schaeffer Mountain, it's called, from here going downriver, it teased us....On the way, it's in front, next thing it's behind you.[9] Then way down by Crow Mountain, beside it is [a mountain] called *Gwak'àn Choo* [Burnt Hill]. Below that is Second Mountain.[10] Long ago, there were stories about the people grieving....When some of the people died, their hair was long....They burnt up on Second Mountain. That's why it's called *Chyah Ddhàa*. Their hair was long; it's called *chyah* in the Gwich'in language.

(CHARLIE THOMAS, King Edward Creek, June 9, 2001,
VG2001-2-15:005-045, Gwich'in)

Long History at Black Fox Creek in *Van Tat*

What I know, what I hear, I'll tell you about that. You want to learn everything, that's why you're taking the elders around here. It's really good that's being done. It's for our children and our grandchildren in the future. They will hear this and they'll use it. That's why when you tell me to come to places like this, I obey you. People would not come around here. Me, I know a little about this place so I will sit here with you.

You see the houses here? A long time ago, a man named John Tizya made a place here. He raised his family. Finally his children were married. They all stayed with him. So really this little place has been used by one family from long ago....

John Tizya really was an Elder. I remember him when I was a child. He raised his children here. They lived here in the winter and trapped. They would go way back through Pete's [Lord] country over to Timber Hill. All the way back, where they call *Dzan Ehłai'* they trapped for mink and fox. They really lived well in winter. In the summer and the fall, they made fish traps here at Black Fox [Creek]. Then in the fall the caribou came back [and] passed by here. They killed caribou, too. So then they did that during the winter.

Then in the spring, there's a big lake located on the riverbank across there called *Sheihtsoondii*. Way back there...there's a lake. Down to Pete's country, too, they trapped and hunted muskrats around there. Really right to underneath the mountain where they call *Pelly K'oo*, all around there....Then after that Peterson came here from Herschel Island. He married [Peter Moses's] daughter Alice....He taught his children to live in the bush well....

Across this river, Cadzow had arrived at Rampart House. They met long afterwards. Fox pelts were a good price. They sold for lots so he asked the people to get him live foxes, so they did that for him....[A man named] John Niliikakti' took two black foxes to him. He killed two black fox so Cadzow called him John Blackfox. He lived around here with the Tizyas. This river is named after him, Blackfox. John Blackfox and John Tizya lived here together. This river takes their name, John Niliikakti' name. So really long ago, the Van Tat Gwich'in around here, when they used to live without the white man, they're from that time: John Tizya, John Niliikakti'....

That story is long. Then, who would know? Around Old Crow, not one person knows. Andrew Tizya was raised around here, Johnny Ross, too. Even they don't know this kind of big story about around here. But me, Peter Moses told me stories about how people lived around here. That's why I come here now and that's what I talk about. I never saw it, that's what I mean.

Across those mountains there, back there, through Black Fox [Creek] and way back there by the mountains, that *Ch'izin* had a caribou fence. People really made use of it. There are stories about all of them. On all those mountains across there, there were caribou fences. Not one caribou fence: when they talked about them, they're not all the same.

(ALFRED CHARLIE, Black Fox Creek, June 24, 2001,
VG2001-2-44:006-175, Gwich'in)

Moving Back and Forth to *Van Tat*

Ah, my grandchildren, we really came through hard times. After New Year's, they moved to those mountains [and] dried meat...in January, February, and March. Then it was Easter, after that, so they moved to *Van Tat* [Crow Flats] with dog teams. The people took their stuff ahead, then they came back again the next day. Finally, some of them, their camps were a long ways away. Us, we camped three nights before we got to our campsite. All that is hard work. We trapped muskrats and then on June 15th, they finished everything. Then they all made canvas boats. They paddled down the long river; there was lots of mosquitoes. When the wind blew, we stopped and landed the boats. It was really nice, but it was bad [too]. In the end they landed here and cooked and danced, really nice! We came down slowly but we never thought of it that way....

Running the rapids on Chyahnjik *(Crow River), 2001.*
[Shirleen Smith ©VGFN (VG2001-6-166)]

They did this [the same, year after year]. How many times, my clothes, my dirty clothes, I was going to wash in a big tub [so] I hauled water. I wonder where my strength is now. Now, I should just sit in a chair but I still work for myself.

(ELLEN BRUCE, March 12, 1997, VG1997-8-07:305-325, Gwich'in)

Van Tat to Rampart House, 1926–86

Yeah. I'll talk with you. Before that I want to say thank you. Thank you, my people. Because of you, the last time I stayed here was in 1986, but I came back in 2001. For that I am happy. I say thank you to God for that.

People lived around here long ago. When the Alaska people came into *Van Tat*, Old Archie [Linklater] had all his children living with him. Clara Tizya was a young girl at that time. I was single. Archie and Charlie Linklater and another two little brothers had a camp here, around 1926. Some Fort Yukon people stayed with them. There were lots of *Ch'ineekaii* [Inuvialuit or Inuit] around there at that time. All the people who stayed there would go to town on hard snow. They knew my father, that's why they came around here.

Around [19]26, there were lots of muskrats all over. My father's place was located on the other side [of Crow River], way across at Potato Creek. That was his muskratting place. For five years, I had this for my muskratting place. I stayed alone. My one dog was tied over

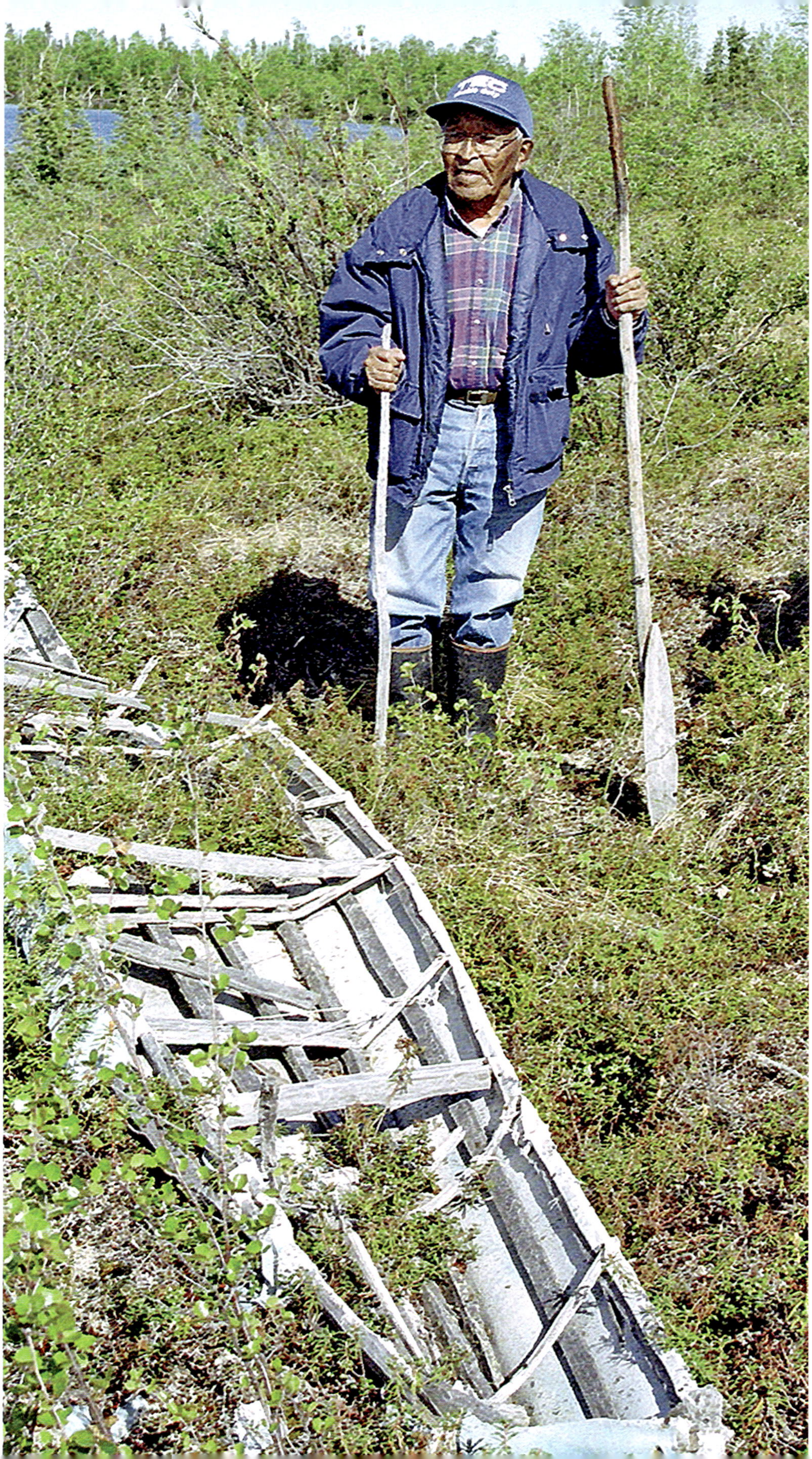

Elder Charlie Thomas and the remains of his canoe at his camp in Van Tat *(Crow flats), 2001.*

[Shirleen Smith ©VGFN (VG2001-6-211)]

there. I opened the radio for him. It was loud; at 1:00 AM it signed off. That kept him company while I paddled around all night shooting muskrats. That's what I did.

Long ago, our parents, all of them, made their living around here. After them, I stayed around here. This is the story I have about it.

You see those mountains down there? Long ago, our parents and their elders before them, all [went there] for caribou and ptarmigan. In the spring the ground squirrels would come out, too. They lived on those. At that time there were lots of people in *Van Tat*. King Edward Mountain, it's called *Ch'anchàł*. Up that way is the trail to Rampart House; they went over that and from there they separated and went different ways....

People were all over. That mountain across there, Timber Mountain; it's called *Dzan Ehłai'* [muskrat caught in a trap] in the Gwich'in language. All around there were people: way down to Pete Lord's country, down at John Moses's place...all down that way were people. Around 1926, after that...for seven year there were no muskrats. Then seven years later there were muskrats again. [Seven year cycle.]...That's what the people lived off.

Way down another 35 miles below Rampart House, there was another village called Old Rampart. My father trapped on the other side of the mountains from there. I was 16 years old when I first started trapping. He taught me how to do all kinds of work....That is how it was long ago.

Down that way...is a lake, and below that is the [Crow] River....When there were boats from here, the plane would fly in and pick us up. We quit [hunting muskrats] and all over *Van Tat*, we waited for the plane, at that time, before 1986. Ah, all the people died off and in the meantime, the white trappers lived around here....

That [hill] is called Potato Hill in English. In Gwich'in it's called *Diniizhòo*.[11] Long ago, around the time of the people who lived before our parents, they say...they gathered on it.

That's how...I [trapped and hunted] muskrats. I had it for a muskrat lake. I wonder how the muskrats are now.

(CHARLIE THOMAS, *Van Tat*, June 22, 2001, VG2001-2-37:008-086, Gwich'in)

The Old Crow Area

I remember sometimes on *Chuuts'aii Nàlk'at* [Crow Mountain] when the caribou came back there, the people would move up. They dried meat. They used dog packs and brought the meat down before winter. In the fall before freeze-up, they set fishnets. They fished for dog salmon and dried it. With that, they went in all directions before Christmas and trapped. Just before Christmas, they moved in and danced. The chief made a feast, and they celebrated New Year's and danced. That was how they had fun. There was nothing wrong in those days. Then, everything was a bit hard, what the people went through, I remember.

In those days, they didn't know about Christmas trees. The minister from Mayo, Julius Kendi was his name, when he first came here, he introduced it to us and we've used it ever since....Before that, when they visited each other in the village, they give each other little presents. They never saw oranges; they only got fresh stuff once a year.

(JOHN JOE KYIKAVICHIK, February 18, 1980, VG2000-8-25:020-038, Gwich'in)

The Mountains Surrounding *Van Tat* (Crow Flats)

Van Tat is a great low bowl of lakes, creeks, and marshland surrounded by mountains and high country on all sides but the southeast, where no major hills intervene between it and the Porcupine River. A number of hills directly overlook *Van Tat* and were important gathering places, vistas, hunting areas, and landmarks along the well-frequented trails. The mountains were important for a number of reasons. People only lived in *Van Tat* in certain seasons (spring muskrat season and when fish were running in spring and summer) and moved to the higher country of the surrounding mountains at other times to hunt caribou and other small and large animals, as well as to gather and travel together along the trails.

Andrew Tizya described one of the most notable landmarks, *Ch'anchàł* or King Edward Mountain. This mountain borders *Van Tat* to the southwest and features a high knob with a long ridge that people crossed on their way from the Porcupine River to *Van Tat* on the main trail known as *Geenu*. It is the northernmost of the series of three mountains along the route, *Ch'anchàł*, *Chyah Ddhàa* or Second Mountain, and *Chuuts'aii Nàlk'at* or Crow Mountain at the confluence of the Porcupine and Crow rivers, overlooking Old Crow. Andrew Tizya recounted the place of *Ch'anchàł* in history, as well as its resources and their management. Mary Kassi spoke of how people lived on *Ch'anchàł*, as well as about *Diniizhòo*, also known as *Tsii'in' Ddhàa*, and in English as Game Mountain or, on maps, Potato Hill. This is the next farthest north, to the west of *Van Tat* adjacent to the U.S.-Canada border. Its central location for all western Gwich'in and its proximity both to *Van Tat* and caribou hunting areas made it a significant gathering place. Hannah Netro noted how *Diniizhòo* was situated with respect to *Tl'oo K'at*, Thomas Creek Caribou Fence, and the trade route to Herschel Island in the Arctic Ocean. Charlie Peter Charlie included *Diniizhòo* along with *Geegoo*, another

Elder Andrew Tizya on Nohddhàa, *2001.*

[Shirleen Smith ©VGFN (VG2001-6-699)]

mountain at the head of *Chyahnjik* (Crow River), among the four most important Gwich'in gathering places.

Ch'anchàl
King Edward Mountain Overlooking Van Tat

Long ago, how our grandfathers lived, I'll tell you about that. Long ago, squirrels, rabbits, muskrats, porcupines, all kinds [of small animals], they gathered together. Under King Edward Mountain, over in Crow Flats side, [people] had camps. There were fish traps—[fish] came from Schaeffer Creek....Our grandfathers lived on the fish they caught in them.

[At King Edward Mountain] long ago, [my grandfather Tizya told me] a lot of people...starved. No food, too many [people] with them. One moose, you killed, even [that] didn't last long. Well, that way people all got stuck without food in those days.

[A lot of people gathered at] King Edward Mountain [because] the grizzly and black bears had lots of dens around here....They didn't kill all of them, maybe sometimes two grizzly bears or two black bears. They kept it for the winter months. The next winter, the cubs were killed and so on. This is a good story....If they killed all of them at one time, they would not have food. That is how they looked after their land.

The Second Generation 185

They gathered at Crow River and at Schaeffer Creek in the winter. They had camps there, mostly at the mouth of Schaeffer Creek. Yeah, good. Lots of people, lots of rabbits and, right there, beaver and muskrat, too. Especially fish, lots of fish all over. Fish traps; only us, we had fish traps that way, you know. [We] travelled around to all different places. [There was] only one place there with lots of fish in the lake. So that way we lived, I remember. I stayed at a fish trap and fished, one year, too.

Ah, lots of people died [on top of this mountain] they said; about million, more [than a] million, I guess. That's what my grandfather told us. He saw it, too. He said when they stopped breathing, [they] just piled them up. That's the way we buried them. Well, in those days, [there were] no axes or anything so [it was] really tough living, you know. [That happened a] long, long time ago. My grandfather Tizya said he was real young [when it] happened; he said he saw it, too.

A lot of caribou came around here. Really, a lot of caribou came around. Today it's not like that. Even I remember...wherever we went, there was always lots of caribou. Today there's nothing.

[They travelled this country]...mostly with dog packs....Winter, they stayed in one place. So they lived that way. Summer, that's the time they moved around lots. Well, there were no tents in them days, hah. They had caribou skin tents, no stoves. All that way, they said [it was] easy to move around. But us, not easy for us. That's right.

(ANDREW TIZYA, *Ch'anchàł*, August 2, 2000, VG2000-4-16:007-069, Gwich'in and English)

Diniizhòo (or *Tsii'in' Ddhàa*), Game Mountain (Potato Hill)

Tsii'in' Ddhàa, *Diniizhòo* they call it but I don't know the name in English. They only call it *Diniizhòo* [or] *Tsii'in' Ddhàa*.

They came from all over. From...Arctic Village [Alaska], Fort McPherson [Northwest Territories], and Arctic Red [now Tsiigehtchic, Northwest Territories]...and Van Tat Gwich'in people. All them, [Fort Yukon people] too, from Rampart House. Long ago, before we were born, in those days they all gathered here, they said.

All around here caribou skin tents were set up, they said....There were lots of people. They came here and worked for their meat. In July ...they prepared all their meat, pemmican, dried meat, even dried fish; everything, even bone grease. They put that all together and fed everybody. Then they played, they said.

Diniizhòo *(Potato Hill/ Game Mountain)* overlooking northwestern Van Tat *(Crow Flats)*, 2004.

[Shirleen Smith ©VGFN (VG2004-6-134)]

[They made games with] everything, drums, long-ago games, [from] anything, they made games....They said they even danced: maybe they jigged. The round bone on the caribou leg, they twirled it. *Nilaiizruk* too, this is the stick pull: two people pull with it....This was a favourite game, they said. Then a round, white hide, on it they put caribou hoofs, which they tried to catch...That's the kind of games they played.

Then they...tied something, maybe your hat, kerchief, anything. Whoever owns it...they say, "What are you going to do for this?" They say [the owner must] do it, it doesn't matter what, even if it's bad, that game [*Neeveede'gooya'*].

They came here only in the summer and fall time, before it got cold. In the summer, they picked berries all around here. In the evening they played games, right on top here, for everything, ducks.

Yes, [they knew they were coming here beforehand]. From all over, from far away they travelled. The leader, what we call chief now, he went among them. In early morning he had a big meeting with all the people and told them, "We are going to do this," and he was to be obeyed. They came here with dog packs, they said....

They came in May, in the springtime when it was melting, on little snow, with dogs and caribou leg toboggans....They dried meat, and

The Second Generation

played games in July....They tanned moose and caribou hides. They made lots of things. They put porcupine quills [decoration] on tanned skin dresses, nice ones. They also tanned caribou hide with the fur left on for blankets. Around the edges, they sewed *jitsoo hah nagankai'* [thin, tanned, caribou hide]. They piled it, they said...and the best would win. Sometimes they just shared, gave it to people [as a] present, good caribou skin. Sometimes a big moose skin, they're easy to tan, even the white ones. They made lots of caribou skin mukluks, caribou mitts, animal hats, that kind of thing. They made a big pile afterward, when they're going to leave, and gave it to each other.

They really made use of this land. All the people who lived long ago, before our parents, their grandmothers, they all came here. All over this land. Arctic Red [Tsiigehtchic], in 1938 my father went there for meat. One old woman about 100 years old said, "That the man from Old Crow, he's to come see me." He went to her and she took his hand, she's poor, 100 years old. "My grandchild, that *Diniizhòo* [Game Mountain], is it still there?" she asked him...."Grandmother, it's still there; it won't go anywhere. Behind there is my country. It's always there. We always see it," he told her. The poor old lady just yelled out crying. He just about cried himself, it was so good.

When we were young, we had good times on [Game Mountain]. They even got married there, they said. There are lots of stories of this place. It's valuable, this mountain. Everybody knows about it....

Yes, my grandmothers all told me about [this place]. Long ago, all my grandmothers, grandfather *Shitsii Ch'eeghwal*, [my grandfather *Ch'eeghwal*[12]] his children, all his relatives—you know some of them died not long ago. They all travelled around here, they all told me stories. *Anits'u',* ["Oh, my goodness!"] beautiful caribou skin dresses, beaded and sewn with porcupine quills. They came with heavy packs from Fort Yukon. *Anjithitii ik* [anorak parka], you know how Eskimos made them, they did, too. They looked beautiful! New shoes, porcupine quill shoes, they dressed up and danced, they said. They had a good time.

[They stayed here] long, maybe all summer, until fall time when it froze up. Then they all left [for]...a mountain where it's good for caribou. They moved around, long-ago people, that's how they lived. That's what they said about them.

It's lucky that when I was a child, my parents and grandmothers told lots of stories in front of me. They said we have to take care of the land, I know....I always wanted to talk about it. This past fall, people were gathered in the hall and I talked about it so now it's known.

Tl'oo K'at, *2004.*

[Shirleen Smith ©VGFN (VG2004-6-88)]

[Along here were round skin tents, all along here]....They got water [from the lake below], down in the timber, *nan chu' gahtsii*: they made a hole in the ground to get water. Down there, those rocks, they put raw meat under the rocks where it's cold. That's what that is, down there. Way down there, there's a bigger rock piles. Sometimes there's two piles. They pile rocks on the meat. That's what they did a long time ago. That's how they kept their meat fresh.

(MARY KASSI, *Diniizhòo*, August 1, 2000, VG2000-4-12:006-135, Gwich'in)

Diniizhòo

Gathering at Game Mountain

In all my life this the first time I see what they call *Diniizhòo*, Game Mountain. Ah, there's lots of berries around here. I'm happy to come here. My father told me stories, but I was small so I forgot lots of them. I don't know the land. *Diniizhòo*, they always said it's special.

They hunted around here for caribou, all over this big country. In the summer there were lots of caribou, lots of small animals around here. Down there is a big lake; there's a lot of whitefish in it. At the same time, the berries grew and so they were not hungry. They walked all over to places they knew. From there, in fall time, they all went down to *Tl'oo K'at*, when the caribou were crossing [the Porcupine River]. In the summer months, they dried meat....

The Second Generation 189

I'll talk about that time. They dried meat at *Tl'oo K'at* and then went to Rampart House for the summer months. At that time Dan Cadzow had a store there, they said. That's not long ago.

This is really a big country....They say [the *Diniizhòo* area is] close to the ocean. They used to go to Herschel Island with dog packs. They took dried meat and bone grease to sell to the Eskimos. With the money they bought a little groceries. [North of *Diniizhòo*] is Thomas Hill: that is Charlie Thomas's grandfather's [place]. You see how big the mountain is? He made a caribou fence there. When the caribou went in the caribou fence, all those people had meat....

When it got warm, before they moved away from here, they had a feast. They got water from that lake down there. They said it's good water....They played different games, all the games they knew. Today, they don't play them, I mean....They taught their children about everything. They tanned hides, cut meat, made drymeat, all that. That is how they lived long ago....

Around here they killed caribou. They made lots of meat: they didn't leave behind even a small piece, they said. They cleaned everything. They took rocks and made big cellars, deep, way down. They kept meat in there, and they said it didn't spoil. That's really good.

How big this lake [below Game Mountain] is. They cleaned off the snow...and made...hockey sticks with birch trees, they said. The women and children shovelled the snow away and they made the ice really clean. Then the moose...arm, the...round part on it, they said they had that for [a ball]. They played with that, too....Wrestling, too....The women, this side, then the men, they played ball....[They competed to see] who could tan skins the quickest. One woman always tanned skins fastest, they said. Then they [competed making] snowshoes, knitting [them and] everything. They raced each other. That one woman, she always won, they said....

(HANNAH NETRO, *Diniizhòo*, August 1, 2000, VG2000-4-13:017-048; 097-140, Gwich'in)

The Mountains on the Main Trail, *Geenu*, from *Van Tat* (Crow Flats) to the Porcupine River

Long ago our grandfathers and grandmothers travelled all this country around here. It's a beautiful country. There's lots of ground squirrels around here; animals live off them. There was a grizzly bear trail here. In the spring we saw the tracks on the snow. He's after the ground squirrels. He eats those ground squirrels.

Long ago when people lived around here, there's a small creek down there. There's a lot of small creeks amongst these mountains. Sometimes there's a lot of fish in them. That's where they stayed....They made their living like that, even on ground squirrels, everything, caribou, too. Sometimes down the side of the mountain, moose, too....

Long ago in our grandfathers' time, people lived around here. When you are trying to get ground squirrels, they stake a stick on one side, not over top so it won't get scared of the stick....Long ago, when it was difficult to get snares, they used babiche and sinew, moose sinew, braided it and used it to kill ground squirrels.

Our grandfather *Deetru'* (Edward Crow)....Right there, *Geenu* [main trail between Van Tat and the Porcupine River], farther down, he used to live around there. He walked all over and walked to the river all the time. That's why they call that mountain Edward [King Edward Mountain]—I don't know where the King comes from. He was a medicine man.

Rampart House is just down here. People lived around here for berries and caribou meat. They lived all over and dried caribou meat. They killed ground squirrels. People know about this area lots. You see that mountain, it's shaped like a head. That's why they call it *Ch'anchàł*....

Chyah Ddhàa [Second Mountain], long ago people had braided hair, huh....That's why the stones are black. They said all the people burned up on that mountain....They call it *Chyah Ddhàa*: braided hair, it [*chyah*] means....

Lots of our elders and grandfathers lived around here, you know. It's a big country. They went down into *Van Tat* for muskratting by the shore. They said they didn't have traps in those days. They set snares made out of sinew to catch muskrats....Those days...sometimes they made deadfall traps. They said deadfall traps were good for ground squirrels, too. That's how the people lived back then, they lived hard lives.

(MARY KASSI, *Ch'anchàł*, August 2, 2000, VG2000-4-17:009-074, Gwich'in)

The Four Important Gathering Places

I'm going to say it in English: only three or four places, they got lots of caribou [and] killed so much and they stay there till summer, that's how much meat. There's lots of people in [the] gathering. There's only three or four places around here: one of the places is *Vihsraii Ddhàa* [Cody Hill]. It means big mountain, high mountain, and this is one of the places where they have this gathering. And...the people came to this gathering from places like Fort Yukon, Dagoo, Fort McPherson, Van Tat Gwich'in, even from Eagle sometime (but before that nobody heard of Eagle). So this is the main place where people gathered. And another place is *Vi'àltl'ii* and another place in *Van Tat* [Crow Flats] at the head of *Chyahnjik* [Crow River] and it is called *Geegoo*. It means so many people go over and back they make like this. So those kind of places, still today they know where [they are]. Even today, when we go to *Van Tat* the young people and even the kids, they want to see this place called *Geegoo*. This gathering place, they want to know about it and they always ask, "Where is *Geegoo*?" So many people gathering. Not too far from there is this little mountain—it is shaped just like a potato so they call it that name. All those people, boys and girls especially, they all go there and play. White people call it Potato Hill but in my language, they call it *Diniizhòo*. It means big mountain and you tear some of the mountain off and put it somewhere. Aw, good one. Still they know that, they still hear about it. And whoever has heard about it, they ask us about it and we tell them.

(CHARLIE PETER CHARLIE, August 26, 1998, VG2001-13-05:017-075, Gwich'in and English)

Upriver on *Ch'oodèenjik* (Porcupine River)

Driftwood Village, LaPierre House, Johnson Creek Village, and Whitestone Village

Ch'oodèenjik (Porcupine River) is the major waterway linking the western Gwich'in peoples and others to the west, and it ultimately flows into the Yukon River and the Pacific Ocean. Upper *Ch'oodèenjik* is the traditional lands of the Dagoo Gwich'in, now dispersed and living primarily among the Vuntut and Teetl'it Gwich'in of Old Crow and Fort McPherson respectively. In the area, *Ch'oodèenjik* flows from the south, fed by rivers and creeks draining the Richardson Mountains to the east and the Nahoni and Keele ranges to the west. The high country of the upper Porcupine is the home to moose, fine fur-bearers, beaver, caribou on their winter ranges in some locations, grizzly bears, and remote salmon runs. Gwich'in—Dagoo, Vuntut, and others—long used the area and established villages on some of the tributary rivers, such as Driftwood Village, Johnson Creek Village, and Whitestone Village. For a time, traders had stores at the latter two locations, as well as at LaPierre House on the Bell River. Ultimately, in the mid-20th century, upper *Ch'oodèenjik* was "cleaned out" of furbearers and food species, due to great trapping pressure. Dick Nukon recorded the use of strychnine by white trappers, and Alfred Charlie noted that many Gwich'in trappers from outside

MAP 6
Dagoo Territory, Upper Porcupine River

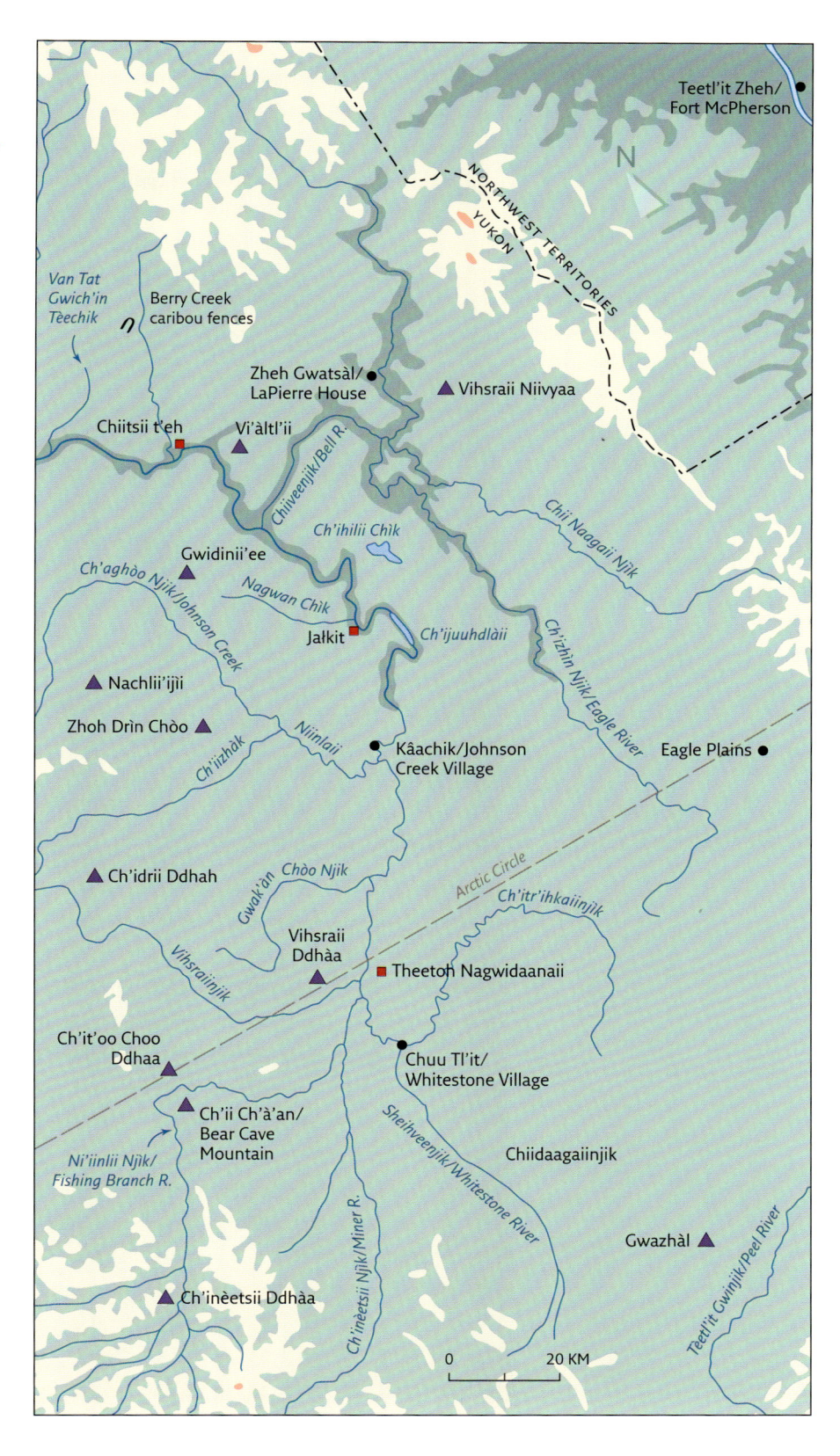

the territory also came there to trap, overwhelming Dagoo conservation and management practices (Alfred Charlie pers. comm. 2005). The Dagoo were forced to leave the area and dispersed amongst their neighbours. Some joined the Vuntut to derive their trapping income from muskrats in *Van Tat* (Crow Flats) and were incorporated into the system of family trapping areas. The area continues to be used, particularly for hunting moose, and many Gwich'in travel up *Ch'oodèenjik* to the old villages when the water is high in the spring. They have monitored the return of wildlife in their former homes.

Various members of the Kyikavichik family described life at *Troo Chòo Njìk* (Driftwood Village), a location convenient to the caribou to the north and fish runs that drew many families. Dick Nukon, originally from Alaska, demonstrated his extensive knowledge of the far upper reaches of *Ch'oodèenjik*, at *Chuu Tl'it* [Whitestone Village] and neighbouring Chance Creek, Miner River, Blackstone River, and Eagle Plains. He described how people from upper *Ch'oodèenjik* would travel to Old Crow and bring meat and wood to the elders there. Hannah Netro referred to John Nukon, father of Dick, who raised his family there, and her husband, Joe Netro, who had a store at *Chuu Tl'it* and trapped around the Fishing Branch River. Andrew Tizya, noted for his hunting ability, told of a time when people were short of food at *Kâachik* but, through good fortune in hunting, managed to celebrate New Year's with a fiddle dance.[13] Alfred Charlie explained that the upper Porcupine area was the homeland of the Dagoo. He also recorded that winter caribou ranged around *Kâachik* [Johnson Creek Village] more regularly than at *Chuu Tl'it*, where the people relied on moose instead.

Troo Chòo Njìk—Driftwood Village

> I remember I was 12 years old and lived at *Troo Chòo Njìk* [Driftwood River; literally: *troo* (wood), *chòo* (big), *njik* (creek)]. At the mouth of *Troo Chòo Njìk* you [can] make a fish trap and...get fish if they're quick. I made a ditch like [and] they spilled [the fish] in there to freeze. After it froze, they cut it up with a saw and squared it. That's the way they handled it; that's dog feed. In the days I talk about, people used [it], even me....We used nets; we got lots of fish. We got about 15 [hundred to] 2,000 dog salmon, besides caribou. [At] that time we tried to get enough caribou, too...even [so] sometimes we ran short after New Year. What we got, we used as dog feed [and for] our family....So them days, it didn't matter where there was a trapping business [trapline], people in different areas [were] going to have a hard time with dog [feed]....One guy or two guys, they said, "Lots of caribou in the trapline." So after New Year everybody

went there to get meat, feed their dogs, come back. By that time, people got a little more [food] and went back again. That much, they were really after caribou in those days, you know.

(JOHN JOE KYIKAVICHIK, June 16, 1997, VG1997-9-11:003-023, English)

I don't know how many years he stayed in *Troo Chòo Njìk*, Grandfather [Big Joe Kaye], quite a few years, you know. He raised Auntie Ellen Bruce, Hannah [Netro], John Joe [Kyikavichik], Ross [Tizya], he raised all these, they said. His cabin is still up there...up the river. Not too long ago, Pete and them were still using it but now it's fallen down....After [his first wife died], I think John Joe was just a baby: he couldn't walk, he just sat in a blanket, eh?...He [Big Joe Kaye] used to go out in fall and trap all winter. He gave meat, clean meat, good and already cut. What fur he got, he used for feasts and all the meat he got, he used for feasts. He was really something.

(ABRAHAM PETER, March 7, 1991, VG1997-2-18A:121-140, English)

Troo Chòo Njìk [Driftwood Village] is where we were raised. Tabitha Kyikavichik and Hannah Netro were born here.[14] In those days when I was a little girl, I dragged a long dress around here, I know that. We were raised around here....

I don't really know this place very well, but they always talked to us about it. You see how big this land is. Toward Dawson and then over to Fort McPherson, up to the Mackenzie, down toward Arctic Village, where they call *Eetr'adadal*, over to the coast, my father's [Big Joe Kaye] tracks [footprints] are there....He was never lazy. Over all that area, he hunted on the land.

In [19]32, I went to Fort McPherson. I came back over in [19]34. He made a house back there when I came back. In those days, we were really scared of our fathers. Then when we got married, we were scared of our husbands. We lived hard lives....

[My father] would make fish traps around here, too. He would catch lots of fish. Many people lived here with him: my friend Mary Firth from Fort McPherson, William Firth's wife, her father, and Walter, and then... Steamboat, a big man, all of them, and Snowshoe. They all had houses here but they're all gone now. I know only that about then....

I was about 10 years old when my mother [Katherine Kyikavichik] died. I remember well when my mother died...We were poor orphans; my father raised us....My father was a smart man. That's why we never went hungry when we were raised....He knew a lot and when the people moved around, drying meat, he made church services wherever he went. He did this all his life. Prayer, he really meant it....

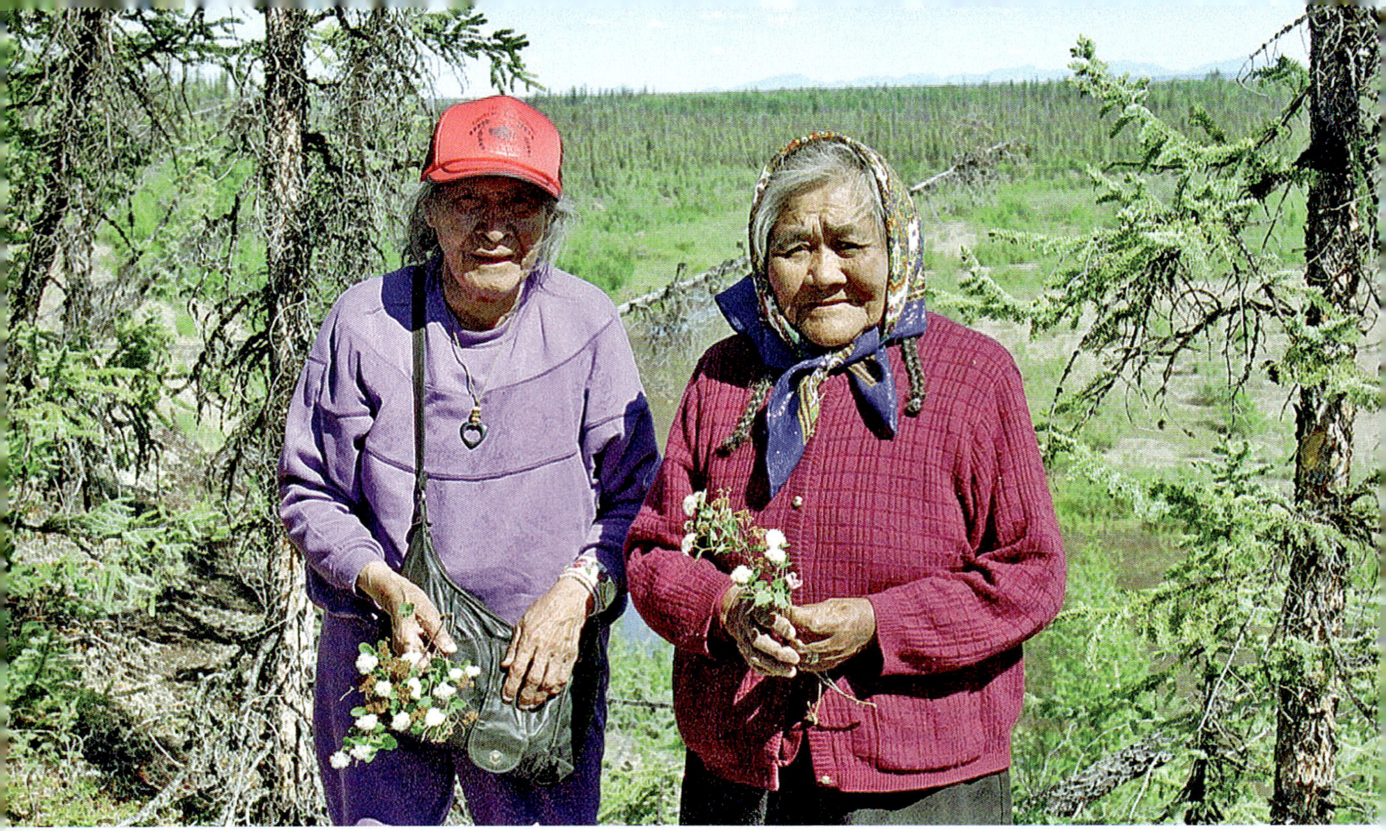

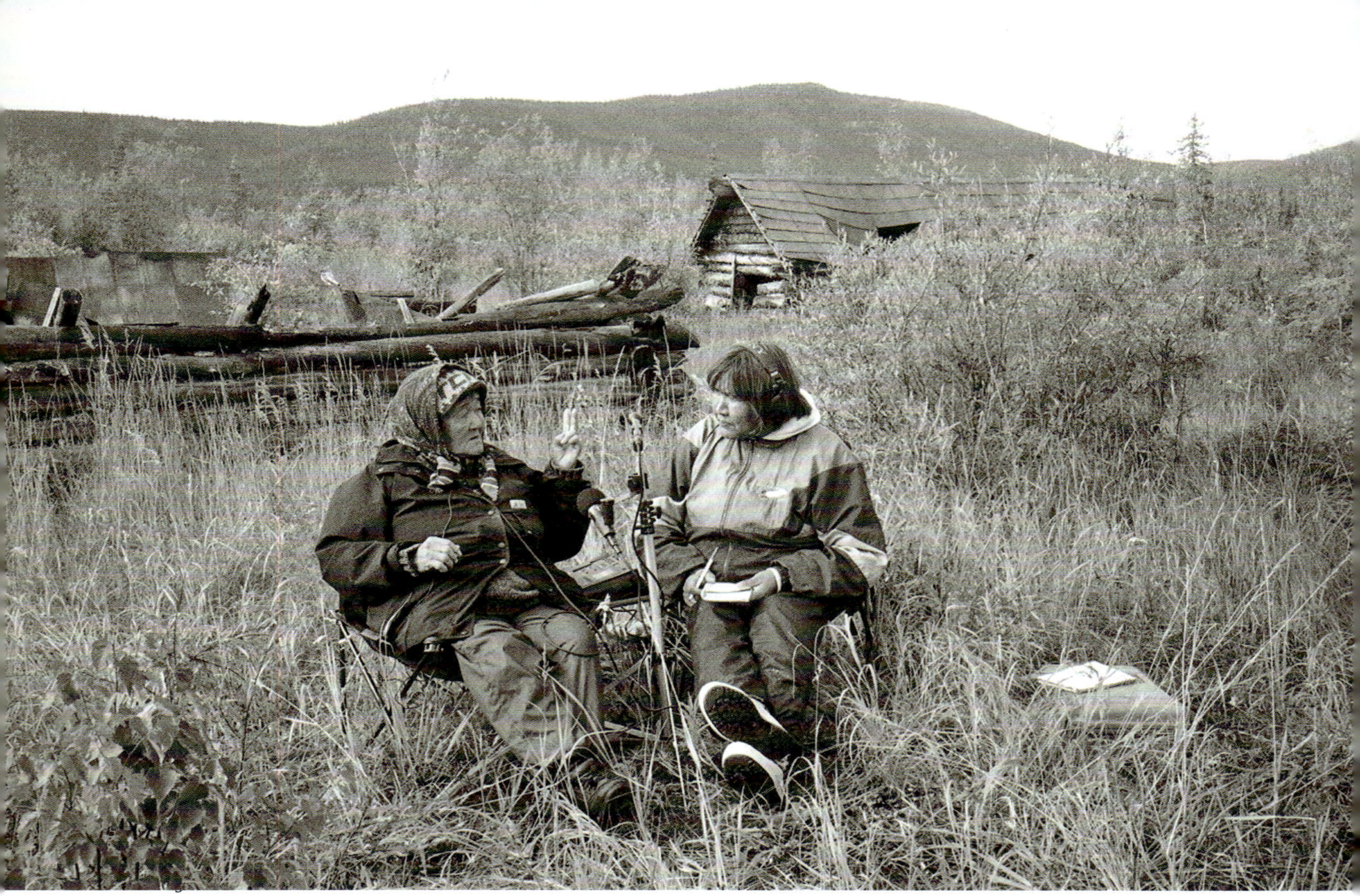

Page 196 (top): Elders Hannah Netro and Lydia Thomas (sisters, née Kyikavichik) at the site of Troo Chòo Njìk *(Driftwood Village) where they grew up, 2001.*
[Shirleen Smith ©VGFN (VG2001-6-502)]

Page 196 (bottom): Elder Mary Kassi and Jane Montgomery at the ruins of LaPierre House, 2002.
[Shirleen Smith ©VGFN (VG2002-5-179)]

They went over toward the coast with the ministers. From there, they went up with boats....he said. That's what he did and wherever I said his footprints are, I say the truth.

I think [my father] raised children three times: first he raised his sisters, then his children, then after that, his grandchildren. He did lots of hard work. If we say so, we are not lying. In those days, the men were very smart. My father [Big Joe Kaye], then my father Elias, and my father John Charlie, Uncle Peter Charlie, Uncle Alfred [Charlie], they all lived around here, [and also] Ben Kassi and Moses Tizya. They were all smart. When the men killed meat they shared with those who were poor, a woman with no husband, elderly women and men, those people were given the choice parts of meat. They wouldn't give out arms [front legs]. Today, only that is given out.

(LYDIA THOMAS, *Troo Chòo Njìk*, June 26, 2001, VG2001-2-52:008-093, Gwich'in)

Zheh Gwatsàl—LaPierre House Village

Zheh Gwatsàl [LaPierre House] is the main place where Gwich'in people used to gather to dry meat and to make their living. They used to just live off the land. A minister used to come from Aklavik...named Jim Edward. My father told me these stories. At that time, we used to stay at Eagle River....

People used to stay at *Zheh Gwatsàl* almost all winter. They stayed around there and hunted and they used to have a big camp and dry meat. People from Old Crow, Aklavik, and Fort McPherson, that's where they used to gather and have big camp and dry meat until spring. [In springtime] when it turned warm then they all separated.

When Gwich'in people got together and were ready to leave each other, they used to trade stuff. When they traded stuff like that, it was to remember one another. That's how people used to treat each other a long time ago. The Gwich'in people, they used to be kind to one another. They used to share land. They used to share whatever they got and Van Tat Gwich'in people used to share land with Fort McPherson people. They used to come over and use the land and share and camp together. They used to socialize together and people used to live along the river. Moses Tizya used to stay at Salmon Cache and other people that lived along the river used to go to *Zheh Gwatsàl* to buy groceries.

The Gwich'in people that used to live along the river...used to trap and that's where Jim Jackson made money. In those days, they didn't have radios. Just certain people had a radio—they used to use batteries. After Jim Jackson moved his store to Old Crow...young people used to go down to visit him and listen to radio. I was one of them—I went down and listened to the radio until one or two in the morning sometimes. I listened to the Carter family sing....On weekends [Jim Jackson] used to make root beer and we used to buy it from him for 25 cents. Way after that, people start getting little radios called transistor radios and from there, people had radio here and there....

[The trail from Old Crow to *Zheh Gwatsàl* to Fort McPherson] is the main trail and that trail has been used for a good many, many years. In my father's days they used to travel back and forth, they used to walk from *Zheh Gwatsàl* over to Fort McPherson. You go past this glacier in the mountain. No matter whether there is water or not, you have to be brave to pass there. There are two cutbanks, on both sides, [and] there is a mountain. There's no way around—you got to go through it. Once they were over the mountain, they could see Fort McPherson from there. When they walked, it took them two days from where they could see Fort McPherson to get there. It took them two days.

There is another trail that goes to Fort McPherson [and another one] to Aklavik. So there are two different trails. The trail to Aklavik goes through Rat Pass. I figure it's 1,000 years or more, that's how many years people used that main trail.

(JOHN JOE KYIKAVICHIK, *LaPierre House Oral History*, 1995:128-132)

Zheh Gwatsàl (LaPierre House) as a Meeting Place

So it happens, [when] people came over to visit [from Rampart House], they set tents at different places [at LaPierre House]....Probably 1927 [or] '26, before we were born. We lived at Driftwood. After New Year my father moved up [to LaPierre House], I remember that, because caribou [were] around here and people [were] coming over. [At the] same time he wanted to meet his brother [Johnny Kaye from Fort McPherson], that's why he moved around.

(JOHN JOE KYIKAVICHIK, *Zheh Gwatsàl*, July 4, 1997,
VG1997-9-15:101-112, English)

The Meat Trade from the *Zheh Gwatsàl* [LaPierre House] Area with the Hudson's Bay Company

Gwich'in people used to, when they had a chance, kill enough caribou or moose and dry the meat and sell it, and also the hides. One of the best parts they bought and they liked is the caribou arm—the caribou shoulder part. That's what they liked. I heard the Hudson's Bay was still buying meat in 1940. I used to get a bunch of caribou around Whitefish Lake and take a load of meat over to Fort McPherson to sell to the Hudson's Bay Company. But after that, they started buying meat from outside and I don't think they bought any more [from us].

The Hudson's Bay in Fort McPherson used to buy meat, fish and keep it and then—I guess they had a freezer—they sold it back to the Native people and made 10 per cent on it in the summertime. I know that because I was over in Fort McPherson one summer and they never had a can of meat in the store.

(ALFRED CHARLIE, *LaPierre House Oral History*, 1995:109-110)

Trading and Caribou Hunting

I was here [LaPierre House] when I was 12 years old. My father moved from Driftwood to look for caribou; they said there was lots of caribou around this area. So he moved his family up. That's the time the Trading Post was here. You know, I remember that....Those white people were trapping and the Jackson brothers were trading here. That's why people came over from Aklavik and Fort McPherson. In those days people really shared the country together. Nobody kicked [complained or disputed], you know. They do what they like trapping, hunting. Van Tat Gwich'in came up here and met each other and they used this area all together. They shared everything on it—caribou, moose, whatever—trapping. Nobody kicked.

(JOHN JOE KYIKAVICHIK, *Zheh Gwatsàl*, July 4, 1997, VG1997-9-15, English)

Kâachik (Johnson Creek Village)[15]

Since I remember, we stayed about 180 miles upriver every year. In September, we started here; we came after breakup, springtime. We were all up there, every one of us, until 1942, '44.

Before gasoline engines we would track the boats upriver. When I was small, I rode in the boats while the adults and dogs walked. Sometimes there was a big fight between all the loose teams. I was 10 years old in 1928-29. At this time John Nukon and his family moved to *Chuu Tl'it* [Whitestone Village] after freezeup. The nearest trading post was LaPierre House. There was not too much white man food, just a little bit of flour, sugar, like that, in the boat. Jim Jackson and his brother had set up a little trading post at LaPierre House so we could

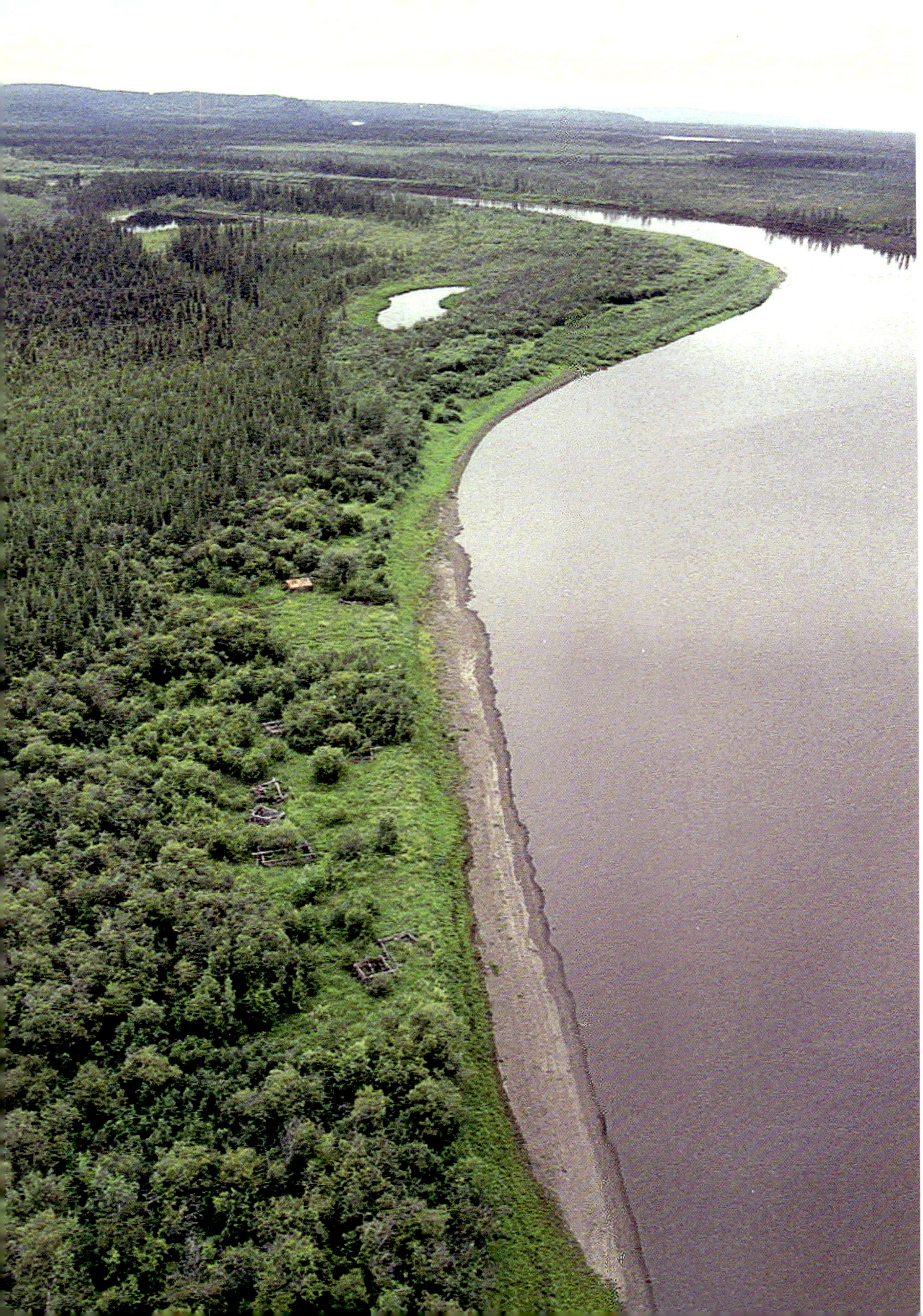

Page 200: Ruins at Kâachik (Johnson Creek Village), 2000.

[Shirleen Smith ©VGFN (VG2000-6-198:)]

Lazarus Charlie, early winter.

[Canadian Museum of Civilization, photo Father Jean-Marie Mouchet S2004-1422]

go there when we were short of something. In the springtime [April], we went to Fort McPherson for shells and tea.

In 1933 my father bought a 12-horsepower inboard motor in Fort Yukon. It was sure slow but pretty good for those days. Around this time, there were six or seven families at Johnson Creek including my uncle John Charlie and Moses Tizya. At Whitestone Village were John Nukon, Uncle Joe Netro, Paul Josie, and John Moses and all his family. In 1944 there was a post at Whitestone [Joe Netro's store], which was a one-day trip from *Kâachik* [Johnson Creek Village]. Travel to Old Crow from Johnson Creek with dog teams, breaking trail, took four days.

(LAZARUS CHARLIE, 1980, VG2000-8-23:002-050, English)

[My family] used to stay in Eagle, Alaska, but we moved back [to Canada] in 1927. When we moved back, Johnson Creek [Village] was already there. My dad told me that Johnson Creek was built before 1927. At that time, some white men were staying upriver already, like Bill Mason and Old Ab [Abraham] Schaeffer. That's why they named

The Second Generation

these places after where those white men stayed. Like Schaeffer Creek up Porcupine River and Bill Mason's cabin and all that.

(DICK NUKON, *LaPierre House Oral History*, 1995:50)

Famine and Feast at *Kâachik*

My father and my mother...sometimes we lived at Johnson Creek.... McPherson people come over [too]. They got all kinds of fish and...well, they pretty near starve....Lucky we was in Johnson Creek, yeah. About three family stay there but they wouldn't help. Them too, they're [having a] hard time, I think. They got to look after their food...They all pretty near starve, you know. But damn lucky, I was just happen. All winter we go all over hunting, never see even old track just once.... Well, my dog [was acting] funny for me. They smell, you know, so I think: "Check, check time." Quiet, so I hitch them up. I don't want them to holler so, quiet, I hitch them up. So I took [my] gun, shell in it, too. I go ahead, put chain on the leader and go ahead. Jeepers! It's downhill, like, low downhill, down at the bottom is flat....

My dog [acted] just like something [was] ahead of me....Go in the bottom, little way, my dog, I look at them and Gee Whiz! They [were looking at a] bunch of caribou, right there! Really lucky I got good gun. Maybe, I don't know, I know how to shoot sure, right there. I got shell on it, just standing there! I just shoot. Nine shot, nine caribou! Boyee oh boyee! So I [was] going home now, so I skin some of them but I cover it, take the guts [out], I clean all the guts good. So I cover [the caribou] with snow. Then two caribou, I want to haul it, so I put [them] alongside the trail and cover [them] with snow again.

So next morning I left early, travel all day. Ah, my dog [were] slow, walk slow and sometimes [found it] hard to pull, too. When I got to Johnson Creek, it's not too late; early I got there....I just start to drink tea. My mother, well it got to be rabbit, no meat huh, rabbit with tea. I eat, while that, dog bark. McPherson [people] come. We have two [caribou], that I brought, two caribou: brought it all the way. I have to go back tomorrow, but I got lots of meat already....Those man [McPherson], they go there and hunt with me, too. Ah, we make good time. After that, they make Christmas and New Year big dance. Gee whiz! Fiddle there, big dance.

(ANDREW TIZYA, Old Crow, July 31, 2000, VG2000-4-18, Gwich'in and English)

Florence and Mary Netro at Kâachik (Johnson Creek Village), 2000.

[Shirleen Smith ©VGFN (VG2000-6-180)]

The Headwaters of *Ch'oodèenjik* (Porcupine River) in the 1930s

In the 1930s, when I was 12 years old, my father trapped at the headwaters of *Ch'oodèenjik* and I went with him. He hunted for meat and trapped for marten around there. He taught me; I really never had any schooling. I was raised only out in the bush...Nowadays the children go to school. I never did that. I always talk to you in my language.

I remember back around 1930, it was a bit hard. The people went through hard times. They lived only on food from the land; in those days there was not much white man's food. They hunted in different directions and trapped. They lived on the meat they hunted....They went way upriver for moose and caribou, too. They made rafts and brought [the animals] home and then they dried them. In those days, Moses Tizya and Peter Charlie had boats. [They would take them] way up where they hunted for food. From there they made caribou rafts to go back down[river]. This is the way people lived long ago, when I was growing up.

(JOHN JOE KYIKAVICHIK, February 18, 1980, VG2000-8-25:005-020, Gwich'in and English)

Chuu Tl'it *(Whitestone Village)*, 2000.

[Shirleen Smith ©VGFN (VG 2000-6-90)]

Trapping Lynx Around *Chuu Tl'it* (Whitestone Village)[16]

A long time ago, around 1940, sometimes there were no lynx, then other times there were many. At first, in 1930–35 around there, there were no lynx. There were lots of rabbits but I never even saw lynx tracks. There was going to be lots of lynx. I went through Chance Creek with a boat. There, [with my] old man [father], we hunted for moose.... There was always moose around there.

[My father] said he heard lynx. When it makes a noise it sounds just like a cat, you know. By Canoe River, he shot a moose. We were going to it. In the early morning he got up, "While we were sleeping, I heard a lynx making noises," he said. Before that I never heard one....When he paddled through Canoe River he said he saw lynx. He said, "I think there's going to be lots of lynx." Before that I never saw any.

That fall, after little snow fall we set rabbit snares. There was just a round track and small ones, little ones. Right there, I snared a young baby lynx in the rabbit snare. Ah, that winter there were lots of lynx. We trapped through Chance Creek, all over, up Cody Creek and *Ni'iinlii Njik*

[Fishing Branch River].[17] There were lynx tracks all over. That winter we killed over 200 lynx. The top price was $100 for a big one.

Lynx, it runs all over for its food, you know, rabbits. If there's no rabbits, there's no lynx. When the rabbits come back, the lynx come back. One time in Fort Yukon when there were lots of rabbits, all the lynx went down there. Right up to today, there's still nothing: a few lynx around here but not too many. That's when there are not many rabbits.

(Dick Nukon, Old Crow, February 15, 2001, VG2001-2-5:006-040, Gwich'in)

People who Trapped in the Upper *Ch'oodèenjik* (Porcupine River) Area and Hunting to Support Elders

Yeah, Eagle Plains, we heard about it. We used to trap around Blackstone. We saw lots of Teetl'it Gwich'in around there and my dad asked them which way they came [over the Richardson Mountains].[18] They said they came up the Peel River and some of them came over the Richardson Mountains right through Eagle Plains and then right through Caribou Mountain, they told us that. They went all over, those Teetl'it Gwich'in, in those days. Some of them went the other direction and then they all came together at the mouth of Blackstone River. They stayed around there and then everybody moved back to Fort McPherson. I was around there then—I was a kid at that time but I remember...John Francis, John Vaneltsi. The last time I went over to McPherson, he told me about that. He was young at that time, too; now he's 98 years old.

I never lived [at Eagle Plains] but I trapped around there [when] I was about 16 or 17 years old, I guess....We were there in 1930; lots of people were there with us. Paul Neiman, that's a white man. And Edward Itsi, William Itsi, and Edward Kaye, Myra Crow, David Elias and his wife....And my dad and all my sisters. Enid John from Fort Yukon, too, was there. Lots of people used to stay there. John Thomas used to be there. Paul Josie's family and Paul George from Fort Yukon, Paul Ben [Kassi] and his wife. Hannah Netro—Joe Netro had a trading post [at Whitestone] for three or four years and two trappers stayed 10 miles this side, Rube Mason and Billy Mason and Nap Norville, Charlie Abel used to trap around there, too; Charlie Linklater, Paul Ben, Charlie Thomas, Kenneth Nukon, and Amos Josie. We got lots of visitors from Old Crow, too. We trapped around Fishing Branch, then went to Whitestone just to buy things from Joe Netro. Police made patrols

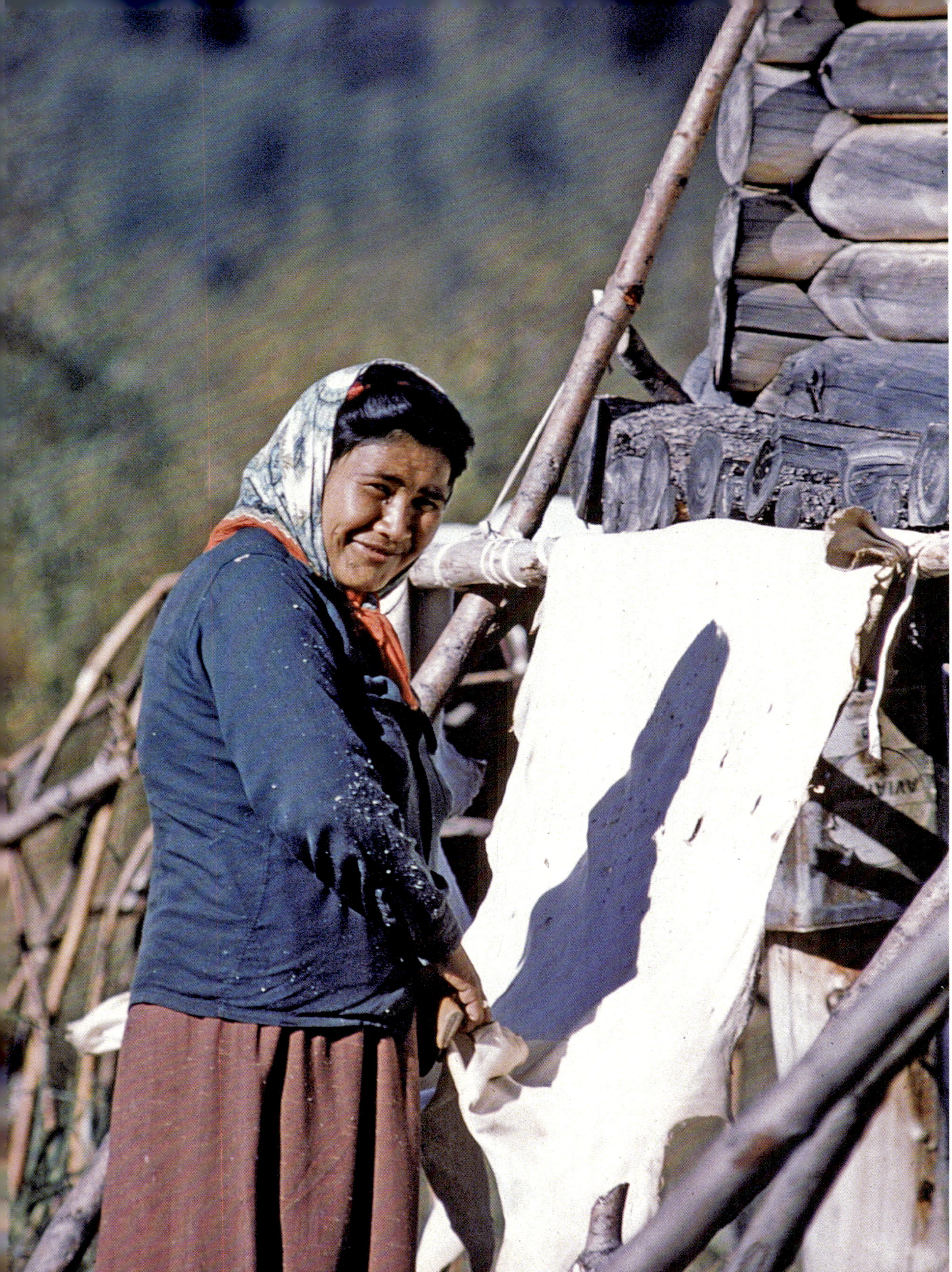

Mrs. Charlie Abel dressing a caribou hide.

[Canadian Museum of Civilization, photo Father Jean-Marie Mouchet S2004-1408]

[with] Special Constables John Moses and Thomas Njootli. Cops named Jim Wade and Tom Hollyhide were there. One time they hired me to [guide them to] Blackstone. Cheap wages in those days: $7.50 a day.

They stayed year round [at Whitestone Village]. Some of them stayed one year then quit when rat season opened and moved down to Crow Flats. Us, we just stayed there until breakup. That's our country so right after breakup, we hunted beaver. We trapped year round, saved all that fur. Right after breakup we hunted beaver and then came down the Porcupine River. At many lakes, we hunted muskrat—anything— beaver, otter, muskrat. In those days people went out to Crow Flats from [Old Crow]. We landed here [and there was] nobody around here, just old people. [There were] lots of caribou around here but it was hard for [the old people] to get it. So when we landed here we went up to Second Island or First Island [near Old Crow] and shot some caribou and brought it back. We just gave it to them, the old people. All those old people, not one of them is alive now. They're all gone.

Yeah, long ago we were in Whitestone and my dad came down to Old Crow. From Johnson Creek; John Charlie and Peter Charlie all came down here [Old Crow] but we stayed up there. They had a big dance around here, "Old time" dance. At New Year's and Christmas they made some kind of games for old timers. They used to pull a toboggan from house to house and they collected anything. Meat, tea, pound of sugar, things like that. Big Joe Kaye was chief at that time. After that Peter Moses was chief for 16 years.

Easter time, that's the time we young men came down here: Peter Benjamin, Alfred Charlie, Lazarus Charlie, Charlie Peter [Charlie]. From Whitestone, me, Charlie Thomas, Charlie Linklater, Paul Ben, Joe Martin—we came down here for Easter. At that time, lots of caribou were coming back this way, lots were around Lone Mountain. Yeah, I remember all those old people used to stay up that way. John Charlie, Peter Charlie, my dad. "We're ready to go tomorrow," he talked to us. "Do this:...there's going to be lots of caribou around. On Lone Mountain, you guys shoot caribou. Haul two or three caribou down. When you get to Old Crow, don't look for pay: just give it out to old people," he said. We did that. In those days, it was hard to get wood, too. There were no snow machines, just dog teams. Everybody had no wood. I hauled lots of wood for old people for nothing. They told us to do that, so we did. We didn't want pay, just gave it to them. They told us "good luck for your life, I hope you get everything you wish for all your life and your family has your own home," they said. Now we have

Peter Benjamin, special constable with the Royal Canadian Mounted Police in Old Crow.

[Canadian Museum of Civilization, photo Father Jean-Marie Mouchet s2004-1331]

our own home, our own family and our family is growing up now. Us, we turn to elders now.

(DICK NUKON, Porcupine-Peel, January 20, 1995, 1995:74-77, English)

Trappers, Traders, and "Ice Bears" at *Chuu Tl'it* (Whitestone Village) and *Ni'iinlii Njik* (Fishing Branch)

Chuu Tl'it [Whitestone Village]...is where I lived. My husband [Joe Netro] trapped at Fishing Branch and Charlie Creek. [Near there] were two white men's cabins, near the mouth of Porcupine River and the Fishing Branch...by a lake. Right there is where two white men lived, real cabins. Their names were Rube Mason and Frank Foster. They were trappers....[Frank] worked for Rube Mason. Rube left and then Frank worked for Jim Jackson. Jim Jackson's cabin is at LaPierre House.

We Gwich'in didn't have cabins, we used tents. We just camped anywhere we wanted, at a good place. And then we took the tents down and went again the next day.

Rube Mason's place was maybe right across from [Whitestone] Village. There's a little cabin, every so many miles they had a cabin.... He used to walk across the river [to Whitestone] to listen to the radio. My old radio, it ran by a big battery. Only they listened to it—I didn't bother with it when I was alone—because it was war time, eh, they listened to news....

So, what are we supposed to do? We have to protect all this, *Etkinjik* [Canoe River]. My grandpa was the first person to paddle down with a little canoe. I wasn't there: my cousin John Nukon told me that story. He came down to John Nukon Village. I call it John Nukon Village: that's where he built his cabin: Whitestone Village, it's a good [name], but I call it John Nukon Village because he lived there, he raised his kids there....

From the Porcupine, the village is right around there....That's where I worked hard. That's where I lived and Mary Kassi lived there, too. Edith [Josie] and her parents, the Josie family, lived there, too....As far as I know two, one girl and one baby [were buried] around there, [on the little hill across from where we lived]. That's where we picked berries; we had to walk across the river and we picked cranberries. But me, I didn't go far away because I had two little kids. Edith and her mother always went someplace; they went far away for berries....My uncle said everything was there but we had to go a long ways for blueberries. They hunted for moose, caribou, trapped for everything. After breakup in June, [it was a] really good place for marten.

We [Hannah and Joe Netro] got a little groceries to sell, you know. People bought lots of groceries from him. He got a licence to do that. That's how we lived in the village. He went so far from Whitefish, and then they killed a moose and when they're trapping they killed caribou, sheep, or moose to use on the trapline. When they got a moose before freezing, that was for us at home. They killed moose [to use on] every trapline. Good idea, eh? And still they never threw anything out, they used it all.

I told a story one time...my old man [husband] said he went to Fishing Branch, that open place to fish king salmon [or the other one, we call it dog salmon. [It] just dies in that open [unfrozen] place. He went past there in wintertime when he was trapping. [There were] lots of grizzly dens close by. Lots of grizzly bears eat and eat and eat in that water. That open place, even looked thick, white, because of [all the dead] fish.

After the grizzly bears eat it all, the water turned good, looked clean. I asked him, "How do you know it's good?" "Because I drank it and I didn't get sick." That's funny, you know. I just think the way God put it down there for us. Really it even stinks there, when you go close, and that's when the grizzly eats it all and then it's clean again....

That's where he trapped from the village. Yeah, it took a month and...it's not a long winter. It warms up quick. A grizzly can travel all winter, and that's what they worried about when they were gone away and we women were alone. Ice bear, we call it...grizzly. [They would be out in winter] because at Fishing Branch, after they clean it, they go to their dens but they're always around, uncle said, because it's warm all winter. We never saw one or anything. Shorter winter [at Whitestone], but cold like Old Crow. So the bears come out for a walk or to look for something to eat....So it's really quite different for me than Old Crow Village.

(HANNAH NETRO, July 21, 1999, VG1999-2-4:043-237, English)

Learning to Trap at *Chiidaagaiinjik* (Head of the River–Whitestone Area)

When I was old enough my dad told me I was going to have to make my own living. He gave me four dogs. It was time to go up to *Chiidaagaiinjik* [Whitestone area] to trap, 1940. I went up with Charlie Abel. To prepare myself, I went to see Jim Jackson [trader] to see if I could get an outfit to trap with and Jim Jackson was going to make a list. I got my outfit and left for *Chiidaagaiinjik*....My outfit from Jim Jackson—material, groceries, tent, stove, traps, everything I needed for trapping—it only cost me $1,800. At that time everything was cheap. I got up there to *Chiidaagaiinjik* and really liked what I saw. I liked the land, I liked the place but I didn't know the country. When it was time to go trapping, Joe Netro was staying up there in *Chiidaagaiinjik* [Whitestone Village] and asked me to go with him. I was really happy to be asked to go trapping with someone. I could set traps and make some money. We trapped all winter around the head of *Ch'oodèenjik* [Porcupine River], up the Miner River and over the mountain. The river called Grayling Creek, which runs into Porcupine or Yukon River, that's where we trapped that winter and we finished trapping in March.[19] In those days we had good dog teams. That winter I got 44 marten and four mink.

That spring when we were ready to come down from *Chiidaagaiinjik* to Old Crow, Joe Netro and the families that stayed up there had boats and they left before me but I came down with one white guy that was staying up there. His name was Rube Mason.

That spring before I came down, I went beaver hunting and got 28 beaver. This was the first time I went on my own to make my own living and to survive. That was the responsibility that my dad gave me because I was old enough. I was young at the time, very young and when I went hunting for beaver, I went alone. I wasn't afraid or anything. I wanted to make money. I had to make my own living so being afraid was not going to do it for me. I had to go out and do it.

The winter I stayed up at *Chiidaagaiinjik* I met my wife. Her name was Jessie Nukon and her dad's name was John Nukon. When I came down in the spring, I was ready to go up *Chyahnjik* [Crow River] to pick up my parents because they were staying in *Van Tat* [Crow Flats]. My dad had a motor and boat here [Old Crow]. It was springtime and I was ready to go up the *Chyahnjik* when my girlfriend proposed to me, to marry her. She said, "Ask my dad if you can marry me," so I did. And the old man told me, "Go ahead, do whatever you want; but all of us are not going to be there someday." That old man meant what he said because now I live alone. There are none of them left and I live by himself. I married my wife in July 1941.

(CHARLIE THOMAS, *LaPierre House Oral History*, 1995:120–123, Gwich'in paraphrased by Alice Frost)

Meeting the *Chuu Tl'it* [Whitestone] People

Well, some people stayed out all winter and went to town maybe at Easter time in order to go to Crow Flats [afterward], and took all their fur. But we were close [Bluefish River]; the people who stayed as close to town as we did made regular trips, like maybe once a month. But people up in Whitestone and up at Black Fox and Gilbert Lord [creeks], Johnson Creek, they took a boatload up. Not a fast boat like we've got now, an inboard motor. They took cases of food so it lasted all winter, yet cheaper: they got it from Fort Yukon. Sometime [when] they had enough money and a boat, they took their fur down to Fort Yukon. [They took] enough food for all winter.

Some of them came [a little] late to Old Crow, like the Charlies, John Nukon, the Nukons (the older ones). That's why they called it Whitestone Village, hah. It was a village by itself, with the surrounding trappers. They had a little store there and the only time they came to town was after breakup. They came down the Porcupine to Old Crow with their winter catch: drymeat. Gee, I remember my mother taking us up to Peter Charlie's and John Nukon's. They had drymeat, caribou skins [which they had taken] the hair off. [They] really cared for that drymeat, you know. It was important and people still do it yet, but you know it's hard now for everybody to do that, hah. They came down with maybe 10 big bales of drymeat, well-preserved, no fly [damage], smoked, dry. They looked after it so good....Drymeat, if you put one piece that's wet in there, it will [mold and] spoil all the rest.

(STEPHEN FROST SR., Porcupine-Bluefish River, June 23, 2001, VG2001-2-41:146-172, English)

The Decline of Animals
Leaving Chuu Tl'it *(Whitestone) and* Kâachik *(Johnson Creek) Villages*

This is a big country. All the country from way up at the headwaters [of *Ch'oodèenjik* or Porcupine River] was cleaned up [denuded of game]. From 1936 till 1955, they cleaned [out] the area around *Chuu Tl'it*. So in *Van Tat* [Crow Flats], they made their living off muskrats. There was no fur. Muskrats, all over the country the people made their living from them. Down to Fort Yukon, these Vuntut Gwitchin, over in Fort McPherson, and down toward Aklavik, everywhere, all the *Ch'ineekaii* [Inuvialuit or Inuit], too, lived off the muskrats.

(CHARLIE THOMAS, *Sriinjik* (Bluefish River), June 23, 2001, VG2001-2-42:075-083, Gwich'in)

The Use of Poison

There was lots of animals but [later] there were no animals. Here it has gotten good again, you know. A long time ago, the white people who trapped around here used bad medicine [poison]. They pretty well spoiled the land. That was about 60, 70 years ago, you know. Now it's gotten better.

(DICK NUKON, *Chuu Tl'it*, July 28, 2000, VG2000-4-4:069-072, Gwich'in)

White man, they use that poison so they buggered up all that country for about 60 or 70 years. Now everything has come out really good. That's why we don't want any white man bothering this area no more....Lots of them want to come here and trap around here: they ask me when I go Whitehorse. I tell them "I can't promise you. If you want to come here you have to phone the band council or chief in Old Crow and they'll tell you, but not me." If they tell them yes, we won't let them bother around here. Used to be people went up the Crow River, and they buggered up all that country.

(DICK NUKON, Porcupine-Peel, January 20, 1995, 1995:78-79, English and Gwich'in)

Elder Dick Nukon at Ch'it'oo Choo Ddhàa *(Big Nest Mountain), 2007.*

[Megan Williams ©VGFN 2007]

Downriver on *Ch'oodèenjik* (Porcupine River)

Bluefish River, Rampart House, and Alaska

The centre of Van Tat Gwich'in territory is *Van Tat*—Crow Flats, and *Chyahnjik* [Crow River] links the region to the main travel artery, *Ch'oodèenjik* [Porcupine River], where Old Crow is today. Before Old Crow became a village with a trading post, Van Tat Gwich'in travelled elsewhere to trade, and Rampart House was the most long-term location in the memory of this generation of elders.[20] Following its establishment by the Hudson's Bay Company in the 1800s and a series of eastward relocations as the site of the U.S.-Canada border was fixed, Rampart House was taken over by Dan Cadzow, who ran a store there from 1904 to 1929. Between Rampart House and Old Crow is the Bluefish River region, an area of high country and rivers, known for its caves and an important habitat for caribou, fish, grizzly bears, and with good access to muskrat trapping at *Van Tat*. Although many families had their winter hunting territories upriver from Old Crow at some distance from traders, some lived closer to present-day Old Crow, such as Charlie Thomas's family, who trapped on both sides of the border until it was enforced, and the Frost family, who lived at *Sriinjik* [Bluefish River].

The Second Generation 213

Rampart House: reconstruction of Dan Cadzow's store, 2004.
[Shirleen Smith ©VGFN (VG2004-6-48)]

Living in the Mountains North of Rampart House

I was born in 1916, June 25, around New Rampart [House], around the border....My parents lived there. Most of the time, we lived out in the bush all the time, dog packing way back in the mountains. We made drymeat over willows—[there was] no timber there in most places. After we made drymeat and cached it, we dug out a bunch of rocks and made a big cellar. That's the way to cache it for winter. Sometimes a bear really got into it and she dug out everything—that's how they used to give people a hard time.

(CHARLIE THOMAS, Porcupine-Peel, January 20, 1995, 1995:97–98, English and Gwich'in)

My parents used to live around Rampart House because Dan Cadzow had a store there....They made their living around there. From Rampart House, they moved to Rapid River [in Alaska, north of Rampart House] in the summer and dried meat all summer. When fall time came and there was a little snow, the men went to Rampart House to pick up stoves and tents because in the summertime when they moved out to dry meat, they didn't carry stoves or anything. They had to carry light stuff....They used to move around with dog packs....They went to town with dog packs and came back with dog teams on the little snow on the ground. They come back fast with dog teams....

I moved to Old Crow in 1937 and since then I've been staying around here.[21] I moved up to Johnson Creek and Whitestone in 1940. At the time Jim Jackson had a store at LaPierre House. He moved it down to Old Crow because hardly anybody came to LaPierre House or lived there anymore.

(CHARLIE THOMAS, *LaPierre House Oral History*, 1995:118–120, Gwich'in paraphrased by Alice Frost)

Hunting and Trapping at *Sriinjik* (Bluefish River) and Trading at Old Crow

We stayed [at the Porcupine and Bluefish rivers] for fish and meat in the fall and then of course, winter trapping. [There were] no jobs that time, nothing. We just lived on fur and if you didn't get fur, why you didn't eat very much at all, but [there was] always fish and meat and rabbit and things like that.

As soon as [it was] March, we came up [to town] and I'm talking about everybody else did that, too. We all went to town so we could be heading to Crow Flats around the first part of March. If I remember right, it's the only time we came to town. If they ran out of certain food then maybe [they made a trip] at Easter, and then back to Crow Flats. And they stayed there till about...June 15th; we moved to [the Crow] River, with dog teams and [it was] tough. It wasn't tough to us; that's the way life was then....

[Around Bluefish River is] timber country, mostly marten. Along the river here is lot of willow and rabbits; you get lynx, mink, anything, wolverine, wolves....In the spring it's known from way back [long ago] that moose, they start from the higher ground and go toward the river. So we get moose, too, along the river in the spring. But during the winter, they stay up in the hills and creeks in the mountains....

Well in them days, they had a couple of trader's stores. We just sold [furs] to the local trader and in return, bought food right there. That was just like cash. This one trader, his name was Harry Healy, if you sell quite a few furs and he couldn't give you cash, so he gave these "bingo" [tokens] they called them, good for one dollar or 50 cents in trade. Aluminum [with] "Harry Healy" on them. A couple of years ago,

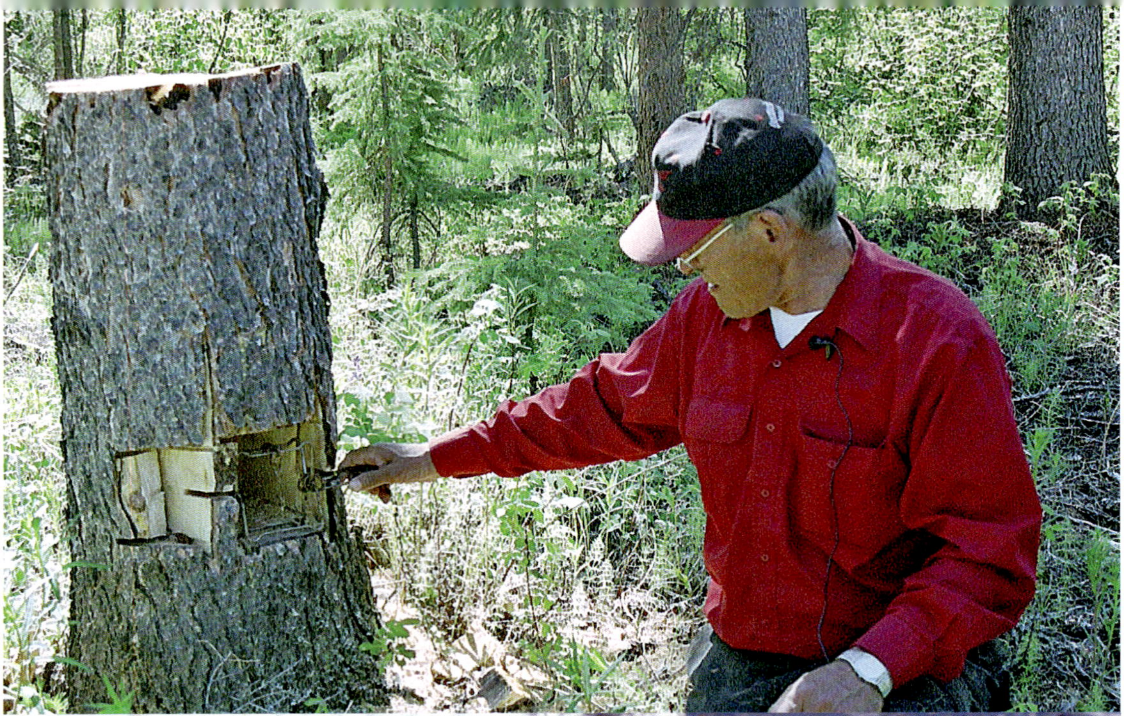

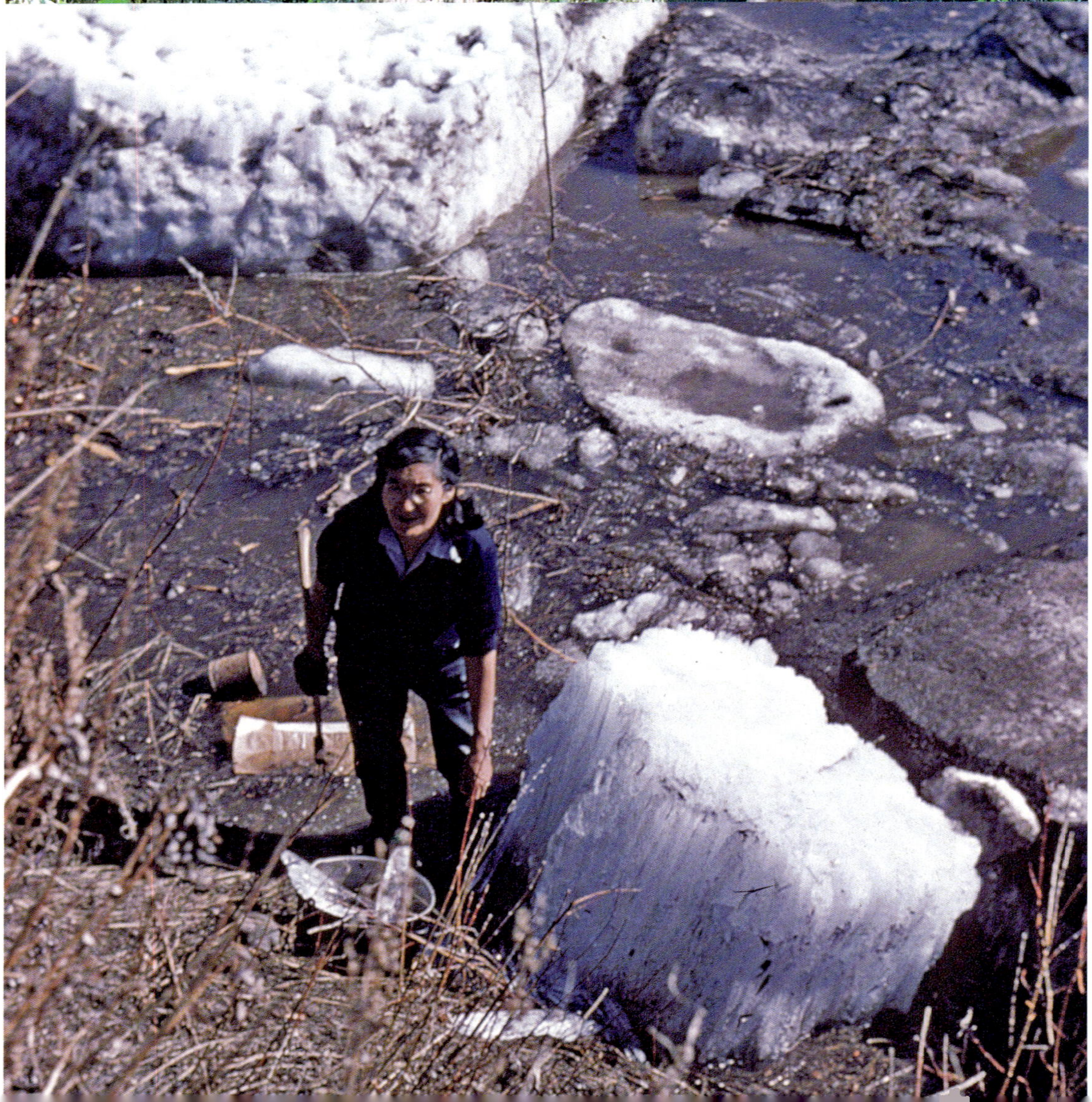

Page 216 (top): Elder Stephen Frost demonstrates setting a trap at his camp at Sriinjik *(Bluefish River), 2001.*
[Shirleen Smith ©VGFN (VG2001-6-311)]

Page 216 (bottom): Clara Frost gathering ice for drinking water after spring breakup.
[Canadian Museum of Civilization, photo Father Jean-Marie Mouchet S2004-1351]

I think...antique people bought them. Hard to collect, you know, we certainly [didn't] throw them away but we lost them sometimes. And no money; as a kid, I never remember [money]. [We were] lucky to get a quarter once in awhile. Our parents, same as today, they give their kids money; at that time we didn't have it, so we got a squirrel, like the one you see on the tree there, or a weasel. They gave us that and we sold it. We bought black Vicks cough drops for candy. No candy, hah? Gee, it tasted good. [Laughter]...

Well I don't remember everything good [fur prices], but I just remember Donald [Frost, older brother] when we was starting to trap, he got a couple of marten. I think our parents allowed him to keep it to get a gun or something like that. He got a $110 for one marten, a black marten. I think so—$90 or 110. Ah, lots of money at that time....

People depended on each other. He [father] had boat [with an] inboard motor. Not every year, but he had boat and Old Peter Tizya or anybody that had a boat, they helped each other, you know. If we were stuck or somebody was stuck down at Rampart House, we went down and got them and they expected [to be] paid well. There was very little pay at that time, but money was valuable. Fifty bucks, you could go a long way.

[In the winter we used] dog teams, dog teams only. Ski-doo, that only came, I don't know, around 1950. [In the] South I guess they had them before that....Some of the older people, they miss that life you know. That's why they always try to go out any chance they get and I do the same thing.

(STEPHEN FROST SR., Porcupine-Bluefish River, June 23, 2001, VG2001-2-41:065-146, 172-205, English)

Rampart House

As time went on, a small village grew up at [New] Rampart House. All the people from *Van Tat* [Crow Flats] and from...around Fort Yukon gathered there. Dan Cadzow landed a small steamboat. Of course, your uncle told stories and said, "Dan has a good name."[22] He always told me stories, your uncle. He said the fur cost lots of money. The black fox, [Cadzow] bought it for $500, he said. The old man [who] trapped a black fox arrived at Rampart House during holidays, before Christmas. They gathered there. He and his wife were dressed up, they said, due to the black fox he sold. He lived at Black Fox [Creek]. He's from there. Now they call it Black Fox Creek—that's how they named it.

Graveyard at Rampart House, 2004.

[Shirleen Smith ©VGFN (VG2004-6-38)]

Around [Rampart House] were lots of people. People from Fort Yukon and all the Arctic Village people gathered there. They came with dog teams. But it was hard times so the Old Crow people went down [to trade] and came back up.

(HANNAH NETRO, Driftwood Village, June 26, 2001, VG2001-2-51:096-116, Gwich'in)

Sriinjik (Bluefish River), Rampart House, Traders, and RCMP

This country [*Sriinjik* area] and across to Old Crow, down to the lake and beyond, they had camps around there....Down [*Sriinjik*] I went trapping. There's muskrats around there on the lakes....We stayed there and went different directions for trapping marten. That's how we lived.

There's a trail up this way, through *Sriinjik* and over to Rampart House....1921 till 1937, I remember, [19]36, people made their living around Rampart House. Cadzow had a store there. That was the only store: other than that there was no store....Jim Jackson had a store way up at the headwaters [upper *Ch'oodèenjik*–Porcupine River]. John Charlie and John Nukon made their living trapping there till they were elders.

This was how it was at Rampart House, too. Way down that mountain there is Old Rampart House. I was raised there....Toward the boundary line, the white men trapped. It's a big country down this way....The Rampart House people made their living off all of it.

Sergeant Dempster made patrols through *Sriinjik*, way over the mountains. I wonder how far he went? He camped; well it's deep snow and it's hard. My father went with him and John Nukon, too, to Rampart House. They made a trail for him. He was going to go to Dawson but they never made it. It was hard going in the deep snow. It's a long way to there. They were going to cross Blackstone but they never even made it there. Across to the head of the Peel River, across that way....

Around here, they just lived on the land. We would never see white men. Cadzow was the only white man, and two policeman at Rampart House, Charlie Young, and Charlie Evanson. I remember them....We were children and we couldn't speak to them in English. We only spoke our language in those days....

That is how it was for us long ago....Peter Moses said, "In the future you will only travel by airplane, you will never see dog teams again," he said. I think about that....Sure, now I see it. We only travel by plane.

This is how it was for us. Around 1940, it was hard to go to Fort McPherson to see relatives. We worked to make our living by trapping muskrats. There were no holidays. It was hard to go to Dawson, also. In the summer, after spring thaw, they trapped for muskrats and beaver to go down to Fort Yukon. It was only then that we saw our relatives.

(CHARLIE THOMAS, *Sriinjik*, June 23, 2001, VG2001-2-42:010-122, Gwich'in)

Farther Afield
Fort Yukon, Dawson, Fort McPherson, and Herschel Island

Van Tat Gwich'in travelled widely beyond their central territory. In the past, there were stories of Gwich'in who went to distant lands to trade, and this generation also travelled for trading purposes by boat and dog team to Fort Yukon, Dawson, Fort McPherson, and Herschel Island, as mentioned in previous interviews. As well, Van Tat Gwich'in individuals guided and broke trail for RCMP on their patrols. In recent times, Van Tat Gwich'in have travelled their lands and the world by aircraft via the air link in Old Crow. Hannah Netro related the stories she was told about trading at distant Herschel Island and Fort McPherson. Andrew Tizya was well-known for his hunting and bush skills. He described guiding the RCMP on a lengthy round trip to Herschel Island.

Page 221 (top): The southern tip of Herschel Island, 2000.
[Shirleen Smith ©VGFN (VG2000-6-268)]

Page 221 (bottom): Elder Andrew Tizya (centre) at Chuu Choo Vee *(Herschel Island), 2000.*
[Shirleen Smith ©VGFN (VG2000-6-260)]

Traders at *Chuu Choo Vee* (Herschel Island), *Chii Tsal Dik* (Fort McPherson), and Alaska

My husband, Joe Netro, his father's name was Charlie Netro. They say he was a strong man....They went to the coast, to *Chuu Choo Vee* [Herschel] [and bought]...wool...It was nice. I don't know who has them today, kettles heavy just like gold....In those days, it was hard to go to the coast, to *Chuu Choo Vee*. I asked my husband [Joe Netro]. He said that [the trade goods were] from Russia. A ship landed at *Chuu Choo Vee* with groceries, dry goods, everything. From there, up *Nagwachoonjik* [the Mackenzie River] to *Chii Tsal Dik* [Fort McPherson], I think, the steamboat came. The ship brought the things that they liked more [than English goods from the Hudson's Bay Company], they said....On the American side, they liked the dry goods from there. They bought stuff from the ship at high prices, they said. Over [*Chii Tsal Dik*] way, there was lots of stuff from the steamboat. The Americans [had] what they really liked and they bought [from] them.

(HANNAH NETRO, *Diniizhòo*, August 1, 2000, VG2000-4-13, Gwich'in)

My mother...my Auntie Annie, too...Mary Elias's mother, they even tanned fur pelts and also made fur clothes. They put lots of big beads on it, big beads; around here they don't know about them. Dan Cadzow had a house; around there was lots of big beads. From over that way, too, Mr. Firth and Dan Cadzow, they helped people with food.[23]

Way down at *Chuu Choo Vee* [Herschel Island], they would go there for a few supplies. The women would sew and tan hides, make babiche, wolverine pelts, animal pelts. They went down with that [and] got a little stuff, from *Chii Tsal Dik* [Fort McPherson], too. Mr. Firth, they say, in a cup he weighed stuff, sugar, flour, two cups for each family. That's no good for nothing! I mean, not enough for big families with kids. They brought beads from *Chuu Choo Vee* and the ladies would sew beaded mitts, moccasins, take it all down [to *Chuu Choo Vee*]. The ship came and the white men in it bought the moccasins....[They traded for] material, for one yard or two yards they made a skirt.... Sometimes those who could afford it bought lots of material to sew a dancing dress.

(HANNAH NETRO, Driftwood River, June 26, 2001, VG2001-2-54:191–224, Gwich'in)

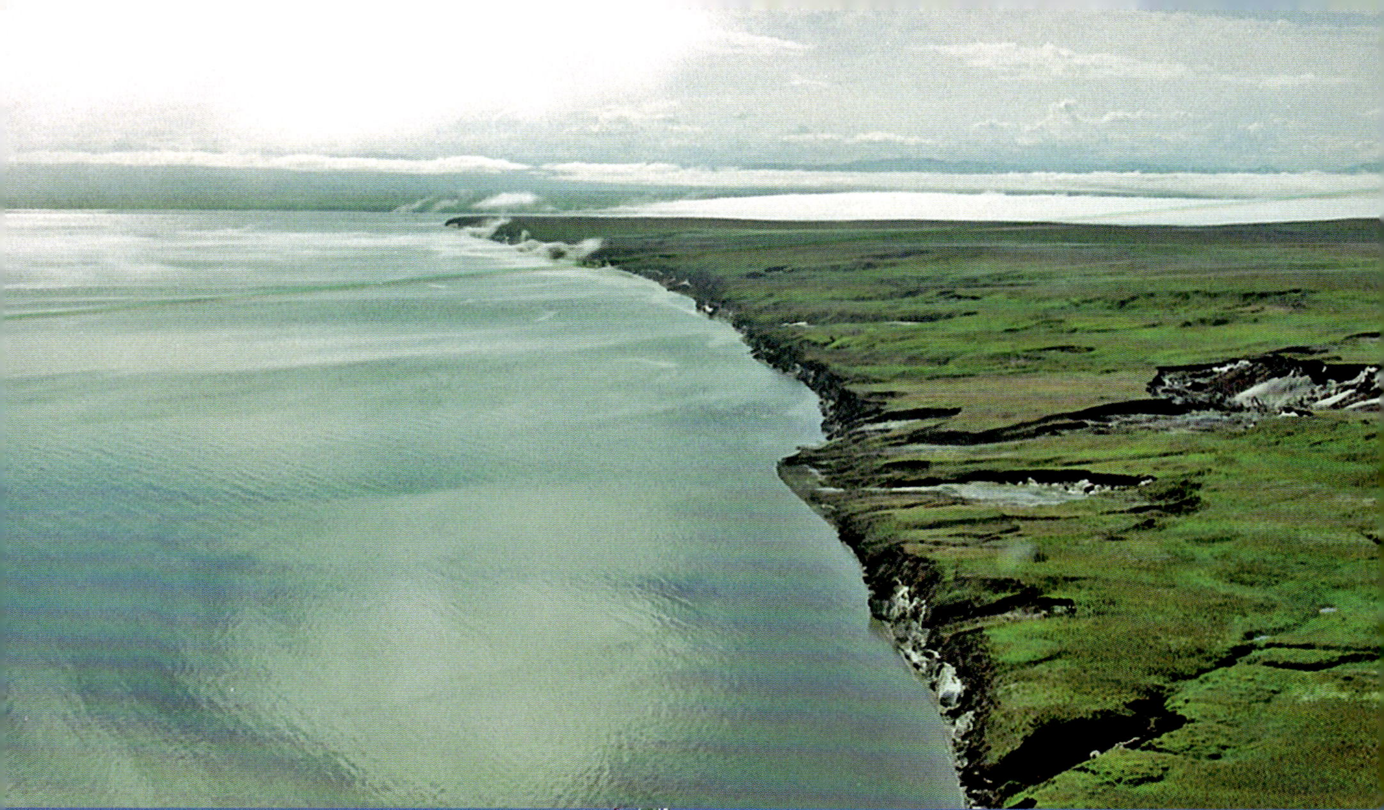

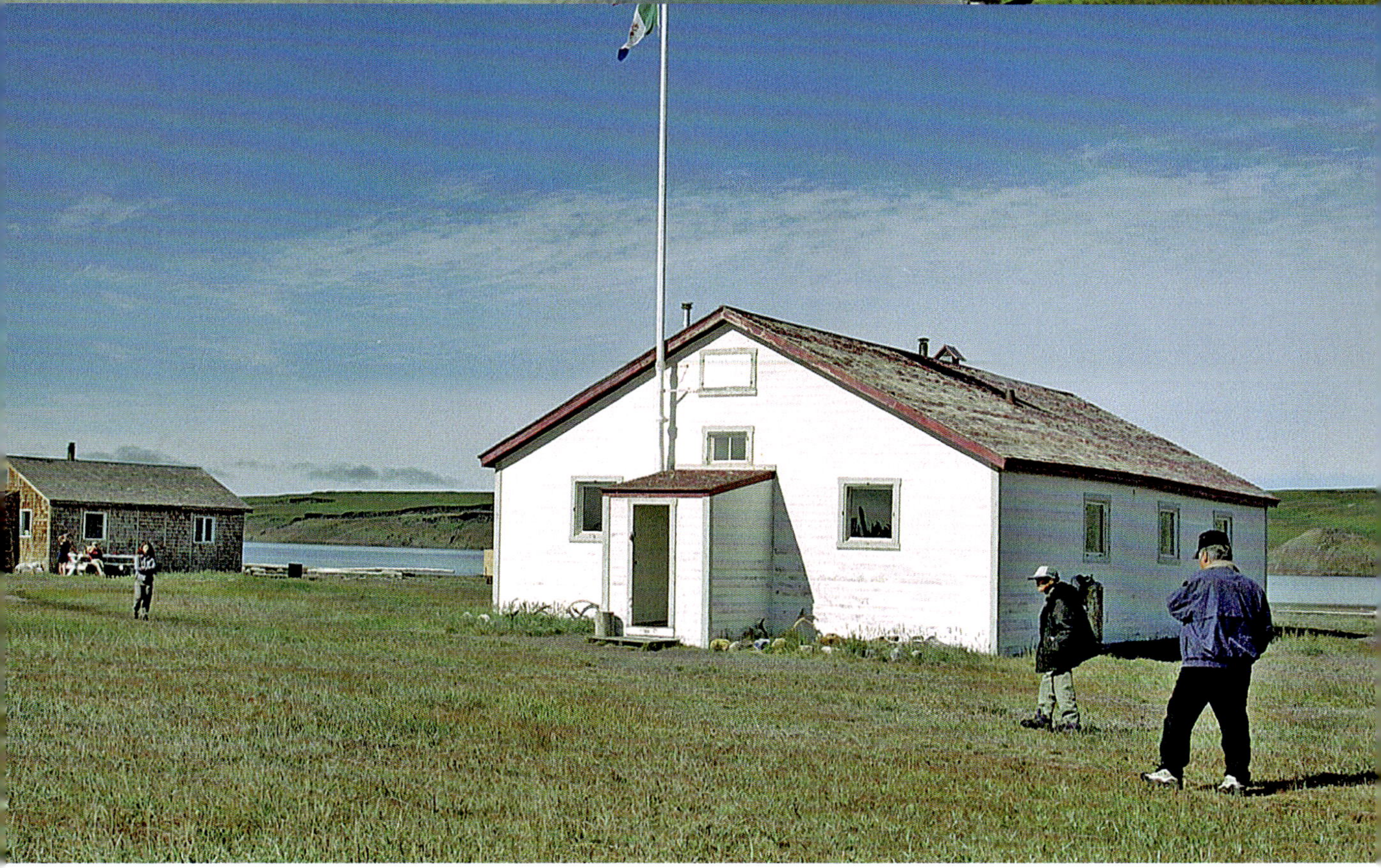

The RCMP Patrol to Herschel Island via Blow River and the Return via Firth River

Roger Moore [patrolled from] Old Crow to Fort McPherson and to the coast [and] I went, too. Then when I came back to Old Crow, myself and Jim Hickling, Herschel Island corporal, they told me to come with him, so…I came [to Herschel Island]. At that time the coast was really hard to go to but the police knew it, so that way I followed to Herschel Island….That's my country but all the time, we knew it from the other side of the mountains, just when we hunted and trapped, that's how we went there long ago….

So I left Old Crow. At that time old Paul Josie stayed [at the] mouth of Driftwood. From there we turned off, from there we follow the dogs all the way to head of Johnson Creek [in Crow Flats] an open place, just little willows. We camped;…went over the mountain and we had to camp there, too. It's a far country but we camped there. The next day, over a big mountain, it's long ways. We went to the head of Blow River, that's where we camped, too, and then just [followed the] river all the way to the mouth, the coast….We had to camp again but this place…we went way around….I [was] going to come over this way…. [At] Isaac's cabin, there's a fishing place there, long bay; there, too, we camped….We left in the morning to Herschel Island and we had to make noon fire. How far we travelled with dog team, gee whiz!

That was good weather; we made a good trip. Only when I left, wind so I turned back. (Two days I left but wind, gee, so I turned back [until there was] no wind. I came back through Firth River.)

I could make it, but that mountain…I had never been there before but I made it….April, month of April. It took 10 days. Well…they thought we got lost—that's why we stayed on the other side of the mountain, for nothing. I told them, "Let's [take the] road here," hah. I could tell [it was a] rat trapper trail. I knew that, even my dogs knew it. My leader just followed it. Well, he smelled gas, oil, so he followed the trail….

Gee, long way, not easy with dog team. I found out, even Ski-doo, soft snow hah! That [time the] snow [was] hard snow, no glacier, just one place is nine mile glacier….I never went ahead of the dogs [to break trail] but you know that wolves and wolverine follow old trails. That really helps, you know. So…I never used no snowshoes, just dogs….We came up a creek and then down [on the] other side. [At the] head of Thomas Creek, the trail is right there, so that way was easy. All the [caribou] fence branches were still there yet, just like willow, dry willow. Some of them were standing up at that time but now I don't

The route to Herschel Island. Father Bulliard and the RCMP on patrol crossing the mountains north of Old Crow.

[Canadian Museum of Civilization, photo Father Jean-Marie Mouchet S2004-1368]

know....Yes, through Firth River, *Antl'it* [valley], I came over there.[24]... Good trail!...

[I went] only one time...just one time. Even then, I made it by myself. I didn't know the country. I never bothered with a map. But long ago, old people told us how Eskimos lived around here. They told me what they do, all that, so [I knew] it's going to be hard to make fire, lots of wood but hard to [find] drift [wood]...to make fire. So, we used a primer [Primus or white gas] stove, only one. But I saw lots of wood. [Voice surprise]...

[It took] ten days, yeah, a long time, long way, you know...from Old Crow.

(ANDREW TIZYA, Herschel Island, July 31, 2000, VG2000-4-11:010-120, English and Gwich'in)

NEIGHBOURS, NEWCOMERS, AND VISITORS

Van Tat Gwich'in have never lived in isolation. They were familiar with other Gwich'in to the east and west, and the Hän and Inuvialuit to the north. More distant Gwich'in travellers encountered other diverse peoples farther down the Yukon River and up the Mackenzie River. As well, other peoples ventured to Van Tat Gwich'in lands. Inuvialuit utilized Crow Flats and traded at Rampart House. A number of white trappers, traders, missionaries, police, nurses, and teachers visited the area, some remaining to marry Gwich'in and raise families.

Inuvialuit in Crow Flats and the Upper Porcupine

The nearest non-Gwich'in neighbours of Van Tat Gwich'in are the Inuvialuit to the north, commonly referred to as *Ch'ineekaii*. Gwich'in long-ago stories record a period of animosity and warfare between the two groups, culminating in *Kò' Ehdanh*'s declaration of peace, and more recently, peace following the hostilities involving *Daachilti'*. Here, the second generation of elders relate friendly experiences with their *Ch'ineekaii* neighbours, while recalling the conflicts of former times and in well-remembered legends. Hannah Netro expressed discomfort when recalling past violence. She, Alfred Charlie, and Dick Nukon recorded the various locations of Van Tat Gwich'in traditional lands where *Ch'ineekaii* used to hunt, trap, trade, and visit in more peaceful times.

War and Peace with *Ch'ineekaii* (Inuvialuit) Neighbours

> Yes, [the *Ch'ineekaii* came to *Diniizhòo*, Game Mountain] too….They even went to *Tl'oo K'at*. Way back in *Van Tat* [Crow Flats]—this is really bad to talk about—but the Gwich'in and the *Ch'ineekaii* fought and killed each other….You see how big *Chyah Ddhàa* [Second Mountain] is? All underneath it people were laying, they said….After that, the *Ch'ineekaii* won so they went back [to their country]. Then one winter, [Gwich'in] got everything ready [and] went after the *Ch'ineekaii*, they said. Over where the largest mountain is located [on the route] to the ocean, they climbed that big mountain while the *Ch'ineekaii* were staying below. They killed all of them. The Gwich'in people won. Then for a long time they were bad to each other. They were not friends.
>
> There are lots of stories about the man called *Kò' Ehdanh* [Man Without Fire]. On the way [by plane] to Whitehorse, you see the big mountains: they're called the Ogilvie Mountains….There, *Kò' Ehdanh* said, "From now on, let's go amongst each other and be good friends." They said he had the last words. That's how [*Ch'ineekaii* and Gwich'in] have become good friends, and still today it's like that….
>
> I saw that *k'ohnjik* [creek]. It runs into the ocean with red water. I didn't know why so I asked the *Ch'ineekaii*. They said, "You see that mountain there? There the Gwich'in people, the Van Tat Gwich'in, killed the *Ch'ineekaii* the last time. That creek runs from the big

mountain. The water is [red with] blood. That's how bad it was, what happened," they said.

"Our land never got destroyed," they said. "They killed lots of people but our land is good."...From that creek the water that runs has man's blood so they [*Ch'ineekaii*] never drink it and they can't drink the ocean water. From long ago, that water never changes, they said...They went for water on a mountain far away. Now they do it with trucks, I guess. They told me about it, the *Ch'ineekaii* over there.

(HANNAH NETRO, *Diniizhòo*, August 1, 2000, VG2000-4-13:048-097, Gwich'in)

Ch'ineekaii (Inuvialuit) in *Van Tat* (Crow Flats)

A long time ago [*Ch'ineekaii*] used to come ratting over on this side of the [British] Mountains. In wintertime they trapped around Timber Hill and David Lord Creek—they came over with dog teams and trapped. I remember they used to come here [Old Crow] for Christmas and New Year's...from Herschel Island.

They didn't go [as far south as Johnson Creek]. One *Ch'ineekaii* named Isaac used to come over every year and he's got family. One guy...says he [was] born in Crow Flats: Ishmail Alunik they call him. Gee, he liked Old Crow people....He was born in Crow Flats so he liked Old Crow people....It's not that far over mountains from Herschel Island.

(ALFRED CHARLIE, Porcupine-Peel, January 19, 1995, 1995:038-039, English)

Most of the time we lived in *Van Tat*—summer and winter. We stayed by *Ch'ineekaii*; lots of *Ch'ineekaii* were around there at that time. We played with *Ch'ineekaii* kids lots of times and snowshoed.

(CHARLIE THOMAS, Porcupine-Peel, January 20, 1995, 1995:99, English and Gwich'in)

Ch'ineekaii in the LaPierre House–Johnson Creek Area

In 1914, Jim Jackson had a trading [post at LaPierre House]. Before that, Ch'ineekaii were around there. But I don't know, even Johnson Creek people never saw them. They talked about that, who saw them from here. They're all gone now. They all died so I don't know.

(DICK NUKON, Porcupine-Peel, January 20, 1995, 1995:71-72, English and Gwich'in)

White Trappers and Other Visitors

There were a number of waves of white trappers into the Van Tat Gwich'in lands, particularly following the Klondike Gold Rush at the turn of the 20th century, and during the Great Depression in the 1930s. Van Tat Gwich'in history of these newcomers varies considerably. Some white trappers and traders are fondly remembered, while others highlighted the difficulties for Gwich'in in protecting and managing their lands and animals. While some newcomers spoiled the area in their efforts at short-term gains, others stayed for a longer duration and married into the community. Ab Schaeffer and Pete Lord, in particular, are remembered for their skill in trapping muskrat so as to increase the muskrat population, and many Gwich'in attribute their own muskrat trapping skills to these two men.

Other white visitors passed through the area, like the explorer Vilhjalmur Stefansson, or are forgotten but for their impact, such as bringing tin cans and radios.[25] Many of the English place names in the area commemorate the white trappers of the 1930s. There are two Johnson Creeks,[26] one in Crow Flats and one near Johnson Creek Village in the upper Porcupine area, and Mount Schaeffer, Schaeffer Creek, and Schaeffer Lake are in Crow Flats. As well, Mason Hill is downstream from the Bell River, and David Lord Creek is upstream from Old Crow. Charlie Thomas and Dick Nukon recalled specific white trappers, some who married into the community and others whose activities were problematic. Hannah Netro spoke of the novelty of the early newcomers. Charlie Linklater related the experiences of his father, a Scottish former policeman. John Joe Kyikavichik described some effects of white trappers' activities in the area around LaPierre House.

White Trappers from Alaska, Whitestone, and LaPierre Areas

> I stayed in Alaska [and] I know lots of white trappers from up there. Rube Mason and Billy Mason. *Altin schoo* [young jackfish]...one *oonjit* [white man] stayed with him. Curtis used to stay there. Schaeffer used to trap around the Johnson Creek area. [He had] two places, that cabin there. [Mostly] they used to trap there....Eagle River, some white people went up there trapping. I forgot all the names of them. I was a kid that time. From Alaska, I known them. [At] LaPierre House, Jim Jackson had store [and] his brother Frank Jackson [was] with him. They took people up there and McPherson people came over [in] wintertime. He helped them with stuff [trade goods], too, [and that] way he got in the hole. Those people, I hear [they] never paid [him] back. They gathered fur from there—Johnson Creek people, some white people around there.

In those days, [they] carried mail with dog team to Rampart House, [and] from Fort Yukon to Rampart. From here police went down and met them and got their mail. They didn't haul much; letters, that's all they hauled I guess, not heavy stuff.

(CHARLIE THOMAS, Porcupine-Peel, January 20, 1995, 1995:105, English and Gwich'in)

Effects of White Trappers in the Whitestone Area

[There] used to be lots of white men fool around that place, lots of them. Ab Schaeffer, Billy Mason, Rube Mason, Curtis. [On] Eagle River—Jim Hawk, Bill Dempsey, Sam Olson, and one white man named Baustom. They stole the country in those days. They used that medicine—poison. They bugger up the country [for the] last 40 years. [It's] getting good now. Everything died off. They spoiled that country so they won't let no white men fool around there no more now.

(DICK NUKON, Porcupine-Peel, January 20, 1995, 1995:62-63, English)

White Trappers Who Married into the Community
Ab Schaeffer, Pete Lord, Victor Peterson

This creek here, in the Gwich'in language, it's called *Ch'anchał Njik*. In English it's Schaeffer Creek. He made a house here, so from a long time ago it's been named Schaeffer. He stayed way down around Fort Yukon. His family was there, too, Margaret, Tommy, and the others. Richard Martin's grandmother, Mary, he married her sister and they had a family. After awhile he arrived around here, I don't know when. He remarried Selena, Esau Thompson's mother, Annie's [sister]....This is where they were raised.

Schaeffer was a good trapper, all over Alaska, here on Crow River, and way up through Johnson Creek. He has a house there, too. That's how much work he did.

In 1924, when I was six years old, I came up this way....In 1936 we came back this way again....From then, I always heard about Schaeffer in Alaska. At New Year's, the muskrat trapping season would open, at that time. There are lots of lakes through Schaeffer Mountain. He was a trapper: he taught Pete Lord how to trap, and his wife, Selena, too. Pete Lord would kill two, three thousand rats a year. Some people got only 1,500 that's all. I was a child yet in Alaska, in the month of February, middle of February, they said Selena had killed 600 rats.

The Second Generation

There was rews all the way down river. He did this every year. Around here in wintertime it was hard; when the muskrat season opened, there was lots of muskrats, every year. This is what they did.

Schaeffer was a good man; he was a man with a good mind. He would tell stories. When they went for muskrats, he had to go there, that's all! He would always talk bad. He didn't mean it, that's the kind of person he was. That's how he was all the time. What a good man, my friend Schaeffer was a good man. There are lots of stories about him.

Peterson who lived back at Black Fox [Creek], there's lots of stories about him, too....I don't know how many years they lived around here, but this is how they lived, long ago, our people. There were lots of white trappers. Good people! Peterson, way back at Black Fox...up at David Lord Creek, David Lord had his place. At LaPierre House, Jim Jackson had a store there. The Fort McPherson people would come over. Them, too, they trapped around there. People used all this land. Two white men were camped around up the Bell River. All of them were good people. At Whitestone, Rube Mason lived for many years, trapping....Since they're gone, all of their camp places have grown over.

(CHARLIE THOMAS, *Ch'anchał Njik* Cabin, June 9, 2001, VG2001-2-16:009-080, Gwich'in)

Early White Trappers

There was lots of white men. There was a white man living in *Van Tat* on the edge of a lake. He only lived on canned stuff, I guess. Ah, they said his camp place was just full of cans. Around there, one Old Crow person was hunting. All of a sudden, he came upon lots of empty cans. He took them away. They say he brought home a big pack of empty cans. Then he used them for dishes and cups. He even cooked in them. He expected bears, so at the riverbank, he strung a rope and tied the cans to it. When the wind blew, it scared the bears. "At first I had no cup. Then I had lots of cups, they were just ringing." He was happy for those cans.

They said that happened when the white man came here....When the miners came, they said it was that time. I wonder what year that happened. Sarah Simon talked about that in front of me. I was a small girl, I stayed with my grandfather. I remember a little bit: she said, "I was afraid of the white man." She said she only stayed by her grandmother. She said that in front of me. Now she's over a hundred years old. They tell the truth, I guess.

(HANNAH NETRO, Driftwood Village, June 26, 2001, VG2001-2-54:113-139, Gwich'in)

An RCMP Officer who became Part of the Community and
an Explorer who Passed Through

It was the year 1918. I barely remember. My dad was a carpenter and he was building whenever he was hired. So this William Stefansson [Vilhjalmur Stefansson] came down the Porcupine River.[27] I don't know how he got there but he landed at New Rampart [House] and the only one that had a rowboat was my dad. My dad was an old ex-policeman. His name was Archie Linklater. His parents came from Aberdeen, Scotland. He was born in Canada. His mother and father emigrated through the Hudson Bay area; this is what I remember.

Stefansson hired my dad to take him down the Yukon River. At that time, the sternwheelers were plying the Yukon and Stefansson had to catch the last boat coming up this way. My dad had to row him down the Porcupine River. In later years, I read Stefansson's book. My dad took him down the Yukon River and he rowed that boat 16 hours a day to get him to Fort Yukon to catch the last boat going out in September. So it was too late to go back. My dad knew he wasn't going to be able to get back up the river [before freeze-up] so he took his dogs and the whole family. We landed in Fort Yukon and my dad built a cabin. He had nothing else to do at that time [but work for the] steamboat and haul wood on the river. So he had to cut wood all winter, and trapping. We only had five dogs. At that time there was lots of rabbits, salmon running up the river, fishnets: sure lots of salmon. But I was only a kid, I barely remember.

I remember my two sisters and brothers went to school and I was raving mad because I didn't go along. I was the only one left at home.... What happened was my dad took that explorer down to Fort Yukon. He got stuck there and spent the winter, and then he stayed around there a year or two until my brother and sister got back. Then [we went] back up to New Rampart House, a village right on the border. While we were there, the residential mission in Fort Yukon burnt down. So we went back down the river again. I didn't know what was going on with my dad, got fired, got hired, I guess, rebuilding that boat [mission].... In 1927, we went back to New Rampart; by the time, my dad was paralyzed....So we moved to Old Crow in 1929. I remember still....Then in 1931, my mother died, drowned. From then on, it was just touch and go. I took care of my father and myself. In that time there was no welfare. I cut wood for five dollars a cord.

(CHARLIE LINKLATER, VG1999-6-2:003-051, English)

Monitoring White Trappers at LaPierre House

> I don't really remember too much about LaPierre House but I am really glad to see it again...and look at it. In some way it might help control this area.
>
> This river here is the Little Bell. On this side, I think a white man stayed. His name was Jim Hawk. He went there every winter [and] trapped...wolf and wolverine, fox, like that. [In those] days those animal were a good price. They fooled around with that medicine [poison—strychnine] for trapping. They got all kinds of fur. Not only him, right down to Old Crow, there's little cabins here and there all the way down, [named for] white people....Indian people don't know about medicine [poison], you know....But that white man up there, he got caught poisoning. I forget what year but police came up from Old Crow and Fort McPherson. They...really caught him and chased him away. That's what happened.
>
> There were so many white people in this country it was getting cleaned [out], so pretty soon Indian people just quit, just like that.
>
> (JOHN JOE KYIKAVICHIK, LaPierre House, July 4, 1997, VG1997-9-15:230-251, English)

Ministers and the Church

The Church of England has been an important presence for Vuntut and Dagoo since the time of Archdeacon McDonald in the late 1800s to the present. The church representatives have been diverse. McDonald created a cadre of lay preachers and some Gwich'in were ordained and preached throughout the region. Later, ministers from elsewhere were stationed in Old Crow for temporary terms. As well, the Roman Catholic Church had a long-term presence in the person of Father Mouchet, OMI, who championed a successful cross-country ski program but did not compete with the Anglicans for converts.

Elders John Joe Kyikavichik, Ellen Bruce, and Hannah Netro revealed the degree of their involvement with the church and Christianity. They considered the church in Old Crow and many of the ministers their own and spoke proudly of them, as well as the strength of their beliefs, the way they adhered to rules, such as the restriction on working on Sundays, and their dedication to church activities, such as the Women's Auxiliary.

Lay Preachers

I remember Julius Kendi. I think he came before 1929 and was here for eleven years. He taught Old Crow people quite awhile, then he left to Mayo and stayed there, I don't know how many years....After that he came back around 1940 and taught in Old Crow. He taught and made his living in Crow Flats at the same time. Julius Kendi worked with Old Crow people with my father, Joe Kaye, beside him, and Ben Kassi: they were lay readers in those days. Somewhere around 1937, Ben Kassi died so Julius Kendi and my father still worked together. And the same time, my father Joe Kaye was chief. Thirty years, and he worked with Julius Kendi that long. Pretty soon he took over the missionary and he worked for 50 years. I think my father learned mostly from Julius Kendi.

Julius Kendi did lots of things for Old Crow. We still remember. I was a kid but I still remember....The first time anybody knew about Christmas trees, and the WA [Women's Auxiliary], Julius Kendi taught all that....He started in the church, this old church right on the left of this mission. Since then, Christmas trees started and Santa Claus is coming all the time....Every house had a tree, a little one, especially the old people. No decorations at that time, no lights, no electricity: they just used coal oil lamps and candles. But anyway, those old people, on their little tree, they cut velvet and yarn in little pieces and put them on the tree. At the bottom, they put a little candle: they say they could see a fancy tree. What little they had, dry prunes or something like that, they gave it to the kids, I remember. Lots of old people gave that to me lots of time.

As far as I know from Julius Kendi, when he was here in 1940, he moved out to Crow Flats, and got some muskrat. Most of the time he taught, travelling around to camps. Part of it is a little bit funny story. Julius Kendi, him and his wife, they went hunting with a canoe, paddling around the edge of the lake. Pretty soon they went to a creek ...a little bit swift water, [and a] little lake there. [It was] Saturday night [and] they were hunting close to 12 o'clock. They started to go home after about half an hour. Julius Kendi paddled down the creek. On the ice, there was a rat [muskrat] sitting there. His wife told him, "Is that a rat there?" Julius Kendi, what he did, he [called] to that rat, "Why don't you sleep all night, sleep on that ice." The rat went into [the water]; he never got it. He went across the little lake, landed, and got out of canoe. He looked at his wife; [she was] still mad at him. That's the way Mr. Kendi made his wife mad just because he didn't shoot that rat.

Because he thought it was Sunday, he never bothered the rat. All day Mrs. Kendi was mad about it. [Chuckles]...

Around 1940...or [19]50, somewhere anyway, Julius Kendi went back to Crow Flats again for the last time. He came down Crow River and he got sick, so they took him down to the Fort Yukon, Alaska, hospital. Not one week, news come back that Julius Kendi is gone. He died of meningitis. We learned lots from Julius Kendi. I know lots of people still remember.

(JOHN JOE KYIKAVICHIK, 1997-02-11:010-100, English)

Ministers in Van Tat Gwich'in Area

I remember the different ministers....Around 1925, the first church minister came around here, Mr. Moody was his name. He was a really good minister. He was the first white minister. He lived here for two winters after that another minister named McCallum came over from Fort McPherson. We had him as a minister for a long time. Those ministers stayed for two years.

At that time, in the summertime and all winter until Christmas, all the people lived by gathering food from the land. In the fall the women worked the skins...caribou and moose skins....Then after New Year, they moved across to those mountains and dried meat and fixed the caribou skins....

After McCallum, a minister by the name of Mr. Ellis was here, too.... This minister, his wife stayed with him. They had children, too.... After that, sometimes in between, there were no ministers here. When that happened, my father Joe Kaye...would be the minister. The Native minister around there, his name was Ben K'ashih [Kassi]. And John Tizya, Joe Kaye, in those days when there was no ministers, they worked in place of the ministers....

After [Mr. Ellis], a minister named Wheeler came here....In between, when there were no minister, a woman who was a nurse made church services with us. My father he helped out a lot. After...Wheeler, then Mr. Hamilton was our minister; then Mr. Exham, Mr. Ferris, [and] John Watts. Altogether 10 ministers were here and left now. In between, James Simon and Julius Kendi came one after another. [Julius Kendi] left and came back again....He got sick and he went back to Dawson and died there. That's a long time ago. That many ministers were here and gone.

Julius Kendi, a lot of white ministers came and went. My uncle Julius Kendi came here in 1929. At that time his wife started the WA

[Women's Auxiliary]....This woman made all the women in Old Crow, WA members. The WA became very strong. Every Friday, we sewed.... There were lots of us, 20 women, 25 in WA. They would all come and cook and eat while they sewed. Nowadays, it's very different....Now it's really different living on this land. The Native work, it's not all being done today. Only a few of them work with skins....The white man's ways of working, they only work that way and our way of life, our work, has come to an end....We think the language is like that, too. Before, the people here, ministers and teachers, all of them didn't want to see the Native language lost. They spent lots of money to teach the Native language....The young people today, they shouldn't think only of the white man's ways. For them to be strong in the Native language, I hope for that.

(ELLEN BRUCE, 1980, VG2000-8-30:003-110, Gwich'in)

Dan Cadzow opened a store at New Rampart. That was in 1904. How do he know [to go there], I wonder to myself? Bishop Stringer, that's how he knew, they said. Bishop Stringer came to this country from Fort McPherson. He taught there....I saw him, Bishop Stringer. He spoke Gwich'in. He was a white man and he spoke good Gwich'in, and Eskimo, too. That is how he taught. He knew lots of languages. Because of him, in 1904 Dan Cadzow opened a store. He never went back down [South] they said.

(HANNAH NETRO, *Diniizhòo*, August 1, 2000, VG2000-4-13:150-180, Gwich'in)

EVENTS AND TRENDS

A number of specific events occurred in the 20th century that would have repercussions for Van Tat Gwich'in. Pressure from non-Gwich'in trappers at various times during the century changed the distribution and availability of game and contributed to the dispersal of the Dagoo amongst the neighbouring Gwich'in nations. The border between Yukon and Alaska came to be enforced with increasing diligence, until ultimately it created a barrier to regular crossing and families came to utilize one side or the other. Later, with the establishment of schools and other services in Old Crow and changes in the fur trade (declining fur prices and rapid increase in trade good prices following World War II), Gwich'in began to move from their villages and camps across their lands to base themselves semi-permanently in town. Finally, one event from the Depression era—the manhunt for Albert Johnson, the "Mad Trapper"— is well-remembered and illustrates a number of events and trends, such as the influx of white trappers and the impact of the new radios they brought with them.

The Dagoo Disperse

The Dagoo Gwich'in lived in the upper reaches of the Porcupine River, at Whitestone and Johnson Creek villages, to LaPierre House. In the mid-20th century, they abandoned the area and dispersed among other Gwich'in groups thereby no longer constituting a separate Dagoo people. The Dagoo descendants Alfred Charlie and Charlie Peter Charlie told the story of where and how they lived prior to this time, and the circumstances of their dispersal.

Chuu Tl'it (Whitestone Village), *Kâachik* (Johnson Creek Village), and the Dagoo

> Yes, [*Chuu Tl'it*] is John Nukon's place. He trapped, hunted, and fished; that's how he made his living. He stayed here a long time alone with his children. His wife had died. He just lived here alone with his children.
>
> Long ago this used to be Dagoo country....In those days they said there were lots of people here. [People lived] over to the Dempster Highway, all around there....At that time, they would go to Dawson in the summertime, in June, I guess. Then in the fall, they came back up [here]....Sometimes too, [they would live] at the place they called *Ts'iizhùu* [Ogilvie] and then go down to Eagle [Alaska] and stay there for the summer [and] some young men worked on the steamboat....In the fall, they would come back up....
>
> They would hunt moose down this way. They came down and stayed here. [Originally the Dagoo were the first to stay in this place, they say]. Then they would sew up the moose skins to make boats. After the ice went out, they...paddled down the river. Down at where they call *Ch'ihilii Chìk* [Whitefish Lake] they would land, and they would set fishnets. There were lots of good whitefish....At Porcupine [River or Lake] they would get grayling and there they stayed. The women would tan the moose skins from the moose skin boats while they waited for them....
>
> Then they would go over to Fort McPherson for the summer. Then in the fall time, [they came] back up again. They would stay down *Kâachik* also and hunted and fished before winter. That was how the Dagoo made their living in those days on this land. There were really lots of people back then, they say....

Elder Alfred Charlie on Chuuts'aii Nàlk'at (Crow Mountain), 2000.
[Shirleen Smith ©VGFN (VG2000-6-162)]

In 1940, around then, Uncle Joe Netro opened a store here. He... would bring in supplies for them and they lived off that for the winter months. Sometimes in the winter, there would be lots of people around here. The people from Old Crow who trapped in this area would stop here, so there was a lot of people here.

Some of them came up to *Kâachik*[28] [Johnson Creek Village] and stayed with us and trapped in the winter....My grandfather *Ch'ichi'Viti'* raised his children at [his place at *Kâachik*]:...Alfred Charlie, Peter Charlie, and John Charlie....They really lived a good life in the winter and made lots of money. They would go to Old Crow. Down at Fort Yukon was the Northern Commercial Store. They would take their fur there and sell them and get supplies for the winter, lots of supplies... enough to last until spring.

Then in the spring after the ice went out, they hunted beavers and sold them in Fort Yukon. In the winter, they killed moose only occasionally. There were lots of caribou around here. They killed caribou in the winter, and in the spring they hunted moose. They dried the meat before the summer. They would land their boats filled with drymeat [and] live on that in the summer in Old Crow.

In those days, there weren't boats like there are today. Sometimes there was no meat in the summer.[29] When they hunted, they used canoes. Up this river [Porcupine] and down toward Old Crow and below there, at the place called *Theetoh Nagwidaanaii*,[30] below there they would hunt with canoes. Sometimes they would kill moose. That's what they did in those days.

Today, there's lots of boats, and lots of caribou, too. Now they have meat freezers that were brought in. That's why we don't run out of meat. In the spring, the caribou migrate near us, and in the fall they do it again, so we don't run out of meat nowadays.

Not long ago there was no school in Old Crow; we just lived alone in the bush. The government didn't know about us, the people [around Old Crow] lived on the land off the animals, small animals, and fish....In those days there was no government [assistance] but it was never hard for them around here. They always lived well....They helped each other and when they got a little something, they looked after each other. I don't remember a time when the people were stuck for anything when I was a child....

This big river is called *Sheihveenjik* [Whitestone River]. Back there is another river just as big. It comes from over that way; it's called *Ch'itr'ihkaiinjik*. In English, they call it Canoe River [now Chance Creek on maps]. All the way to Eagle Plains, they trapped in winter....John Nukon,...Joe Netro, my uncle Paul [Josie], sometimes Peter Tizya, too, and lots of people besides them....

Grandfather John Nukon and my father, too, [trapped] below the Eagle River, up at *Nan ihlah juuka* [Burnt Hill], they call it, above there to Eagle Plains. Where they have the house [Eagle Plains Lodge] at Eagle Plains, around there they would set up their tents....It is a big country up that way. They trapped all over....

(ALFRED CHARLIE, *Chuu Tl'it*, June 25, 2001, VG2001-2-47:005-167, Gwich'in)

Dagoo Territory

The most important thing they came to *Zhoh Drìn Chòo* [White Snow Mountain] for was meat, hah? There is always lots of caribou here, don't matter when: even in wintertime some of the caribou stop here. Caribou stay till next spring, all winter there's caribou here. That is how we are okay. And then pretty soon up [around] *Chuu Tl'it* [Whitestone] and across this way, all that is caribou. Before that, the first time we moved here, they never did that, you know. Then after that, there was always lots of caribou.

Brenda Kay interviewing elders Charlie Peter Charlie and Fanny Charlie on Zhoh Drìn Chòo *(White Snow Mountain), 2001.*

[Shirleen Smith ©VGFN (VG2001-6-654)]

There's three different kinds of caribou. One is the Old Crow caribou, and one is way up at the headwaters of this river: that caribou they call *davadzaii* caribou. It, too, is a big caribou. In the *Nagwachoonjik* [Mackenzie River] area there's lots of small caribou, they call it dog rib. You hear about it? They are small caribou: the caribou cow is just like a calf....

They call this Snow Mountain because there's always lots of caribou on it. Sometimes they even have to come here from Old Crow when there's no caribou there, even Fort McPherson. It must be good food. There's caribou on it every year, mostly bulls, too. It was a good mountain. All the people knew about it. Even Old Crow [people], they came here for meat. Across that way, [*Nagwachoonjik*] runs: that way there are caribou, too...the *davadzaii*,...big caribou. That caribou has calves just like young bulls. That big! So, when we lived on it...we were busy all the time.

And [there were] lots of moose here. In the fall they killed lots of moose and dried the moose meat, not quite dry, just half-raw. When it's like that they put it in the cache for the winter. First of May, they took it out and...then it's dried for summer. Lots of dried meat, moose meat, caribou, too.

The Second Generation

At *Kâachik* [Johnson Creek] we never ran out of food. This mountain, too, they hunted here even from Old Crow when there were no caribou there. One winter, lots of people from the other side [of the mountains], made drymeat here; lots of McPherson people, about 15 families I guess. So it's an important mountain, this one. In the summer and in the fall, people from Old Crow hunted way up [*Nagwachoonjik*] for moose—not [usually] to *Kâachik*, just a very few times—mostly to the mouth of Bell River. We never ran out of people around here, always people here.

(CHARLIE PETER CHARLIE, *Zhoh Drìn Chòo*, June 29, 2001,
VG2001-2-63:007-062, Gwich'in)

Long ago, they said a lot of people lived around here [upper Porcupine River], the Dagoo people. From here, the Dagoo people scattered all over: Dawson, Eagle, lots went over to Fort McPherson. My grandfather *Ch'ichi'Viti'* along with his children, he stayed behind and lived here. He made his living around here with his children during the winter. In the summer, they went down to Rampart House. They came back in the fall time and stayed here all winter. That's how the people lived in this country. Then sometimes they went to Fort McPherson. Around *Zheh Gwatsàl* [LaPierre House], they all moved there, all of them. My uncles, my father, all of them. They all went over to Fort McPherson. They lived all summer in Fort McPherson, then in the fall, as it was freezing up, then they came back over to *Kâachik*. Then every year they did the same thing. Ah, they lived good; I remember as a child....

(ALFRED CHARLIE, *Ch'ii Ch'à'an*, July 29, 2000,
VG2000-4-8:041-061, Gwich'in)

The Dagoo People and Life around *Ni'iinlii Njik* (Fishing Branch River)

I said there were lots of Dagoo people. Now they're all [gone], there's no more. Only Edith [Josie] is Dagoo around Old Crow. At Dawson, Joe Henry and his wife, only they are Dagoo now. Our father Peter Charlie was raised at Johnson Creek. My mother was from Arctic Village and we're from there, too, so we're not Dagoo. Dick Nukon was raised around there. They call us Dagoo now, too. They all went back around McPherson so there's no more [Dagoo] people. Peter Alexie, Abraham Alexie, only their children and William Vittrekwa's wife, Mary Esau, and her children: they're all from around here. Then my uncle [John Charlie] children, they are Dagoo now and they live in Fort McPherson. Peter and Abraham Alexie, sometimes they trap way up around Eagle Plains

Donald Frost on Ch'ii Ch'à'an *(Bear Cave Mountain), 2005.*
[Shirleen Smith ©VGFN (VG2005-3-271)]

in winter and their children go, too. That's all. Long ago they said there was a lot of people.

In the winter when they had no meat around here, the Dagoo people had a hard time hunting. There wasn't many moose up at *Sheenjik* [Fishing Branch River].[30] In the middle is a spawning place for chum salmon. They knew this so they moved there and set up camp. [The next day] they went to fish but a grizzly bear lived up above there, where it's called Bear Cave Mountain. I guess sometimes it's warm during the winter, so the grizzly bear doesn't go into his den early. There were two of them.

So there was no food and the grizzly bears were taking the fish. They went after them and found Bear Cave Mountain. When an animal is in his den, they say he doesn't fight. They knew that so they went inside *Ch'ii Ch'à'an* [Bear Cave Mountain]. It was dark so they felt around for the bear. My grandfather *Ch'ichi' Viti'* said, "I touched the grizzly bear, I touched its ears. I told them to give me the gun so they gave me the gun. Where I thought his neck was, I shot." That's how they killed the two grizzly bears inside Bear Cave Mountain. They tied a rope to the bears and pulled them out.

There's lots of stories about *Ch'ii Ch'à'an* in those days. At that time there were no candles. Way down at the river they would get dry wood and make wood shavings and kindling. They went inside the caves with that but it was never a strong enough light. There were lots of people then living in skin tents, made of caribou skins....

Sometimes around here the Dagoo went down to Rampart House when they built the houses, they heard that....There they would pick up supplies and live around here in the summer and winter. Before the Hudson's Bay [Company] first put the store at Fort McPherson, there was really no stuff [trade goods]. The Dagoo around here and the Fort McPherson people didn't know about tea, tobacco, and things like that....At that time it was really far to Fort McPherson from here, to Dawson, too.

In those days the young men were smart. Those they thought were smart, they would send to Fort McPherson. Then animal fur wasn't sold: dried meat and tanned hides were traded for tobacco and tea. There was no brush so they could see them coming a long way. The people would meet them. The women would put on water inside the skin tents to make tea. The young men would be walking and they gathered to meet them. The first young man who was coming, when he got close to the people, he would put tobacco in a pipe and light it. He would approach the people and the first person standing there, he would give him the pipe. They would puff two times on it and pass it on to the others. That's how they came home [with] tobacco. Then the second young man coming, inside the women were boiling water, [and he] took the tea inside and they made tea. After all the people had smoked they went inside and drank tea. They took one cup, passed it around and drank it. But they didn't bring lots of tobacco or tea home. Sometimes it lasted only two days. After that there was no more, only meat broth. That's how it was long ago when our grandfathers first got trade goods. They lived off the land and carried on.

(ALFRED CHARLIE, *Chuu Tl'it*, June 25, 2001,
VG2001-2-47:167-363, Gwich'in)

The Effects of the Border with Alaska

Although Alaska was purchased from Russia by the Americans in 1867, it was not until 1911 that the border with Canada was formally surveyed and subsequently enforced. Fairly immediately, the border affected trade in the region. The initial consequences were felt by the Hudson's Bay Company, which was required to abandon Fort Yukon and move eastward to British-Canadian territory a number of times before ultimately abandoning the

Yukon Territory. Trade was impacted in the longer term because the easiest accessible river access to southern trade goods, the Yukon River, eventually became unavailable to Canadian traders. The boundary survey itself affected the area when the survey party arrived at Rampart House, bringing with it a disease initially resembling smallpox. A quarantined "hospital" was set up on an island in the river, and the homes and possessions of those suspected of infection were destroyed. Later, a customs checkpoint restricted the amount and kinds of goods that could pass over the line, and imposed levies that restricted free travel. Ultimately, although on their own lands, Gwich'in had to decide which country they preferred to live in, and some families relocated. The border caused a number of restrictions in land use and made it gradually more difficult for Gwich'in to associate regularly with their relatives and friends across the line. Currently Gwich'in traditional territory is in the jurisdictions of Alaska and two territories in Canada. Charlie Thomas, Clara Tizya, and Dick Nukon spoke of the effects of the border on Gwich'in life before and after it was enforced. Mary Kassi described the remains left behind by the survey party.

When the Border was not Enforced

> New Rampart, that's [on the] Alaska Border. Most of them that stayed there were American, but no border [was enforced] for Indians in them days. [People] moved back and forth, no customs. A policeman was there at New Rampart—but they didn't bother Indians.
> (CHARLIE THOMAS, Porcupine-Peel, January 20, 1995, 1995:102, English and Gwich'in)

How the Border Limited Hunting

> [When people moved from Rampart to Old Crow a lot of it had to do with fish and wildlife rules.] After the boundary was set in, for a long time nobody bothered about borders or boundaries, you know. So the people just continued with hunting and everything they were doing, trapping. They went over the border...But just before we moved, a couple of years, the game wardens started patrolling so we couldn't go over the border anymore without taxes or licences or whatever. So the last few people moved up, moved away. But I always thought it [Rampart House area, right on the border] would be a nice place for a couple of people to make a living, you know, because they can trap over that way.

A lot of our people used to trap across that way. There was a lot of marten and things. My dad used to go over that way. [It's] really good hunting for moose but it's over the border. The men used to go [over the border] and kill moose in the fall...We didn't care then but later we had to be careful. When dog salmon come, it is the time you just get them by the hundreds. They used to just throw them up on the beach because it was already cold, you know. We used them for dog feed and we ate them, too. And then we brought them up and put them in the cache [when they were] frozen. Frozen fresh, they are good. We used to get king salmon in the summer but just enough to eat. My aunt used to dry quite a bit because she was alone.

(CLARA TIZYA, June 5, 1997, VG1997-9-07:102-129, English)

Signs of the Surveyors

Then there were surveyors here, down to Rampart House mountain: it leads to Rampart House, you know. Up there is where the border is; the Alaska border crosses there. Long ago, they came up there with horses...Then out in *Van Tat* [Crow Flats], I don't know how they died, [but] down around the river, you can find horse bones. Along this mountain, the surveyors made a trail through right toward this mountain. They marked it with lots of stones; [now] they're all gone. When the boys [young Gwich'in hunters] came around they probably knocked them down, I guess.

Rampart House is just down there. People came up and lived around here, for berries and caribou meat. They lived all over and dried caribou meat. They killed ground squirrels. People knew this area well.

(MARY KASSI, *Ch'anchàl*, August 2, 2000, VG2000-4-17:042-055, Gwich'in)

Customs, Licences, and Fees

In 1926, around then, the Fort Yukon people would go to Crow Flats. They had to pay a $100 licence. There was customs at Rampart House. If they killed a dog, if they had a broken toboggans, broken snowshoes, and they left it behind there, they had to pay for that. Custom gave them the order. They reported it; that was how. Lots of Fort Yukon people lived around here.

(CHARLIE THOMAS, *Van Tat*, June 10, 2001, VG2001-2-20:150-157, Gwich'in)

The Effects of Borders and Boundaries

> In those days, people moved around all over—no border in those days....Alaska people could come up to Canada. Canadian people could go down to the American side. No problem. Then the border line started so they watched for that. You can't do what you like, where you want to go. You can't go to the Alaska side. Our land right here, the McPherson people, they start the land [claims], you know. That's why we wouldn't let them come to the Yukon side. They sold their land so they got no place to go. That's why they bother this land. One year they asked for land—just to lend it to them. Around Eagle Plains, we lent them land. They made a meeting for it. They gave them that area. You could do what you like: hunting trapping like that....After you finish, then you finish. And then, they trapped and hunted like that, and they came back here again and they wanted more land. We said, "No way. You asked for land, we lent it to you and you trapped on it and then you want some more. No way." That area, the Eagle Plain area right up to Blackstone [River] and way down to Hungry Lake—that's the Northwest Territories side—I [travelled] around there, me and my dad. I walked with snowshoe every day, all over. I don't think I'm ever going to go back to that area any more till I die—finish.
>
> (DICK NUKON, Porcupine-Peel, January 20, 1995, 1995:81–82, English and Gwich'in)

Moving to Town

Van Tat Gwich'in and some of the Dagoo people make their homes in Old Crow today. People moved from various locations on the land, such as Whitestone Village, Driftwood Village, Johnson Creek Village, and Rampart House, to Old Crow, beginning in the 1920s with the closure of trading at Rampart House. During the 1950s, the remaining villages were abandoned due to lack of game and furs and people relocated in Old Crow and relied on muskrat trapping in Crow Flats for their income. Gradually services, such as the RCMP, churches, health, and education, were established in Old Crow. Elders described the gradual growth of Old Crow as a semi-permanent settlement. John Kendi described what he saw in the early days of the town. Edith Josie, Dick Nukon, and Kenneth Nukon all moved from the Whitestone River area to Old Crow. Both Dick Nukon and Alfred Charlie identified the school as a factor in remaining in Old Crow.

Martha Benjamin (wife of Special Constable Peter Benjamin) and her dog team that she raced annually at the Sourdough Rendezvous in Whitehorse, Yukon, ca. 1960.

[Yukon Archives, Richard Harrington fonds 85/25 #4]

Changes in Old Crow in the 1950s

When I first came to Old Crow [in] 1929, there was hardly anything around here: nothing, just a few houses. No government help [for] people at that time. People work for their own living. The old people get their pension from the government, only $5.00 a month. That's not very much compared to what we get now. And then Erik Neilson[32] came to Old Crow around 1957 and then we started to going up a little all the time. He put our pensions way up. All the old people got a good pension. And then we got everything: all the airport and airplanes, everything.

So we're doing a little better now but the [price of] groceries is a little too high around here. But I hope Neilson do something about that soon. [Laughter]

(JOHN KENDI, 1980, VG2000-8-27:091-100, English)

Relocating from *Chuu Tl'it* [Whitestone Village] to Old Crow, and Early Health Services

1940, [was the] first year I got to Old Crow. We got to Whitestone [Village] and stayed there the spring. After breakup, we [came] down to Old Crow with skin boats. The first time I was in Old Crow, by that time [there were] quite a few people [there], over about 200 people. In those days there was hardly any nurse, only the RCMP [officer] and his wife, Corporal Kirk and Mrs. Kirk. No nurse so Mrs. Kirk looked after the patients. And there was no way they could take patients to hospital, [only] by boat and by dog team in wintertime. So when they took patients to hospital, down to Fort Yukon with dog team, it was getting too late...

1940-42, that year some kind of flu [came] around Old Crow and [there was] no hospital, too. So I think over 20 people, man, boys, and girls, passed away. If a nursing station or nurse was here, and if they know which way to take the patient to hospital, those people would live yet. But there was no way to send them out so quite a few passed away.

During summertime we stayed here, and last of August, we took a winter outfit and went up to Whitestone....It took us about one week.... We stayed at the mouth of the Whitestone [River], if the water [was] not high....We stayed there till freeze-up. After freeze-up and snow, we moved up to Whitestone [Village] with dog team. We spent [the winter] there and...after breakup we came down to Old Crow [by] boat....

After three years, every one of us stayed in Old Crow. I think that started from 1949, we started to stay in Old Crow. 1950 we stayed in Old Crow, we spent [wintertime] here in Old Crow. Next summer...1951, that's the first year they sent a nurse here. And then...they worked out so they sent some patients to Aklavik hospital. Since that people never pass away.

(EDITH JOSIE, January 1980, VG2000-8-19E, English)

Trapping and Rising Prices for Supplies

The fur we got during the winter, [my father] took to Fort Yukon. They bought the fur in Fort Yukon and Fairbanks. I went to Dawson with him. Dawson NC [Northern Commercial] store was there, and he was selling stuff cheap. We bought lots of supplies. He brought the cargo by the steamer *Yukon*, down to Fort Yukon. Then my daddy got his own boat, and we came upriver with that. From Fort Yukon to Old Crow; it took us four days. We stayed here four or five days and then went right up to *Chuu Tl'it* [Whitestone] for the winter.

Then we went up to Dawson City. The fur buyer there bought his fur. There were six of them [fur buyers] there. I remember who bought his fur, his name was Kay Wilson. I remember [my father] made $17,000 one year. My dad bought a boat and kicker [outboard motor]. That time my brother Kenneth Nukon stayed at Old Crow and looked after 23 dogs all summer. [Laughs] From 1927 till 1949, the last time we were at *Chuu Tl'it*....Supplies were getting too high so [it cost] too much money to go up there. So everything happened gradually in Old Crow: school started, lots of work. People quit what they used to do and worked for wages. So, they don't do much trapping now.

(DICK NUKON, August 9, 1994, VG1997-7-4:138-176, Gwich'in)

Moving to Old Crow for School

Before that there was no school, so the first year [there was] going to be school [1950], that's when Whitestone and Johnson Creek Village, all those people moved down here [to Old Crow]. Since then, nobody goes back there. Just once in a while some winter we go up there trapping, while [the children] go to school. The mothers have to stay home and look after the kids. They go to school today yet. That's how we left that country. We didn't leave it, really—we go up there once in a while hunting for moose with boats. We try to go up there with dog teams [but] since then kids go to school, so people never go out.

(ALFRED CHARLIE, Porcupine-Peel, January 19, 1995, 1995:42-43, English)

Leaving Whitestone to Live Near Old Crow

I lived in a tent a long time, you know....1941, we left Whitestone, your mother [Hannah Netro], too. We moved down here. After that I went up to Goose Camp with a tracking line, me and my Annie. We were poor, too, I remember: no tea, no nothing. We stopped at Caribou Lookout. I set a net and we got jack fish, that's all we got. That time my [son] Peter was small, my John was small. My Peter just ate all the jack fish, that's all we had and when we got to Goose Camp, we had a poor tent, too. We got there and...stayed all winter...and I started to build a house. In two weeks, I built a house....From that time, I stayed up there every year, you know.

(KENNETH NUKON, August 1979, VG2000-8-02, English)

The Mad Trapper Incident

Elders tell of an event in 1932 that caused unusual concern among Van Tat Gwich'in and other residents, the local RCMP, and beyond. The trapper Albert Johnson entered the Rat River area and following complaints from his neighbours, he shot an investigating RCMP officer. A manhunt ensued, which ended in Dagoo and Van Tat Gwich'in country. The story highlights some novel ways in which the Gwich'in were linked to the outside world at the time, such as the worldwide depression that brought an influx of white southerners, some with few other options, to try their hand at trapping in the North, the various relationships between Gwich'in and these newcomers, and the technology they brought with them to "keep in touch": the radio. As well, the Mad Trapper story tells of the co-operation between Gwich'in and the RCMP and with other white trappers, in monitoring the land and serves as a temporal "marker" to Gwich'in oral history of the early 20th century. A succession of Elders laid out the story, from Alfred Charlie's description of Albert Johnson and the initial incident that sparked the manhunt, to Dick Nukon and Hannah Netro's recollections of the tension and fear that resulted, and Dolly Josie's account of the climax and aftermath.

Albert Johnson, the "Mad Trapper"

> He came to Aklavik with a raft and moved to Rat River. Albert Johnson put a cabin right on somebody's trapline. That winter somebody went to set traps on his trapline and Albert Johnson went on that guy's trapline and sprung some traps. When that guy went back to look at his traps and they were sprung, he went to Aklavik and reported Albert Johnson. Then…the RCMP they went to his cabin to talk to him and that's where he shot one of them. Somehow he got away from his cabin and came all the way over to this side, into the Yukon, and crossed the trail above LaPierre House. All that time the RCMP were chasing him around with dog teams but Albert Johnson had to pack and him, he walked. The RCMP from Aklavik and Fort McPherson and other guides and helpers assisted them to look for Albert Johnson. Shortly after the RCMP from Old Crow and the special constable went to help them. There were about 50 teams.
>
> They got Albert Johnson on Eagle River…by a long bend. He was on that long point when he heard a noise and thought that the RCMP surrounded him, but what he heard was the echo over the portage. He made a place there in the snow low enough to hide, and that's where he was stuck and that's where they got him….
>
> (ALFRED CHARLIE, January 20, 1995, *LaPierre House Oral History*, 110–111, Gwich'in)

Spreading the News by Radio

The year the Mad Trapper cause trouble, 1932....I never saw him, but we heard about it. You know what happened. At that time we were on the Whitestone River and two trappers were staying below us, ten miles, two white guys [one was Frank Foster]. They were good friends of my dad.

We wanted to go to Eagle by dog team. So, [my father] went to let those white men know, he said. He went down to see them, just 10 miles. He hitched up the dogs and then went down and when he came back, he brought the news. One guy had a big radio....When he came back he told us he heard on the radio last night that a man name Johnson shot that RCMP last night in Aklavik. That was the Mad Trapper. The next day we just left. It took us one month to go down there. We took our time. So when we got to Eagle, the people there had heard all that happened. They hunted for the Mad Trapper, people from there, they hunted for that guy too, eh. They all heard on the radio, they told my father that I guess.

We stayed down there [Eagle, Alaska] almost a month and then came back to Whitestone. The next day my dad went down to see those two white guys again. When he got down there, they told my dad that the guy who shot the police, they got him yesterday. He got shot yesterday on Eagle River. I know where he got shot, you know. Yeah, he got shot on February 20. So, you saw the news about him I guess?

(DICK NUKON, August 9, 1994, VG1997-7-4:208-239, Gwich'in)

Fear on the Trails

I remember that when we were coming back [from Eagle] I ran in snowshoes behind my father. At that time...I was running after my dad...[after] we heard about Albert Johnson in Eagle on the radio, and when we were coming over the mountain, somebody was hollering to us and they were wondering what was going on. We were all scared, somebody was hollering and we stopped and waited and pretty soon that person was coming toward us. For sure we thought it was Albert Johnson. We were scared and even hid, and my dad stood there and this guy and my dad talked back and forth. And my dad hollered to that guy, "Who are you?" The guy said "Alfred Kendi." Alfred Kendi was from Fort McPherson. He was just going back to Fort McPherson from Dawson....When we stopped and waited for that guy for sure we thought it was Albert Johnson. My dad and the other guy even had guns ready. The other guy thought the same because him, too, he heard about Albert Johnson around Aklavik.

After we came back to Johnson Creek, my dad went to find out what was happening with Albert Johnson and when he got there he heard that they shot [him]. They started looking for him in January and when they shot him, it was February 20. I remember good. There were lots of people helping to search for him and they caught him up Eagle River. On Eagle River there is one big bluff: that's where they shot him, on that long stretch under the big bluff. They had a hard time getting him. When they saw him under that bluff, the dogs made noise and the echo of the dog was the other way. He thought it was upriver and when he was running back away from the noise, he ran right into them. He ran right under the place where they were waiting for him; they waited on top of the bluff and he was down on the river. And that's where they shot him.

Albert Johnson was a good shot so they were kind of afraid of him. There were lots of people; white people that stayed up river like Rube Mason and Jim Hogg and all those people, those white men that stayed upriver, they helped to hunt for him. Johnny Moses was there and there were some people from Fort McPherson [and] the RCMP....Johnny Moses was there and they were afraid of Albert Johnson because he was a good shot and they thought he might kill them. Johnny Moses was...among those people when they were shooting at him....Johnny Moses is from Old Crow and he was a special constable then. And he's the one who shot Albert Johnson. When they did kill him, they said that Albert Johnson had a gun and lots of shells.

(DICK NUKON, March 1994, *LaPierre House Oral History*, 52–54, Gwich'in)

Fear in the Camps

You heard about that Mad Trapper, they got him here at Eagle Lodge?... Yeah, they call it *Chii Vee*, Grey Rock. You could see it from lodge, that's where they got him. All the way from McPherson, he came by Rat River....

[He had a gold ring] from his mom, or that's what he said. So they sent that ring out to his family. It's true, his mom got that ring for him. So that part is okay.

Eagle Lodge, maybe we were around there, my dad's family....My mom was there, my sister Ellen Bruce, she was grown up. I had three [sisters]. I was about 10 years old, I think....We were there January till March, I guess. So while we were there, a long away out [the Mad Trapper was there].

We didn't know [about it] until my brother came back to town to get groceries. When he came back, the RCMP talked to him about the Mad Trapper...Albert Johnson. We had to watch out. My dad talked to us, scary, but he told us if we see the guy to talk nice to him and give him tea or whatever [if he comes around] when [my dad] was gone hunting, trapping, or when we were alone....So, we had to do that. If he didn't want tea, whatever he needs, maybe matches, we should give it to him, he said. But we didn't see him. They got him over here.

(HANNAH NETRO, July 21, 1999, VG1999-2-4:293-360, English)

After the Shooting

Even though I was very young at the time I remember a lot of what was going on at that time. This man had started acting strange and knew that people were beginning to work with him. I don't remember how many police were behind him. I do know that Uncle John Moses was with them. And he had started following the river. Uncle John Moses was a special constable for the RCMP at that time and he was on the manhunt. He was the one who killed him.

After that a year passed and the following summer John Moses had some problems. The manhunt that he was on had affected his personal life. He went away and stayed in the bush for one month. Peter Moses held a meeting for John Moses with the people of Old Crow and requested that they leave items that he would need in the bush on a trail behind the village. Items like food and mosquito nets, which he picked up when...there wasn't anyone there. People kept a watch out for him but whenever he was approaching and saw anyone, he disappeared back into the bush. For about a week no one did anything about it and finally one day...John returned to his home and to his wife and children. At that time Peter Moses asked him some questions about his behaviour. John Moses explained that he was a special constable following orders, performing his duties. "In the course of my work I have performed the duty that did not agree with me and this had some serious effect on my mentality and that is why I had some problems. The thought of this had gone to my head and I had some serious mental problems." And this is what he told Peter Moses and this is what I remember.

(DOLLY JOSIE, March 19, 1994, *LaPierre House Oral History*, 59-60)[33]

Endurance and Change

Elders from the second generation emphasized the changes that have occurred between what their parents and grandparents told them of the past, their own youth, and their later years, and between their lives and those of their children and grandchildren. The greatest change is the amount of time people spend in town now versus when the elders and previous generations spent their lives entirely on the land. The elders expressed sadness about this change, but they emphasized that the land and animals remain pivotal in Van Tat Gwich'in life: they continue to rely on the caribou, fish, moose, birds, and other animals; plants, such as berries, "bush tea," and wild rhubarb; wood for heating and building homes; and clean, local water sources. Elders often expressed concern for the future, in the context of great changes in their lifetime and their experiences with uncertainty. They say that during hard times to come, the land will continue to provide salvation for future generations of Van Tat Gwich'in.

Second-generation elders like John Joe Kyikavichik reflected on the importance of Crow Flats and the mountains around it for Van Tat Gwich'in survival in the past and possibly in the future. Charlie Thomas repeated his grandmother's information on the last caribou fence and its importance, as well as the position of his grandfather who was the last keeper of the fence. Lydia Thomas illustrated the continuity between her early life and that of her grandparents' generation: hard but rewarding times. Ellen Bruce's commentary is about social life: the way a proper feast was held in the past and present, and the way family disputes were resolved by the community. Dick Nukon related changes that occurred in his family's lives—and those of many others—over a century in the past, with the Klondike Gold Rush. Charlie Thomas provided detailed knowledge of caribou, reflecting his concern about the connection between the past and future importance of caribou for Van Tat Gwich'in. Finally, Alfred Charlie stressed the overarching importance of the land and his message for the younger generations: monetary wealth is transitory, but there is always a living to be made from the land—if you take care of it.

The Past and Future in the Heartland

> In this country around here, since a long, long time ago our grandfathers and grandmothers, who we knew, lived around here on the land, here in *Van Tat* [Crow Flats]. Before that, their parents all lived around here. You see the mountains up there? Caribou fences are located at different places and they have names. Up there, you see the big valley? It's called Caribou Fence Valley….Down that way…is Thomas [Creek]

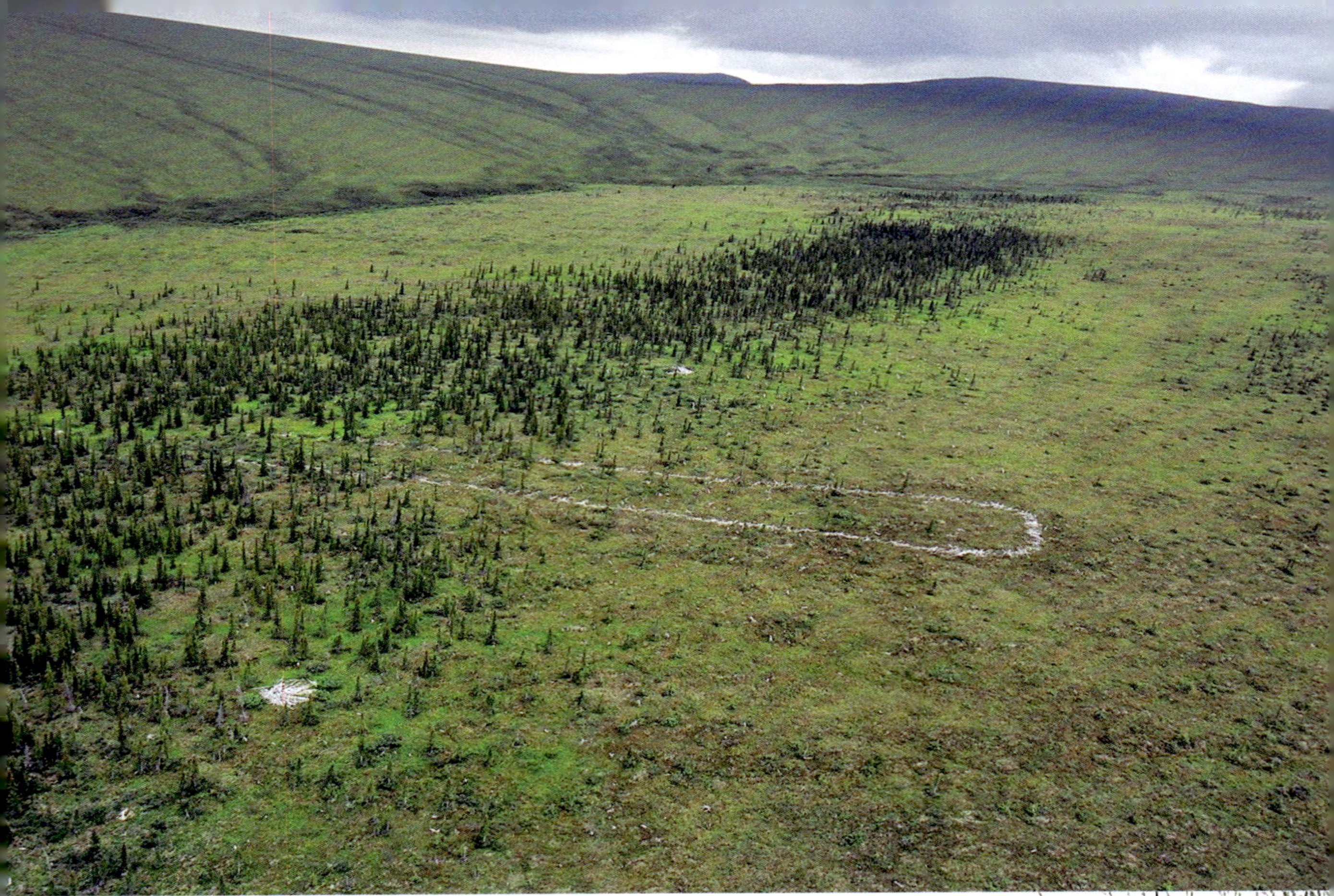

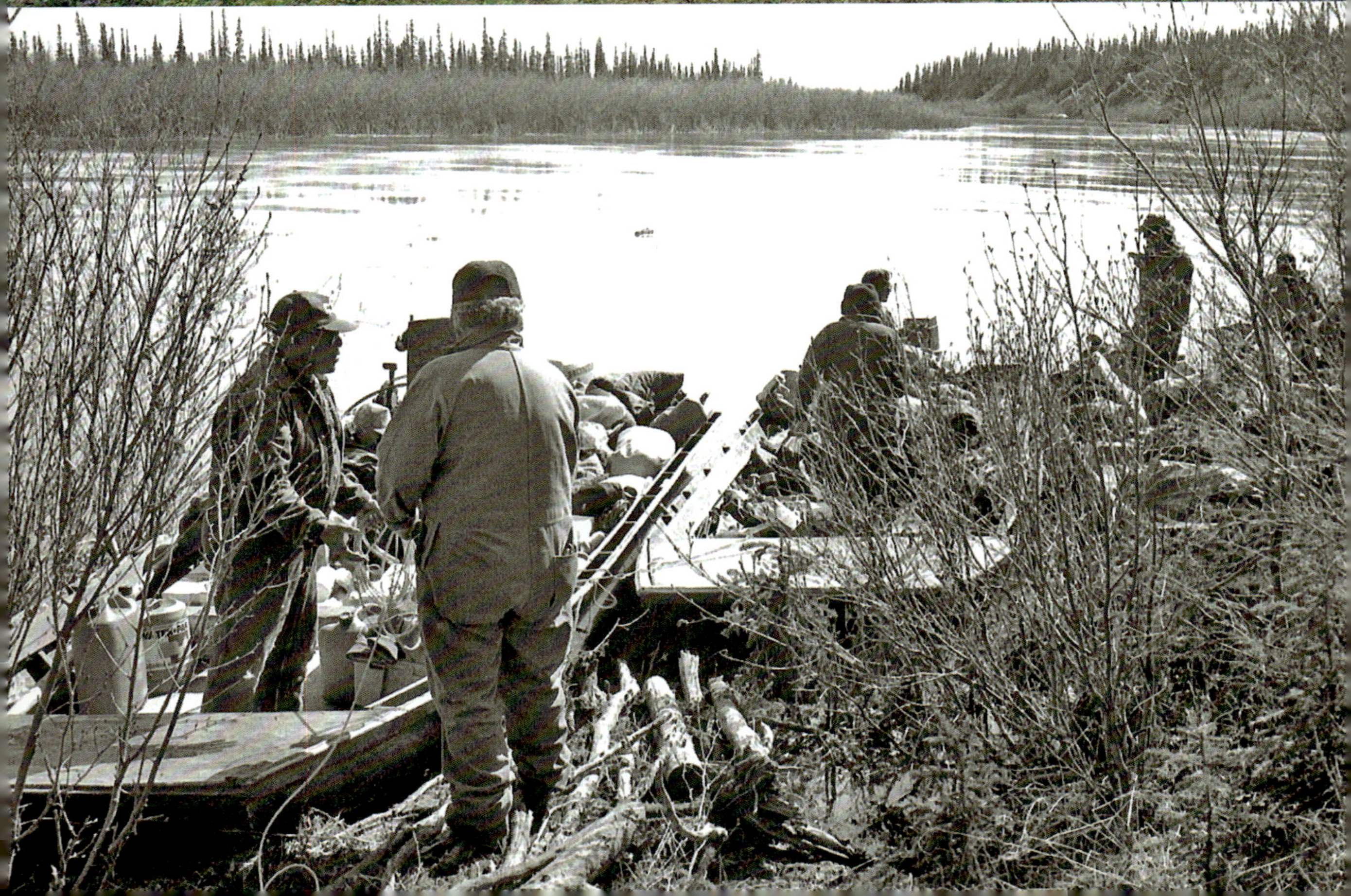

Page 252 (top): Black Fox Creek Caribou Fence #2, 2004.
[Shirleen Smith ©VGFN (VG2004-6-270)]

Page 252 (bottom): Boats at Cook's Camp, Chyahnjik *(Crow River). Foreground (L–R) John Joe Kyikavichik, Robert Bruce Jr., 2001.*
[Shirleen Smith ©VGFN (VG2001-6-369)]

caribou fence. All this was done by our great, great grandfathers who worked so hard to build all the caribou fences. From then and we used this area as a family; we made our living this way and were still do that today yet.

Families, how our parents taught us, today we still follow that and work for ourselves. That's why when I talk in meetings about that time, I always say that the land is different to me. I say that. How is it going to be in the future? Nowadays our children are going by white man's ways. This land is just nice around here, now you see there's no one out here. There's no people. It used to be noisy in *Van Tat*....

Here today, I see my father's place again. Long ago, our grandfathers, our fathers, and our grandmothers were strong. You see that lake up that way? You see how big the lake is? My grandmother used to walk along the lakeshore trapping muskrats. She would trap ducks and bring them home. She would feed us well, we children. When they raised us, that's how they made a living, lots of hard work. We were not raised like today. They did not even have rubber [boots], just canvas boots, and they walked along lakeshores. Even when their shoes tore, they never gave up. That's how, long ago, our elders raised their families...and this is why we live so good now. You see the mountain, it goes all the way to Fort McPherson and land claims. We talked about it for a long time and we're still talking about it. Maybe some day people might use *Van Tat* again. Maybe they might listen to us. And if they do, they may see what happened long ago, the way they used to work. And if they see all the old camps and the canoes, then it might be a good thing, and hard, too. And this all I'm going to say.

(JOHN JOE KYIKAVICHIK, *Van Tat*, June 11, 2001, VG2001-2-31:046-096, Gwich'in)

The Last Caribou Fence

This is my grandfather Thomas's [Domas] country, Van Tat Gwich'in.... This is where my grandfather had a caribou fence....When my grandfather had a caribou fence here, my father's mother packed him around, I heard. He was a child then. They picked berries, my grandmother told stories, I see it and I say thank you. It is called *Antl'it Tthał* in Gwich'in. In English, it is called Thomas [Creek] Fence. [Thomas Creek flows]... toward Crow Flats.

All the people made use of [the caribou fence]. Way down at Fort Yukon, Van Tat Gwich'in, up there, the Dagoo, even they came here for meat, they said. They killed lots of caribou, people all over the land made use of it. Thomas Fence, it is a big name. The Eskimos also came over here from Herschel Island. He [his grandfather, Domas] went down and got supplies [and] the Eskimos had him for a friend....In the winter when it was hard to get meat they would all come here. He would give them meat. Wherever they came from, they would go back with their meat. They hunted and lived on the meat during the winter, they said. That is what my grandfather, Thomas did a long time ago. His name was famous.

Now, there have been many geologists who have worked around here. I know them all....*Shih Ddhàa Tsal* [Little Grizzly Bear Mountain; literally: *shih* (grizzly bear); *ddhàa* (mountain); and *tsal* (little or small)], down that way are the Arctic Village people. They come up this way. At that time, we only lived on meat. From around Timber Creek, head of Black Fox Creek, are two caribou fences. Way up at the head of Driftwood River there is a caribou fence. Even that, this caribou fence, has the only name in all this country. People used it. My grandmother told me stories, I remember, when I was a child. That way, I know this much. This is about all I know, that I can tell you about....

Lots of people stayed with him [Domas], his relatives....People who travelled back and forth all stayed there and he gave them meat, and they went back home. During the winter, they lived off the meat....All summer...he just stayed by the caribou fence. He took good care of it: he made it in good shape all the time for another year when the caribou come. [August till November, the caribou came.] Across that way, a flag is at the end. Over the mountain, all [the poles had] flags on them. That's so if the caribou come up that way, they have to come here. They went into the fence and he snared them, speared them, took then out of the snare, pulled them right out [of the fence] to where they had a cache. We kept it clean in there so the caribou wouldn't smell anything....Somebody watched all the caribou go in and said, "Woo, woo, woo, woo," so we kept them inside. We did this, we caught them this way....

Year round, [Domas] stayed around here....That's all he depended on for meat, so he kept it in shape, kept it strong. I don't know how many years he was here, most of his life, anyway. He has a grave in Fort Yukon. I guess, after he finished here, he moved down to Alaska. He died there....My grandmother has a grave at Old Rampart, Alaska, 35 miles past the borderline.

Their camp [at the caribou fence] where they stayed, they couldn't find it. Bill Irving [archaeologist] looked all over. The campsite is some place but they couldn't find that place.

My grandmother told me these stories when I was a child, that's how I know these stories that I just told you. That's all I know. Long ago, all the elders who know have all died. Everything was hard, long ago when those people lived....However it [the caribou fence] was made, we'll never know, but long ago people knew it. Not one of them is alive....This is all I know. I only saw this after it had fallen down. Everybody only [saw it] after it had fallen down....

[Cache], they made it like a house [with small logs], it's high. They put a roof on it for the winter. They call it *tsiik'it*...in the Gwich'in language. Yeah, they put meat in it.

(CHARLIE THOMAS, *Antl'it Tthał* [Thomas Creek Caribou Fence], July 27, 2000, VG2000-4-3:009-215, Gwich'in)

Hard times, Good times

In those days, people lived off the land. Before they made camp, they set snares for rabbits....The people sometimes got a porcupine, a ptarmigan, one rabbit, only that little and they would bring it home. Even so, many people ate it, its juice [broth], too. This is the way they lived long ago. The land you see, all of it, the people made their living off of it. Up that way at Johnson Creek is rough country. The people lived there. Now, they [don't see] that country even though there's lots of snowmobiles. The people then did lots of work with their dog teams. Even me, I remember doing all that.

We came out of hard times, but we lived a good life, now that I look back on it. There wasn't much white man's food around but we lived good on our own food. The dogs, too. When the dogs swing you around, it was nice. It was like that. Recently when we go around where the people were always happy, now they are all underground, all buried underground. The way they did it long ago, my grandmothers and grandfathers, when they come upon a camp or sign of people, they would jump with joy.

(LYDIA THOMAS, *Troo Chòo Njìk* [Driftwood Village], June 26, 2001, VG2001-2-52:095-117, Gwich'in)

How to Hold a Feast

When you make a feast [today], there's all kinds of different salads. I don't like it. I remember [in the past]...they boiled meat and whoever had flour, gave it out and [made] gravy. They made soup with that. It was hard to get vegetables....Then, too, sometimes there was no baking powder so they wet [the flour] and cooked it in grease and made brown bannock. We never saw cake, one bit.

At Christmas, my father made a feast with just straight meat, gravy [flour soup], with grease bannock. Neil McDonald, lots of times he made, a New Year's feast, you know. A 50-pound flour bag of cloth, in that he made a raisin pudding, a big one. He cut it into small pieces, just like cake. He made them thin and gave out small pieces to all the people. Ah, I was in a hurry to eat it. It was going to taste good. Lots of people know him for when he made pudding. That's the way they made a feast. Today they do it the white man's way, I guess.

They landed here and danced. They dressed up. The women, even the girls, wore long dresses and brown moccasins; they looked so nice. The elders had ribbons on them. Combs with beads, they put in their hair. Ah, they looked so beautiful when they swung way out.

(ELLEN BRUCE, March 21, 1997, VG1997-8-07:403-440, Gwich'in)

Resolving Family Difficulties

Not too long ago, when there was family trouble the people all gathered in one place....Then the woman and man, they were put out there in the middle. The elders talked to them. They talked to them, in the Lord's words and they made everything good again. No family trouble again. In those days, for everything bad, they had meetings. They don't do that today. Only the minister married people and now the JP [Justice of the Peace] marries people....I don't like that but I can't talk against it either.

(ELLEN BRUCE, March 21, 1997, VG1997-8-07:240-247, Gwich'in)

The Dawson Gold Rush and Wage Work

First of all I'm going to tell you about where my parents come from. I wasn't born in Canada [but in]...Eagle, Alaska, in 1925. My dad came from the Northwest Territories—Teetl'it Gwich'in...In those days, people moved around in the bush and used skin houses. And it happened they found Eagle, Alaska. [There were] many white men around there so they asked people, "Why [are] so many white men around here?" They said, "It's mining in Dawson City." [It was] 1898. So they stayed around the Ogilvie [Mountains] and then at the head of Twelve Mile River, and then they found Dawson City. So [there was] mining there in 1898. In those days they didn't know what year it was. Until 1919 or 1901, like that, they didn't count the year. That summer my dad stayed around there, he wasn't married, too. In Dawson, so many white men were frostbitten so they wanted meat, any kind of meat: moose, caribou, soup or anything, rabbit, ptarmigan. They bought meat from the Indian who got paid a dollar a pound. So Indian people hunted caribou, moose and they hauled it down to Dawson and [sold it].

1898, all the time my dad was around there he wasn't married. The steamer *Yukon* worked on the Yukon River between Anchorage and Dawson. He got a contract cutting wood for the steamer *Yukon*. They needed wood. It was only eight dollars a cord, too. He cut 300 cords one year. Every year he did that, him and one guy but that guy, [after] not even one year, he quit—too hard for him, I guess. My dad kept on getting wood and cut 300 cords a year.

Then he trapped around the Ogilvies and Blackstone and [happened to] go down to Eagle, Alaska, and stayed down there about 20 years: that's where I was born. We were eight in the family: six sisters, one brother, and myself. They're are all gone....I was born in 1925 and then in 1928 he [his father, John Nukon] wanted to come back to the Yukon, so we came through the Ogilvie [Mountains] and to the head of Porcupine River, the whole family, my mom, all my sisters. I was a kid that time and I don't really remember it, just part of it. We stayed there till breakup. My dad went down to Eagle to get some more groceries and then after breakup, we make a skin boat and floated down the Porcupine River right to Old Crow. At that time way up Porcupine River, we saw Johnson Creek [Village]. That's where the Charlie Tetlichi family stayed: Peter Charlie, Charlie Charlie, Alfred Charlie, and that old man, Charlie Tetlichi they called him. So we came to Old Crow. I spoke way different than Van Tat Gwich'in: all my sisters [and I] talked Hän Gwich'in. We didn't understand Van Tat Gwich'in, what they talked about and they didn't understand us, what we talked about. My dad and mom knew how to talk Van Tat Gwich'in.

(DICK NUKON, Porcupine-Peel, January 20, 1995, 1995:93-95, English and Gwich'in)

The Continuing Importance of Caribou

Caribou hair changes in March; it turns grey: moose is the same. They also get rid of their horns and eventually grow them back. In April when they return to the calving grounds their hair gets old and they lose it. In August when they start to return south the hair is short, but in September it grows long for the winter months. Bull caribou have

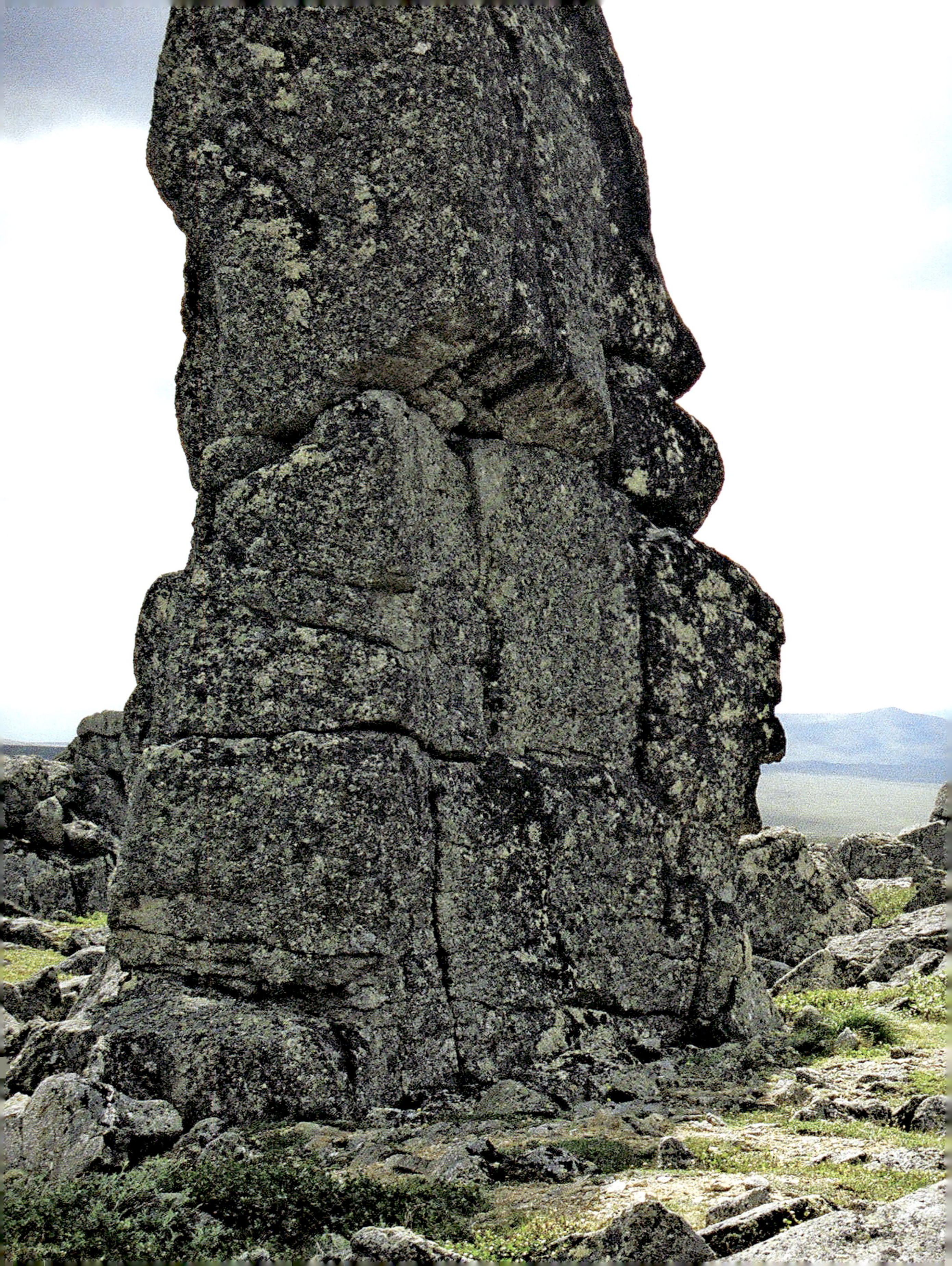

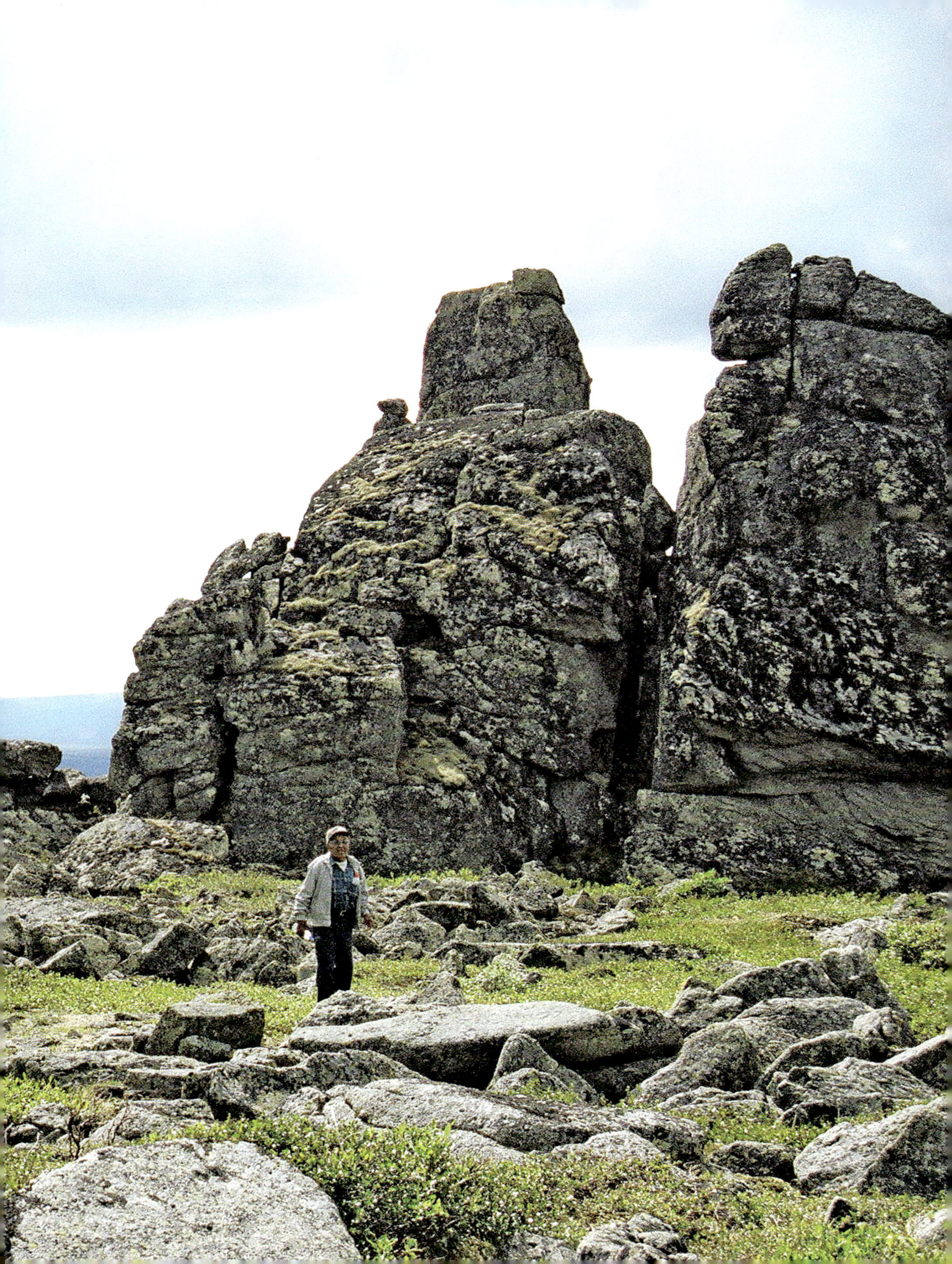

Pages 258–259: Elder Charlie Thomas at Ddhàa Chah Khai *(Flat Mountain), 2006.*
[Megan Williams ©VGFN 2006]

big horns and the hair under their chins is long. We know by looking at the caribou if it's female by this feature.

The older people know what is a good caribou to shoot. Today young people just shoot any kind of caribou; it's not like a long time ago....If it has no calf and it looks fat, that is the caribou we killed a long time ago. We knew by looking at the caribou if it's bull, female, young, or calf. A calf that was born in spring and passed a winter, the next spring we no longer call it a calf.[93] Then it is a female, or fall-time caribou. When we trap for fur we see the caribou tracks: that's how we know where to find them. Caribou travel in herds and a caribou that stays in one place is call *ni'daachik*. This doesn't happen every year.

We lived on caribou all our lives—that is why we still depend on caribou today. When we were living up in Whitestone, we hunted for caribou around Cody Creek. We knew where to look for caribou. Especially when we went trapping; when we saw caribou, we killed it. In those days we only travelled by dog team. Sometimes we brought home loads of meat. In preparation for hunting we woke up early in the morning. We got a teapot and whatever we were going to drink tea with ready. Sometimes we came across lots of caribou and killed it and sometimes there was no caribou. We hunted for moose only when it was windy....When there is no wind, we can't come close to the moose.

Today young people hunt for caribou with snowmobiles. They come up close to the caribou and shoot it. We didn't hunt like this in the past. We used to hunt for caribou with only snowshoes and if it was a long way from camp we used a dog team....In those days we used dog teams and they also ate caribou meat so we needed lots of meat. I sometimes killed about 40 caribou and after New Year's I had to go hunting for more meat. People ate the kidneys, caribou legs, and roasted the ribs on the fire. Sometimes they came home in the evenings and cooked the best parts.

In those days young boys didn't eat fresh caribou, and they never ate too much caribou head. Young people never ate calf caribou. I only ate calf after I became an elder. In those days we killed caribou when we saw it but we always left one caribou, we never killed them all. We also depended on rabbit and ptarmigan. In the springtime when the ground squirrel came out we killed it, too. We killed whatever game we saw. When we saw caribou on the mountain we went up there to hunt. Also people long ago use shamans. Long ago they had a name for people who went into the woods to kill caribou easily. They called them *dinjii shishanaghà*. Caribou eat white moss and grass. In the wintertime the caribou dig for their food; they know where there is food. When we go hunting we look for places where caribou dig up snow; that is how we know if there are caribou around, too. Beside people, wolves hunt the caribou down. Wherever there is caribou, there is bound to be wolves. In the past people lived where there was game: it's the same with wolves. In the summer the caribou go up on the mountain, and in the fall they travel south toward the Dempster Highway. When wolves kill caribou for food, other animals eat from the kill, like ravens, foxes, and martens.

When I worked with geologists I travelled to Black Fox [Creek] and Edward Creek. My grandfather Domas [Thomas] used to live in this area [where] the people used to build caribou fences. They moved the caribou toward the fence; once inside the caribou were caught in snares made from caribou hide...[and then] the people speared them. People living in the area would travel to Black Fox [caribou fence] and they would receive meat.

In those days when we hunted for caribou the snow was deep. The people used to travel fast with snowshoes then. We usually killed caribou in the fall. The caribou hide was used for clothing, such as caribou-fur pants and parka. In those days people used only fur clothing. In the beginning of August we started to hunt for caribou. When we lived around New Rampart [House] we went into the mountains to hunt. We dried the caribou to preserve it....

Every part of the caribou was used, even the eye was taken out to dry. The meat was used to eat; the hide was use for clothing. The caribou leg hide was also tanned and use for making dog packs. The bones from the caribou were use for making bone grease, and the broth was use for drinking. Bones were also for tanning hides: bone scrapers were made from the leg bone. None of the caribou parts were used for medicine.

Long ago people respected the caribou or any animal. They didn't make fun of the animals. In those days there was not much food around, only flour, lard, butter, sometimes syrup and oats. I'm not sure if people sell the caribou meat, they probably won't say. That is the only way they would get a little money.

If other people travel the Dempster Highway to hunt I'm sure the game wardens watch them carefully. It is not right to leave part of the caribou behind, we never experienced this before. Nowadays they put collars on caribou. I think they should stop this. They drop a net on the caribou from a helicopter and then they put a collar on it and because of this caribou suffer. I hear the caribou that are collared are poor. This has to stop. People that hunt on the Dempster Highway should be monitored carefully. The people from Whitehorse should only kill one or two caribou; that is sufficient.

(CHARLIE THOMAS, August 24, 1998, VG2001-13-37, Gwich'in)

Taking Care of the Land in the Future

They really dirtied our land with garbage. I worked for them and I watched what they were doing to our land. Not only for us, but think about the animals. Lots animals moved out of the country. Roots, grass: moose gets willows and birch, same with beaver. They don't think about that as long as they want to get money. A long time ago our great, great grandfathers told us, "You don't need money for your land. If you look after your land, you will survive. Keep your land clean." That's what we are trying to do....

Lucky we stopped them from coming in here. Otherwise...Old Crow [would] be nothing now. Our water were going be polluted, our animals going to die off. See? A long time ago...between 1940 [and] '50, this were not many animals around here. Because around...Rampart House, lots of white people [were] up here [and] they went out trapping [and] used poison. They didn't keep it clean and they really cleaned [out] this country. And then they're all gone, they all died off.

But lucky Corporal Kirk was [the] police here. He didn't let white people come around here trapping [any] more. That's why [in] our country, all the animals [have] come back now. See, lots of birds, how many thousand caribou we got, moose. All the animals [are] back now....That's why we have to keep our land clean: to keep our animals here, healthy....

[Did] you hear me yesterday on the radio? They want to put a pipeline through here and all the way up to, I don't know where, all the way north....Where [are] our caribou going to migrate? They can't cross that pipeline. They're going to block everything up on us. They don't care what they do to Indians, you know. Not as long as they get money. But lucky I was right there. Tom Berger, I told him, "Tommy, you put pipeline through here, you going to get your gas cheap and oil cheap." I told him, "We could still pay [what] we pay for it, because I don't want a pipeline through here. Because you're going to just ruin my country and block my caribou from grazing, and where am I going to get caribou?"

So you guys [speaking to young men] don't ask for money. Don't sell your land. That's one big mistake you're going to make. [The] government [will] tell you, "I'll give you money." Money's no good for a young person. You keep your land clean and look after it, [and] you [will] survive. Money, you won't survive with money. Now, today, you do but later on it [will] be no more. You see? Chrétien, he was minister of Indian Affairs at that time. He came here twice. He [asked] me, "Why don't you let anybody come to your land to look for oil?" I told him, "If you find oil in my country, you're going to give my people how [ever] much they want a year?" He said, "We can't do that." "Okay, keep your money. I'll keep my land." That's why he doesn't come here no more....Government, [they] just want money, but us, we have to keep our land....

Northwest [Territories], those Gwich'in people sold their land because they wanted money. But they don't know they made a mistake. Yeah, they ruined their country....[One] time I told them, "I don't want [an] oil company [on] my land because my people [are] living out there." I told them, "Nobody destroy it. If you make scrambled eggs out of my land and you don't find nothing, you won't even say goodbye to me and you're going to leave....Where [are] my kids going to make a living?"

[Jason Benjamin: You think there'll be many jobs in the future for people in Old Crow?] That's a good question. [Laughs] You know, like I said, if you look after your land, if [there's] no more jobs, still you're going to have a living. [You] don't need jobs. As long as your animals [are] there, you'll [have] something to eat. This land is your store. Yeah, so that's a hard question to ask.

(ALFRED CHARLIE, August 8, 1997, VG1997-8-8:156–236, English)

4 | The Oral History of Today

Van Tat Gwich'in Commentary on the Past, Present, and Future

Contents

269 **THE PRESENT AND FUTURE**

270 Continuity
  The Importance of Passing on Stories

274 Stories and Relationships Between People

276 Passing on Stories, Experience, and Knowledge of the Land

284 Reflecting from the Present
  Acknowledging the Ancestors

290 Relationships in the Future
  Concern for the Next Generations

294 The Youth Speak about the Future

302 **ORAL HISTORY FROM ANCESTORS TO YOUTH**

302 Collecting and Communicating Oral History

305 Van Tat Gwich'in History and the Northern Yukon

307 Events, People, Responses
  The 19th and 20th Centuries

311 The Non-historical
  Other Elements of Van Tat Gwich'in Oral Tradition

It's important for young people to know; it's part of their culture, part of their heritage and everything. A lot of these old stories that old people know are really good stories and pretty useful. It's good for one's identity and that kind of stuff because of changes in lifestyle today. Today, a lot of changes in lifestyle.

(STANLEY NJOOTLI SR., July 2003, VG2002-3-20:080-085, English)

THE THREE CHAPTERS OF ORAL HISTORY showcase the long-ago stories—*yeenoo dài' googwandak*—and the history of two generations of Van Tat Gwich'in and reveal much about their lives and times, their perspectives and values. The people and events they described were of the 19th and 20th centuries, a time of immense changes that ultimately made their way to Van Tat Gwich'in country. Running through their accounts, the themes of the relationship of Gwich'in to the land and nature, and their relationships with Gwich'in and other people unselfconsciously speak to the heart of their identity as a people.

But what of the present and future? What stories do the adults and youth of today tell about what it is to be Van Tat Gwich'in? What old stories are being passed on; what are the topics of the new stories; what is the oral history of today? Van Tat Gwich'in are no strangers to change nor with integrating the new with the ancient while retaining their distinctive identity. The Van Tat Gwich'in Oral History Collection contains materials from "young elders" (people now in their 40s to 60s) and some interviews with youth (people in their teens and early 20s). A representative sample of their

Elder John Joe Kyikavichik explaining the use of ground caches (foreground) near Diniizhòo (Potato Hill/ Game Mountain), 2007. (L–R) Michelle Kendi-Rispin, Irwin Linklater, John Joe Kyikavichik, Tracy Rispin, Fanny Charlie, Phillip Rispin, Brandon Kyikavichik, Frances Bruce.

[Shirleen Smith ©VGFN (VG2007-3-174)]

stories shows the challenges of life in the late 20th and early 21st centuries: shared and disparate ways of life, language and values, continuity with the past, and hopes for the generations to come.

The history presented here and in previous chapters demonstrates both the details of Van Tat Gwich'in history and their perceptions of it. Through this historical journey, the connection between the remote past and the immediate present can be traced. Also clear is the connection between documentary, archaeological, and other independent sources of Van Tat Gwich'in history and their oral history. The oral history adds detail and insights into the motivations and consequences of past events, and it touches on the background to more recent issues, such as political autonomy, land rights and use, ongoing efforts to save the caribou herd, language, and culture. This history explains, in part, the continuing vitality of Van Tat Gwich'in society, the busy community of Old Crow, and the tradition of public expression to promote a wider understanding of Van Tat Gwich'in (for example, speaking out about preserving the caribou and care of the natural world, Edith Josie's long-running newspaper column, and working with scientists and filmmakers). They describe the lessons of their history: how to live in a sustainable way on the land and maintain a healthy society, while at the same time seeking to make the best of a time of the incursion of rapid and profound external influences.

Three boys roasting caribou ribs.

[Yukon Archives, Father Jean-Marie Mouchet fonds 91/51R #215]

THE PRESENT AND FUTURE

The majority of the material in the Van Tat Gwich'in Oral History Collection was from two generations of Van Tat Gwich'in. However, the collection also contains some interviews from others, such as those now in their 40s to 60s, and young people. These comment on the more recent way of life of Van Tat Gwich'in and suggest values and directions for the future.

The oral history of Van Tat Gwich'in in their 40s to 60s and the voices from the youth detail Van Tat Gwich'in life in the more recent past. The young elders spoke of spending considerable time on the land in their youth and young adulthood, learning from their elders. Their history has much continuity with that of the previous generations, but it is also framed by their experiences from schooling and other influences (such as land claims and politics). They related some specific changes, such as the incursion of wage labour and decline of the fur trade, which caused many people to spend more time away from the land and in town, starting in the 1980s, and which remain factors in going on the land today. Here it must be emphasized that in 2008, people still were going on the land to: travel, hunt, fish, collect firewood, run their dog teams, pick berries, conduct and assist with research and filmmaking, participate in youth-school camps, take their children on the land, go to their spring camps and winter cabins, and some live out of town on the land for a significant part of the year. Like the elders before them, the young elders and middle-aged people spoke of the values and practices they would like to pass on to the youth, and they look realistically at the problems they will encounter while doing this. They discussed the pleasures of the way of life of their own youth, compared to today's life. Although they emphasized that life in the past was physically difficult, it had other important benefits: social cohesion, grounding in nature, satisfying (albeit difficult) work, personal freedom, and better health. The youth interviewed also spoke of the way their experiences on the land brought a new appreciation and attachment to it, along with respect for their elders, as well as specific knowledge (for example, muskrat behaviour). Their views echoed those of their elders and predecessors who wish to continue the age-old relationship between Van Tat Gwich'in and their land.

Taken as a whole, Van Tat Gwich'in oral history depicts themes, perspectives, values, events, trends, causes, and effects. It also reveals not only what it is to be Van Tat Gwich'in, in the past and today, but also a glimpse of the future.

Continuity

The Importance of Passing on Stories

The mature, active Van Tat Gwich'in of today have had many life experiences different from those of their elders. Many, but not all, are fluent in Gwich'in as well as English, and all had formal schooling. Some were active in politics, education, or other ways of working for their people and have a sophisticated awareness of life outside the northern Yukon. Yet until as late as the 1980s (and beyond), trapping and travelling on the land were also part of their lives and those of their family members. They know many of the old stories and the context of the oral history of their elders. They are also familiar with the world of their children—today's youth—and are well placed to have an interesting perspective on the past and future of Van Tat Gwich'in, and to both transmit and reflect upon the history of their people.

Van Tat Gwich'in currently in their 50s recall the values, as well as the stories, of their parents and grandparents. Stanley Njootli Sr. and Robert Bruce Jr. spoke of the importance attached to passing on the stories. Stanley Njootli Sr. related how his elders intentionally told him stories.

The Importance of Passing on Stories

> Elders talk about...what was passed on to our elders here, elders before them, you know. They know these old stories about the different areas,

Elder Alfred Charlie and granddaughter Brianna Tetlichi on Ch'oodèenjik *(Porcupine River) near* Kâachik *(Johnson Creek Village), 2005.*
[Shirleen Smith ©VGFN (VG2005-3-26)]

different names, for this whole area....The elders know a lot of stories about our old people from the past...they ask me to speak on some of these and some of my life experience, too, so I'm going to do that.

(STANLEY NJOOTLI SR., July 2003, VG2002-3-20:001–005, English)

Old People's Stories and How They Lived

Long ago when I was a kid, Joe Kaye, Peter Charlie, John Moses, Peter Moses, Elias [Kwatlatyi], all of them, they tell us stories at night. They talked about this land. Sometimes they talked about Miner River, Cody River, and Eagle River, too; they would talk about LaPierre House, too.

Those days what they said, which direction, I wondered which direction they meant. Today I see that country: Cody River, Miner River, up that way, I went with boat, around Whitestone, too. I also went around there with helicopter. They travelled over a big country. When they trapped, sometimes they were gone for one month. Those days there was also no dog food: if they didn't do anything, their dogs wouldn't eat, too. Us, too, we wouldn't be able to eat, too. Whatever animals they killed, they lived off that.

(ROBERT BRUCE JR., Bell River, July 2003, VG2002-3-12:130–149, English)

The Oral History of Today

Stephen Frost Sr. and Robert Bruce Jr. at Babbage River falls, 2005.
[Shirleen Smith ©VGFN (VG2005-3-136)]

Page 273: At the pocket of Antl'it (Thomas Creek Caribou Fence), 2007. (L–R) Irwin Linklater, Sherrie Frost, Dr. Ray Le Blanc (archaeologist), Brandon Kyikavichik, Jane Montgomery, Mary Jane Moses, Brenda Frost.
[Shirleen Smith ©VGFN (VG2007-3-287)]

Learning about Van Tat Gwich'in Leaders from the Elders

I was walking downtown here and I sat with Sarah Abel and Myra Moses. They sit there telling me stories. She told me stories about *Shahnuuti'*. She didn't tell me the whole story, she just wanted to let me know their names, I guess. She told me the short story, the short version of it.

There's *Shahnuuti'* and *Ch'eeghwalti'*—he lived here. And *Shahvyah*: according to her, *Shahvyah* moved to the Circle, Alaska, area. And *Shahnuuti'*, he moved to Fort Yukon. *Ch'eeghwalti'* stayed here and he had another brother, but she didn't remember his name. So these were the three main guys back during the time of contact. They were probably in their prime just before contact...when Alexander Murray came into the country...they were the leaders.

Shahvyah was the leader in Circle. He used to make moose fences for his people. That's how he got moose and fed his people.... *Shahnuuti'* made fishtraps for salmon down the Yukon River and that's how he took care of his people. And *Ch'eeghwalti'*, he fished for fresh water fish in Little Flats [*Van Tat Gwatsàl*] in the Crow Flats area and made caribou fences.

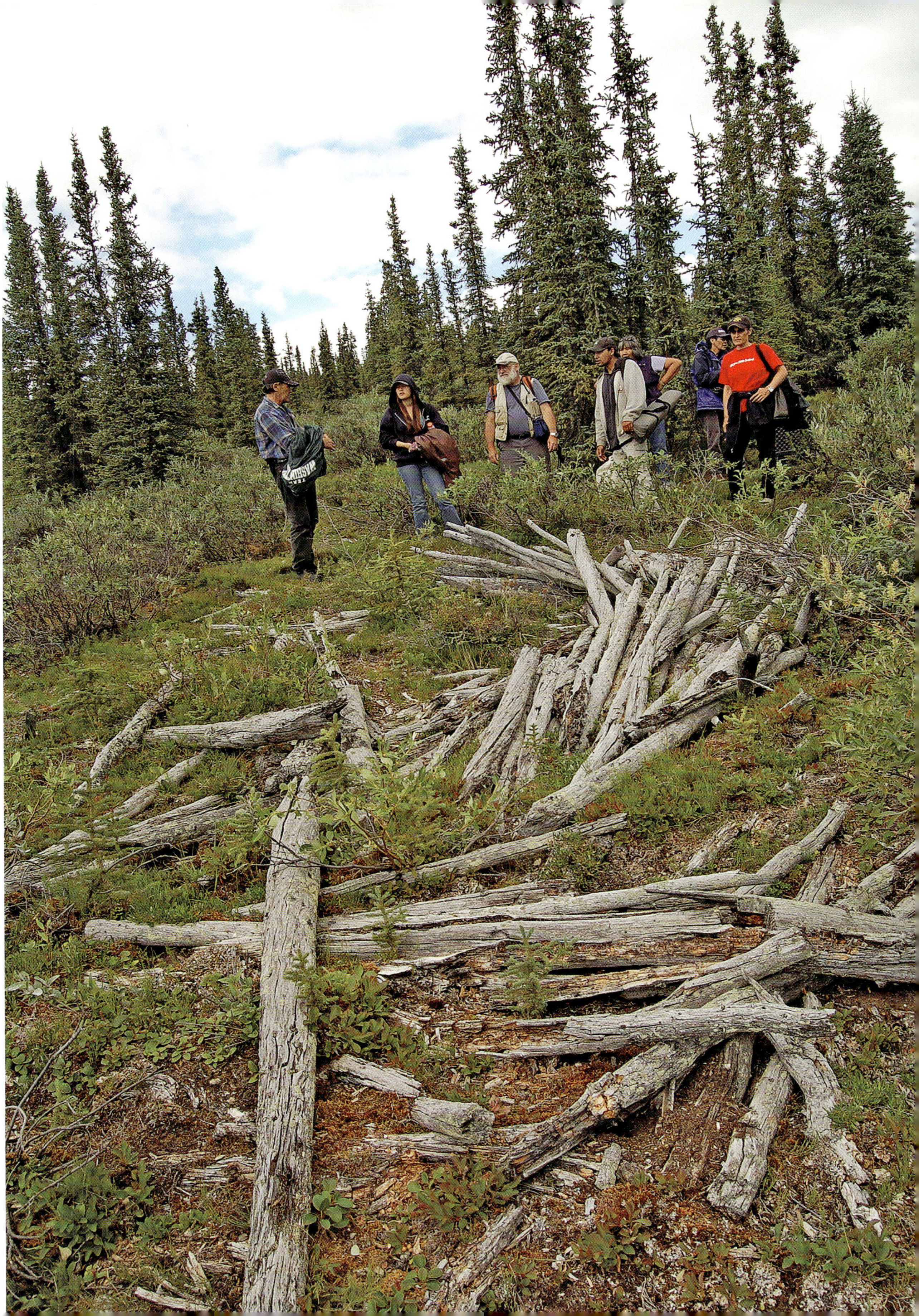

So those were the three brothers and they lived a long time and did quite well. Sometimes they had gatherings....The oldest was *Shahvyah*, [in] Circle, and he asked for the people to get together and they all [went] over to Circle. So from around Crow Flats, they would walk over to Circle. He gave them a lot of notice. They would get their stuff together and dry meat and make all the best food available....They took that down there and he [*Shahvyah*] did he same thing...probably had a good winter so asked his brothers to come down...so they had a big feast. [They] gathered down there for the summer in Circle and spent lots of time there. Fall starts to come in August, so they start heading back up this way. Everybody went back to their own area and start to work for the winter again, gathering food, berries, and setting fish traps in the *Van Tat Gwatsàl* [Little Flats] area....

Back in the old days, they didn't keep still very much, those old people. The month of July is like a holiday for them. After they had a good winter, they sort of stayed around in camps and they had a gathering sometimes.

(STANLEY NJOOTLI SR., July 2003, VG2002-3-20:034-069, English)

Stories and Relationships Between People

How to behave toward other people—kith and kin, one's own people and others—is both culturally specific in its expressions and universal in that all societies have their codes, procedures, and mores. As their oral history chronicles, certain relationships have distinctive expression in Gwich'in society: the relationship between youth and elders, the place of the *shanaghàn* (old women), the alliance of brothers, and partnerships. Bella Greenland (née Bruce) recounted the importance of friendships between brothers-in-law, told a story of a friendship, a bear injury, and how people looked after each other. Irwin Linklater described the elders' role in choosing a marriage partner.

Strong Friendships between Brothers-in-law

My grandfather Big Joe [Kyikavichik] was expecting my grandfather John Nukon.[1] He said, "I hear a boat. Maybe it is my brother-in-law." They called him *Vidzii shuh* [John Nukon].[2] They must have told each other: if he shoots twice, then that is my brother-in-law, *Vidzii shuh* [a wart in his ear]. Not long after that we heard two shots. In front of the house they were drying meat. He was looking through that. He took fat brisket and said, "I am going to put this in a pot to boil for my brother-in-law *Vidzii shuh* outside." So he boiled it, and meanwhile he was watching for him. He saw him coming so he went down to him. They came to one another and just hugged each other. They wrestled but didn't fall down and started walking up with their arms around each other's neck. That is how much people cared for each other long ago. They got to the tent and he said, "Brother-in-law, inside the tent we will sit with each other and eat and tell stories." So they went in and started eating.

Me and Abraham sat there. I sat down and Abraham, he just went really close to him and started looking in his ear. [Laughs] "My brother-in-law, someone must have called me *Vidzii shuh* in front of this kid. What is he doing?" [Laughs] It was just like he didn't know where to look. [Laughs] I remember this.

(BELLA GREENLAND, April 19, 2003, VG2004-01-03, Gwich'in)

Long-ago Courtship

I told the young people a story about long ago. When a woman was going to marry a man, they used to hang their pants out on poles. This is just because the elders told them to do this, I guess, so that is what they did. They would hang their caribou-skin pants out and the woman would go and pick out a [pair of] pants and they grabbed the first pair of pants before the other women. This one woman was raising her grandchild: she told her grandchild to get the one that's all wrinkled up. Even though she didn't want to, she had to. Here it was the pants of a hardworking man. This young man, he did more work than all the other men. The men came back to camp and were looking for their pants and here this poor woman had his pants.

(IRWIN LINKLATER, Crow Mountain, August 12, 2004, VG2004-4-13, English)

Caring for a Bear Injury

My grandfather [Big Joe Kyikavichik], he called that Albert Ross *shijaa*, *shitlih* ["my friend"].[3] They really liked each other, just like you say my friend, or my relative, they called each other *shitlih* [my friend]. Big Joe [Kyikavichik] said we were staying someplace and they were going to go hunting, Big Joe and Albert Ross. They were going to walk around this mountain and he put his gun down. Big Joe asked, "*Shijaa* [my friend], what are you doing with your gun?" And he said, "It is too heavy for me to carry. I am tired so I am leaving it here and when we come back this way, I will pick it up later." And he told him, "*Shijaa*, in the fall you don't know what you will run into. It is not right that you

The Oral History of Today 275

Gwich'in elders, youth, and researchers hiking to Antl'it (Thomas Creek Caribou Fence), 2007.

[Shirleen Smith ©VGFN (VG2007-3-278)]

leave your gun behind." He had a little axe and he said, "Just this is good enough." I don't remember what he said he would do.

So, Big Joe took his gun and they started walking around that mountain and they came to a bear den and he told him, "*Shijaa*, we only have one gun. We expect bear. He is in his den and we probably should expect it." Meanwhile I don't know what he threw in front of the bear's den and the bear growled and it was very loud. He started running up the side of the mountain and the bear grabbed him and pulled him down the mountain and started attacking him. He didn't know what to do; he just shouted and finally [the bear] left him alone. He told the bear, "Our relatives are hungry and they hunt around here. We travel around hunting for food, so leave us alone," he told the bear. So the bear started walking away and once in awhile, he looked back.

Meanwhile, *shijaa* was lying there full of blood, after the bear left. [Big Joe said:] "Right where he was lying, I made a place for him by the campfire. I got lots of wood on both sides of him and I told him, '*Shitlih*, put this in the fire once in awhile and even though it is hard for you, so you won't fall asleep, move around lots,' he said. So I left and left my gun with him and where he left his gun, it was quite far away so I started running without a gun. So I ran to where he left his gun all night and all day. I walked and ran and finally got to where we had the camp. I told my father and he said something to me and all the men went and got trees. And they tied caribou mattresses to the trees—in those days they never had nails. And that is what they went to pick him up with. Even how tired I was, I went back with them. Right where I left him, there was still smoke coming out. While we went back for him the women picked wood [spruce] gum, and when we got back to camp, the women put wood gum all over his wounds, and that is how they healed him."

(BELLA GREENLAND, April 19, 2003, VG2004-01-03, Gwich'in)

Passing on Stories, Experience, and Knowledge of the Land

In the course of millennia living on their lands, Van Tat Gwich'in amassed an encyclopedic store of knowledge, including details about specific places, which is the foundation for making a living and many other aspects of society. The stories of younger elders and middle-aged people, such as Robert Bruce Jr., Bella Greenland, Stanley Njootli Sr., and Irwin Linklater, revealed the knowledge they learned from their elders, as well as their own experiences on the land. Their information connects their detailed knowledge of geography with long-ago history, such as the *K'aiiheenjik* story, and with accounts of how past and present generations make a living—or augment

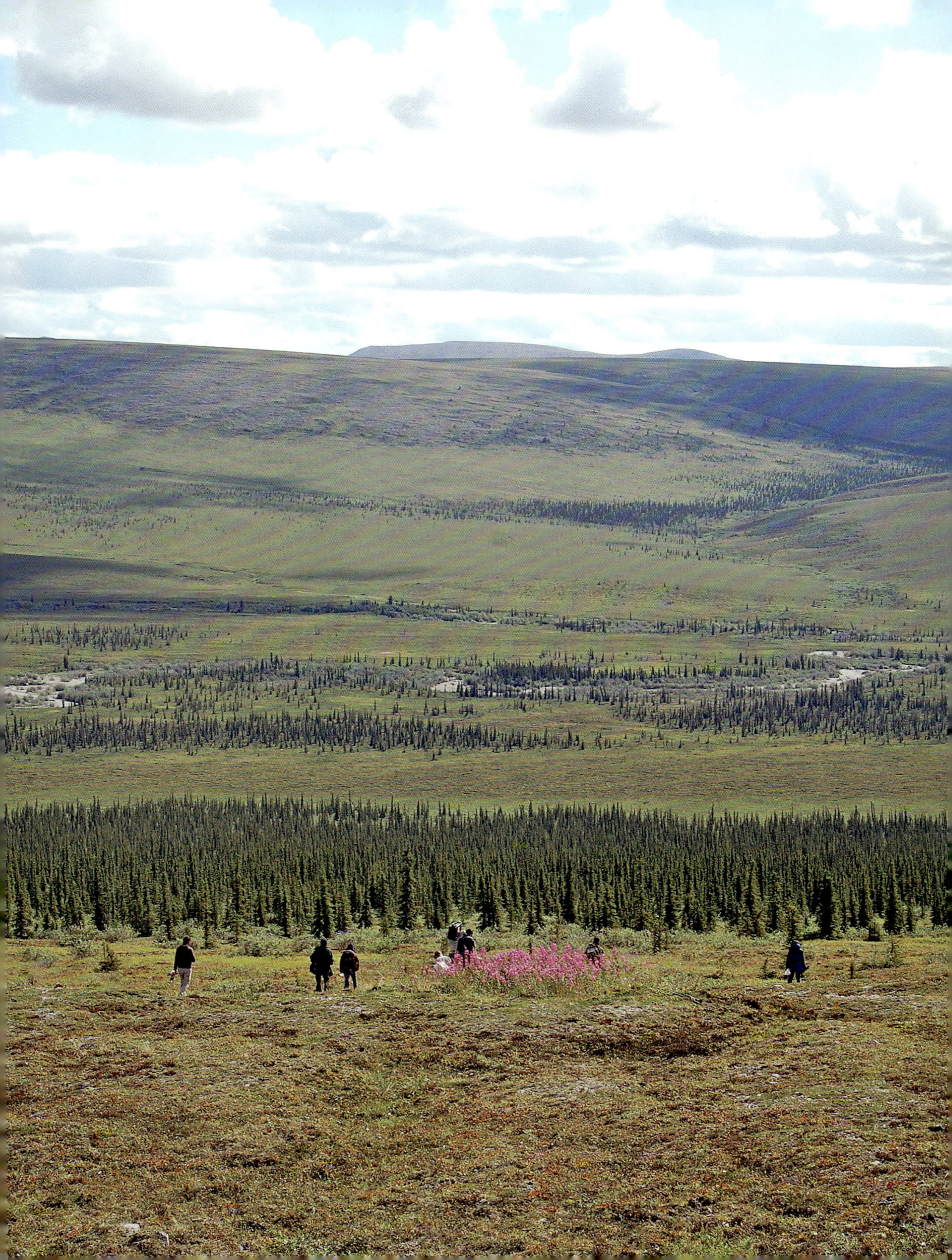

their livelihood—from the land. Stanley Njootli spoke of the strategic importance (both in terms of security and subsistence) of *Tl'oo K'at*, and Irwin Linklater referred to managing the resources at their camp at *Van Tat*. Robert Bruce Jr. and Bella Greenland told of the importance of two mountains: *Zhoh Drìn Chòo* [White Snow Mountain] and *Chuuts'aii Nàlk'at* [Crow Mountain], respectively, following in the tradition of educating youth and others about where to go and how to work to ensure survival. Stanley Njootli Sr. and Irwin Linklater related stories of *Ch'ii Ch'à'an* [Bear Cave Mountain] and *Diniinvee Njik* Caribou Fence [Black Fox Creek Caribou Fence] that tie to their grandparents' generation or before.

History of *Tl'oo K'at*

> There's a little bit of history of *Tl'oo K'at* area. People used to gather there in the springtime. The reason for that is [it's] a strategic point of the area because there's a lake behind and then there's a strip of land, then there's the river. So it's a good place to spend the summer [because] people used to have wars a long time ago. That's why people used to spend summer up there and visit with each other at *Tl'oo K'at*. Then in August, September, caribou start crossing and up at Caribou Lookout, eight miles, six, four miles above…*Tl'oo K'at*….They used to get their caribou with bow and arrow and spears when they cross. Then they put a fence right on the opposite bank and on the same side where they are. And then the caribou run up and whatever they miss, they come down again. They have a chance to get enough for the winter. Then they dry meat and raft it down with their canoes to *Tl'oo K'at* and they dry meat for the winter. So, Gwichyàa Gwich'in [Fort Yukon people], when they get enough [meat], they made a raft. They want to go up to *Trozhyah*[4]…There used to be a big pile of driftwood all the time and they made driftwood rafts and then they land at *Tl'oo K'at* and put all their stuff on it. Then they went back down to Fort Yukon with drymeat for the winter. That's what they used to do.
>
> (STANLEY NJOOTLI SR., July 2003, VG2002-3-20:090-109, English)

Life at *Van Tat*
Managing the Land by Staying Elsewhere every Three to Four Years, and the Supply of Wood for Canvas Boat Frames

> Yeah. This here place, I remember back since 1944. That's as far as I can remember back. I'm actually born 1940, January 8. And far as I can remember, I used to come down the river on our way back to Old

Elders and community members hiking to Robert Bruce Lake in Van Tat *(Crow Flats), 2001. Foreground (L–R) Megan Williams, John Joe Kyikavichik.*

[Shirleen Smith ©VGFN (VG2001-6-22)]

Crow from behind the hills there. That's where the lakes are where we have our spring camp. Sometimes we don't come here [for] about three years because there's no muskrats and we live different places like Potato Creek and over at Mary Kassi's place, under King Edward Mountain, places like that. And then when the [musk]rat comes back, we move back here again. Sometimes there's no muskrats for about three to four years.

I was here last spring with my mother. This hill back here, that's where we used to build the boat frame to wrap canvas around. There's a tree about 24 foot long. And toward the end it's getting hard to get [long enough trees for the frame] because we come down here. Most the time we go along the hill there. We start packing it from way down. And that ran out, so we had to go upriver here, little bend up. We build a boat there and bring it down and then we load on and keep going....

I seen lots of people who come through here because they're way over, far away from river, so this is only closest to Crow River. It take them two days to get here. Like I said before, when Lazarus [Charlie] got no muskrat [at] his place, he stays down that way. He comes through here. Charlie Thomas, we're close together by lake, just a portage away, but where we move to river it take hours, winding, this river.

(IRWIN LINKLATER, his camp on Crow River, June 10, 2001, VG2001-2-21:003-025, English)

New Trails due to Erosion from Dog Teams

My mother...she told me a story. She was just a little girl when they first moved here, probably around two or three years old, I guess. Ever since they been moving down here. Onto my left here is an old trail that comes down over here. We had to build new trail coming down this side because it's all worn out by dog team. Dog in there, using same footprint, it just digs into ground. It starts erosion and then we can't use it anymore, so we had to make another trail.

(IRWIN LINKLATER, his camp on Crow River, June 10, 2001, VG2001-2-21:045-050, English)

The Importance of White Snow Mountain (*Zhoh Drìn Chòo*)[5]

Snow White Mountain [*Zhoh Drìn Chòo*], that's really an important mountain. When there was no caribou [anywhere else] there would always be caribou there, they said. Abraham [Peter], on account of that he stayed above Johnson Creek...for two years. One time I went to visit him. That first year, he took his supplies up, [and] he left it on the beach, while the water was coming up [rising]. We landed there by him [and] helped him take his supplies up the [river]bank. He was gone up the river to Whitestone. He was gone all night. It was dark [but] he had a small electric plant. We started it up and had the electricity on all night. Then the next morning he was still gone. Freddie [Frost] and Johnny [Abel] went up with boat. Up there they got to him. Here he had shot eight moose. He was working with all that while the water was rising. He didn't even remember his supplies. [Laughter] Then after that, he came back down. We had put his supplies on top of the riverbank. He was really happy....

White Mountain [*Zhoh Drìn Chòo*] is across from Johnson Creek, about 40 miles across from Johnson Creek. White Mountain is long: there's a big airstrip on it. It's close to Porcupine Lake, about 30 miles. Porcupine Lake, Abraham stayed there with him and Albert for the winter. They got nearly 200 marten that winter. While that [at that time] Charlie Abel and I stayed at Dempster Highway, trapping. There, too, we killed nearly 200 marten at that time. That time there was lots of marten.

Now, up there two winters ago, I travelled around. There is no animals. All that country is burnt so that's what happened and it's hard. Soon, they say it will be hard times. If the children experience that, it's going to be hard for them. That's why, the young men, when they travel around, they make me happy. I came up every fall, when boat come up. When it's young men, I'm really happy for them. They try.

(ROBERT BRUCE JR., Bell River, July 2003, VG2002-3-12:172-217, English)

How People Lived at *Gwitr'uu* on *Chuuts'aii Nàlk'at* (Crow Mountain), Working with Meat and Storing Food for Winter, and a Boy's First Hunt

Up at *Gwitr'uu*,[6] that is where my mother and them would camp and my grandfather and his wife Myra would stay beside us. And just above us in the timber was my grandfather Paul Josie; he would move there with his family. And a little farther over, a lot of people stayed there also: the Thomas boys and their mother and little farther was Eliza *Tsal* [small Eliza; Eliza Ben Kassi, mother of Paul Ben Kassi], and my uncle Paul Ben Kassi stayed with her. Ahh, lots of people stayed around there. All below the mountain was just white with tents, and they all had caches by their tents.

During the day we would cut meat. We would never waste meat; they would dry all the meat on the caribou. After they finished cutting up the meat and putting it away they would pick berries. My father would dig out rocks from the side of the mountain and put two wooden barrels in there and we would put blueberries in them. Not only us, everybody. We picked blueberries and cranberries for the winter. With some of the meat they dried, they made *ch'itsùh* [pemmican] from dried meat and bone grease. Then they would make babiche with the skin, and also tan skins and make backpacks with them. All these things they made to put drymeat in later on. Our grandmothers and grandfathers took good care with caribou and worked hard. All this I remember.

Then in the fall, they would go across [the Porcupine River to the flats on the south side] and there, too, we worked with meat. They would kill moose and fix the skins....In the fall they would start making toboggans, right around where Neil [McDonald] stayed. He had a barrel outside and made a fire in that big tank. They would boil water for the toboggan boards and boil them. Then they would nail together the boards that were bent. They all helped each other and made toboggans. They would also make baskets for the back of the toboggan and [dog] harnesses from moose skins. Everything we had was made from things on this earth, I remember.

When a young boy killed his first moose or caribou they would have a feast, I remember. That was for his first time killing an animal. Abraham [Peter] was at that age. My father made him a toboggan with a basket at the back and they bought him a gun....They also raised five pups for him and made harnesses from moose skin for the dogs. My father made a sleigh for him. So he went to set traps. His dogs chewed the harness and he broke his sleigh and his gun, and he came back. This is what they did, I remember. [Laughter]

(BELLA GREENLAND, April 19, 2003, VG2004-01-03, Gwich'in)

The History of *Ch'ii Ch'à'an* (Bear Cave Mountain) and *Ni'iinlii Njik* (Fishing Branch River)

Up around Bear Cave Mountain—*Shih Ddhàa*[7]—that place has lots of history for the Gwich'in people, a lot of history. First of all, that's where *K'aiiheenjik*—he's Van Tat Gwich'in—and there's a long story about him, how he ended up living there. He got in a fight with his people....He was a very strong man and his own people up at *Tl'oo K'at*, in springtime they got in a fight with him. So with his brothers...lots of stuff happened and he ended up living in Bear Cave. That's where he was for years and years so people couldn't find him....

That was a nice area to be....[There are] a lot of sheep up there, a lot of wildlife, salmon spawn and they just gave it a name, [official name] too, *Ni'iinlii Njik* [Fishing Branch]—[referring to] salmon spawning, that means replacing, it's a big high word I guess, and it's an area where everything gets replaced. So that's what it means, salmon go there to die, spawn, and new life begins.

That's the name of that river and it has a history of a couple of names according to one elder. One point in time they called it *K'aiiheenjik Gwinjik*, *K'aiiheenjik* River, and they found artifacts in that cave....You know, [there] is a lot of history with the Vuntut people in this area and there's been a lot of heroes like *K'aiiheenjik*, *Kò' Ehdanh* and—I'm not sure of her name—smart woman...something like *Nehleteedyaa*...lots of wars over her, too.

(STANLEY NJOOTLI SR., July 2003, VG2002-3-20:126-156, English)

Diniinvee Njik Caribou Fence and Learning from Grandmother

Òaii niinlaii, *Diniinvee*, that's what they call Black Fox [Caribou Fence]: they call it *Diniinvee* in the Gwich'in language.[8] *Diniinvee Njik*, my grandmother used to always talk about it when I was a kid, that [caribou] fence and Thomas fence, too. She was always moving around, my grandmother Eliza Steamboat. She was the one who raised me. Sarah Baalam and Myra Deetru', I am her godchild and Rachel Cadzow,

Lance Nagwan at the fish weir at Ni'iinlii Njik *(Fishing Branch River), 2007.*

[Lance Nagwan photo]

they all used to sit with each other and tell stories. They used to talk about that fence. The mountains out that way, she would name all the place names for them. She would always point to the Black Fox fence, "When I was a young woman, we used to stay near the fence," she said. She would look at me once in awhile and ask me if I was listening. She must have done this because she knew I was going to talk about it in the future. I went there in a helicopter and you could see Crow Flats from there. It takes about 20 minutes. I saw that lookout place and the caribou fence….

Chiizheh is on this side of that fence by that mountain. One man had a lookout place there. From the rain and snow it rotted and fell down. They used to keep food in the rocks and there were logs around that place where they kept their food. In one place the logs were still in place and the person who made it or who it belonged to must have never come back. He put food in it just like a cellar. It was left just the way it was. There was just bones in there. My grandmother used to

The Oral History of Today 283

> talk about it and I seen it. At that time they used to just wear calf-skin parkas and use bows and arrows and spears. The caribou would go into the fence and that snare, they called it *niivyaa*; they would put snares on both sides of the fences. The caribou got caught in the snares and would pull, trying to get out. The young men would kill them with spears and bows and arrows. The women would wear caribou pants and parkas and stand on the side of the fence and chase the caribou into it. Sometimes even when the caribou got snared it got out and sometimes she talked about old broke-up fences. She must mean that they just stampede right through the fence, I guess. Long ago people talk, we wouldn't understand them, but me, my grandmother talked to me so that is why I understand. It's just high language: in English, same thing....
>
> (IRWIN LINKLATER, Crow Mountain, August 12, 2004, VG2004-4-13, English)

Reflecting from the Present
Acknowledging the Ancestors

Van Tat Gwich'in in their 40s to 60s emphasize that their lives are different from their ancestors and that life in the past, while rewarding, was also difficult. The change to present lifestyles was gradual, involving the development of communities like Old Crow, wage-labour jobs, schools that keep children in town for much of the year, and the changing economy of the fur trade.

The perspectives of Roger Kaye, Robert Bruce Jr., Marion Schafer, and Joel Peter derive from working for their people in government and religious capacities, as well as from familiarity with the land. They all spoke of the humbling effect of visiting places on the land where their ancestors lived and travelled, and thinking of their hard work and wise stewardship. They repeated the crucially important lessons of taking care of the land and animals and ensuring the water remains clean. They felt that fulfilling these lessons and passing them on are their responsibility to the future.

The Still-untouched Land of the Grandfathers and Taking Care of the Land and Water

> Today I had the opportunity to walk on the land where my grandfather told stories about. I had no idea which country he was talking about, but now I see, and this I can share with my children. I'll be proud of my son that he comes from the Kyikavichik family. I would hope that he would come here some day to look at it and say this is my great,

great grandfather's grave, and be proud to say that this is where I came from.

Great man, hunt with bows and arrows. What a wonderful feeling. It's kind of hard to try and explain how one feels about this journey we made today. To hear stories is great but to come to the actual site is more, greater. It makes me feel proud.

And for the younger generation out there that's suffering from alcohol abuse, drug abuse: you listen to your grandparents' stories and you come to the site that they talk about, it will help you to find a better way of life.

It's so wonderful to see this whole great land that all our ancestors have taken care of, and today is still the same....There's no development, the land is untouched, pure, and that's what they wanted, and we're still fighting for it.

I would like to thank them all, all our ancestors for the great work. Our grandfathers, our fathers, that taught us to take care of this land. They taught us only to take what we need. They taught us, take care of the waters, and that's what they were taught by our grandfathers.

(ROGER KAYE, Top of the Hill Mountain, June 22, 2001, VG2001-3-39:034-065, English)

Sitting in Ancestors' Places and Living Differently from Them

Now, here I'm sitting here on Sharp Mountain. It's really good for me but I got a bit of a lump in my throat. Long ago when I was a child, my grandfather, my father, my uncles, all of them, they talked about this mountain. Now I'm sitting on it. I look all around, what they talked about, I see it clearly now. On this side of Old Crow [south] is a big land. Long ago, my father, Robert Bruce Sr., said he trapped on it. Also he said lots of times he hunted around here. He said he sat here one time, on Sharp Mountain.

These elders, they talked, I listened to them good, and I also went with them. What they talked about, really, they lived like that....How our grandfathers long ago lived, he said they lived like that. They [father's and his generation] said they only lived a bit like them. That's how I am. Me, too, on this land, I came around here with dog team, too. I didn't do like my elders. Even though I was a young boy, I walked a long ways with snowshoes, but I never did like them. On account of that, they make these tapes. So in the future if the children see them, maybe they'll try even harder. So, I sit here now.

(ROBERT BRUCE JR., Sharp Mountain, June 27, 2001, VG2001-2-56:004-011,126-148, Gwich'in)

Muskrats, Caribou, Bone Grease, and Water Boots

When we used to stay in Crow Flats with my mother and father, I remember they worked very hard. My dad would hunt muskrats and bring lots of them back home. My mother would skin them and then work with them and it was a lot of work. Both of them worked hard.

Then in the springtime, father would kill many caribou and my mother, how she worked, sometimes I remember that. She dried lots of meat and she also made bone grease. My sister, Alice, and I watched her. She made bone grease and poured it into the caribou stomach and she would freeze it. She did lots of work, I remember that. Then father would bring home ducks and how well my mother used to prepare them. The ducks, she would prepare them [pluck, gut, cut up]. Then she would store them underground [under the moss on permafrost]. That was for when they moved to the river, for lunches. I remember her telling us that.

In those days, too, she made water boots....Today they call them gumboots. In those days there were no gumboots... She would melt candle wax and coat them with it. That was water boots, similar to gumboots.

(MARION SCHAFER, Old Crow, April 2003, VG2002-3-19:050-074, Gwich'in)

How Going Out on the Land has Changed, Difficulties Today, and Importance for the Future

It was very important, this Crow Flats, to the people of Old Crow. Right up until 1970s, I remember we used to come to Crow Flats. [There] used to be lots of people here in them days. Nighttime, we used to visit around to each other. About 1974–75, Crow Flats start to die off a little bit. Young boys start to get job and I remember, even myself, I used to work at airport. I maintained the airport thirteen and a half years. Every spring I wanted to go to Crow Flats, so I just take off. Come out with airplane and stay the spring and come back in the spring and work back at the airport.

But now it's not like that. The younger boys are not interested in that lifestyle. That's too bad because part of it, I blame myself for it, too, because the job was too important and politics was too important. Crow Flats, I forgot all about Crow Flats. Now I got a 22-year-old boy and he doesn't even know his area where we been raised up....Even though I'm not healthy enough, I always think to myself: I sure like to bring him out one day or one time and show him the country.

Like I say, we travel around at night after it turn hot during the day and snow melt. At nighttime it turn cold—[you] could walk on the snow without breaking through and that's the time you can go anywhere and that's the time people visit around. And I'd like to show him that—how if people lived out here you know we could visit each other, sit around overnight and talk and tell stories about Crow Flats, and that's another way of getting our culture across to the young people. You know a lot of young boys in Old Crow, some of them went to Crow Flats and they sure like to go back.

Today's society, world that we live in today, price are so high to move to Crow Flats, it cost money to move back to what we used to do. So the stuff [price of supplies] are so high, gas price are up, Ski-doo price are high. Nobody uses dog team anymore, so all these we take into account to get anyone out on the land. Not only talking about Crow Flats: people want to trap across the river from Old Crow toward White Mountain, Johnson Creek, Salmon Cache, Bell River. You can't do it. That's just because prices are too high and you can't make any money when price of fur don't come up to pay off your bill.

The way Charlie talk before, when I remember my grandfather talk about it a lot. When I was growing up, we come out here to live good. We don't come out here to make money, we just come out here to live our traditional way that we live off animal. When we get back to Crow Flats, to Old Crow, we'll do the same thing. So he was right.

I remember that later on things start to change. In 1964, I could remember *Brainstorm* [supply barge] come up the Porcupine and start to make record of freight run: three or four times in the summer, five trips a summer and everybody used to get fresh groceries. Anything fresh, you get it on that boat and it stay fresh and then from there on things start to change. We start to live off pop and all kinds of good candies, stuff like that. Today's society, we live off beef meat. We got fridge; we got freezer. So it's a big change.

Even as far back as 1964, we never had freezers like that or fridge. We had a walk-in freezer where everybody put their meat in the spring. If you live in Crow Flats, you had no meat in Old Crow because you weren't there to kill the caribou and put it in the walk-in freezer. But I must tell you: people was good. People them days, they share with each other. People who live in Crow Flats, we don't have to worry because the people who live in Old Crow, them days, they kill caribou and they put meat away for people that live in Crow Flats. Maybe couple caribou ham, couple ribs and some brisket, they put your name on it and when you get back they tell you you got meat in the walk-in freezer and that was helpful. You have to give something for that. Black

ducks—we call it black ducks here but the real name is black scoter—
and we used to kill lots of that. And our mother make lots of good
drymeat, bone grease, marrow. We take the things back like that and
when somebody do that, too, they get treated good.

(ROBERT BRUCE JR., *Diniizhòo* (Game Mountain or Potato Hill), July 25, 2004,
VG2004-4-06, English)

When Muskrats are Scarce, how Family Areas in Crow Flats Developed,
and the Future

[To sell muskrat skins] there's a trader, his name is Joe Netro. He's
pretty well-known and he's been providing all the people with groceries to go Crow Flats every spring and everybody give him his muskrats
and pay off their debt. So he's the one that's buying it. We accept
whatever he give us. [Laughter]...Just give him the whole muskrats,
whatever you get, and you accept whatever he give you because
there's no other buyer. And sometime we don't know what the price
is, even till we get back down.

[The most muskrats I trapped] just myself, I got 800. Billy Bruce, we
used to trap together. We used to get a thousand, 1,200. And the least
is probably about 300 when muskrat were pretty well scarce.

[When there's no muskrats] well, like grandfather, you have another
place, across from Old Crow and that's where he go and trap a few
beavers. And, mostly, drymeat is an important thing. So I think it's
pretty hard when muskrats die off and it last for a few years.

[To move from the camp to the river took] a couple of nights. We
usually work couple nights [to move] all the stuff. And we had to cut
down trees and build a canvas boat...Yeah, every spring we made a
new one. You haul that canvas out every year. It's a pretty risky thing
but that's the only way, the only transportation you have. Can't make
skin boat....

Crow Flats, in the late 1800s people used to come from Rampart
House. There was no Old Crow in them days. And there's no boundary....People from Fort Yukon [Alaska] used to come out to Crow Flats
and they used to stay anywhere, just pitch tent anywhere. There was
no "my area," that sort of thing. Then later on, the government pitch
in and there's a boundary, there's a law [saying] you can't trap on this
side, especially for them. Then in probably 1920s, maybe, people start
going to one certain area and they sort of claim it and they go in that
area every year. So that's how people got certain area: they go every

Preparing to cover a canvas boat frame on Van Tat *(Crow Flats), 2001. (L–R) Harvey Kassi, Freddy Frost.*
[Shirleen Smith ©VGFN (VG2001-6-91)]

year because they got trapping things [which] they left [in] that specific area. And that's how you get to know your country and where to trap...

[There were] always people around here. They're all gone and they're deceased. Just me and Shawn [Bruce], [another] couple of boys, I guess, come out there sometimes. I'm still looking forward to carry on this place, amongst my lakes.

(JOEL PETER, his cabin at Crow Flats, June 25, 2001, VG2001-2-49:069-140, English)

Reasons for the Decline of Muskrats in *Van Tat* (Crow Flats) and Hopes for their Return in the Future

We all stayed here. While it is like this [spring], they killed lots of caribou and dried lots of meat....When [there was] no ice, we hunted muskrat with canoe. Before that, we trapped muskrat on clear ice and we killed lots that way. We also used canoes and killed lots of muskrats, too. And from here we moved to the river; there was lots of stuff to move. We moved dry muskrat...and muskrat skin, drymeat and all our stuff, and I know why we take it to town and the next spring, we bring it all back out....

The Oral History of Today 289

But one thing...now we're standing here, there's no muskrats and no muskrat houses on the lake. As I look around, there's no muskrats, [I saw only] four muskrats sitting on the ice. And nowadays people don't get to *Van Tat* [Crow Flats]. We don't do things like long ago. We used to trap muskrats every year. And this is why I think there are no muskrats.[9] [i.e., because of changes in trapping patterns]

One elder said this in a meeting in Old Crow: after 10 years the muskrats start coming back....If people don't come out to *Van Tat*, and also at Schaeffer Lake, this is why I think there's not too many muskrats.

Now we come up with boats this spring to where people used to stay long ago. We stopped here and there, and no one stays there at this time. Today this is why we travel to *Van Tat*: to tell stories about what we used to do long ago. Maybe if the young people see this tape and stories they might try to go to *Van Tat*.

The only way is: we have to talk a lot about *Van Tat* to young people before young people can go *Van Tat*. If we come out with them, I think it will help a lot....

Twenty-three years ago, that was the last time I came here to this old spring camp and that's where I stayed for last time 23 years ago.... There was lots of muskrats at that time: I killed 1,200 muskrats sometimes, too. At that time there were lots of us here...but still we killed lots of muskrats....Now there's no muskrats in *Van Tat*....

Now that I'm here, I'm happy and sometimes I'm a little sad. It makes me think of what we used to do here long ago and I'm happy to be here. We do this trip to see if there's any change in muskrats. It looks like there's no muskrats.

(ROBERT BRUCE JR., Robert Bruce Lake, Crow Flats, June 10, 2001, VG2001-2-30, Gwich'in)

Relationships in the Future

Concern for the Next Generations

The single greatest prevailing theme for all generations of Van Tat Gwich'in is concern for future generations. Elders spoke of hard times in the past and believe they will return. Current concerns are that the youth don't know the land as well as their predecessors and are therefore vulnerable. As well, they see that for future generations of Van Tat Gwich'in to live satisfying, healthy lives, they need to maintain the fundamental relationships with their past and their land.

Esau Schafer with replica fish lure he made, Diniizhòo *(Potato Hill/ Game Mountain), 2007.*

[Shirleen Smith ©VGFN (VG2007-3-376)]

Marion Schafer, David Lord, and Robert Bruce Jr. expressed their belief that the youth need to go out on the land and learn some of the knowledge and skills of their ancestors in order to live better lives and continue their culture. They described how they were trained when they were young and the foundation this provided for their lives, as well as their wish that young people today could benefit from some of the same opportunities.

The Past and Future of how the People Worked on the Land

When we travelled around with my mother and father, in those days they worked really hard. But today there are lots of jobs and people do not live out on the land anymore. The days when I was a child being brought up, we only lived out in the bush. There my mother taught me how to work. Today I still remember all that. There was lots of work with meat preparation, and my father harvested muskrats. It was hard work. Today I remember his work. We were brought up well. Now as I look back, today people don't go out on the land too much.

What I wish for is for our children to live out on the land and learn our traditional ways and skills. They would set traps, hunt and learn all these skills so that they will use them in the future. They would also learn the place names on the land. If we talk to them about all that, they will live a good life and have a good future.

(MARION SCHAFER, Old Crow, April 2003, VG2002-3-19:022-039, Gwich'in)

Hunting Then and Now

The elders say that "Wherever you travel, take the young men with you, it will be good." Well, that's what they did to me. When I was a young boy, whenever they go hunting, I went with them. In those days it was only with dog teams, [and] we hunt only with snowshoes....They would go up on the hills. From there, we see it good, that's why it was done that way. We leave our dog teams and we walk a long way. These days it's only with Ski-doo that they travel around. When they hunt [now] they only stay on the trail. They think they see the country—they don't see the country!

(ROBERT BRUCE JR., Bell River, July 2003, VG2002-3-12:112-130, English)

Growing Up at Crow Flats and Reasons to Return

My father, he take me all over Crow Flats. Even [when I was] two to three years old, I go with him. He carry me in canoe to every lake, show me everything, shoot [musk]rat. [Emotional]

Ah, nowadays nobody comes here....[It's] not like it used to be. When I was kid growing up, [it was] noisy, this Crow Flats. Lots of people! Everybody busy! Hear shoot all over, and springtime, we hurry to come here, to Cook Cabin [family camp]. And then we go to the other end of the bluff there. He show us how to make canvas boat and everything. [Sound of geese passing by]

My grandmother Sarah Abel used to come out with us, too. That's the one [who] show me lots, take me all over those lake. We walk around lake, and she tell me where it's good for muskrat, set trap along the shore, tell me stories.

People used to come here all the time and wait for my father [Peter Lord]. But him, he's hard working man: he make everybody wait, all the time. People want to go to town but he stay right till [musk]rat go in, him. He don't: muskrat swim around, he stay till it's gone.

This is where he really train me. This is where I learn everything, out here in Crow Flats. That's how come, today I come here and know what to do. If I'm going to make canoe, I know how to do it; canvas boat, anything. This was all taught to me. He teach me all that.

So, we need to come back to this Crow Flat and bring young people out here, teach them all this. Even [though] trapping is no good now, still you come back out here; you feel good, eat good, sleep good and enjoy life. Just like coming home for me, feel good here. Lots of times, he tell stories and then when you come out here is no worries. Everything is here, what you need. Stay, live out on the land and we got no worry. You want to eat, it's right there. So it would be good to come back here, bring young people back here and show them all these things I talk about, teach them. Because hard time is coming around and not too far [in the future] is going to be hard time again....Young people need to know all this Crow Flat and where all their place is. Learn their country, live off the land. Don't have to depend on store all the time. Come out on the land, it's just like a store here, too.

(DAVID LORD, Cook's Cabin (Pete Lord's place), Crow River, June 10, 2001, VG2001-2-25:024-070, English)

Teaching Younger Generations to Look after the Land Because Hard Times are Coming

Today when we get caribou, I dry meat the way my mother taught us. "Whenever you go out in the bush, when you kill caribou, don't leave any parts behind," she told us. She also said, "Always look after your caribou meat well." This is what I learned from her. We would never throw away any meat. She also talked to us about hard times coming back. Today, my mother was telling the truth, I think to myself.

She told us, "When you go out on the land, look after the land well. That land is sacred," she said this, too....She said it will be hard times coming; today we see it. That's why it's important to teach our children

Page 295 (top): Jeffrey Peter and his grandmother Lydia Thomas on upper Neegoo Zràii Njik *(Black Fox Creek) by the Barns Range, 2006.*

[Shirleen Smith ©VGFN (VG2006-11-377)]

Page 295 (bottom): Youth participants in oral history research near Diniizhòo *(Potato Hill/Game Mountain), 2007. (L-R) Front: Michelle Kendi-Rispin, Melissa Frost, Brandon Kyikavichik. Back: Frances Bruce, Tracy Rispin, Phillip Rispin.*

[Shirleen Smith ©VGFN (VG2007-3-220)]

how to hunt, how to work with meat. If they're taught all that today, that will be good.

(MARION SCHAFER, Old Crow, April 2003, VG2002-3-19:090-105, Gwich'in)

The Youth Speak about the Future

The future of Van Tat Gwich'in will be in the hands of the youth of today and subsequent generations, so concern for the welfare of youth also speaks to the future of Van Tat Gwich'in in general. Clearly, the experience of growing up in Old Crow today is very different from that of all the generations of elders, and even the middle-aged people, before them. While their lives may resemble those of youth elsewhere in Canada in a number of ways—access to schools, satellite television, computers, politics, and the popular culture of the day—Van Tat Gwich'in youth also live among their elders and families, the timeless cycles of caribou migrations and salmon runs, dog teams, snowmobiles, wood-burning stoves, and Gwich'in language classes at school. It is difficult to predict the futures they will choose. Looking to the Van Tat Gwich'in Oral History Collection, a sample of interviews with youth gives their thoughts about what it may mean to be Van Tat Gwich'in in their future.

Brandon Kyikavichik was seventeen years old and attending high school in Whitehorse, Yukon, at the time of his interview. Erika Tizya-Tramm, Tammy Josie, Cheryl Charlie, and Melissa Frost were in their early 20s and, along with teenagers Natasha Frost and Kathie Marie Charlie, participated in oral history-cultural geography research in 2005-2007 and travelled by helicopter on the land with their elders. Their brief comments provide an insight into what their heritage and land mean to them.

Brandon Kyikavichik, His Grandfather, His Land, and His Future

My grandpa's [John Joe Kyikavichik] camp is across the river about 16 miles west of Old Crow. We go out in the springtime, around April, and we set up camp. We just go there to fool around, just for the living, I guess. We hunt black ducks and trap muskrats. We hunt beaver, too. He tells us about beaver, he say: if that beaver come up and he smell you, he gonna go away and you'll never see him again. But if he see you, it's okay, he'll probably come back....You gotta sit there, long time, too, you gotta be quiet. Then we sit there and we hunt beaver. We watch those muskrat, cause we can't shoot, gotta be quiet. We just watch them. Quite the thing to see. We watch them fight, too. They go up to that muskrat house. If there's a muskrat sitting there, then

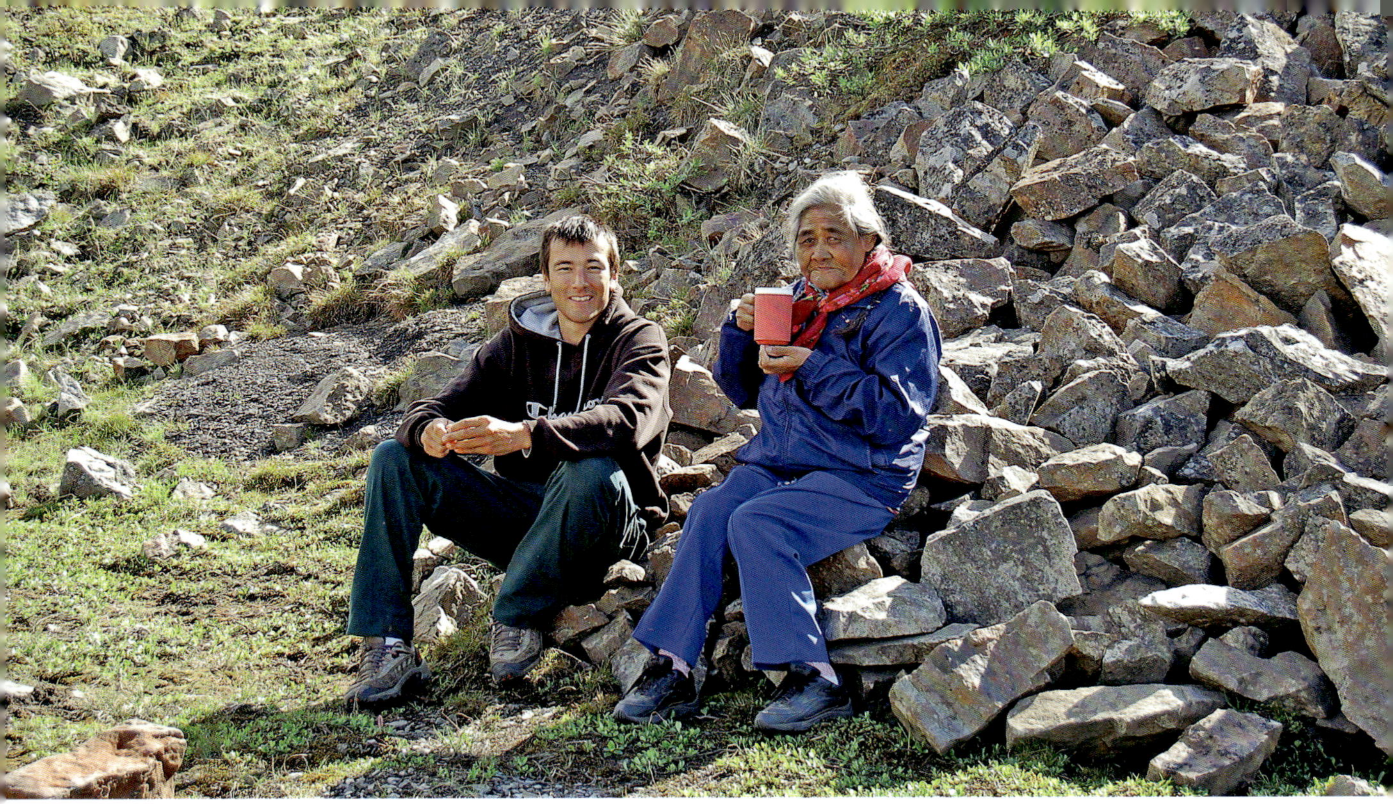

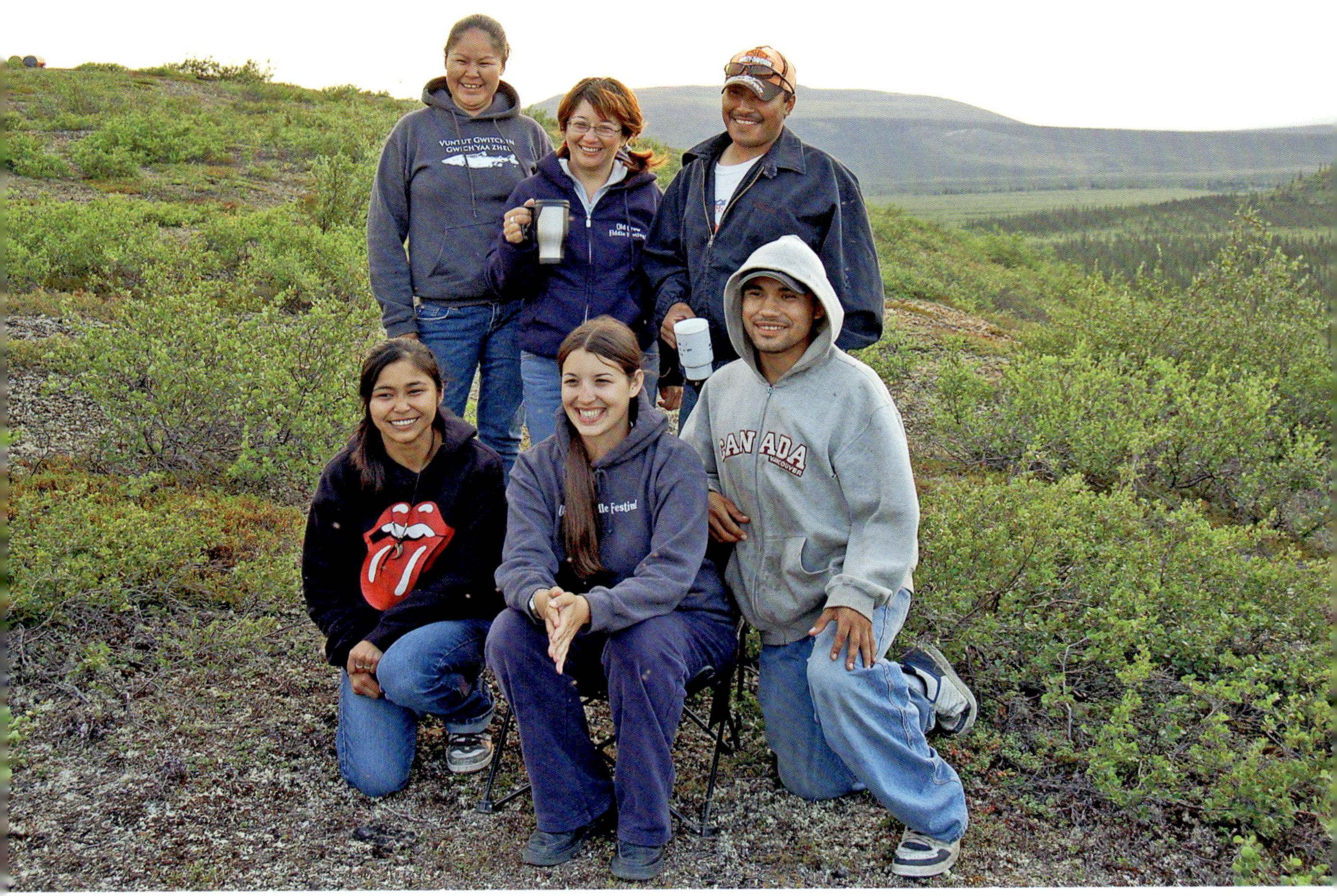
VUNTUT GWITCHIN
GWICH'YAA ZHEE

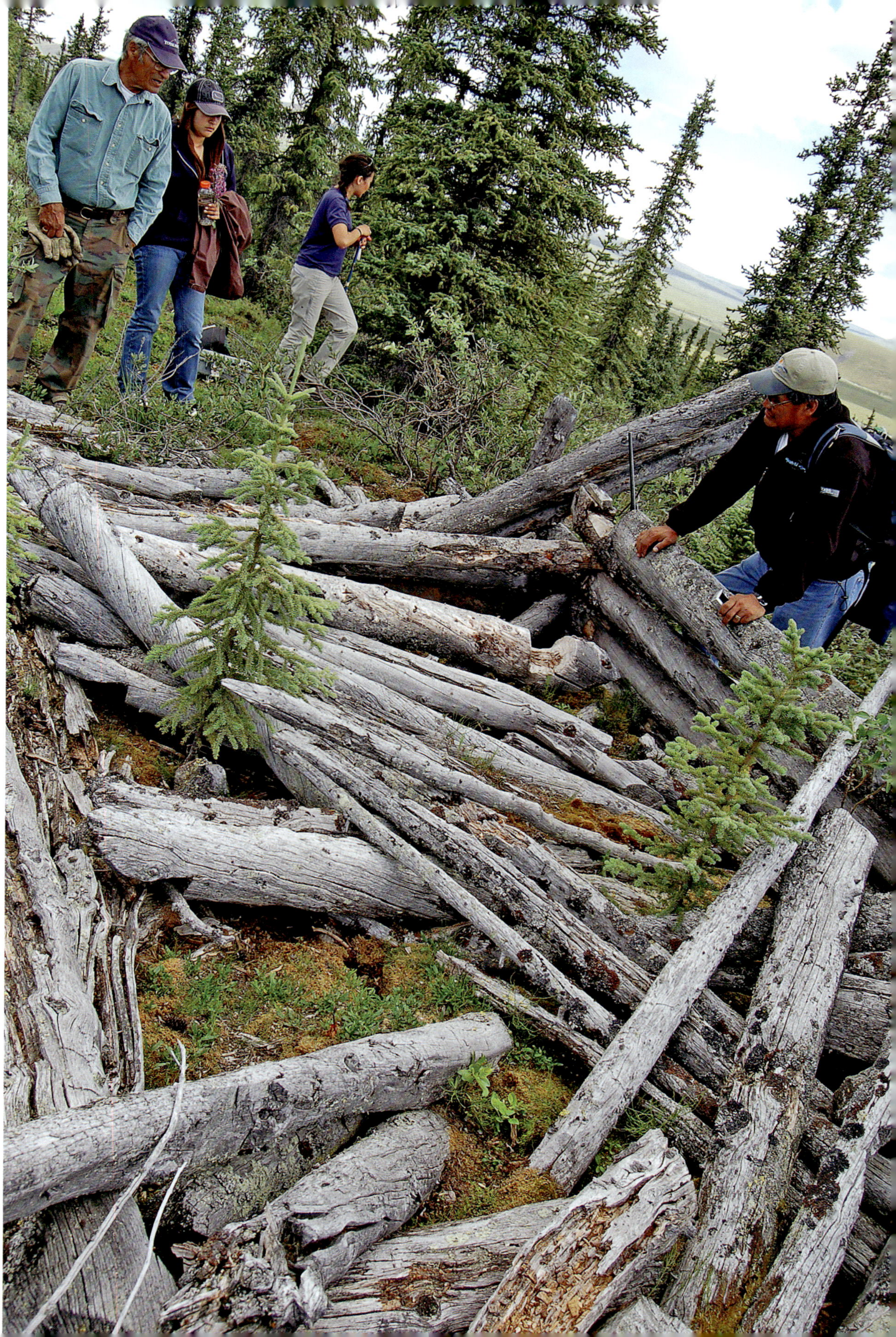

Page 296: Cache at Antl'it (Thomas Creek Caribou Fence), 2007. (L–R) Stephen Frost Sr., Sherrie Frost, Erika Tizya-Tramm, Esau Schafer.
[Shirleen Smith ©VGFN (VG2007-3-283)]

Donald Frost and granddaughter Natasha Frost at Sriinjik (Bluefish River), 2005.
[Shirleen Smith ©VGFN (VG2005-3-50)]

another muskrat come, they like that sitting spot, he gonna try take it over. So he go there and fight, fast, too. Just like that—all over. And usually when they take over, they usually fight to the death. Quite the thing to see….

[How do you feel about going to school in Whitehorse and then you don't go hunting and stuff—do you miss it?] Oh yeah, especially springtime. Springtime, I can't stop thinking about my camp, cause I just feel like, ah, you know, even when I was gone this year, too, nobody went [there] for spring. My grandpa always want it to be used, hah. He said if you don't use it, the roof gonna fall in and all that. So I think about that: gotta use it all the time. So maybe when I graduate, I'll come back and stay there.

[Who taught you about your culture?] My grandpa, all my grandpa. He's the only one who ever took me out.

(BRANDON KYIKAVICHIK, Bell River, August 18, 2002, VG2002-3-13:090–105, English)

The Oral History of Today

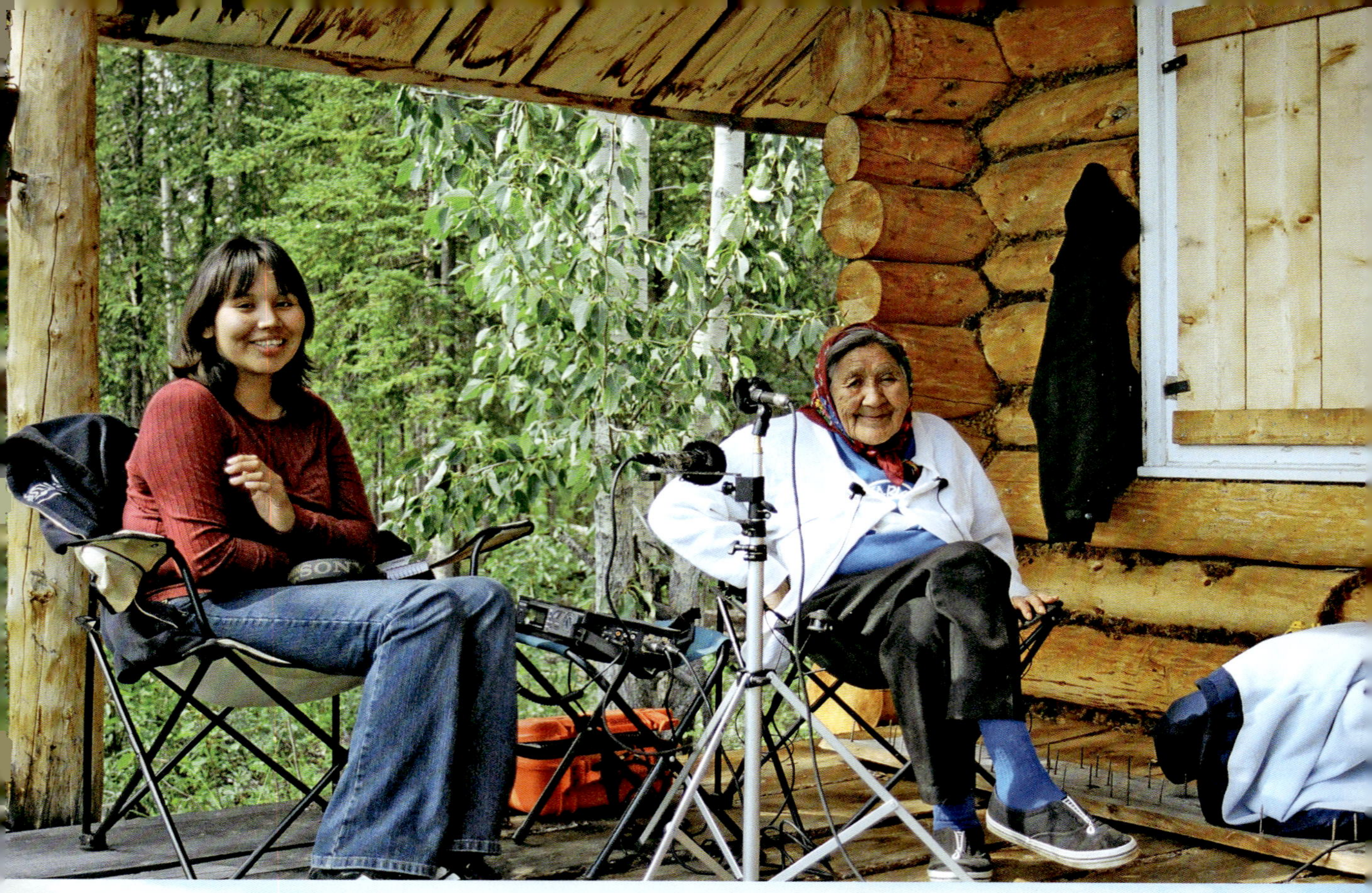
SONY

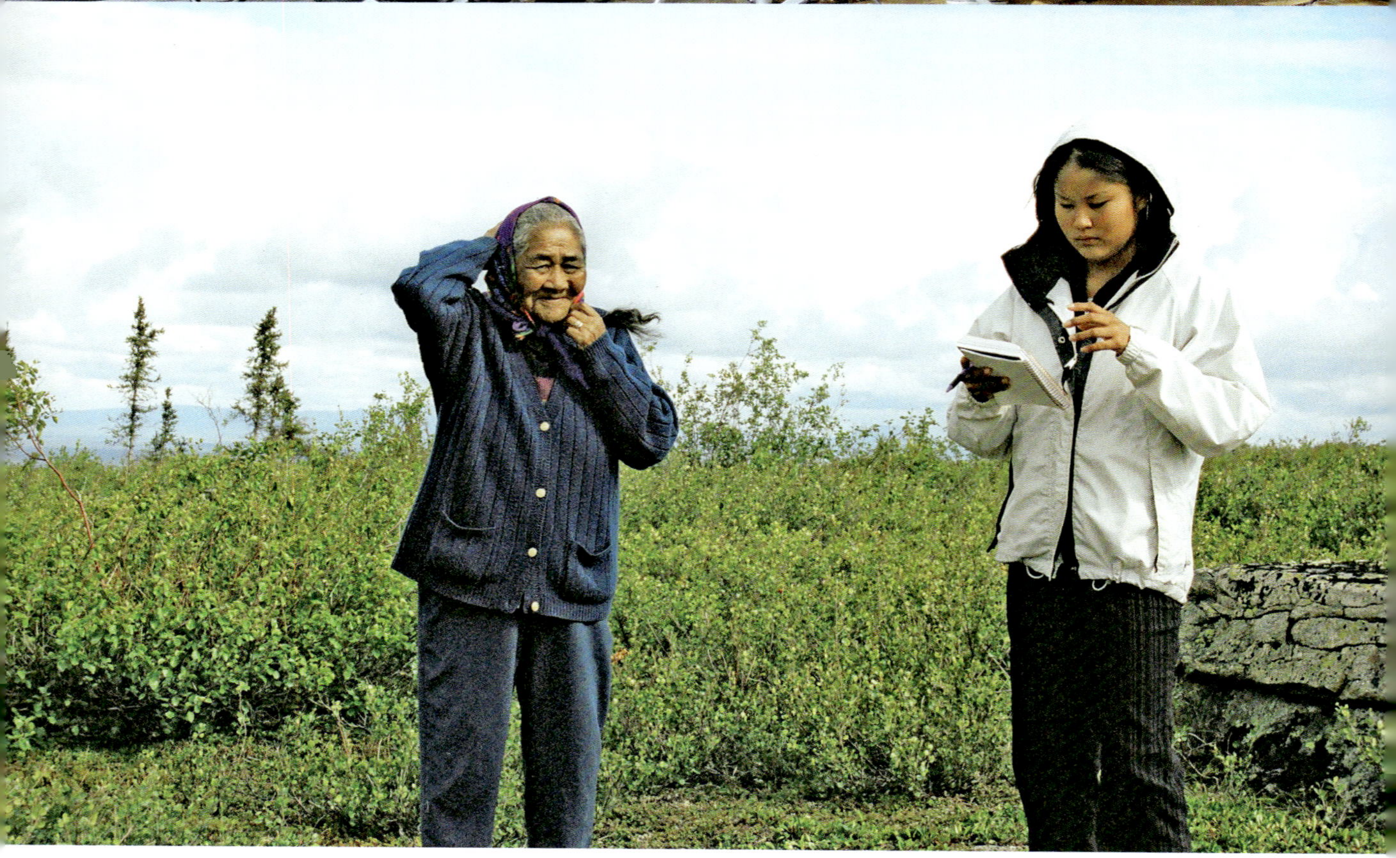

Page 298 (top): Tammy Josie and her grandmother Edith Josie at Chuu Tl'it *(Whitestone Village), 2005.*
[Shirleen Smith ©VGFN (VG2005-3-185)]

Page 298 (bottom): Elder Lydia Thomas and Kathie Charlie at Gèegook'yuu, *2005.*
[Shirleen Smith ©VGFN (VG2005-3-232)]

Erika Tizya-Tramm's Visit to *Van Tat* and Black Fox Creek

Today I had the opportunity to visit a few places within the Van Tat Gwich'in traditional territory…It's phenomenal to think that I have walked in the footsteps of my ancestors because it was their strength and knowledge that allowed me to be here. These places are very important to our culture….The land has provided us with food and a home so that we can carry our culture on to future generations. Our people settled here for a reason, which is why it's so important to protect and honour its existence. I feel this experience has reinforced a lot of my values and beliefs as a First Nations person. And it's also strengthened a lot of my hopes for the future.

(ERIKA TIZYA-TRAMM, Black Fox Creek, July 2005, English)

Natasha Frost at *Sriinjik* (Bluefish River)

Bluefish is an important place to me because it's where my family is from; it's part of where I'm from. I've learned a lot today from my grandpa [Donald Frost], from the stories he tells me…Being at those places is amazing. It's not like looking at a picture, it's actually there…

(NATASHA FROST, *Sriinjik*, July 2005, English)

Cheryl Charlie at *Zhoh Drìn Chòo* (White Snow Mountain)

When we were there…my grandma [Fanny Charlie] showed me different plants used for medicine…It was a good experience to see where grandparents grew up and were raised…

(CHERYL CHARLIE, *Zhoh Drìn Chòo*, July 2005, English)

Tammy Josie at *Chuu Tl'it* (Whitestone Village)

Chuu Tl'it was an important gathering place for the Dagoo people… there used to be lots of people in this area, *Chuu Tl'it* area. There were many fur-bearing animals in this area that made survival possible for the Dagoo people, *Takidah*. Looking at *Chuu Tl'it* today, all the fallen cabins, the tall grass and willows…I can only imagine a vibrant village… I feel a sense of belonging and I feel so privileged.

(TAMMY JOSIE, *Chuu Tl'it*, July 2005, English)

Kathie Marie Charlie at *Gèegook'yuu*[10]

It's important to me to see where my family was raised...
(KATHIE MARIE CHARLIE, *Gèegook'yuu*, July 2005, English)

Melissa Frost at *Diniizhòo* (Potato Hill or Game Mountain)

...You know, reading those stories is an amazing thing and seeing all the pictures but actually coming here and being here, you know it's hard to explain. You could feel the power of our ancestors, the power of the land....I mean, this is the best view that you can get. I see why they came here for camp in the summer, you know. Look at this beautiful view, all the mountains in the back. I mean, like I said, it's very powerful.

Not only is it a good experience, getting to sit around with elders and they tell you stories and they show us different kind of tools that were used and how we made them then, like bone scraper, caribou legbone scraper and how they made it. Robert Bruce and Fanny [Charlie] and John Joe [Kyikavichik], they all explain that to us just earlier and tell us stories about long ago and they say that Game Mountain or Potato Hill or *Diniizhòo*, as we call it, they would go there for summer gatherings, they get married, celebrate, summertime, good living and feasts and just be all together and it's good that we get to experience that as a group...

Being here I remember my Grandma Alice a lot, Alice Frost. She taught me a lot growing up, up until I was 13 [years old], till she passed away. She taught me lots about the land and she would always take me on trips and tell me about different plants and different medicines and I remember her while I'm here. And those teachings are carried on through our other elders and through everyone, everyone teaches us something. I made these tobacco ties, I remember her, my Grandma Alice, she took me up to top of Crow Mountain one time. I was sick and she took spruce tree, little spruce tree and she chopped it down, she end up making tea for me with it but first she said, "You got to give back to the land." It's about balance, keeping balance and that is something that our ancestors have taught us since time immemorial, since we have been here, since we grew from the land. And it's about balance and giving back so being here and being able to be at this camp I had to give back something and tobacco is good medicine to give. So I, she taught me to make tobacco ties, just tie it on a

Mary Jane Moses sewing a moose-hide ball at Diniizhòo (Potato Hill/ Game Mountain), 2007.

[Shirleen Smith ©VGFN (VG2007-3-316)]

willow and just say a prayer with it so that's what I'm going to do here. And once again I just want to say thank you. I've learnt, it's unexplainable how much I've learnt and how much I've grown, just being these couple of days here. Ah, *Mahsi' Cho.*

(MELISSA FROST, *Diniizhòo*, July 14, 2007, VG2007-02-11:165-215, English)

ORAL HISTORY FROM ANCESTORS TO YOUTH

The oral history from the "young elders," middle-aged, and youth reveal very different ways of life and communication styles from those of their ancestors, as well as notably consistent themes. The central message is about passing on—and receiving—the basic tenets of Van Tat Gwich'in identity, found in the ways of relating to the land/nature and society. The middle-aged speakers are well aware of the differences between their elders' lives (aspects of which they experienced themselves as children) and those of the youth of today. For their part, the youth express the importance of their connections to their ancestors and the land as a foundation of values and identity in their diverse and complex lives.

Taken collectively, the elders created a cycle of stories that began with *yeenoo dài' googwandak* (long-ago stories) that described creation and the organization of the Gwich'in world and society. The first generation of elders spoke about life in relationship with this world but with the beginnings of European involvement in their economy, as well. The second generation continued to live on and manage their lands and experienced the most intensive period of the fur trade. During their time, the influence of the polity of Canada came to their lives, bringing institutions such as schools, police, health care, and the infrastructure of permanent communities. The cycle was completed with the concerns expressed by current elders and middle-aged Gwich'in (and youth) about the importance of the continuity of the lessons that reach back to the long-ago period, and in passing them to the future.

Collecting and Communicating Oral History

The primary reason for assembling this history of Van Tat Gwich'in is for the future generations. This is the mandate from the elders. Those who worked to collect the interviews, translate them, assemble historical and recent photographs and film footage, develop educational materials, and work to identify Gwich'in place names and promote the use of the language are all committed to this purpose. The second objective is to foster a wider understanding of Van Tat Gwich'in, along with messages such as the importance of caring for the natural world, animals, water, and of sharing their knowledge of ways of living well with other people. This book is part of the work they have been pursuing for decades to protect the land and animals for which they feel responsible and to foster a healthy society, in the face of challenges that at times have been monumental.

This history is assembled from a significant—but finite—collection of oral history transcripts. The over 350 transcripts are only a sample of the

Van Tat Gwich'in elders and community members singing Gwich'in hymns on Ch'anchàł (King Edward Mountain), 2000.
[Shirleen Smith ©VGFN (VG2000-6-353)]

entirety of Van Tat Gwich'in oral history: that part which happened to be recorded in relatively recent times. As such, this history does not claim to represent everything about Van Tat Gwich'in but rather a slice of the history and culture. It is also only one of many approaches to the material; not all stories could be included, and different perspectives could have been taken. However, the diversity and richness of this fragment—from long-ago stories to environmental knowledge to the history of the 19th and 20th centuries in the northern Yukon—gives a sense of the scope and breadth of Van Tat Gwich'in oral history, the rich detail of specifics and broad sweep of themes, from how to live in the natural world to family life to dealing with external authorities. The history presented here is undoubtedly not the final word on Van Tat Gwich'in history, nor is it the only possible interpretation or organization.

The approach taken toward Van Tat Gwich'in history in this book has been to focus on the speakers: their identity, age, generation, and social networks (where and with whom they were born, grew up, and later lived). While some topics became spread between chapters, the purpose of this organization was to show Van Tat Gwich'in over time, as well as Van Tat

The Oral History of Today 303

Gwich'in commentary and values on their history and culture. The primary objective is Van Tat Gwich'in history: to collect and present their history for subsequent generations and to forefront a source and subject of history that has been viewed previously only as a backdrop or on the margins of major historical events. As such, the significance of this book is the voices of the people themselves. Although these voices pass through the filters of translation from Gwich'in to English, oral to written, and in-context oral events to decontextualized written fragments, the sheer number, detail, nature, and sweep of the voices is preserved. Taken as a whole, Van Tat Gwich'in oral history is a chorus of individual, intimate voices that speak of more than 150 years of events, people, places, values, and changes, to give us a unique sense of their history from the "inside."

The history related by the first generation of elders is dominated by how they made their living from the land: the individual labour, activities, knowledge, and technology, as well as the collective effort and satisfaction. What emerges is a story of a group of people working to continue through time to exist in a place and way of life that to some extent defines them. The second generation encountered some new and unique challenges that formed the backdrop to their history: an increase in the influx of non-Native trappers and traders brought by, for example, the Klondike Gold Rush, the attraction of trapping during the Depression of the 1930s, and whaling. These newcomers had a number of impacts: some married into the community and raised families, some trapped amicably, while others are remembered for poisoning areas and rendering them useless for making a living for decades following their presence. A very few are recalled for their unco-operative or threatening presence (for example, the Mad Trapper incident). As well, change in the form of new technology (such as snowmobiles, outboard motors, reliable guns, nylon nets) began to have greater effects on the way of living than previously, where new technology could be said to have assisted customary tasks rather than transforming them. Finally, the crisis in the fur trade of the 1980s, along with the rapid increase in the cost of consumer goods, resulted in previously unexperienced ways of life for the second generation. The history of the third generation and youth reveals this in more detail and raises some important questions about the future.

Each generation of Van Tat Gwich'in spoke not only of their own experiences but of those of their predecessors, and the history ultimately spanned a timeframe of about a century and a half, from the mid-1800s to 2007. The experiences of this group and their knowledge emphasize the vagaries and pleasures of making a living in the far northern reaches of continental North America during times of great global and local change. On one level, their history is of everyday life and everyday people. When the context of the challenging climate and remarkable social, technological, and political change is taken into consideration, the broader significance of Van Tat Gwich'in history emerges.

Van Tat Gwich'in History and the Northern Yukon

Many of the earliest stories in the Van Tat Gwich'in Oral History Collection revolve around the history of making a living in a land of radically fluctuating resources, in a time of considerable change. The backdrop to this history is the northern Yukon, which, historically speaking, represents one of the farthest outposts of the fur trade system of eastern North America, following upon its even earlier remote links to the European (Russian) fur trade. The Hudson's Bay Company presence began relatively late—1845—and ended in 1873, followed by a series of private traders. Logistically speaking, the lands of Van Tat Gwich'in are remote: a mountain range separates the northern Yukon from the Mackenzie River fur-trade routes. Goods travelled either over the Richardson Mountains to the east, or to the west upstream on the Porcupine River from its confluence with the Yukon River, in Alaska, which poses both physical and bureaucratic difficulties. Using alternative trading locations involved long and difficult overland journeys: to Herschel Island and the whalers and traders to the north, or to the more distant and difficult trading centres, such as Eagle, Alaska, and Dawson (which elders seldom reported visiting) to the south. Elder Alfred Charlie illustrates the relative isolation of Van Tat Gwich'in:

> Lots of elders nowadays speak good English. They went to school. It was not like this for us. We saw non-Natives in this area later than other communities. Now people my age [80s], when we go to different communities, it's just like we don't speak English as well as other people our age. Myself, I never went to school. I have a hard time speaking English and understanding English.
>
> (ALFRED CHARLIE, Moses Hill, July 27, 2004, VG2004-4-09, Gwich'in)

The land of the Van Tat Gwich'in is a complex place to make a living. Added to its isolation, the northern Yukon is a land of extremes. At high latitudes (Old Crow is at 67°31' N latitude), the seasons alternate between extreme dark, cold winters and hot summers of almost continual light. As well, many of the main species of food animals are migratory: caribou, salmon (various species), waterfowl. Other species remain year round but hibernate, such as bear and ground squirrel (but this attribute is variable too, as in stories of "ice bears," grizzly bears that don't hibernate [see Chapters One and Two]). Still others, such as snowshoe hare and ptarmigan, experience regular population cycles, which in turn affects the population dynamics of the species that rely upon them. Plants are naturally affected by the seasonal variation and produce berries or other edible or useful parts mainly in the brief spring and summer seasons. These are just some of the factors that Van Tat Gwich'in had to consider to come up with a strategy for personal and social survival.

As well as the seasonal fluctuation in the availability of resources, the land of Van Tat Gwich'in is diverse. The heartland—*Van Tat* or Crow Flats— is a large, complex area of lakes, streams, rivers, and lowlands of about 7,500 square kilometres. It is surrounded to the north, east, and west by mountains, to the south by the Porcupine River and more flats and then mountains. The rivers around Crow Flats drain into the Yukon River system to the west; slightly farther north, they drain to the coastal plain and the Arctic Ocean. Immediately north of Crow Flats is the northern extent of the treeline, beyond which the scarcity of wood for fuel, tools, shelter, and other construction requires technologies adapted specifically to these conditions. In addition, the topography of the entire area is influenced by permafrost, which is subject to difficult, boggy ground in low-lying areas, rapid erosion when disturbed, yet can also provide convenient refrigeration.

A significant theme of the oral history is the way people coped with the challenges of climate, geography, and biology. The stories are distinct from straight "traditional knowledge" by being enacted within a social context. Elders not only presented knowledge and technologies but they set this information in its historical, cultural, and social setting. Examples abound: not only does the history include stories of the techniques of making and using snares to hunt everything from moose to hare, but the social organization of who made and used the snares and the historical period and reasons for decline in the use of snares are all discussed. The social roles of old men and women in manufacturing snowshoes and dogsleds and assisting the people through their ingenuity and experience are described in history and long-ago stories, as was the way they were assisted by children, who performed chores and received stories in return. The way people moved on the land in response to fluctuating resources and times of shortages was an important theme, emphasized repeatedly by warnings of the return of hard times in the future.

In the oral history, people spoke of how they worked together to assist each other and survive as a society. Survival was not a matter of individual strategies but of collective responsibilities. Van Tat Gwich'in described the values of sharing, industriousness, and caring for each other that guided their lives. They noted that in the past, people shared with the entire group "like one family," even if only a small amount of food was available, thereby sharing both benefits and risks. Stories that reiterated this strategy include examples of how a group of people survived difficult times in this manner and also the long-ago history of a group of people who all perished. The centrality of the sharing ethic is echoed in the description of *nanaa'in'* or bushmen, beings who were said to derive from people who refused to share and thereby removed themselves from society. Furthermore, the manner by which Van Tat Gwich'in relations with other peoples was conditioned by sharing (trade, partnerships, intermarriage, feasting) in times of peace—and as a measure of peace—drew attention to the role of sharing in their international relations.

Events, People, Responses
The 19th and 20th Centuries

Aside from the major theme of making a living on the land, Van Tat Gwich'in history described a number of other topics: war and peace with neighbours; the coming of new outsiders and the various views and responses by Van Tat Gwich'in; decisions about changes to how people moved and lived on the land; responses to world events, such as wars and borders; the fur trade; religion; policing; diseases and health; and political relations (for example, with Canada).

A series of novel occurrences are described in the oral history, starting in the 19th century. They began as small changes in the normal order of things: new trade goods described in the *yeenoo dài' googwandak* [long-ago stories] came to the Van Tat Gwich'in by trading with the *Ch'ineekaii* or making the long journey across the mountains to the east and up the Mackenzie River. These stories were followed by descriptions of early traders like *Kheh Kai' Zhoo* ("Bearded Chief-Trader" John Firth, trader at LaPierre House and Rampart House from 1880 to 1893). During the same period, Gwich'in relate the story of the coming of the early missionaries *Giikhii Danahch'i* (Robert McDonald), Bompas, and Stringer, the lay readers, and Gwich'in ministers, and their responses to these newcomers, which ranged from welcoming acceptance to reluctance to adopt new beliefs and practices, such as monogamy (see the story of *Shahnuuti'* on pages 109-110).

While describing the early newcomers and the goods and ideas they brought, the oral history also reveals that life on the land was little changed during this period: activities revolved around the changes of the seasons, patterns of animal movement, and ability to amass a surplus for social activities in the summer; people were still using *tthał* (caribou fences, known as "deer barriers" to the Anglican missionary Robert McDonald in the 1860s), as well as bows and arrows, spears, and fish traps; people were living according to their own laws, customs, and practices as they had always done. The new tools and ideas were gradually incorporated into the existing system

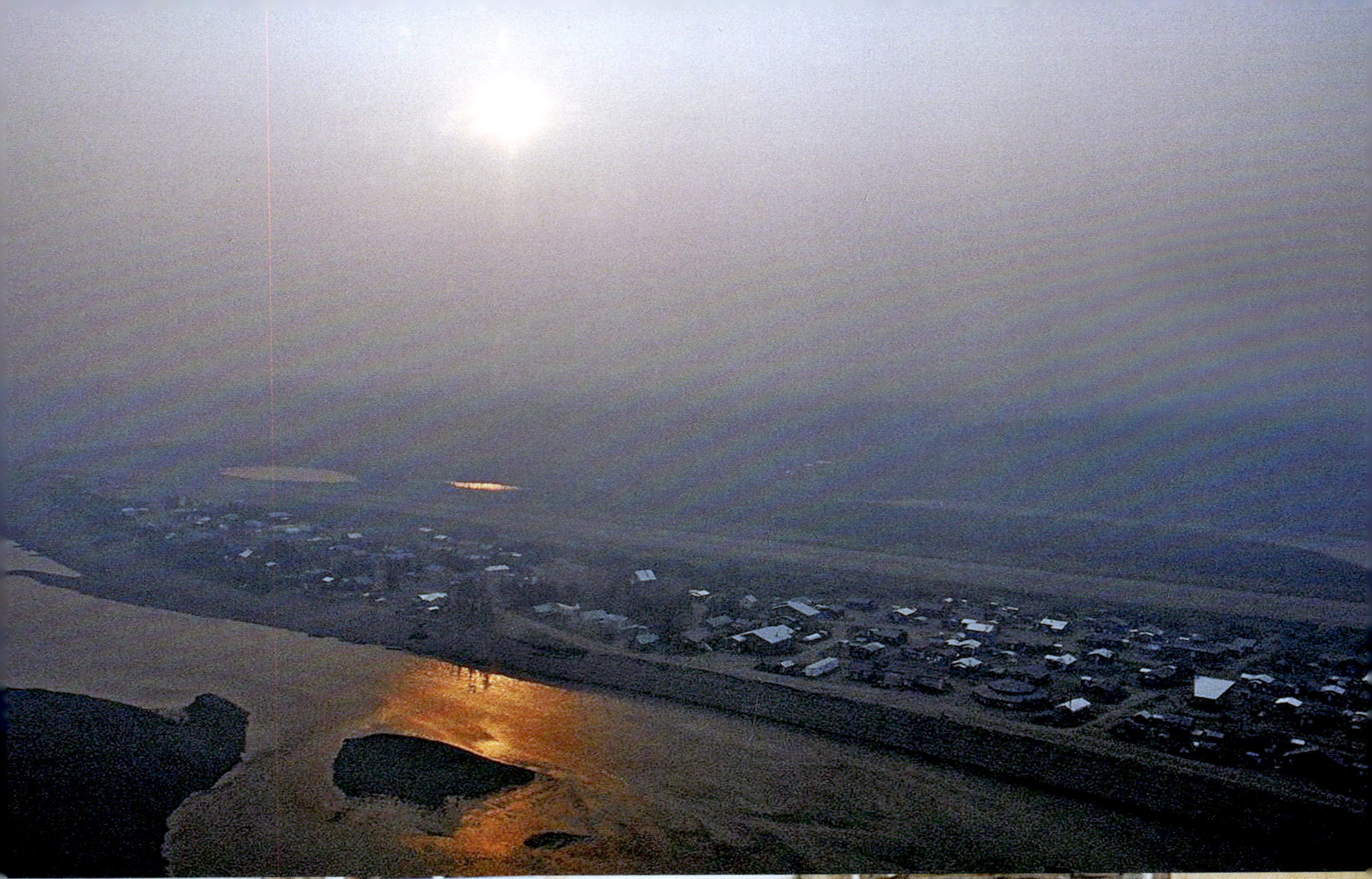

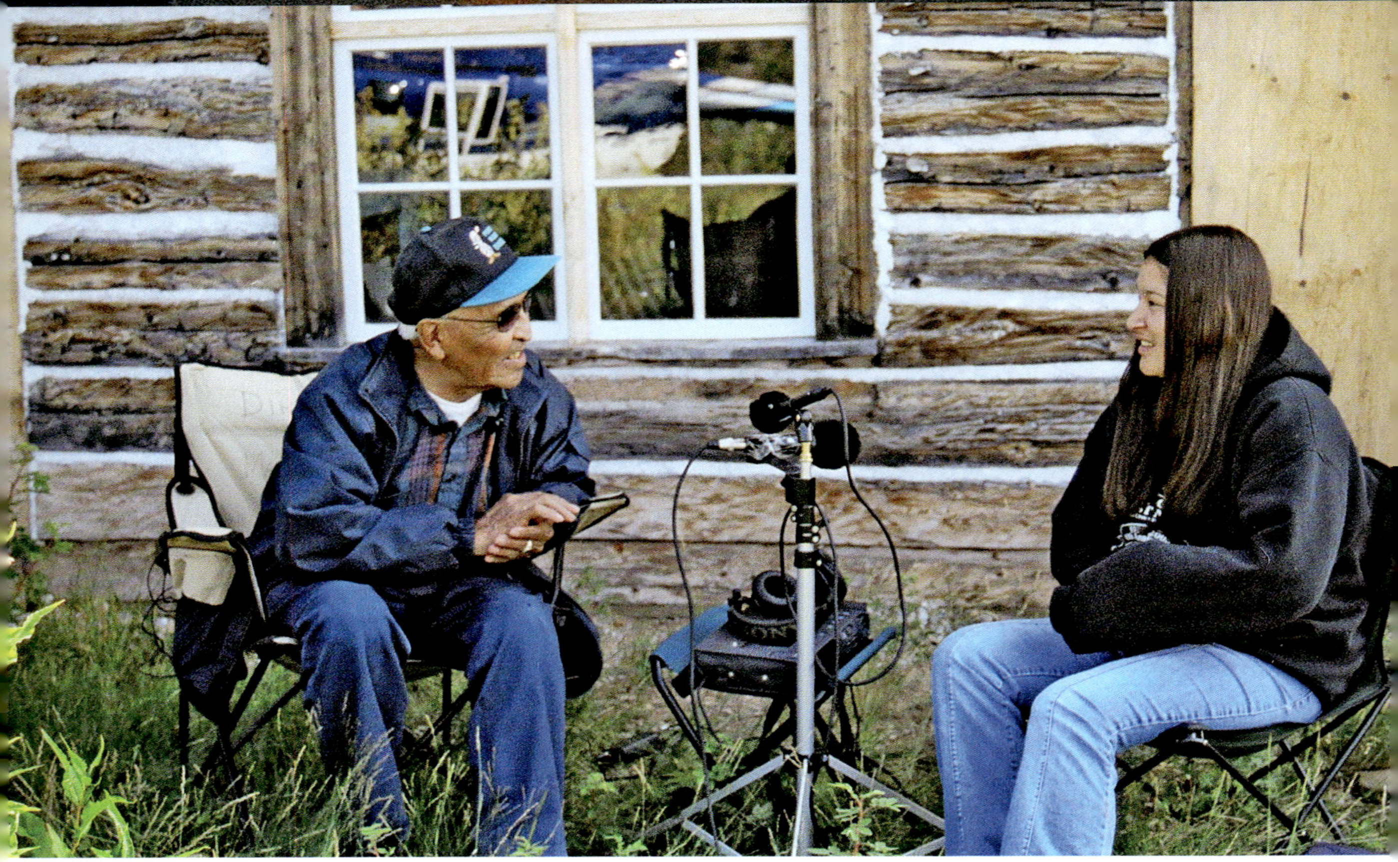

Page 308 (top): Old Crow in smoke from forest fires, 2004.
[Shirleen Smith ©VGFN (VG2004-6-200)]

Page 308 (bottom): Elder Charlie Thomas and Sherrie Frost at Rampart House, 2005.
[Shirleen Smith ©VGFN (VG2005-3-492)]

for some time (for example, the changing technology of rifles). According to Elders Sarah Abel, Moses Tizya, Myra Moses, and Joe Netro, more significant changes were brought about by diseases that reduced the population of Gwich'in, the imposition of the international border through Gwich'in country, and the shifting loci of trade (temporary trading centres were established at LaPierre House, Fort Yukon, Howling Dog Village, the two Rampart Houses, Herschel Island, and short-term private trading stores, such as that of Joe Netro at Whitestone Village before the more enduring trading store at Old Crow was established).

The oral history tells of the events of the time from a Van Tat Gwich'in perspective, which is sufficient to render it unique. Moreover, individuals from the past emerge through their history. Not only historical events, but their consequences are brought into focus. The experience of the first generation of the pullout of the Hudson's Bay Company in 1893 following about 50 years of trading in the area is a case in point. Over 70 years after the event, elders spoke of causes and effects: the trade with whalers (and later, traders) at Herschel Island, the coming of many independent traders, some having ventured to the North for the Klondike Gold Rush of 1898. Elders recalled specific individuals and their stories, as well as the impacts of these events on Gwich'in families. Their history foreshadows events that became important in the future: the effects of the U.S.-Canada border that divided families and local Gwich'in First Nations, and restricted Gwich'in from their millennium-old access to their lands. Abandoning Rampart House for Old Crow as a trading centre and seasonal residence was partly due to the border, and the new home base for Van Tat Gwich'in for at least part of the year was to assume greater significance in more recent decades when people's lives increasingly centred on the community.

The second generation of elders (the current elders at the time of writing) echoed a significant amount of what their elders experienced. They, too, grew up on the land and spent their adulthood there. Like previous generations, *Van Tat* was centrally important, and it was there that they met kin and neighbouring groups, both in times of scarcity and plenty. However, the history they told is also different from that of their elders. They spoke of a greater emphasis on trapping for trade, life in the villages of the upper Porcupine River, and the white trappers who became problems or became family. They "set the scene" of that area and that time with stories of "ice bears" and meeting Gwich'in trappers from across the mountains to the east. They tell of the excitement of the Mad Trapper incident, not a significant occurrence in the long run but one that served as a chronological marker in the oral history and highlighted a number of other events: the influx of white trappers at that time, the role of the police, the co-operation between Gwich'in and police, the effects of new technology—radio—in

Van Tat Gwich'in and researchers at Diniizhòo *(Potato Hill/Game Mountain) with replica Gwich'in bow and arrow, 2007. (L–R) Standing: Ray Le Blanc, Cheryl Charlie, Michelle Kendi-Rispin, Sherrie Frost, Melissa Frost, Brenda Frost, Tracy Rispin, Jane Montgomery, Mary Jane Moses. Kneeling: Shirleen Smith, Phillip Rispin, Brandon Kyikavichik, Erika Tizya-Tramm, Esau Schafer, Irwin Linklater.*

[Jim Broadbent ©VGFN 2007 (VG2007-3-240)]

the unprecedented spread of news to people dispersed on the land, and the effects on individuals and the community from the outcome of the event. Ultimately, the second generation also related the abandonment of the upper Porcupine once it was decimated of fur and game and the scattering of the Dagoo as a people.

Finally, the oral history of the young elders and younger people described the more familiar world of today, bridging the current reality with the past, and revealing peoples' hopes and thoughts about the future. The stories of this chapter are clearly part of a continuum along with those of past and youth generations. The distinctiveness of the Van Tat Gwich'in voice is readily identifiable: people speak of the land and life there in familiar ways, albeit with some different tools and time frames. Their lives are based in the community more so than at any time in the past, yet they also travel the world. They continue to be concerned about the land, the animals, such as salmon and caribou, and their desire for young people to know their land and history as Van Tat Gwich'in. The distinctiveness of these generations is their modern sophistication: they also have experiences with school, work, media, and technology from outside the Van Tat Gwich'in realm, including how they are depicted by the outside world. They are able to reflect on their history and society as insiders while also realizing their distinctiveness in a broader context.

The Non-historical

Other Elements of Van Tat Gwich'in Oral Tradition

The emphasis in this book has been Van Tat Gwich'in history. The reason is that no reliable source of Van Tat Gwich'in oral history is available, and those who are able to span the time from the present back to before significant European contact are elderly, or, in the case of the first generation of elders presented here, deceased. For the present and future Van Tat Gwich'in, as with all other peoples, it is critically important to know the past for many diverse and important reasons: identity, culture, survival, and decisions about the future.

However, history is not the only topic covered in Van Tat Gwich'in oral tradition, as the chapter on *yeenoo dài' googwandak* [long-ago stories] attests. Students of culture, religion and belief, oral traditions, comparative mythology, folklore, comparative psychology, and other disciplines specialize in examining these kinds of stories for what they reveal about the people to whom they belong. For example, certain stories—*Kò' Ehdanh*, the Blind Man and the Loon, the old women stories, and parts of the *Ch'ataiiyuukaih* stories about changing animals—have been studied and parallels found in different parts of northern North America. Different versions of the stories recorded decades and even centuries apart, or across great distances, have been compared to look for what is essential about each story (see commentary by Slobodin, Mishler, and Wallis in the Introduction). Others have looked for the way stories such as these are used: as commentary ethics, instruction, observation on the natural or social world, socialization (for example, Cruikshank 1998).

We felt it important to include *yeenoo dài' googwandak* here as the backdrop to appreciating Van Tat Gwich'in history. The stories in Chapter One are some of the essential stories in the oral tradition, stories "everyone should know," the major links to the very distant past. They provide the ideological context of much of the oral history and give a sense of how some aspects of the history might be framed.[11] For example, the *shanaghàn* or old women stories echo the importance of the knowledge of elders, the values of sharing "like one family," and the ability to overcome adversity through ingenuity. Historically, living on the land and dealing with the variables that entailed were essential skills, and the importance of learning from the elders is echoed through each generation of oral history presented here, including that of the youth. Stories of revenge, such as that of *Kò' Ehdanh*, are echoed in the tales of warfare with the *Ch'ineekaii* from the 19th century, where key individuals led their people in attacks to avenge the deaths of their relatives, particularly brothers. This story has strong parallels with the more recent story of the strong man, *K'aiiheenjik*. Stories of the importance of strong leaders are carried through in descriptions of *Shahnuuti', Ch'eeghwalti',* and *Shahvyah* and, more recently, Chief Peter Moses. All were known for their energetic work for their people and their ability to support many people.

Taken together, the *yeenoo dài' googwandak* and the oral history give a detailed and nuanced picture of the Van Tat Gwich'in and their past. This body of history and oral tradition is a unique and significant contribution to the history of this region of North America.

NOTES

Preface

1   The community of Old Crow and the Vuntut Gwitchin First Nation Heritage Department fully owned and conducted all aspects of the project, which involved approximately 65 community members and the co-ordination and assistance of anthropologist Shirleen Smith.

2   A number of independent recordings/transcriptions of some of the older stories and *yeenoo dài' googwandak* reveal a high degree of consistency in the main story elements although they were recorded in distant locations, up to a century apart in time, and even translated into different European languages (usually French and English) (e.g., see Chapter One, *Kò' Ehdanh* and Blind Man and the Loon stories).

Introduction

1   Generally when Van Tat Gwich'in elders refer to locations as "up" or "down" they mean upriver (up the Porcupine River) or downriver, respectively, not north or south. The Porcupine River flows north from its headwaters and turns west to flow past the Crow River confluence at Old Crow, ultimately to join the Yukon River in Alaska. So, in general, "up" often means east or south and "down," west or north, depending upon where one is on the river.

2   Four agreements were completed in 1995, three in 1997, one each in 2002, 2003, 2004, and 2005 (totaling eleven), and by spring 2009, three more remain.

3   Many authors have employed a variety of definitions of "oral history" and "oral tradition" (for example, Jan Vansina and others base the distinction between the two on the age of the material, 1965:12). Here a more general approach is used because a time-based distinction is narrow and its relevance and significance requires demonstration. Thus, oral tradition encompasses all aspects of culture: songs, poems, ritual, education, life stories, as well as history

and the context of transmission. This book could be seen as oral tradition because some of the stories are akin to parables (for example, how the loon and crow got their colours). However, the focus is history, and stories, such as parables, myths, and legends grouped as *yeeno d'ài' googwandak* are included to complement the history and highlight Van Tat Gwich'in perspectives on their history and its place in their culture.

4   Two spellings of "Gwich'in" are used in Old Crow. The Vuntut Gwitchin First Nation follows Archdeacon McDonald's spelling of "Gwitchin." The modern orthographic spelling, "Gwich'in," will be used here except when referring to the Vuntut Gwitchin First Nation.

5   According to geologists, there were two major time periods during the Pleistocene era when glaciers covered an extensive area, from about 120,000 to 65,000 years ago, and again from approximately 38,000 to 12,000 years ago (Hughes 1989). During this time, the area from the northern Yukon west through central Alaska to Siberia, known as Beringia, was free of ice.

6   The Pleistocene is the time period defined by geologists as from about 2,000,000 to 10,000 years ago, characterized by a succession of ice ages and the evolution of modern humans. The most populous ice age species were mammoths, horses, and bison (R. Gotthardt 2005:pers. comm.).

7   As Greer noted: "Several stories or versions of a story refer to times when the area was covered with water (e.g., Cass 1959; Barbeau and Camsell 1915)."

8   Camsell (1954:196) provided additional clarification for this story, noting that Mr. Peter Ross of Fort McPherson told him that Crow's walking stick was to be found atop Crow Mountain (overlooking Old Crow).

9   Yukon archaeologist Ruth Gotthardt explained that 1,250 years ago is a critical date in Yukon prehistory because the White River volcanic eruption (dated now to about 1150) likely disrupted human populations. It may have triggered significant population movements and brought people into contact with new neighbours (R. Gotthardt 2005:pers. comm.).

10 Archaeologist Sheila Greer summarized the archaeological research of this period: "The evidence from these sites allows us to say with considerable certainty that the Yukon Gwitchin have been associated with the Porcupine [caribou] herd for a long time—hundreds if not thousands of years. In addition to the spring hunts along the river, they are also believed to have taken caribou at other times of the year elsewhere in their territory, using devices such as surrounds or fences" (Greer 1999:9).

11 *Ch'ineekaii* is a general term that refers to the Eskimoan peoples bordering the Gwich'in to the north and northwest, such as Inuvialuit, Inuit, Yupik, and Inupiat.

12 The story of *Khach'oodaayu'* (Hatodaiu) was also told to anthropologist Asen Balikci by a Dagoo elder in 1961.

13 In 1863, Strachan Jones was factor of Fort Yukon and was succeeded by James McDougall in 1866.

14 The Turner survey party reported in 1889-90 that Gwich'in suffered from pneumonia and consumption that winter, initially receiving treatment from the

surveyor's doctor until deaths prompted them to lose trust in him (Mendenhall et al. 1893:191-194).

15   The Vuntut Gwitchin Government and the Historic Sites Program of the Yukon Heritage Resources Unit has conducted a reconstruction project at Rampart House for a number of years. The trader's store, residence, and a number of other buildings dating from about 1904 are undergoing stabilization and reconstruction. Rampart House is visited mostly by hunting parties from Old Crow and Fort Yukon, as well as river-borne travellers.

16   Murray's observations that the Gwich'in desired beads and traded "Eskimo spears" among themselves are echoed in the long-ago stories of *Olti'* and *Kò' Ehdanh*, in Chapter One.

17   John Firth is known to Gwich'in as *Kheh Kai' Zhoo* meaning Bearded Chief, a reference to his full beard.

18   Archdeacon McDonald later paid homage to Henry Venn by baptizing a Dagoo Gwich'in leader with his name.

19   Stringer became known as "The Bishop who ate his Boots" after a period of privation in the north (Peake 1966).

20   Van Tat Gwich'in also had residences in Alaska (for example, John Thomas's cabin at Rapid River) prior to the enforcement of the border and are familiar with the Porcupine River and its history to Fort Yukon.

21   For an analysis of the factors that caused the widespread move off the land and into towns across northern Canada in the 1950s, see Asch 1979.

1 | Long-ago Stories

1   For further discussion of analytical categories of oral history and maintaining the ability to differentiate history, (for example, from other categories) see Preface. Note that here we maintain the Gwich'in category of *yeenoo dài' googwandak* and use it as they do, which doesn't conflate it with their history.

2   There are a number of alternative pronunciations and spellings of *Ch'ataiiyuukaih,* sometimes omitting the initial "ch" sound: *Ataachookaii* (McClellan et al. 1987:258) and *A-ta-tco-kai-yo* (Osgood 1970[1936]:164).

3   Arctic Red River, Northwest Territories, is now known as Tsiigehtchic.

4   Edith Josie uses an alternative pronunciation for *Ch'ataiiyuukaih.*

5   Here the story of *Ch'ataiiyuukaih* and the Loon, and the Mouse and Otter, are often told as part of the series of stories about how *Ch'ataiiyuukaih* fixed the world.

6   *Atocok'ái* refers to the Gwich'in culture hero *Ch'ataiiyuukaih* (Paddled a Different Route) discussed previously.

7   The narrative structure of the Inuit story of the film *Atanarjuat: The Fast Runner* directed by Zacharius Kanuk (2002) contains parallel plot elements and many similar details to *Kò' Ehdanh* (Man Without Fire).

8   See the publication of a different translation of Jim Fell's recording of Sarah Abel in McClellan et al. 1987.

9   Henry Nukon's interviews are copyright Canadian Museum of Civilization.

10　In a later version, Sarah Abel said the attack took place in the upper Porcupine region: "Way up around *Chuu Tl'it* [Whitestone Village], I think it happened around there" (Sarah Abel, VG2003-3-01:210).

11　In his research on "Man Without Fire," Slobodin noted similar variations in the early part of the 20th century: the enemy was identified as either from the Pacific Coast or Inuvialuit from the Mackenzie Delta.

12　For a more recent use of *shitlih* and *shijaa*, see Chapter Four.

13　There are many variations and apparent contradictions to certain aspects of the *Kò' Ehdanh* story, as well as great consistency in key story elements. In this case, Sarah Abel's story was recorded in two interviews. In the first part, she told of *Kò' Ehdanh* finding an old fire and eating caribou feet, and later that he had not seen fire since the massacre. There are many possible reasons for this discrepancy, perhaps due to the break between interviews or another artifact of the interview, or that she considered one cooked caribou leg insignificant.

14　Slobodin points out that lone survivors occupied a special status and had to be carefully reintegrated into society, because if a person was isolated long enough, they could turn into a semi-supernatural bushman. "It was said to be the practice of Kutchin [Gwich'in] and of the neighboring people with whom they warred to leave alive by design one man of the camp that was attacked. He was to spread the news among his people….he assumed, as a matter of course, the formal status of chief mourner for his slaughtered kin and camp-mates, and would be expected to organize a revenge raid in due time" (Slobodin 1971:284).

15　Myra Moses recorded that the Gwich'in name for war is "*navèh*" (Myra Moses, VG2000-8-14A:306).

16　The importance of beads to Gwich'in in the mid-1800s was reported by the trader Murray (see Introduction), and researched by anthropologist Cornelius Osgood in the 1930s: "The wealth of the family, consisting of beads, the husband controls" (Osgood 1970[1936]:113).

17　There are a number of variations of the name of *Kò' Ehdanh's* wife.

18　Here *K'aiiheenjik* is referring to the deaths of his family members that left him bereft and wanting to die.

19　Also see *Two Old Women* (Wallis 1993) for an example from Fort Yukon, Alaska, Gwich'in.

20　Sarah Abel is describing the characteristics of bears when they don't go into their customary winter hibernation. They may remain active throughout the winter for some reason, such as age, infirmity, or insufficient food to enable them to amass adequate fat reserves for hibernation, because of warm weather, or to take advantage of very late autumn salmon runs, such as on the Fishing Branch River by Bear Cave Mountain (Van Tat Gwich'in information about bears, 2002).

21　Fish traps were made of sticks lashed together to block a stream and trap the fish in a cylindrical structure that prevented their escape.

22　Slobodin records similar Gwich'in stories from both the Mackenzie River and upper Yukon River regions. After noticing peculiar wood chips (made with a steel axe) floating down the river, the head of a Gwich'in family investigates and encounters a large camp of strange people (Fort Good Hope on the Mackenzie or Fort Yukon on the Yukon River). He remains among the strangers, receives gifts and instructions on how to use them and how to procure and prepare the specific kinds of furs the strangers seek. He returns to his people wearing a kind of garment made from the sides of a wicker Chinese tea chest, hence the name "Grass Pants" or "Straw Pants" (Slobodin 1962:23).

2 | The First Generation

1. Myra Kaye was referring to the age of interviewer Linda Netro, who was 21 in 1980.
2. *Gwatl'ahti's* descendants in the Old Crow area took his name as a surname (e.g., John Kwatlatyi) and later the practice of using the Christian name as a surname gave some of Elias Kwatlatyi's descendants the name Elias as a surname. *Gwatl'ahti'* is the spelling of Kwatlatyi in modern Gwich'in orthography.
3. Myra Kyikavichik was known as Myra *Choo*, or Big Myra. Myra Moses (born in the Fort Yukon area, daughter of John Englishoe or *Vikaiitruu*) was called Myra *Tsal* (Small Myra).
4. The Klondike Gold Rush brought thousands of white prospectors to the Dawson area in 1898.
5. John Firth was the Hudson's Bay Company trader at LaPierre House from 1880-94 and later at Old and New Rampart Houses and Fort McPherson. He married into the Gwich'in community and was known as *Kheh Kai' Zhoo* (literally "leader or trader bearded") with reference to his full beard.
6. In a meeting about caribou fences in 2002, Elder Alfred Charlie described the time of year the summer fences were used and some details of their operation:

   > They go in there and lots of caribou get caught in the snares. Then after that, [whatever is left over, they chase back out of the fence]. Then with spears they kill them. They did not [use] arrows inside the fence, only spears....This happened in August. They skin them all and fix up all the meat. Then they start tanning caribou hides. The August caribou hides are good and are used for making clothing...winter clothing. Whatever is left over they make winter skin tents out of them. The big [bull] caribou hides, they made babiche, and made lots of skin tents out of them. When they made snowshoes they used some there, too, toboggans, too.
   >
   > (ALFRED CHARLIE, March 8, 2002, VG2003-02-01:212-250, Gwich'in)

7. He is likely referring to Dr. William Irving, the archaeologist who worked in the Old Crow area from the 1960s to the 1980s.
8. *Ch'iitsii Vihtr'ih* is in the vicinity of the headwaters of the Driftwood River. The remains of two large caribou fences [*tthał*] are in this area.
9. *Ch'eeghwalti'* was an important leader, ancestor of many Van Tat Gwich'in families, and brother of the influential leaders *Shahnuuti'* and *Shahvyah*. See the discussion of leaders later in this chapter.

10 "Gate end" may be a reference to the entry side of the fence or to the way the fences were used: the end was taken down when not in use to avoid unintentionally trapping any animals inside (Van Tat Gwich'in Elders meeting on caribou fences, March 2002).

11 The Gwich'in name for Second Mountain is *Chyah Ddhàa*. In Gwich'in, *ddhàa* denotes a specific "mountain." *Chyah* means long braided hair. In 2001 Hannah Netro described the events that gave *Chyah Ddhàa* its name. "All the way down were lots of people. People were killed, Vuntut Gwitchin, that's why it's called *Chyah Ddhàa*. *Chyah* is, in those days, even men had long hair, they braided it, that's what it means: long hair, they braided it and fancied it up. That's what they call *chyah*." She goes on to describe how those who died at Second Mountain were buried by a big rock slide in the days when people had long hair (Hannah Netro, Driftwood River, June 26, 2001, VG2001-2-54B:002-024, Gwich'in).

12 In cases such as this when no one speaks, it is not because they disagree or are uninterested but quite the opposite: they concur to the extent that they cannot state the case better and greatly respect the speaker and his views.

13 When only one or two people had gasoline boat motors, all the other families would join their canvas boats together like a raft and the motor boat would propel them all down the Crow River: much easier than days of rowing. There are a number of photographs and film footage of the festive atmosphere of rafting into town with families, dogs, and the spring catch of muskrat fur.

14 Although outdated and not the currently preferred term, the name "Eskimo" is sometimes used here because it is the term the elders use when speaking English and the closest translation of the term they use when speaking Gwich'in, *Ch'ineekaii*, which does not specify which group of Inuit, Inuvialuit, Inupiat, Siglit. "Eskimo" is used as a general, non-specific term. The usage is not intended as derogatory in any way.

15 Neil McDonald's father, the missionary Archdeacon Robert McDonald, was Métis-Cree from southern Manitoba, and Neil spent time there as a child. In his travels he encountered northern Cree in the Athabasca-Mackenzie district (see McDonald 1869).

16 Neil McDonald had a more detailed interpretation of *Zzeh Gittlit*: "The chief at the time, the Hudson's Bay Company was here, Crow [May] I Walk, but his other name is *Zzeh Gittlit*. *Zzeh Gittlit* means when they move they make their round [skin] tents, they always tore a hole through at the back so the air comes through and keeps the smoke going up in the centre, through the hole at the top" (Neil McDonald, VG2000-8-7A:052-058, English).

17 Murray's and Dall's drawings are reproduced in McClellan's *Part of the Land; Part of the Water* (1987:66, 72).

18 "Old Man Minister," Archdeacon McDonald, described negotiating with *Shahnuuti'* to give up his wives and take up the Christian practice of monogamy, as well as *Shahnuuti*'s concern that the abandoned wives would suffer or even starve (McDonald 1869).

19 *Chyahnjik* is named for the same story as *Chyah Ddhàa*, because the Crow River (*Chyahnjik*) flows past Second Mountain (*Chyah Ddhàa*).

20 "He sleeps to caribou" is the way the elders describe a shamanic relationship to caribou, which was in the form of dreaming.

21 Free trader Dan Cadzow was at Rampart House from 1904 to 1929.

22 Chief Peter Moses collected money to assist World War II war orphans in England and was later awarded a British Empire Medal from the British government.

23 The *Olti'* and *Khach'oodaayu'* stories fit within the *yeenoo dài' googwandak* (long-ago story) genre of Chapter One but are included here as part of the history of Gwich'in trade with Europeans.

24 He may be referring to the major portage (about ten miles or sixteen kilometres) around the Rapids of the Drowned between Smith's Landing and Fort Smith on the Slave River. The next big portage on the fur-trade route to the southeast was Methye Portage on the height of land between the Arctic and Hudson Bay drainage systems.

25 *Nishuunii* is an old Gwich'in word for a small cache or warehouse added onto the corner of a house (Jane Montgomery and Robert Bruce Jr., personal communication, January and February 2004).

26 Tracking is the method of travelling upstream with boats pulled by people on shore using ropes.

27 Born in 1872, Amos Njootli was a respected member of the network of Gwich'in ministers and lay readers trained by Archdeacon McDonald. He was ordained in 1911 and ministered to Van Tat Gwich'in (Sax and Linklater 1990:69, 91).

28 Probably Elias *Gwahtl'ahti'*.

29 From the perspective of the early 21st century, the prices for "staples" such as flour and sugar in Old Crow are still very high due to the cost of air transport, as there is no road access to Old Crow except for a periodic winter road (every five years or more).

30 "Rachel Cadzow was married previously to William Blackfox. They had one boy, and Joanne [later Joanne Njootli] and her sister [Nellie]. I think they had three" (Neil McDonald, VG2000-8-40:278, English). Rachel and William Blackfox had two children, Joanne and Abraham. Then Rachel married Dan Cadzow and they had one daughter, Nellie.

31 She likely means reading Dagoo from the Bible, hymn, and prayer books translated into that language by Archdeacon McDonald.

32 Arctic Red River, Northwest Territories, has been renamed Tsiigehtchic.

33 This is one of a number of common ways to say "in the 1800s," possibly the meaning he intended.

34 Jim Oliver's camp is believed to have been between Rampart House and Fort Yukon.

35 *Cheesih* is remembered as an Elder of the generation before Sarah Abel's, an aunt of the mother of current Elder Mary Kassi.

36 See Dick North, 1978, *The Lost Patrol*.

37 *Chuu Tl'it* is Gwich'in for Whitestone Village. *Sheihveenjik* is the Whitestone River. *Chiidaagaiinjik* refers to the area around the head of the Porcupine River in the vicinity of the Whitestone River and Whitestone Village.

3 | The Second Generation

1. She is referring to the calving grounds of the Porcupine caribou herd on the north slope of Alaska, an area that is outside of Van Tat Gwich'in lands but critically important to the survival of the caribou and, hence, Van Tat Gwich'in culture and way of life.
2. Before the coming of missionaries, Gwich'in customarily had a single name. Missionaries began baptizing people in the area in the late- to mid-1800s. They introduced surnames, which began a patrilineal system of reckoning kinship overlaid on the Gwich'in matrilineal clans. Some of the surnames derive from early Gwich'in names, such as Kyikavichik (often shortened to Kaye) and Tetlichi (now commonly Charlie). Others stem from the Christian names of the men, such as Elias (from Elias Kwatlatyi). At one time, it was normal for a woman to take both of her husband's names as her surname (Eliza Ben Kassi), or for her and her children to take her husband's first name as their surname (Mary Elias).
3. Four-wheeled open all-terrain vehicles.
4. Families would trap in their areas dispersed among the lakes in Crow Flats, and then after the muskrat season closed in mid-June, they hauled their belongings to their customary locations along Crow River to raft downriver to Old Crow or Rampart House on the Porcupine River. Usually families travelled together and these journeys are fondly remembered events.
5. Muskrat trapping season closed in mid-June.
6. The Crow River meanders greatly and a traveller must cover a great distance along the river to go a much shorter linear distance.
7. The *yuu, yuu* game involved standing in a circle and guessing what is put on your head. "After that is all finished we hold hands, we really hold hands, whoever runs through we chased them and the person who grabs him or her is next [to stand in the middle and try to break through the circle]....Everyone has a turn.... It was lots of fun" (Lydia Thomas, May 3, 2004, Gwich'in).
8. "Vuntut" is derived from Archdeacon McDonald's spelling of *Van Tat*.
9. Because of the curves and meanders of the Crow River, landmarks such as Schaeffer Mountain appear first on one side, then the other, back and forth as travellers proceed along the river.
10. *Chyah Ddhàa* is literally "Hair Mountain," a reference to the long braided hair of Gwich'in of the past. The Gwich'in name for Crow River, *Chyahnjik*, shares this reference. It is the second of three mountains between Old Crow on the Porcupine River and Crow Flats.
11. *Diniizhòo* is also known as *Tsii'in' Ddhàa* in Gwich'in and Game Mountain in English.
12. *Ch'eeghwal* was a descendant of *Ch'eeghwalti'*, the brother of *Shahnuuti'* and *Shahvyah* described in Chapter Two. Gwich'in named parents for their first child by adding "ti" (father of) to the end of the name, hence *Ch'eeghwalti'* means father of *Ch'eeghwal*.
13. See the *Kò' Ehdanh* story in Chapter One for a reference to Andrew Tizya's reputation as a hunter and provider.

14   Hannah Netro's maiden name was Kyikavichik and she was the sister of Ellen Bruce, John Joe Kyikavichik, Tabitha Kyikavichik, and Lydia Thomas.

15   Johnson Creek Village is also known as *Tâachik* in the dialect spoken in Alaska, for example by Charlie Thomas.

16   Whitestone River is *Sheihveenjik*.

17   *Ni'iinlii Gwinjik* is the name Dick Nukon uses for Fishing Branch River. *Ni'iinlii Njik* is currently the official name.

18   Teetl'it Gwich'in are the people of the Peel River area in the Northwest Territories. The principal community is Fort McPherson.

19   Grayling Creek is also known as Charlie Creek (Charlie Thomas, Old Crow, August 24, 1998, VG2001-13-37:124, Gwich'in).

20   Van Tat Gwich'in have no name for Rampart House in their own language. *Gindèh Chik* (and *Giideechik*) is the name for a camp area near Rampart House.

21   He is referring to moving from the Rampart House-Rapid River, Alaska, area to the Old Crow area. He does not mean he lived only in the town of Old Crow, but in the territory of the people of Old Crow—actually a large region. In other interviews, he emphasizes that he moved from Alaska to Canada, illustrating the greater role the border came to play in Gwich'in lives.

22   Hannah Netro was speaking to Robert Bruce, her nephew. His uncle was her husband, Joe Netro.

23   Firth was at Fort McPherson and Cadzow traded at Rampart House.

24   *Antl'it* or *Antl'it Tthał* is the name of the Valley Caribou Fence or Thomas Creek Caribou Fence.

25   See the story of Albert Johnson, the Mad Trapper, in this chapter for other impacts of white trappers.

26   The Johnson Creek in Crow Flats is *Aadrìi Njik* in Gwich'in (Charlie Thomas) and the Johnson Creek on the upper Porcupine River is *Ch'aghòo Njik* (Dick Nukon). Schaeffer Lake is *K'ii Zhìt* (Hannah Netro), Schaeffer Creek is *Neet'ai* (Charlie Thomas), and Schaeffer Mountain is *Ch'icheechih* (Dick Nukon). Mason Hill is *Vialtli'* and David Lord Creek is *Tl'iiyeenjik* (Dick Nukon).

27   Vilhjalmur Stefansson, renowned Arctic explorer and author, travelled down the Porcupine River in 1907 in a considerable hurry to reach Eagle, Alaska, to send a despatch to southern newspapers forestalling the erroneous report of the deaths of three Arctic explorers (Leffingwell, Mikkelson, and Storkerrson). He said of Archie Linklater, "I had thought of hiring Indians, but Cadzow said that Linklater would take me to Fort Yukon much more rapidly than any Indian. Linklater undertook the job, and in a few hours he and his family were on their way with me in a flat-bottomed rowboat. I have never seen a man who could work as Linklater did. He was over six feet in height, powerfully built and used to the roughest kind of work. For years he had been a member of the Royal Northwest Mounted Police at Dawson, at which time he had gained a reputation as a traveller. He had never been a sailor, but he must have done a good deal of rowing in his time, for he kept steadily at the oars something like sixteen hours a day" (Stefansson 1922:237-238).

28 Gwich'in speakers in Old Crow speak a number of dialects. Johnson Creek Village is known both as *Kâachik* and *Tâachik*.

29 The Porcupine caribou herd spends the summer on its calving grounds on the coastal north slope of Alaska.

30 On the Porcupine River between Old Crow and Caribou Lookout.

31 *Sheenjik* is an alternate Gwich'in name for the Fishing Branch River. The commonly used name is *Ni'iinlii Njik*.

32 Eric Neilson, federal cabinet minister and brother of actor Leslie Neilson.

33 The interviews from the LaPierre House Oral History project were translated differently than others in this book, more as summaries of the speaker's words or intended meaning. See the preface for a brief note on translation, transcription, and excerpting.

34 Gwich'in names for caribou: Bull caribou: *Vadzaih choo*; Young caribou: *vadzaih dazhoo*; Cow caribou: *ch'iyaht'ok*; Female caribou: *vadzaih tr'ik*; Fall-time caribou: *khadatsan*.

4 | The Oral History of Today

1 Bella Greenland referred to John Nukon, who was her grandfather's brother-in-law (likely her great-uncle) as "grandfather" because in the Gwich'in kinship system he was a relative in her grandfathers' generation. Joking relationships between siblings-in-law are another characteristic of the system (Slobodin 1981:519).

2 In Gwich'in, *Vidzii* means "his ear." *Vidzii shuh* means "a wart in his ear," a humorous nickname. John Nukon's other nickname from the Dawson area was "Meat Juice Father."

3 Both *shijaa* and *shitlih* mean "my friend." *Shitlih* refers to a closer friendship. See Moses Tizya's use of *shitlih* in the *Kò' Ehdanh* story, Chapter One. Moses Tizya would be in Bella Greenland's grandfather's generation.

4 *Trozhyah* is the location of Alfred Charlie's camp upstream of Old Crow between Caribou Lookout and Goose Camp (within about 15 miles or 25 kilometres east of Old Crow).

5 On maps, *Zhoh Drìn Chòo* is called White Snow Mountain. When speaking English, Gwich'in speakers refer to the mountain as White Snow Mountain or Snow White Mountain (or even White Mountain) interchangeably.

6 *Gwitr'uu* is where a fireplace is located on *Chuuts'aii Nàlk'at* (Crow Mountain).

7 *Shih Ddhàa* is an alternate name for Bear Cave Mountain, meaning literally grizzly bear (*shih*) mountain (*ddhàa*). *Ch'ii Ch'à'an* refers to stone or rock (*chii*) cave (*ch'à'an*).

8 *Diniinvee Njik* is a tributary of *Negoo Zràii Njik* (Black Fox Creek) and is the location of a caribou fence.

9 He is referring to changing trapping patterns as a reason for the decline in muskrat numbers. Van Tat Gwich'in talk about building up muskrat populations by judicious trapping methods that reduce the excess muskrats before they can deplete their food supply, thereby enabling considerably greater muskrat

harvests. This management method was combined with resting specific lakes periodically for a number of years, described previously.

10 *Gèegook'yuu* is a large hill on the south side of the Porcupine River across from the Driftwood River. There is no English name for this hill.

11 For links between forms of plots common to both literature and history, see Porter 1981. Using examples from English-North American literature and history, he describes common concepts used to describe human experience (both in fiction and non-fiction), such as 14 types of plots dealing with, for example, action, pathos, tragedy, admiration, maturation, degeneration, education, revelation, and disillusionment. The relationship between how literature and history are structured suggests there may be plot and ideological structures common to both *yeenoo dài' googwandak* and Van Tat Gwich'in oral history.

GLOSSARY

Pronunciation

There are 45 consonant sounds in Gwich'in, not all of which are represented by a single letter in the modern orthography (for example: ch, ddh, dz, dzh, gh, ghw, kh, khw, nj, tl, tth). Vowels can be long or short (represented by double or single letters: a, aa, e, ee, etc.) and can have a high or low tone. High tone is unmarked and low tone has a grave accent (a or à). Only the first vowel of a long vowel is marked to indicate a low tone (àa). Additionally, an apostrophe indicates a glottal stop (the sound is stopped at the back of the throat) (aat'oo) and a hook under a vowel indicates it is nasalized (ą). The vowel sounds are pronounced:

- **a**: short a as in English "around"
- **aa**: long aa like English "father"
- **e**: short e as in English "set"
- **ee**: long ee is similar to the *a* in English "make," except the sound changes less from start to finish
- **i**: short i as in English "fit"
- **ii**: long ii like English "see"
- **o**: short o like English "vote"
- **oo**: long oo as in English "vote" but held for a longer duration
- **u**: short u like English "duke"
- **uu**: long uu as in English "duke" but held for a longer duration
- **aii**: sound varies depending on whether it's written aih, ai', or with nothing at the end. All are similar to the ie in English "pie"
- **aih**: similar to *ie* in English "pie"
- **ai'**: similar to *ie* in English "pie" with a glottal stop at the end
- **eii**: similar to *ay* in English "gay"
- **ao**: similar to *ow* in English "now"

325

Gwich'in to English

A

Aachin	Slavey people
Aadrìi Njik	Johnson Creek (up the Crow River)
aak'ii	cow
aak'ii ghai' tsòo	butter
aat'oo	birch
àazrùk	shaving
ah, thoochyàh	spruce bough
ah'ąąlak, ah'ànlak	old squaw duck
ahchin	it's raining
ahchin'	it rained
ahshii	it's snowing
ahshu'	it snowed
Ahtr'aih Zrii	February
ahtr'aii	wind
ahtr'aii vii	whirlwind
aih	snowshoe
aih ch'ok	pointed snowshoe
aih ghat, aih tr'aghat	netting snowshoe
aih shin'	snowshoe frame
aih vał	chisel (flat head)
aih vał	snowshoe needle
aih zheii	round snowshoe
ak'ii t'òk	cow's milk
akoo diginuu	they said
altin	jackfish, pike
ałts'ik k'anahtii	nurse
ałts'ik zheh	hospital
andaii	candy
Anits'u'	Oh, my goodness!
anjithitii ik	anorak, parka
antl'it	valley
Antl'it Tthał	Thomas Creek Caribou Fence
athitl'ii	cloth, material
athitl'ii chuu	flannel
athitl'ii vàalaii	silk
Atr'ididaagaii	Lent
Atr'ididaagaii Drin	Ash Wednesday
avii	weasel

B

bèebii	baby
beebìi dehk'it	crib
bèebii zhìi	baby food

C

ch'aachii	two-year-old beaver
ch'aadrìh nùu	moonlight
ch'a'an	cave
ch'a'àn	den
ch'achàn	stump
Ch'adachoo Zrii	July
Ch'adaghòo Zrii	June
ch'adhat	liver
ch'adhòh tr'ìhchòo	skin boat
ch'adhòh tthàh tsal	skin needle (triangular)
ch'adhòh zheh	skin house
ch'adhòo	hindquarter
ch'adizhoo	grasshopper
ch'adzoh zheh	dance hall
Ch'aghòo	Choho Hill
Ch'aghòonjik	Johnson Creek
ch'agòondaih	medicine
ch'akaiiłaih	foot straps
ch'ak'èh	fat
ch'ak'oh	cold weather
ch'ak'oh	neck
Ch'ak'oh Zrii	January
chàlvii	widgeon
ch'anàn	backbone
ch'ananhgyu'	worm under caribou skin
Ch'anchàł	King Edward Mountain
ch'anchàł gyù'	worm in caribou head
Ch'anchał Njik	Schaeffer Creek
ch'ànchàn	rump
ch'àndòonagwàl	leg (front)
ch'àneeluh	unripe berries
ch'ànghwah, ch'ich'yàa	tanning scraper
ch'ąngwàl	leg (back)
ch'ànjòo	elder
ch'ankaii	blood soup
ch'ànluh	hail
ch'at	tendons

326 *Glossary*

ch'at'àn	leaf
ch'at'an nizii	flower
ch'at'òo	nest
ch'atr'a'aa zheh	restaurant
ch'atr'ał	fog
ch'atthaii	caribou or moose
ch'edoovii	three-year-old beaver
chèe	river (bottom)
chèet'it, shìchèet'it	pocket
cheezrilchit	ashes
chèhchìi	sinkers
chèhgyù'	bloodsucker
chèhlùk	loche, burbot
chehtsì'	water beetle
ch'èzhùr	moose (bull)
ch'ichèe	falcon
Ch'ichee Zrii	April
Ch'icheechih	Schaeffer Mountain
ch'ichèezhuh	fat
ch'ichi'	head
ch'ichì', ch'itshì'	tail
ch'ichìidruu	great grey owl
ch'ichìidrùu	collarbone
ch'ichik	ribs
ch'ichòo, tsèe choo	largest beaver
ch'ich'yàa	white fox
Ch'ichyàa	Wolf Clan
ch'ichyàa	tongue
ch'idajòl, ch'îi'ijiòl	sandfly, gnat
ch'idàk ik	jacket
ch'idèeghàn	chest
ch'idingwat'an	Canada jay
ch'ìdinìichii	shreds on bark
ch'idrèedhòh	caribou leg hide
ch'idrèedhòh vał	toboggan (skin)
ch'idrihdòk	lungs
ch'idrìi	heart
Ch'idzèe Njik	Caribou Bar Creek
ch'idzigyek	chickadee
ch'ìdzìt	Bible
ch'igèechàn	moose caller
ch'igèechàn	shoulder blade
ch'igii	calf
ch'igìn	arm
ch'ìh	thread

ch'ih khanìidòo	sinew
ch'ihłak	one (1)
ch'ihłak juutin	one zero (10)
ch'ihłak juutin juutin	one zero zero (100)
ch'ihłak juutin juutin juutin	one zero zero zero (1,000)
ch'ihłak juutin ts'at ch'ihłak	one zero and one (11)
ch'ihłak juutin ts'at ch'ihłoogwinli'	one zero and five (15)
ch'ihłak juutin ts'at ch'iteech'ii neekaii	one zero and seven (17)
ch'ihłak juutin ts'at daang	one zero and four (14)
ch'ihłak juutin ts'at neekaii	one zero and two (12)
ch'ihłak juutin ts'at nihk'ii daang	one zero and twice four (18)
ch'ihłak juutin ts'at nihk'ii tik	one zero and twice three (16)
ch'ihłak juutin ts'at tik	one zero and three (13)
ch'ihłoogwinli'	five (5)
ch'ihłoogwinli' juutin	five zero (50)
Chihshòo	Whitefish Lake
chihshòo	broad whitefish
chihthee, chìhjùu	mink
chihvyàh	fishnet
chihvyàh vàh di'ke'tr'ahchuu	fishnet needle (big)
ch'ii	mosquito
chii	rock, stone
Ch'ii Ch'à'an	Bear Cave Mountain
ch'ii ch'agoondaih	mosquito repellant
chii daa'aii	stone axe
chii gwik'ih	sharpening stone
Chii Tsal Dik	Fort McPherson
Chiidaagaiinjik	area around the head of the Porcupine River near Whitestone River and Whitestone Village
ch'iidhèeghwàt	tripe
ch'iidhòh	mosquito net
chiitat gwilùk	harlequin duck
chìitee	orphan
ch'iitii nândit'èe	airplane
ch'iitsii	stove

ch'iitsii ahtsii	blacksmith
ch'iitsìi edlii	fiddle
ch'iitsii khał	car, truck
ch'iitsii khał	snowmobile
ch'iitsii khyah	steel trap
ch'iitsii laii'	bell
ch'iitsii nândit'èe	airplane
ch'iitsii t'èh gwich'ìk	oven pan
ch'iitsii tl'yàh	dog chain
ch'iitsii tyah	tin can
ch'iitsii vah k'e'tr'ajahkaii	sewing machine
ch'iitsii zhik	stovepipe
ch'iitsiida'al	scissors
Chiitsiighe'	Salmon Cache
ch'iitsiigwał	fork
Chiiveenjik	Bell River
ch'iiyàht'òk	caribou (cow)
Chiizràiinjìk	Blackstone River
ch'iizrìi	spear
chiizrùk	comb
ch'ijì'	horn
chik	smoke hole
ch'ìk	plate
ch'ìk dòhsròo	dishtowel
ch'ìk ghoo	bowl
chik hijùu'èe	ridgepole
ch'ìk k'it	cupboard
chìk lùu	ashes
ch'ìk tsal	saucer
ch'ik'èh tthai'	bacon
ch'ił	diapers
chin'	rain
chin k'òh	rain clouds
ch'ìndèe	eye
ch'ìndohgyù'	intestines
ch'ineedzit	bee
ch'ineedzit t'òo	bee nest
ch'ineedzit ts'ik	wasp
Ch'ineekaii	Inuit or Inuvialuit
Ch'inèetsii Njìk	Miner River
ch'ineezit soogaii	honey
chinìitràn	hawk
ch'ìntsih	nose
ch'iriinjòo, ch'ak'ohnjùh	pintail duck

chit nilii	boss
ch'iteech'ii neekaii	seven (7)
ch'itl'ak, nin tl'ak	parasites, fleas
ch'itl'òo	scent gland
ch'itòo	brisket
Ch'itr'ihkaiinjìk	Canoe River (Chance Creek on maps)
ch'itr'òo	kidneys
ch'itr'ùu	Arctic tern
ch'its'igighòo, łuk ts'ìk	fish guts
ch'its'ik	ice crystal
ch'its'ik tàn	frost
ch'itsùh	pemmican
ch'ivat	stomach
ch'ivèedzyàa	dried apples
ch'ivìt, shivìt	sleeve
ch'izhèe	marrow
ch'izhìn	golden eagle
Ch'izhìn Njik	Eagle River
Ch'izhìn Zrii	March
ch'izhuutsoo	baby duck
Ch'oodèenjik	Porcupine River
ch'ookat zheh	store
chuh	bird feather
ch'ùh	charcoal
chùh	pillow
chuh ts'at	eiderdown
chuk	pucker, ruffle
chuu	water
chuu choo	ocean
Chuu Choo Vee	Herschel Island
chuu daa'il	water (dropped)
chuu dhah	hot water
chuu drin'	water (clear)
chuu jùughàl	water (calm)
chuu juuka'	gas
chuu k'oh	cold water
chuu niingyu'	warm water
chuu niint'aii	rapids
Chuu Tl'it	Whitestone Village
chuu tyah	cup
Chuuts'aii Nàlk'at	Crow Mountain
chyaa	boy
chyaa tsal	boy (little)
chyah	mattress, rug

ch'yàh	snowshoe lace
Chyah Ddhàa	Hair Mountain (Second Mountain)
Chyahnjik	Crow River

D

daa'aii	axe
daa'aii nihk'yùu vèek'i'	double axe
daa'aii tai'	axe handle
daadzaii	common loon
daagoo	ptarmigan
daagoo kài'	clubs
daang	four (4)
daang juutin	four zero (40)
dàatlih	soap
daats'at	sucker
daatsoo	mouse
daazraii	swan
daazraii gahkhàa	green-winged teal
dachan	wood
dachan ahghòo	termites (woodworm)
dachan ch'anhgwàh	hand plane
dachan ch'ìk	wooden scoop
dachan chyàa	woodpecker
dachan khyàh	deadfall
dachan srii	knife (crooked)
Dachan Tat Gwich'in	Mayo people
dachan tyah	wooden box
dachan zheh	cabin
dachànchyàh	floor
dahshàa	rotten wood
daih	spruce grouse
daii	spring
daii gwichu'	spring water
daii'	fly
danahch'i'	old man
dandaih	stoneberries
danzhìt	canyon
dats'an	duck
dazhoo	caribou (young bull)
dazhòo thał	caribou-skin pants
dazhoo tsoo	caribou (two-year-old male)
ddhah	mountain (unspecified)
ddhah dee	mountain berries
ddhah deechan	foothills
ddhah lùk	Arctic char
ddhah tòh	mountain pass
dèeddhòo	stone scraper
deek'it, dehk'it	bed
de'elah	floaters
dèetl'yàh	dip net
deetree'aa	scoter (fish duck)
deetrù'	raven, crow
deetrù' jak	juniper
dehdrah	cache (platform)
dèhzhòo	snow on branches
didich'eii	dry branch
dii ahtr'aii	west wind
diik'ee	gun, rifle
diik'ee chì'	bullets
diik'ee choo	large gun (.30–.30 rifle)
diik'èe kaihtał	gunstock
diik'èe kàiidràl	trigger
diik'ee k'èegòo	gunsight (rear)
diik'ee teenjìr	gunsight (front)
diik'ee tsal	small gun (.22 rifle)
dineech'ùu	black currant
dineedzìl	spruce cone
dinèhtl'eh	book, paper
dinèhtl'eh choo	Bible
dinehtl'eh k'anàhtii	mailman
dinèhtl'eh tai'	pen, pencil
dinèhtl'eh tyàh	box (paper)
dinèhtl'eh zheh	post office
Diniizhòo (Tsii'in' Ddhàa)	Potato Hill (Game Mountain)
dinjii	man
dinjii chìl'èe	rich man
dinjii dazhan	medicine man
dinjii kat	people
dinjii khehkai'	chief
dinjii zhùh	Native person
dinjik	moose
dinjik dhòh	moose hide
dinjik nilìi	moose meat
Dinjik Zrii	September
ditsik	young moose
divii	sheep
divii choo	large ram

divii gii	lamb
divii tr'ik	ewe
Divii Zrii	November
dizhùu	moose (cow)
dlak	squirrel
dlak gii	squirrel (baby)
dlìt	water moss
dlòodèetthah	shrew
dohsròo	canvas
dòhsròo	towel
dohsròo kaiichàn	canvas boots
dòhsròo tr'ihchoo	canvas boat
doo	driftwood
doo'ii ahshii	puffball
drah	cache
drijahtsai'	stormy weather
drin	day
drin	daylight
Drin Ch'ihłoogwinli'	Friday
Drin choo	New Year's Day
Drin Daang	Thursday
drin gwiniidhàa	warm weather
drin k'ideetak ch'ihłak	one week
drin k'ideetak neekaii	two weeks
Drin Neekaii	Tuesday
Drin Tik	Wednesday
drin tl'an	noon
Drin Tł'ee	Monday
Drin Tsal	Christmas
Drin Yeet'ìi, Drin Ts'ò'	Saturday
Drin Zhit	Sunday
duh	sandpiper (long legs)
dzan	muskrat
dzan dhòh zhìt tâii'ii'ee	muskrat stretcher
Dzan Ehłai'	Timber Mountain (muskrat caught in a trap)
dzhii choo	goshawk
dzhii tsal ghòo	eggs
dzìh	gum
dzìh kò'	spruce gum (chewable)
dzìh tl'ùu	spruce gum (soft)

E

ee ahtr'aii	north wind
ehdanh	without
ehdii	timber stand

G

gał	stick, club
ga'oonahtan	teacher
ge'ha'aii	sunrise
ge'tr'oonahtan zheh	school
geek'ii	mountain ridge
geh	rabbit
gihdaiivyàa	door
giikhii	minister
Giikhii Choo	Bishop
Gindèh Chik	Rampart House
git	glacier
git chu'	glacial water
googeh	snow goose
googwandak	story
gugèh zhùu	snow bunting
gwàatr'al	thick bushes
gwajàt	dust
Gwak'àn Choo	Burnt Hill
gwànzhih	carrots
gwànzhìh	potatoes
gwatl'ak	flea
gwatsak	nails
gwatsak tsal	tacks
Gwazhàl Njik	Ogilvie River
gwich'àa	clothes
gwich'àa eenjit tl'yàh niniint'aii	clothesline
Gwichyàa Gwich'in	Fort Yukon people
gwichyah	plateau
Gwichyah Gwich'in	Arctic Red River people
gwìdaiiyùhdlàii	water (low)
gwidèedrìi'	spider
gwidèedrìi' vyaa	spiderweb
gwik'ih	file
gwikak dàłchuu	tarp
Gwilùu Zrii	May
gyàh	snare
gyùhk'ah	black worm with white head

gyùhtsanh	wormwood
gyuu	worm
gyùu zhòo	caterpillar

H

hah	and
Hai' Gwintl'atr'ada'aii Drin	Thanksgiving
han	river
Hän Gwich'in	Eagle and Dawson people
hiłchin'	it started to rain
hiłshu'	it started to snow

I

ik	dress
ik tsàk	button

Ì

ìk tsàk k'it	buttonhole

J

jah	crane
jah	wedge
jak	berries
jak choo	dried prunes
Jak Ddhah	Berry Mountain
jak gaii	raisin
jak tloo	berries (boiled)
jak zraii	blueberries
jał	fish hook
Jesus Gatr'ałtsak Drìn	Good Friday
jidii ch'ahtl'oo	green
jidii dagaii	white
jidii datl'òo	blue
jidii dich'ik	pink
jidii dich'ìk	orange
jidii ditsik	red
jidii tsoo	yellow
jidii tthoo	brown
jidii vee	grey
jidii zraii	black
jii tsal t'òo, dzhii tsal t'òo	bird's nest
jii, dzhii	bird
jirh	mitts
jitsoo hah nagankai'	thin, tanned caribou hide

jùh toh	pole for boat
juk drin	today

K

Kâachik	Johnson Creek Village
k'àii'	willow
k'àii dzhùh	willow shoot
k'àii yuuzhù'	bark whistle
kaiichàn	mukluks
kaiik'it	village, place, site
kaiitrih	moccasins
k'eejit kat	youth
k'eejit khaii	last year
k'eejit khaii gwichih khaii	year before last
k'ehdai'	yesterday
k'ehdai' gehnòo	day before yesterday
khada'ahtsan, khadatsàn	yearling
khadatsan	fall-time caribou
khàh	club
khah zhak	short winter day
Khah Zhak Dha'aii	December
khaii	grease, lard
khaii	winter
khaii juuk'a'	candle
khaii juuk'a'	oil
khaii łùh ch'ùh	grease bannock
khaiits'ò', nagwidik'ii	autumn
khał	sleigh
khèechiigwijìłk'a'	sundog
kheh	Canada goose
khoh	thorn
khòo	raft
khyah	trap
khyàh zhìi	bait
k'i'	arrow
k'idèechì'	arrowhead
k'ii	birchbark
k'ii ch'ìk	birchbark plate
k'ii chu'	syrup
k'ìi tr'ih	birchbark canoe
K'ìi Zhìt	Schaeffer Lake
k'il	dry willow
k'iłtai'	bow
k'iłtai' tl'yàa	bowstring

kò'	fire, matches
ko tanh	flint
ko'gàł, ch'iitsii gał	stove poker
k'oh	alder
k'oh	clouds
k'oh dagaii dok	spring clouds
k'ohnjik	creek
k'ohnjik chu'	spring water
k'oo	fish trap
k'oonaiit'aii	handkerchief
kwàn chit	red coals
kwàn deek'it	fireplace
kwànchit hijàa	spark

L

lagar	playing cards
lagùusrùu	pig
lagwìizràk	dog straps
lazraa dhòh	wallet
lazraa zheh	bank
lazraa, tsèe dhòh	money
lèelat	fog on water
lesel, doahghwai'	salt
lidii	tea
lidii masgit	Labrador tea
lidii tyah	teapot
lidlii	key

Ł

łaii	dog
łaii choo	horse
łaii ghàa	dog pack
łaii tl'yàa	dog harness
łaii tl'yah dadàach'ii	dog team
łaii tsal	puppy
łaii ts'ì'	dog (female)
łaii viitrii	dog whip
łaii zheh	dog house
łaii zhìi	dog food
łaii zhinadha'èe	dog collar
łat	smoke
łintsùutlìi aih	sharp snowshoe
łit ts'ìh	smoke dust
łùh	flour

łùh andaii	cookies
łuh ch'ant'at	mud (sticky)
łuh chìl	wood chips
łùh ch'ùh	bannock
łùh dàn	bread
łùh gaii	crackers
łuh jik	kindling wood
łùh tlok	pancakes
łùh tlòo	gravy
łùh vah niituu	baking powder
łùk	fish
łùk chì'	fish head
łùk chì'	fish tail
łùk choo	king salmon
łùk ch'ùh	fried fish
łùk dagàii	whitefish
łùk deek'it tr'agwich'ii	fish camp
łùk gaii	dried fish
łùk gyù'	fish fins
łùk k'yù'	fish eggs
łùk nàn	fish backbone
łùk ni'iinlii	spawning
łùk tl'ì'	tail fin
łùk tl'ùu	fish slime
łùk vìrh, łùk vìr	boiled fish
łùu	ice
łùu dril	ice (thin)
łùu dril ch'òk	icicles
łùu drin'	ice (clear)
łùu dzyah	ice chisel
łùu hijìi	breakup
łùu tìl k'ìt	ice (cracked)

N

naadoo ts'eh	tongue
nàagàii	beads
nàagàii tthah tsal	bead needle
nàazhùk	yarn
nàazùu	striped clothes
nadinii'èe	crosspiece
Nagwachoonjik	Mackenzie River
nagwidhah ìindìi	chinook wind
na'iida'aii	first quarter
nakàł	salmonberries

Nakał Vàn	Salmonberry Lake
nan chyàh, teet'ih	meadow
nan ghòo khàak'at	pingo
Nan ihlah juuka	Burnt Hill, by Eagle River
Nanaa'in Ddhàa	Bushman Mountain
nanaa'in'	bushman
Nanagwaalii Drin	Easter
nanh, nan	land, earth
nanùht'ee	butterfly
natąįįlaii	waterfall
nataniihaii	water (overflow)
natl'at	cranberries (low bush)
Natr'agwaazhii Drin	Halloween
navèh	war, soldiers
navèh t'ah'in	police
navèh t'ah'in zheh	police station
ne'a'aii	sunset
neeghaii	frog
neegoo	fox
neegoo chì'	fox tail
neegoo gii	fox pup
neegoo ninìlzraii	cross fox
neegoo tsoo	red fox
neegoo zraii	black or silver fox
neejìi	ant
neekaii	two (2)
neekaii juutin juutin	two zero zero (200)
neekaii juutin juutin juutin	two zero zero zero (2,000)
neekòk juutin	two zero (20)
neet'ak choo	mallard duck
Neetaii	Schaeffer Creek
Neets'ik Gwich'in	Arctic Village people
Neetsaih	Crow Clan
nèevyaa zheh	round tent
nee'yùu	red currant
neezhì'	one-year-old beaver
neezhìn'	snow-blind
nèhdlii	coho (silver) salmon
nèhkak	ball
nèhtanh	thunder
nèhtanh kwàn	lightning
nèhtrùh	wolverine
Nèhtrùh Vavàn	Wolverine Lake
nichìh	rosehips
nich'it	girl
nich'it tsal	girl (little)
ni'dinìltsi'	fancy
Nigoonlii Drin	birthday
nihkàa	tomorrow
nihkàa gehndòo	day after tomorrow
nihk'ii daang	twice four (8)
nihk'ii tik	twice three (6)
nii ahtr'aii	south wind
Ni'iinlii Njik	Fishing Branch River
niinjii	lynx
niinjii gii	lynx cub
niinjii zhuu	cat
niinjii zhuu gii	kitten
nilaiizruk	the stick pull (a long-ago game)
nilèediik'èe	shotgun (pistol)
nilèejirh	gloves
nilèetth'ak	ring
nilii	meat
nilii gaii	dried meat
nin	animals
nin dhòh	animal pelt
njàa	white-winged scoter (black duck)
njùu	island
nootl'ii	herd of caribou
nù'	moss

O

òk	eddy
oonjit	white man
oonjìt shìi	food, grub

S

saban	spoon
shaa	his brother-in-law
sha'àt, shitr'ìinjòo	my wife
shahanh, na'àa	my mother
shał k'it	holes for babiche
shanaghàn	old woman
shèedèenuh	her daughter-in-law
sheejii	my older sister
sheek'aii	my aunt (father's sister)
sheek'aii	my aunt (mother's sister)

Glossary 333

Sheenjik	Fishing Branch River (alternate name)
sheih	gravel, sand
sheihtsoo	swallow
Sheihveenjik	Whitestone River
shichaa	my younger brother
shih	food
shih	grizzly bear
shih eenjit tr'agwich'ii	meat camp
shih gii	bear cub
shih nihtat ts'at dhavìr	stew
shii	chum (dog) salmon
Shiidàatsik	Cadzow Lake, Fish Lake
shijaa, shijyaa, shalak	friend, partner
shijùu	my younger sister
shijyàa	my friend
shijyàa	my partner
shikai', shidanahch'i'	my husband
shilak	my relatives
shilik	my dog
shin	summer
shitì', ti'yàa	my father
shitii	my uncle (father's brother)
shitlih	my friend
shitr'igijiinjiizhee	flycatcher
shitsii	my grandfather
shitsuu	my grandmother
shoh	bear
shòh tsòo	brown bear
shoh zraii	black bear
shoo'ii	my uncle (mother's brother)
shoondee	my older brother
Shriijaa Njik	Bluefish Creek
shùh	drum
shùh tr'ahghàa	drumstick
shuu	my nephew (brother's boy)
shuu	my nephew (sister's boy)
shuu	my niece (brother's girl)
shuu	my niece (sister's girl)
sittichinlii	spruce tree standing with branches spread out
so'	star
so' choo	morning star
so' nadàadhàk	falling star
so' tsal	evening star
soongaii	sugar
sree	sun
sree dhàa	sunrays
sree drìn	calendar
sree gwit'ąįį'aii	eclipse
sree ka'ahchaa	clock
sree nanh	month
sree ne'nìlt'aii	ring around sun
sreendit, gwałgo', daii, gwąhgo'	spring
sreevyàa	rainbow
srii	knife
srii dhòh	knife case
srii gwàt	knife (dull)
srii jiinin	knife (sharp)
srii tr'ijiigwàt	knife (table)
srii tsal	knife (pocket)
sriijaa	grayling
sriits'aii, nanhdaih ts'aii	right side
sroo	dew
sruh	coney
srùh	robin

T

taa'aih	paddle
tadèedàtan, tadìdìchii	freeze-up
tah	socks
taih	hill
taih gwidadlàn	hill (steep)
taii	path, trail
tajìltin	puddle
tan dagaii	white ice
tan ts'ih	ice (clear; when snow melts on lakes to reveal only the ice)
tan zrùh	candle ice
tanèedichìt, lageevirh	pepper
Teechih Gwich'in	Tanana people
Teechik	mouth of the Crow River
teechik	river (mouth of)
teechik	slough
Teechik Gwatsàl	Big Joe Creek
tèeddhàa	water hole
teedhàh zràa	steam (from kettle)
teeghèets'ìl	sandpiper (short legs)

teekai'	red-necked grebe
Teenjiraatsyaa	the middle clan
Teetł'it Gwich'in	Fort McPherson people
teevee	shore
te'itreh	red-throated loon
thał	pants
thał gwàn	shorts
Than Natha'aii	Lone Mountain
theetoh	portage
theetru'	copper
thoh	belt
ti'il ts'ik	snowshoe babiche
tik	three (3)
tik juutin	three zero (30)
tik juutin juutin	three zero zero (300)
tit	waves
tl'agoot'aii	baby strap
tl'aii'iival	swing for baby
tl'eedik, vihzràii dik	riverbank
tlèefàa	perfume
tl'èethoh	skirt
tl'il	babiche
Tl'iyèenjik	David Lord Creek
tl'ohts'aii	left side
tl'oo	grass
tl'oo go'wal	swampy place
tl'oo hànzhu'	tussock
tl'oodrik	wild onion
tl'uu	bullfly, horsefly
tl'yah tr'an	dragonfly
tl'yàh tr'ichyàa	flint
tlyàh ts'ik	string
toh	cane
t'oo	cottonwood
too	night
too oozrii	moon
too oozrìi ch'iilèetl'at	half moon
too oozrii k'inyàazhìi	full moon
too tl'an	midnight
trah	merganser
tr'ahgyùu	fish scales
trèelùk	herring
tr'igiikhii zheh	church
tr'ih	canoe
trih	roots
tr'ih tl'i'	canoe (rear)
tr'ihchoo	boat
tr'iinin	child
tr'ìinin ch'ik	umbilical cord, his
tr'iinin kat	children
tr'ìinjòo	woman
tri'itthòh	dock roots
tr'il	fish wheel
tr'inìihàa zheh	hotel
troo	firewood
Troo Chòo Njìk	Driftwood River, Driftwood Village
tr'òochii zheh	bedroom
trùh	otter
tsaih	red ochre
tsaih zhyàa	snow under crust
tsàiidhòh thał datl'òo	blue jeans
tsal	little, small
ts'ałvit	Arctic loon
ts'at	blanket
ts'at tah	duffle
tsèe	beaver
tsèe dhòh	beaver pelt
tsèe dinjii	beaver (male)
tsèe jirh	beaver mitts
tsèe kàn	beaver house
tsèe lìn	beaver castor
tsèe nanìi'wal	beaver dam
tsèe tr'ik	beaver (female)
tsèe zhìi, kaiitràlt'ùu	water lily
ts'èenakał	raspberries
ts'èet'it	tobacco
ts'èet'it shik tr'alchìt	chewing tobacco
ts'èet'itchì'	pipe (smoking)
ts'eh	cap, hat
ts'eh zraii	black
ts'èhch'ìn	girl (just become a woman)
ts'iigyùu	rhubarb
ts'iiheenjoo	tamarack
Tsii'ideh	Kind Edward Ridge
Tsii'ideh Njik	King Edward Creek
Tsii'in' Ddhàa	Potato Hill, Game Mountain, Diniizhòo
tsiik'it	cache

Glossary 335

ts'iivii	green wood
ts'iivii	spruce
ts'iivii leegàk	spruce needle
ts'iivii nèech'ùu	spruce bark
Ts'iivii Shùh	Timber Hill
ts'iiviijìl	small spruce
Ts'iizhùu	Ogilvie
tsił	snowdrift
tsìlch'ùu	blackbird
ts'it	porcupine
ts'it ch'òo, ch'oh	porcupine quills
ts'oh, gyùu	maggots
tsuk	marten
tsuk zraii	black marten
tthaa	gopher, ground squirrel
tthah	awl
tthah tsal	sewing needle
tthah tsal dhòh	sewing bag
tthak	fringe
tthał	caribou fence
tth'an chù'	bone juice
tth'an ghài', ch'aghwàaghai'	bone grease
tth'e'tthai'	tenderloin
tthòochàn	spruce branch
tyah	pot (for cooking)
tyàh di'diniintin	lid
tyàh vizhìt chuu dhakaii	pail (for water)

V

vadzaih	caribou
vadzaih choo	caribou (largest male)
vadzaih dazhoo	caribou (young)
vadzaih dehgaii	reindeer
vadzaih dhòh	caribou hide
vadzaih dhòh chyay	caribou hide mattress
vadzaih nilìi	caribou meat
vadzaih tr'ik	caribou (female)
vadzaih zhìi, ch'oodèezhùh	lichen
Vadzaih Zrii	October
vaghaii	her brother-in-law
vaghaii	her sister-in-law
vaghaii	his sister-in-law
vaghàn	his spine
vaghò'	his teeth
vaghòhgwat	his shoulder
vaghòo	his testicles
vagwat	his knee
vah chanchyah k'eech'atr'atryaa	mop
vah chihvyàh tr'itl'uu	fishnet needle (small)
vah ch'itr'idi'ee	crayons
vah chuu dizhìt tr'ìnjàa	dipper, ladle
vah di'ke'tr'ahchùu	net rope, twine
vah gijiitìi	hand drill
vah gwìitr'at	rake
vah gwìitthàt	hammer
vah tr'igwaht'an	glue
vah troo tr'it'ii	saw
vahgi'łi'tr'adatan	broom
vajohk'it	his navel
vakai' tth'àn	his foot (bone)
vakak ch'atr'adantl'òo	writing paper
vakak ch'ik'èech'atr'ahtryàa	washboard
vakak ii'aa	table
Vakak Te'nithinìi	Drown Lake
vakak tr'oodii	chair, couch
vał, dachàavał	toboggan
vamà, vit'ok	her breast
vamà chì'	her nipple
van	lake
Van Tat	Crow Flats
Van Tat Gwich'in	Old Crow people
Van Tat Gwich'in Teechik	Rat Indian Creek
van vee	lakeshore
Vanagwàandàii Drin	Remembrance Day
Vanàł'ee	Donut Lake
vanàn	his back
vanành k'òo	his backside
Vananh Ne'ni'dajaa Zrii	August
vanchàn	his rump
vanchòh	his thumb
vanh	morning
vànvoh	his cheek
vants'at	his forehead
vànzhàł	his nose (ridge)
vatł'òo	his gallbladder
vatsàn	her vagina

vats'at	her womb
vats'oh	his elbow
vatthàl	his anus
vazhàk yu'hùch'ù'	binoculars
vazrak, vitrìl, vichìt	his belly
veedèenùh	her son-in-law
vich'at	his tendons
vicheii	her grandchild
vicheii	his grandchild
vichi'	his daughter
vichì'	his head
vichì' nìltl'àa	hair braids
vichii	his daughter-in-law
vichiidrùu	his collarbone
vichiighàii	his brain
vichiighè'	his hair
vichiikai'	his son-in-law
vichìk	his ribs
vichìt	his belly
vich'ùu	his veins
vichyàa	his tongue
vidàa	his blood
vidèeghàn	his chest
vidèeghàn	his rib cage
vidèevàa	his lips
vidèezhòo	his beard
vidhàt	his liver
vidhòh	his skin
vidìl	his penis
vidinji'	his son
vidizhùu	his upper arm
vidòo	his calf
vidrihdòk	his lungs
vidrìi	his heart
vidzèe	his ear
vidzìi	his ear (inner)
vigèe	his armpit
vigèechàn	his shoulder blade
vighè'	his body hair
vighòo ch'àtlok	his gum
vigìn	his arm
vihchyàa	his larynx
vihdàii	his throat
vihdì'	bird's beak
vihdì'	his chin
vihk'ah	bluff, rampart
Vihsraii Ddhàa	Cody Hill
Vihsraii Njik	Cody Creek
vihtl'èekòo	his neck (glands)
vihtth'àn	his jaw
vihzràii dik	riverbank
vii'idzèe	great horned owl
vijì'zhòo	velvet on caribou antler
vikai'	his foot
vikaiidràl	his toes
vikaiigàii	his toenail
vikàiitl'èe	his foot (sole)
vikaiits'at	his toe (big)
vikàntik	his foot (top)
vik'eh	his fat
vikèhtàl	his heel
vik'oh	his neck
vinchàat'ìi	his hand (back)
vindèe	his eye
vindèezhìi	eyeglasses
vinèedòo	his eyelashes
vinèedòoghe'	his eyebrows
vinèevyàa	his uvula
vinèezrìh	his eyeball
vinin'	his face
vinjaa'yaa	window
vinjaa'yàa gidinìivyàa	curtain
vinlèedràl, vinlèetth'ak	his finger
vinlèegaii	his fingernail
vinlèegòo	his finger (between)
vinlèets'ihtth'ak	his finger (small)
vinlì'	his hand
vintl'èe	his hand (palm)
vintsìh	his nose
visàiidavee	snowy owl
vit'èe	bird's wing
vitl'ì'	his buttocks
vitlèe	his knee (cartilage)
vitr'òo	his kidney
vits'edèhtth'àn	his knee (bone)
vitsii	her father-in-law
vits'ik	his guts
vitth'àn	his bone

Glossary 337

vitth'àn	his leg
vitthai'	his flesh
viyeets'i'	her daughter
viyùughwàn	his father-in-law
vizhèe	his marrow
vizhìk	his mouth
vizhìn	his body
vizhìt adi'tr'anàa'in	mirror
vizhìt ch'ik'èech'atr'ahtryàa	washtub
vizhìt nilèetth'ak ii'ee	thimble
vizhìt shih tr'achu'uu	roaster
vizhìt shih tr'ahch'ùu	frying pan
vizhìt tl'yah zhìt tr'igi̱ikhii	telephone
vizhuhchyàa	her breastbone
vizhuu	her son
vootr'ì'	her mother-in-law
vootr'ì'	his mother-in-law
vyah	big snare (for caribou)
vyuh	seagull

Y

yahkee	dawn
yeendoo khaii	next year
yeenoo dài' googwandak	long-ago stories
yùhdii	dipper
yùhdìi choo	big dipper
yùhdìi tsal	little dipper
yukaih	northern lights

Z

zheetìi	sky
zhèezhàh	skylark
zheh	house
zheh gwàazraii	jail
Zheh Gwatsàl	LaPierre House
zheh gwichiit'ik	roof
zheh ts'at	house (corner)
zhehgwadhòh	tent
zhì'	lice
zhìnadhat'aii	scarf
zhinanùut'aii	necklace
zhoh	snow
zhòh	wolf
zhoh chàt	snow (powder)
zhoh ch'ik	snow scoop
zhoh ch'ìk	shovel
Zhoh Drìn Chòo	White Snow Mountain
zhòh gii	wolf cub
zhoh kahn	snow houses
zhoh tl'ak	snow bug
zhoh trah	snow (wet)
zree	moon

English to Gwich'in

A

airplane	ch'iitsii nândit'èe
alder	k'oh
and	hah
animal pelt	nin dhòo
animals	nin
anorak, parka	anjithitii ik
ant	neejìi
anus, his	vatthàl
apples (dried)	ch'ivèedzyàa
April	Ch'ichee Zrii
Arctic char	ddhah lùk
Arctic loon	ts'ałvit
Arctic Red River people	Gwichyah Gwich'in
Arctic tern	ch'itr'ùu
Arctic Village people	Neets'ik Gwich'in
arm	ch'igìn
arm (upper), his	vidizhùu
arm, his	vigìn
armpit, his	vigèe
arrow	k'i'
arrowhead	k'idèechì'
Ash Wednesday	Atr'ididaagaii Ddrin
ashes	chìk lùu, cheezrilchit
August	Vananh Ne'ni'dajaa Zrii
aunt (father's sister), my	sheek'aii
aunt (mother's sister), my	sheek'aii
autumn	khaiits'ò', nagwidik'ii
awl	tthah
axe	daa'aii
axe (double)	daa'aii nihk'yùu vèek'i'
axe (stone)	chii daa'aii
axe handle	daa'aii tai'

B

babiche	tl'il
babiche (snowshoe)	ti'il ts'ik
babiche, holes for	shał k'it
baby	bèebii
baby food	bèebii zhìi
baby strap	tl'agoot'aii
back, his	vanàn
backbone	ch'anàn
backside, his	vanành k'òo
bacon	ch'ik'èh tthai'
bait	khyàh zhìi
baking powder	łùh vah niituu
ball	nèhkak
bank	lazraa zheh
bannock	łùh ch'ùh
bannock (grease)	khaii łùh chùh
bark (shreds on)	ch'idìnìichii
bark whistle	k'àii yuuzhù'
bead needle	nàagàii tthah tsal
beads	nàagàii
bear	shoh
bear (black)	shoh zraii
bear (brown)	shòh tsòo
bear (grizzly)	shih
Bear Cave Mountain	Ch'ii Ch'à'an
bear cub	shih gii
beard, his	vidèezhòo
beaver	tsèe
beaver (female)	tsèe tr'ik
beaver (largest)	ch'ìchòo, tsèe choo
beaver (male)	tsèe dinjii
beaver (one-year-old)	neezhì'
beaver (three-year-old)	ch'edoovii
beaver (two-year-old)	ch'aachii
beaver castor	tsèe lìn
beaver dam	tsèe nanìi'wal
beaver house	tsèe kàn
beaver mitts	tsèe jirh
beaver pelt	tsèe dhòh
bed	deek'it, dehk'it
bedroom	tr'òochii zheh
bee	ch'ineedzit
bee nest	ch'ineedzit t'òo
bell	ch'iitsii laii'
Bell River	Chiiveenjik
belly, his	vichìt
belt	thoh
berries	jak
berries (boiled)	jak tloo
berries (mountain)	ddhah dee

Glossary 339

berries (unripe)	ch'àneeluh
Berry Mountain	Jak Ddhah
Bible	dinèhtl'eh choo, ch'ìdzìt
big dipper	yùhdìi choo
Big Joe Creek	Teechik Gwatsàl
big snare (for caribou)	vyah
binoculars	vazhàk yu'hùhch'ù'
birch	aat'oo
birchbark	k'ii
birchbark canoe	k'ìi tr'ih
bird	jii, dzhii
bird feather	chuh
bird's beak	vihdì'
bird's nest	jii tsal t'òo, dzhii tsal t'òo
bird's wing	vit'èe
birthday	Nigoonlii Drin
Bishop	Giikhii Choo
black	jidii zraii, ts'eh zraii
black bear	shoh zraii
black currant	dineech'ùu
black marten	tsuk zraii
black or silver fox	neegoo zraii
black worm with white head	gyùhk'ah
blackbird	tsìlch'ùu
blacksmith	ch'iitsii ahtsii
Blackstone River	Chiizràiinjìk
blanket	ts'at
blood soup	ch'ankaii
blood, his	vidàa
bloodsucker	chèhgyù'
blue	jidii datl'òo
blue jeans	tsàiidhòh thał datl'òo
blueberries	jak zraii
Bluefish Creek	Shriijaa Njik
bluff, rampart	vihk'ah
boat	tr'ihchoo
boat (canvas)	dòhsròo tr'ihchoo
boat (skin)	ch'adhòh tr'ihchòo
boat, pole for	jùh toh
body hair, his	vighè'
body, his	vizhìn
bone grease	tth'an ghài', ch'aghwàaghai'
bone juice	tth'an chù'
bone, his	vitth'àn
book, paper	dinèhtl'eh
boots (canvas)	dohsròo kaiichàn
boss	chit nilii
bow	k'iłtai'
bowl	ch'ìk ghoo
bowstring	k'iłtài' tl'yàa
box (paper)	dinèhtl'eh tyàh
box (wooden)	dachan tyah
boy	chyaa
boy (little)	chyaa tsal
brain, his	vichiighàii
bread	łùh dàn
breakup	łùu hijii
breast, her	vamà, vit'ok
breastbone, her	vizhuhchyàa
brisket	ch'itòo
broad whitefish	chihshòo
broom	vahgi'łi'tr'adatan
brother-in-law, her	vaghaii
brother-in-law, his	shaa
brother (older), my	shoondee
brother (younger), my	shichaa
brown	jidii tthoo
brown bear	shòh tsòo
bullets	diik'ee chì'
bullfly, horsefly	tl'uu
bunting (snow)	gugèh zhùu
burbot, loche	chèhlùk
Burnt Hill	Gwak'àn Choo
Burnt Hill by Eagle River	Nan ihlah juuka
Burnt Hill Creek above Johnson Creek	Gwak'àn Choo Njik
bushes (thick)	gwàatr'al
bushman	nanaa'in'
Bushman Mountain	Nanaa'in Ddhàa
butter	aak'ii ghai' tsòo
butterfly	nanùht'ee
buttocks, his	vitl'ì'
button	ik tsàk
buttonhole	ìk tsàk k'it

C

cabin	dachan zheh
cache	drah, tsiik'it
cache (platform)	dehdrah

Cadzow Lake, Fish Lake	Shiidàatsik
calendar	sree drìn
calf	ch'igii
calf, his	vidòo
Canada goose	kheh
Canada jay	ch'idingwat'an
candle	khaii juuk'a'
candle ice	tan zrùh
candy	andaii
cane	toh
canoe	tr'ih
canoe (birchbark)	k'ìi tr'ih
canoe (rear)	tr'ih tl'i'
Canoe River/ Chance Creek	Ch'itr'ihkaiinjìk
canvas	dohsròo
canvas boat	dòhsròo tr'ihchoo
canvas boots	dohsròo kaiichàn
canyon	danzhìt
cap, hat	ts'eh
car, truck	ch'iitsii khał
cards (playing)	lagar
caribou	vadzaih
caribou (fall-time)	khadatsan
caribou (female)	ch'iiyàht'òk, vadzaih tr'ik
caribou (largest male)	vadzaih choo
caribou (two-year-old male)	dazhoo tsoo
caribou (worm on hide)	ch'anàngyuh
caribou (young bull)	dazhoo
caribou (young)	vadzaih dazhoo
Caribou Bar Creek	Ch'idzèe Njik
caribou fence (corral)	tthał
caribou herd	nootl'ii
caribou hide	vadzaih dhòh
caribou hide (thin, tanned)	jitsoo hah nagankai'
caribou leg hide	ch'idrèedhòh
caribou meat	vadzaih nilìi
caribou or moose	ch'atthaii
caribou-skin pants	dazhòo thał
carrots	gwànzhih
cat	niinjii zhuu
caterpillar	gyùu zhòo
cave	ch'a'an
chair, couch	vakak tr'oodii
charcoal	ch'ùh
cheek, his	vànvòh
chest	ch'idèeghàn
chest, his	vidèeghàn
chewing tobacco	ts'èet'it shik tr'alchìt
chickadee	ch'idzigyek
chief	dinjii khehkai'
child	tr'iinin
children	tr'iinin kat
chin, his	vihdì'
chinook wind	nagwidhah ìindìi
chisel (flat head)	aih vał
chisel (ice)	łùu dzyah
Choho Hill	Ch'aghòo
Christmas	Drin Tsal
chum salmon	shii
church	tr'igiikhii zheh
clock	sree ka'ahchaa
cloth, material	athitl'ii
clothes	gwich'àa
clothes (striped)	nàazùu
clothesline	gwich'àa eenjit tl'yàh ninìint'aii
clouds	k'oh
clouds (rain)	chin k'òh
clouds (spring)	k'oh dagaii dok
club	khàh
clubs	daagoo kài'
coals (red)	kwàn chìt
Cody Creek	Vihsraii Njik
Cody Hill	Vihsraii Ddhàa
coho salmon	nèhdlii
cold water	chuu k'oh
cold weather	ch'ak'oh
collarbone	ch'ichìidrùu
collarbone, his	vichiidrùu
comb	chiizrùk
common loon	daadzaii
coney	sruh
cookies	łuh andaii
copper	theetru'
cottonwood	t'oo
couch, chair	vakak tr'oodii
cow	aak'ii

Glossary 341

cow's milk	ak'ii t'òk
crackers	łùh gaii
cranberries (low bush)	natl'at
crane	jah
crayons	vah ch'itr'idi'ee
creek	k'ohnjik
crib	beebìi dehk'it
cross fox	neegoo ninìlzraii
crosspiece	nadinii'èe
Crow Clan	Neetsaih
Crow Flats	Van Tat
Crow Mountain	Chuuts'aii Nàlk'at
Crow River	Chyahnjik
Crow River, mouth of	Teechik
cup	chuu tyah
cupboard	ch'ìk k'it
currant (black)	dineech'ùu
currant (red)	nee'yùu
curtain	vinjaa'yàa gidinìivyàa

D

dance hall	ch'adzoh zheh
daughter-in-law, her	shèedèenuh
daughter-in-law, his	vichii
daughter, her	viyeets'i'
daughter, his	vichi'
David Lord Creek	Tl'iyèenjik
dawn	yahkee
day	drin
day after tomorrow	nihkàa gehndòo
day before yesterday	k'ehdai' gehnòo
daylight	drin
deadfall	dachan khyàh
December	Khah Zhak Dha'aii
den	ch'a'àn
dew	sroo
diapers	ch'ił
dip net	dèetl'yàh
dipper	yùhdii
dipper, ladle	vah chuu dizhìt tr'ìnjaa
dishtowel	ch'ìk dòhsròo
dock roots	tri'itthòh
dog	łaii
dog (female)	łaii ts'ì'

dog chain	ch'iitsii tl'yàh
dog collar	łaii zhinadha'èe
dog food	łaii zhìi
dog harness	łaii tl'yàa
dog house	łaii zheh
dog pack	łaii ghàa
dog salmon	shii
dog straps	lagwìizràk
dog team	łaii tl'yah dadàach'ii
dog whip	łaii viitrii
dog, my	shilik
Donut Lake	Vanàł'ee
door	gihdaiivyàa
double axe	daa'aii nihk'yùu vèek'i'
dragonfly	tl'yah tr'an
dress	ik
dried apples	ch'ivèedzyàa
dried fish	łùk gaii
dried meat	nilii gaii
dried prunes	jak choo
driftwood	doo
Driftwood River	Troo Chòo Njìk
Driftwood Village	Troo Chòo Njìk
Drown Lake	Vakak Te'nithinìi
drum	shùh
drumstick	shùh tr'ahghàa
dry branch	didich'eii
dry willow	k'il
duck	dats'an
duck (baby)	ch'izhuutsoo
duck (harlequin)	chiitat gwilùk
duck (mallard)	neet'ak choo
duck (old squaw)	ah'ąąlak, ah'ànlak
duck (pintail)	ch'iriinjòo, ch'ak'ohnjùh
duffle	ts'at tah
dust	gwajàt

E

Eagle and Dawson people	Hän Gwich'in
eagle (golden)	ch'izhìn
Eagle River	Ch'izhìn Njik
ear (inner), his	vidzìi
ear, his	vidzèe
earth, land	nanh, nan

342   *Glossary*

Easter	Nanagwaalii Drin
eclipse	sree gwit'ąįį'aii
eddy	òk
eggs	dzhii tsal ghòo
eiderdown	chuh ts'at
eight (8)	nihk'ii daang
eighteen (one zero and twice four; 18)	ch'ihłak juutin ts'at nihk'ii daang
elbow, his	vats'oh
elder	ch'ànjòo
eleven (11)	ch'ihłak juutin ts'at ch'ihłak
evening star	so' tsal
ewe	divii tr'ik
eye	ch'ìndèe
eye, his	vindèe
eyeball, his	vinèezrìh
eyebrows, his	vinèedòoghe'
eyeglasses	vindèezhìi
eyelashes, his	vinèedòo

F

face, his	vinin'
falcon	ch'ichèe
falling star	so' nadàadhàk
fancy	ni'dinìltsi'
fat	ch'ak'èh, ch'ichèezhuh
fat, his	vik'eh
father-in-law, her	vitsii
father-in-law, his	viyùughwàn
father, my	shitì', ti'yàa
February	Ahtr'aih Zrii
fiddle	ch'iitsìi edlii
fifteen (one zero and five; 15)	ch'ihłak juutin ts'at ch'ihłoogwinli'
fifty (five zero; 50)	ch'ihłoogwinli' juutin
file	gwik'ih
finger (between), his	vinlèegòo
finger (small), his	vinlèets'ihtth'ak
finger, his	vinlèedràl, vinlèetth'ak
fingernail, his	vinlèegaii
fire, matches	kò'
fireplace	kwàn deek'it
firewood	troo
first quarter	na'iida'aii
fish	łuk
fish (boiled)	łùk vìrh, łùk vìr
fish (dried)	łùk gaii
fish (fried)	łùk ch'ùh
fish backbone	łùk nàn
fish camp	łùk deek'it tr'agwich'ii
fish eggs	łùk k'yù'
fish fins	łùk gyù'
fish guts	ch'its'igighòo, łùk ts'ik
fish head	łùk chì'
fish hook	jał
fish scales	tr'ahgyùu
fish slime	łùk tl'ùu
fish tail	łùk chì'
fish trap	k'oo
fish wheel	tr'il
Fishing Branch River	Ni'iinlii Njik, Sheenjik
fishnet	chihvyàh
fishnet needle (big)	chihvyàh vàh di'ke'tr'ahchuu
fishnet needle (small)	vah chihvyàh tr'itl'uu
five (5)	ch'ihłoogwinli'
flannel	athitl'ii chuu
flea	gwatl'ak
flesh, his	vitthai'
flint	tl'yàh tr'ichyàa, ko tanh
floaters	de'elah
floor	dachànchyàh
flour	łuh
flower	ch'at'an nizii
fly	daii'
flycatcher	shitr'igijiinjiizhee
fog	ch'atr'ał
fog on water	lèelat
food, grub	oonjìt shìi
foot (bone), his	vakai' tth'àn
foot (sole), his	vikàiitl'èe
foot (top), his	vikàntik
foot straps	ch'akaiłaih
foot, his	vikai'
foothills	ddhah deechan
forehead, his	vants'at
fork	ch'iitsiigwał
Fort McPherson	Chii Tsal Dik
Fort McPherson people	Teetl'it Gwich'in

Glossary 343

English	Gwich'in
Fort Yukon people	Gwichyàa Gwich'in
forty (four zero; 40)	daang juutin
four (4)	daang
fourteen (one zero and four; 14)	ch'ihłak juutin ts'at daang
fox	neegoo
fox (black or silver)	neegoo zraii
fox (cross)	neegoo ninìlzraii
fox (red)	neegoo tsoo
fox (white)	ch'ich'yàa
fox pup	neegoo gii
fox tail	neegoo chì'
freeze-up	tadèedàtan, tadìdìchii
Friday	Drin Ch'ihłoogwinli'
friend	shijaa, shijyaa, shalak, shitlih
friend, my	shijyàa, shitlih
fringe	tthak
frog	neeghaii
frost	ch'its'ik tàn
frying pan	vizhìt shih tr'ahch'ùu
full moon	too oozrii k'inyàazhìi

G

English	Gwich'in
gallbladder, his	vatł'òo
gas	chuu juuka'
girl	nich'it
girl (just become a woman)	ts'èhch'ìn
girl (little)	nich'it tsal
glacial water	git chu'
glacier	git
gloves	nilèejirh
glue	vah tr'igwaht'an
gnat, sandfly	ch'idajòl, ch'îi'ijòl
golden eagle	ch'izhìn
Good Friday	Jesus Gatr'ałtsak Drìn
goose (Canada)	kheh
goose (snow)	googeh
gopher, ground squirrel	tthaa
goshawk	dzhii choo
grandchild, her	vicheii
grandchild, his	vicheii
grandfather, my	shitsii
grandmother, my	shitsuu

English	Gwich'in
grass	tl'oo
grasshopper	ch'adizhoo
gravel	sheih
gravy	łùh tlòo
grayling	sriijaa
grease bannock	khaii łùh ch'ùh
grease, lard	khaii
great grey owl	ch'ichìidruu
great horned owl	vii'idzèe
grebe (red-necked)	teekai'
green	jidii ch'ahtl'oo
green wood	ts'ìivii
green-winged teal	daazraii gahkhàa
grey	jidii vee
grizzly bear	shih
grouse (spruce)	daih
gum	dzìh
gum, his	vighòo ch'àtlok
gun, rifle	diik'ee
gun, rifle (.22 rifle; small gun)	diik'ee tsal
gun, rifle (.30-.30 rifle; large gun)	diik'ee choo
gunsight (front)	diik'èe teenjìr
gunsight (rear)	diik'èe k'èegòo
gunstock	diik'èe kaihtał
guts, his	vits'ik

H

English	Gwich'in
hail	ch'ànluh
hair braids	vichì' nìltl'àa
hair, his	vichiighè'
Hair Mountain	Chyah Ddhàa
half moon	too oozrìi ch'iilèetl'at
Halloween	Natr'agwaazhii Drin
hammer	vah gwìitthàt
hand (back), his	vinchàat'ii
hand (palm), his	vintl'èe
hand drill	vah gijiitìi
hand plane	dachan ch'anhgwàh
hand, his	vinlì'
handkerchief	k'oonaiit'aii
harlequin duck	chiitat gwilùk
hawk	chinìitràn

head	ch'ichì'
head, his	vichì'
heart	ch'idrìi
heart, his	vidrìi
hearts	ch'idrìi
heel, his	vikèhtàł
herd of caribou	nootl'ii
herring	trèelùk
Herschel Island	Chuu Choo Vee
hide (caribou)	vadzaih dhòh
hide (moose)	dinjik dhòh
hill	taih
hill (steep)	taih gwidadlàn
hindquarter	ch'adhòo
holes for babiche	shał k'it
honey	ch'ineedzit soogaii
horn	ch'ijì'
horse	łaii choo
hospital	ałts'ik zheh
hot water	chuu dhah
hotel	tr'inìihàa zheh
house	zheh
house (corner)	zheh ts'at
house (skin)	ch'adhòh zheh
husband, my	shikai', shidanahch'i'

I

ice	łùu
ice (clear)	tan ts'ih, łùu drin'
ice (cracked)	łùu tìl k'ìt
ice (thin)	łùu dril
ice (white)	tan dagaii
ice chisel	łùu dzyah
ice crystal	ch'its'ik
icicles	łùu dril ch'òk
intestines	ch'ìndohgyù'
Inuit or Inuvialuit	Ch'ineekaii
island	njùu
it rained	ahchin'
it snowed	ahshu'
it started to rain	hiłchin'
it started to snow	hiłshu'
it's raining	ahchin
it's snowing	ahshii

J

jacket	ch'idàk ik
jackfish, pike	altin
jail	zheh gwàazraii
January	Ch'ak'oh Zrii
jaw, his	vihtth'àn
Johnson Creek (up the Crow River)	Aadrìi Njik
Johnson Creek	Ch'aghòonjik
Johnson Creek Village	Kâachik
July	Ch'adachoo Zrii
June	Ch'adaghòo Zrii
juniper	deetrù' jak

K

key	lidlii
kidney, his	vitr'òo
kidneys	ch'itr'òo
kindling wood	łuh jik
King Edward Creek	Tsii'ideh Njik
King Edward Mountain	Ch'anchàl
King Edward Ridge	Tsii'ideh
king salmon	łùk choo
kitten	niinjii zhuu gii
knee (bone), his	vits'edèhtth'àn
knee (cartilage), his	vitlèe
knee, his	vagwat
knife	srii
knife (crooked)	dachan srii
knife (dull)	srii gwàt
knife (pocket)	srii tsal
knife (sharp)	srii jiinin
knife (table)	srii tr'ijiigwàt
knife case	srii dhòh

L

Labrador tea	lidii masgit
ladle, dipper	vah chuu dizhìt tr'ìnjàa
lake	van
lakeshore	van vee
lamb	divii gii
land, earth	nanh, nan
LaPierre House	Zheh Gwatsàl
larynx, his	vihchyàa

last year	k'eejit khaii
leaf	ch'at'àn
left side	tl'ohts'aii
leg (back)	ch'ąngwàl
leg (front)	ch'àndòonagwàl
leg, his	vitth'àn
Lent	Atr'ididaagaii
lice	zhì'
lichen	vadzaih zhìi, ch'oodèezhùh
lid	tyàh di'diniintin
lightning	nèhtanh kwàn
lips, his	vidèevàa
little dipper	yùhdìi tsal
little, small	tsal
liver	ch'adhat
liver, his	vidhàt
loche, burbot	chèhlùk
Lone Mountain	Than Natha'aii
long-ago stories	yeenoo dài' googwandak
loon (Arctic)	ts'ałvit
loon (common)	daadzaii
loon (red-throated)	te'itreh
lungs	ch'idrihdòk
lungs, his	vidrihdòk
lynx	niinjii
lynx cub	niinjii gii

M

Mackenzie River	Nagwachoonjik
maggots	ts'oh, gyùu
mailman	dinehtl'eh k'anàhtii
mallard duck	neet'ak choo
man	dinjii
man (old)	danahch'i'
man (rich)	dinjii chìl'èe
man (white)	oonjit
March	Ch'izhìn Zrii
marrow	ch'izhèe
marrow, his	vizhèe
marten	tsuk
marten (black)	tsuk zraii
material, cloth	athitl'ii
mattress (caribou hide)	vadzaih dhòh chyah
mattress, rug	chyah

May	Gwilùu Zrii
Mayo people	Dachan Tat Gwich'in
meadow	nan chyàh, teet'ih
meat	nilii
meat (caribou)	vadzaih nìlii
meat (dried)	nilii gaii
meat camp	shih eenjit tr'agwich'ii
medicine	ch'agòondaih
medicine man	dinjii dazhan
merganser	trah
middle clan, the	Teenjiraatsyaa
midnight	too tl'an
milk (cow's)	ak'ii t'òk
Miner River	Ch'inèetsii Njìk
minister	giikhii
mink	chihthee, chìhjùu
mirror	vizhìt adi'tr'anàa'in
mitts	jirh
mitts (beaver)	tsèe jirh
moccasins	kaiitrih
Monday	Drin Tl'ee
money	lazraa, tsèe dhòh
month	sree nanh
moon	too oozrii, zree
moon (full)	too oozrii k'inyàazhìi
moon (half)	too oozrìi ch'iilèetl'at
moonlight	ch'aadrìh nùu
moose	dinjik
moose (bull)	ch'èzhùr
moose (cow)	dizhùu
moose (young)	ditsik
moose caller	ch'igèechàn
moose hide	dinjik dhòh
moose meat	dinjik nìlii
mop	vah chanchyah k'eech'atr'atryaa
morning	vanh
morning star	so' choo
mosquito	ch'ii
mosquito net	ch'iidhòh
mosquito repellant	ch'ii ch'agoondaih
moss	nù'
mother-in-law, her	vootr'ì'
mother-in-law, his	vootr'ì'

mother, my	shahanh, na'àa
mountain	ddhah
mountain berries	ddhah dee
mountain pass	ddhah tòh
mountain ridge	geek'ii
mouse	daatsoo
mouth of Crow River	Teechik
mouth, his	vizhìk
mud (sticky)	łuh ch'ant'at
mukluks	kaiichàn
muskrat	dzan
muskrat stretcher	dzan dhòh zhìt tâii'ii'ee

N

nails	gwatsak
Native person	dinjii zhùh
navel, his	vajohk'it
neck	ch'ak'oh
neck (glands), his	vihtl'èekòo
neck, his	vik'oh
necklace	zhinanùut'aii
needle (bead)	nàagàii tthah tsal
needle (fishnet, big)	chihvyàh vàh di'ke'tr'ahchuu
needle (fishnet, small)	vah chihvyàh tr'itl'uu
needle (sewing)	tthah tsal
needle (skin, triangular)	ch'adhòh tthàh tsal
needle (snowshoe)	aih vał
needle (spruce)	ts'iivii leegàk
nephew (brother's boy), my	shuu
nephew (sister's boy), my	shuu
nest	ch'at'òo
net rope, twine	vah di'ke'tr'ahchùu
netting snowshoe	aih ghat, aih tr'aghat
New Year's Day	Drin Choo
next year	yeendoo khaii
niece (brother's girl), my	shuu
niece (sister's girl), my	shuu
night	too
nipple, her	vamà chì'
noon	drin tl'an
north wind	ee ahtr'aii
northern lights	yukaih
nose	ch'ìntsih
nose (cartilage), his	vanchàł
nose (ridge), his	vànzhàł
nose, his	vintsìh
November	Divii Zrii
nurse	ałts'ik k'anahtii

O

ocean	chuu choo
ochre (red)	tsaih
October	Vadzaih Zrii
Ogilvie	Ts'ìizhùu
Ogilvie River	Gwazhàl Njik
Oh, my goodness!	Anits'u'
oil	khaii juuk'a'
Old Crow people	Van Tat Gwich'in
old man	danahch'i'
old squaw duck	ah'ąąlak, ah'ànlak
old woman	shanaghàn
older brother, my	shoondee
older sister, my	sheejii
one (1)	ch'ihłak
one hundred (100)	ch'ihłak juutin juutin
one thousand (1,000)	ch'ihłak juutin juutin juutin
onion (wild)	tl'oodrik
orange	jidii dich'ìk
orphan	chìitee
otter	trùh
owl (great grey)	ch'ichìidruu
owl (great horned)	vii'idzèe
owl (snowy)	visàiidavee
oven pan	ch'iitsii t'èh gwich'ik

P

paddle	taa'aih
pail (for water)	tyàh vizhìt chuu dhakaii
pan (frying)	vizhìt shih tr'ach'ùu
pan (oven)	ch'iitsii t'èh gwich'ik
pancakes	łùh tlok
pants	thał
paper, book	dinèhtl'eh
paper (writing)	vakak ch'atr'adantl'òo
parasites, fleas	ch'itl'ak, nin tl'ak
parka, anorak	anjithitii ik

partner, my	shijyàa
path, trail	taii
pemmican	ch'itsùh
pen, pencil	dinèhtl'eh tai'
penis, his	vidìl
people	dinjii kat
pepper	tanèedichìt, lageevirh
perfume	tlèefàa
pig	lagùusrùu
pike, jackfish	altin
pillow	chùh
pingo	nan ghòo khàak'at
pink	jidii dich'ik
pintail duck	ch'iriinjòo, ch'ak'ohnjùh
pipe (smoking)	ts'èet'itchì'
plate	ch'ìk
plate (birchbark)	k'ii ch'ìk
plateau	gwichyah
playing cards	lagar
pocket	ch'èet'it, shìchèet'it
pointed snowshoe	aih ch'ok
pole for boat	jùh toh
police	navèh t'ah'in
police station	navèh t'ah'in zheh
porcupine	ts'it
porcupine quills	ts'it ch'òo, ch'oh
Porcupine River	Ch'oodèenjik
portage	theetoh
post office	dinehtl'eh zheh
pot (cooking)	tyah
Potato Hill (Game Mountain)	Diniizhòo, Tsii'in' Ddhàa
potatoes	gwànzhìh
powder snow	zhoh chàt
prunes (dried)	jak choo
ptarmigan	daagoo
pucker, ruffle	chuk
puddle	tajìłtin
puffball	doo'ii ahshii
puppy	łaii tsal

R

rabbit	geh
raft	khòo
rain	chin'
rainbow	sreevyàa
raisin	jak gaii
rake	vah gwìitr'at
ram (large)	divii choo
rampart, bluff	vihk'ah
Rampart House	Gindèh Chik
rapids	chuu niint'aii
raspberries	ts'èenakał
Rat Indian Creek	Van Tat Gwich'in Teechik
raven	deetrù'
red	jidii ditsik
red coals	kwàn chìt
red currant	nee'yùu
red fox	neegoo tsoo
red ochre	tsaih
red-necked grebe	teekai'
red-throated loon	te'itreh
reindeer	vadzaih dehgaii
relatives, my	shilak
Remembrance Day	Vanagwàandàii Drin
restaurant	ch'atr'a'aa zheh
rhubarb	ts'iigyùu
rib cage, his	vidèeghàn
ribs	ch'ìchìk
ribs, his	vichìk
rich man	dinjii chìl'èe
ridgepole	chìk hijùu'èe
rifle, gun	diik'ee
rifle, gun (.22 rifle; small gun)	diik'ee tsal
rifle, gun (.30-.30 rifle; large gun)	diik'ee choo
right side	sriits'aii, nanhdaih ts'aii
ring	nilèetth'ak
ring around sun	sree ne'nìlt'aii
river	han
river (bottom)	chèe
river (mouth of)	teechik
riverbank	tl'eedik, vihzràii dik
roaster	vizhìt shih tr'ahch'uu
robin	srùh
rock, stone	chii
roof	zheh gwichiit'ik
roots	trih
rosehips	nichìh

rotten wood	dahshàa
round snowshoe	aih zheii
round tent	nèevyaa zheh
ruffle, pucker	chuk
rump	ch'ànchàn
rump, his	vanchàn

S

salmon (chum; dog)	shii
salmon (coho; silver)	nèhdlii
salmon (king)	łuk choo
Salmon Cache	Chiitsiighe'
salmonberries	nakàł
Salmonberry Lake	Nakał Vàn
salt	lesel, doahghwai'
sand	sheih
sandfly, gnat	ch'idajòl, ch'îi'ijòl
sandpiper (long legs)	duh
sandpiper (short legs)	teeghèets'ìl
Saturday	Drin Yeet'ìi, Drin Ts'ò'
saucer	ch'ìk tsal
saw	vah troo tr'it'ii
scarf	zhìnadhat'aii
scent gland	ch'itl'òo
Schaeffer Creek	Ch'anchał Njik, Neetaii
Schaeffer Lake	K'ìi Zhìt
Schaeffer Mountain	Ch'icheechih
school	ge'tr'oonahtan zheh
scissors	ch'iitsiida'al
scoop (snow)	zhoh ch'ik
scoop (wooden)	dachan ch'ìk
scoter (fish duck)	deetree'aa
scoter, white-winged (black duck)	njàa
scraper (stone)	dèeddhòo
scraper (tanning)	ch'ànghwah, ch'ich'yàa
seagull	vyuh
Second Mountain	Chyah Ddhàa
September	Dinjik Zrii
seven (7)	ch'iteech'ii neekaii
seventeen (17)	ch'ihłak juutin ts'at ch'iteech'ii neekaii
sewing bag	tthah tsal dhòh
sewing machine	ch'iitsii vah k'e'tr'ajahkaii
sewing needle	tthah tsal
sharp snowshoe	łintsùutlìi aih
sharpening stone	chii gwik'ih
shaving	àazrùk
sheep	divii
shore	teevee
short winter day	khah zhak
shorts	thał gwàn
shotgun (pistol)	nilèediik'èe
shoulder blade	ch'igèechàn
shoulder blade, his	vigèechàn
shoulder, his	vaghòhgwat
shovel	zhoh ch'ìk
shreds on bark	ch'ìdìnìichii
shrew	dlòodèetthah
silk	athitl'ii vàalaii
silver salmon	nèhdlii
sinew	ch'ih khanìidòo
sinkers	chèhchii
sister-in-law, her	vaghaii
sister-in-law, his	vaghaii
sister (older), my	sheejii
sister (younger), my	shijùu
six (6)	nihk'ii tik
sixteen (16)	ch'ihłak juutin ts'at nihk'ii tik
skin boat	ch'adhòh tr'ìhchòo
skin house	ch'adhòh zheh
skin needle (triangular)	ch'adhòh tthàh tsal
skin, his	vidhòh
skirt	tl'èethoh
sky	zheetìi
skylark	zhèezhàh
Slavey people	Aachin
sleeve	ch'ivìt, shivìt
sleigh	khał
slough	teechik
small, little	tsal
smoke	łat
smoke dust	łit ts'ìh
smoke hole	chik
snare	gyàh
snare (big, for caribou)	vyah
snow	zhoh
snow (powder)	zhoh chàt

Glossary 349

snow (wet)	zhoh trah
snow bug	zhoh tl'ak
snow bunting	gugèh zhùu
snow goose	googeh
snow houses	zhoh kahn
snow on branches	dèhzhòo
snow scoop	zhoh ch'ik
snow under crust	tsaih zhyàa
snow-blind	neezhìn'
snowdrift	tsił
snowmobile	ch'iitsii khał
snowshoe	aih
snowshoe (netting)	aih ghat, aih tr'aghat
snowshoe (pointed)	aih ch'ok
snowshoe (round)	aih zheii
snowshoe (sharp)	łintsùutlìi aih
snowshoe babiche	ti'il ts'ik
snowshoe frame	aih shin'
snowshoe lace	ch'yàh
snowshoe needle	aih vał
snowy owl	visàiidavee
soap	dàatlih
socks	tah
son-in-law, her	veedèenùh
son-in-law, his	vichiikai'
son, her	vizhuu
son, his	vidinji'
south wind	nii ahtr'aii
spark	kwànchit hijàa
spawning	łùk ni'iinlii
spear	ch'iizrìi
spider	gwidèedrìi'
spiderweb	gwidèedrìi' vyaa
spine, his	vaghàn
spoon	saban
spring	sreendit, gwałgo', daii, gwąhgo'
spring clouds	k'oh dagaii dok
spring water	k'ohnjik chu' chu', daii gwichu'
spruce	ts'ìivii
spruce (small)	ts'ìiviijil
spruce bark	ts'ìivii nèech'ùu
spruce bough	ah, thoochyàh
spruce branch	tthòochàn

spruce cone	dineedzìl
spruce grouse	daih
spruce gum (chewable)	dzìh kò'
spruce gum (soft)	dzìh tl'ùu
spruce needle	ts'ìivii leegàk
spruce tree standing with branches spread out	sittichinlii
squirrel	dlak
squirrel (baby)	dlak gii
star	so'
star (evening)	so' tsal
star (falling)	so' nadàadhàk
star (morning)	so' choo
steam (from kettle)	teedhàh zràa
steel trap	ch'iitsii khyah
stew	shih nihtat ts'at dhavìr
stick pull, the (a long-ago game)	nilaiizruk
stick, club	gał
stomach	ch'ivat
stone, rock	chii
stone (sharpening)	chii gwik'ih
stone axe	chii daa'aii
stone scraper	dèeddhòo
stoneberries	dandaih
store	ch'ookat zheh
stormy weather	drijahtsai'
stories (long-ago)	yeenoo dài' googwandak
story	googwandak
stove	ch'iitsii
stove poker	ko'gàl, ch'iitsii gał
stovepipe	ch'iitsii zhik
string	tlyàh ts'ik
striped clothes	nàazùu
stump	ch'achàn
sucker	daats'at
sugar	soongaii
summer	shin
sun	sree
sun (ring around)	sree ne'nìlt'aii
Sunday	Drin Zhit
sundog	khèechiigwijìłk'a'
sunrays	sree dhàa
sunrise	ge'ha'aii
sunset	ne'a'aii

swallow	sheihtsoo
swampy place	tl'oo go'wal
swan	daazraii
swing for baby	tl'aii'iival
syrup	k'ii chu'

T

table	vakak ii'aa
tacks	gwatsak tsal
tail	ch'ichì', ch'itshì'
tail fin	łùk tl'ì'
tamarack	ts'iiheenjoo
Tanana people	Teechih Gwich'in
tanning scraper	ch'ànghwah, ch'ich'yàa
tarp	gwikak dàłchuu
tea	lidii
teacher	ga'oonahtan
teal (green-winged)	daazraii gahkhàa
teapot	lidii tyah
teeth, his	vaghò'
telephone	vizhìt tl'yah zhìt tr'igjikhii
ten (10)	ch'ihłak juutin
tenderloin	tth'e'tthai'
tendons	ch'at
tendons, his	vich'at
tent	zhehgwadhòh
tent (round)	nèevyaa zheh
termites (woodworm)	dachan ahghòo
tern (Arctic)	ch'itr'ùu
testicles, his	vaghòo
Thanksgiving	Hai' Gwintl'atr'ada'aii Drin
they said	akoo diginuu
thick bushes	gwàatr'al
thimble	vizhìt nilèetth'ak ii'ee
thirteen (13)	ch'ihłak juutin ts'at tik
thirty (30)	tik juutin
Thomas Creek Caribou Fence	Antl'it Tthał
thorn	khoh
thread	ch'ìh
three (3)	tik
three hundred (300)	tik juutin juutin
throat, his	vihdàii
thumb, his	vanchòh

thunder	nèhtanh
Thursday	Drin Daang
Timber Hill	Ts'ìivii Shùh
Timber Mountain (muskrat caught in a trap)	Dzan Ehłai'
timber stand	ehdii
tin can	ch'iitsii tyah
tobacco	ts'èet'it
tobacco (chewing)	ts'èet'it shik tr'alchìt
toboggan	vał, dachàavał
toboggan (skin)	ch'idrèedhòh vał
today	juk drin
toe (big), his	vikaiits'at
toenail, his	vikaiigàii
toes, his	vikaiidràl
tomorrow	nihkàa
tongue	ch'ichyàa, naadoo ts'eh
tongue, his	vichyàa
towel	dòhsròo
trail, path	taii
trap	khyah
trap (steel)	ch'iitsii khyah
trigger	diik'èe kàiidràl
tripe	ch'iidhèeghwàt
truck, car	ch'iitsii khał
Tuesday	Drin Neekaii
tussock	tl'oo hànzhu'
twelve (12)	ch'ihłak juutin ts'at neekaii
twenty (20)	neekòk juutin
twenty-one (21)	neekòk juutin ts'at ch'ihłak
twine, net rope	vah di'ke'tr'ahchùu
two (2)	neekaii
two hundred (200)	neekaii juutin juutin
two thousand (2,000)	neekaii juutin juutin juutin

U

umbilical cord, his	tr'ìinin ch'ìk
uncle (father's brother), my	shitii
uncle (mother's brother), my	shoo'ii
unripe berries	ch'àneeluh
upper arm, his	vidizhùu
uvula, his	vinèevyàa

V

vagina, her	vatsàn
valley	antl'it
veins, his	vich'ùu
velvet on caribou horn	vijì' zhòo
village, place, site	kaiik'it

W

wallet	lazraa dhòh
war, soldiers	navèh
washboard	vakak ch'ik'èech'atr'ahtryàa
washtub	vizhìt ch'ik'èech'atr'ahtryàa
wasp	ch'ineedzit ts'ik
water	chuu
water (calm)	chuu jùughàl
water (clear)	chuu drin'
water (cold)	chuu k'oh
water (dropped)	chuu daa'il
water (glacial)	git chu'
water (hot)	chuu dhah
water (low)	gwìdaiiyùhdlàii
water (overflow)	nataniihaii
water (spring)	k'ǫhnjik chu', daii gwichu'
water (warm)	chuu niingyu'
water beetle	chehtsì'
water hole	tèeddhàa
water lily	tsèe zhìi, kaiitràlt'ùu
water moss	dlìt
waterfall	natąįįlaii
waves	tit
weasel	avii
weather (cold)	ch'ak'oh
weather (stormy)	drijahtsai'
weather (warm)	drin gwiniidhàa
wedge	jah
Wednesday	Drin Tik
week (one)	drin k'ideetak ch'ihłak
weeks (two)	drin k'ideetak neekaii
west wind	dii ahtr'aii
wet snow	zhoh trah
whirlwind	ahtr'aii vii
white	jidii dagaii
white fox	ch'ich'yàa
white man	oonjit
White Snow Mountain	Zhoh Drìn Chòo
whitefish	łuk dagàii
whitefish (broad)	chihshòo
Whitefish Lake	Chihshòo
Whitestone River	Sheihveenjik
Whitestone Village	Chuu Tl'it
widgeon	chàlvii
wife, my	sha'àt, shitr'ìinjòo
wild onion	tl'oodrik
willow	k'àii'
willow (dry)	k'il
willow shoot	k'àii dzhùh
wind	ahtr'aii
wind (chinook)	nagwidhah ìindìi
wind (north)	ee ahtr'aii
wind (south)	nii ahtr'aii
wind (west)	dii ahtr'aii
window	vinjaa'yaa
winter	khaii
winter day (short)	khah zhak
without	ehdanh
wolf	zhòh
Wolf Clan	Ch'ichyàa
wolf cub	zhòh gii
wolverine	nèhtrùh
Wolverine Lake	Nèhtrùh Vavàn
woman	tr'ìinjòo
woman (old)	shanaghàn
womb, her	vats'at
wood	dachan
wood (green)	ts'iivii
wood (kindling)	łuh jik
wood (rotten)	dahshàa
wood chips	łuh chìl
wooden box	dachan tyah
wooden scoop	dachan ch'ik
woodpecker	dachan chyàa
worm	gyuu
worm (black, with white head)	gyùhk'ah
worm in caribou head	ch'anchàl gyù'
worm under caribou skin	ch'ananhgyù
wormwood	gyùhtsanh
writing paper	vakak ch'atr'adantl'òo

Y

yarn	nàazhùk
year (last)	k'eejit khaii
year (next)	yeendoo khaii
year before last	k'eejit khaii gwichih khaii
yearling	khada'ahtsan, khadatsàn
yellow	jidii tsoo
yesterday	k'ehdai'
younger brother, my	shichaa
younger sister, my	shijùu
youth	k'eejit kat

BIBLIOGRAPHY

Acheson, Anne Welsh

1977 Nomads in Town: The Kutchin of Old Crow, Yukon Territory. PH.D. dissertation, Department of sAnthropology, Cornell University, Ithaca, NY.

1981 Old Crow, Yukon Territory. In Volume 6, Subarctic, Handbook of North American Indians. June Helm, ed. Pp. 694-703. Washington, DC: Smithsonian Institution.

Allen, Barbara and William L. Montell

1981 From Memory to History: Using Oral Sources in Local Historical Research. Nashville: The American Association for State and Local History.

Anderson, F.W.

1994[1986] The Saga of Albert Johnson: The Mad Trapper of Rat River. Saskatoon: Gopher Books.

Asch, Michael

1979 The Economics of Dene Self-determination. In Challenging Anthropology. David Turner and Gavin Smith, eds. Toronto: McGraw-Hill Ryerson.

Balikci, Asen

1963 Vuntut Kutchin Social Change: A Study of the People of Old Crow, Yukon Territory. Ottawa: Northern Co-ordination and Research Centre, Department of Northern Affairs and National Resources.

Barbeau, Charles Marius and Charles Camsell
1915   Loucheux myths. collected by Charles Camsell and prepared for publication by Charles Marius Barbeau. Journal of American Folklore 109 (28): 249-257.

Bauman, Richard and Joel Sherzer, eds.
1989   Explorations in the Ethnography of Speaking. Second edition. Cambridge: Cambridge University Press.

Beairsto, Colin
1997   Making Camp: Rampart House on the Porcupine River. MS on file, Yukon Heritage Branch.

Berger, Thomas
1988[1977] Northern Frontier, Northern Homeland: The Report of the Mackenzie Valley Pipeline Inquiry. Revised edition. Vancouver: Douglas and McIntyre.

Bockstoce, John
1986   Whales, Ice and Men: The History of Whaling in the Western Arctic. Seattle: University of Washington Press.

Burch, Ernest S. Jr.
1971   The Non-empirical World of the Arctic Alaskan Eskimos. Southwestern Journal of Anthropology 27(2):148-165.

1981   Studies of Native History as a Contribution to Alaska's Future. Special lecture presented to the thirty-second Alaska Science Conference, Fairbanks, Alaska, August 25, 1981.

1991   From Skeptic to Believer: The Making of an Oral Historian. Alaska History 6(1) Spring 1991.

Cass, E.E.
1959   Some Observations on the Loucheux Indians, Their Customs and Stories. MS and audiotapes. Northern Lights Museum, Fort Smith, NT and Canadian Museum of Civilization, Ottawa.

Cinq-Mars, Jacques
1979   Bluefish Cave: Late Pleistocene Eastern Beringian Cave Deposit in the Northern Yukon. Canadian Journal of Archaeology 3:1-32.

Cinq-Mars, Jacques and Richard. E. Morlan
1999   Bluefish Caves and Old Crow Basin: New Rapport. In Ice Age Peoples of North America. Environments, Origins, and Adaptations of the First Americans. Robson Bonnichsen and Karen L. Turnmire, eds. Pp. 200-212.

Corvallis, OR: Oregon State University Press for the Center for the Study of the First Americans.

Clifford, James
1997   Fort Ross Meditation. In Routes: Travel and Translations in Late Twentieth Century. Cambridge: Harvard University Press.

Coates, Kenneth
1982   Furs Along the Yukon: Hudson's Bay Company-Native Trade in the Yukon River Basin, 1830-1893. B.C. Studies 55:50-78.

1991   Best Left as Indians: Native-White Relations in the Yukon Territory, 1840-1973. Kingston: McGill-Queens University Press.

Coates, K. and W. Morrison
1988   Land of the Midnight Sun: A History of the Yukon. Edmonton: Hurtig.

Cody, H.A.
1913   Apostle of the North: Biography of Archbishop William Carpenter Bompas. New York: Dutton and Co.

Cruikshank, Julie
1990   Life Lived Like a Story: Life Stories of Three Yukon Native Elders. Lincoln: University of Nebraska Press.

1996   Discovery of Gold on the Klondike: Perspectives From Oral Tradition. In Reading Beyond Words: Contexts for Native History. Jennifer Brown and Elizabeth Vibert, eds. Toronto: Broadview.

1998   The Social Life of Stories: Narrative and Knowledge in the Yukon Territory. Lincoln: University of Nebraska Press.

Downs, Art, ed.
2000[1982]   The Death of Albert Johnson, Mad Trapper of Rat River. Nanoose Bay, BC: Heritage House.

Finnegan, Ruth
1970   Oral Literature in Africa. Nairobi: Oxford University Press.

1992   Oral Traditions and the Verbal Arts. London: Routledge.

Gotthardt, Ruth
1990   The Archaeological Sequence in the Northern Cordillera: A Consideration of Typology and Traditions. Occasional Papers in Archaeology No. 1, Heritage Branch, Yukon Tourism. Whitehorse.

Greer, Sheila
1999   Historic Summary (contributions from Colin Beairsto). Rampart House Historic Site, LaPierre House Historic Site: Management Plan. Prepared for the Vuntut Gwitchin First Nation and Government of Yukon. Wells, BC: Ecogistics Consulting.

Greer, Sheila and Raymond Le Blanc
1992   Background Heritage Studies: Proposed Vuntut National Park. Report prepared for Parks Canada. Whitehorse.

Hadleigh-West, Frederick
1963   The Netsi Kutchin: An Essay in Human Ecology. PH.D. dissertation, Department of Geography, Louisiana State University. Ann Arbor, MI: University Microfilms.

Hardisty, William
1872   The Loucheux Indians. In Notes on the Tinneh or Chepewyan Indians of British and Russian America. Annual Report of the Smithsonian Institution for the Year 1866. Washington, DC.

Harington, C. Richard
1989   Pleistocene Vertebrate Localities in the Yukon. In Late Cenozoic History of the Interior Basins of Alaska and the Yukon. L. David Carter, T.D. Hamilton and J.P. Galloway, eds. Pp. 93-98. U.S. Geological Survey Circular 1026. Washington, DC: United States Government Printing Office.

Harington, C. Richard, Robson Bonnichsen, and Richard Morlan
1975   Bones Say Man Lived in Yukon 27,000 Years Ago. Canadian Geographical Journal 91(1-2):42-48.

Helm, June and Beryl Gillespie
1981   Dogrib Oral Tradition as History: War and Peace in the 1820s. Journal of Anthropological Research 37:8-27.

Hensel, Chase
1996   Telling Our Selves: Ethnicity and Discourse in Southwestern Alaska. New York: Oxford University Press.

Hughes, Owen L.
1989   Quaternary Chronology, Yukon and Western District of Mackenzie. In Late Cenozoic History of the Interior Basins of Alaska and the Yukon. L. David Carter, T.D. Hamilton, and J.P. Galloway eds. Pp. 25-29. U.S. Geological Survey Circular 1026.

Ingram, R. and H. Dobrowolsky
1989   Waves Upon the Shore: An Historical Profile of Herschel Island. Whitehorse: Yukon Heritage Branch.

Irving, William and Jacques Cinq-Mars
1974   A Tentative Archaeological Sequence for Old Crow Flats, Yukon Territory. Arctic Anthropology 11:65-81.

Jones, Strachan
1872   The Kutchin Tribes. In Notes on the Tinneh or Chepewyan Indians of British and Russian America. Annual Report of the Smithsonian Institution for the Year 1866. Washington, DC.

Josie, Edith
1963   Old Crow News: The Best of Edith Josie. Whitehorse: Whitehorse Star.

1965   Christmas in Old Crow. North 12(6):26-27.

1966   Here Are the News. Toronto: Clark, Irwin.

1970   The Best of Edith Josie, 1969-1970. Whitehorse: Whitehorse Star.

1973   Life in Old Crow Village. Part 1: Old Crow Village. North 20(5):22.

Kassi, Tracy
2003   Personal communication. VGFN Enrollment Information. Biographical information about elders.

Kelley, Thomas P.
1972   Rat River Trapper: The Story of Albert Johnson, the Mad Trapper. Don Mills, ON: Paperjacks.

Kirkby, William
1865   A Journey to the Youcan, Russian America. In Annual Report of the Smithsonian Institution for the Year 1864. Washington, DC.

Larsen, Helge and Froelich Rainey
1948   Ipiutak and the Arctic Whale Hunting Culture. Anthropological Papers of the American Museum of Natural History. 42. New York.

Le Blanc, Raymond J.
1984   The Rat Indian Creek Site and the Late Prehistoric Period in the Interior Northern Yukon. National Museums of Canada, National Museum of Man Mercury Series, Archaeological Survey of Canada Paper No. 120. Ottawa.

1997   The 1997 Archaeological Investigations at New Rampart House, Northern Yukon. MS on file. Yukon Heritage Branch.

Leechman, Douglas
1949   The Vanta Kutchin. National Museums of Canada Bulletin 126, Anthropological Series 33. Ottawa.

McClellan, Catherine
1970   Indian Stories About the First Whites in Northwestern North America. In Ethnohistory in Southwestern Alaska and Southern Yukon: Method and Content. Margaret Lantis, ed. Lexington: University Press of Kentucky.

1981   History of Research in the Subarctic Cordillera. In Volume 6: Subarctic, Handbook of North American Indians. June Helm, ed. Washington, DC: Smithsonian Institution.

McClellan, Catharine, L. Birckel, R. Bringhurst, J.A. Fall, C. McCarthy, and J.R. Sheppard
1987   Part of the Land, Part of the Water: A history of the Yukon Indians. Vancouver: Douglas and McIntyre.

McDonald, Archdeacon Robert
1869   Journal of Archdeacon Robert McDonald. Unpublished manuscript, Archives of the Ecclesiastical Province of Rupert's Land, Manitoba Provincial Archives, Winnipeg.

McKennan, Robert A.
1965   The Chandalar Kutchin. Arctic Institute of North America, Technical Paper 17. Arctic Institue of North America, Calgary.

McSkimming, Robert J.
1973   Territory, Territoriality, and Culture Change in and Indigenous Society: Old Crow, Yukon Territory. Master's thesis, Department of Geography, University of British Columbia, Vancouver.

Mendenhall, T., J. McGrath, and J. Turner
1893   The Alaskan Boundary Survey. The National Geographic Magazine IV, February 8, 1893:177-199.

Mishler, Craig
1973   The Crooked Stovepipe: Athapaskan Fiddle Music and Square Dancing in Northeast Alaska and Northwest Canada. Urbana: University of Illinois Press.

2003   Diving Down: Ritual Healing in the Tale of the Blind Man and the Loon. Arctic Anthropology 40(2):49-55.

Montgomery, Jane, Florence Netro, and Brenda Kay,
2000   Van Tat Gwich'in Ginjik Noun Dictionary. Old Crow, YT: Gwich'in Cultural Society.

Morgan, Lewis Henry
1967[1877]   Ancient Society. Cleveland and New York: Meridian Books.

Morlan, Richard
1973   The Later Prehistory of the Middle Porcupine Drainage, Northern Yukon Territory. National Museums of Canada, National Museum of Man, Archaeological Survey of Canada Paper No.11. Ottawa.

Morlan, Richard, D. Nelson, T. Brown, J. Vogel, and J. Southon
1990   Accelerator Mass Spectrometry Dates on Bones from Old Crow Basin, Northern Yukon Territory. Canadian Journal of Archaeology 14:75-92.

Murray, Alexander Hunter
1910   Journal of the Yukon, 1847-48. Publications of the Canadian archives, No. 4. Government Printing Bureau, Ottawa.

Nabokov, Peter
2002   A Forest of Time: American Indian Ways of History. Cambridge: Cambridge University Press.

Nelson, Richard
1983   Make Prayers to the Raven: A Koyukon View of the Northern Forest. University of Chicago Press, Chicago.

Nelson, D., R. Morlan, J. Vogel, J. Southon, and C. Harington
1991   New Dates on Northern Yukon Artifacts: Holocene not Upper Pleistocene. Science 232(4751):749-751.

Netro, Joe
1973   A book of Indian legends and stories from Old Crow, Yukon Territory. Whitehorse: Whitehorse Star.

North, Dick
1972   Mad Trapper of Rat River. Toronto: McMillan.

1978   The Lost Patrol. Anchorage: Alaska Northwest Publishing Company.

Ong, Walter
1958 Ramus, Method, and the Decay of Dialogue. Cambridge: Cambridge University Press.

1982 Orality and Literacy: The Technologizing of the Word. London: Routledge.

Osgood, Cornelius
1970[1936] Contributions to the Ethnography of the Kutchin. Yale University Publications in Anthropology No. 14. Reprint. New Haven, CT: Human Relations Area Files Press.

Peake, F.A.
1966 The Bishop Who Ate His Boots: A Biography of Isaac O. Stringer. Don Mills, ON: Anglican Church of Canada.

Petitot, Émile
1876 Dictionnaire de la langue Dènè-dindjié. E. Leroux, Paris.

1888 Traditions indiennes du Canada Nord-ouest. Textes originaux et traduction littérale. Alencon: E. Renaut-de Broise.

1889 Quinze ans sous le Cercle Polaire. Tome 1. Mackenzie, Anderson et Youkon. Paris: E. Reuter.

Porter, Dale
1981 The Emergence of the Past: A Theory of Historical Explanation. Chicago: University of Chicago Press.

Richardson, Sir John
1851 Arctic Searching Expedition: a journal of a boat-voyage through Rupert's Land and the Arctic Sea in search of the discovery ships under command of Sir John Franklin London: Longman, Brown, Green, and Longman.

Riggs, Thomas
1945 Running the Alaska Boundary. The Beaver. September 1945:41-42.

Sax, Lee and Effie Linklater
1990 Gikhyi: One Who Speaks the Word of God. True and Remarkable Story of the Arctic Kutchin Christian Leaders. Whitehorse: Anglican Diocese of Yukon.

Schneider, William
1995 Lessons from Alaska Natives about Oral Tradition and Recording. In When Our Words Return: Writing, Hearing, and Remembering Oral

Traditions of Alaska and the Yukon. Phyllis Morrow and William Schneider. Logan: Utah State University Press.

2002   So They Understand: Cultural Issues in Oral History. Logan: Utah State University Press.

Schweger, Charles
1989   The Old Crow and Bluefish Basin, Northern Yukon: Development of the Quaternary History. In Late Cenozoic History of the Interior Basins of Alaska and the Yukon. Washington, DC: U.S. Geological Survey Circular 1026: 30-33.

Sherry, Erin and Vuntut Gwitchin First Nation
1999   The Land Still Speaks: Gwitchin Words about Life in Dempster Country. Old Crow, YT: Vuntut Gwitchin First Nation.

Simpson, Sir George
1845   Letter to John Bell, dated Ft. McPherson, August 1, 1845. HBC Archives, Winnipeg.

Slobodin, Richard
1962   Band Organization of the Peel River Kutchin. National Museum of Canada Bulletin No. 179, Department of Northern Affairs and National Resources, Canada.

1971   Without Fire: A Kutchin Tale of Warfare, Survival and Vengeance. In Proceedings: Northern Athapaskan Conference. A. McFadyen Clark, ed. Vol. 1. National Museum of Man, Mercury Series, Ethnology Service Paper 27. Ottawa.

1981   Kutchin. In Volume 6, Subarctic, Handbook of North American Indians. June Helm, ed. Pp. 515-532. Washington, DC: Smithsonian Institution.

Stager, John
1974   Old Crow, Y.T. and the Proposed Northern Gas Pipeline. Report of the Environmental-Social Committee, Task Force on Northern Oil Development, 74-21. Ottawa.

Stefansson, Vilhjalmur
1922   Hunters of the Great North. New York: Harcourt, Brace and Co.

Tedlock, Dennis
1983   The Spoken Word and the Work of Interpretation. Philadelphia: University of Pennsylvania Press.

Te'sek Gehtr'oonatun Zzeh, Students

1997   Recollections: Old Crow Elders Tell of Change in the Community. An oral history project by the students of Te'sek Gehtr'oonatun Zzeh. Old Crow, YT.

Thornthwaite, Corporal Arthur

     Audio interview. Collection Part 5 (61-2). Yukon Archives.

Vansina, Jan

1961   Oral Tradition: A Study in Historical Methodology. Translated from French by H M. Wright. London: Routledge and Kegan Paul.

1985   Oral Tradition as History. Madison: University of Wisconsin Press.

Vuntut Gwich'in First Nation

1995a   LaPierre House Oral History: Interviews with Vuntut Gwitchin Elders. Prepared for Parks Canada by Vuntut Gwitchin First Nation. Old Crow, YT.

1995b   Oral History in the Porcupine-Peel landscape. Porcupine-Peel Landscape: Traditional Values Study. Yukon Government Contract #SS-9413-3037-00752. Old Crow, YT.

Vuntut Gwitchin First Nation Heritage Committee

1999   Heritage Committee Report, first meeting. February 23, 1999.

Wallis, Velma

1993   Two Old Women: An Alaskan Legend of Betrayal, Courage and Survival. New York: HarperPerrenial.

Wright, Allen

1992   Prelude to the Klondike. Sidney, BC: Gray's Publishing.

INDEX

Italic locators indicate illustrations; "n" indicates endnotes.

Abel, Alice, *167*
Abel, Charlie, *83*, 205, 210, 280
Abel, Johnny, *167*, 280
Abel, Mrs. Charlie, *206*
Abel, Sarah
    life of, 62, 66-67
    pictures of, *17, 42*
    quotations, xiv, 23, 30, 34, 41-42, 44-48, 56-57, 64-68, 78, 84, 93, 99, 110, 111-14, 132, 147-48
    teaching about trapping, 293
    telling stories, 272, 293
airplanes, *lvi*, 134, 183, 219, 286
airports and airstrips, lxi, 219, 244, 280
Aklavik, 197, 198, 199, 245, 247, 249
Alaska
    American purchase of, li, 240
    Ch'ineekaii in, xlvii
    Hudson's Bay Company in, 126
    location of, *lviii*
    oil industry in, lxi
    people of, 65, 105, 109-10, 163, 181, 226, 256, 315n20
    trade routes through, 118
    U.S. purchase of, 118, 142
    wildlife reserve, xxxii
    see also international border

alcohol, 285
Alexie family, 238-39
ammunition, xlix, 120, 123, 130, 131, 152, 201
ancestors, connection with, 284-85, 291-92, 299-302
Anglicanism, lii-liv, lxi, 64, 119, 137, 230
animals
    attacking people, 7-8, 12, 14, 15, 17-18, 276
    characteristics of explained, 6-7, 12-16
    Ch'ataiiyuukaih changing, xli, xlv
    conservation of, xxxii, *lviii*, lxi, 16, 185, 194, 260-62, 268, 284, 302, 322n9
    conversations with people, 17-18, 20, 276
    cycles of, 183, 205, 288, 290, 305-06
    dreaming to, 34, 111, 113, 117-18, 141, 319n20
    medicine animals, 140
    modern, xlv
    populations, 119, 163, 168, 212, 227, 230, 262, 279, 280
    prehistoric, xli, xlii, xliv-xlvi
    respect for, 261
    see also animals by name
Anthony, Harry, 136
anthropologists, 12, 21, 313n1(preface)
Antl'it Tthał
    cache at, 11, *296*
    camp at, 254
    and *Diniizhòo*, 184
    location of, *lviii*, 88, 251, 253, 277
    ruins of, 222, 223, 254, *273*
    stories about, 282
    use of, 89, 251, 253-54
archaeology
    and hunting, xlvii
    in Old Crow, 317n7
    reports on, xxxvii-xxxviii
    research, xl, xliv-xlvi, 254, *273*, 282, 314n9-10
    stories related to sites, 4
Archdeacon McDonald Memorial Church, 145
archetypes, 41-51
Arctic National Wildlife Refuge, *lviii*
Arctic Red River (Tsiigehtchic)
    Christianity at, lii
    current name of, 315n3
    people of, 106, 142, 186
    in stories, 13
    travels to, 116, 188

Arctic Village
    caribou migration, xxviii, 153
    people of, 4, 76, 84, 126, 131, 153, 186, 218, 238, 254
    stories set in, 51
arrows. *See* bows and arrows

Baalam, Sarah, *104*, 282
babiche
    making, 91, 95, 220, 281, 317n6
    for sale, 74, 75, 220
    using, 81, 91, *95*, 99, 123, 191
Balaam, 127-28
bannock, 96, 125, 126, 256
baptisms, 143, 144, 147, 314n18, 320n2
barges, 77
baskets, 281, 282
beads
    beadwork, xxxix, xlviii, *l*, 25, 40, *109*, 114, 188, 220
    as valuables, xlix, lii, 29, 315n16, 316n16
Bear Cave Mountain
    bears at, 316n20
    caves in, xlv, 239, 240
    history of, 282
    location of, *lviii*, *193*
    names of, 322n7
    pictures of, *12*, *239*
    stories set at, 37, 39, 173, 240
bears
    attacking people, 276
    black, 93, 185
    breaking into caches, 214
    brown, 14
    fishing, 239, 316n20
    grizzly, 17-18, 39, 41, 45-46, 93, 185, 190, 209-10, 213, *239*
    hunting, 16, 18, 93, 239
    "ice bears", 210, 305, 316n20
    people impersonating, 39
    scaring, 228
beaver
    hunting, 207, 210-11, 288, 294
    stories about, 5-6
    uses of, 26
beliefs, pre-Christian, 137, 138
Bell River, *lviii*, 75, 173, *193*
Benjamin, Jason, 263

Benjamin, Martha, *244*
Benjamin, Peter, 207, *208*
Berger Inquiry. *See* Mackenzie Valley Pipeline Inquiry
Berger, Thomas, xxxi, 262
Beringia, xli, 314n5
berries
    importance of, 251
    places for, 189, 191, 242, 253, 281
    seasons for, 76, 187, 306
    storage of, 281
    types, 209, 281
    women and children picking, 143, 165, 209
Berry Creek caribou fences, *lviii*, 88, *193*
betrayal, 19-20
the Bible, xxxviii, 137, 141, 143
Big Nest Mountain, *213*
Birch Creek, location of, *xxvii*
birchbark
    canoes, 15, 74, 83, 142
    dishes, 102
    water containers, 20
birds
    populations of, 168, 262
    stories about, 6-7, 12-14, 16, 314n3
Black Fox Creek
    caribou fences, *lviii*, 88, 180, *252*, *254*, 282-84, 322n8
    name of, 217
    people of, 168, 178, 179-80, 211, 228
    pictures of, *7*, *295*
    travel to, 261, 299
Black River
    location of, *xxvii*
    missionaries at, 144, 145
    name of, 180
    people of, 73, 133, 135, 180
    stories at, 23
    trapping at, 115, 180
    travels to, 76, 77, 144
Blackfox, John, 180
Blackfox, William, 319n30
Blackfox, Margaret, *45*
Blackfox, Mrs., *80*
Blackstone, 205, 243, 257
blankets
    caribou-skin, 26, 30, 70, 148, 188

    Hudson's Bay Company, 133
    for transportation, 69, 70, 82
Blind Man and the Loon, 4, 19-20
blindness, 19-20
blood soup, 84
blueberries, 209, 281
Bluefish Caves, xlv, *lviii*
Bluefish River, 163, 173, 211, 213, 215, *297*, 299
boats
    canvas, xix, *103*, 105, 169-70, 180, 279, 288, *289*, 292
    in the fur trade, 122, 124-26, 154
    for hunting, 203, 246
    launches, 117, 137
    launching, *lvii*
    making, 103, 169, *171*, 179, 180, 234, 257, 279, 288, *289*, 292
    motors, xix, 104, 105, 201, 211, 217, 246, 304
    moving buildings, 154
    pictures of, *63*, *73*, *83*, *85*, *103*, *181*, *252*
    rafted together, 318n13
    rowing, 152, 229
    scows, 133, 155-56
    skin, xlvi, 74, 234, 245, 257
    tracking, 124, 130, 133, 155-56, 199, 246, 319n26
    traders', 130, 131
    travel by, 210, 211, 217, 235, 245, 279
    see also canoes; rafts; steamboats
Bompas, W.C. (Bishop), liv, 51, 125, 142, 144-45, 153, 307
bone grease
    making, 74-76, 186, 261, 281, 286, 288
    for trade, 190
bone juice, 29
bones, xliv, 83, 91, 99, 107, 166, 261, 300
border. *See* international border
boundary. *See* international border
bows and arrows
    hunting with, xxix, 15, 19, 71, 74, 82, 93, 95, 165, 278, 284, 307
    making, 29
    pictures of, *l*, *25*, *310*
    as poor people's weapons, 74, 82
    for war, 55, 107
Boy in the Moon, xlvii, 9, 11, 67
British Empire Medal, *lix*, 110, 115
brothers, 35, 40, 274
Bruce, Billy, 288

Bruce, Ellen
    family, 195, 249
    pictures of, *19*
    quotations, 19-20, 164-66, 180-81, 232-33, 256
Bruce, Frances, *268*, *295*
Bruce, Robert, lii
Bruce, Robert Jr., *xxxiv*, *252*, *271*, *272*, *276*, 280-81, *285*, 287-91, *292*, 300
Bruce, Robert Sr., 285
Bruce, Shawn, 289
Burnt Hill, 179, 236
bushmen, 47-51, 307, 316n14

cabins. *See* houses
caches
    of berries, 281
    at caribou fences, 91, 254-55, *296*
    destroyed by bears, 214
    elevated, *162*, 255, *296*
    of fish, 86, 166, 242
    ground, 78, 79, 86, 189, 190, 214, *268*, 283, 286
    log, 91, *162*, *296*
    natural refrigeration in, 79, 189, 306
    process, 237
    at tents or houses, 281, 319n25
    see also death rituals
Cadzow, Dan
    about, lxi, 134, *135*
    arrival of, 233
    church building, 132
    employees, 133
    at Old Crow, 133
    origin of, 133
    at Rampart House, liv, 115, 130, 131-35, 155-56, 164, 180, 213, 217-19, 319n21
    reputation, 217, 220
    sharing food, 220
Cadzow, Rachel, lxi, 134, 282, 319n30
camps
    modern, lxii
    pictures of, *96*
    seasonal, 279
    setting up, 66-67
    sites of, *96*, 288-89, 290, 292, 294, 297
    visiting at, 169

Camsell, Charlie, 155
candles, 147, 231
Canoe River, 209, 236
    see also Chance Creek
canoes
    fishing in, 166
    hunting in, 83, 103, 183, 231, 236, 289
    in long-ago stories, 8, 12-13, 15
    making, 15, 74, *75*, 83, 84, 145
    pictures of, *77*, *182*
    travel by, *75*, 142, 209
    see also boats
canvas. *See* boats; tents
Carcross School, 152
caribou
    characteristics of, 257, 260-61
    collars, 261-62
    cooking, 73, 260, 261, *269*
    importance of, *xxxiii*, *xlvii*, 260
    migration, *xxviii–xxix*, 78, 86, 91, 236, 257, 260-62, 294, 305
    people transformed into, *xlvii*
    pictures of, *xlvi*, *96*, *235*
    population, *xxviii*, 186, 236, 262
    relationship with, 109
    respect for, 261
    seasonal changes, 257
    snaring, 82, 83, 89-91, 93, 94, *95*, 261, 284
    types of, 237, 322n34
    uses of, 24, 26, 42, 55, 73, 74, 83, 165, 187, 261, 281, 286
    see also caribou fences; caribou hunting; caribou skins; hides; meat drying; Porcupine caribou herd
caribou fences
    archaeology of, *xl*, 314n10
    caches at, 91, 254-55, *296*
    and caribou trails, *xxix*
    decline of, 89, 90, 251
    described, 86, *87*, 160, 254
    early accounts of, 89
    locations of, *xxvii*, *xxix*, *lviii*, *88*, 94, 165, 180, 190, *193*, 251, 253, 254, 278
    making, 68, 86, 89, 95, 272
    mending, *xxix*, 91, 251, 254
    names of, 251

368   *Index*

ownership of, 91
preservation of, xxxiii
productivity of, 89, 91, 92, 129-30
recounting the history of, 160
ruins of, 90, *252*, 273
seasonal, 68-70, 86, 89-92
in stories, 9, 23
summer, 86-87, 90-91, 317n6
using, xxix, 90, 93, 94, 165, 254, 261, 284, 307, 318n10
see also Antl'it Tthał
caribou hunting
    pictures of, *xlvi, 73, 85*
    in rivers, 74, 78, 83, 189, 278
    seasons for, 68-70, 165, 172, 235, 261
    selection, 260
    sites, 203, 207, 236, 280
    in stories, 9, 11
    for trade, liv, 122, 123, 257, 261
    transporting the kill, 203
    see also caribou fences
Caribou Lookout, lxi, 173, 246, 278
"Caribou Month", 68
caribou skins
    clothing, 24, 66, 70, 76, 81, 82, 165-66, 261, 284, 317n6
    cooking in, 71
    eating, 77, 85
    preparing, 74-76, 81, 95, 121, 166, *207*, 211, 232, 317n6
    for trade, 74, 75, 77, 119
    for transportation, 82
    using, 94, 165
    see also babiche
Carroll, Nellie, 134
catechists, 142, 145, 155
Catholic Church. *See* Roman Catholic Church
caves, xlv, *lviii*, 213
celebrations. *See* Christmas; marriage; New Year's
Chance Creek, 204, 236
    see also Canoe River
Ch'anchàl. *See* King Edward Mountain
change
    approach to, xxxvi, 251, 268
    degree of, 62-63, 160-61, 163, 284, 285, 287, 307-09
    technologies and tools, 78, 127-29, 304, 309
    in travel, 219
Charlie, Alfred

    camp, 322n4
    as chief, xxx
    family, xxx
    home, 197, 235, 257
    hunting, 207
    pictures of, *12, 72, 177, 235, 271*
    quotations, xii, xiii-xiv, xviii, xxviii-xxix, xxx-xxxi, 13-14, 128-29, 179-80, 194, 225, 234-36, 238-40, 246, 247, 263, 305, 317n6
Charlie, Andrew, 72
Charlie, Charlie Peter, 72, *171*, 191-92, 236-38, *237*
Charlie, Cheryl, 299, *310*
Charlie Creek, 208
Charlie, Dorothy, *72*
Charlie family. *See* Tetlichi-Charlie family
Charlie, Fanny, *237*, *268*, 299, 300
Charlie, John
    family, 238
    giving feasts, 117, 118
    home of, 201, 207, 235
    hunting, 207
    pictures of, *lvii*
    trapping, 218
Charlie, Kathie, *298*, 300
Charlie, Lazarus, 72, 199, 201, *201*, 207, 279
Charlie, Mary, 71, *72*, 134
Charlie, Peter, *lvii*, 71, *72*, 106
    giving feasts, 117
    home of, 207, 211, 235, 238, 257
    hunting, 117-18, 203, 207
    and illnesses, 134
    telling stories, 271
Charlie, Peter Sr., *80*, 170
Ch'ataiiyuukaih, xli, xlv, 12-16, 315n2, 315n4, 315n5
Ch'eeghwalti', 109, 111, 113-14, 188, 272, 317n9, 320n12
Chief Zzeh Gittlit School, 109
chiefs
    named, xxx, xlix, lix, lxi, 66, *83*, 108-10, 123, 171, 172, 207
    non-Gwich'in, 123-24
    use of the word, 170, 172
    see also leaders; trading chiefs
children
    education, 151-53
    growing up, 14-15
    hunting, 152

learning, 64, 86, 138, 179, 183, 190, 203, 253, 269, 276, 281-82, 292-94, 297, 300-01. *See also* education; school
and parents' names, 320n12
playing, 169, 225
relationships with fathers, 195
and surnames, 320n2
transporting, *xxxix*, 78, 103, 105, 132, 147, 165, 199
trapping, 217
treats for, 165-66, 217, 231
work of, 69, 86, 114
see also education
Ch'ineekaii
at *Antl'it Tthał*, 254
camps, *53*
conflict with, *xlvii*, 23-25, 30-35, 51, 53-55, 93, 107, 224, 312
at Herschel Island, 223
location of, *xxvii*
meaning of term, 314n11
peace with, 55, 107-08, 131, 224
songs, 116
trade with, *xlviii*, *liv*, 119-20, 190, 307, 314n16
in *Van Tat*, *xlvii*, 104, 106, 168, 181, 223, 224-25
Chitze, Old Abel, *108*
Chitzi family, 111
Christianity, xix-xx, 137, 140
see also churches; religion
Christmas
celebrations at, 164, 172, 202, 207
Christmas trees and Santa Claus, 231
games at, 207
gatherings for, 225
presents, 184
supplies for, 131, 172, 207
Church Missionary Society, lii
churches
collection in, 151
helpers in, 147, 151
hymns, *303*
at Old Crow, *lx*, 145-46, 155, 156, 231-33, 243
people's relationship with, 230
pictures of, *146*
services, 147-48, 169, 195, 232
workers' travel, 137, 142, 150-51, 153
see also religion

Chyah Ddhàa, 99, 179, 184, 191, 224, 318n11
Circle, Alaska, 77, 109, 272, 274
clan system, 13-14, 49, 320n2
climate, 305
clothing
beaver-skin, 26
caribou-skin, 24, 66, 70, 76, 81, 82, 165, 166, 261, 284, 317n6
children's, *xxxix*, 9, 76, 166
coats, 26
in courtship ritual, 275
decoration, *xxxix*, 40, 188, 256. *See also* beadwork
fabric, 76, 82, 133, 220
footwear, *17*, *80*, *81*, *101*, *146*, 165, 188, 220, 244, 253, 256, 286
fur, 220
men's, *xlviii*, 24, *25*, 92, 109, *128*, 133, *146*, *149*, *201*
mitts, 26, *146*, 165, 188, 220
rabbit-skin, 27, 66, 76
for sale, 220
season for making, 76
sheep-skin, 81
trade goods, *lii*, 133, 220
washing, 181
women's, *xxxix*, *l*, *10*, *17*, *45*, *48*, *80*, *128*, 133, *161*, 165, 188, 256
clubs, 25, 32, 34-37, 55
Co-op, 137
Cody, Bill, 132
Cody Creek, xxx, 204, 260, 271
Cody Hill, 191
Communion services, 151
competitions, 190
conflicts
social, 21
see also war
conservation
of animals, *xxxii*, *lviii*, lxi, 16, 185, 194, 260-62, 268, 284, 302, 322n9
of heritage, *xxxii*, lxii, 268, 291-94, 297, 299-301
of the land, xxxiii, 194, 251, 263, 284, 293, 302
of water, xxxiii, 262, 284, 302
cooking
caribou, 73, 260, 261, *269*
methods, 70-71, 74, 78, 84, 86, 102, 255-56, 274-75

370   Index

moose, 35
rabbits, 47, 48, 76, 125
utensils, *l*, 70-71, 78
while travelling, 84
Cook's Camp, *252*, 292
co-operation
as continuing value, 64, 72, 84, 111, 137-38, 306-07, 311
food collection, 61-62
making things, 281
operating caribou fences, 89-91, 93
sharing land, 197, 199
see also sharing food
councillors, 172
counting, 54
cranberries, 209, 281
credit. *See* debt and credit
Crow, Edward, 191
Crow Flats. *See* Van Tat
Crow May I Walk, lxi, 108-09, 110, 154, 318n16
Crow Mountain, 165, 179, 183, 184, *235*, 280-81, 314n8
Crow River
course of, 320n6, 320n9
fishing at, 99
gathering at, 186, 192
location of, *xxvii*
name, 108, 320n10
pictures of, *174-75, 177, 181, 252*
travel on, 279
travel to, 215
crows, 6-7, 12-13
customs checkpoints, 241, 242

Daachilti', 53-55
Dagoo Gwich'in
dispersal of, xxix-xxxi, lxi, 154, 192, 194, 233-36, 238, 310
individuals, 62, 106, 238
language, xxxviii, 137
location of, *xxvii*, 234, 236-40
ministers serving, 150
stories, 314n12
territory, xxx-xxxi, lxi, 192, *193*, 299
trading sites, liv
trapping, lvii
travelling to hunt, 192, 253

dances
on arrival at *Van Tat*, 180
at Christmas and New Year's, 116, 164, 184, 202, 207
clothing for, 188, 220, 256
at feasts, 76, 116, 117
at Old Rampart House, 125
traditional, *xlviii*, xlix, 187-88
David Lord Creek, 117, 135, 143, 226, 228
Dawson
move to, lxi, 232, 238, 256-57
in stories, 15
travel to, 219, 234, 245, 246, 257, 305
see also Klondike Gold Rush
death
burial sites, 113, *218*
graves, 113, 209, *218*, 254, 285
grieving, 179
rituals, 20, 99, 105, 316n14
suicide, 39-40
debt and credit, 134, 168-69, 226, 288
deception, 19-20
Deetru' K'avihdik. See Crow May I Walk
Deetru', Myra, 282
Dempster Highway area, xli, 234, 261-62, 280
Dempster, Sergeant, 219
Dendoo Gwich'in, *xxvii*
Dene, 30
depopulation, liv, 64, 65, 89, 90, 93, 183, 309
Depression, 161, 226, 233, 247
Diniizhòo
gathering on, 183, 186, 189-90, 192, 300
location of, 98
name, 320n11
people at, 184
pictures of, *187, 268, 291, 295, 301, 310*
visiting, 300-01
diseases
instances of, liv, lvi-lvii, 63, 133, 241, 245, 314n14
and move to Old Crow, lvii
and population decline, 91, 309
dishes, 78, 79, 83, 102
dog teams
breaking trail for, 114, 201, 219
decline of, 219, 246, 287
eroding trails, 280

harnesses, 281, 282
Hudson's Bay Company, 126
hunting with, 260, 292
mail, 114, 227
modern use of, 269, 294
pictures of, *xxxv*, 67, 92, 223
racing, *244*
school attendance and use of, 246
travel with, 18, 67, 105, 131-32, 144, 168, 178, 180, 201, 207, 215, 217-18, 222, 245, 246

dogs
carrying packs, 68, 75, 76, 84, 131, 165, 166, 178, 183, 187, 214, 215, 261
characteristics of, 26
damage by, 282
feed for, 74, 166, 168, 172, 194-95, 242, 260
fighting, 199
finding the way, 222
hunting with, 202
listening to a radio, 183
numbers of, 24
pictures of, *10, 128*
raising, 282
sounds of, 169
starvation of, 77, 130, 271
summer care of, 246
time before dogs, 67, 70
travelling by boat, *63*, 169, 318n13
see also dog teams

Domas, 89, 253-54, 261
Draanjik Gwich'in, *xxvii*
dreams and dreamers, 34, 111, 113-14, 117-18, 138, 141, 319n20
driftwood, 13, 223, 278
Driftwood caribou fences, *lviii*, *88*, 254, 317n8
Driftwood Village
missionaries at, 143
move from, 173, 243
people at, 66, 163, 164, 169, 176, 194-97, 198, 199, 222
pictures of, *196*
productivity of, 194

drug abuse, 285
drums, 116, 187
drymeat. *See* meat drying
ducks, 121, 130, 168, 176, 253, 286-88, 305

Eagle, Alaska, liv, 113, 192, 201, 234, 238, 248, 256, 257, 305
Eagle Plains, *193*, 205, 236, 238-39, 243
Eagle River, 197, 226, 227, 247, 248, 271
eagles, 16
Easter, 207, 211, 215
education
Gwich'in language and history, xx, xxxiii-xxxiv, 294
and language use, 160
by ministers, 141, 145
modern, xx, 246, 269, 310
self-taught, 137
through stories, 4
traditional, 151
see also literacy; schools

Edward, King, 15
elders
advice for hunting, 165
care of, 61, 77, 84-86, 114, 115, 125, 137-38, 151, 194, 197, 207
fishing, 46-48, 97, 102
food for, 51
learning from, 64, 86, 138, 179, 183, 190, 203, 253, 269, 276, 281-82, 292-94, 297, 300-01
making toboggans, 81, 102
pensions, 244
relationship with youth, 274, 293-301
warnings of, 41, 45-46

electricity, 280
English language
and intermarriage, 160
learning, 151, 152, 160, 162
Old Crow dialect, xxxvi
use of, xxxv, 270, 305

entertainment, 4
epidemics. *See* diseases
episodic stories, 4
ethics. *See* values
ethnology, xxxvii-xxxviii
explorers, 229

families
brothers, 35, 40, 274
food sharing, 74
and the international border, 241
kin-based social system, 13-14, 49, 320n2

372   Index

relationships in, 111, 256, 274-76, 316n16, 322n1
size of, 64
territories of, 194, 253, 288, 289, 320n4
travelling together, 320n4
visiting, 219, 241
see also clan system; intermarriage; marriage; matrilineal identity

feasting
activities at, 76
after buying imported food, 77
after hunting, 23, 116-18, 274
food for, 73, 76, 207, 255-56
at funerals, 105
little feasts, 86
as seasonal activities, 164, 169, 300
as sharing, 307
sponsors of, 108, 117, 118, 184, 195, 256
see also Christmas; New Year's

fiddling, 76, 116, 202
filmmaking, 268, 269, 302
fire
in homes, 66, 72-73, 82, 86, 128, 147, 318n16
making, 26, 46, 56-57, 74, 79, 143, 240
transporting, 27
see also stoves

firearms. *See* guns
firewood
collection, 62, 207
driftwood, 223
for ministers, 125
modern use of, 160, 251, 269, 294
pictures of, *lvii, 10, 45, 101*
steamboat fuel, 173, 229, 257
wood chips, 86

Firth, John, lii, 81, 94, 123-24, 220, 307, 317n5
Firth, Mary, 19
Firth River, 222, 223
fish
caches, 86, 166, 242
cooking, 84, 99, 102
dog feed, 168, 184, 194-95, 242
drying, 48, 76, 79, 84, 101, 124, 164, 166, 172, 184, 186, 242
frozen, 101, 194, 242
oil, 102
relationship with, 109

for trade, 124, 135
see also fishing; salmon

fish and wildlife regulations, 241
Fish Hook Town, 135
Fish Lake, 139-40
fishing
activity for the elderly and infirm, 46, 97, 102, 242
co-operative, 61
fish hooks, 82, 108
historic remains of, xlvii
lures, *291*
modern, 269
nets, 76, 81, 82, 84, 99, *100*, 123, 166, 304
pictures of, *47*
regulations, 241
seasons for, 166, 172, 179, 184
sites, 99, 130, 154, 176, 179, 191, 194, 195, 205, 234, 274
spearing, 71, 102
trapping, 46, 49-50, 65, 71, 76, 101, 102, 109, 121, 176, 179, 185, 186, 195, 272, 307, 316n21
weirs, *283*
winter, 166
see also fish

Fishing Branch River
bears at, 316n20
fishing at, 205
history of, 282
hunting at, 239
location of, *lviii, 193*
name, 321n17
people of, xxx
pictures of, *38, 283*
protected area, xxxiii
stories set at, 35, 40
trapping at, 204-05, 208-10

Five, Jimmy, 133
Flat Mountain, *259*
Flett, Andrew, lii
Flett, William, lii
flint, 56-57, 79
flood, xli-xliv, 314n7
folktales, lxii, 4
food
co-operative preparation, 67

imported, 56, 61, 68, 74, 77, 94, 123, 125, 132, 133, 145, 163-66, 199, 220, 287
modern diet, lxii, 287
modern gathering of, lxii, 160
preservation, 30, 48, 68, 75, 79, 101, 166, 187, 189, 190, 194, 236, 286, 306. *See also* caches; meat drying
at school, 152
see also berries; cooking; fishing; hunting; pemmican; scarcity; sharing food; starvation

Fort McPherson
church at, 143
founding of, xlviii
Hudson's Bay Company at, liv, 118, 121, 126, 129, 199
location of, lviii, 122
ministers at, 148, 150
move to, lxi, 205, 238
people of, xxx, 55, 75, 106, 109, 115-16, 120, 137, 155, 159, 169, 186, 192, 197, 226, 228, 238, 243
stories from, xliv
traders at, lii, 137
travel to, 173, 176, 198, 201, 219, 220, 234

Fort Simpson, 31, 119, 120

Fort Yukon
fur trade, li, 211, 235, 245, 314n13
hospital at, 232, 245
Hudson's Bay Company at, li, 76, 118, 121, 142, 240-41
location of, 122
missionaries at, 143, 144
people of, 73, 105, 106, 109, 111, 113, 115, 186, 192, 218, 242
stores at, 137, 211
stories at, 23, 130, 235
travel to, 173, 176, 178, 219, 229, 278

Foster, Frank, lvii, 208, 248

four-wheelers, 165

foxes
poisoning, 133
trading, 180, 217
trapping, lvii, 92, 168, 179, 180

Francis, James, *lvii*

Fredson, Annie, *xxxix*, 178

Fredson, Daniel, *xlvi*, 170

Fredson, Donald, 178, *297*, 299

friends
relationship, 274-76
and war, 25-26, 33, 34-35

Frost, Alice, 21, 79, 82-84, 300-01
Frost, Brenda, 273, *310*
Frost, Clara, 160, *217*
Frost, Donald, *177*, 217, *239*
Frost, Ethel, 113
Frost family, 163, 213
Frost, Freddy, 134, 280, *289*
Frost, Harold "Jack", lii, lvi, 75, 160
Frost, Melissa, *295*, 300-01, *310*
Frost, Natasha, *297*, 299
Frost, Sherrie, 273, *296*, *308*, *310*
Frost, Stephen Sr.
pictures of, 7, *216*, *272*, *296*
quotations, 6-7, 211-12, 215, 217

fuel. *See* firewood

fur trade
decline of, 176, 269, 284, 304
disruption due to, xlvii
early, li, 120
economy, lxi, 215, 235, 246, 284, 287
tokens, 215, 217
and Van Tat Gwich'in territory, 118, 305
wage work in, 122, 162, 173
see also furs; trade; trading chiefs; trading posts

furs
clothing, 220
decline in animal populations, 119
fine, lvii, 163, 192, 205
prices, lvii, lxi, 74, 103, 122, 133, 163, 180, 205, 217, 233, 235, 246, 287, 288
processing, *115*
sources, 101

the future
elders' concerns for, 162, 176-78, 253, 270, 280-81, 290-94, 302
jobs, 263
and language, 233
predictions of, 219
recording stories for, 285, 302
use of *Van Tat*, 290
youth on, 293-94, 297, 299-301
see also hard times coming; stories

gambling, 117
game wardens, 241, 261

games, xlix, li, 32, 74, 169, 186-88, 190, 207, *301*, 320n7
gatherings
    places, 169-70, 183-92, 197-99, 205, 278, 299, 300, 309
    seasonal, 274
    see also Christmas; meetings; New Year's; visiting
Geegoo, *98*, 192
Geegooky'uu, *88*, *298*, 300, 323n10
Geenu, 184, 191
generators, 280
generosity. *See* looking after each other
geologists, 261
Giikhii Danahch'. *See* McDonald, Robert
Gilbert Lord Creek, 211
Gilbert, Maggie, 4
glaciers, 70, 314n5
gold rush. *See* Klondike Gold Rush
Goose Camp, 117, 246
government, and development, 263
    see also self-government
Grass Pants, xlvii, 4, 56-57, 316n22
graves, 113, 209, *218*, 254, 285
Grayling Creek, 210, 321n19
Great Depression, 161, 226, 233, 247
Great Slave Lake, 30
Greenland, Bella, 274-76, 281-82
Greer, Sheila, xxxvii-xxxviii, xl-xli
ground squirrels
    animals eating, 190
    hunting, 69, 79, 102, 183, 191, 242, 260
guns
    ammunition, lii, 120, 123, 130, 131, 152, 201
    arrival of, 56-57
    and decline of caribou fences, 89, 90
    early, 74, 94
    earning in fur-trade work, 122
    hunting with, 57, 127, 202, 239, 275-76, 304, 309
    pictures of, *25*
    trading for, lii, 75, 120, 122, 127, 130, 217, 282
    types of, 152
Gwatl'ahti', 127, 129
Gwichaa Gwich'in, *xxvii*, 106, 278
Gwich'in language
    characteristics of, xxxviii-xl, 160
    protection of, 268, 294
    publications in, xix-xx, xxxviii, *303*
    spelling, xix-xx, xxxvii, xxxviii, 314n4, 315n2, 317n2, 320n8
    structure of, xxxvi
    teaching, xxxiii-xxxiv, 233, 294
    use of, 160, 162, 210, 219, 270, 305
    value of, 233
    varieties of, 106, 257, 322n28
Gwich'in Social and Cultural Institute, 21
Gwichya Gwich'in, *xxvii*, 21, 142

hairstyles, *25*, *33*, 179, 191, 318n11
Hän, xlvii, liv, 106, 116, 223, 257
hard times coming, 176, 290, 293-94, 306
Harrington, C.R., *xlii*
healing
    by doctors, 314n14
    medicine, 134
    by medicine men and women, 138, 139, 140
    by missionaries, 143, 144
    see also nurses
health
    care of infirm people, 84
    quality of, 268, 270, 290, 302
    transportation to services, 245
    see also diseases; healing; hospitals; medicine; nurses
Healy, Harry, 168, 215
Here Are the News, xiii, *5*
heritage, conservation of, lxii, 268, 291-94, 297, 299-301
heroes, 41, 282
    see also legendary narratives
Herschel Island
    location of, *lviii*
    people of, 53-55, 119, 179, 225
    pictures of, *221*
    RCMP at, *222*
    trading at, 114, 118, 119, 129-31, 190, 220, 305, 309
    travel to, 173, 176, 184, 219-23
    whalers at, liv, 118, 129, 131, 309
hibernation, 305, 316n20
hides
    modern work with, 233
    preparation of, *17*, *80*, 166, 188, 190, *205*, 220, 232, 234, 281
    for trade, 198, 220, 240
    see also caribou skins; moose
historic sites, xxxii, xl, 314n15

history
    oral, xv-xvi, 268, 302-03, 313n3, 322n11
    sources of, 268
    stories, 21, 51-57, 62, 160
    see also prehistory
homes. *See* houses
horses, 242
Horton and Morris Company, 134, 135, 155
hospitals, 133, 232, 241, 245
houses
    Hudson's Bay Company, 127
    log, *xxxv*, xlvi, *lix*, *17*, *43*, *72*, 72, *80*, *128*, 135, 146, *171*, *173*, *196*, *205*, *298*, *308*
    moss, xlvi, 173
    round, xlix, 86, 92, 128, 147, 166, 173
    seasonal use of, lvii
    snow, 69
    sod, 81
    use of fire in, 66, 72-73, 82, 86, 128, 147, 318n16
    winter, *10*, 72-73
    see also tents
Howling Dog Village
    ministers at, 142
    traders at, li, 118, 121, 124, 126
Hudson's Bay Company
    arrival of, xlviii, 118, 121, 122, 305
    boats, 124-25, 126
    buildings, 127, 154
    buying from, 61, 94
    dances at stores, 76
    departure of, liv, 126, 129-30, 142, 305, 309
    and dog teams, 67
    Gwich'in people's relationship with, 126, 130
    and the international border, 154, 240
    missionaries travelling with, 137
    and Russian traders, li
    sharing food, 125
    stock at, 61, 66, 74, 122, 133, 199, 220
    supplies for staff, 125, 126-27
    transporting goods, 123, 126
    see also trading chiefs
hunting
    with dogs, 202
    elders' advice, 165
    with guns, 57, 127, 202, 239, 275-76, 304, 309

    and the international border, 241-42
    leaders' roles, 110, 111, 114-16
    learning about, 281-82, 292, 293-94
    medicine men and women's roles, 138, 141, 260
    modern, 269
    moose, 18, 19, 76, 93, 117-18, 124, 130, 191, 194, 203, 215, 235-37, 242, 246, 260, 281
    organizing, 170, 172
    regulations, 241, 261
    selling meat, 257, 261
    small game, 61, 93, 104, 176, 185, 191, 255
    on snowmobiles, 260
    travel for, 44, 68, 70, 93, 101, 132, 153, 173, 176, 183, 188, 195, 199, 237, 261
    travelling by airplane, 183, 286
    while trapping, 209
    see also caribou; conservation

identity, xxx, lxii, 299-302, 320n2
infirm people, care of, 84
    see also health
intermarriage
    examples of, lii-lvi, 123, 179, 226, 227-29
    and language, 160
    RCMP, 229
    traders, lii, 304
    trappers, liv, 227-28, 304
international border
    arrival of, 119, 240
    crossing, 114, 215
    effects of, lvii, 114, 153, 213, 233, 240-43, 288, 309
    enforcement of, 240, 241, 242
    location of, *lviii*
    see also surveyors
International Boundary Survey, lvi-lvii
Inuit. *See Ch'ineekaii*
Inuvialuit. *See Ch'ineekaii*
Irving, Bill, 254, 317n7
Itsi family, 111
Itsi, William, 12, 21, 205
Ivvavik National Park, xxxii, *lviii*, lxi

Jackson, Frank, 226
Jackson, Jim, lvii, 131, 134-36, 168, 197-99, 208, 210, 215, 217, 225, 226, 228

376 *Index*

Jackson, John, lvii, 134, 135, 136, 199
Jhudi, Balaam, 127-28
jobs, 263
    see also wage work
John Nukon Village, 209
Johnson, Albert, lix, lxi, 138, 233-34, 247-50, 304
Johnson Creek (upper Porcupine River), 139, *193*, 226, 249, 255, 280, 321n26
Johnson Creek (in *Van Tat*), 226, 321n26
Johnson Creek Village (*Kâachik*)
    decline of trapping, lxi, 212
    hunting at, 238
    location of, *lviii*, *193*, 201
    move from, 212, 243, 246
    people of, 135, 163, 173, 199, 201-02, 215, 234-35, 238
    pictures of, *200*, *203*
    population of, 129
    stores at, 118
    trapping at, lvii, 226
Johnson (storekeeper in Old Crow), 155
Josie, Amos, 205
Josie, Dolly, 250
Josie, Edith
    Dagoo origin, 238
    family, 209
    homes, 209
    interpretations by, 79, 81, 86, 94, 95, 315n3
    newspaper column, xiii, xxxi, 268
    pictures of, *5*, *298*
    quotations, 5-8, 7-8, 14-16, 245
    writing style, 12
Josie, Paul, 135, 201, 205, 222, 236, 281
Josie, Tammy, *298*, 299

Kâachik. *See* Johnson Creek Village
K'aiiheenjik, 282
K'ashih. *See* Kassi
Kassi, Ben, *112*, 197, 232
Kassi, Ben Jr., *112*
Kassi, Charlie, *112*
Kassi, Eliza, *112*
Kassi, Eliza Ben, *112*, 281
Kassi, Hannah, *112*
Kassi, Harvey, *289*
Kassi, Mary

    family, 319n35
    home, 209, 279
    pictures of, *161*, *177*, *196*
    quotations, 114, 186-91, 242
Kassi, Paul Ben, 168, 205, 281
Kay, Brenda, 237
Kaye, Big Joe, 154, 195, 197, 207
Kaye, Elias, 197
Kaye (Kyikavichik) family
    alternate name form, 163, 320n2
    home of, 163, 205
Kaye, Joe, *53*, 102, 117, 159, 231, 271
Kaye, Joe, Reverend, *149*, 232
Kaye, John Charlie, 197
Kaye, Johnny, 159, 198
Kaye, Myra
    life of, 62
    pictures of, *52*
    quotations, 35, 36-37, 39, 51, 69-70, 79, 81, 84, 92-93, 102, 123-24, 127, 153
Kaye, Roger, *xxxix*, 285
Kendi, Alfred, 248
Kendi, John, 117, *146*, 244
Kendi, Julius, 184, 231-32
Kendi-Rispin, Michelle, 268, *295*, 310
kettles. *See* pots
Khach'oodaayu', xlviii, 119, 120, 314n12
kidnappings, 48, 107, 120
kin-based social system, 13-14, 49, 320n2
King Edward Creek, 178
King Edward Mountain (*Ch'anchàl*), 138, 178, 183, 184-86, 191, 279, *303*
Kirk, Corporal (RCMP), 172, 245, 262
Kirk, Mrs., 245
Kirkby, Reverend, xxxvii, lii, 137
Klondike Gold Rush
    about, liv, 317n4
    and missionaries, 143
    and surveyors, 155
    and traders, 118, 130-31, 135, 304, 309
    and trappers, 226, 304
    and wage work, 256-57
knitting
    fishnets, 81, 99, *100*, 123
    snowshoes, 83, 190

Kò' Ehdanh. *See* Man Without Fire
Kutug, Julia, liii, 137, 143, 168
Kwatlatyi, modern spelling of, 317n2
Kwatlatyi, Annie, *128*
Kwatlatyi, Elias, *128*, 155, 178-79, 271
Kwatlatyi, Old John, 155
Kyikavichik, Big Joe, 143, 164, 274-76
Kyikavichik, Brandon, *268, 273*, 294, *295*, 297, *310*
Kyikavichik (Kay/Kaye) family
    alternate name form, 163, 320n2
    home of, 163, 195, 197
    members of, 197, 284
Kyikavichik, Hannah (Netro), *136*
Kyikavichik, Joe, 172
Kyikavichik, John Joe
    camp, 294
    family, 109, 195, 294
    pictures of, *19, 177, 252, 258, 279*
    quotations, xviii, 170, 172, 176-77, 183-84, 194-95, 197-99, 203, 230, 251, 253
    telling stories, 300
Kyikavichik, Katherine, 195
Kyikavichik, Myra, 73, 317n3
Kyikavichik, Tabitha, 92, 195

Labrador tea, 92
lamps, 231
land
    attachment to, 188, 190, 251, 270, 293, 299, 300, 310
    claims, 243, 269
    conservation of, xxxiii, 194, 251, 263, 284, 293, 302
    giving back to, 300
    importance of, lxii, 160, 251, 262-63, 293-94, 299-300
    knowledge of, 163, 276, 278
    living from, 64, 65-67, 162-64, 203, 240, 251, 255, 263, 269, 292-94
    modern use of, lxii, 160, 263, 269-70, 286, 287, 292
    moving off, 161, 251
    protection of, xviii, xxxiii, 159, 188, 209, 262-63
    relating to, 302
    rights, 268
    sharing, 197, 199, 243
    see also conservation
land claims, 243, 269
landmarks, 184

language
    changing, xii, xxxv, 233
    English, 151, 152, 160, 162, 219, 270, 305
    for history collection, xxxiii
    see also Gwich'in language; translations
LaPierre House
    archaeology of, xl
    Ch'ineekaii at, 225
    church at, 75, 129
    founding of, xviii, xlviii, 173
    historic site, xxxii
    Hudson's Bay Company at, liv, 75, 118, 126-27, 129, 130
    location of, *lviii, 122, 193*
    missionaries at, lii, 142, 143, 145, 151
    move from, liv, lxi, 154-55, 215
    people of, 66, 75, 106, 126, 198-99
    pictures of, *196*
    population of, 129
    seasonal visits to, 238
    stories about, 271
    traders at, lii, lvii, 118, 136, 197-99, 208, 215, 226, 228, 317n5
    trading at, 197-99
    trapping at, 176, 230
LaPierre House Oral History Project, xvi, 322n33
lay readers and preachers, Gwich'in, 119, 137, 148, 151, 230-32, 307, 319n27
Le Blanc, Raymond, xxxvii-xxxviii, xl-xli, *273, 310*
leaders
    and hunting, 110, 111, 114-16
    roles and qualities of, 61, 108, 110, 184, 187, 312
    selection of, 28, 164, 170, 172
    stories about, 272, 274, 312
    see also chiefs
learning
    from family, 64, 86, 138, 179, 183, 190, 203, 253, 269, 276, 281-82, 292-94, 297, 300-01
    see also education; literacy; schools
legendary narratives, lxii, 3-4, 21-41
Letter Carrier, xlix
licences, 242
light. *See* candles; lamps
Linklater, Archie, lii, liv, lvi, 132, 144, 168, 181, 229, 321n27
Linklater, Charlie, 181, 205, 207, 229
Linklater, Effie, quotations, 9, 11

Linklater, Irwin
    life of, 278-79
    pictures of, *268, 273, 310*
    quotations, 275, 276, 279-80, 282-84
literacy, 137, 141, 151
Little Bell River, 230
Little Flats, *19, 98,* 272, 274
Lone Mountain, 169, 207
long-ago stories
    animals in, 5-7, 12-16
    connected with history and geography, 276, 278, 311-12
    defined, xiv, lxii
    parallels found elsewhere, 311, 313n2 (preface)
    themes of, xlvii, 323n11
    time scope of, xxxvi-xxxvii
    types of, 3-4, 51
    see also histories; legendary narratives
looking after each other
    the elderly, 61, 77, 84-86, 114, 115, 125, 137-38
    orphans, 85, 94, 110, 113, 115
    poor people, 65, 76, 84, 86, 93, 115, 116, 125, 137-38
    as traditional value, 137-38, 163
lookouts, 283
    see also Caribou Lookout
Loolah, William, 145
Loon and Crow, 4, 6-7
loons, 6-7, 19-20
Lord, David, *xxxv, 42,* 293
Lord, David, (white trapper), liv, lvi, 228
Lord, Pete, 134, 168, 179, 183, 226, 227-28, 293
Loucheux, xxxviii, xliii, *xlviii*
loyalty, 17-18
lying, 34
lynx, lvii, 132, 204-05, 215

Mackenzie Flats, *xxvii*
Mackenzie Valley Pipeline Inquiry, xxxi, lxi
"Mad Trapper of Rat River." *See* Johnson, Albert
mail delivery, 114, 227
Man Without Fire, 4, 21, 23-35, 224, 282, 316n11, 316n13
marriage
    arranged, 14-15
    ceremonies, 143, 188, 256, 300
    courtship, 275
    performed by ministers, 143, 256
    polygamy, liv, 23, 110, 113, 137, 307, 318n18
    proposals, 211, 275
    relationships in, 111, 195, 256
    and religion, liv, 110
    to supernatural beings, 8-9
    and surnames, 320n2
    see also families; intermarriage
marrow, 288
marten
    clothing made from, 9
    fur sales, 74, 122
    origin of, lvii, 8
    population, 280
    and pre-Christian beliefs, 138
    trapping, 82, 115, 168, 203, 209, 210, 215, 217, 242, 280
Mason, Billy, liv, 132, 201, 205, 226, 227
Mason Hill, 226
Mason, Reuben, *liv,* 205, 208-10, 226-28, 249
Mason, Shirley, liv
matches, 74
matrilineal identity, xxx, 320n2
Mayo, 184, 231
McDonald, Julia. *See* Kutug, Julia
McDonald, Kenneth, 142
McDonald, Neil
    family, 138, 167, 318n15
    giving feasts, 256
    home of, 281
    hunting, 117-18
    life of, 62, 137, 167-68
    pictures of, *liii, 101, 135*
    quotations, 67, 99, 101-02, 106-07, 117-18, 132-35, 139-40, 145-46
    territory of, 167-68, 281
    as trader, *135, 136*
McDonald, Robert
    arrival of, 119, 141, 307
    on caribou fences, 89
    departure of, 145
    and diseases, 91
    and dreamers, 113-14
    family, lii-liv, 138, 142, 143, 145
    and Gwich'in language, xix-xx, xxxviii, 314n4, 320n8
    homes of, 125, 142, 143
    legacy of, 137, 138, 143, 230

pictures of, *liii*
respect for, 141, 143, 145
training lay readers and ministers, 148, 150
meat drying
containers for, 281
importance of, 164, 165, 169
modern, 293
pictures of, *10*
process, 211-12, 214, 237, 261, 281
seasons for, 68, 69, 75, 78, 79, 172, 180, 186, 189, 197, 214, 232
sites of, 197
for trade, 74, 75, 77, 124, 126, 190, 198-99, 240, 257, 261
transportation of, 123, 183, 211-12, 235, 278, 281
see also caches; fish
medicine
delivery of, 134
as trade goods, 122
traditional, lxii, 261, 276, 299, 300
medicine men and women
belief in, liv, 137, 138-41
and Christianity, 140
named, 191
paying, 140
powers of, 37, 39, 137-41
process, 141
see also dreams and dreamers; shamans
meetings, 101-02, 159, 170, 172, 187, 256, 268
see also gatherings
menstruation, 14-15
mice, 7-8
migration, caribou, xxviii-xxix, 91
see also travel
Miner River, *lviii*, 173, *193*, 210, 271
miners, 228, 256
ministers
attitudes to, 141
boats of, 124-25, 197
care of, 141
Gwich'in, *19*, 119, 132, 137, 145-51, 184, 230, 232, 307
helpers of, 147, 151
and marriage, liv, 143, 256
named, 232-33
receiving medicine deliveries, 134
services, 143

supplies for, 124-25
travel, 142-44, 197, 231
see also catechists; churches; lay readers and preachers; missionaries
mink, lvii, 8, 115, 168, 179, 210, 215
missionaries, liv, 64, 89
arrival of, 137, 138, 141
and the Hudson's Bay Company, 137, 142
at schools, 152
teaching, 141, 150, 151, 153
see also ministers
money, 217, 262-63, 287
see also beads; fur, prices; wage work
Montgomery, Jane, *xxxiv*, *23*, *196*, *273*, *310*
the moon, 9, 11
Moore, Billy, 156
moose
butchering, *108*
characteristics, 257
cooking, 35
drying, 237
feasts and dances, 117-18
fences, 272
hunting, 18, 19, 76, 93, 117-18, 124, 130, 191, 194, 203, 215, 235, 236, 237, 242, 246, 260, 281
migration, 215
population, 262
relationship with, 109
skins, 77, 85, 93, 130, 188, 232, 234, 281, *301*
snaring, 71, 94, *95*
trading, 124, 257
morality stories, 9, 21
Moses, John, 6, 183, 201, 207, 249, 250, 271
Moses, Mary Jane, *xxxiv*, *23*, *273*, *301*, *310*
Moses, Myra
family, 71, 114-16
life of, 62, 65-66
nickname of, 317n3
pictures of, *lix*, *22*
quotations, 27, 29-32, 61-62, 65-66, 71-78, 81-86, 94-97, 107, 114-17, 124-25, 129-30, 131, 141-45, 153, 155-56
telling stories, 272
on traditional values, 13-18
Moses, Peter
after shooting of Albert Johnson, 250

    as chief, 110, 114-16, 172, 207, 312
    family, 179
    on future travel methods, 219
    giving feasts, 117
    hunting, 66, 71
    meetings about the land, 159
    pictures of, *115*
    telling stories, 180, 271
    trading, 178
Moses, Roy, xi, 21
mosquitoes, 13, 31-32, 65, 117, 180
Mouchet, Father, 230
mountain sheep. *See* sheep
mountains, 183, 184-92
Mounties. *See* RCMP
Murray, Alexander Hunter
    arrival of, 272
    illustrations by, *xlviii, xlix, li, 10, 25*, 109
    as trader, xlviii-lii
    writings by, xlix, li, 106, 315n16, 316n16
music, 76, 116-18, 198
    see also fiddling; singing
muskrat hunting
    camps, *96*, 99
    dependence on, 163, 212, 243
    for dog feed, 172
    equipment for, *75*, 99, *101, 103*, 115
    fur prices, lvii, 103
    historic remains of, xlvii
    at night, 183
    places for, 66, 97, 99, 101-05, 177-79, 191, 218, 286
    processing furs, *115*, 167
    season, lvii, 163, 169, 180, 227, 320n5
    techniques, 191, 253, 289
    for trade, 120
muskrats
    drying, 172, 289
    population of, 103, 168, 177-78, 181, 183, 279, 288, 290, 322n9
    stories about, 5-6
myths, lxii, 4

Nagwan, Lance, *283*
names
    before missionaries' arrival, 320n2
    of parents, 320n12
    see also place names
nanaa'in'. *See* bushmen
national parks, xxxii, xxxiv
Neets'aii Gwich'in, *xxvii*, 106
neighbouring peoples
    existence of, xlvii, 223-24
    relations with, 106-08, 305, 314n9
Neilson, Eric, 244
Nerysoo, William, xi
Netro, Charlie, 220
Netro, Elsie, *136*
Netro, Florence, *203*
Netro, Hannah, *136*, 159, *161*, 189-90
    family, 195, 205, 246, 321n14
    move to Old Crow, 246
    pictures of, *136, 161, 197*
    quotations, 159, 189-90, 208-10, 217-18, 220, 224-25, 228, 233, 249-50
Netro, Joe, *liv*
    family, 220
    home of, 201
    life of, 62
    pictures of, *135, 136*
    quotations, 14, 110, 120-22, 130, 140, 141
    stories written down by, 35, 36-37
    as trader, 134, 136-37, 168, 201, 205, 235
    as trapper, 135, 137, 208, 210, 236
Netro, Kathy, *136*
Netro, Mary, 172, *203*
Netro, Minnie, *136*
New Rampart House. *See* Rampart House
New Year's
    celebrations, 116-17, 164, 184, 202, 256
    games at, 207
    gathering for, 225
    supplies for, 125, 172, 256
    travel after, 81
Niliikakti', John, 180
Njootli, Amos, 132, 319n27
Njootli, David, 117, 168
Njootli, Stanley Sr., 267, 270-72, 274, 276, 278, 282
Njootli, Thomas, 207
Njootli, William, 147, 148
Nohddhàa, *98*, 185

non-human characters, 4
Northern Commercial Company, 136, 137, 235, 245
Northwest Company, 67
Nospeak, Henry, 140
Nukon, Christine, *36*
Nukon, Dick
    family, 204, 257
    home of, 238
    pictures of, *36, 177, 213*
    quotations, 35-36, 40-41, 204-05, 207-08, 212, 225, 227, 243-46, 248-49, 256-57
Nukon family, *63*, 135, 211
Nukon, Henry, 21
Nukon, Jessie, 211
Nukon, John
    family, 211, 234
    friendship, 274-75
    guiding police, 219
    home of, 199, 201, 211, 234
    life of, 256-57
    pictures of, *63*
    store, lix, 211
    trapping, 218, 236
Nukon, Kenneth, *63*, 205, 246
nurses, 133, 151, 224, 232, 245
NWMP, lii

Oblates, lii, 21, 137
ochre, 39, 40
Ogilvie Mountains, viii, xlv, 224, 234, 256, 257
oil and gas development, xxxi-xxxii, lxi, 101-02, 262
Old Crow
    airport, 219, 244
    bringing meat to, 207, 235
    Ch'ineekaii at, 225
    church at, *lx*, 145-46, 155, 156, 231-33, 243
    climate, 210
    English dialect, xxxvi
    funerals at, 99, 105
    growth of, lxi, 132, 156, 243-44, 246, 284
    health services, 245
    jobs in, 263
    location of, xxvi, *lviii*, 154, 305
    ministers at, 148, 150
    missionaries at, 143, 155
    modern life, 268, 294
    move to, lvii, 134, 145, 154-56, 163, 207, 211, 215, 229, 238, 241, 243-46, 257, 309
    name of, 108, 110
    people of, 109, 111, 114, 238
    pictures of, *lvi, lvii, lx, 77, 128, 308*
    prices in, 244, 245-46, 287, 304, 319n29
    RCMP at, 230, 243, 244
    school at, lxi, 109, 246
    services at, lxi, 233, 243, 246
    as site of stories, 6
    stores at, lxi, 118, 132-34, 136, 155, 156, 198, 215, 217, 309
    teachers at, 231
Old Man Minister. *See* McDonald, Robert
Old Rampart House
    church at, 124, 125
    establishment of, li
    feasts at, 76
    Hudson's Bay Company at, 76, 121, 124-26
    location of, *lviii, 122,* 183
    missionaries at, 142, 143, 153
    move from, 154, 156
    people of, 73, 219
    traders at, lii, 317n5
    trapping at, 74
"Old Steamboat", *100*
old women. *See* elders; *shanaghàn*
Olti', 119-20
oral history, xv-xvi, 268, 302-03, 313n3, 322n11
Order of Canada, *170*
orphans, 85, 94, 110, 113, 115, 195
orthography, xx, xxxviii, 314n4, 315n2, 317n2, 320n8
Ottawa, 15, 16
otters, 7-8, 207

packsacks, 120, 123, 144, 281
    see also dogs, carrying packs
Paddled a Different Route. *See Ch'ataiiyuukaih*
paddles, 75, 105, 145, *149*, 166, *182*
palaeontology, xli-xlii
parables, lxii, 314n3
parks. *See* national parks
partners, 25-26, 33-35, 274-75
Paul, Sophie, 110
peace, 17-18, 34, 55, 307

Peel River, *xxvii*, *lviii*, 13, 106, 205
Peel River Post, xlviii, 118, 121
   see also Fort McPherson
pemmican, 29, 73, 77, 102, 186, 281
permafrost, 306
permanent communities. *See* settlements
Peter, Abraham, 195, 280, 281-82
Peter, Jeffrey, *295*
Peter, Joel, 288-89
Peterson, Victor, lii, 168, 178, 227, 228
Petitot, Émile, 21, 48
pipelines, xxxi-xxxii, xxxviii, lxi, 262
pipes, 51
place names
   of caribou fences, 251
   learning, 292
   origins of, liv, 131, 201-02, 226, 230
   study of, xiii
plants
   uses of, lxii, 92, 102, 251, 299-301, 306
   see also berries; roots
playing. *See* games
Pleistocene era, xli, *xlii*, 314n6
Point Barrow, Alaska, 120-21
poison, lvi, lxi, 132-33, 192, 212, 227, 230, 262, 304
police, at the international border, 241
   see also RCMP
politics, xxxiii, 268, 269, 270, 286, 294
   see also government; land claims; self-government
polygamy, liv, 23, 110, 113, 137, 307, 318n18
poor people
   helping, 65, 76, 84, 86, 93, 115, 116, 125, 137-38, 197
   life of, 246
   weapons of, 74, 82-83
   women, 41
population
   decline of, liv, 64, 65, 89, 90, 93, 183, 309
   in the past, 66, 70-72, 91-94, 183, 186, 234, 239, 281
Porcupine caribou herd
   calving grounds, 320n1, 322n29
   hunting, xxviii-xxix
   location of, *xxvii*, 322n29
   and pipelines, lxi
   protection of, xxxi-xxxii
   Van Tat Gwich'in relationship with, xlvii, 314n10

Porcupine Lake, 280
Porcupine River
   hunting on, 236
   modern camps on, lxii
   pictures of, *xxx*, *lx*, *73*, *189*
   pre-glacial, xli
   route of, xliv, 313n1(introduction)
   site of stories, 5
   as trade route, 305
   see also upper Porcupine River
porcupines
   hunting, 185, 255
   quills, 188
Potato Creek, 102-05, 163, 181, 279
Potato Hill. *See* Diniizhòo
pots, 70, 78, 125, 220
prayer, 141, 195, 301
predictions. *See* dreams and dreamers; medicine men and women
prehistory, xxxvii-xxxviii, lxii
presents, 184, 188, 197
prices
   of fur, lvii, lxi, 74, 103, 122, 133, 163, 180, 205, 217, 233, 235, 246, 287, 288
   of supplies, 161, 244, 245-46, 287, 304, 319n29
"prize women", 49-51
ptarmigan
   cycles, 305
   hunting, 44, 85, 260
   importance of, 70, 85, 255, 260
   places for, 183
   snaring, 64, 70
public expression, 268
   see also meetings

rabbit drives, 23, 91
rabbits
   cooking, 47, 48, 76, 125
   hunting during caribou shortage, 125, 176, 255, 260
   population of, 205
   rabbit-skin, clothing, 27, 66, 76
   snaring, 47, 64, 85, 91, 125, 132, 166, 204
   uses of, 27, 66, 79
   see also rabbit drives

radios
- effects of, 226, 234, 247
- keeping dog company, 183
- music on, 198
- news on, 209, 247, 248, 309-10
- Gwich'in people on, 262

rafts, 75, 76, 119, 123, 154, 164, 169, 203, 278
- *see also* boats

Rampart House
- archaeology of, xl
- celebrations at, 116-18
- Ch'ineekaii trading at, 106, 224
- church at, 155
- closing of, lii
- customs checkpoint at, 242
- diseases at, lvi-lvii, 133, 241
- dogs of, 132
- establishment of, li, 154, 217
- explorer at, 229
- historic site, xxxii, 314n15
- hospital at, 133, 241
- Hudson's Bay Company at, liv, 66, 86, 118, 121, 213
- hunting at, 261
- and the International Boundary Survey, lvi, 213
- location of, *lviii*, *122*
- missionaries at, 142, 143, 153, 154
- move from, lxi, 134, 135, 145, 155-56, 241
- original, li
- people at, 86, 155, 164, 167, 168, 170, 214, 240
- pictures of, *214*, *218*, *308*
- police at, 133, 219, 241
- population, 71, 218
- productivity of, 242
- school at, 153
- settlement at, 173
- traders at, lii, liv, 94, 118, 130, 131, 146, 155-56, 180, 213, *214*, 217, 218-19, 317n5
- trading at, 106, 213, 224
- visits to, 190, 238, 315n15
- *see also* Old Rampart House

Rat Indian Creek, xlvi, 37, *38*
Rat Indians, 106
Rat Pass, 198
RCMP
- and Albert Johnson, 139, 247-50
- breaking trail for, 114, 219
- co-operation with, 247-49, 309
- dealing with poison use, 230
- deaths of, 150
- former, 75
- guiding, 207, 219
- intermarriage, lii, 229
- and medicine delivery, 134
- at Old Crow, lxi, *208*, 243
- patrols, 114, 150, 205, 207, 219, 222-23
- pictures of, *223*
- at Rampart House, 133, 219
- special constables, 207, *208*
- travel with, 222
- *see also* NWMP

relationships between people, 111, 256, 274-76, 302

religion
- Christianity and traditional, 113-14, 141
- importance of, 230
- and marriage, 110
- printed works, xxxviii, 137, 141, 143
- *see also* Anglicanism; churches; lay readers and preachers; ministers; missionaries

retribution. *See* vengeance
revenge. *See* vengeance
Richardson, John, 89
Richardson Mountains, 192, 205, 305
Rispin, Phillip, *268*, *295*, *310*
Rispin, Tracy, *268*, *295*, *310*
Robert Bruce Lake, *279*
Rock River, xlv
Roman Catholic Church, lii, 230
- *see also* Oblates

roots, 102
Ross, Albert, 275-76
Ross, Johnny, 180
ruins
- caribou fences, 90, 222-23
- villages, 173, *196*, *200*

Russians
- coming of, xlvii, 121
- and the Hudson's Bay Company, li, lii
- trade with, xlviii, 119-20, 305

salmon, 166, 192, 194, 209, 239, 242, 272, 282, 294, 305, 316n20
    see also fishing
Salmon Cache, 66, 75, 143, 173, 197
Santa Claus, 231
scarcity
    episodes of, 71, 76-77, 147, 202, 271
    places to go in time of, 97, 99, 176, 306
    sharing during, 85
    storing surpluses for, 84, 91
    see also starvation
scars, 34, 35
Schaeffer, Ab, lii, liv, 132, 201, 226, 227, 228
Schaeffer Creek, 132-33, 169, 185, 186, 201, 226, 227
Schaeffer Lake, *162*, 169, 178, 226, 290
Schaeffer Mountain, 179, 226, 227
Schaeffer, Selena, 227
Schafer, Esau, *291*, *296*, *310*
Schafer, Marion, *xxxiv*, 286, 292, 293-94
schools
    arrival of, 119
    attendance at, 270, 305
    effect on going out on the land, 246, 284
    at Fort Yukon, 229
    going away to, 68, 152, 297
    Gwich'in language and history, xxxiii-xxxiv, 294
    high school, 297
    at Old Crow, lxi, 109, 246
    residential, 152, 229
    years before schools were established, 66
    see also education
scientists, 268
seagulls, 14
seasonal activities
    arrow-making, 29
    autumn, 68
    boat building, 169, 289
    camp visits, lxii, 169
    camps, 279
    caribou fence use, xxix, 68, 68-70, 86, 89-92
    caribou hunting, xlvii, 68-70, 73, 165, 172, 235, 261
    drymeat transportation, 183
    duck hunting, 121
    fishing, 71, 166, 172, 179, 184
    food gathering, 187, 189
    food preservation, 68, 187, 189
    hide preparation, 166, 232
    house-building, 72-73
    marten trapping, 209
    meat drying, 68, 69, 75, 78, 79, 172, 180, 186, 189, 197, 214, 232
    muskrat trapping, lvii, lix, 163, 169, 227
    snowshoe and toboggan making, 68
    spring, xlvii, 69, 279
    squirrel hunting, 183, 260
    summer, 69-71, 307
    trading, 173
    travel, 61, 173, 184, 186, 190, 215, 219, 234
    visiting, 169, 178, 219, 287, 300
    winter, 61, 68, 71, 76, 93, 186
    see also Christmas; Easter; New Year's
Second Mountain. *See Chyah Ddhàa*
self-government, xxxiii, 268
    see also politics
settlements, lix, 119, 161, 163, 173, 176
    see also settlements by name
sewing, 232, *301*
    see also clothing
Shahnuuti', 109-10, 111, 113, 272, 318n18
Shahvyah, 109, 111, 114, 272, 274
shamans, 34, 70, 109, 111, 137, 138, 260
    see also dreams and dreamers; medicine men and women
shanaghàn, 28, 41-51, 69-70, 274, 311
sharing food
    after a hunt, 61-62, 85, 90, 93, 94, 172, 236
    capable hunters, 30
    from caribou fences, 254
    fishing, 76
    with Hudson's Bay Company employees, 125
    with ministers, 147
    and *nanaa'in'*, 49-51
    at Old Crow, 287
    with poor people, 65, 86, 197
    with relatives, 74
    as social value, 41, 49-51, 64, 84, 93, 137-38, 287, 311
    by traders, 125, 220
    see also co-operation; elders
Sharp Mountain, 285
sheep, 37, 81, 120, 282
Shingle Point, *53*, 54, 55, 178

Simon, Sarah, 228
singing, xlix, 34, 106, 116, *303*
Sittichinlii, Edward, 148, 150
Sittichinlii, Lazarus, 148, 149-50
Ski-doos. *See* snowmobiles
skiing, 230
sleighs
    making, 282
    pictures of, *10, 67, 92, 96, 128, 223*
    use of, *xxxv*, 67, 282
Slobodin, Richard, 12, 21, 41, 48, 53, 316n11, 316n14, 316n22
"smart women", 23, 30-32, 41-42, 44-51, 84, 107, 132, 282
Smith, Shirleen, *310*, 313n1 (preface)
smoking hides, *80*, 166
snares
    caribou, 82, 83, 89-91, 93, 94, *95*, 261, 284
    lynx, 132
    making, 82, 83, 85, 91, 94, 95, 191, 261
    moose, 71, 94, *95*
    muskrat, 99
    preserving, 95
    ptarmigan, 70, 132
    rabbits, 47, 64, 82, 83, 85, 91, 125, 132, 166, 204
Snow Mountain. *See* White Snow Mountain
Snow White Mountain. *See* White Snow Mountain
snowmobiles, 217, 222, 255, 260, 287, 292, 294
Snowshoe, 195
snowshoes, 24, 40
    broken, 242
    hunting on, 260, 292
    making, 68, *80*, 81, 83, 145, 190, 306, 317n6
    pictures of, *128*
    travel on, 144, 261
social mores. *See* values
songs. *See* singing
spears
    fishing, 71, 102
    hunting, 16, 74, 83, 89, 91, 261, 284
    trading for, 119, 314n16
special constables, 207, *208*, 247, 249, 250
spelling, xx, xxxviii, 314n4, 315n2, 317n2, 320n8
spirituality, and *Van Tat*, 97
    see also religion
spruce, 83, 84, 150
square dances, 116

squirrels. *See* ground squirrels
St. Barnabas Mission, lii
starvation
    dealing with, 85, 101, 130, 202
    frequency of, 44, 57, 93, 99, 101, 185
    and population decline, 93
    in stories, 9, 41-42, 44-46
    see also scarcity
Steamboat, 168, 195
Steamboat, Eliza, *43*, 282-83
steamboats
    honouring *Shahnuuti'*, 113
    traders', 77, 134, 155, 156, 217, 220
    travel on, 152, 229, 245
    and wage work, 173, 229, 234, 257
Stefansson, Vilhjalmur, 229, 321n27
stone tools, 107
stores
    debt and credit, 134, 168-69, 226, 288
    establishment of, 118
    pictures of, *135, 214*
    trading to, 75-76, 77
    see also traders
stories
    historical versus long-ago, xiv, 51, 53
    passing on, xi-xv, xviii, 163, 270-72, 276-77, 282-85, 287, 290, 300
    recording, xxxi, 285
    and relationships between people, 274-76
    sources, xiv, xviii
    value of, xii, xviii, 53, 56, 179, 267, 270-71, 285, 287, 312
    wording of, xiv
stoves, 62, *80*, 127-28, *146*, 173, 210, 223, 294
Stringer, I.O. (Bishop), liv, 143, 152, 233, 307, 315n19
strong men, 35-37, 38, 41, 282, 312
strychnine. *See* poison
suicide, 39-40
Sundays, liv, 127, 231-32
supernatural stories, 8-9
supplies, prices of, 244, 245-46, 287, 304, 319n29
surplus
    storage of, 84, 307
    see also caches
surveyors, *liv*, 155, 242, 314n14
    see also international border

taking care of each other. *See* co-operation; elders; sharing food
tea
    drinking before hunting, 260
    drinking together, 86, 92, 240
    as gifts from ministers, 125
    reusing, 86
    scarcity of, 74, 240
    trading for, 76, 122, 130, 201, 240
    wild plants, 92, 251
teachers, 224, 231
    see also education; literacy; schools
teepees, 66
Teetl'it Gwich'in
    Dagoo Gwich'in integrated into, xxx
    hunting for trade, liv
    individuals, 169, 205, 256
    location of, *xxvii*, 205
    move to Fort McPherson, 205
    name, 106
    trapping, lvii, 205
tents
    buying, 210
    canvas, 62, 127-29, 173
    church services in, 147-48
    frames, *162*
    pictures of, *17, 50, 80, 96, 162*
    skin, 24, 65, 66, 72, 76, 81-82, 121, 173, 186, 189, 240, 256, 317n6
    trading for, 120, 128-29
    use of fire in, 318n16
Tetlichi, Brianna, 271
Tetlichi, Charlie, 257
Tetlichi-Charlie family, 163, 257, 320n2
Tetlichi, Randall, 165
Thomas, Charlie
    family, 190, 210, 211. *See also* Domas
    home of, 163, 205, 213, 225, 279
    hunting, 207
    pictures of, *xlii, 182, 259, 308*
    quotations, xiv, 167-69, 178-79, 181, 183, 210-12, 214-15, 218-19, 225, 227-28, 241-42, 253-55, 257, 260-62
Thomas Creek Caribou Fence. *See* Antl'it Tthał
Thomas Hill, 190
Thomas, John, 104, 105, 205, 315n20

Thomas, Lydia
    pictures of, *170, 196, 295, 298*
    quotations, 169-70, 195, 197, 255
Thomas, Mary, xix, 102-05, *104*
Thompson, Peter, 6
Timber Creek caribou fences, *lviii, 88*, 254
Timber Mountain, 183
tin cans, 228
Tizya, Andrew
    home of, 180
    as hunter, 30, 320n13
    pictures of, *185, 221*
    quotations, 185-86, 202
Tizya, Clara, 181, 241-42
Tizya, Jacob, 143
Tizya, John, lxi, 142, 145-46, 155, 179-80, 232
Tizya, Martha, 50, 62, 82, 85
Tizya, Moses
    education of, 152, 160
    family, 30, *50*, 142, 145
    home of, 197, 201
    hunting, 117-18, 129, 203
    as leader, 172
    life of, 62, 152
    pictures of, *50, 108*
    quotations, xi, xlvii, liv, 3, 23-30, 33-35, 49-51, 53-56, 108, 119-20, 126-27, 136-37, 141, 142, 152, 154-55
    stories from, 82
Tizya, Peter, *96*, 117-18, 217, 236
Tizya, Ross, 195
Tizya-Tramm, Erika, *296, 299, 310*
Tl'oo K'at
    Ch'ineekaii at, 224
    and *Diniizhòo*, 184, 189
    history and importance of, 278
    hunting at, 189
    location of, *88*
    people at, 74-75, 78, 173
    pictures of, *189*
    prehistoric remains, xlvi, xlvii, lxi
    stories set at, 37, 127
Tl'oo Thał. See Grass Pants
tobacco, 51, 74, 76, 122, 125, 130, 151, 240
tobacco ties, 300-01

toboggans
    baskets for, 281-82
    broken, 242
    caribou-skin, 82
    children in, 67
    dancing on, 116
    making, 42, 50, 68, 69, 81, 102, 145, 187, 281, 306, 317n6
    pictures of, 96
    travel with, 77, 78
    women pulling, 130
tools
    making, xliv, 83, 300
    trading for, 120
    using, 99, 101, 107
tracking methods, 30
trade
    early, 119-20
    fighting over, 107, 120
    of hides, 198, 220, 240
    and the international boundary, 241
    prehistoric, xlvii-xlviii, 219
    of presents, 188, 197
    Van Tat Gwich'in as middlemen, xlvii, xlviii, li-lii
    see also debt and credit; fur trade; stores; trade goods; traders
trade goods
    as change, 307
    clothing, lii, 133, 220
    early, xlix, li, lii
    Hudson's Bay Company stock, 61, 66, 74, 122, 133, 199, 220
    prices of, 161, 233
    transportation of, 122-23, 136-37, 305
traders
    cultural contributions of, 116
    freight hauling, 136, 137, 173
    Gwich'in, 136-37, 163
    intermarriage, lii
    pictures of, liv
    private, 118, 130, 131-37, 305, 309
    wage work for, 122, 162, 173
    see also Hudson's Bay Company; Russians; stores; traders by name
trading chiefs, li-lii, 108, 109
trading posts
    growth of settlements around, 173
    see also posts by name
trails
    bears', 190
    breaking, 114, 201, 219
    caribou's, xxviii, xxix
    erosion of, 280
    landmarks on, 184
    routes, 183, 198, 222
    snowmobile, 292
    surveyors', 242
    winter, 91
    see also Geenu
transformation stories, xlvii
translations, xvi, xxxv
trapping
    by children, 217
    deadfall, 82, 115, 191
    decline of, lxi, 192, 194, 243, 246, 284, 287
    early, li-lii
    fish, 46, 49-50, 65, 71, 76, 101, 102, 109, 121, 176, 179, 185, 186, 195, 272, 307, 316n21
    for food, 64
    learning about, 168, 183, 210-11, 226, 227
    organizing, 172
    overtrapping, 192, 194, 212, 230, 233, 262
    pictures of, 216
    supplies for, 210
    by women, 105, 132, 168, 177, 227, 253, 293
    see also beaver; muskrats; poison; rabbits; snares; trapping, fur; white trappers
travel
    by air, lvi, 134, 183, 219, 286
    camp setting, 66-67
    church workers, 137, 142, 150-51, 153
    cooking, 84
    extent of, xxvi, 219, 223
    and fire making, 79
    frequency of, 46, 64, 66, 208, 238
    for hunting, 44, 68, 70, 93, 101, 132, 153, 173, 176, 183, 188, 195, 199, 237, 261
    and the international border, 153, 241, 243
    ministers, 142-43, 144, 197, 231
    modern, 160, 165, 280-81
    spring, 287

388   Index

summer, *xlvi*, 75, 76, 131, 164-65
winter, *xxxv*, 10, 18, 42, 44, 54-55, 61, 67, 68, 74, *92*, 93, 104, 131, 144, 150, 169, 201, 217, 261. *See also* dog teams; snowmobiles; snowshoes
see also boats; canoes; dogs; rafts; steamboats; trails
trickery, 6, 38, 40
Tukudh. *See* Dagoo Gwich'in

upper Porcupine River
   about, 192, 194
   Ch'ineekaii in, 225
   hunting and trapping at, 203-07, 210
   location of, *xxvii*, *193*
   modern visits to, 194
   move from, 310
   overtrapping of, 192, 194, 212, 230
   people of, xxix
   productivity of, 163, 192, 203
   stories set on, 35
   traders in, 218
   see also Porcupine River

Valley Caribou Fence. *See* Antl'it Tthał
values
   continuing, 64, 84, 137-38, 141, 270, 302, 306-07
   educating children about, 151
   in long-ago stories, 17-18, 19, 21
   relationships, 274
   see also co-operation
Van Tat
   camps in, *96*, 288-90, 292, 294, 297
   Ch'ineekaii in, xlvii, 104, 106, 168, 181, 223, 224-25
   decline in use of, 286, 290
   description of, xxvii, 97, 306
   family areas in, 288-89
   gatherings at, 169-70, 309
   historic use of, 66, 97, 115, 121, 130, 163, 168, 172, 181, 191, 243, 286, 288-89, 292
   importance of, 97, 99, 101-02, 176, 286, 293
   location of, *lviii*
   map of, *98*
   modern use of, lxii, 176-77, 253, 287
   mountains around, 183, 184-92
   moving to and from, 180-81, 215, 278-79, 288-89
   name, 97

   pictures of, *xxvi*, *67*, *96*, *103*, *162*, *174-75*, *182*, *187*, *279*, *289*
   productivity of, 97, 168, 288, 290
   protection of, xxxiii
   seasonal use of, 184, 225, 286, 292
   as site of stories, 6
   visitors to, 56-57, 62
   see also Little Flats
Van Tat Gwich'in
   history of, xxvi-lxii
   lands of, *xxvii*, xxxi, xxxviii, 173, 176
   names, xx, xxxviii, 97
   neighbours of, xlvii, 106-08
   people integrated into, xxix
   pre-historic flood, xli-xliv, xlv, 314n7
   see also Gwich'in language
Van Tat Gwich'in Cultural Geography Project, xiii
Van Tat Gwich'in Heritage Committee, xxxiv
Van Tat Gwich'in Oral History Project, xiii, xxxiii, xxxiv-xxxvi, xl-xli, 4, 62, 302-12
variations in stories, 4
vengeance, 17-18, 19-20, 35, 312, 316n14
Vuntut Gwitchin Final Agreement, xxxii-xxxiii, xl
Victoria, Queen, 15
villages. *See* settlements
visiting
   at camps, 169
   children and elders, 86
   exchange of presents, 184
   and the international border, 241
   seasonal, 169, 178, 219, 278, 287, 300, 307
   see also gatherings; meetings
Vuntut Gwitchin First Nation, xxxii-xxxiii, xl, 313n1 (preface), 315n15
Vuntut National Park, xxxii, *lviii*, lxi

wage work
   at the airport, 286
   effect on going out on the land, 292
   effect on trapping, 246
   and Klondike Gold Rush, 256-57
   learning English through, 162
   with police, 207
   rise of, 163, 269, 284
   school children, 152
   on steamboats, 234

    with traders, 122, 162, 173
    woodcutting, 229, 257
Walking Crow. *See* Crow May I Walk
war
    extent of, 93
    food supplies for, 30
    frequency of, 28, 50
    lone survivors, 316n14
    over trade, 107, 120
    people left behind, 30
    prizes, 49
    Second World War, 115, 209
    stories about, 21, 28, 51, 53-56, 224-25
washing, 66, 79, 181
water
    conservation of, xxxiii, 262, 284, 302
    containers, 20, 78
    drinking, 78, 109, 217, 225
    hauling, 86, 181
    red, 225
    sources, 189, 190, 209-10, 217, 251
    see also flood
weapons
    bear hunting, 16
    caribou hunting, xxix, 90, 165
    making, 29-30
    moose hunting, 15
    pictures of, *25*
    trade for, xlviii, 119-20
    for war, 25, 54-55, 107
    see also bows and arrows; clubs; guns; spears
weasels, 7-8
whalers, liv, 118, 129, 131, 305, 309
Wheeler, Reverend, 134
White Mountain. *See* White Snow Mountain
white people
    arrival of, xlvii, 4, 56-57
    speaking the Gwich'in language, 233
    time before arrival of, 93
    see also intermarriage; white trappers
White Snow Mountain, 236-37, *237*, 280-81, 299, 322n5
white trappers, lvi, lxi, 132-33, 178, 179, 183, 199, 205, 208, 212, 219, 224, 226-28, 230, 234, 247, 248, 249, 304
    see also intermarriage; poison
whitefish, 234

Whitefish Lake, 234
Whitehorse, 68, *244*, 297
Whitehorse Star, xiii, xxxi
Whitestone River, 236
Whitestone Village
    climate, 210
    and Dagoo people, 299
    decline of trapping, lxi, 212, 243
    hunting at, 236, 260
    location of, *lviii*, *193*, 201
    modern use of, 173, 271
    move from, 212, 243, 245, 246
    people of, 163, 199, 201, 207, 209, 211-12, 215, 228, 234-36
    pictures of, *204*, *298*
    police at, 150
    population of, 129
    ruins of, 299
    store at, lix, 118, 121, 134, 135, 136, 173, 205, 211, 235
    stories set at, 316n10
    trapping at, lvii, 204-05, 210-11, 228
    visits to, *298*, 299
Whittaker, Archdeacon, 150
widespread stories, 4
Williams, Megan, *279*
willow
    in caches, 79
    for fish traps, 102
    for fishnets, 82, 84, 99
    for house frames, 81, 92
    for meat drying, 81, 214
    and tobacco ties, 300-01
Willow Man, 4, 35-41
wolverines, 215, 220, 230
wolves, 16, 138, 215, 230, 261
women
    social position of, 42, 274
    trapping, 105, 132, 168, 177, 227, 253, 293
    work of, 64, 67, 75, 78, 81, 91, 95, 105, 124, 165, 166, *205*, 286
    see also clothing, women's; marriage; "prize women"; *shanaghàn*; "smart women"
Women's Auxiliary, 231, 232-33

yeenoo dài' googwandak. *See* long-ago stories
youth
    concern for the land, 299-301, 310

defined, 267
on the future, 293-94, 297, 299-301
knowledge of the land and past, 290-301
lives of, 302
passing stories to, xii
problems of, 285
relationship with elders, 274, 293-301

Yukon, northern, 305-07
Yukon Comprehensive Claim Umbrella Final Agreement, lxi
Yukon Flats, *xxvii*

Zzeh Gittlit. *See* Crow May I Walk